The Conservative Party and Europe

by
Ben Patterson

JOHN HARPER
PUBLISHING

The Conservative Party and Europe

Published by John Harper Publishing
27 Palace Gates Road
London N22 7BW, United Kingdom.

www.johnharperpublishing.co.uk
www.europesparliament.com

ISBN 978-0-9564508-7-6

© John Harper Publishing 2011

Printed and Bound in Malta at the Gutenberg Press

Contents

Acknowledgements vii
Foreword ix
About the author x
Preface xi

1   The Churchill Legacy 1
"A kind of United States of Europe" 1
Intersecting circles 4
The Eden view 8
"It'll never happen" 10
Sixes and sevens. 12
Free trade, fair trade 14

2   The Macmillan Application 18
"If the terms are right" 18
Opinion during the negotiations. 21
Immigration and sovereignty 23
The geopolitical dimension 25
The General says "Non!" 27
Conservative responses. 29

3   Finding a Role 34
"A dead duck" 34
Bow Group views: the case for Europe. 35
Bow Group views: the case against. 38
In opposition. 41
What kind of Europe? 42
What alternatives? 44

4   Preparing the Ground 46
Under new management 46
Conflicting voices. 48
Conservative Gaullism 50
Constituency opinion 52
Preparing for office 54

Powell on Europe. 58
Wooing Conservatives 62
Wooing the French. 67
The balance of rebellion 69
Conservative federalists 72
A consensus 73

5   **Membership and Referendum**. **78**
Parliament. 78
Commission and Council 80
Problems at home 82
Party politics suspended. 85
Human rights 88

6   **Direct Elections** **91**
Electoral systems and alliances 91
Organisation and candidates 95
Issues and policies 98
The campaign. 101
The results. 103

7   **The Years of "Maggie's Money"** **108**
In the EDG. 108
Changing the Rules 111
The battle of the Budget 112
Widening and deepening 115
Crocodiles and Kangaroos 118
Constituency issues 121
"True to Britain and true to Europe". 125

8   **Towards the Single Market**. **129**
"1992" 129
The Cockfield White Paper. 133
The Single European Act. 136
Second thoughts. 138
Business opinion 141
Lobbying in Brussels 145

9   **Bruges and After** **149**
"A diet of Brussels" 149
The Bruges speech 151
Rise of the Eurosceptics. 154
Joining the EPP Group 156

10 **ERM and EMU**. **160**
Werner, Jenkins and Delors 160
Common or single? 163

Into the Exchange Rate Mechanism 165
Changes at home and abroad. 168
The opt-in solution 171

11 The Battle for Maastricht. 174
"Game, set and match" 174
The Party divides 176
The General Election of 1992 and after 179
"Black Wednesday": causes and consequences 182
The Maastricht rebellion 185
Activist opinion: conflicting evidence 188

12 Into the Cold 193
"Europe: Right or Left?" 193
Luxembourg, CJD and BSE 197
A "vote-free recovery" 200

13 No Longer the Party of Europe. 205
The Party in opposition. 205
Evidence from the CPS 208
Establishing a policy 212
"Unelected Commissioners ..." 216
"... and unelected bankers" 218
"In Europe, but not run by Europe" 220
Saving the pound 224
The defence dimension 227
"No European defence without a federal Europe". 229
Retrospect: the Westland affair and after 231

14 The Constitutional Treaty 235
Amsterdam, Nice and beyond 235
The proceedings of the Convention on the Future of Europe 237
What the Constitution said. 240
The criminal law and the Charter of Fundamental Rights 242
"A Constitution in all but name". 244

15 The Road to Recovery 247
Elections in 2004 and 2005 247
Cameron Conservatism. 251
Where to sit? 253
Moats and duck-islands: the European Elections of 2009 257
Conservatives and Reformists 259
The Lisbon Treaty. 261
The 2010 election and after. 264

16 1945 to 2010 – An Analysis 269
Europe and the parties 269

Switchers 271
"I thought we were only joining a Common Market" 273
What is a Common Market? 277
A federal super-state? 278
The state, the nation and the nation state 281
International society 285
Centralism and subsidiarity 288
Conservative Europeanism examined 292
The post-Maastricht problems 296
Public opinion 299
… and the media 301
The influence of Labour 304
Conservative Euroscepticism examined 306
The democratic deficit 309
The alternatives 313
Conclusions 316

17 **Conservative European Policy and the Future** 322
Party policy in coalition 322
Coherence and contradiction 325
Referendum lock and Sovereignty Act 329
Pragmatism, conservatism and ideology 331
Three scenarios 335
The bottom line 340

Appendix 1: Conservatism and Christian Democracy 343
The search for allies 343
Christian Democrat and Conservative philosophies 344
The Social Market Economy 348
Charity and the voluntary sector 350
The federal project 352
Joining and leaving the EPP Group 354
The Future 356

Appendix 2: Chronology of Main Events 359

Appendix 3 369
Chart 1 British public opinion on membership of the European
     Communities/European Union, 1960–2010 369
Table 1 Results of Elections to the European Parliament in
     Great Britain, 1979-2009: seats won and % of votes 370

Bibliography of works cited 371
Index 383

Acknowledgements

I should like to thank the staff of the Bodleian Library in Oxford for their help in tracing various documents from the 1960s and 1970s; and also the European Parliament's London Office for access to its records. My thanks, too, to many former colleagues in the European Parliament for their contributions and comments, in particular my fellow MEP for Kent, Christopher Jackson, and the sitting MEP for the East Midlands, Bill Newton-Dunn. I am also grateful to my former boss at the Conservative Political Centre, Russell Lewis, for his insights over years, both as an early supporter of Common Market membership and then from a more sceptical position.

My thanks to my wife, Felicity, and my daughter, Olivia, for reading through the early drafts of this book; for their suggestions and corrections; and for their patience as the final text slowly took shape.

And finally, I thank my publisher, John Harper, for his support and enthusiasm in getting this work into print.

Ben Patterson
Hawkhurst, October 2011

Permission to reprint extracts from other works is acknowledged as follows:

Quotations from *British Politics and European Elections 1994* by David Butler and Martin Westlake (St.Martin's Press, 1995) reproduced by kind permission of Palgrave Macmillan.

Quotation from *Europe: the State of the Union* by Prof. Anand Menon (Atlantic Books, 2008) reproduced by kind permission of Atlantic Books.

Quotations from *A Stranger in Europe* by Sir Stephen Wall (Oxford University Press, 2008) reproduced by kind permission of Oxford University Press.

Quotations from *The Tories and Europe* by John Turner (Manchester University Press, 2000) reproduced by kind permission of Manchester University Press.

Quotation from *Diaries* by Alan Clark (Phoenix paperback, 1993) reproduced by kind permission of the Orion Publishing Group.

Quotations from *Memories of the first elected European Parliament* (Allendale, 2008) reproduced by kind permission of Allendale Publishing.

Related books from John Harper Publishing

Those interested in the relationships between British politics and the European Union, and especially the European Parliament, may wish to consult these related titles from John Harper Publishing:

Building a Liberal Europe: The ALDE Project, by Graham Watson. Published in 2010. ISBN 978-0-9564508-1-4.

"Graham Watson chronicles a fascinating period in the EU's development with the humanity and humour which were a hallmark of his leadership of the EU's Liberal MEPs."
Romano Prodi, former President of the European Commission

Wreckers or Builders?: A History of Labour MEPs, 1979-1999, by Anita Pollack. Published in 2009. ISBN 978-0-9556202-9-4.

"At last we have a history of Labour MEPs in the first twenty years of the directly elected Parliament... a well-researched record – warts and all."
Neil Kinnock, former leader of the Labour Party and Vice-President of the European Commission

For full details of these and other titles, visit
www.europesparliament.com

Foreword

by the Rt. Hon. Kenneth Clarke, QC, MP

The subject of Europe has caused endless controversy inside the Conservative Party for the last sixty years. It could hardly be said that the Party shows much sign of becoming any calmer or totally agreed on the subject. My old friend, Ben Patterson, and I have spent our entire political careers living in the middle of this. Ben and I were active Conservative students at Cambridge in the early sixties, when Harold Macmillan first announced that Britain would be applying for membership of the Common Market. Ben and I were – and still are – keen supporters of Britain's role at the heart of what has become the European Union. We both had the privilege and excitement of being constantly involved in the debate.

Ben found himself in Brussels and Strasbourg as a Member of the European Parliament, with a closer and more detailed view of the many events there than I had from Westminster and Whitehall. His account is an accurate account of key events and debates in the European Parliament in particular over the years. He writes it from the standpoint of a fair-minded participant and of someone whose views, like mine, represented the mainstream majority of the Conservative Party for most of the relevant time.

I commend the book to anybody who wants to have an insight into how Conservative politicians were engaged in and participated in this debate over the last few decades.

House of Commons
26 October 2011

About the Author

Ben Patterson has played an active part in the Conservative Party's policy towards Europe since reading languages at Trinity College, Cambridge in the late 1950s. His first job was as a tutor at Swinton Conservative College in Yorkshire, with special responsibility for lecturing on the then topical and controversial issue of Britain's first application to join the Common Market. In 1965 he moved to Conservative Central Office, where he was involved in the Party's preparations for the eventually successful negotiations to join the Community. In the 1970 general election he stood, though unsuccessfully, as the Conservative candidate for Wrexham.

In 1973 he became Deputy Head of the European Parliament's London Office, accompanying the first, largely Conservative, British delegation to the Parliament's sittings in Strasbourg and Luxembourg; and in 1979 became the Conservative Member for Kent West in the first directly-elected European Parliament. He served in the Parliament for three terms, where his activities included being *rapporteur* on the Single Market project and on the events surrounding "Black Wednesday". Between 1994 and 2004, he was research officer for the Parliament with responsibility for, among other things, preparations for the Euro. He is currently Chairman of the Conservative Party's Kent Area Management Executive Committee.

Preface

When in June 1979 I became the MEP for Kent West in the first directly-elected European Parliament it was as the candidate of the "party of Europe". The main opposition was moving rapidly in a Eurosceptic direction, and would soon have, as official policy, complete withdrawal from what was then called the European Community. By contrast, my party's manifesto noted that for almost two decades we had "believed that Britain's future is best assured as a member of a free, strong and democratic European Community".[1] In the earlier general election in the same year, the party's manifesto had stated that "we must ... work honestly and genuinely with our partners in the European Community. There is much that we can achieve together, much more than we can achieve alone".[2]

What was my party? Surprising as it may seem to those who have only experienced British politics during the last ten years, it was the Conservative Party. We were the ones who had taken the UK into the European Community in 1973. Now we were the ones who would campaign throughout the 1980s, and successfully, for "1992" – a real Single Market. Supporting the next step, a Single Currency, was only considered mildly heretical.

Today, the positions of the two largest British parties have been almost entirely reversed. True, the Conservative Party is not in favour of British withdrawal from what is now the European Union. In opposition, however, it adopted a number of positions which threatened to make membership somewhat semi-detached – though coalition government with the Liberal Democrats has now made their implementation unlikely. Meanwhile, the New Labour party which won the General Election of 1997 rapidly ditched its Euroscepticism and moved smartly into the vacated "party of Europe" slot – even, at one time, seriously proposing the abolition of the pound sterling in favour of the euro.

Such a changeover is remarkable enough. But my memory goes back well before 1979; and what is perhaps even more remarkable is that this had happened at least twice before. When in the early 1960s the Conservative Government of Harold Macmillan opened negotiations for UK accession to the newly-created European Economic Community (EEC), together with the older European Coal and Steel Community (ECSC) and with Euratom, the Labour leader Hugh Gaitskell accused Macmillan of betraying "a thousand years of history". Yet only a few years later – the application having foundered on de Gaulle's "Non" – the Labour Prime Minister Harold Wilson and his Foreign Secretary George Brown were touring the capitals of Europe in a new bid to join. And the Conservative Party? Europe, Macmillan's successor Sir Alec Douglas-Home was said to have remarked, was a "dead duck".

The Conservative leader who followed Sir Alec, Ted Heath, having won the General Election of 1970, nevertheless brought the negotiations started by Wilson and Brown to a rapid and successful conclusion. Official Labour policy, almost overnight, then turned against membership (though the European Communities Act 1972 which implemented the Accession Treaty was supported by a dedicated group of Labour pro-Europeans led by Roy Jenkins). The Labour Government of 1974 came in pledged to "renegotiate" the terms of British membership; and a number of now forgotten changes were indeed made, enabling Wilson to recommend a "Yes" vote in the 1975 referendum.

Both the Labour and Conservative Parties have a core vote of some five million, and usually poll around ten million each in a general election. How is it that the opinions of these voters concerning Europe are apparently so malleable? One possible explanation is that Europhiles and Europhobes retain their views, but switch *en masse* between the parties at election time. This is not what the long series of election studies by David Butler and others have shown to have occurred. There can be large switches in and out of abstention and some in and out of third parties; but, broadly, loyal supporters of both Conservative and Labour seem quite happy to switch their views on Europe in accordance with the current policies of their parties.

The history of such movements of opinion within the Labour Party has been written by others; and, as the party of Michael Foot became the party of Tony Blair, it certainly provided the most striking example of how attitudes to Europe can alter over quite a short period.

This book, however, is about the history of similar changes within the Conservative Party. As a (just) pre-Second World War baby my first memories of a political kind are of Winston Churchill – a voice on the radio to be listened to in silent awe, and photos in the papers and on posters of a man with a chubby face smoking a cigar and holding up two fingers. And Winston Churchill is, indeed, a good starting point for any study of the Conservative Party and Europe.

Notes

1   *Conservative Manifesto for Europe 1979* (Conservative Central Office, May 1979).
2   *The Conservative Manifesto 1979* (Conservative Central Office, April 1979).

1   The Churchill Legacy

"A kind of United States of Europe"

In the official histories of the European Union, Churchill sits securely in the pantheon of founding fathers, alongside Monnet and Schuman, Spaak, Adenauer and de Gasperi. This is partly based on his wartime role as liberator of Europe from the Nazis; but more on his campaign after the war in support of European unity.

This campaign was formally launched in a speech delivered at Zurich University on the 19th September 1946. He began by describing the then current state of Continental Europe.

> Over wide areas a vast quivering mass of tormented, hungry, care-worn and bewildered human beings gape at the ruins of their cities and homes, and scan the dark horizons for the approach of some new peril, tyranny or terror ...
>
> Yet all the while, *he continued*, there is a remedy which, if it were generally and spontaneously adopted, would as if by a miracle transform the whole scene, and would in a few years make all Europe, or the greater part of it, as free and as happy as Switzerland is today. What is this sovereign remedy? It is to re-create the European Family, or as much of it as we can, and provide it with a structure under which it can dwell in peace, in safety and in freedom. We must build a kind of United States of Europe.

Churchill's Zurich speech has been much analysed by both supporters and opponents of British European Union membership. Opponents have observed that, though Churchill may have repeatedly called for "a United States of Europe", he never explicitly stated that the UK would be an integral part of it. In the Zurich speech itself, indeed, he referred to "Great Britain, the British Commonwealth of Nations", together with "mighty America, and Soviet Russia" acting as "the friends and sponsors of the new Europe".

There is no doubt, however, about the political impact of the speech. It put centre-stage what had previously been the cause of only a few dedicated campaigners. Moreover, it contained evidence that Churchill had given the matter some thought. The first step in the re-creation of the European family, he declared, "must be a partnership between France and Germany. ... There can be no revival of Europe without a spiritually great France and a spiritually great Germany". As Roy Jenkins observed in his biography of Churchill[1], this "proclaimed a doctrine which was at least premature to many people, but which was to become axiomatic within a few years".

In the Zurich speech Churchill also announced a principle which has been fundamental to the subsequent development of European unity.

> The structure of the United States of Europe, if well and truly built, will be such as to make the material strength of a single state less important. Small nations will count as much as large ones and gain their honour by their contribution to the common cause.

Some have advanced the view that Churchill's campaign for European unity was one of his sudden enthusiasms, a cause to occupy him after he had unexpectedly lost power in Britain. The evidence does not bear this out. Already in 1945, addressing a joint meeting of the Belgian Senate and Chamber on the 16th November, he had called for a "United States of Europe" which would "unify this Continent in a manner never known since the fall of the Roman Empire, and within which all its peoples may dwell together in prosperity, in justice, and in peace".[2] Earlier still, in October 1942, he had sent a memo to the Foreign Secretary, Anthony Eden, outlining his hope for "the revival of the glory of Europe" once the war was over.

> I look forward to a United States of Europe in which the barriers between the nations will be greatly minimised and unrestricted travel will be possible. I hope to see the economy of Europe studied as a whole. I hope to see a Council ... which would possess an international police. ... [3]

His support for European unity, moreover, was not just a reaction to the Second World War. In 1930 he had written in the American periodical, the *Saturday Evening Post*, that "the conception of a United States of Europe is right. Every step taken to that end which appeases the obsolete hatreds and vanished oppressions ... is good in itself".[4]

Churchill's campaign was not limited to great speeches. As Jenkins notes, he was the organisational force behind the Hague Conference of May 1948, which was convened by his son-in-law Duncan Sandys, chairman of the newly-formed European Movement. In the following year this resulted in the establishment of the Council of Europe Assembly in Strasbourg. Not only did Churchill personally address both the initial sessions of the Assembly, but in August 1949 he spoke to a crowd of some

20,000 in Strasbourg's Place Kléber. "Such spontaneous enthusiasm for the European cause had never been seen in Strasbourg before; nor has it been since", Jenkins ironically comments.

Jenkins also casts doubt on the belief that Churchill was only telling others to unite, and did not really envisage full British participation. He observes that, in his speech at The Hague, Churchill referred to "sixteen European states now associated for economic purposes" and five which had "entered into close economic and military relationship". "As he counted Britain not merely among the sixteen but among the five, he was obviously then regarding his country as not merely part of Europe but part of its core."[5] In 1946 he had spoken of "a united Europe in which our country will play a decisive part".

More significantly, perhaps, when in 1950 the Schuman Plan for a European Coal and Steel Community (ECSC) was launched – the first embodiment of what is now the European Union – Churchill led the Conservative Party in June of that year into the pro-Schuman division lobby. The future Conservative Prime Minister Ted Heath, in his maiden speech, enthusiastically supported British participation, and probably reflected the views of many younger Conservative MPs at the time, particularly those, like Heath himself and the future Chancellor of the Exchequer and later Party Chairman under Margaret Thatcher, Peter Thorneycroft, who had seen at first hand the consequences of war in Europe. Schuman, after all, had stated that the objective of the plan was to make war "not merely unthinkable, but materially impossible".[6]

Julian Amery, son of the great Tory imperialist Leo Amery and son-in-law of Harold Macmillan, argued for participation in the Schuman Plan on grounds of "Imperial interest"; and Quintin Hogg (later Lord Hailsham) on grounds of Commonwealth interest – remarkable arguments in view of the debates that were to take place within the Conservative Party some years later. Harold Macmillan himself recalled that, though "the world was startled" by the sudden launching of the Plan, the idea of coordinating the coal and steel industries at a supra-national level had been under discussion for some time: for example within the European League for Economic Cooperation (ELEC), of whose British committee he was himself a member.[7] In the same year, in Strasbourg, Churchill also proposed and carried a resolution calling for "a unified European army" under the authority of a European Minister of Defence and subject to European democratic control. This was an important initiative in view of the Pleven Plan of the following year for a European Defence Community (EDC). Perhaps of even greater significance was Churchill's statement during his speech that "we would all play an honourable and active part" in the proposed army.

On the other hand, as the late Hugo Young observed in his history of Britain and Europe since the Second World War,[8] "the last begetter of British greatness ... was also the prime exponent of British ambiguity". Churchill had "encouraged Europe to misunderstand Britain, and Britain

to misunderstand herself. ... His oracular pronouncements were as ambiv-
alent as those of the goddess-seer at Delphi ... ".

An even more cynical view is advanced by N. J. Crowson in a study
of Conservative attitudes towards European integration: Churchill's pro-
Europeanism was largely for domestic consumption, "a purely rhetorical
exercise" and a useful stick for beating the Labour Government. "With
a Conservative return to office the European unity issue had served its
purpose. ... "[9] In contrast with Churchill's speeches in Strasbourg while
the Conservative Party was in opposition, those delivered by the Home
Secretary, David Maxwell Fyfe, and the Foreign Secretary, Anthony Eden,
in the first Assembly session after the Party had returned to power, were
widely considered disappointing exercises in backtracking. Eden made
it clear that Britain would not participate in a European army on any
conceivable terms.

And it is indeed true that the most serious objections to Churchill's
pro-European credentials arise from the actions of his second government after the 1951 general election. His health was already dete-
riorating sharply, and he increasingly left foreign policy to Eden. Yet
hopes had been high both among European leaders and British pro-
Europeans that the incoming Conservatives would take the UK wholeheartedly into the mainstream of European unification. The ECSC was
proving a success; the much more ambitious project of the European
Economic Community (EEC) was soon to be launched, building both on
the ECSC itself and on the "Benelux" common market which Belgium,
Luxembourg and the Netherlands had already established at the beginning of 1948.

Instead, as the history books of the period note, British foreign policy
became embroiled in what Peter Hennessy in his account of the 1950s[10]
calls "The Geometric Conceit".

Intersecting circles

If you had asked any Conservative activist during the 1950s and early
1960s, and perhaps even later, what were the foundations of the Party's
foreign policy, he or she would probably have come up with some version
of Churchill's "three circles". These were the Empire and Commonwealth;
Europe; and the "English-speaking peoples" (which was understood to
mean a "special relationship" with the United States). Britain was strategically located where the three overlapped.

Both Crowson and another recent writer on the Conservative Party and
Europe, John Turner, take a sceptical view of this "Churchillian vision"
too. For Crowson it was "as much a compromise designed to hold the
party together as it was a sham in *Realpolitik* terms".[11] For Turner it was
an "obfuscation", designed to appease all factions, which "assumed that
no real decisions needed to be made between these different spheres of
influence".[12]

This, though, is taking cynicism too far. Hennessy is more convincing in arguing that not only did Churchill genuinely believe in Britain's "special place at the triangulation point of Atlantic/Empire-Commonwealth/European relationships", but that it was a plausible view of international realities at the time.

> In 1951, or even 1955, only the greatest pessimist could have antici-pated the scale of the economic and industrial undertow pulling against national resources, including those accumulations which, together, shape a country's influence abroad.[13]

Events during the nineteen-fifties resulted in each circle receiving espe-cial emphasis at different times. For older Conservatives brought up before the war (and perhaps having been members of the Junior Imperial League, predecessor of the Young Conservatives), the Empire and Commonwealth generally took priority. For others, as the Cold War began and continued until nearly the end of the century, the Atlantic Alliance became para-mount. For others again, economic reality and the success of the European Community eventually made Europe the key relationship. The important thing, however, was for Britain to maintain its role in all three.

The Conservative manifesto at the 1951 general election,[14] signed and possibly written by Churchill himself, faithfully reflected the "three circles" concept. Priority was given to "the safety, progress, and cohesion of the British Empire and Commonwealth of Nations". Second came "the unity of the English-speaking peoples". Third came the need for a United Europe, including – an important point, this, in view of developments forty years later – the countries then behind the Iron Curtain. The mani-festo was amplified in a longer document, published a few days later: *Britain, Strong and Free.*[15] Churchill's successor, Anthony Eden, faithfully continued to promote the "three circles" model, making it the main theme of his speech as Foreign Secretary to the 1953 Conservative Party confer-ence in Margate.

My own family background was an illustration of how the three circles could be combined. My mother, Dr. Ethel Patterson (*née* Simkins), whose first degree in geography was from Liverpool University, had been a Commonwealth fellow, and had studied for her doctorate at Clark University in Boston, Mass.. She had met my father, Professor Eric Patterson, in the 1930s when lecturing at Exeter University (then called the University College of the South West) where he was head of the departments of international politics and of extra-mural studies. From her I acquired an early belief that the Empire and Commonwealth were Britain's finest achievements, the existence of which automatically put us at the international top table; and also a belief that Britain and the US were basically "family".

My father's field, however, was international affairs, with a special focus on central Europe. He had written books on Yugoslavia and Poland,[16] and

also on the Polish leader, Marshal Pilsudski.* When the First World War
had broken out he had been at the University of Freiburg, doing a "gap
year" from Cambridge University, and had actually been able to continue
his studies there for some months "as it will all be over by Christmas".†
In the Second World War he was attached to Special Forces, involved (I
think) in operations in the Balkans – at any rate, our marmalade cat when
I was small was called Marshal Tito. From him I acquired a feeling for
the complexity and awfulness of European politics and history, but also a
belief that it *was* possible to make things better.

It was not until Suez‡ that I, like a large number of Conservatives, began
to suspect that Britain's imperial pretensions were something of an illusion. Indeed James Morris, in his monumental three-volume history of the
British Empire,[17] suggests that Suez, at least symbolically, marked its end.
Right into the 1960s, however – in particular during the Macmillan negotiations to join the European Economic Community – a sizeable group
within the Conservative Party insisted that the imperial illusion continued
to be reality. Members of the League of Empire Loyalists toured the country
heckling Conservative speakers who supported EEC membership.

Suez also put the second priority, the "special relationship" with the
United States, into perspective. It became clear that the Sterling Area – once
the economic dimension of Empire – was becoming a source of weakness

---

*   When in the 1990s I myself went to Poland to give a number of lectures at the European
     Institute in Łódź I quoted from the first of these books, published in 1934: "The economic
     reconstruction of Poland has astonished even its friends, while it has dumbfounded its
     enemies and made them take stock anew of the Polish situation". History had come full
     circle.

†   He later wrote an account of his escape across Germany to the neutral territory of the
     Netherlands, which was published in the journal of his College at Cambridge University,
     Peterhouse.

‡   It is an indication of how events can disappear from public memory which, to those
     around at the time, appeared historic, that I was asked by a reader from a younger gener-
     ation (who saw this text in draft) to explain what "Suez" meant. Briefly, following the
     announcement in July 1956 by the revolutionary President of Egypt, Gamal Abdel Nasser,
     that the Suez Canal would be nationalised (the UK government owned a substantial
     number of the shares – purchased in 1875 by, as it happened, Prime Minister Disraeli – and
     France also had a large holding), in October British and French aircraft bombed Egyptian
     airfields and their troops later occupied part of the canal zone. Some days earlier, Israel
     had invaded Egypt and captured the Sinai peninsula. The claims of Prime Minister Eden
     that Britain and France had gone in to "separate the combatants" and safeguard naviga-
     tion through the canal were not believed, particularly when it came out that the action had
     been planned at a secret meeting between Eden and the Prime Ministers of France and
     Israel, Guy Mollet and David Ben-Gurion. The United States refused to back the British
     and French action, and joined the Soviet Union in calling for a cease-fire; a Sterling crisis
     threatened; and both Eden and Mollet soon lost their jobs. For the Conservative Party it
     was a shattering experience, with most Conservatives loyal but uneasy at the time, and
     eventually reconciled to the outcome. Some, like the Minister of State for Foreign Affairs,
     Anthony Nutting and the Economic Secretary to the Treasury, Sir Edward Boyle, who
     resigned in protest, opposed the action. Others claimed to the end that Eden had been
     right, and only betrayal by the US had prevented a victorious outcome. The Chief Whip at
     the time, Ted Heath, was given credit for holding the parliamentary Party together.

rather than an asset. The US Secretary of State, John Foster Dulles, had no compunction in exploiting this weakness in order to bring Britain to heel.

Moreover, whatever we in Britain thought, the Americans themselves were all for European unity, and more or less assumed that Britain would be included. The Marshall Plan for massive financial aid to post-war Europe had come with the clear condition that the different national governments should get their act together, so giving rise in 1948 to the Organisation for European Economic Cooperation (OEEC). On the 4th July 1962 (American Independence Day), President Kennedy left little room for doubt when he called for "a declaration of interdependence".

> We believe that a United Europe will be capable of playing a greater role in the common defence, of responding more generously to the needs of poorer nations, of joining with the United States and others in lowering trade barriers, resolving problems of currency and commodities, and developing co-ordinated policies in all other economic, diplomatic, and political areas. We see in Europe a partner with whom we could deal on a basis of full equality in all the great and burdensome tasks of building and defending a community of free nations.[18]

The priority given by Conservative Governments to the Empire and Commonwealth, and to the "special relationship", also made in difficult to remain fully within the third circle, Europe, as Denis Judd observes in his study of the British Empire.[19]

> One of the most damaging effects of the imperial inheritance was that Britain, at least until the mid-1960s, was able to distance itself from the development of the European Economic Community, on the pretext that its traditional 'special relationship' with its first great ex-colony, the United States of America, and its continuing close financial and commercial relationships with so much of the expanding independent Empire, were of more significance and promise than an uncertain involvement in the movement for European unity.

Perception by others of that inheritance, indeed, wrecked the policy towards Europe of the Macmillan government. General de Gaulle remembered only too well Churchill's remark to him in 1944 that "each time we have to choose between Europe and the open sea, we shall always choose the open sea"; or, as he put it in his *Mémoires*, Churchill could not help feeling "*quelque souffle de l'âme de Pitt*".*[20] De Gaulle also read the Suez episode as proving that Britain would always, in the last resort, capitulate to American pressure, and would prove an "Anglo-Saxon Trojan horse" (or, as it has been put more recently and more unkindly, "Trojan poodle") within the EEC. After all, his own ambition after the war had

---

* "a whiff of the spirit of Pitt".

been to group together, with the later addition of former enemies Italy and Germany, "*aux points de vue politique, économiques, stratégique, les Etats qui touchent au Rhin, aux Alpes, aux Pyrénées. Faire de cette organisation l'une des trois puissances planétaire et, s'il le faut un jour, l'arbitre entre les deux camps soviétique et anglo-saxon*".*[21]

Later he had articulated an even grander vision: "*Oui, c'est l'Europe, depuis l'Atlantique jusqu'à l'Oural, c'est toute l'Europe, qui décidera du destin du monde.*"[22]†

The Eden view

The 1950s were, in any case, "confusing times for the Conservatives on the issue of Europe".[23] The flame of Churchillian enthusiasm for European unity was kept alight by several leading party members who had been close to him, such as Duncan Sandys and Bob Boothby. But as the young Bow-Grouper, David Howell – later Director of the Conservative Political Centre, then MP for Guildford and a Minister, and now a Minister again in the House of Lords – complained in 1960, " ... if ever a band of active idealists has sunk without trace, it is the fiery group of Conservatives who provided the driving force behind the European movement while Labour was in power".[24] In a "pathetic debate on Europe in the House of Commons", only seven Conservatives (together with eight Labour Members and four Liberals) had signed a statement asking the Government to initiate negotiations with a view to full membership of the Common Market. They represented "all that is left of the party which was once going to lead Britain forward at the head of Europe".

As was soon to become clear, the pro-European cause was very much less in the doldrums than Howell perceived at the time; and, indeed, he ended his article with the hope that Macmillan would "lead the country back to Europe with patience and skill". Moreover, a new generation of pro-European Conservatives was waiting in the wings – some, like Ted Heath, Peter Kirk and Geoffrey Rippon already MPs.

During the 1950's, however, most Conservatives (like most members of the Labour party) agreed with the policy summed up in a Conservative Political Centre discussion pamphlet published in February 1957,[25] just before the Rome Treaty was signed by the six countries already in the ECSC. Successive British Governments had appreciated the strength of "the European idea" and had sympathised with the efforts made to give concrete expression to it. But Britain had not felt able to join in some of those efforts, in particular those which envisaged the transfer of national

---

*   "politically, economically and strategically, those States bounded by the Rhine, the Alps and the Pyrenees. Make of this organization one of the three world powers and, if it becomes necessary one day, the referee between the two camps of the Soviets and the Anglo-Saxons."

†   "Yes, it is Europe, from the Atlantic to the Urals, it is the whole of Europe, that will decide the destiny of the world."

sovereignty to supra-national European bodies. "Thus Britain's leadership in an *inter*-national body such as the Organisation for European Economic Cooperation (O.E.E.C.) stands in contrast to Britain's refusal to join a *supra*-national body such as the European Coal and Steel Community."

Moreover, most Conservatives at the time seem to have followed Eden, Foreign Secretary and then Prime Minister, in considering moves towards European unity really rather a bore – certainly when compared to the increasingly threatening Cold War, with nuclear weapons deployed on both sides, and Britain's imperial and other world-wide interests. In Eden's memoirs covering the period between 1951 and 1957[26] there is one passing reference to the Messina Conference (which eventually led to the creation of the Common Market); and that is in the context of discussions in Washington. His policy following the creation of the ECSC (though he had supported engagement with the Schuman Plan in the June 1950 debate) had been to emphasise the roles of the wider and much looser Council of Europe and OEEC as the main vehicles for British influence. Indeed, in March 1952 he had put forward the "Eden Plan" for placing the supra-national ECSC, together with all other existing European bodies, under the authority of the safely inter-governmental Council.

Eden was aware that Britain's attitude towards the "European idea" had been "a constant source for criticism by our allies, who complained that our practice fell short of our precepts". We had encouraged European unity, "but from the reserve position that we would not accept a sovereign European authority, from which our Commonwealth ties precluded us". He went on to develop a theme which has been a constant thread in the more Eurosceptic Conservative school of thought.

> Perhaps as a result of our island tradition, we have a different instinct and outlook on constitutional questions from our European neighbours. We have no written constitution and this is not due merely to obstinacy or to suspicion of legal form. It is because, as a people, we like to proceed by trial and error. We prefer to see how a principle works in practice before we enshrine it, if we ever do.[27]

Thoughts like this have not been confined to Eurosceptics. Macmillan himself in on record as musing that

> The continental tradition likes to reason a priori from the top downwards, from the general principle to the practical application. It is the tradition of St Thomas of Aquinas, of the schoolmen, and of the great continental scholars and thinkers. The Anglo-Saxons like to argue a posteriori from the bottom upwards, from practical experience. It is the tradition of Bacon and Newton.[28]

Even Churchill had in 1953 cryptically described Britain's position as being "with Europe, but not of it. We are linked but not comprised".

In any case, for Eden the main European issue was Germany: how could the rapidly recovering Federal Republic (West Germany) be integrated into the North Atlantic Treaty defence structure without stirring up unpleasant memories among neighbouring countries? Behind this question was the fear that West Germany would be tempted into a deal with the Soviet Union, in which reunification with the East would be offered in exchange for permanent neutrality – in effect, buffer zone status.

"It'll never happen"

Paradoxically, it looked at one time as though the "European idea" was going to provide an ideal solution to the German question: the Pleven Plan, already mentioned, for a European Defence Community in which the *Bundeswehr* would be safely integrated into a supranational organisation on the lines of the existing European Coal and Steel Community. Then the plan was rejected, at the last moment, by the French Parliament. The debates and subsequent recriminations threw up a number of reasons, but one inescapably stood out: the unwillingness of the French to proceed without full UK participation. The Labour Government of Clement Attlee had stated in 1950 that the UK was only willing to become an associate member of the Community; and Churchill, on taking over as Prime Minister in 1951, with Eden as Foreign Secretary, endorsed the same policy.

Eden was widely credited with saving the day by organising the creation of the Western European Union (WEU), a much more inter-governmental solution which nevertheless allowed the integration of West Germany into the North Atlantic Treaty Organisation (NATO). As the Conservative Party manifesto at the 1955 general election[29] proudly maintained:

> In Western European Union we have undertaken an act of faith without precedent in British history, in that we are pledged to keep our forces on the Continent so long as they are needed by our European allies. This British pledge, following the French rejection of E.D.C., led to the London and Paris Agreements. It has restored the basis of European unity. It has strengthened N.A.T.O. by giving America and Canada added confidence in their European partners. It holds out the hope of a new and friendly relationship between France and Germany.

Britain seemed to have achieved what Oliver Franks in his 1954 Reith Lecture for the BBC (quoted by Peter Hennessy[30]) described as "a country membership" of Europe. "We pay our subscription and take on our obligations, but not the full subscription nor all the obligations of the regular members, our continental neighbours."

Yet the episode had two unfortunate effects.

The first was on opinion on the Continent, and in France in particular. It finally put to rest the hopes raised in the post-war years by Churchill that Britain was ready to join wholeheartedly in, and even lead, the United

Europe project. According to the then Home Secretary, Sir David Maxwell Fyfe (later Lord Kilmuir), failure to participate in the European Defence Community project was "the single act which above all others destroyed Britain's name on the continent".

The other effect was on British opinion, particularly within the Conservative Party. The success of Eden in creating Western European Union convinced most that the traditional inter-governmental model of cooperation between European States was more likely to bear fruit than anything advocated by ardent "United Europeanists". Granted, the European Coal and Steel Community (ECSC) was working; but the collapse of the European Defence Community indicated the more likely outcome if the subject matter was really crucial. As a result, the plans of Monnet and others to build on the ECSC by creating an integrated European Economic Community were taken far less seriously than they should have been. Officials in the Foreign Office confidently predicted that the Conference of Foreign Ministers of the Six, called at Messina to discuss the proposals, would lead to nothing.

This advice was, of course, horribly wrong. A committee chaired by the Belgian Prime Minister, Paul-Henri Spaak, was established to work out in detail the steps necessary to create a full customs union, including a common external tariff, and the institutions which would administer it. Britain was invited to participate; and the Eden government faced the dilemma of whether to send a "representative" (who might commit Britain to something) or merely an "observer" (who would be unable to influence any decisions).

The story of the civil servant from the Board of Trade, Russell Bretherton, who was eventually selected to attend the Spaak Committee on behalf of the whole British government, has entered into political folk-lore. Hugo Young contradicts the often-held view that he was merely a junior official of little weight (he was, after all, the Board representative on the Organisation for European Economic Cooperation, and had taught economics at Wadham College, Oxford, one of his pupils being the future Labour Prime Minister, Harold Wilson); and also doubts whether he really walked out of the Committee with the final words: "Gentlemen, you are trying to negotiate something you will never be able to negotiate. But if negotiated, it will not be ratified. And if ratified, it will not work."

On the other hand it probably *is* true that he was sent, as Nora Beloff put it, with the brief to "go out and see what little Tommy is doing and tell him to stop".[31] In his memoirs the Foreign Secretary at the time, Harold Macmillan, confesses that the decision not to participate in the negotiations was "influenced by two considerations, in both of which we were proved wrong. We thought they would not succeed – or, if they did, that we could work out a satisfactory association".[32] Bretherton had actually reported that the negotiations *were* going to succeed; and a study carried out by the Treasury had concluded that it *would* be in Britain's interests to participate.

Certainly those events gave rise to a perception – repeated ever since in countless speeches by semi-friendly Continental politicians – that British policy towards the "European club" always follows a traditional path. "First you say it will never happen. Then, when it does, you say it won't work. But in the end, when it does work, you join – and then grumble about the rules!"

In the event, of course, the Messina Conference led to the publication in April 1956 of the Spaak Report, which, in turn, led to the Rome Treaty, signed by France, Germany, Italy and the three Benelux countries in a solemn ceremony on the 25th March 1958.

Sixes and sevens

My own active political life began at Cambridge University, in the three years leading up to the Macmillan government's application to become a Member State of the "Common Market". When I joined the Cambridge University Conservative Association (CUCA) the echoes of Suez were dying away. Instead, the build-up was beginning to the you've-never-had-it-so-good* General Election of 1959, in which Harold Macmillan entirely restored Conservative morale with a decisive victory.

As I remember it, the foreign affairs issue which caused the most controversy among Conservative students afterwards was not Europe, but Africa, and in particular South Africa. Macmillan's "wind of change" speech to the South African parliament in February 1960 was rightly felt to be a key event.

I did, however, also join the Cambridge University Liberal Club largely in order to hear the British Liberal Party's very popular leader, Jo Grimond. There, Europe was a more important topic – the just-retired former British ambassador in Paris and future Liberal MEP, Sir Gladwyn Jebb (by then Lord Gladwyn), had already founded a Common Market Campaign Committee to promote British EEC membership. As a modern linguist, I had visited France and Germany quite a lot, and had some knowledge of the political issues in those countries (I was in Paris when, in 1958, all the car horns were sounding the rhythm of *"Algérie française"*, paving the way for de Gaulle's return to power). I knew about the movement towards European unity, expressed in Britain through Federal Union, the UK Council of the European Movement and another organisation, set up in 1957, as a campaigning body for membership of the European Economic Community, Britain in Europe.

If the "European club" jibe described above were entirely accurate, it would have come as a great surprise to Britain that the EEC, together with Euratom, successfully came into existence at the beginning of 1958.

---

* A phrase which Macmillan never uttered. It is, in fact, a misquotation from a speech he made in Bedford in 1957, in which he said ""Let us be frank about it: most of our people have never had it so good", going on, however, to observe that this was not true of everyone, and warn of impending economic problems.

Actually, the Conservative government had earlier acknowledged the possibility of this happening, and had made some attempts to prevent it, or at least to modify its effects. In 1956 it had proposed turning Western Europe into an industrial Free Trade Area – "Plan G", one of seven options devised in the Treasury – and repeated the idea more formally when the EEC became inevitable. There was even a scheme, agreed at an unofficial Commonwealth conference in New Zealand, to bring together in a single system the Commonwealth and the potential free trade countries of Europe.

Negotiations for a European Free Trade Area were conducted by a committee under a cabinet minister without portfolio, Reginald Maudling, until they were brought to an abrupt halt at the end of 1958. Despite the fact that the Spaak Report had specifically stated that creation of a customs union "does not exclude the possibility of superimposing on it a Free Trade Area", the proposal was turned down flat by President de Gaulle – the first of his three vetoes.

De Gaulle, however, was not on this occasion out on his own. As a Bow Group pamphlet published in 1957[33] had already observed, "because the attitude of the Common Market towards Britain is hardening, it now seems less likely than it did some months ago that the Free Trade Area proposals will go through. The proposal to limit the scheme purely to manufactures is increasingly regarded as a means by which Britain gets the most by sacrificing the least."

Following the veto, the future Conservative cabinet minister Patrick Jenkin (now Baron Jenkin of Roding), writing in the Spring 1960 edition of the Bow Group magazine *Crossbow*, was even more blunt. What had been surprising "was not that the talks failed, but that they ever started".

> If you want to join a club, you usually have to agree to abide by the rules; if you make it clear either that you intend to contract out of most of the rules, or that you really want a different sort of club altogether, you have no right to complain of 'intransigence' when your application for membership is firmly turned down.

The rest of Jenkin's article outlined in some detail the economic case for full membership of the EEC; but there was no attempt to overlook the political dimension. The only entity able to confront the USA, Russia and China on equal terms would be a United States of Europe.

> We must recognize that unless we are prepared gradually to sink to the status of Europe's off-shore island, we must identify our interests with those of our nearest neighbours and form a single, coherent unity which can stand on its own and compete with the other major powers. If this involves a surrender of sovereignty, then so be it. ...

The next move by the government, however, was to form a Free Trade Area anyway, together with a number of other non-EEC European countries – although, as the Party's 1959 general election manifesto[34] noted, "our aim remains an industrial free market embracing all Western Europe". The Stockholm Convention of May 1960 established EFTA (the European Free Trade Association), which came to be known as the "Seven"* (in effect eight, since Ireland formed part of the UK monetary area). The popular press had a field day, describing Europe as now being "at sixes and sevens".

This division between the integrationist Six and the free-trade Seven was also symbolic of the situation within the Conservative Party, both then and since.

Free trade, fair trade

From time to time in the history of the Conservative Party, and that of the Tories before it, there have been divisions of opinion which have had the effect of keeping them out of government for long periods. This has happened when the contending factions have put their beliefs before party unity, and even before office. In the early 18th century the issue was Jacobitism. In the mid-19th century, and again in the early years of the 20th century, it was Protection.

Since the early 1990s, the issue has been "Europe". So long as this was thought to be about getting rid of barriers to trade, most Conservatives were happy to support it. But as soon as it became "political" – or rather, as soon as the political aspects were brought to their attention – large numbers appeared to turn against it.

To be in favour of free trade within Europe – and indeed throughout the world – is an honourable position, and finds theoretical justification in the works of economists from Adam Smith and Ricardo onwards. The case for free trade has also had a powerful moral dimension. It has been seen as a means for making war less likely and for bringing people in different parts of the world together in brotherhood. The great 19th century free-trader Richard Cobden campaigned against the Corn Laws in the 1840s with the watchword "Free Trade is the International Law of God".

Conservatives, however, have only intermittently been free traders. Many of those who had supported Peel's abolition of the Corn Laws in 1846, like Gladstone, soon moved to the new Liberal Party, while the Conservatives returned to support for agricultural protection. By the end of the century, led by Disraeli and then Lord Salisbury, the Party fell in with the prevailing free-trade orthodoxy. But at the beginning of the following century the campaign by Joseph Chamberlain for Imperial

---

* Austria, Denmark, Ireland, Norway, Portugal, Sweden, Switzerland and the UK. Finland and Iceland became associate members, both later becoming full members, as did Liechtenstein.

Preference – though at first a disaster for the Party, with some free traders, like Winston Churchill, again going over to the Liberal Party – eventually bore fruit in 1932 with the introduction of Commonwealth Preference.

Within the 20th century Conservative Party, nevertheless, there has always been a strand of thinking true to the free trade, free market traditions of classical 19th century Liberalism. Its most influential exponent over the last fifty years has been the Institute of Economic Affairs (IEA); and in 1962 one of the IEA's founders, the Liberal Oliver Smedley, helped to found an anti-Market organisation, Keep Britain Out, on the grounds that joining the EEC would be incompatible with free trade on a wider basis. The IEA itself initially supported Common Market membership, but would eventually turn against what it perceived as the Community's growing *dirigiste* tendencies.

Yet the problem has been, both in the 1960s (as the Macmillan government discovered) and indeed ever since, that pure free trade has just not been on offer.

The counter-argument to the cause of unconstrained free trade is that "free trade must be fair trade": there must be no "cheating" to steal a competitive advantage. For this reason the EEC was bound to develop an active competition policy, limiting, for example, government subsidies. Later, the Single Market was also bound to involve a large amount of legislation to prevent the use of health regulations or technical standards as protectionist devices. In addition, though mainly on the political left, there was the fear of "social dumping": relatively lax health and safety or employment legislation, giving those with lower standards a competitive advantage.

Added to the pressure for legislation to set the framework for free trade is the pressure to create institutions to police it. Both a Commission tasked with ensuring that Member States fulfil their treaty obligations and a Court of Justice applying common commercial law follow from "free trade must be fair trade". To anticipate later chapters, Conservative dislike of "political" Europe has been subject to the same criticism that has been made of "Thatcherism" in general: that it "resembled Marxism in the way it grossly underestimated the importance of political institutions."[35] A similar point is made by Professor Anand Menon in a recent study of the European Union (as it now is).[36] Commenting on the widespread Conservative belief in the Single Market, but without "Brussels", he observes that "it is curious how, so often, those most in favour of the market are those who understand it least. Without the Court and the Commission, there would be no single market".[37]

In the early 1960s, the conclusion was reluctantly reached that, if a Free Trade Area could not be negotiated from outside the EEC, the best option was to join and argue from within. There was strong US pressure on the Macmillan government to do so, and the all-party campaign for membership, which included some senior Conservative figures such as the ex-Chancellor of the Exchequer, Peter Thorneycroft, was gathering momentum. Many Conservative MPs, too, had come to the conclusion that it was time to test the waters of EEC membership – as early as October 1956 a resolution calling for British participation had been signed by eighty-nine Conservatives (among whom was the future cabinet minister Sir Keith Joseph).

Much of the Conservative Party as a whole, however, was taken by surprise. A few days before Macmillan's announcement on the 31st July 1961 the official *Conservative News Letter* had confidently stated that

> The Liberals call on the Government to apply forthwith to join the Common Market. It is foolish advice which the Government are wise to reject.

Moreover, the recorded motives of those behind the move were a long way from the spirit of Churchill in the post-war years. Macmillan's Foreign Secretary, Selwyn Lloyd, wrote unenthusiastically that the problem was "how to live with the Common Market economically and turn its political effects into channels harmless to us."[38] Indeed, within the Conservative Party itself one important reason for acceptance of the policy was a somewhat complacent confidence that, once inside the EEC, Britain would have no difficulty in thwarting the integrationist plans of the existing Member States. Many years later, in 1981, the policy would be unforgettably lampooned in the television series *Yes Minister*.[39]

The Foreign Office is considering the introduction of identity cards in the form of a "Europass". Didn't the FO realise, asks the minister James Hacker of his senior civil servant, Sir Humphrey Appleby, "how damaging this would be to the European ideal?"

SIR HUMPHREY APPLEBY: I'm sure they do, Minister. That's why they support it.

HACKER: I'd always been under the impression that the FO is pro-Europe. Is it or isn't it?

APPLEBY: Yes and no, if you'll pardon the expression. The Foreign Office is pro-Europe because it is really anti-Europe. In fact the Civil Service was united in its desire to make sure the Common Market didn't work. That's why we went into it.

Notes

1   *Churchill* by Roy Jenkins, (Macmillan 2001) p. 814.
2   *Churchill, a Life*, by Martin Gilbert, Chapter 36. (William Heinemann, 1991) p. 996.
3   *The Second World War, Vol. 4: The Hinge of Fate*, by Winston S. Churchill, Chapter 31, 'Suspense and Strain', p. 452.
4   *Saturday Evening Post*, February 1930.
5   Jenkins *op.cit.* p. 815.
6   In the Schuman Declaration delivered at the Quai d'Orsay (French Foreign Office) on 9 May 1950.

7 See in *Tides of Fortune: 1945–55* by Harold Macmillan (Macmillan 1969) pp. 154 and 186.

8 *This Blessed Plot: Britain and Europe from Churchill to Blair* by Hugo Young (Macmillan 1998) pp. 6 and 25.

9 *The Conservative Party and European Integration since 1945: At the heart of Europe?* by N.J.Crowson (Routledge, 2009) p. 17.

10 *Having it so good: Britain in the fifties* by Peter Hennessy (Allen Lane, 2006).

11 Crowson *op.cit.* p. 72.

12 *The Tories and Europe* by John Turner (Manchester University Press, 2000) p. 49.

13 Hennessy *op.cit.* p. 279.

14 *Conservative Party: 1951* (Conservative and Unionist Central Office, September 1951).

15 *Britain Strong and Free: a statement of Conservative and Unionist policy* (Conservative and Unionist Central Office, September 1951).

16 *Poland* (Arrowsmith 1934) and *Yugoslavia* by Eric J. Patterson (Arrowsmith 1936).

17 *Heaven's Command, Pax Britannica* and *Farewell the Trumpets* by James Morris (Faber and Faber, 1973–8).

18 Quoted in *A History of the Twentieth Century, Volume Three: 1952–1999* by Martin Gilbert (HarperCollins, 1999).

19 *Empire: the British Imperial Experience from 1765 to the Present* by Denis Judd (HarperCollins, 1996) pp. 428–9.

20 *Mémoires: Le Salut 1944–1946* by Général de Gaulle (Plon, Livre de Poche, 1959) p. 239.

21 *ibid.* p. 211.

22 Speech in Strasbourg November 1959.

23 Turner *op.cit.* p. 49.

24 *Crossbow*, Autumn 1960 (Bow Group).

25 *Our Trade with Europe* by James Driscoll (Conservative Political Centre, February 1957).

26 *Full Circle* by Sir Anthony Eden (Cassell, 1960) p. 337.

27 Eden *op.cit..* Book 1, Chapter III, 'The Pangs of E.D.C.', p. 29.

28 At Strasbourg on 15 August 1950. Quoted by Nora Beloff in *The General Says No* (Penguin, 1963) p. 60.

29 *United for Peace and Progress: The Conservative and Unionist Party's Policy* (Conservative and Unionist Central Office, 1955).

30 Hennessy *op.cit.* p. 297.

31 Beloff *op.cit.* p. 74.

32 *At the End of the Day: 1961–63* by Harold Macmillan (Macmillan 1973). Chapter 1, 'Europe and Britain', p. 15.

33 *Challenge from Europe: Britain, the Commonwealth and the Free Trade Area* by Russell Lewis (Bow Group 1957).

34 *The Next Five Years* (Conservative and Unionist Central Office, 1959).

35 *Democracy in Europe* by Larry Siedentop (Allen Lane, 2000).

36 *Europe: the State of the Union* by Prof. Anand Menon (Atlantic Books, 2008).

37 Menon *op.cit.* p. 152.

38 Quoted in *That Sweet Enemy: the French and the British from the Sun King to the present* by Robert and Isabelle Tombs (William Heinemann, 2006), p. 622.

39 *Yes Minister: the diaries of a Cabinet Minister by the Rt.Hon.James Hacker MP, Volume One* by Jonathan Lynn and Antony Jay (BBC, 1981).

2 The Macmillan Application

"If the terms are right"

From my personal point of view, the application to join the EEC in 1961 could not have come at a better time. I had come down from Cambridge with my II(1) in Modern and Medieval Languages; but no job. Then, at my local branch of the Young Conservatives in Exeter, I heard that there was a vacancy for a Tutor at the Swinton Conservative College in Yorkshire.* I was due to go there anyway to attend a Federation of University Conservative and Unionist Associations (FUCUA) course, so I applied for the post. The Principal of the College was the powerfully eloquent old-style Tory and Cambridge economist Sir Reginald Northam, who agreed to employ me; and also to act as my supervisor as I studied for a BSc(Econ) at the London School of Economics.

Although Swinton primarily existed to run courses for various Conservative Party groups and to train Conservative agents, a considerable number of "industrial courses" were run for the employees of local firms, notably Imperial Chemical Industries (ICI) and Yorkshire Imperial Metals (YIM). The impending negotiations to join the EEC became a major element in the agendas of both kinds of course; and this was the principal subject on which I was to lecture.

For the Conservative Party at the time, Swinton also provided something more than a training ground and an intellectual centre. The College occupied the larger part of the 19th century gothic Swinton Castle, the rest being the home of the Earl and Countess of Swinton. Lord Swinton – born Philip Lloyd-Graham, but having taken his wife's name of Cunliffe-Lister in 1924 – had had a distinguished career in pre-war, war-time and post-war governments, and was credited with having commissioned the Spitfire when Secretary of State for Air between 1935 and 1938. In the 1960s he and the Countess regularly played host to senior Conservatives

---

* Swinton was originally the Conservative College of the North. That of the South was the Bonar Law "College of Citizenship" at Ashridge in Hertfordshire, where my father was Principal before the outbreak of the Second World War. After the war Ashridge was briefly re-launched, but eventually became a business school unconnected with the Conservative Party. Swinton itself ceased to operate as a Conservative College in 1975, and the whole Castle was sold in 1980. It is now a hotel.

looking for relaxation on the Yorkshire moors, shooting or fishing. One quite frequent visitor was the Prime Minister, Harold Macmillan.

Some doubts have been expressed about the pro-European credentials of Harold Macmillan. For Jenkins, "he was only partially a European".

> He possessed the vision to seen the dangers of Britain being excluded from a united Europe. But if Britain were outside, he did not want Europe to achieve unity. He wanted the EDC to fail, and he thought much the same about the early move towards the Economic Community. ... In a sense his position was the reverse of Churchill's. Churchill in government wanted European unity to succeed with Britain benevolently on the outside. Macmillan preferred it to fail unless Britain was satisfactorily even if somewhat reluctantly on the inside.[1]

This is rather unfair – Macmillan's earlier record shows genuine support for Churchill's European vision. In his memoirs, the failure of the British Government to join the ECSC in 1951 is recalled with the added word "alas". He even contemplated resignation from the government in May 1952 over its failure to change the previous Labour government's stance on the EDC proposals. It can also be said that "the conversion of the Conservative party to the Common Market was one of the more remarkable of Macmillan's political achievements, for the whole enterprise stood in flat contradiction to all the traditional instincts of the party. ... "[2]

However, Jenkins' perception does fit the attempts to create a Free Trade Area, already described; and also the public stance of extreme caution when accession negotiations were opened. For Hugo Young he was "a European only of his time and place, which is to say a tormented and indecisive one."[3] In his memoirs, Macmillan describes the cabinet decision of the 27th July 1961 to make a formal application to join the EEC as "a turning point in our history."[4] Yet we would only join, Conservatives were told – by me among others – if satisfactory arrangements were made in a number of areas: Commonwealth trade, in particular New Zealand butter and West Indian sugar; British agriculture; and the interests of fellow EFTA countries.

The main argument of those opposing the policy – as expressed by, for example, the young unit trust whiz-kid, chairman of the YCs at its peak and founder, in 1961, of the Anti-Common Market League, Peter Walker* – was that seeking Common Market membership constituted a betrayal of Empire and Commonwealth. This view was supported to the last ditch by the Beaverbrook newspapers, the *Daily Express, Sunday Express* and *Evening Standard*, which portrayed Europeans as "Catholic, undemocratic and unclean".[5]

---

* He became Lord Walker of Worcester after his retirement from the House of Commons in 1992, having been MP for Worcester since 1961. He died in June 2010.

Macmillan recalls, however, that the rest of the Conservative-inclined press – *The Times, Daily Telegraph* and *Daily Mail*, together with the Labour-inclined *Daily Mirror* – were sympathetic to the government's application. The House of Commons vote following a two-day debate in August resulted in only one Conservative MP, Anthony Fell, voting against the Government with just over twenty abstaining. These abstainers, Macmillan noted at the time, "are of two kinds – earnest Imperialists [and] the disgusted group". Earlier in May, however, he had also noted that "there are very many anxious Conservatives. It is getting terribly like 1846." His consolation was that there was "no Disraeli to my Peel".[6]

For a long time it was a cliché of political commentary that "loyalty is the Conservative Party's secret weapon". This is especially true when a general election is appearing over the horizon. Accordingly, there was little opposition to the Common Market application at the 1961 Conservative Party conference at Brighton that October – the first of nearly fifty which I attended over the years. Macmillan recalled that only "thirty or forty voted against, in a huge assembly of four thousand or more".

A second debate took place at the Conservative Party Conference in Llandudno in the following year. The former health minister, Sir Derek Walker-Smith MP (later a distinguished President of the European Parliament's Legal Affairs Committee) moved a hostile amendment to the pro-Common Market motion, dwelling chiefly on the Commonwealth and sovereignty issues. Echoing the thoughts of Eden and Macmillan, quoted earlier, he argued that Britain did not really belong in Europe: the evolution of the Common Market countries had been "continental and collective", whereas Britain's had been "insular and imperial".

This amendment, too, was heavily defeated by much the same majority as at Brighton; and Macmillan recorded at the time that "Butler and Heath seem to have made excellent speeches" (though I myself recall Butler, ironically at best a lukewarm supporter of Common Market membership,[*] being somewhat put out by the heckling throughout by infiltrators from the League of Empire Loyalists). Ted Heath, in his autobiography,[7] recalled receiving a survey of Conservative backbenchers in June 1962 showing 189 in favour of Common Market entry with 77 against; and only forty-seven MPs signed an anti-Common Market motion in December 1962 – much the same number that were to oppose membership when it was about to become a reality in 1971.

"We had … surmounted triumphantly any hostile opinion in the Conservative Party", Macmillan's Memoirs recall. "We were now 'in the straight'." By late 1962, "the opposition of the 'anti-Marketeers', as they would now be called, had proved a complete, almost ludicrous failure."[8] Opinion within the Conservative Party was also reflecting wider public

---

[*] Despite the fact that Butler was Foreign Secretary between 1963 and 1964, his autobiography, *The Art of the Possible*, contains no reference to the Common Market issue at all.

opinion: a Gallup poll that October found support for Common Market membership at 58%, with only 22% against and 20% "don't know".

Opinion during the negotiations

As a tutor at Swinton Conservative College between 1961 and 1965 I was in a good position to monitor, and even perhaps influence, the opinion of Conservative activists concerning Common Market entry. Not only members of the government, but a wide variety of back-benchers, journalists, industrialists and other opinion-formers lectured at the College; and one of the tutors' duties was to record and summarise these lectures for later distribution. There were also discussion groups and question-and-answer sessions where the balance and shifts of argument became evident.

Interestingly, one of the first lectures on which I took notes, in mid-1961, was given by the Hon. Patrick Maitland – later the Earl of Lauderdale, who died in December 2008, aged 97 – from the Expanding Commonwealth Group. This accurately reflected the somewhat hesitant nature of the Macmillan application, at least as presented to the Conservative Party. The arrangements negotiated for the Commonwealth, said Maitland, would be the critical issue. "Let us ... keep in mind that we have not yet authorised negotiation of our entry, but have merely asked that the terms of entry be ascertained."

Other lecturers emphasised that entry into the Common Market should be seen as only an element of wider policies. Col. (later Sir) Douglas Dodds-Parker MP – who would in 1973 become part of the first UK delegation in the European Parliament – told a seminar on "Can the West Win?" in December 1961 that one of the aims was to prevent the EEC from becoming "economically and politically self-sufficient. ... Ultimately, we must go on to consider some form of Atlantic Union ... ".

By the beginning of 1962, however, a coherent party line had been established, which was cogently presented to a March course on "Britain in the Modern World" by the then MP for Sevenoaks, John Rodgers (also later knighted), a member of the One Nation Group in the House of Commons.

Contrary to the view of many Conservatives today (and also of many academics: for example Anthony Forster in *Euroscepticism in Contemporary British Politics*[9]), the case for Common Market membership was *not* made exclusively in economic terms. "The political aspect is as important, if not more important, than the economic one," Rodgers began. The Cold War had made it clear that "cooperation, both political and economic," was essential if the challenge of Soviet Communism was to be met.

In making the economic case for Common Market membership Rodgers emphasised the changing pattern of Britain's trade. Although the 1959 manifesto had proclaimed that "half our trade is with the Commonwealth, and the new Commonwealth Economic Consultative Council will provide further opportunities for expansion," it had become clear shortly afterwards (if not at the time) that the Commonwealth proportion was falling as that of the EEC countries rose. The EEC, Rodgers noted, was the fastest-growing trade area in the world. By the end of the year, tariffs between the Six would be cut by up to 50%, and some major British exports – he mentioned motor cars, textiles and machinery – would have to pay a higher tariff in the EEC than goods produced inside it. Excluded from the Six, the prospect in front of the country was "indeed bleak".

The economic case for EEC membership also reflected more general fears: notably that Britain was falling behind in terms of growth and living standards. Though of course starting from a lower base, income per head in Germany, Italy, France and the Benelux countries was year after year rising faster than in the UK – in the case of the first two, more than twice as fast. The British economy, in stark contrast to – for example – the German *Wirtschaftswunder*, seemed stuck in a low-growth groove; and there was a hope that Britain could somehow "catch" economic success from its ECC partners. As Turner observes, "Europe seemed to offer a way of breaking out of the traditional cycle of stop-go economic policies".[10]

These arguments, though subject to objections on theoretical economic grounds, proved powerful politically. When Labour came to power in 1964, it was not long before they were accepted by the new government. By 1966, according to opinion polls, 43% of the public believed that joining the EEC would make Britain more prosperous, as opposed to only 16% who thought prosperity would fall.

Rodgers concluded his lecture by examining briefly the state of play in the three areas where Britain was seeking "adequate safeguards". Commonwealth trade would have to be dealt with on a commodity-by-commodity basis, and there would be "hard bargaining", particularly on temperate foodstuffs. He echoed, however, the conclusion of a Conservative Political Centre (CPC) discussion brief published in January 1962[11] that there was "no question of choosing between the Commonwealth and Europe, nor any reason why, given satisfactory arrangements for our entry, our membership of the Common Market should not be complementary to our role in the Commonwealth". Europe, the brief pointed out, was the Commonwealth's most important market, absorbing about a third of total Commonwealth exports.

As far as agriculture was concerned, Rodgers continued, farmers would still get guaranteed prices; but these would come from the market rather than the taxpayer. Food prices would rise; but £270 million in deficiency payments would be saved.

On safeguards for the other EFTA countries Rodgers said little. It had already become clear at the time, indeed, that the original idea of negotiating "six to seven" had quickly been shelved, and that – although the EEC continued to negotiate as a bloc, working out a common position in advance – each EFTA country was looking after its own interests as best it could. The general attitude to EFTA among Conservatives at this time seemed to be that it was "the European accident of the 1960s. It was a marriage on the rebound. ... The Seven, feeling rebuffed by the Six, sought solace in each other's charms. But ... were as much concerned to provoke jealousy in the beloved as to make a success of their own venture."[12] In any case, as the then Paris correspondent of the *Financial Times* pointed out in 1961,[13] "the formation of EFTA was meant to facilitate an agreement with the Six". Instead, it had made it more difficult.

Immigration and sovereignty

Rodgers also dealt with an issue which seemed to loom large at the time, but which, in the event, did not become any kind of reality until over forty years later: the fear that Britain would be "swamped by foreign labour" from other EEC counties, in particular Italy. Though often raised at the time by opponents of Common Market membership, this issue in fact hardly registered among most Conservatives, and not at all by comparison with the growing contemporary concern about immigration from the "new Commonwealth".

It has to be admitted, indeed, that the immigration issue did much to reduce the once overwhelming support for the Commonwealth among Conservatives, and helped to reconcile them to the Common Market. An opinion was more than once expressed by participants in Swinton discussions which today would almost certainly result in the suspension of party membership: "At least the people in the EEC are white and democratic. Better that than a lot of blacks run by dictators." A Bill to regulate immigration from the Commonwealth was before Parliament in 1962,* which was attacked by the future Conservative minister, John MacGregor in the New Year 1962 number of the Bow Group magazine *Crossbow*.[14] The evidence was strong "that despite Government denials the Bill has an anti-colour effect, and the attitudes of many of its supporters both in Parliament and in certain parts of the country show that this is their main reason for welcoming it".

One indication of how far Conservative interest in the Commonwealth declined and that in Europe rose during this period is provided by figures on subjects covered in Conservative publications. Between 1950 and 1959, for example, there were 7 CPC pamphlets dealing with the Commonwealth as opposed to 2 on Europe. Between 1959 and 1964, however, and between 1964 and 1969, there was only one on the Commonwealth in each period. The equivalent figures for Europe were 5 and 9. In *Crossbow* there were no fewer than 23 articles on Europe in the 1960–1964, but only 4 on the Commonwealth.

In any case, most Conservative activists were by this time fully behind the government's policy. As I myself began to point out in my own

---

* The Bill in due course became the 1962 Commonwealth Immigrants Act, which took away the right to enter the UK from all Commonwealth countries except those issued with work vouchers, and their dependants. The Act was to be strengthened in 1968, under the Wilson Labour Government, to include colonial citizens who had been issued passports by the UK government rather than that of another Commonwealth country.

lectures, the economic issues were clear-cut, and the identified problems were being resolved satisfactorily in the negotiations being conducted by Ted Heath. I did also reflect the concerns of my audiences, however, in referring to some political uncertainties. In April 1962, for example, I devoted some time to the issue of "sovereignty". Signing the Rome Treaty, I said, was not like signing any other treaty.

> It commits a country not only to actions stated in the Treaty itself, but to actions which may subsequently be advanced against the will of its own government. Though this may mean not so much a loss of sovereignty as a pooling of sovereignty, it means that a great deal will turn on the powers and voting arrangements in the various institutions of the Common Market.

Rodgers himself made a point of noting that one objective of the Rome Treaty was "ever-closer union", though the form this might take was still vague.

> Some, like de Gaulle, are in favour of a Confederation; others, like M. Spaak, favour a complete Federation on the model of the U.S. What matters is that, if we become a member, we shall be able to veto on the Council any developments we do not wish to see.

Other lecturers felt able to treat the sovereignty issue with less caution. Martin Madden MP – one of David Howell's brave seven who had voted for Common Market membership *before* the application – approvingly quoted M. Alain Peyrefitte, a confidant of de Gaulle's: "*aujourd'hui l'Europe des patries; demain la patrie européenne,*"* and concluded that "we must show that we are not hidebound by the ideas of the past, but are moving into and with the new world that is being built up for the future." "Ever-closer union" was to be welcomed, not swept under the carpet.

Not surprisingly, opinions such as these prompted lively exchanges of views. As in the many debates on Europe which would take place within the Conservative Party in the years to come, it was generally accepted that EEC membership involved a trade-off: economic benefits and greater Western unity on the one hand, limitations on national freedom of action on the other. Views as to which side of the equation weighed most heavily would of course vary.

It is therefore as untrue to say today that the issue of sovereignty and the EEC's "federal objectives" were ignored at the time as to say this of the political dimension. In 1960 the Lord Chancellor, Lord Kilmuir (who had been a pro-European of the first hour when in the House of Commons as Sir David Maxwell Fyfe) had cogently analysed the constitutional implications of signing the Treaty for Britain's sovereignty – as it happens, at the

---

* "Today the Europe of nations, tomorrow the European nation."

request of the Minister of State for Europe, Ted Heath. Later, he put them on public record in the House of Lords.

Kilmuir did not play down the importance of these implications, nor their potential for future conflict. On the primacy of Community law, he observed:

> In my view the surrenders of sovereignty involved are serious ones, and I think that, as a matter of practical politics, it will not be easy to persuade Parliament or the British public to accept them. I am sure that it would be a great mistake to underestimate the force of the objections to them. But these objections should be brought out into the open now because, if we attempt to gloss over them at this stage, those who are opposed to the whole idea of joining the Community will certainly seize on them with more damaging effect later on.[15]

The issue of "sovereignty" would in fact be a constant source of concern for Conservatives both during the debate on whether to join the Common Market and afterwards. As Crowson observes, "academics would appear unable to reach unanimity about what it is".[16] Nevertheless, anti-market-eers and later Eurosceptics would complain unremittingly about it being "lost" or "sacrificed", while pro-Europeans would repeatedly give assurances that it was really being "pooled" or "shared". In more intellectual circles, lawyers on both sides would attempt to define the term to their advantage (see, for example, "The Party divides" in Chapter Eleven). There would also be some confusion between the concepts of "national sovereignty" and "parliamentary sovereignty", except in cases like that of Enoch Powell for whom the two were inseparable.

For ordinary party members, the term meant roughly a combination of "exercising power in the world" and "running our own affairs". But these concepts were potentially in conflict. It would be a constant source of anxiety for Conservatives whether involvement in Europe meant gaining "real" sovereignty over decisions affecting us; or whether the power to take those decisions was being given away.

The geopolitical dimension

By April 1962 William Rees-Mogg – later editor of *The Times* and now, in the House of Lords, something of a Eurosceptic – was able to give a very upbeat presentation at a discussion week-end for industrialists. Mr. Heath had gone a long way towards ensuring the ultimate success of the negotiations.

As far as British industry was concerned, there was nothing at all to fear. "By joining we stand to increase our home market by 340%, whereas it only means an increase of 30% to the Common Market countries". In a stout defence of the Common Agricultural Policy (CAP), Rees-Mogg observed that "it would not be easy under this system to sacrifice the

British farmer to demands for cheap food, as has happened in the past". In any case, Britain's deficiency payment system would have to change, whether we joined the Common Market or not. Like Rodgers earlier, he spent little time on EFTA: "a problem we have put round our own necks". The problems of the Commonwealth were more serious, but soluble: association under the same terms as French overseas territories for the developing counties, special arrangements for New Zealand.

As to the political issues, Rees-Mogg forecast that "Britain was quite likely to take the lead in political developments", notably in ensuring "democratic control over a well-intentioned but uncontrolled bureaucracy". Moreover, his attitude to national sovereignty contrasted starkly with the views he was to express forty years later. Throughout history, he told a Conservative Political Centre Summer School in July 1962,[17] there had been a trend towards "the organization of economies and industries in larger units". The visible result had been that "economic power in the world has shifted towards the continental economies and away from the nation states, however highly developed". The experience of being occupied in the war had convinced most Continental countries "that the nation state was no longer an effective political defence". But Britain, "which did not go through the same experience, still tended to feel the nation state had a validity when militarily, economically and politically this had become seriously undermined".

In a later lecture at Swinton, Rees-Mogg drew the geopolitical conclusions.

> In the not-so-distant future there are likely to be four great powers in the world: the United States, the USSR, China and Europe. If we are not members of the European group, its strength will be less, but it will nevertheless occupy a powerful position, in many respects hostile to British interests. If, on the other hand, we join, we ourselves will be in a position to add to European power and to influence world events. … In the end, peace is maintained by authority; in the modern world by the authority of the Great Powers; and it is essential that in the future Britain should be a member of one of those Great Powers.

This was as clear a presentation as any of the "Europe as substitute for Empire" argument, which played a significant part in support for Common Market entry among many senior Conservatives. One, the then chairman of the Party, Lord Hailsham, was later to write: "For myself, I have never doubted that, given the dissolution of Empire, we must endeavour to create a power base in Europe adequate to solve our international and economic problems on an international scale."[18] It also echoed the arguments advanced during the post-war years by those Conservatives who believed, like Churchill, in European Union; but who, unlike Churchill, had no doubts that Britain should be part of it. One of these, Bob Boothby, had written in 1947:

Try as I do, I can see no other answer to the problems which now press upon a war-torn and distracted world than the organization of regional groups. Call them United States, Federations, Unions, Commonwealths, blocs – what you will; they should be something less than a single sovereign State, something more than a League of sovereign States.[19]

The discussion following Rees-Mogg's first lecture immediately brought out a theme which has continued ever since: the general public's (perceived) lack of information about Europe. A number of participants complained that "on the shop floor all they know about the Common Market is that it will put up food prices".

There was also a discussion on an issue which became central to the Europe debate many years later: did the government have a mandate to join the Common Market if the negotiations were successful, or would there have to be a general election? No-one mentioned a referendum.

As the negotiations progressed, it became possible to give more detailed presentations on the likely consequences of Common Market membership. The notes I took, and my own lectures, include extensive descriptions of the arrangements for different agricultural and industrial product categories. The negotiations were apparently succeeding, as the chief negotiator Ted Heath put it,[20] in reconciling "the new movements in Europe with our historic duties in the Commonwealth, to the enrichment of both". The upbeat mood was maintained in lectures by, among others, Ralph Harris (later Lord Harris) from the Institute of Economic Affairs.

The General says "Non!"

Interestingly, however, a much more cautious assessment was given in September 1962 by the future Cabinet Minister, James Prior MP (now a Baron), who noted that "the Commonwealth Prime Ministers have been unexpectedly critical; and the public opinion polls have been showing that there is undoubtedly less support for membership than there used to be".

In retrospect, this shift of opinion can be seen as only one element of the more widespread problems beginning to face the Macmillan government. In July 1962 there had been the "night of the long knives", when the Prime Minister had sacked a third of his Cabinet. The Profumo Affair – which had begun in 1961 when the then Secretary of State for War, John Profumo, had started a relationship with a London showgirl, Christine Keeler, who was also, as it happened, the mistress of a Soviet spy – was beginning to go public. The economy was going badly. Sharp political satire had moved out of its birthplaces in the Universities of Cambridge and Oxford onto television and was beginning to sap morale. Conservative activists were calling on the government to do more to "get its message across" (as do the activists of all parties when things are going wrong).

In the context of the Common Market negotiations, Prior responded that the government, throughout the negotiations, had been in considerable difficulty.

> It cannot appear too keen on joining, since this would weaken our bargaining position; nor can it appear too reticent, since it must exhibit some real will to get the problems settled. This has meant that a considerable atmosphere of uncertainty has surrounded the issue, and it has not been possible to put the case over to the country with any conviction.

In addition, the Labour Party was coming out against Common Market membership, particularly after Opposition leader Hugh Gaitskell's "thousand years of history" speech to the 1962 Labour Party Conference. Labour was using the issue to harass the government, and Conservatives in the constituencies were beginning to fear that "Europe" was a vote-loser. That November, F. F. Pearson MP also observed in a lecture that the focus of discussion about Europe was changing. In the early stages of the negotiations, public interest had largely centred on the economic aspects of the Common Market. "Now it is the political side which is the principal centre of discussion."

And it was, of course, the political side which, in January 1963, brought the negotiations to an abrupt end – "brutally, publicly and ruthlessly", as Andrew Marr describes it in his recent history of the period.[21] De Gaulle, now in an impregnable political position in France after the introduction of the Fifth Republic Constitution and a massive win by his supporters in elections to the French parliament, felt he could act as he felt fit within the context of the Six. He decided that Britain was not yet ready to join even a "*Europe des patries*". For Macmillan it was a hurtful blow: Europe had been his ace, a senior Party official was quoted as saying,[22] "and de Gaulle had trumped it". "All our policies at home and abroad are in ruins", Macmillan himself despairingly recorded.[23]

For a time, the hope was kept alive that the "friendly five" would come to Britain's rescue. This turned out to be an illusion. To begin with, some of the five were not as friendly as all that. Even the Dutch, who provided the stiffest opposition to de Gaulle for some time afterwards, gave up carrying the torch for Britain when, having won the General Election of 1964, Harold Wilson's Labour government introduced a treaty-breaking 15% import surcharge. The German Chancellor, Adenauer, was not going to put at risk the historic *rapprochement* with France – according to Churchill, after all, the key to European unity. Instead, Adenauer signed, with de Gaulle, a Treaty which effectively set up a "Franco-German axis" within the Common Market, a system which was to be continued by subsequent French Presidents and German Chancellors until the present day.

There were residual hopes that when the more free-market Ludwig Erhard, architect of the West German economic miracle, took over from

Adenauer in October Germany might prove more helpful. That, too, turned out to be wishful thinking.

In any case, the Six were soon too busy with internal problems of their own to worry greatly about Britain's position. The EEC was certainly proving an economic success: the dismantling of internal tariffs was proceeding ahead of schedule, and economic growth was, by comparison with Britain's at least, healthy. Politically, however, the tensions were mounting. Most of the six governments, together with the Commission, supported the aims of the founding fathers for full political union. De Gaulle had very different ideas. The tension would culminate in a show-down between the Commission, which had put forward ambitious plans on EEC finance, and the French government, resulting in the "empty chair" boycott of the Common Market's institutions by France between July 1965 and January 1966.

Conservative responses

The records of a Swinton course for constituency officers in March 1963 provide a good indication of the effect of de Gaulle's veto on Conservative opinion. As one lecturer, Richard Bailey, observed, there appeared to be three schools of thought, believing respectively

1   that the negotiations were succeeding and that ending them was all the fault of the French;
2   that the negotiations would not, regrettably, have succeeded as the remaining issues were intractable; and
3   that we had had a lucky escape.

All these opinions were represented, though of course the main concern of constituency officers was the effect on the Conservative vote at the approaching general election. I myself, lecturing on the completely different subject of opposition policies, remarked that at least there was one silver lining: the veto had removed hostility to the Common Market as a Labour weapon.

At the time, the first school of thought was in the majority: the episode triggered a lot of anti-French feeling. Macmillan and Heath had discussed tactics in the negotiations in May of 1962, and had concluded (as recorded by Macmillan)[24] that "the strange feature of the present situation is the paradox that de Gaulle wants a kind of Europe we would be able readily to join, but he doesn't want us in it (*L'Europe à l'anglais sans les anglais*). ... He hates England – still more America – because of the war, because of Churchill and Roosevelt, because of the nuclear weapons."

From the start, indeed, those involved had clearly considered the possi-bility of a French veto. Ted Heath's great friend from university days, Madron Seligman – who, in 1979 would become one of the first elected Members of the European Parliament – recalled that Heath prepared for the negotiations by "studying de Gaulle as an adversary, reading all his memoirs and speeches". It is true that Macmillan had later recorded that "I find it difficult to be sure about de Gaulle's attitude";[25] but it was the earlier perception that became the standard opinion in the Party following the veto.

Even at this time, however, some expressed a more detached view: that de Gaulle's action was not entirely unjustified. Given his known opinions about "Anglo-Saxons", part of the negotiating strategy should have been to allay his fears that Britain was an American fifth column. The signing of the Nassau Agreement with the United States in late 1962, under which the US undertook to supply Britain with the Polaris submarine-based missile system,[*] so tying Britain inextricably with the US in the field of nuclear weapons, was bound to have exactly the opposite effect. As Jock Bruce-Gardyne (who had spent three and a half years as the Paris correspondent of the *Financial Times*) wrote in the Spring edition of the Bow Group magazine *Crossbow*: "It is the 'special relationship', and nothing else, which has kept us out of Europe."[26] Paul-Henri Spaak, at the heart of the negotiations on the EEC side, had no doubts. He told a Greater London Area Young Conservatives conference in 1967 that "nobody can contest that the *volte face* of 1963 was a consequence of the Nassau Agreement".[27] Henry Kissinger, no less, has written that the Agreement "could not have been timed more disastrously for Britain's application for membership of the Common Market".[28]

Yet Macmillan claimed in his memoirs[29] that Nassau could not have been the cause of the veto, since he had told de Gaulle about Britain's position well in advance in a meeting at the President's official residence at Rambouillet. It is, in fact, conceivable that the whole episode was the result of a terrible and fatal misunderstanding: Macmillan thought he had told de Gaulle about Polaris, whereas de Gaulle thought Macmillan was ready to co-operate on a Franco-British system. But nobody can check on the record because "the vital conversations were held *à deux* without an interpreter there, and were conducted in French".[30] Even more alarming, the French ambassador to London at the time, Jean Chauvel, later told Ted Heath that it was "such a pity that Macmillan went to sleep when de Gaulle was talking to him after lunch!".[31]

More seriously, in Nora Beloff's view it was "doubtful whether there was ever any real meeting of minds ... and their mutual habit of speaking in generalities and surveying the world from Himalayan heights may well have led them to imagine themselves much closer than they really were".[32]

It can also be plausibly argued, however, that the Polaris agreement played no part in de Gaulle's thinking, "as he had already made up his

---

[*] Britain had originally intended to equip its V-bombers with the air-launched Skybolt system, which was being developed jointly with the US. Following a series of test failures, however, the US decided to cancel the project, leaving Britain without a credible warhead delivery system. Equipping the Royal Navy with Polaris missiles and the submarines to launch them eventually resolved the crisis.

mind to keep Britain out".[33] According to Heath, de Gaulle was worried that the British application to join the Common Market was "just a game".[34] On the other hand, the Polaris affair *did* "provide him with a splendid justification of his view".

As I myself discovered many years later in discussions with French politicians, the French objection to Nassau was not so much to the purchase of an American system, as to the conditions for its use. Polaris was "assigned" to NATO in normal circumstances. Only when "supreme national interests were at stake" would this not be so. "But are you absolutely certain," the French would ask me, "that, in the event, you could fire a nuclear weapon – for example, at the United States?"

In retrospect, had we been really determined on Common Market entry, we *would* have offered to co-operate in developing an Anglo-French deterrent. But not many Conservatives at the time were willing to contemplate a move that radical.

As far as the second school of thought was concerned, it is true that, as F. F. Pearson MP had pointed out, "the further the negotiations progress, the more difficult are the outstanding items". The problem of Australian soft wheat, which was in direct competition with French wheat, was proving particularly difficult to resolve. The EFTA dossier, although not given very high priority, had hardly been opened. On the other hand, there was no reason to believe that Heath's indefatigable team would not have eventually arrived at solutions. Pearson had forecast tough negotiations "through the next five or six months". Macmillan, clearly of the first school of thought, held the view that "the end did not come because the discussions were menaced with failure. On the contrary, it was because they threatened to succeed".[35]

A sub-group in the second school of thought, however, believed that the negotiations would probably have succeeded, but that they would not have been approved by Parliament: Labour MPs would have combined with Conservative rebels to defeat implementing legislation. Here the state of public opinion could have been significant. The Gallup poll had shown that Macmillan's decision to open negotiations was supported by a margin of four to one. As the negotiations proceeded, however, the polls had revealed an interesting pattern. When the news from Brussels was good, i.e. when the negotiations were going well, a steady 55% favoured Britain's entry, while when the negotiations were going badly, this figure fell to 45%.[36]

It was therefore reasonable to conclude that, had the negotiations ended in success, this fact would in itself have favourably affected public attitudes. On the other hand, there was no doubt that the country, and to a lesser extent, the Conservative Party, was seriously split. Could the momentous step into the Common Market be taken, when the numbers supporting membership never outnumbered the "antis" and "don't knows" together?

This was a point emphasised by those who had opposed membership all along, to whom the collapse of the accession negotiations proved a great fillip. Apart from those with open links to the League of Empire Loyalists, anti-Market Conservatives had kept reasonably quiet during the negotiations in order not to rock the party boat. Now they were able to put their case without fear of being thought disloyal. Essentially their belief was that Britain could now go back to the *status quo ante*, develop Commonwealth trade and continue some version of the three circles.

But this, as all governments since have had to realise in the end, was already little more than nostalgia. The negotiations had in themselves changed the situation, and made a return to the past impossible. As an anti-Market pamphlet[37] (to be discussed more fully later) itself put it, Britain's policy of seeking Common Market membership "leaves the Commonwealth in no doubt that the belief in this relationship as anything more than a pleasant anachronism has died in Britain and that other arrangements must be made".

Notes

1 Jenkins *op.cit.* p. 856.
2 *The Conservative Party 1918–1970* by T. F. Lindsay and Michael Harrington (Macmillan, 1974) p. 214.
3 *This Blessed Plot* by Hugo Young, Chapter 4, "Harold Macmillan: agonizing for Britain" (Macmillan 1998) p. 114.
4 Macmillan *At the End of the Day*, p. 1.
5 Crowson *op.cit.* p. 186.
6 Macmillan *At the End of the Day*, p. 8.
7 *The Course of My Life: the autobiography of Edward Heath* (Hodder and Stoughton 1998).
8 Macmillan *At the End of the Day*, p. 333.
9 *Euroscepticism in Contemporary British Politics* by Anthony Forster (Routledge, 2002).
10 Turner *op.cit.* p. 52.
11 *The Commonwealth and the Common Market: a brief for CPC discussion groups* by Peter Minoprio (Conservative Political Centre, January 1962). Minoprio later became Secretary-General of the European Democratic Group in the elected European Parliament.
12 "EFTA" by Geoffrey Smith in *Crossbow*, October–December 1964.
13 "The Common Market: way in for Britain?" by Christopher Johnson in *Crossbow*, New Year 1961.
14 "Immigration and Europe" by John Macgregor in *Crossbow*, New Year 1962 (Bow Group).
15 Public Records Office (PRO), FO 371/150369.
16 Crowson *op.cit.* p. 85.
17 "Industry and the Common Market" in *The New Europe* by the Rt. Hon Edward Heath, Dr. Hans Nord, Emile Noël, William Rees-Mogg, William Clark and Richard Bailey (CPC, August 1962).
18 *The Door Wherein I Went* by Lord Hailsham (Collins, 1975) p.106.
19 *I Fight to Live* by Robert Boothby MP (Victor Gollancz, 1947) p. 370.
20 Introduction to *The New Europe*.
21 *A History of Modern Britain* by Andrew Marr (Macmillan, 2007), p. 205.
22 In *The British General Election of 1964* by David Butler and Anthony King (Macmillan 1965).
23 Macmillan *At the End of the Day*, p. 367.
24 Macmillan *At the End of the Day*, p. 118.
25 Macmillan *At the End of the Day*, p. 121.
26 "Should we join the USA?" by John Bruce-Gardyne (aka Jock Bruce-Gardyne). Article in *Crossbow*, April–June 1963 (Bow Group).

27 *Face to Face with Europe* by Paul-Henri Spaak (CPC, May 1967).

28 *The Troubled Partnership* by Henry Kissinger (McGraw-Hill, 1965) p. 84.

29 Macmillan *At the End of the Day*, p. 367.

30 The journalist and author Kenneth Young in his biography *Sir Alec Douglas-Home* (J.M.Dent & Sons, 1970).

31 *The Course of My Life, the autobiography of Edward Heath*, p. 239.

32 Beloff *op.cit.* p. 150.

33 *A Smaller Stage* by Leon Brittan, Julian Critchley, Hugh Dykes, Russell Lewis and David Walder MP (Bow Group, December 1965).

34 Heath *op.cit.* p. 225.

35 Speech on 11 February, 1963.

36 *Britain and Europe since the Breakdown* by Hugh Beesley, Political Counsellor at the Council of Europe (*Swinton Journal*, March 1964). The article was based on a talk given at the College in December 1993.

37 *No Tame or Minor Role* by Leonard Beaton, Michael McNair-Wilson, Timothy Raison, Geoffrey Smith, John Wakelin and Sir Robin Williams (Bow Group, 1963).

3   Finding a Role

"A dead duck"

"Since the negotiations at Brussels came to an end," Russell Lewis (journalist and later also Director of the Conservative Political Centre) began a lecture on "Britain, Europe and the Commonwealth" in May 1963, "there has been a tendency in this country to view the problem of the Common Market as a dead issue." This view was certainly widespread in the Conservative Party, even among its leadership: Sir Alec Douglas-Home, who took over from Harold Macmillan as PM later that year, was reported to have described it as "a dead duck".

One reaction, reflected in lectures and discussions at Swinton, was to conclude that the "European solution" was perhaps already out of date, and to focus instead on the wider international context. A course in June 1963 covered the Kennedy Round of proposed cuts in tariffs through the GATT, the Triffin Plan to expand the role of the IMF, the Basle agreement between European Central Banks and even the COMECON (the Council for Mutual Economic Assistance of the Soviet bloc), to which British exports were rising. The Rt. Hon. Dame Patricia Hornsby-Smith, DBE, MP, spoke on the United Nations (not always Conservatives' favourite body), which had to be "made to work" in keeping peace throughout the world, but which had also had great success "in the far less publicised field of the war on poverty, want and disease".

Salt had been rubbed into the wound – admittedly a short time in advance – by the celebrated remark of US Secretary of State Dean Acheson in December 1962 that Britain had "lost an Empire and (had) not yet found a role." I was reflecting the reaction of many Conservatives when I said in a lecture in July 1965 (as it happened, my last as a Swinton tutor) that we should have been even angrier at his later assertion that Britain had been "banished" from Europe "at the time of the Plantagenets". "Waterloo, the trenches and the Liberation are evidence that we have been very much part of Europe since then," I said. "The fault lies in thinking that Europe consists of only the Common Market."

Yet, as Russell Lewis went on to observe in his earlier lecture, "the emergence of the European Community of the Six, and the changed position of

Britain in the world, are facts which still face us, and give rise to problems of increasing importance". It had been a mistake to emphasise trade as the main economic argument for Common Market membership, he said. The real reason for joining was to "take part in formulating the common policies needed by the West and by Western Europe".

As the Common Market was completed, and the Six began take further steps towards economic integration, this argument was to grow in importance. European countries outside the EEC increasingly had to adapt to decisions taken by the Six in which they had played no part. One good, if technical, example was the adoption by the Common Market of Value Added Tax (VAT) as the common indirect tax system. This enabled businesses based in the Six selling into third-country markets to rebate all indirect tax on exports, thus giving them a competitive edge over businesses based in countries like Britain which retained Purchase Tax. As a result, Britain was already planning a switch-over to VAT in the 1970s, whether inside or outside the EEC.*

Nevertheless, though the reality was as Lewis described it, interest in, and support for, Common Market membership fell off markedly in the following years. The movements of opinion are well documented by two pamphlets published by the Bow Group: the first, *Britain into Europe,*[1] in August 1962; the second, *No Tame or Minor Role,*[2] in September 1963. Both, as Crowson records,[3] were only approved for publication by narrow majorities in the Group's publications committee.

Bow Group views: the case for Europe

Of all the groupings within the Conservative Party, the Bow Group has probably been, over the years, the most influential. The One Nation Group, formed in 1950 and comprising most of the leading Conservatives of subsequent years, was critical in the development of Conservative thinking in the 1950s, but was confined to existing MPs. Others – the Monday Club, Pressure for Economic and Social Toryism (PEST), the Selsdon Group, the Bruges Group, the Tory Reform Group (TRG) – have all had their moments. But ever since its formation in February 1951 at the Bow and Bromley Constitutional Club, the Bow Group has influenced Conservative policy through a steady stream of pamphlets, reports and research papers and its magazine *Crossbow*. A steady stream of Bow Groupers, too, has

---

* N.J.Crowson, in *The Conservative Party and European Integration since 1945*, considers that the adoption of VAT in the UK "is entirely due to EEC entry" (p.99); and he quotes party sources from 1969 urging that the adoption VAT should be Conservative policy as evidence of "meaning business" on Europe. However, my own experience, as someone working at Conservative Central Office at the time, and on occasions responsible for preparing briefings on VAT, is that EEC entry was only a minor factor. More important were the considerations of international competitivity described here. In fact, the adoption of VAT had been recommended by "Neddy" – the National Economic Development Council (NEDC) – as early as 1963. Within the Conservative Party, the arguments for adoption were outlined in a 1967 pamphlet published by the CPC: *A Tax for Our Time* by Anthony Mitton.

found its way into the House of Commons, and then into Conservative Governments. Indeed one of the original Bow-groupers, Geoffrey Howe, wrote in 1982[4] – when he had become the Rt. Hon. Sir Geoffrey Howe QC, MP and Chancellor of the Exchequer – that "in more than one way, today's Conservative government represents the 'Bow Group' generation".

The formation of the Group derived from a resolution passed at the 1950 annual conference of FUCUA (the Federation of University Conservative and Unionist Associations), which had called for "an effective counter to 'intellectual' Socialism and the Fabian Society"; and members have been mainly recruited in the universities (I myself was interviewed and subsequently admitted to membership by Leon Brittan at Cambridge in 1959). At its height, the Group had some thousand members. The Group's aim has been "to gather together younger Conservatives in an independent research society", and it has always claimed to be "in no sense a pressure group" and not to stand "for any special kind of Conservatism – left, right or centre". In the 1950s and 1960s, nevertheless, it was generally considered to be on the "progressive" wing of the Party, broadly supporting, for example, the stance of Iain Macleod on such issues as decolonisation and race relations. In later years its image shifted towards the centre – or perhaps the Conservative Party itself shifted. A study of Bow Group publications and articles, at all events, provides an excellent guide to the changing strands of thinking within the Conservative Party over the last sixty years.

In the case of the Common Market issue, the two pamphlets noted above had been preceded by one which was published when the Free Trade Area proposals were still on the table, and which has been quoted earlier.[5] The author was Russell Lewis. One of his main arguments was "the fillip which increased competition in the home market will give to British industry".

This argument appears only briefly, and tangentially, in *Britain into Europe*: "In the big European market, for almost every industry, competition can be maintained concurrently with the full exploitation of economies of scale." The chapter on "Why Britain must join" concentrates instead on the political dimension, which it makes no attempt to play down.

> It is important to recognise that, though the Common Market is concerned almost exclusively with economic affairs, it aims at European political unity. ... The argument for Britain's joining cannot therefore be confined to the implications of the Treaty of Rome alone, but must justify joining a movement directed at creating a political unity as well.

A number of arguments for British membership follow.

First, the authors go back to the original case for the European Defence Community: the German question. "It is of the greatest importance for the peace and stability of the world that the Germans should aspire to a European ideal rather than espouse the cause of pan-Germanism. ... " The alternative, a deal with the Soviet Union for a neutralised Germany, "would make the defence of Western Europe impossible".

It then refers to a need to "provide a more solid base from which to negotiate a settlement with the Soviet bloc", quoting Churchill's memorandum of 1942 that "it would be a measureless disaster if Russian barbarism overlaid the culture and independence of the ancient States or Europe". The Western alliance would be a healthier structure, "if the Western European nations were united".

There then follows an economic argument which can only strike one today as bizarre.

> If the West is to rival the rapid rates of industrial growth accomplished in the Soviet bloc it will be necessary to take a leaf out of their book. For it is an interesting fact that planning in Russia and her satellites ... is now carried out at the regional level. Comecon, the Soviet equivalent of the Common Market, draws up production plans on the basis that each part of the area will specialise in those goods which its endowment of natural resources and human skills best qualifies it to make. The doctrine of specialisation applies with equal force to Western Europe, and it is the Common Market programme which can carry it into effect.

Although the pamphlet later notes that "the Community already has some experience of planning", particularly the High Authority of the ECSC, it is doubtful if the EEC Commission, even in its heady early days under its first President, the German Professor Walter Hallstein, ever aspired to such powers. It is necessary to remember, however, that this was the period when economic planning, particularly the "indicative planning" pioneered by Jean Monnet in France, was at the peak of its popularity. Even a Conservative Government in Britain had created a framework for its own version of Госплан,* with "Neddy" (the National Economic Development Council, containing "Neddo", an office of some forty economists) and "Nicky" (the National Incomes Commission). That it would all end in tears – more spectacularly in the Soviet bloc than in Britain – was not widely predicted at the time.

The final main argument of *Britain into Europe* is that Britain, together with EFTA countries, had a great deal to add to the Common Market. "Fortified by Britain and Scandinavia, where stable democratic arrangements have strong roots, European institutions could prove an anchor of political stability."

Almost as an afterthought, the pamphlet adds an argument which, in retrospect, has proved of some importance: "Britain's membership of a united Europe will also help to solve one of the West's most pressing

---

* *Gosplan*, the State Planning Committee of the USSR.

problems – that of aid to underdeveloped countries." The problem at the time, for Africa in particular, was the existence of two competing preference areas: that of Britain and the Commonwealth; and that of countries associated with the EEC. The eventual merging of these into the present African, Caribbean and Pacific (ACP) grouping has arguably been one of the Common Market's most useful achievements. The European Union, as it now is, is the world's largest giver of aid to what are now called developing countries.

The rest of the pamphlet is largely taken up with an outline of the Common Market policies and their likely impact in Britain. This concludes by an examination of the sovereignty issue. Over a large area of policy it emphasises that unanimity in the Council of Ministers would be required: i.e. the UK would have a veto. On the issue of majority voting it correctly points out that this "is in practice a last resort, and the Council machinery is looked upon as a means of reaching a generally accepted agreement".

The final section deals with likely future developments. One possibility would be an increasingly energetic and powerful Commission, though "not everyone would ... wish to see the growth of a Federation linked with the rise to power of a federal bureaucracy". Direct elections to the European Parliament* represented another way forward. Finally, on the table was the Fouchet Plan for common foreign and defence policies. On all these proposals the pamphlet limits itself to the cautious "wait-and-see" attitude on political union expressed in the negotiations by Heath.

Bow Group views: the case against

One can find in the second Bow Group pamphlet most of the arguments, particularly on the political dimension, which have survived intact within the Conservative Party until today.

No Tame or Minor Role begins by noting that failure to get into the Common Market had "left the country in considerable confusion". It had become widely believed that prosperity and the best political and military future lay in the creation of unified Western Europe, and that Britain would face isolation outside. But "in politics, myths have a way of returning to haunt their authors. There is an urgent need to dispose of the myth that some sort of calamity faced the country if it did not join the EEC."

The first section then consists of a quite detailed analysis of the terms which had already been agreed during the accession negotiations. It notes that there had been an assumption from the start that the Rome Treaty would not be amended, but that the solutions to the problems of British accession would be essentially transitional arrangements. Hence the answer to the problem of imports from the Commonwealth largely concerned the rate at which Britain would impose the Common External

---

* Still at this time formally the "Assembly", though calling itself the "Parliament". The pamphlet used both terms at different points.

Tariff (CET). The EEC had agreed to cut this to zero on only a limited group of products, especially sensitive for the British, including "tea, cricket bats, polo sticks, kangaroo meat and tinned and frozen rabbit". In the case of the African and Caribbean Commonwealth countries, where association status was on offer, only the West Indian states had welcomed it whole-heartedly. Ghana, Nigeria and Tanganyika had rejected it, largely because they "feared a resurgence of outside domination – not from a Britain they know well but from a new and unknown European great power".

In the case of British agriculture, substantial savings for the Exchequer on deficiency payments would be offset by a heavy cost to the consumer, less prosperity for the farmer (whose cost of imported feed from Commonwealth countries would rise) and a heavy burden on the balance of payments under the Financial Regulation. This last issue, not much discussed at the time, nevertheless returned in spades during the 1970s in the form of Harold Wilson's "renegotiation" and in the 1980s in the form of "Maggie's money".

These terms, the authors concluded, "taken together, were as bad as the French could make them". Accepting them would be inconsistent with the pledges given on "vital Commonwealth interests".

The second section of the pamphlet covers the political issues; and this is where the authors' real objections to Common Market membership clearly lay. They met head-on the argument that Britain would only be able to maintain its influence in the world by joining a larger grouping.

> If Britain had a special part to play with the Americans, the Commonwealth or the Communist world, it would be played through European institutions and in the name of Europe. But there is a strong chance that our views would, so to speak, be eliminated in the European preliminary. In that event, we might find ourselves forced to accept a policy which was uncongenial to the British people.

This now reads rather oddly in the light of the Blair Labour Government's ability to conduct a completely independent policy on Iraq, and the ability of "new Europe" to cock a snook at the position of "old Europe" on the issue. It does, however, chime in with recent Conservative reservations on the foreign policy implications of the Lisbon Treaty.

No Tame or Minor Role also casts doubt on the argument that Britain would naturally be taking a leading role – for example, in democratising the institutions.

> The continuing and ever-surprising failure of the French, Germans and Italians to adopt the methods of government in which the British can operate with any satisfaction is not a misfortune associated with the shortcomings of their present leadership: it is a difference of temperamental outlook which they have no intention of remedying.

This is, in fact, a slightly more down-to-earth version of the views expressed by Eden and Macmillan, quoted earlier; or, indeed, of de Gaulle at the press conference of the 14th January 1963 at which he vetoed the Macmillan government's application.

The section continues by outlining what would emerge as the crucial "sovereignty" argument, later developed in its most cogent form by Enoch Powell. The British people would find themselves in "a new political complex".

> The point is not that the powers of the national parliaments and governments would be circumscribed – they have always been by the realities of international power politics – but that the laws and regulations would be made on behalf of the people and decisions taken in their name by organs of government which were not accountable to them alone. There is a strong possibility that the British would find themselves in a political complex which they did not understand and which did not yet have the homogeneity and common allegiance which is needed to sustain constitutional politics.

The section next examines the idea that a united Europe would help strengthen the Atlantic Alliance and the security of Europe in the face of the Soviet threat. The Kennedy/Monnet idea of NATO based on the "twin pillars" of the US and a united Europe nevertheless created the risk that the US might withdraw from the European pillar, leaving it to fend for itself against a Russian army "half way to the Bay of Biscay".

Finally, the section raises the dangers of creating a *Nineteen Eighty-four*-like world divided into antagonistic blocs: "the triumph of continentalism over the mercantile tradition". As 1984 has come and gone, Britain already for some years inside the EEC, without anything like George Orwell's predictions coming to pass, this argument may now seem fanciful. The reality has, in fact, been the opposite: "globalisation", the triumph of the mercantile tradition over continentalism. At the time, however, it was taken seriously. In the mid-1960s I happened to find myself on the anti-Market side of a debate between Fulham YCs and Chelsea YCs, and used the spectre of *Nineteen Eighty-four* as my main argument. I won without difficulty.

It is when the pamphlet starts outlining policy for a Britain outside the Common Market that it begins to grow vague. While admitting that Commonwealth trade had accounted for a declining proportion of British exports – down from 40.8% in 1952 to 32% in 1962 (and sales to the EEC in the decade had risen by more than 100% compared to 20% in the case of the Commonwealth) – it expresses a hope that the Commonwealth might "provide expanding markets in the future." The best alternative to Europe for Britain might be the Kennedy Round of tariff cuts under the GATT; and there is the suggestion of a "new free trade area" including both EFTA and the US. If free trade led to balance of payments problem and currency instability there might be an "Atlantic Payments Union".

As to the political dimension, the authors stated their view that "Britain should openly and frankly return to the three circles ... " As far as the European pillar was concerned, "our duty ... will best be done by cultivating our particular character and seeking genuine cooperation from a position of strength." And they concluded with the stirring words:

> Britain, through her unique relationship with the Commonwealth, the United States and Western Europe has the opportunity to become the linchpin of the free world. ... To become side-tracked into the creation of a European great power is to sacrifice a unique destiny.

In opposition

Mainstream opinion in the Conservative Party, however, soon recovered from de Gaulle's veto, and returned to support for Common Market entry. This was particularly true when, in 1965, Ted Heath became leader of the Party. The One Nation Group of MPs in that year published a pamphlet, *One Europe*,[6] under the editorship of Nicholas Ridley – then a self-confessed "federalist", but who would in 1990 be forced to resign from the Thatcher government by describing the proposal for a Single Currency, in an interview with *Spectator* editor Dominic Lawson, son of Nigel Lawson, as "a German racket designed to take over the whole of Europe".[7] *One Europe* restated the argument that "we can no longer develop our economy, our defences, our influence from outside the Common Market".

Andrew Roth, in a book published in 1970,[8] claimed that 25% of *One Europe* was written by Enoch Powell; and Hugo Young adds that Powell "never denied it". His name does not appear as one of the listed authors. On the other hand, his name *is* listed as a supporting member of the One Nation Group, so that it can at least be assumed that, at the time, he agreed with its conclusions. One explanation offered is that, as a member of the shadow cabinet, he was prevented from signing as an author.

Most of the themes in this pamphlet are the familiar ones from the time of the negotiations, with perhaps a greater emphasis on the need for cooperation on defence – even for the creation of a European nuclear deterrent based on a pooling of resources by Britain and France. There is a significant new element, however: a fear that, having "missed the bus" in 1963, Britain would find it increasingly difficult to get on another one. The EEC, indeed, was implementing the Rome Treaty even more rapidly than the timetable laid down. Each new agreement, *One Europe* notes, "leaves the Six more complete, making it harder for Britain to adjust herself. ... Each decision is the result of a compromise between the different member countries, leaving less room for a further compromise with a newcomer such as Britain." This problem, which would come to be known as that of the *acquis communautaire*, was to become of increasing importance as the Six both "widened and deepened" in later years. By the beginning of the twenty-first century, the newest arrivals from Central and Eastern Europe had little option but to adopt it lock, stock and barrel.

Meanwhile, *One Europe* observes, Commonwealth trade had continued to decline, "despite the preferences"; and trade with Europe had continued to expand, "despite the Common External Tariff. ... How much greater might [the European trade] expand if the tariff were no more?"

The second new element in the pamphlet followed on from the first. "The first major line of advance ... must be to prepare Britain for entry by starting to make some of the alterations to our economic life which will bring us more into line with Europe. ... " Arrangements for agriculture, coal, steel and other industries would have to change. Anti-cartel and monopoly laws would need to be tightened up on similar lines to the EEC's competition policy. Above all, every effort should be made to co-operate with EEC countries on specific projects, of which Concorde provided an example. The enormous R&D costs of high-technology projects in any case required both spreading the load of development, and a wider market for the eventual products.

On the political dimension of *One Europe*, however, the authors were less bold. It was not necessary to "take sides in the dispute between the Federalists and the Confederalists, even though we might prefer a looser association to start with. Once we are members we can share with the others the task of working out the solution to this problem."

This position – which of course continued the attitude of the Conservative Government in the early 1960s, and was to continue as that of the next Conservative Government during the successful negotiations in the early 1970s – seemed eminently practical and pragmatic at the time. It did nevertheless contain the seeds of future trouble. By having no, or very few, firm views on the future political development of the Common Market in the run-up to accession, the leadership of the Party left itself open to the charge in future years that it had misled voters.

What kind of Europe?

This is not to say that thinking about the possible political development of the Common Market was absent in the Conservative Party. In the Spring of 1962, when the negotiations were still taking place, an article in *Crossbow* by Gordon Pears (who had earlier worked in the WEU) observed that "there is no inevitability about the movement towards European unity." De Gaulle's "*Europe des patries*" he described as "essentially a negative approach, concerned more with what should not develop than what should." Uncertainty about the political future was likely to persist for some time. On the other hand, if countries surrendered their control of economic policy to the extent required to implement the Rome Treaty, the surrender of political independence was bound to follow, whether planned or not. Political Europe would be "an organic growth – and as such should endear itself to Tory intellectuals at least".

Much of the first number of *Crossbow* in the following year was devoted to articles on the theme "beyond the nation state". In it, Gordon Pears turned to the question: "What will happen if our state becomes part of a super-state?"

He dealt first with the question of the Monarchy, and concluded that there was no reason to believe that it would be affected, since the headship of state in Britain was "separated from the exercise of power". Nor would the Common Law be affected, except where "the continued existence of more than one law ... covering the same field would frustrate the efficient working of the Treaty". His treatment of the "sovereignty of the House of Commons", however, was more controversial.

> As parliamentarians are treated with contempt in all European countries (including this one), they may turn to the new supra-national institutions and find that there is the opportunity for genuine democratic control.

The real issue, however, would be "the extent of real power which Brussels will possess;" and the best way of assessing this would be "who will do the taxing". His answer (apart from defence expenditure, which would have to be "organised collectively") was, first, that "the big government expenditure will continue to be on things among which it can be allotted on a strictly national basis". But secondly, taxation was "a major weapon of economic policy and substantial differences in its incidence ... could distort the pattern of the Community's trade or economic development. ... By and large, diversities among national taxation systems can be permitted as far as their effect on individual incomes are concerned; but company tax will have to be harmonised quickly, and so will most general sales taxes."

It is interesting to compare this assessment in 1963 with what has actually occurred. The Common Market has not developed into anything like a super-state. On the other hand, many of the matters raised by Pears became the subject of intense debate within the Conservative Party in the context of the European Community of the 1970s and 1980s and now of the European Union of the 1990s and early twenty-first century.

On the future of the Monarchy, an issue which aroused intense passions, the assessment has turned out correct, as it has on the matter of the Common Law (though this has perhaps begun to be an issue in the context of the Lisbon Treaty). On the House of Commons – though public contempt for MPs has certainly grown – Pears' prediction has been fulfilled only very partially. The European Parliament has gained power over the Commission and legislation, and was directly elected from 1979 onwards, it is true; but still has a long way to go before justifying the claim of the first Chairman of its Rules and Petitions Committee – amazingly the left-wing British Labour MP Willie Hamilton – that "the power is here, the museum's at Westminster".

The most interesting divergence, however, is on the question of the power of "Brussels". Apart from the completely unfulfilled prediction that defence expenditure would be pooled, the forecasts on taxation have turned out nearly correct. The whole EU budget has remained at only about 1% of GDP, and for most of its history has only been important in the field of agriculture. VAT has replaced all Purchase and Sales Taxes; but corporate taxes have been harmonised only to the extent needed to prevent blatantly unfair practices (and that mostly through inter-govern-mental coordination rather than legislation).

Yet this has not prevented a belief, recently widespread in the Conservative Party, that Britain is being "run from Brussels" – or at least that there is a danger of this happening. Concentrating on the classical attribute of national parliamentary sovereignty, the Power of the Purse, Pears overlooked the much more complex matter of the regulatory envi-ronment – what a future Conservative Foreign Secretary, Douglas Hurd, would describe as interference in the "nooks and crannies of everyday life"; and Lord Denning, in a famous judgment in 1972, as "an incoming tide" that "cannot be held back".

What alternatives?

Inspiring though their rhetoric may have been, the Achilles heel of those Conservatives who opposed British entry into the Common Market in the 1960s was their inability to come up with a convincing alternative. It was not enough to say that the alternative to joining was *not* joining. Britain's increasingly serious economic difficulties, the changing pattern of trade, the Cold War and the melting away of the Empire appeared to require some vision of the way forward.

Writing in the Autumn 1963 edition of *Crossbow*, another former Paris correspondent of the *Financial Times*, Christopher Johnson, criticised the pamphlet *No Tame or Minor Role* precisely for having advanced only a "rag-bag of simultaneous alternatives". The Commonwealth as an alternative came up against the problem that "Commonwealth countries, developed or undeveloped, all want to protect their industries". EFTA was "relatively small, and Sweden and Switzerland are traditionally low-tariff countries, so that any preferences they give British exports is of marginal value". GATT tariff cuts and world monetary reform were policies which should be pursued anyway, and were not genuine alternatives. As for being "the linchpin of the free world" at the intersection of the three circles, this would actually condemn Britain to "shrink to a geometer's point".

The one serious alternative which tempted Conservatives at this time seems to have been an extension of the "special relationship" with the United States. Writing in the January-March *Crossbow*, the future Conservative Minister and future European Commissioner Leon Brittan observed that "talking to an American of a comparable background, an Englishman will often feel that he is on the same intellectual wavelength after an astonishingly short time. Only a handful of Englishmen can honestly say that they feel this so readily in the case of Europeans."[9] Britain and the United States shared "certain unique features in the *distribution* of their international efforts. ... The instinctive common understanding that tends to emerge from this is assisted by the historical fact that it is broadly speaking Britain's role in the world that the United States has taken over." Under the cross-head "Kennedy Toryism", Brittan also noted "the essential compatibility of the Kennedy and Macmillan administrations".

It was, however, precisely this view that Jock Bruce-Gardyne, writing in the following edition of *Crossbow*, accused of "keeping us out of Europe". As proof that de Gaulle had not been alone in doubting Britain's European credentials he drew attention to the vote in the European Parliament – then composed of members nominated from the six national parliaments – where a motion criticising the General, tabled immediately after the veto, had failed to carry. He concluded that those who believed that our future was inextricably tied up with the US "should have the courage of their convictions".

They should recognise that these will inevitably involve turning our backs on Europe; and that the only logical basis for the sort of relationship with America which they desire is full membership of the American Union. We might be only another Texas or California.

Notes

1 *Britain into Europe* by William Russell, Jock Bruce-Gardyne, John Macgregor, Patrick Jenkin, Robert Erith and Talbot Hainault (CPC for the Bow Group 1962).
2 *No Tame or Minor Role* by Leonard Beaton, Michael McNair-Wilson, Timothy Raison, Geoffrey Smith, John Wakelin and Sir Robin Williams (Bow Group, 1963).
3 Crowson *op.cit.* p. 123.
4 *Conservatism in the Eighties* by The Rt.Hon.Sir Geoffrey Howe, QC, MP (CPC, September 1982).
5 *Challenge from Europe: Britain, the Commonwealth and Free Trade Area* by Russell Lewis (Bow Group, 1957).
6 *One Europe* by Lord Balniel, Robert Carr, Paul Channon, Christopher Chataway, William Deedes, Charles Fletcher-Cooke, Ian Gilmour, Philip Goodhart, Brian Harrison, John Hill, John Hobson, Charles Longbottom, Gilbert Longden, James Ramsden, Nicholas Ridley, John Rodgers, Anthony Royle and John Vaughan-Morgan (CPC, April 1965).
7 *The Spectator*, 14 July 1990.
8 *Enoch Powell* by Andrew Roth (Macdonald, 1970).
9 "The special relationship" by Leon Brittan in *Crossbow* January–March 1963 (Bow Group).

4   Preparing the Ground

Under new management

Until 1965, leaders of the Conservative Party had been chosen in a variety of ways, none of them very democratic. Churchill had been more or less imposed on the Party by an alliance of the Labour Party and Conservative MPs opposed to the appeasement of Nazi Germany. Eden had succeeded as the obvious heir-apparent. Macmillan had "emerged" instead of Butler, it is said as a result of decisive support from "Bobbety", the 5th Marquess of Salisbury. Sir Alec Douglas-Home had also "emerged" instead of Butler as a result of the "customary processes of consultation"* with various sections of the party – or alternatively, as alleged by Iain Macleod in a famous *Spectator* article, pushed into the job by a Tory "magic circle".[1]

Ted Heath, in July 1965, was the first to be elected by a poll of his peers: the Conservative MPs. Unexpectedly, he defeated the former Chancellor and shadow Foreign Secretary Reginald Maudling by 150 votes to 133. The third candidate, Enoch Powell, got 15. One of Heath's strengths, commentators later observed, was the reputation he had gained as the negotiator in Britain's attempt to join the Common Market, as well as his success in defying the small-shopkeeper lobby to abolish Resale Price Maintenance, and his earlier success as Chief Whip in holding the parliamentary party together during the Suez crisis.

The first statement of policy[2] under the new leadership was entirely clear about Common Market membership.

> When the present difficulties and uncertainties in Europe are resolved, we believe it would be right to take the first favourable opportunity to join the Community and to assist others who wish, in the Commonwealth and EFTA, to seek closer association with it. Until this becomes possible a future Conservative Government will co-operate with other European countries in joint policies in the common interest.

---

* The phrase used by Macmillan setting the processes in train. Actually, there were no such "customary" processes.

A Bow Group pamphlet, *A Smaller Stage*[3] published in December of the same year, went even further. Britain should not only "re-affirm our belief in European unity" but also "in the Community's institutional method of achieving it". Though there "was some admiration in this country for the way in which de Gaulle has played his cards", we should come out against his vision for Europe in favour of the "Atlanticist" (and "federal") alternative. One of the authors, Hugh Dykes,* had earlier argued in *Crossbow*[4] that "tearing down tariffs and impediments to trade will never be enough on its own – ... a close matching and fusion of monetary and economic measures is the essential framework".

In a section on "How to join the club", *A Smaller Stage* also outlined a three point "formula for action": first, a "declaration of intent"; secondly a "pre-membership alignment policy"; and finally an "association agreement on technology". This final point was, in the following year, developed by Sir Anthony Meyer, Bart.† (who was temporarily out of the House of Commons, having lost his seat of Eton and Slough in the General Election of 1966) in a CPC pamphlet.[5] The EEC, he wrote, "is a moving target, and we shall never hit it unless we aim well ahead of it. The only chance now is to adopt a new, a dynamic approach; to look at the EEC as it will be, and to decide how we can help to ... improve its future."

The idea of a European Technological Community (ETC) had, in fact, been launched by Labour Prime Minister Harold Wilson in November of that year (he had already committed Labour to the "the white heat" of a technological revolution at home), but without details. Meyer's pamphlet outlined a way in which it could be done. Although the Common Market was working well for more traditional industries, "the reason for the relatively poor showing of the EEC as a whole in the newer technologies lies in the half-hearted efforts which member governments have made to work together in this field." France was doing well in nuclear energy, and had a thriving aircraft industry; but Germany, was "already virtually an American colony" in the field of new technologies. An OECD survey had found that "the US was devoting two and a half times as much effort, in men and money, to research and development as the whole of Western Europe, including the UK".

The Meyer proposal was for a new Community, modelled on the existing ECSC, EEC and Euratom Treaties, but covering all the countries of both the EEC and EFTA. Of course, it did not happen; but the description of the ETC's tasks bears a prophetic resemblance to much of the Single

---

* Like me, Hugh Dykes had studied both languages and economics. As an MP, he would in the 1970s also become a member of the Conservative delegation to the nominated European Parliament. Later still he would join the Liberal Democrats and sit in the House of Lords.

† Sir Anthony, who had spent fifteen years in the Foreign Office, was one of the most confirmed pro-Europeans in the Conservative Party. He was later, in December 1989, to be the "stalking horse" standing against Prime Minister Margaret Thatcher for the party leadership.

Market programme of 1985–92, when the EEC and EFTA had virtually merged: a "European Company", subject to European Company Law and a European company tax; the removal of obstacles to cross-frontier mergers; a patents convention; joint arms procurement and production; a European space programme; and the removal of "obstacles caused by local regulations governing health, safety, right of domicile, etc." – what would be known later as the "non-tariff barriers to trade". Some of these proposals are still under active consideration, over forty years later.

The new leadership, in fact, gave pro-Europeans within the Conservative Party the confidence and incentive to aim, as Meyer put it, well ahead of the target. Addressing the Young Conservative national conference in February 1966,[6] Heath declared that "when the opportunity does come for our entry into Europe then we must be ready"; and he drew attention to the Party's policies to change the system of agricultural support and to adopt the metric system. The manifesto for the General Election of 1966, *Action not Words*,[7] was as clear on Common Market membership as *Putting Britain Right Ahead* had been. "We are determined to give Britain a respected place in the world again and lead her into the European Community" it said. A Conservative government would "seize the first favourable opportunity of becoming a member of the Community".

Conflicting voices

The clarity of the policy concerning Europe on which the Conservatives fought the General Election of 1966, however, perhaps gave a misleading picture of the state of opinion within the party on the issue. At that year's party conference, the policy was endorsed, but with nearly a quarter of those attending voting against.

To begin with, there were diverse views at the time about future defence policy, and the implications for policy towards Europe. This was linked with what became known as the "East of Suez" question: whether or not Britain should continue to maintain a military presence in the Middle East – for example in Aden and the surrounding Aden protectorate, where British troops were becoming the target of both sides in a struggle for post-independence control – and in the Far East. In March 1965, for example, the future cabinet Minister Geoffrey Rippon argued that "we should seek agreement in WEU and in NATO to a reduction of our commitments to provide … substantial land forces in Europe as the threat to peace and security shifts to other theatres".[8]

Yet an article[9] in the following year by the foreign editor of the *Spectator* at the time, Malcolm Rutherford, observed that a willingness to abandon British defence commitments "East of Suez", as a necessary price for entering the Common Market, seemed to be "fairly sweeping the Conservative Party at the moment. … We are running the risk of abandoning everything else for the sake of an entry to Europe that may never come."

There was also a new group within the party which had views differing sharply from most of those in the Bow Group. This was the Monday Club – so called because its founding members initially met informally on Monday evenings – which came into formal existence on the 1st January 1961 with the aim of forcing constituency associations "to discuss and debate party policies". Like the Bow Group it described itself as an "independent research group composed of Conservative Party members", and similarly published a newsletter, later a magazine, *Monday World*; and pamphlets outlining the findings of its research groups.

Where the Monday Club differed from the Bow Group was in its clear political stance. Its founders, so it stated on the early Club publications, had been "concerned at the tendency shown by the Government to embark on policies which in many respects appeared to depart from Conservative principles". In particular, it opposed the Macmillan government's policies of decolonisation in Africa, and would later provide the main organised support within the Party for Ian Smith's Unilateral Declaration of Independence (UDI) in Southern Rhodesia.

On Europe, however, the Monday Club, like the Bow Group, contained a variety of views. In 1963 it opposed EEC entry and suggested development of the Commonwealth instead. Later it had no official policy on the issue – indeed, one prominent member, Geoffrey Rippon, was to be the chief negotiator of Britain's successful bid to join at the beginning of the 1970s and would later lead the Conservative Group in the European Parliament. In the House of Commons, members like Julian Amery and John Biggs-Davison were in favour; others, like Teddy Taylor, strongly against. A history of the Club's first ten years, published in 1972,[10] states that "there have been no pro-E.E.C. or anti-E.E.C. campaign committees in the Club. The Executive Council prohibited the forming of such groups within the Monday Club." It also, however, records a vote taken at a meeting in October 1971 which resulted in 47 supporting entry into the European Community, and 66 against.

Evidence that the divisions on Europe in the Conservative Party, even at this time, went deeper than economics or worries about the Commonwealth is provided by the pamphlet *Europe: Should Britain Join?* which was published by the Monday Club in 1966.[11] This took the form of an exchange of letters between representatives of positions at opposite poles: on the one side Sir Anthony Meyer; on the other Victor Montagu, formerly Viscount Hinchingbrooke and generally known as "Hinch", one of most inveterate opponents of Common Market membership.*

Much of the exchange between the two treads the fairly conventional territory of how Britain is to find markets for science-based and technologically-advanced industries. Meyer argues that one advantage of the

---

* Hinch had read economics at the London School of Economics (LSE) and had been Stanley Baldwin's private secretary from 1932 to 1934. He entered Parliament in 1941, but was obliged to give up his seat on succeeding to the Earldom of Sandwich in 1962. He disclaimed the peerage in 1964 in an (unsuccessful) attempt to re-enter the Commons.

Common Market is that it is "irreversible": entrepreneurs can invest in the expectation that tariffs cannot be suddenly re-imposed on their products. Hinch counters with the prediction that "the Common Market will melt away, as its constituent states recover their historic stance".

The contrasting "historic stances" of the authors, however, provide the most interesting feature of their letters. "I suppose that most of us spend our time inventing good intellectual reasons for justifying the course to which our emotions bid us," Meyer begins his first letter. "It is certainly so in my case over Europe." In the Second World War "virtually all my friends were killed, and the absolute conviction that untrammelled national sovereignty is the cause of war ... made me enthusiastic about a united Europe, and what made me want my country to join in".

For Hinch, however, it was precisely from "untrammelled national sovereignty" that "the glories of ancient and present Europe" had sprung. He preferred

> Europe to shine and attract the attention of the world like the facets of a diamond, by its many-sided aspects of living, by its different and colliding cultures and its separate nationalities. I do not want it to be rebuilt as a monstrous power-house of concrete and brass.

The potential for serious and lasting divisions within the Conservative Party on the issue of "sovereignty" is apparent from the fact that the arguments of the two sides were exactly those "to which our emotions bid us".

Conservative Gaullism

Earlier, in October 1965, the Cambridge University branch of the Monday Club had produced *A Europe of Nations*,[12] edited by a future Conservative cabinet minister, Peter Lilley (another contributor, Roger Helmer, eventually became a Conservative Member of the European Parliament). It was not enough, it argued, to adopt a "wait-and-see" attitude to the future political development of the Common Market: it *was* necessary to take sides as between Federalists and Confederalists, Atlanticists and Europeans.

The pamphlet begins by coming down firmly against federalism and federal institutions, using arguments drawn from the then young branch of economics, public choice theory. It was a mistake, they argued, to think that bureaucracies like the Commission would inevitably pursue the common interests of the states they superseded. Instead, they would try to increase their own power and "sacrifice the common cause to administrative convenience". Rather than a federation, "Britain should aim to create a confederation of independent states in Western Europe". There was nothing wrong with maintaining national sovereignty: "nationalism, like any other human emotion, can be good or bad according to circumstances".

But in the dispute between Atlanticists and Europeans, *A Europe of Nations* comes down equally firmly on the European side. "If moves towards closer unity are seen as merely a more efficient way of organising an American hegemony they will lose their attraction." The GATT, it argues, inevitably "conforms more to American interests and ideas than to those of other countries". The same was true of the Kennedy Round, which would leave America "with the only large protected market in the world".

When the authors come to their specific policy proposals, there is considerable overlap with those of other Conservatives, outlined earlier. There should be more joint industrial projects, like Concorde and the European Space Launcher. "We should work to remove as quickly as possible those institutional differences which impede private firms who wish to operate in several national markets", including "different legal, administrative and tax systems". Together, Britain and France could create a credible European nuclear deterrent; and there should be "a European military bloc within the Atlantic Alliance". The view in *A Europe of Nations* might be described now as "Gaullism plus the Single Market"; and, with the exception of the anti-Atlanticism – an attitude prevalent among those older members of the Monday Club who could never forgive America for Suez – it is not a bad outline of recent Conservative policy.

Ironically, the "Soames Affair", four years later in 1969, briefly opened up the possibility of just that kind of Europe. De Gaulle, in a *tête-à-tête* with the newly-appointed British ambassador to Paris, Christopher Soames, effectively proposed that Britain and France should act together to replace the Common Market with a much looser body more to his taste. The conversation, however, was leaked by the Foreign Office, which by that time was working to a policy of full EEC membership – though some Labour ministers like Dick Crossman and Douglas Jay thought the offer should have been accepted as a heaven-sent opportunity. (De Gaulle himself believed the actions of the British government to have been an "act of revenge").

The divergences of view within the Conservative Party at the time, indeed, were mirrored by a very similar situation in the Labour Party. The leadership, like that of the Conservative Party, was cautiously in favour of Common Market membership. Roy Jenkins led a group strongly in favour. On the left of the party the Common Market was regarded it as a "capitalist plot". Others again were Commonwealth loyalists, Atlanticists or full internationalists for whom the United Nations was the key organisation.

Despite these divisions, not long after his victory in the General Election of 1966 Prime Minister Wilson made a new tentative move to join the European Economic Community. He and the strongly pro-Europe Foreign Secretary, George Brown, began a process of "sounding out" continental opinion, in preparation for a new application to join. This application de Gaulle felt obliged to derail with another veto, at another press conference, on the 16th May 1967. This time he gave as his main reason the inability of the British economy to pay the probable price of entry – a claim which had some credibility, given the forced devaluation of the "pound in your pocket"[*] some weeks earlier.

Just before the negotiations were halted, the decision to apply for Common Market membership had been approved by a large majority in the House of Commons: 488 votes to 62. The "no" voters included only twenty-four Conservatives, as against thirty-four Labour MPs, with another fifty abstaining. A comparison of these statistics with those of the similar vote in 1971, this time with the Conservative Party in government, is of some interest.

Constituency opinion

At almost exactly the same time as Heath became leader of the Party, I found myself joining the staff of Conservative Central Office as assistant to the new Director of the Conservative Political Centre (CPC), David Howell.

The CPC[13] began in 1945, on the initiative of R.A. Butler ("Rab"), as an independent political education movement. In 1964, however, it had been fully integrated into the party organisation, with a National Advisory Committee and committees at area and constituency level. Its first function was to act as the Party's main publishing house, producing pamphlets especially written for the CPC or published on behalf of groups within the party. Though there was often confusion as to how far these documents were "official", most began by stating that "this pamphlet is a personal contribution by the author to discussion and not an official Party pronouncement." CPC subscribers also received a *CPC Monthly Report*, which I edited.

The second function was the "Three-Way Contact Programme", designed to promote an exchange of ideas between the leadership of the party and Conservatives in the constituencies, and then get these across to the general public. This programme operated through a network of discussion groups throughout the country. In this context, my main task was to prepare a "Masterbrief" (later re-named "Contact Brief") for discussion each month; and also, later, tape recorded interviews with shadow ministers (after 1970 real ones). The answers were sent back to Central Office; collated and analysed; the summary sent to Conservative Research Department and appropriate shadow minister, later minister, for comment. The results were then distributed to the discussion groups. These varied in number, but were usually at just below the one per constituency level, though the distribution was uneven across the country, reflecting the level of Party support. The South East Area, for example, regularly produced more

---

[*] Wilson had made a television broadcast in which he maintained that devaluation did not mean that "the pound in your pocket" had been devalued – a phrase effectively used against him when the rate of domestic inflation rose.

than two reports per constituency, with Wessex and Eastern producing nearly two. At the other end of the scale Northern and North Western, and Scotland, were sending in fewer than one for every two constituencies.

The Contact Programme during May to August 1967 provides data on the state of opinion on Europe within the Conservative Party at the time. Three consecutive briefs appeared on the theme of "Britain in Europe": *Britain's Place in Europe,*[14] *What Joining Would Mean,*[15] and *Britain, Europe and the World*[16] (the first two at 4d. each, the third at 6d. – inflation was at work). The first of these outlined the standard arguments for Common Market membership, in particular the declining importance of Commonwealth trade and the superior growth rates in EEC countries. The second covered the well-trodden ground of Commonwealth preferences, EFTA, British agriculture and the balance of payments, ending with brief questions on the political issues. The final brief covered general trade liberalisation; the world monetary system; development aid; and defence, in particular the "East of Suez" issue.

The results of these consultations provided no great surprises. Majorities in all areas were behind the Party's policy of seeking Common Market membership, provided the usual safeguards were obtained for the Commonwealth and British agriculture. The dissenting minorities also rehearsed the familiar themes of loyalty to the Commonwealth, suspicion of foreign entanglements and defence of national sovereignty. This balance of opinion within the Party confirmed the vote at the 1969 Party Conference, which adopted by 1,452 votes to 475 a motion declaring that " … joining the European Economic Community (EEC) would make a major contribution to the security and prosperity of Britain".

Not surprisingly, the economic benefits of removing barriers to trade with countries whose growth rates were higher than that of the UK was a frequent theme on the pro-Market side. The advantages of greater political unity in Western Europe, also featured prominently, though not support for full "federal" union. The general attitude was that already described as "Conservative Gaullism" without the anti-Americanism. The old Imperial allegiance was maintained in general support for maintaining British forces "East of Suez", no doubt partly in reaction to the Labour Government's "scandalous programme of withdrawal".

One pro-Market argument worthy of especial note reflected the political situation at the time: that joining a free-market organisation would prevent the imposition of Socialism by Labour governments. This was, of course, a mirror-image of the anti-Market arguments on the Labour left – indeed, the description of the Common Market as a "capitalist club" did a lot to endear it to Conservatives. The argument contrasts strikingly with that which became prevalent within the Party forty years later, when the EU was thought to be a *source* of "Socialism" rather than a defence against it.

Preparing for office

As the Conservative Party prepared for a General Election and the possibility of being in government, the policy of seeking European Community* membership meant exercising persuasion in two directions. The most obvious field of action was the British electorate. In the late 1960s public opinion in Britain had turned sharply against joining the Community: whereas a Gallup poll taken in July 1966 had found 71% per cent approving of entry, one taken in April 1970 found only 19% of voters in favour, with more than half rejecting even the idea of even getting into talks.[17]

The most significant source of this opposition was not the fear of political union or loss of sovereignty, but the bread-and-butter issue of food prices. A government White Paper, published in February 1970,[18] had estimated that these would be 18% to 26% higher within the EEC, pushing up the overall cost of living by 4% to 5%. The Conservative Party's 1970 *Campaign Guide* accordingly emphasised the importance of "a satisfactory transition period in which to adjust".

Less obvious, but perhaps just as critical, was opinion among French politicians and opinion-formers. In 1969 de Gaulle lost a referendum on constitutional reform and resigned, eventually to be succeeded by the Prime Minister who had capably handled the *événements* of 1968, Georges Pompidou. The Gaullists, however, were still effectively in power.

Hugo Young, covering the same period, describes in some detail the preparatory work that was going on behind the scenes at civil service and diplomat level. "A conspiracy of like-minded men" centred on the European Integration Department of the Foreign Office was whittling away at opposition to British membership, both within the Community abroad and within Whitehall at home. It was also preparing in detail for renewed accession negotiations, to take place whether Wilson or Heath found themselves in Downing Street after the election.

A number of channels existed for the exchange of information and coordination of these various actions. All major political parties were theoretically in favour of British Common Market membership; and in October 1968 the Conservative, Labour and Liberal Parties formally joined the Action Committee for the United States of Europe, a body which had been established by Jean Monnet in 1955 – and which, as its name implied, made no secret of its central objective.

While Wilson was in office, the pro-Europeans in the Labour Party were clearly in the best position to link what was happening at ministerial and civil service level with action at public level. In 1969 the rather sedate UK Council of the European Movement, on the executive of which sat a number of pro-Europe Conservative MPs, was effectively taken over by the more

---

*   The official term for the "Common Market", until the Merger Treaty of 1965 (which came into force at the beginning of 1967), had been the "European Communities", meaning the ECSC, the EEC and Euratom. After the Merger Treaty it was generally called the "European Community" until changing again to the "European Union" under the Maastricht Treaty.

militant Britain in Europe, to form an activist European Movement under the Directorship of a Labour supporter, Ernest Wistrich. This provided one important channel of communication, both in the run-up to EC accession and also, later, in the 1975 referendum campaign. Research and linkage to academic opinion was provided by the Federal Trust – the Director from 1967, Diarmid McLaughlin, was a friend from Cambridge days[*] – and by Political and Economic Planning (PEP),[†] whose Director, John Pinder, was a longstanding campaigner for European integration. The London Office of the Commission under Derek Prag (later an elected Conservative MEP), Russell Lewis and Roy Price also provided briefing and organised visits to Brussels. The Foreign Office did its bit by holding seminars at its country house at Steyning. My job at the CPC resulted in my being involved one way or another in all these activities.

As far as the French dimension was concerned, one promising field of action was the Independent Republican Party, led by the former French Finance Minister Valéry Giscard d'Estaing. De Gaulle had dismissed "VGE" from the government in 1966, largely as a result of disagreement about Europe. Attached to this party was a Bow-Group-like body, *Perspectives et Réalités*; and in 1968 I was invited to attend its annual conference in Lyon. The Giscardiens proved enthusiastic about British accession to the Community, and seemed happy to be in contact with British Conservatives – though his party, including Giscard himself, would eventually sit with the Liberals in the European Parliament.

During this period, however, the campaign for Community accession was not the political issue which occupied most of my time. On moving to London in 1965 to take up my job at Conservative Central Office I joined the Chelsea Young Conservatives (although actually living in Barons Court) and shortly afterwards became a committee member of the Greater London Area Young Conservatives: "GLYC".

It is difficult to visualize today – when the YCs as such have been disbanded, and replaced by the much smaller Conservative Future – how significant a force the YCs were during the 1960s. Chelsea alone, at its peak, had over 850 paid up members; and the neighbouring South Kensington branch much the same. The number of Greater London Area Young Conservatives was far above the total current 15,000 national membership of Conservative Future.

Moreover, the YCs of this period – and certainly the YCs of GLYC – were far from being the purely social movement of caricature. Though there were, of course, dances at the Conservative Club in the Kings Road, the Chelsea YCs held at least two political meetings a week. The GLYC

---

[*] While there he had chaired the Cambridge University Federal Union. He would later become a senior Community official.

[†] Political and Economic Planning (PEP) was a think tank founded in 1931 to act as "a bridge between research on the one hand and policy-making on the other". In 1978 it merged with the Centre for the Study of Social Policy (CSSP), and became the Policy Studies Institute (PSI).

committee itself acquired a reputation as a militant force on the left of the Conservative Party, broadly looking to Iain Macleod for inspiration on social issues, but also to Enoch Powell on economics. YCs in other parts of the country did not, of course, necessarily share these views: an article on the "The YCs today" in the June 1974 *Crossbow* would refer to "the left-wing, arch-trendy attitudes" of the Greater London Area Young Conservatives.

Europe was, of course, one important political issue concerning YCs at the time. In 1967 Conservative Central Office published a brief for YC discussion groups and branches on "Britain & Europe: the theme of YC activity in 1967"[19]; and it was clear that enthusiasm for Community membership was greater within the YC movement than within the party as a whole. Paul-Henri Spaak was well received at the Greater London Area Young Conservatives' Conference in Bognor Regis in March 1967.[*]

The most contentious issues of the time, however, did not concern Europe: they were the Southern Rhodesian Unilateral Declaration of Independence (UDI); and the Vietnam War. In the case of Rhodesia there was considerable opposition within the Conservative Party to the Wilson Government's policy of economic sanctions – and quite a lot of support for the Rhodesian Prime Minister Ian Smith, too. At the 1968 Conservative Party Conference in Blackpool constituency parties tabled twenty-five resolutions on Rhodesia, most, like that selected for debate, opposing sanctions and rejecting "no independence before majority rule". Only three resolutions were tabled referring even tangentially to European Community membership (two, as it happens, by future cabinet ministers Patrick Mayhew and John Selwyn Gummer).

The Vietnam War, in which Britain was not directly involved, was fought out by proxy on the streets and in debate. A group of mainly YCs, the Hyde Park Tories, spoke every Sunday from a stand at Speakers' Corner, attracting larger audiences and applause as the popularity of the Wilson Government waned. Our support for the US in Vietnam, however, resulted in two stands being kicked apart beneath us. The European Community was hardly ever mentioned.

By 1968 the Labour Government was at a nadir of unpopularity. At the London Borough elections of that year there was a massive swing to the Conservatives, with the Party gaining control of councils where, previously, there had been no elected Conservatives at all. In some cases an element of continuity was only ensured through the aldermen, who were soon to be abolished. A large number of YCs stood in marginal or "unwinnable" wards and found themselves elected councillors, in my case for the London Borough of Hammersmith. In Lambeth one of the YCs swept into power was the future Prime Minister, John Major.

---

[*] Where I started going out with fellow Chelsea YC Felicity Raybould. We would be married in 1970.

In retrospect, the heady political atmosphere I experienced in London during those years before the General Election of 1970 may have given a somewhat misleading impression, both of the strength of support for the Conservative Party and of support for European Community membership within it. The fact that Ted Heath was, in the event, elected with a reasonable majority obscures the fact that Wilson was generally expected to win, not least by himself. (Whether the Conservative victory was due to a "late swing", or whether the Party had a hidden organisational advantage is discussed in the study of the election by David Butler and Michael Pinto-Duschinsky[20]). In the same way, the successful conclusion afterwards of the negotiations to join the Community, and the successful passage of the necessary legislation in Parliament, obscured the fact that some sections of the Party were anything but enthusiastic.

The main currents of thought within the party, though, still supported Community membership. On the political right, a trenchant article in *Monday World*[21] by its Literary Editor, David Levy, asserted that "whether we like it or not our future is intimately involved with that of our European neighbours".

> Every day we abstain from the making of multinational Europe our real independence is whittled away. Cooperation with our European equals is surely closer to self-government than our present slide into the economic slavery of American domination.

In *Crossbow*,[22] Russell Lewis – by now my boss as Director of the CPC – argued that "the case for entry is as strong as it ever was", and attacked the "anti-Europe backlash". He observed that opponents of Community membership had come up with a new alternative, a North Atlantic Free Trade Area (NAFTA). "Yet when all is said and done, NAFTA does not exist and shows little sign of doing so." The Bow Group published another supportive pamphlet, *Our Future in Europe: the Long-Term Case for going in*,[23] one of whose authors, Leon Brittan would one day become a European Commissioner, another, Derek Prag, an elected MEP. "Britons tend to be sceptics, and take pride in their pragmatism," it concluded. But "we have surely missed enough buses to exorcise both our scepticism and our so-called pragmatism".

And yet ... compare the clear text of 1966 with the extreme caution of the manifesto for 1970.[24]

> There would be short-term disadvantages in Britain going into the European Economic Community which must be weighed against the long-term benefits. Obviously there is a price we would not be prepared to pay. Only when we negotiate will it be possible to determine whether the balance is a fair one, and in the interests of Britain.

Our sole commitment is to negotiate: no more, no less. As the negotiations proceed we will report regularly through Parliament to the country.

A Conservative Government would not be prepared to recommend to Parliament, nor would Members of Parliament approve, a settlement which was unequal or unfair. In making this judgement, Ministers and Members will listen to the views of their constituents and have in mind, as is natural and legitimate, primarily the effect of entry upon the standard of living of the individual citizens whom they represent.

A myth appears to have grown up in recent years that this manifesto also contained a pledge not to join the Community without the "full-hearted consent of the British people" (this mistake is made, for example, by Anthony Forster in *Euroscepticism in Contemporary British Politics*[25]). Actually the phrase occurred in an earlier speech by Heath to the British Chamber of Commerce in Paris.

The shadow Foreign Secretary at the time was former Prime Minister Sir Alec Douglas-Home. In August 1969 the CPC had published a short pamphlet, *Britain's Place in the World*,[26] in which he outlined Conservative foreign policy, including that towards Europe, giving a foretaste of the more cautious approach. In the face of the Soviet threat Europe needed to combine economically; and there was a "powerful case for Britain's entry into the Common Market if we can get economic conditions which are acceptable". But there were risks, and the Common Market was "not an answer to our troubles in the short run". Presciently, Sir Alec particularly singled out the possible strain on the balance of payments, which would be too great "unless we are able to get a substantial proportion of what we subscribe returned to us".

The Party leadership was also obliged to look back over its shoulder at a new threat. Having refused, together with Macleod, to serve under Sir Alec Douglas-Home, Enoch Powell had been brought back into the shadow cabinet by Heath in 1965. But his removal from it again in 1968 had not only given him the freedom openly to attack the policy of seeking European Community membership, but had also ensured that he would be listened to by a large following, both in the Party and the country.

Powell on Europe

Despite his poor showing in the 1965 leadership contest, Enoch Powell exerted considerable influence over Conservative thinking in the 1960s. This, at least at first, was overwhelmingly in the field of economics. Despite having read Classics at Trinity College, Cambridge – or perhaps because of it – he became fascinated with the intellectual rigour of classical economics. Indeed, according to an early biography by the journalist T. E. Utley,[27] his support for market forces had an almost religious dimension.

"Powell believes not only that it is legitimate to buy in the cheapest market and sell in the dearest, but that it is positively immoral to do otherwise."

Even when still serving in the Macmillan government, he was an opponent of the, for him, woolly thinking that had led to "Conservative planning". He rejected attempts to control inflation through an "incomes policy", arguing instead for control of the money supply; and became a supporter of floating exchange rates.[28] Much later, both were to become orthodox Conservative policy.

On the issue of the Common Market, however, he did change his mind, possibly twice. In 1950 he was one of five Conservatives to vote against participation in the Schuman Plan for a European Coal and Steel Community (ECSC) because, as he later maintained, it implied political union. Yet in 1971 he wrote that "I was not an opponent of British membership of the European Economic Community in 1961–62. I was prepared to accept it, on the grounds of trade, as the lesser evil, compared to being excluded."[29]

He supported British membership in his 1966 election address; and as late as May 1967 he voted in favour of the Wilson-Brown initiative to join the Community, apparently willing to accept the political implications of the EEC which he had once rejected in the lesser case of the ECSC. It was not until that initiative ran into the third de Gaulle veto that he later recorded reaching the conclusion that it was time "to take new stock and make a break with 1962 and all that".

Yet until 1968, as shadow minister of defence, he was forcefully advocating the controversial policy of withdrawing from "East of Suez" in favour of committing Britain's main forces to the defence of Europe (the opposite of the policy advocated by Geoffrey Rippon). In a speech at the 1967 Conservative Party conference, which earned him a standing ovation from a nevertheless somewhat puzzled audience, he had argued that "the security of the British Isles is bound up with Western Europe".

> It would be idle to pretend that this presence (of British troops in Europe) is not closely relevant to Britain's aspiration to join in the economic cooperation of Western Europe which has found expression in our recent application to join the European Economic Community. … Political unity is inseparable from defensive unity. And to move towards the one is to move towards the other …

Nor did Powell have illusions, like many other anti-Marketeers of the time, about a Commonwealth and Empire alternative.

Interestingly, there is no mention at all in the Utley biography, published in 1968, of Powell's views on the Common Market. As associate editor of the *Spectator* and then a leader writer on the *Daily Telegraph*, Utley knew Powell well; and, the dust cover observes, "has analysed with him his political outlook in all directions and at all levels". This leads to the conclusion that for Powell, at this time, whether Britain joined the EEC was not the all-consuming issue he made it in later years.

Indeed, Powell only became a convert to the anti-Market cause after he had turned to a completely different subject, effectively ending his political career: immigration. The "rivers of blood" speech in April 1968 – delivered at a CPC meeting in Birmingham – resulted in his removal from the Shadow Cabinet, to which he never returned. Eventually, in 1974, he would call on the electorate to vote Labour, leave the Conservative Party itself for the Ulster Unionists, and finally lose a place in the House of Commons for good.

Whether this foray into the field of race relations strengthened or weakened Powell's impact in the field of Europe is a matter for debate. On the one hand, the 1968 speech made him a national figure in a way that no amount of speeches on economic policy or the Common Market could have done. On the other, there was always attached to him afterwards a whiff of the lunatic fringe. When, in 1975, he formed part of the all-party team calling for a "no" vote in the referendum on continued Community membership, this was a factor of which the "yes" campaign made good use. By 1978, in evidence to the House of Lords Select Committee on the European Communities,[30] he confessed that Europe had become an obsession. "To help destroy, or radically modify that membership [UK membership of the EEC] is my principal object in the remainder of my political life."

The central argument which Powell deployed throughout those later years was one which had already been used in 1963 in the Bow Group pamphlet *No Tame or Minor Role*: the need for a "common allegiance" if constitutional politics was to be sustained. In 1971 Powell gave speeches in Frankfurt, Turin, Lyon and The Hague in an attempt to get across the message that

> the greater part of the people of Britain are profoundly opposed to British accession to the Community. ... Can we be, and will we be, one electorate, one constituency, one nation, with you and with the rest of the people of the Community? I do not believe that anyone who knows Britain can doubt that the answer to that question is No.[31]

According to Powell, it had become clear "that the Community ... would be something quite different from a free trade area, and something to which Britain could not belong".[32] In consequence, he rashly predicted, that "the first and most important thing to say about British entry into the European Economic Community is that it is not going to happen".[33]

Yet it has to be said – as in the case of virtually all those Conservative pro-Europeans who have later converted to Euroscepticism – that maintaining "I thought we were joining a free trade area, not a political union" is highly disingenuous. Even if what is actually in the Treaties has somehow been overlooked, the events of the late 1950s described earlier should have made it very clear that the EEC was not just about free trade, which was specifically rejected. Nor, as the speeches and pamphlets quoted in previous chapters make clear, was the political dimension of Community membership somehow swept under the carpet. Finally, the pressure within a Common Market for free trade also to be fair trade, also mentioned earlier, in itself made a "political" dimension inevitable. Hugo Young, in *This Blessed Plot*, accordingly describes Powell as "an apologist for amnesia".[34]

As it happens, Enoch Powell was the only senior member of the party who came during the General Election of 1970 to support my candidature for the parliamentary constituency of Wrexham, for which I had been selected earlier in 1970. This was then still a mining seat, and the Labour candidate, Tom Ellis, was considered to be a shoo-in. Ironically, he was later to leave the Labour Party for the Social Democrat Party (SDP) after sitting in the nominated European Parliament in the late 1970s.

The meeting at which Powell spoke was held in the miners' hall, and was standing-room-only (though I doubt if more than a handful of those present actually voted Conservative). When I came to speak I gave my opinion that Britain should join the European Community, apologising for having to disagree with the main speaker. "Don't apologise", Powell broke in. "If that's what you believe, stick to your beliefs."

So I did. But I note that my election address reflected the caution of the 1970 manifesto rather than that of 1966: "*Common Market*", it said. "Start negotiations for British entry. But not entry regardless of conditions." Yet this was considerably less cautious than the manifestos of over 60% of Conservative candidates at the election, who didn't mention the European Community at all! It had by now become received wisdom among party workers that "there are no votes in Europe".

Next door to Wrexham was the constituency of Oswestry, where the sitting MP was John Biffen, with whom Felicity – by now my fiancée – and I stayed on one or two occasions. He was widely considered at the time to be Powell's disciple, and indeed was to vote more consistently against the implementing legislation for Common Market membership, the European Communities Act 1972, even than Powell himself. Unlike Powell, though, he would eventually become a Conservative cabinet minister in the government of Margaret Thatcher, even as Leader of the House steering the Single European Act through the Commons. Biffen's position on Europe was almost entirely based on political rather than economic arguments. Like Powell, and like a number of Conservatives who studied history at Cambridge University,* he was a firm believer in the nation state as the only basis for true democratic government. Like Powell, too, he was a "House of Commons man", seeing the issue of British

---

* Those Conservatives who studied history at Cambridge under Maurice Cowling, were later described as belonging to a school of "black Conservatism". John Biffen, however, was far too nice a person ever to attract such an adjective.

sovereignty inextricably bound up with sovereignty of Parliament. As a member of the Bow Group, he was part of the early minority opposing Common Market membership; and later almost certainly one of the influences which shifted the Group's general position. In the 1990s he was to become, according to Hugo Young, "a teacher and strategist" for a new intake of young, less pro-Community MPs, describing himself as "the Fagin of Euroscepticism".[35]

Wooing Conservatives

Despite the caution expressed in the manifesto for the General Election of 1970, Ted Heath's victory meant that the drive to join the European Community was immediately pursued with a new determination. Hugo Young's *This Blessed Plot*, relying substantially on the account of the chief official negotiator, Sir Con O'Neill, observes that most of the "negotiating modalities" were already in place by the time the new government took office.[36] As far as detailed, technical matters were concerned, there had been "unremitting work" within the civil service to prepare the ground for whichever party came in. The outgoing Labour Government had in fact decided to open negotiations at ministerial level on the 30th June, and the incoming Conservative Government had merely to confirm the date and "pick up the hand which their predecessors had prepared".[37]

The political dimension, however, was a different matter. Public opinion was not particularly favourable: private research carried out for Conservative Central Office before the 1970 election found support as low as 18%. Among Conservative MPs, the group resolutely opposed to membership on any conceivable terms was small. However, there was also a much larger group worried about the consequences, but disinclined to rock the Party boat. The same was true of the Party's membership as a whole. At the 1971 Party conference only four out of nearly a hundred resolutions tabled on the Common Market were hostile – a figure, however, which was probably as much a reflection of loyalty as of firm conviction.

Finally, there was still the problem of the French. Support from the Giscardiens would not be enough. Could the Gaullists be convinced that Britain under a Conservative Government would be ready to join the Community? Was there now sufficient common ground between the French and British parties – both, after all, ostensibly of the centre right?

In the case of public opinion, a renewed effort at persuasion, initially targeted at "opinion formers", was launched. British industry and commerce were strongly in favour of Common Market membership, and the European Movement found itself well-funded. *Europe: The Case for Going In*,[38] published in 1971, contained sections by representatives of the three major political parties: Christopher Mayhew for Labour, Jeremy Thorpe for the Liberals, and Geoffrey Rippon, Lord Harlech, and Duncan Sandys for the Conservatives.

This book is interesting in view of later claims that the campaign for Common Market membership ignored the political consequences and the issue of national sovereignty. Lord Harlech – who had previously, as David Ormsby-Gore, been the Conservative MP for, as it happens, Oswestry – affirmed the objective of political unity in almost Hegelian terms.

The history of the human race has been the evolution of society from family to tribe, from tribe to principality or city-state, from state to nation, and then from the nation towards some larger unit of continental proportions.

The Sandys article on "The Political Case" (which I had "ghosted") examined the issue of sovereignty in some detail, distinguishing between the theoretical, legal concept and the practical limitations on national freedom of action. The limitations on national sovereignty in Europe had been brought home three years earlier by the crushing of the "Prague Spring".

When ... Soviet tanks rolled into Czechoslovakia ... Western Europe was able to do little more than stand by to receive refugees. It was accepted – by the Soviet Union as much as in the West – that only the United States was in any position to influence events. Once the Soviet Union had decided that the 'Brezhnev doctrine' (the freedom of the Soviet Union to interfere in its own sphere of influence) would be tacitly accepted by America, the invasion of Czechoslovakia was inevitable. ... Czechoslovakia illustrated the extent to which European nations on both sides of the Iron Curtain have lost control over their own decisions.

The article also took up a theme which had been developed by the French journalist and politician Jean-Jacques Servan-Schreiber in the hugely influential *Le Défi Américain* of 1967: that theoretical national sovereignty could become an illusion if large sections of an economy were controlled from abroad.

Neither Britain nor the other countries of Western Europe are anything like on the way to becoming banana republics ... (but) foreign-owned companies (70 per cent of which are American-owned) account for over 50 per cent of British production in cake-mixes, cosmetics and toilet preparations, electric switches, ethical proprietaries (drugs sold to the National Health Service), frozen foods, foundation garments, pens and pencils, motor-cars, pet foods, petroleum-refinery construction equipment, refrigerators, rubber tyres, tractors, vacuum cleaners; over 60 per cent in agricultural implements, aluminium semi-manufactures, breakfast cereals, calculating machines, cigarette lighters, domestic boilers, electric shavers, instant coffee, potato chips, razor

blades and safety razors, refined petroleum products, soaps and
detergents, spark plugs and tinned milk; and over 80 per cent in boot
and shoe machinery, carbon black, colour films, custard powder and
starch, sewing-machines, tinned baby foods and typewriters.

A key issue for the antis was whether the replacement of unanimity in
the Council of Ministers (i.e. the veto) by weighted majority voting would
mean that Britain could be overruled on important national issues. The
answer turned on the so-called "Luxembourg compromise" of January
1966. Where "very important interests of one or more partners were at
stake" the Council would try "to reach solutions which can be adopted by
all members".

There was, however, a "gentleman's disagreement" on how this
compromise was to be interpreted. For the majority, the solution had to be
reached "within a reasonable time". For the French, the discussions would
have to continue "until unanimous agreement is reached". In practice, the
analysis in the Sandys article concluded, "the outvoting of a member state
on a vital matter was out of the question"; and this, in fact, has virtually
always turned out to be the case.

However, the Luxembourg compromise had no legal base in the
Treaties – it was that very British device, a "constitutional conven-
tion". When, in 1982, the Council of Agriculture Ministers overruled a
British declaration of "important national interest" when voting on the
Annual Farm Price Review, the then British Minister of Agriculture, Peter
Walker, reported angrily to the House of Commons that the Council of
Ministers had "violated an accepted convention ... the established practice of the Community".[39] In this case, however, it was clear that other
countries doubted whether the issue was actually covered by the compromise. Agricultural prices were in fact only a proxy for the real issue at
the time, the UK's net contribution to the Community Budget, with the
British Government hoping to use the Price Review as a hostage in the
budget battle. Others argued that the compromise should only be invoked
on matters to which it was directly related. In his coverage of the issue,
the one-time British Ambassador to the Community, Sir Stephen Wall,
concludes that "a defeat for Britain which had seemed cataclysmic only a
month before was resolved by an agreement to disagree, which is what, in
practice, the Luxembourg compromise had always been".[40]*

As far as the Conservative Party itself was concerned in 1971, another
Contact Brief[41] published for discussion groups in September/October of
that year asked the straightforward question: "Are you in favour of British
entry into the European Community on the conditions negotiated by the
Government?" A White Paper[42] had been published in July setting out in

---

* Sir Stephen also recalls that the Conservative Members of the European Parliament at the
time (of which I was one) voted to decide the Price Review by weighted majority vote in
Council.

detail what those conditions were, together with background information. In addition, the CPC had earlier provided groups with an extensive reading list on the issues, including – it should be noted – not only factual material and publications favouring British entry, but also anti-entry documents from bodies like the Common Market Safeguards Committee, and on alternatives to joining.

The answer of the CPC discussion groups was an overwhelming "yes". Out of the 576 reports received, 491 supported Common Market entry, 23 were against, and 55 were either undecided or gave no definitive answer. Of the 6,433 participants, 4,775 were recorded as voting "yes" as against 730 "no". The opinions of 847 were either unrecorded or recorded as undecided.

The detailed analysis of the reports carried out by the CPC showed broad acceptance of the government's main economic case for entry: access to the UK's fastest-growing market and the linked need to attract inward investment. Among the main political arguments were "ensuring that there will be no more wars", and building "a prosperous and united Europe as a barrier to Communism". The main arguments for those voting "no" were "the cost of entry" – food prices and payments into the Community budget – and "sovereignty" (although the analysis commented that "there appeared to be some confusion as to what would actually be lost").

One issue, however, was unexpectedly prominent: over half the groups, both positive and negative, expressed anxiety about territorial fishing rights; and this perhaps helps to explain a feature of the regional variations. The least positive region was Western, where nearly 20% of participants were against. The most positive, with fewer than 10% against, were London, the North West, Yorkshire, the East Midlands, the South East and Wessex. Community entry also received massive backing at the October party conference in Brighton, where there was a card vote: 2474 to 324.

Entry was also strongly supported by some members of the party with interesting pasts or futures. In 1971 the CPC published a pamphlet on *A Europe for the Regions*,[43] which argued that "immense gains await Britain's less prosperous regions inside the Common Market." The author was the journalist George Gardiner who, as the MP for Reigate in 1997, would leave the Conservative Party to fight his seat as the Eurosceptic Referendum Party candidate. A foreword was contributed by the founder of the Anti-Common Market League who was now Secretary of State for the Environment, Peter Walker.

The most acute problem lay in the House of Commons. The Party's majority at the General Election of 1970 was 30 – adequate for most purposes, but not for that of Community membership. In addition to irreconcilable opponents like Powell and Biffen, enough MPs were likely to have doubts about the terms negotiated to make it impossible for the government to get the necessary legislation through without Labour support. Indeed an Early Day Motion indicating that the probable terms would be unacceptable was signed by 44 Conservatives. In addition to the

Anti-Common Market League, a dining club called the "1970 Group", led by Sir Derek Walker-Smith and Neil Marten, had fifty or so anti-Market members.

Meanwhile the Labour Party was rapidly moving into a position of opposing membership on the terms in the process of being agreed. An all-party Common Market Safeguards Committee was formed in 1970, with a parliamentary section headed by a Conservative, Sir Robin Turton. Also still in existence was the all-party free-trade organisation, Keep Britain Out, whose committee included the Conservative MP Richard Body and a co-founder of the Institute of Economic Affairs, Oliver Smedley.

The various initiatives which the Party leadership took in the 1961–63 period, and again in the early 1970s, to keep Conservative MPs in line has been well documented by N. J. Crowson.[44] Committees were established to promote the case for Europe at critical junctures: for example a Parliamentary Group on the Common Market in 1962, a European "Tactical" Group in 1966, a Co-ordinating Committee on Europe in 1967. MPs were liberally supplied with briefing material prepared by Conservative Research Department.

One important development was the formation, within the umbrella of the European Movement, of a Conservative Group for Europe (CGE), initially launched in 1969 as the European Forum, but which changed its name at the 1970 AGM. This carried out a vigorous recruiting campaign, particularly among Conservative MPs, with over 200 of these eventually signing up. Its magazine, *Tory European*, was edited by none other than George Gardiner.

The formal constitution of the Group, eventually adopted in May 1973, stated its aims as:

a to work for a united Europe based on Conservative principles;
b to promote awareness and knowledge about European matters within the Conservative Party;
c to support and encourage all forms of European activity within the Party and in the country at large;
d to give expression to ideas and views on the future of a united Europe, and in this respect, to spur on the Party and the British Government;
e to set up study groups and to publish their findings;
f to encourage close links with like-minded parties within Europe;
g to operate in close concert with the Party organisation, though remaining outside it;
h to maintain close links with the European Movement, including full representation on the Movement committees.

The first chairman of the CGE was Sir Tufton Beamish MP (who would later achieve immortality as "Sir Tufton Bufton", *Private Eye*'s semi-fictitious member of the nominated European Parliament). In 1971 the CPC published a short study on the sovereignty issue,[45] written by Tufton

Beamish together with the future cabinet minister Norman St John-Stevas. One of the subjects discussed was the primacy of Community over domestic law. It was true that "Community laws embodying policies approved by the representatives of national governments would take precedence over the domestic law of member states, and that British legislation in the fields covered by them would have to be consistent with Community rules".

There followed a number of reassurances. This situation "would be no innovation": the GATT, the European Convention on Human Rights and the UN Charter imposed similar restraints on the powers of the UK Parliament. "Community law operates only in a limited number of fields of non-criminal law". Finally, there were "no grounds for fear that entry would entail submission to arbitrary legislation arbitrarily imposed". There was the right of appeal to the European Court of Justice; and "so far as Community law directly affects individuals in their private capacities it confers rights more than it imposes obligations".

More important than these reassurances, however, is the fact that the primacy of Community law, and the consequent restrictions on the right of Parliament to legislate, *was* being clearly spelled out *before* British entry. This puts into perspective both the later claim by Eurosceptics that the country was misled on the issue, and the objections to the primacy being re-affirmed in the Lisbon Treaty.

In his memoirs,[46] Geoffrey Howe (who in 1971 was Solicitor General, and responsible for drafting the European Communities Bill) draws attention to an extensive paper on *The Rome Treaty and the Law*,[47] which had been published in July 1962 as a supplement to the Bow Group magazine *Crossbow*. This had stated clearly that the Community had "power to make laws that are binding on the citizens of the Member States"; and continues, (though this is not quoted by Howe): "the national parliaments therefore give up their right to legislate in these particular fields … ".

The fact that, as Hugo Young maintained, ministers did not state categorically in the House of Commons that "the law of the European Community would have supremacy over British law" seems to imply that MPs hear and read nothing except what appears in *Hansard*. If anybody was unclear on the matter, lawyers in the Conservative Party could have pointed to rulings of the European Court of Justice (ECJ)[48] which left no room for doubt. Indeed, the Society of Conservative Lawyers did examine in some detail the legal consequences of Community membership, and published, through the CPC, a collection of papers in 1968.[49] This described, in particular, the status and functions of the ECJ.

Wooing the French

Hugo Young, in *This Blessed Plot*, observes that "the moment that decided everything" in securing British entry into the European Community took place in Paris on 19th and 20th May 1971.[50] This was when Prime

Minister Heath and President Pompidou met "in twelve hours of deeply private talks", following which Pompidou made it clear that there would be no further French veto. A political decision had been taken that the Community would be enlarged: Denmark and Ireland would both join at the same time as the UK, and it was also envisaged that Norway would join. The negotiators were now merely required to make the necessary deals.

The head of the Leader of the Opposition's office at the time, future Foreign Secretary Douglas Hurd (now Baron Hurd of Westwell), observes in his memoirs that this was very much Ted Heath's own initiative. Not only the Foreign Office, but even veteran pro-Europeans like Duncan Sandys and Peter Kirk too, thought the most fruitful tactic would be "rallying the other five existing members against France". But "Ted was sure that Britain could enter the EEC only by persuading the French. ... It was pointless to try to isolate France, since there could be no Europe without France."[51]

However, it would not have been possible for Pompidou to have been so positive if a large majority of those supporting him had remained opposed to British entry. For this reason, the Conservative Group for Europe became active in forming contacts with leaders of opinion on the French centre and centre-right. A number of meetings took place where Conservative MPs, officials and other party members exchanged views with Gaullist officials and members of the *Assemblée française* and the *Sénat*.

Two French politicians stand out in my memory: the Gaullist "of the first hour" and former minister Raymond Triboulet, at that time a Member of the nominated European Parliament; and the more centrist Michel Habib-Deloncle, who had links to Geoffrey Rippon through the European Documentation and Information Centre (*Centre Européen de Documentation et d'Information*, CEDI), a body set up after the war to unite different Christian and conservative movements. CEDI had, in fact, already done a great deal to form links between the Conservative Party and other centre-right parties in Europe during the 1950s and 60s.

These meetings established a meeting of minds on at least three issues. The first was general support for a *Europe des patries* rather than more integrationist models; the second that Europe, or at least Britain and France, should be able to stand on their own feet in the field of defence rather than rely entirely on the United States; and the third, more controversial but perhaps decisive, that European farming needed to be supported. The atmosphere of cooperation was greatly enhanced by the presence of the CGE's elegant organiser, Caroline de Courcy-Ireland.*

---

* It was at one of these meetings that an event occurred which has become an entry in various political joke books. One of the British MPs made a short speech in English, which was received in polite silence. He was followed by a French speaker, whose remarks were punctuated by frequent rounds of applause, in which the MP, rather put out, nevertheless joined. His neighbour turned to him and said: "I wouldn't bother to clap if I were you. It's the translation of your speech."

There was also some talk of whether Conservative Party MEPs would sit with the Gaullists in the European Parliament, once they got there – in the Council of Europe Assembly, the Conservatives had sat as Independents, as had the Gaullists. This was not, in fact, to be the case: the Conservative MEPs from the House of Commons and the House of Lords who took their seats in 1973 were to form their own group, the European Conservative Group. The closest cooperation in the Parliament turned out in the end to be with the Christian Democrats, in particular the German *Christlich Demokratische Union* (CDU) /*Christlich Soziale Union* (CSU)* members; and this was eventually to lead to the merger with the Group of the European People's Party (EPP) – as the Christian Democrats eventually became – in 1992.

There was always a minority view within the Party, however, that our real allies were the Gaullists – and certainly it was important to give that impression during the 1970–73 period. Had the French Gaullists in the European Parliament not linked up with the most nationalist of the Irish parties, *Fianna Fáil*, and had the troubles in Northern Ireland not been a major political issue (to say nothing of the fact that the Ulster Unionists, off and on, sat with the British Conservatives), more might have come of it.

The balance of rebellion

The White Paper of July 1971, *The United Kingdom and the European Communities*, has been subjected to intense scrutiny in subsequent years. Eurosceptics have maintained that it glossed over the political consequences of Community membership, pointing in particular to the phrase: "There is no question of any erosion of essential national sovereignty".

Apart from the interventions of Conservative antis like Powell, Walker-Smith and Biffen, however, the debates leading up to Parliament's "decision in principle" in the House of Commons of 28 October focused, not on "sovereignty", but on whether the detailed terms negotiated were, or were not, acceptable. The official Labour position – reached more for tactical reasons than for reasons of principle – was that they were not. This meant that the decision rested on the balance of rebellion in the two major parties. A free vote on the Conservative side resulted in thirty-nine voting against, and two abstaining. But sixty-nine Labour MPs then felt able to vote with the Government, with another twenty abstaining; and the principle of joining the Community was approved by 356 votes to 244, a healthy majority of 112. In the House of Lords the majority was overwhelming: 451 to 58.

---

* In the State of Bavaria, the Christian Democrat Party is the CSU: *Christlich Soziale Union* (Christian Social Union). In the rest of Germany it is the CDU: *Christlich Demokratische Union* (Christian Democrat Union (CDU)).

The same group of Labour pro-European MPs, led by Roy Jenkins, also ensured the subsequent passage of the European Communities Act 1972, which provides the legal base for the UK's Community membership. Passage of the legislation was also helped by the fact that the Conservative rebels "unlike their heirs of the 1990s, the Maastricht rebels, ... never voted against their own government on procedural questions".[52] There were 104 separate divisions, none of which were lost by the pro-Europeans (though the majority on one occasion fell to four, as a result – according to Howe – of some Conservatives being at a Duncan Sandys party). It has also been noted[53] that, of the forty-one Conservatives who failed to support the principle of Community entry in October 1971, fourteen – including the future elected MEP Harmar Nicholls – thereafter cast no vote against. This has in part been attributed to pressure from their constituency Conservative Associations, which, though not necessarily all strongly pro-Europe, did not wish to see the Government fall.

Passage of the Act meant that the way was now clear for the UK to sign the Treaty of Accession to the Community, which it did on the 22nd January 1972. The Rome Treaty was amended to provide for the institutional and other changes made necessary by the enlargement of the Community to nine Member States: English and Danish, for example, became official Community languages. A special Protocol covered the positions of the Isle of Man and the Channel Islands, which did *not* join the Community, a situation which was soon to prove controversial (see Chapter Six) and also many years later when the issue of "tax havens" became topical. On the 1st January 1973, the UK became a full Member State of the European Community.

One consequence of this was that a large number of new posts were created in the Community institutions in Brussels and Luxembourg, specifically for UK, Danish and Irish personnel. The Foreign Office and the Treasury had compiled lists of suitable candidates for the UK posts, and several of us working at Conservative Central Office or Conservative Research Department saw new opportunities opening up. At Research Department, Stanley Johnson – whose son, Boris, would later be elected London's Mayor – had been advising the Party on environmental policy, and quickly secured an appropriate key job in the Commission. He would later become the first elected MEP for Wight and Hampshire East.

In my case, in the freezing December of 1972, I turned up at Alexandra Palace, together with some thousand others, to sit the first *concours* for aspiring British Eurocrats. The circumstances did not make a good first impression. There was no heating of any kind. The Commission staff committee had called a strike, with the result that the examination was being organised by a small number of personnel from the Commission's London embassy and information office. One of the papers, I recall, involved summarising a document written in a language other than English; and we were asked at the start to choose which Community language we wished to take it in. A few put up their hands for Dutch and Italian, a few more for German; and finally about 90% for French. Aghast, the organisers discovered that they hadn't nearly enough French papers to go round; we had to take the exam in two sittings.

Although I did pass this exam, the job I actually got was not with the Commission in Brussels or Luxembourg, but with the newly-established European Parliament Information Office in London. This was the indirect result of the Labour Party having refused to take up any seats in the Parliament (although, inconsistently, it did agree to George Thomson becoming a Labour Commissioner).

The Parliament had appointed as head of the office an established Commission official, Roger Broad, who was also, however, a member of the Labour Party. As a result, it was thought expedient to appoint as Deputy Head someone with Conservative credentials. Luckily, the then Director of the Conservative Group for Europe, Jim Spicer, had also been National Chairman of the CPC; and when he was consulted, he put my name forward. By the beginning of 1974, I had left Conservative Central Office in Smith Square for Kensington Palace Gardens – an up-market work-place if ever there was one, where porters with yellow bands round their top hats saluted my battered car as it was driven through the gates each morning.

One of my last tasks at the CPC in connection with Europe was writing another Contact brief for discussion groups.[54] Among the questions was one concerning the strengthening of the European Parliament's powers over legislation and appointment of the Commission, and whether it should be directly elected. The groups were substantially in favour.

What is perhaps more interesting, however, is that, under the general heading "The next steps", the brief advanced the idea of Economic and Monetary Union (EMU). Prime Minister Heath had earlier, in an interview, stated that this was likely to be the main topic for a "summit" of the nine member, or future member, countries.

> Movable exchange rates, *the brief said*, are not compatible with a fully integrated economic Community: no-one, for example, would argue that there should be different currencies for Yorkshire or Cornwall, because the inconvenience and waste of effort in constant resort to the exchanges is so obvious. In the same way, the ultimate replacement of the different national currencies by a single Community currency is a desirable goal.

The first steps in this direction were, of course, already in preparation: the Werner Plan for the gradual alignment of exchange rates through the "snake in the tunnel" mechanism, in which the pound sterling would briefly participate (see Chapter Ten). The Paris Summit agreed that "the second stage of the economic and monetary union would be implemented on January 1, 1974, and the full union completed by December 31, 1980".

The single community currency, however, would not become a reality until after the passage of the Maastricht Treaty some twenty years later – and then with Britain, under a Conservative government, once again "opting out". Today, it is difficult to conceive of Conservative Campaign Headquarters (CCHQ), as Central Office has become, putting out a document including the passage quoted above.

Conservative federalists

Nor, even in the early 1970s, would Central Office have put out *Towards a European Identity*,[55] a pamphlet issued, as British Community membership drew near, by another Conservative pressure group, Pressure for Economic and Social Toryism (PEST). The Group had been formed in 1963 by members of the Cambridge University Conservative Association (CUCA), but soon spread to other universities, and with associate membership in the wider Party. PEST's formation, like that of the Monday Club, had been a reaction to the Party leadership; but in this case to that of Sir Alec Douglas-Home, and in the opposite direction. Avowedly on the left of the Party – its stated objective was to remedy the "lack of coherence in progressive Tory thought" – it expressed early solidarity with those who declined to serve under Sir Alec, more particularly Iain Macleod. It stood for economic policies in the tradition of One Nation Toryism and the Harold Macmillan of the "Middle Way".[56] Its founder was Michael Spicer, later Sir Michael Spicer MP, chairman of the Conservative backbench "1922 Committee", and now in the House of Lords.

Towards a European Identity is a clear, and in places lyrical, statement of the case for a federal Europe – indeed, one going well beyond federalism.

> This pamphlet is not concerned with a 'partnership agreement in a trade of pepper and coffee' but with the fulfilment of an ideal. ... We ... question the existing basis of the European institutions, which is a contract between the sovereign states. ... Our contention (is) that the British people will experience the greatest possible freedom in our time within the setting of an integrated European nation.

Such a nation, fulfilling the Tory philosophy of Edmund Burke, would be "a partnership not only between those who are living, but between those who are dead, and those who are to be born ... a clause in the great primeval contract of eternal society".[57] It would embody "a European – not just a British – civilisation," the ethos of which embodied two philosophical streams: "the empirical approach and the humanist tradition". Not Churchill, but Erasmus, Rousseau, Bentham, Cobden, Kant and Victor Hugo are cited as the "founding fathers" of a "Europe of Venice and Florence, Paris and Geneva, Copenhagen and London ... of Proust, Thomas Mann and Shakespeare, of Goethe, T. S. Eliot and Picasso, and of Beethoven, Rossini and Michael Tippett".

Among the pamphlet's practical recommendations were not only that the European Parliament should be directly elected, but that "the Chief Executive in Europe must be an elected chief minister of the European Parliament".

PEST pamphlets, unlike those of the Bow Group, were "the corporate view of PEST": in this case on "the aims and ideals of a future European Union". It is therefore interesting to see the list of those associated with it, which included some fifty Conservative MPs. There is some overlap with pro-Europe Bow Groupers: Chris Chataway, Ken Clarke, Hugh Dykes, David Howell and Patrick Jenkin, for example. Other well-known names from the left of the party include Norman Fowler, Ian Gilmour, John Gummer, Michael Heseltine and PEST President Nick Scott.

What, though, is one to make of the name at the top of the list, Pressure for Economic and Social Toryism's Patron the Rt. Hon. Peter Walker? Or one of the authors of the Bow Group's anti-Common Market pamphlet of 1963 (see Chapter Three), *No Tame or Minor Role*, Tim Raison? Or, in the light of his later opinions on Europe, PEST's founder Michael Spicer himself?

In 1975 Pressure for Economic and Social Toryism would merge with three other Conservative groups on the left of the party – the Macleod Group, the Social Tory Action Group and the Manchester Tory Reform Group – to form the Tory Reform Group (TRG). This would maintain a strong pro-European stance within the party, but lose a number of its members in the 1990s through defection to the Liberal Democrats in reaction to the rise of Conservative Euroscepticism.

A consensus

Given the wide gap between the views of Pressure for Economic and Social Toryism on the one hand and those of Powell, Biffen and Conservative anti-Marketeers on the other, it is perhaps surprising that the Party held together so successfully during the run-up to European Community accession. There was, however, a consensus at the broad centre of the Party which enabled the leadership to implement the policy of membership with only the minimum of dissent.

This consensus brought together two main themes.

First, there was the view most clearly and consistently expressed by the Foreign Secretary, Lord Home of the Hirsel (as Sir Alec Douglas-Home had become): that it was necessary for European nations to pull together in a dangerous world. During his first term of duty as Foreign Secretary, when he was still the Earl of Home and on the eve of the Macmillan government's application to join the Common Market, he had told a CPC meeting that "the political division of Europe has twice this century brought Britain and the Commonwealth within sight of ruin. There is no greater British and Commonwealth interest than the economic, political and military cohesion of the Continent."[58]

This was, of course, a restatement of Churchill's analysis in the 1940s
– but with the important difference that British participation was explicitly advocated. "It should be possible," Home had continued, "to arrive
at a political and economic arrangement with the European Economic
Community which would greatly add to the wealth and strength of the
whole". Eight years later, in the run-up to the General Election of 1970,
Home had succinctly outlined the consequent Conservative policy. The
"broad British objectives in relation to the continent of Europe" were
reasonably clear: "support of NATO, Europe carrying a greater responsibility for its defence in future years and partnership in the Common
Market, which will be in practice confederal rather than federal, because
in practice no one is as yet prepared to drown the conception of the nation
state".[59]

The second element of the consensus concerned the economic dimension. The huge backing for Common Market membership in the business community both conditioned and reflected the views of those
Conservatives who saw joining the EEC largely in terms of freer trade and
wider competition. For these, applying the Rome Treaty would have "a
tonic effect on free enterprise capitalism".[60]

It should be noted, however, that support for Common Market membership among free market Conservatives was not unconditional. As an
Institute of Economic Affairs paper concluded in 1970[61] "the UK could and
should join the EEC if it has real promise of becoming a liberal, outward-
looking institution. But she should not join if it is designed as a tight, paro-
chial European bloc".

In addition to being outward-looking, the Community would also need
to resist the temptations of French-style *dirigisme*. The free-marketeers, at
this point, were optimistic. As Russell Lewis put it in another IEA booklet,
Rome or Brussels … ?, "the attention which the Treaty of Rome devotes to
the economics of control are minimal compared to that which it lavishes
on the economics of freedom".

Rome or Brussels..? also reviewed favourably the record of the Community
in implementing the Treaty. The tariff-free movement of goods within the
Common Market had become a reality in 1968, and a common external
tariff introduced at the same time, based on the average of those applied
by the participating nations. Taking into account subsequent multilateral
reductions within the GATT, "the EEC's common external tariff, at least
on industrial goods, was below those of America, the United Kingdom
and Japan".

In the case of agriculture, the CAP was clearly protectionist, was
creating surpluses like the infamous "butter mountain", and indulging in
subsidised dumping on world markets. Yet "as the CAP was only in effect
an amalgamation of several national policies – the sum of its previously
protected parts – it is probable that surpluses would have arisen even if
it had never been born". The Conservative Government was, in any case,
pledged to switch to the EEC system of agricultural support instead of

the taxpayer-funded deficiency payment system (a return to which, it was calculated in 1979, would cost the British taxpayer £1 billion a year).

It is interesting to note that *Rome or Brussels..?* also saw "little cause to fear economic authoritarianism from Brussels on the record to date". It was "the free market aspects of the Rome Treaty which have been the most successful, and the potentially *dirigiste* and centralising common policy aspects which have been the worst failures". "Harmonisation" was not being equated with "equalisation" – though there were dangers that this might change in the field of social policy. The Treaty objective of an equalisation of social conditions "in an upward direction" was worthwhile, but this would "be better accomplished democratically by the market than paternalistically, clumsily and insensitively by legislation".

Russell Lewis' analysis in *Rome or Brussels..?* reflected well the prevailing attitude to the economic issues among most Conservatives at the time. Sovereignty was a minority interest. The majority believed that, even if some transfer of powers from nation states to Brussels was unavoidable, this could be limited and controlled. There was quiet confidence that the tradition of Adam Smith would find no difficulty in seeing off that of Colbert. For this reason, and in the light of later divisions within the Party, it is interesting to find Lewis arguing powerfully for eventual Monetary Union. During a transitional period of adaptation, flexibility of exchange rates "should have a useful part to play". But "in a fully integrated Community movable exchange rates would be a contradiction in terms".

> The basic idea of the customs union is that economic unification shall be accomplished through the free movement of price and through other forms of competition in merchandise and the factors of production. If national exchange rates were to move freely the mutual adjustment of goods and factors would be considerably reduced, as exchange rate fluctuations would add an exchange cost to hamper the flow.

With the (near) completion of the Single Market at the beginning of 1993, the logic of this argument should have become even more compelling.

Notes

1 I. Macleod, 'The Tory Leadership', *Spectator*, the 17th January 1964.
2 *Putting Britain right ahead: a statement of Conservative aims* (Conservative and Unionist Central Office, October 1965).
3 *A Smaller Stage* by Leon Brittan, Julian Critchley, Hugh Dykes, Russell Lewis and David Walder MP (Bow Group, December 1965).
4 "Europe: the reason why" in *Crossbow,* April–June 1965 (Bow Group).
5 *A European Technological Community* by Sir Anthony Meyer BT (CPC) New Tasks, New Techniques series, New Techniques No. 7, December 1966).
6 *The Conservative Goal: a call to Action* by the Rt. Hon. Edward Heath MBE, MP (CPC, March 1966).
7 *Action not Words: the new Conservative Programme* (Conservative and Unionist Central Office, March 1966).

8   *Britain's World Role* by The Rt. Hon. Geoffrey Rippon Q.C. (CPC New Tasks series, no. 3, March 1965).

9   "This is no way to get into Europe" by Malcolm Rutherford (*Crossbow*, July–September 1966).

10 *The Story of the Monday Club* by Robert Copping (Monday Club, April 1972).

11 *Europe: Should Britain Join?* by Sir Anthony Meyer and Mr. Victor Montagu (Monday Club, November 1966).

12 *A Europe of Nations* by Spenser Batiste, Alec Berry, John H.Davies, Anthony Dove, Roger Helmer, Gordon Kingsbury, William Meakin and Charles Tracey, ed. Peter Lilley (CPC for the Monday Club, October 1965).

13 See *CPC in action* (CPC, October 1967, republished January 1972).

14 *Britain's Place in Europe*, Masterbrief 7 (CPC, May 1967).

15 *What Joining Would Mean*, Masterbrief 8 (CPC, June 1967).

16 *Britain, Europe and the World*, Masterbrief 9 (CPC August 1967).

17 See Hugo Young *op.cit.* p. 223.

18 *Britain and the European Communities – An Economic Assessment* (HMSO, 1970).

19 *Britain & Europe* by Ben Patterson (CCO for the YCs, March 1967).

20 *The British General Election of 1970* by David Butler and Michael Pinto-Duschinsky (Macmillan, 1971).

21 *"The European Perspective"* by David Levy *(Monday World*, Summer 1970).

22 "Europe Third Time Round" by Russell Lewis (*Crossbow*, October–December 1969).

23 *Our Future in Europe: the Long-Term Case for going in* by Leon Brittan, Jock Bruce-Gardyne, John Macgregor, Archie Hamilton, Howell, Harris Hughes and Derek Prag (Bow Group, February 1970, reprinted August 1970).

24 *A Better Tomorrow: The Conservative programme for the next 5 years* (CCO, 1970).

25 Forster *op.cit.* p. 49.

26 *Britain's Place in the World* by Sir Alec Douglas Home (CPC, August 1969).

27 *Enoch Powell: the man and his thinking* by T.E.Utley (William Kimber, 1968).

28 See the collection of essays and speeches *Freedom and Reality* by Enoch Powell edited by John Wood (B.T.Batsford, Ltd. 1969).

29 *The Common Market: the case against* by Enoch Powell (Elliot Right Way Books, 1971) p. 9.

30 *Relations between the United Kingdom Parliament and the European Parliament after Direct Elections* (House of Lords Select Committee on the European Communities, Vol. II, Minutes of Evidence. HMSO, July 1978).

31 See "The Common Market" in *Still to Decide* by Enoch Powell, edited by John Wood (B.T.Batsford Ltd., 1972)., p. 216.

32 Powell *The Common Market: the case against*, p. 9.

33 Powell *Still to Decide*, p. 230.

34 Hugo Young *op.cit.* p. 243.

35 Hugo Young *op.cit.* p. 377.

36 *op.cit.* pp. 223–7.

37 See "Negotiations with the Communities" in *The United Kingdom and the European Communities* (Cmnd. 4715, HMSO July 1971).

38 *Europe: The Case For Going In* (George G. Harrap & Co for the European Movement (British Council), 1971).

39 *Hansard*, 19 May 1982, Col. 352.

40 *A Stranger in Europe* by Sir Stephen Wall (Oxford University Press, 2008) p. 17.

41 *The Common Market*, Contact Brief 42 (CPC, September/October 1971).

42 *The United Kingdom and the European Communities* (Cmnd. 4715, HMSO July 1971).

43 *A Europe for the Regions* by George Gardiner (CPC, August 1971).

44 Crowson *op.cit.*, especially Chapter 5, "Selling Europe".

45 *Sovereignty: substance or shadow* by Tufton Beamish and Norman St John-Stevas (CPC, July 1971).

46 *Conflict of Loyalty* by Geoffrey Howe (Macmillan, 1994).

47 *The Rome Treaty and the Law* by Dennis Thompson (supplement to *Crossbow* Bow Group, July–September 1962).

48 For example Case 6/64, *Falminio Costa v. ENEL* [1964] ECR 585, 593.

49 *Europe and the law* by Maurice Bathurst, Desmond Miller, Philip Turl, Alan Campbell, Derek Hene and Edward Wall (CPC, February 1968).

50 Hugo Young *op.cit.* p. 234.

51 *Memoirs* by Douglas Hurd (Little Brown Abacus paperback, 2003) p. 194.

52 Howe, *op.cit.* p. 68.

53 *Conservative Dissidents: Dissent within the Parliamentary Conservative Party, 1970–1974* by Philip Norton (Temple Smith 1978) quoted by Forster, *op.cit.*

54 *Fitting into Europe*, Contact Brief 51 (CPC, November 1972).

55 *Towards a European Identity* by William Shearman, Nicholas Beacock and Reginald Watts (PEST, 1972).

56 *The Middle Way*, subtitled *A Study of the Problems of Economic and Social Progress in a Free and Democratic Society*, was a book by Harold Macmillan published (by Macmillan & Co.) in 1938.

57 Quotation from *Reflections on the French Revolution* (1790). Burke was commenting on the theory that society was founded on a "social contract".

58 Published as *Great Britain's Foreign Policy* by The Earl of Home (CPC, April 1961).

59 *Britain's Place in the World* by Sir Alec Douglas Home (CPC, 1969), pp. 9–10.

60 See *Rome or Brussels … ?* by W.R.Lewis (Institute of Economic Affairs, Hobart Paperback, 1971).

61 *UK, Commonwealth and Common Market: a Reappraisal* by James E.Meade, Professor of Political Economy, University of Cambridge (Institute of Economic Affairs 1970).

5 Membership and Referendum

Parliament

The first UK Members of the European Parliament were not, as they should have been, fully representative of the British Parliament. The UK was entitled to thirty-six seats; but, of the major parties, only the Conservative and Liberal Parties took them up. Pending a referendum on continued Common Market membership, the Labour Party boycotted the Parliament, and was joined by the Scottish National Party. The Ulster Unionists initially sent one MP in the person of Rafton Pounder; but after he had lost his Belfast South seat in the General Election of February 1974, the Unionists did not replace him. On the other hand a Social Democrat for a short while formed a single British representative in the Parliament's Socialist Group: Dick Taverne, the MP for Lincoln, who had left the Labour Party on the issue of Europe.

The membership of the nominated European Parliament was indeed extremely unstable: the same Members[*] rarely, if ever, met from month to month. This was in part because national elections frequently changed the political balance of the national delegations, partly because individual parliamentarians might find themselves in government (and therefore ineligible as members of another institution, the Council of Ministers), or otherwise indisposed. The European Conservative Group in the Parliament initially consisted of eighteen British Members, making it – with two Danish Conservatives, and, briefly, Rafton Pounder – the fourth largest after the Christian Democrats, the Socialists and the Liberals and Allies.

Members of the Group already had considerable experience of, and contacts in, the European political scene, half having already served in the Council of Europe or WEU Assemblies. The Group was headed, until his sudden death in 1977, by one of these, the MP for Saffron Walden, Sir Peter Kirk, whose maiden speech was greeted with enormous enthusiasm, and great expectations.

During the period before the Labour Party took up its seats following the 1975 referendum, there were quite a few changes in the British

---

[*] The nominal total number of Members at the time was 198; but a number of seats were generally left vacant, including fourteen UK seats.

Conservative delegation, many as a result of the two general elections of 1974. The first members from the House of Commons included some, like Sir Tufton Beamish (later Lord Chelwood) and Sir Douglas Dodds-Parker, who knew Strasbourg well from the British delegation to the Council of Europe. Others would one day sit in the elected Parliament, some with a dual mandate, some having given up their House of Commons seats: Elaine Kellett-Bowman, Tom Normanton, Sir Brandon Rhys-Williams and James Scott-Hopkins; and many years later John Corrie. They included the ardent pro-Europe Bow Grouper, Hugh Dykes; and the long-standing anti-Marketeer, Sir Derek Walker-Smith. Among other Members was the MP for Norfolk North, Ralph Howell, whose son Paul Howell would sit in the elected Parliament after 1979 as the MEP for Norfolk.

The delegation from the House of Lords aroused great curiosity. Alone among those from other nations, some were, in effect, hereditary MEPs. There were eminent-looking figures like Deputy Conservative leader Lord Bessborough and the Liberal Peer Lord Gladwyn and the tall, gaunt Lord Reay. There was the suitably eccentric figure of Lord Rowley St. Oswald, who had escaped a Communist firing-squad during the Spanish Civil War while covering it for the *Daily Telegraph*. Almost as eccentric was the position of Lord Charles O'Hagan, who represented the cross-bench peers in the Lords, but who found himself seated just behind the Communists, and was widely assumed to belong there. When he turned up as the elected Conservative Member for Devonshire in 1979, many heads were scratched. Lord Bethell would also be elected to the Parliament in 1979, as would Baroness Elles, a founder of the European Union of Women; and so, later, would her son James Elles.

Reporting on the first year of Community membership in a CPC pamphlet, *Three Views of Europe*,[1] Kirk observed that the Conservative Group, on its arrival in the European Parliament in Strasbourg in January 1973, "decided not to hide its light under a bushel".

> To a certain extent, of course, the main thing we had to contribute was style – the slightly improvised forceful style of the House of Commons. … And here we were greatly helped by the fact that the original Six had already agreed among themselves to introduce Westminster-style Question Time. … This has turned out to be one of the best ways of getting at both Commission and Council.

Even more important, Kirk goes on, "was the necessity to move as quickly as possible in the field of financial and budgetary control". Springing from the idea of a public accounts system on Westminster lines, the Parliament decided to set up what would eventually be the Budgetary Control Committee, and to turn the ineffective Audit Board into a Court of Auditors, responsible to Parliament through the Control Committee. The importance of this move would become clear over twenty years later, when the refusal by Parliament to grant discharge on the Community

Budget would lead to the fall of the Santer Commission. Kirk prophetically commented at the time that "this is probably the Conservative
group's biggest single achievement to date".

The Conservative Group, however, also set in motion a large number
of other changes which, sooner or later, were to come into effect. The
Parliament already had "a system which many of us at Westminster have
been groping for for years": a system of "pre-legislative committees".
These, Kirk suggested, could take on an "inquisitorial" role similar to
those of the US Congressional committee system, holding open, investiga-
tory hearings. Sir Derek Walker-Smith contributed a key proposal which
has only recently come to pass (and that only partially): that the Council
of Ministers should meet in public when legislating.

In one field, however, there was complete failure: ending "the absurd
pantomime of a peripatetic Parliament". It is still the case that the
Parliament is obliged to hold twelve sittings a year in Strasbourg, hold
its committee meetings (and now additional sittings) in Brussels, while
the seat of its Secretariat and a large proportion of its staff remains in
Luxembourg (for an explanation see Chapter Eleven).

Commission and Council

Appropriately, the first Conservative Commissioner was the son-in-law of
Winston Churchill, Christopher Soames. He was a large personality, both
in size and experience, having been an MP, a cabinet minister, Governor of
Southern Rhodesia and British Ambassador in Paris. As Vice-President of
the Commission he had special responsibility for External Relations from
January 1973 to January 1977.

There is a tendency, particularly in the media, to refer to British
Commissioners as "our" Commissioners. In theory at least, however,
Commissioners are required to act completely independently of national
interests and national governments, in particular that of their own country
of origin – indeed, they take an oath to that effect. They are *not*, however,
required to give up their political affiliations. Soames was therefore able
to contribute to the CPC pamphlet at the end of 1973 reporting back on the
first year of Community membership.

It becomes clear in this that Soames had without effort found himself
completely at home.

> George Thomson keeps his links with the Labour Party, as I do mine
> with the Tory Party: and both of us, regardless of party, have to keep in
> touch with British government thinking no less than public opinion.
> ... Each of us ... must be able to tell our colleagues where the bounds
> of political possibility lie and where the trends of domestic thinking in
> our respective countries seem to be moving. ... (But) it is in the nature
> of things that the Commission will, from time to time, make proposals
> that will be thought to run counter to one or other vested national

interests. Governments should not be surprised at that or take offence. For to seek the long-term interest of the Community as a whole rather than to protect short-term national interests – that, surely, is what the Commission is for.

Yet there was never any complaint that Soames had "gone native", as there would be in later years about both Conservative Commissioners and Conservative MEPs.

The third article in *Three Views of Europe* was by the Minister with special responsibility for European Affairs (and Chancellor of the Duchy of Lancaster), John Davies, who had previously been Managing Director of Shell Mex and BP, and then Director General of the Confederation of British Industry (CBI). His tone was considerably more downbeat. "Britain entered the European Community with a fanfare," he began. "Today the sounds of Community construction have become more muted." There was "a sense of anti-climax in Britain".

This tone, it is possible to detect, is partly the result of his experiences at Council of Ministers meetings in Brussels. The Community, he says, "is, in effect, a non-stop negotiating machine" and "the average newspaper reader could scarcely be blamed for believing that the Community … has staggered from one verbal battle to another"; adding, "to some extent, of course, it has".

It is also clear that, in Brussels, the Conservative Government was not getting the rapturous welcome that Conservative Members of Parliament received in Luxembourg and Strasbourg. "Our critics from the other Member States," Davies wrote, "accuse us, with varying degrees of severity, of pursuing purely British interests in Brussels, of trying to undermine the Common Agricultural Policy, and of acting as a Trojan Horse for America and the Commonwealth. … I contest most strongly the thesis that we have been excessively nationalists in our approach to Community affairs."

Yet in Britain, he added, "our critics condemn us on the grounds that we are doing precisely the opposite;" and concluded that "there is still a great deal to be done to spread basic information about the Community. … The Community is not a faceless monster imposing its will on an unwilling population", nor "'them' imposing their will on 'us'".

Some of this view is understandable in a businessman used to taking clear decisions within a reasonable period of time. It is one, however, that many future Conservative ministers would also come to hold, including – as reported in their memoirs – John Nott and Kenneth Baker. I remember Peter Lilley, during the intense and vital negotiations over Value Added Tax and excise duties in the run-up to the Single Market, describing the proceedings as "faffing around". Political analysts have attributed much of the problem to the – at least until now – unfamiliarity of British politicians, as compared to those from other Member States, with the need to compromise in coalition governments, itself a result of the electoral system.

Other ministers, however, found their experiences in Council more stimulating. As already observed, they resulted in Peter Walker finally abandoning his residual opposition to Common Market membership. Even Norman Tebbit, later an arch Eurosceptic, records that he "enjoyed the challenge of negotiations and dealing inherent in the Community system and first became aware of the extent to which Ministers and officials were benefiting from the cross-fertilisation of ideas and experience".[2]

The perception that ministers' efforts on behalf of the country were not appreciated at home also became a continuing theme. Despite the passage of time, the public always seemed in need of basic information about the Community; and Conservative activists in the constituencies would regularly complain that they were not being told enough about the Party's policy on Europe to pass it on to voters. The British press was perceived as insular, if not downright hostile (but see the section on the Media in Chapter Sixteen).

The result would be the gradual habit of presenting negotiations within the Community as a sporting contest, out of which Britain would emerge victorious: John Major's "game, set and match" after Maastricht became perhaps the most notorious example. This fatally distorted the message that the Community was all about "pooling" sovereignty and "achieving together what we cannot do apart".

Problems at home

Within the Party, nevertheless, membership of the Community initially proved popular and stimulating. In particular, in constituencies where there were links to business and commerce, there were seminars, conferences and dinners on the new opportunities opening up. Visits to Brussels, Strasbourg and Luxembourg for party members (as for those of other parties, for journalists and for other opinion-formers) were organised through the Commission and Parliament information offices in Kensington Palace Gardens.

The Bow Group set up a European Liaison Committee, with former Vice-Chairman of the Greater London Area Young Conservatives, Christine Stewart-Munro as liaison officer. A branch of the Bow Group was established in Paris, with a membership that was broadly one-third French, two-thirds British. Links with the Christian Democratic Parties, particularly at youth level, were also strengthened: the European and Christian Democratic Students had held a conference in London in July 1972.

Almost as soon as Community membership had become a reality, however, the economic and political situation turned sour. This was the direct effect of the October 1973 Yom Kippur War in the Middle East, and of the oil embargo and energy crisis that succeeded it. The Bretton Woods currency system negotiated after the war collapsed as the dollar/gold link was broken. Prices rose, bringing higher wage demands and the threat of an escalating wage-price spiral, which the government attempted to prevent by introducing a statutory incomes policy. The miners went on strike, resulting in the "three-day week".

Within the Conservative Party, Heath's reputation was severely damaged by the charge that he had done a "U-turn" from the free market policies advanced at the General Election of 1970. Another Conservative pressure group, the Selsdon Group,* was created by Nicholas Ridley to promote the free-market economic policies which had been adopted following a shadow cabinet meeting at the Selsdon Park Hotel in 1970. It would soon be chaired by another former tutor at Swinton Conservative College, David Alexander.

These were not good circumstances in which to demonstrate the economic benefits of joining the European Community. Although world food prices (as in the case of all commodity prices) were soaring, it was particularly difficult to argue that this had nothing to do with the CAP, as it had been predicted that precisely such rises would occur. The best estimates at the time were that the UK had paid about £150 million into the EEC Budget and got back about £65 million, resulting in a net contribution of £85 million. This looked bad in the light of a rising balance of payments deficit. So did the fact that, although exports to the rest of the Community had risen by 37% over the previous year, imports had risen by 47%.

In so far as factors due to Community membership could be disentangled from those due to the oil crisis, the situation was in fact not that bad. The net budget contribution was partially offset, for example, by an inflow of capital via European Investment Bank loans. There had also been an inflow of private investment, creating thousands of new jobs. In any case, the transitional period had only just started, and the long-term dynamic effects of membership for the economy were not expected to be significant for some years.

One effect of the dire economic climate was to lend some credence to the Labour Party's claim that the terms of entry had been unfavourable, and should be renegotiated. Another was that sceptics within the Conservative Party began, once again, to question whether the acceptance of a loss of sovereignty in exchange for economic gains had really been worthwhile. In January 1974 the Bow Group published a short pamphlet on *Europe: The First Year*,[3] which contained a section on "the most fundamental impact of the Common Market: its destruction of national sovereignty" by a barrister, Mary Colton.

This made a distinction between treaties concluded under international law and the Rome Treaty. In the former case, any effects on English law had to be the subject of an Act of Parliament, which could be repealed in the normal way. In the case of the Community, however, the European Communities Act 1972 had provided that Community regulations would have the force of law without further national enactment; and also that

---

* The name was in part a defiant reaction to the disparaging use of the term "Selsdon Man" by Harold Wilson. As in the case of the word "Tory" several centuries before, the insult was proudly adopted by its targets.

English courts would be bound by the rulings of the European Court of Justice. Normally, no Parliament could bind its successors. Yet the 1972 Act, it could be argued, had "permanently surrendered power upwards". If there had in fact been an irrevocable transfer, "then any Act of Parliament inconsistent with Community legislation would be held invalid by the English courts, as of course would any Act which purported to repeal the European Communities Act but which was not sanctioned by parallel Community legislation."* The author's conclusion was that "in essence, the United Kingdom's present relationship to the Communities is that of a province within a federation". Sovereignty had been "abandoned not by conscious decision but in a fit of absence of mind".

This legal opinion would reappear, in more or less sophisticated forms, in many more speeches and publications in the years that followed. For the antis, it would lead to the conclusion that there should at least be a referendum on future Community membership, if not withdrawal. For the pros it would be evidence of the Community's "democratic deficit", an argument for restoring parliamentary sovereignty through an elected European Parliament.

Only just over a year after Britain's accession to the Community, the domestic situation led Heath to call the "who runs Britain" election. The Conservative Manifesto, *Firm Action for a Fair Britain*,[4] not surprisingly, led on the energy crisis and the problem of halting a wage-price spiral. Europe appeared only as one item in the final section but one, "Britain, Europe and the World".

The text on Europe, however, is very interesting in the light of Conservative attitudes thirty years later. "We have made it clear that we are not satisfied with every aspect of Community arrangements, and have sought ... changes where these are desirable," it says. Yet is does not go on to call for "less Europe" or the repatriation of powers. A Conservative Government would

> urge on our Community partners the need to extend the scope of Community action into industrial policy, technological questions and social and environmental questions. This is necessary if the full benefits of the larger market are to be reaped, and if we are to realise the full potential of the Community as an instrument for improving the life of the people.

The reference to "social and environmental questions" is of especial significance in view of the debates that would one day take place in the context of the Single Market programme, and later as the Conservative Party moved towards Euroscepticism.

---

* This opinion is of considerable interest in view of the Conservative Party's policy in 2010 of adopting an Act which would affirm that Westminster retained the right to amend (or repeal) the European Communities Act 1972 (see Chapters 15 and 17).

The result of the General Election of February 1974 was a hung parliament. The Conservative Party polled the most votes; but as a result of the decision of the Ulster Unionists to withdraw their support in protest over the Sunningdale Agreement on power-sharing in Northern Ireland, Labour had the most seats. Negotiations between Heath and the Liberal Party leader, Jeremy Thorpe, failed to produce any agreement; and Wilson came back into office. The second election of the year took place in October, with Labour again returned, but with an overall majority of only three.

At the elections Labour had committed itself to a "fundamental re-negotiation" of the terms on which Britain had entered the Community, and also to "consult the people through the ballot box" on the new terms. Although, according to the polls, only 10% of the electorate believed the matter to be "an important question", the potential for catastrophe was high.

Party politics suspended

In 1975 my wife Felicity and I were living in a small terraced house in Putney. We had been married at the end of 1970 and moved across the river the following year. By that time I had lost my seat on Hammersmith Borough Council in the swing-back to Labour. I remember the Labour MP for Barons Court at the time, the future European Commissioner Ivor Richard, telling me at the count: "You know how to get back again? Vote in a Labour Government!"

In the run up to the referendum on continued Community membership in June 1975 our house was the local committee-room for the "Yes" campaign. On the day of the vote, the 5th, a sizeable group of knockers-up operated out of the front room. They included local Conservatives, Liberals (Peter Hain, no less, was the local Liberal standard-bearer), and a section from the Young European Left (YEL). The enthusiasm surpassed anything I can recall from normal elections.

The "renegotiation" carried out by the Wilson government had initially identified seventeen unacceptable items in the terms on which the UK had joined the Community. Only one assumed any importance: the mechanism for ensuring that the UK did not pay an unfair amount into the Community budget; and the resulting agreement on a rebate, based on the UK's GNP as a proportion of the Community average, later turned out to be useless. Moreover, as the recently-appointed Deputy leader of the Conservative Party, Willie Whitelaw, pointed out, the renegotiation produced nothing which could not have been obtained "in the course of the Community's normal development".[5]

Most accounts of Wilson's period as leader of the Labour Party agree that his renegotiation pledge was more a device to keep the Party united than a consequence of real objections to the terms negotiated by Heath. The same is certainly true of the decision to hold a referendum. Crowson records[6] that there was considerable support, even within the Conservative Party, for a referendum on possible Common Market membership in the lead-up to the General Election of 1970; but that this was never seriously considered as an option by the Party leadership, conflicting as it did with belief in the sovereignty of Parliament. Wilson himself almost certainly held much the same opinion; but in his case the alternative to a referendum was the probable collapse of his government.

Moreover, Wilson was not acting blindly. A later study[7] of the campaign by David Butler and Uwe Kitzinger drew attention to a private poll conducted for the government in August 1974 which found massive (76%) support for holding a referendum. It also, however, found that "if the Government renegotiated new terms for Britain's membership of the Common Market", the electorate would vote by 69% to 31% to stay in. This was remarkably close to the actual result.

The renegotiated terms nevertheless played little part in the campaign. Indeed, another subsequent study[8] observed that there was no correlation at all between changes of attitude towards the Community and knowledge or views about the terms. So, rather than to details, the arguments on both sides appealed to gut feelings.

The organisation set up to fight for a "Yes", Britain in Europe, chaired by Roy Jenkins, was massively supported by business: around 80% of Britain's largest companies, according to an *Economist* poll, expected to be harmed by withdrawal from the Community. The Council of the British Institute of Management (BIM), according to its Chairman at the time, the future Conservative MEP Sir Fred Catherwood, voted 47 to 2 to support British membership.[9] The treasurer of Britain in Europe was Alistair McAlpine from the European League for Economic Cooperation (ELEC), who would in the 1990s join Sir James Goldsmith's virulently Eurosceptic Referendum Party. The "Yes" campaign was able to argue for keeping the *status quo* in difficult economic circumstances. "This is no time for Britain to be considering leaving a Christmas club, let alone the Common Market", Commissioner Soames was widely quoted as saying.

On the "No" side, Conservatives – following Powell, now an Ulster Unionist MP – emphasised the sovereignty issue; but opinion polls showed that fewer than 10% of the electorate were actually concerned about such legal points (any more than they were with the argument on the Labour left that the Community was a "capitalist conspiracy"). Rather, the strongest card for the "No" campaign was the fear of rising prices, just as the strongest for the "Yes" campaign the fear of unemployment.

Three leaflets were, theoretically, distributed to every household before the vote. The first, entitled *Britain's New Deal in Europe*,[10] was issued by the Government, and had on the cover the message: "Her Majesty's Government have decided to recommend to the British people to vote for staying in the Community. HAROLD WILSON, PRIME MINISTER". This reflected the 16:7 positive vote in the Cabinet. In a section devoted to the question: "Will Parliament lose its power?" it observed that the House of Commons itself had, in April, voted by 396 to 170 in favour of staying in;

and also made the more controversial point that "the British Parliament in Westminster retains the final right to repeal the Act which took us into the Market".

Despite the evidence that most people were not interested in sovereignty, this was the main theme of the "NO" leaflet, issued by the National Referendum Campaign.[11] The Community "sets out by stages to merge Britain with France, Germany, Italy and other countries into a single nation", it said. Laws were enacted and taxes raised by "unelected Commissioners in Brussels".

By contrast, the "YES" leaflet from Britain in Europe[12] made its major points protecting jobs and "secure food at fair prices". An impressive list of supporters on the back page included Lord Feather, former General Secretary of the Trades Union Congress (TUC), and Sir Henry Plumb, at the time President of the National Farmers Union, but who would one day become the first Conservative President of the European Parliament (and now a Lord).

In most – though not all – constituencies, the Conservative Party played an active part in the "Yes" campaign, encouraged by the strongly pro-European Party chairman Peter Thorneycroft. Local party offices were used by "Yes" supporters, with constituency agents often involved. Central Office issued pro-"Yes" *Campaign Notes*; and the Party organisation was also the conduit for distributing material issued by Britain in Europe and the European Community's own London Information Office. The Head of the Commission section of that office at the time was the one-time director of the Action Committee for the United States of Europe and disciple of Jean Monnet, Richard Mayne; and, as his obituary in *The Times* observed, "while holding to his brief of fairness to both sides ... he undoubtedly helped to swing British opinion towards remaining in the European Community".[13]

Participation in the campaign by the Conservative leadership, however, was muted. Shortly before the referendum, the Party had been through a leadership contest, with Margaret Thatcher replacing Ted Heath. Though the decision had been up to Conservatives in the House of Commons, the constituency parties had been consulted, and most had voted to retain Heath. At the time there was some resentment that the MPs had not listened. Though the new leader did support a "Yes" vote – Douglas Hurd records that "Margaret did not at that time have a definite view on the future of Europe"[14] – she, like Wilson, did not take a lead in the campaign. Conservative support inevitably centred on those around the former leader, Heath. This, in turn, meant that those Conservatives who had been most in favour of a leadership change were less inclined to get involved.

On the other hand, Conservatives were conspicuously absent from the "No" campaign. Of the forty-one rebels in October 1971, only Ronald Bell (a member of whose local party, Hugh Simmonds, started Conservatives Against the Common Market to campaign at constituency association level), Richard Body, Neil Marten, Teddy Taylor and Robin Turton (now in the Lords), played a major role.

One senior Conservative campaigner on the "Yes" side was Geoffrey Rippon. Towards the end of 1974 he published a summary of the case for staying in the Community, *Our Future in Europe*.[15] This emphasised the advantages of being in the Community in the light of "a new world of global inflation, resource scarcity and economic uncertainty". It met head-on the argument about food prices which played a large part in the anti-Market case. The Common Agricultural Policy had made "a real contribution ... to stability of prices and security of supply. ... It has already helped to contain the price of butter, cheese, bread, beef and sugar for the British housewife. ... There is now no more cheap food in the world."

It also met head-on the sovereignty argument. The whole history of political progress was "a history of gradual abandonment of national sovereignty. ... The question is not whether sovereignty remains absolute or not, but in what way one is prepared to sacrifice sovereignty, to whom and for what purpose." It concluded by calling for "a revival of the European ideal".

Britain in Europe had clearly outgunned the National Referendum Campaign; but the result was even more decisive than initially expected: 17.38 million (67.2%) "Yes", 8.47 million (32.8%) "No", on a respectable turnout of 64.5%. We all heaved a huge sigh of relief and had a big party.

Human rights

Europe did not play a major part in the politics of Britain in the four years between the referendum and the European and General Elections of 1979. Wilson unexpectedly handed over to James Callaghan as Prime Minister, Roy Jenkins became the first British President of the Commission, and the Labour Party at last took up its eighteen seats in the European Parliament. The Conservative MEPs were reduced to sixteen; the Scottish National Party, also ending its boycott, sent Winnie Ewing; and there was still one Liberal, Russell Johnston, another Scot.

One European issue that did arouse controversy, however, was that of Human Rights, and the jurisdiction of the European Court of Human Rights in Strasbourg. This gained added prominence because, as a CPC pamphlet of 1977, *Human Rights and Foreign Policy* by Richard Luce MP and John Ranelagh,[16] put it, "in Northern Ireland, terrorism inevitably strains our ability to observe the full range of Human Rights".

> For the past three years Britain has been the most prosecuted of the thirteen countries that have ratified the Convention allowing individual cases to be brought to the European Court of Human Rights. In 1976 there were 153 individual applications made against Britain. ... Since 1974, Britain has faced 200 cases brought on behalf of holders of British passports in East Africa. ... Other cases range from protests that corporal punishment in schools is a breach of article 3 relating to inhuman treatment, to a case that the closed shop contravenes article

11 relating to freedom of association. In addition, Britain is facing the protracted torture case brought by the Irish government.

In December of that year, in fact, the Court ruled that the UK government was guilty of the "inhuman and degrading treatment" of men interned without trial in Northern Ireland.

At the time, and ever since, prosecution of the UK in Strasbourg has been cited by anti-Marketeers and Eurosceptics as evidence of "interference" by the European Community in our domestic affairs.* Attempts to point out that the Court of Human Rights in Strasbourg is *not* the European Court of Justice in Luxembourg – indeed, has nothing whatsoever to do with the European Community or European Union – have been in vain. As an MEP, I was frequently contacted to take up a case with the Strasbourg Court, as were my colleagues. We had to explain that MEPs have no special status in relation to the Court, a body set up under the 1950 European Convention on Human Rights under the auspices of the Council of Europe (and drafted, as it happens, by a Conservative Minister, Sir David Maxwell Fyfe). One member of the British Labour delegation in the late 1970s, Tam Dalyell, once proved the point by being escorted out of a Court hearing when he attempted to intervene.

Not all European countries had given individuals the right of access to the Court, although all the nine Community countries of the time had done so. In the UK, the situation was complicated by the fact that the Convention had not been incorporated into domestic law, which resulted in a disproportionate number of cases going to Strasbourg rather than being settled in national courts. Incorporation was one of the solutions suggested by Luce and Ranelagh; but this was not to happen until the year 2000 under the Human Rights Act 1998. Meanwhile, there would be periodic calls for the UK to remove itself from the jurisdiction of the Court (as there are today, following the Court's insistence that the UK should not deprive certain prisoners of the vote).

The case of the treatment of Northern Ireland internees was clearly the most serious of the cases faced by the UK in Strasbourg. Another that caused almost as much controversy, however, arose from a case in the Isle of Man when, in 1972, four schoolboys were birched for assaulting a prefect. As a Crown Dependency, and not part of the UK, the IoM had not followed the UK in abolishing judicial corporal punishment in 1948. Indeed, the Manx tourist board was using this as a selling point, attributing the low crime rate on the Island to the fact that juvenile offenders there were liable to face a birching. One of the schoolboys had appealed, but lost

---

* One typical example was the claim by the *Daily Mail* on the 30th April 2002, under the heading "Corgis to be banned by EU", that "certain breeds of the Queen's favourite dog could be outlawed under a controversial EU convention … ". The measure referred to was actually a voluntary agreement, the European Convention for the Protection of Pet Animals, drawn up in 1987 by a panel of animal protection experts acting for the Council of Europe. The UK, moreover, was not even a signatory to this Convention.

the appeal, with the result that the birching took place many weeks after the offence. These were the grounds on which the case eventually arrived at the European Court of Human Rights. Its judgement, however, was not delivered until 1978, when, by a 6 to 1 majority, it found that birching was degrading and hence in breach of the Convention.

Within the Conservative Party the affair re-awakened old passions. Those caricatured as the "hang-'em-and-flog-'em brigade" had never accepted the effective ending of capital punishment for murder, and there was also substantial support for the return of corporal punishment for juvenile offenders, as an alternative to incarceration. What was not readily admitted was that backing for these positions was actually greater among Labour voters than among Conservatives.

For the Government, however, the main complication was constitutional. It was responsible for the Crown Dependencies' external relations and hence for their international treaty obligations. On the other hand, the Isle of Man had – and still has – its own parliament and made its own laws. The birching law accordingly remained on the Island statute book until 1993, although the last attempt to carry out corporal punishment under its provisions took place in 1981. (The sentence was turned down on appeal by a judge from the mainland, although the offender, a holiday-maker from Glasgow, actually stated that he would rather be birched than go to a borstal).

The European Court of Justice in Luxembourg, meanwhile, was not yet causing comparable controversy. Indeed, the National Referendum Campaign leaflet, *Why you should vote NO*, had not mentioned it at all.

Notes

1 *Three Views of Europe* by Peter Kirk MP, the Rt. Hon. Sir Christopher Soames and the Rt. Hon. John Davies MP (CPC), December 1973).

2 *Upwardly Mobile* by Norman Tebbit (Weidenfeld and Nicolson, 1988) p. 168.

3 *Europe: The First Year* by Nick Brittain, Mary Colton, Richard Barber and Nicholas Lyell (Bow Group, January 1974).

4 *Firm Action for a Fair Britain: the Conservative Manifesto 1974* (Conservative Central Office).

5 *Hansard*, the 7th April 1975, Col. 840.

6 Crowson *op.cit.* p. 90.

7 *The 1975 Referendum* by David Butler and Uwe Kitzinger (Macmillan, 1976).

8 *Britain Says Yes: The 1975 Referendum on the Common Market* by Anthony King (American Enterprise Institute for Public Policy Research, 1977).

9 See "Trade" in *Here to Stay* by Lord Carrington, Poul Møller, Christopher Tugendhat, Sir Fred Catherwood, David Curry and Adam Fergusson (European Democratic Group, 1983).

10 *Britain's New Deal in Europe* (HMSO for HMG, 1975).

11 *Why you should vote NO* (HMSO for the National Referendum Campaign, 1975).

12 *Why you should vote YES* (HMSO for Britain in Europe, 1975).

13 *The Times*, the 10th December 2009.

14 Hurd *op.cit.* p. 263.

15 *Our Future in Europe* by the Rt. Hon. Geoffrey Rippon (CPC, September 1974).

16 *Human Rights and Foreign Policy* by Richard Luce MP and John Ranelagh (CPC, 1977).

6 Direct Elections

Electoral systems and alliances

The first comprehensive statement of Conservative policy under the Thatcher leadership appeared in October 1976: *The Right Approach*.[1] The section on Europe gave no hint of any incipient Euroscepticism.

> For the last fifteen years, the Conservative Party has consistently believed that the best hope for Britain lay in membership of a free, strong and democratic European Community. In both Government and opposition we have fought successfully to bring Britain within the European fold and, when that membership was threatened, to keep her there.

The statement then dealt with a subject which had already become topical: the prospect that Members of the European Parliament would be directly elected by the voters of the nine Member States rather than nominated from their national parliaments. The Conservative Party's policy was that it hoped "that these elections will now be held in 1978".

An enormous amount of background work had already been carried out on direct elections,[2] and in 1975 the Parliament itself, acting under Article 138 of the Rome Treaty (later renumbered 190), had made proposals, drafted by a Dutch Socialist, Schelto Patijn. The Parliament had, in fact, already drawn up a Convention for direct elections as early as 1960; but it was not until 1976 the Council of Ministers formally adopted the necessary Act.[3] In Britain, anti-Marketeers then argued that, though the Treaty required the Parliament and Council to lay down provisions for direct elections, there was no Treaty obligation on Member States to accept them. This point was answered in the House of Commons by no less a figure than Sir Derek Walker-Smith, who argued that the Member States and their national parliaments had a duty to consider the proposals "until an acceptable form is achieved and adopted".

Within the Conservative Party there was of course significant opposition to direct elections. For some, the reasons were largely practical: the powers of the European Parliament were not enough to justify the trouble and expense of electing it; continuing to nominate its members from national parliaments would ensure that they stayed "on side"; and constituencies would in any case be too big to allow proper representation. Others were against for reasons which were essentially the opposite: that a directly-elected Parliament would soon gain greater power, and be a step on the road to a "supra-national", federal European Union. Westminster would be "reduced to the status of a County Council".*

Curiously, this latter view had already, in some measure, been refuted by Enoch Powell, who had advanced a more sophisticated objection to direct elections: that they would only create an *illusion* of political union, since they would not be underpinned by a common polity.

> A nation politically united can have an elected sovereign parliament … but that does not mean that a politically united nation can be created or promoted by creating an elected parliament. This is the same fallacy as to suppose that, as rich people frequent nightclubs, we ourselves have only to go to a nightclub in order to become rich.[4]

Apart from such issues of principle, two technical matters had also proved controversial. First, how were the seats to be divided up? And, secondly, what exactly did the phrase in the Treaty, "a uniform electoral procedure" imply? On the first question, the compromise reached at Community level was that seats would be allocated on the principle of "diminishing progressivity" (i.e. small countries would get more seats in relation to their population). On the second there was a lot of tortuous legal hair-splitting. "Uniformity" was not the same as "identity". Countries would be able to adopt their own voting *system*, provided the *procedure* was uniform. In the end the compromise established a number of common principles, allowing the implementing measures, in particular the system of voting, to be referred back to the domestic law of each country.

The UK, uniquely, was to choose *two* voting systems: single member constituencies with voting by simple majority (i.e. first-past-the-post) in England, Scotland and Wales; and Single Transferable Vote (STV) in Northern Ireland, the same system as that to be used in the Irish Republic. This was the culmination of complex negotiations between the parties, in particular between Labour and the Liberals.

In February 1976 the Labour Government of James Callaghan published a Green Paper[5] which assumed a commitment to direct elections, though doubting – wisely as it turned out – whether the 1978 target date was feasible. That October, however, the Labour Party conference decisively rejected the principle of any direct elections at all. This put the government in an embarrassing position. It was dependent on the support of

---

* As the veteran anti-marketeer, Neil Marten, had once put it when speaking on the Thames Television programme, *Europe: the Great Debate* in 1970.

Liberal MPs, to whom Callaghan had given a pledge not only to hold direct elections, but to do so on the basis of Proportional Representation.

When the European Assembly Election Bill was published in June 1977, it provided that the UK's 81 MEPs should be elected on regional party lists, though leaving the way open for single-member constituencies. Labour being severely split on the issue of whether election should take place at all, the decision on electoral system was effectively left to the Conservative Party.

The Shadow Cabinet had already appointed a Policy Group under Sir Anthony Royle MP (later Baron Fanshawe of Richmond) to look into the matter. There was significant support in the Party for some form of Proportional Representation – Ted Heath himself voted for it in the House of Commons – and the Conservative Group for Europe submitted a memo to the House of Commons Select Committee on the subject recommending the Additional Member System.[6]* The Royle Committee, however, reported[7] that there was "a great deal to be said for keeping the procedures as familiar as possible". Single-member constituencies would be large, but "no larger than an American congressional district". Other research carried out for the Party also indicated that many more seats would be won with single-member constituencies than under PR – as proved to be the case.

A series of votes eventually resulted in the single-member seat system being adopted, by a majority of 114 votes, in February 1978. The Boundary Commissions then acted rapidly, dividing up Britain into 78 Euro-constituencies by that November. Northern Ireland was made a single, three-member constituency. Polling in the UK was fixed for Thursday 7 June 1979.

The Conservative Party had already drawn one important political conclusion.

> As Mrs. Thatcher has pointed out, the prospect of direct elections makes the creation of a working alliance of Centre and Right democratic parties in Europe a matter of urgency. ... The parties of the Centre and Right have found themselves hampered in their dealings with each other by many myths and misunderstandings. In particular, there have been obstacles in the way of cooperation between parties calling themselves 'Conservative' and parties calling themselves 'Christian Democrat'.

---

* The choice of system was based on an earlier study carried out by a working party of the European Movement, of which I had been *rapporteur: Direct Elections to the European Parliament* (European Movement, 1974). This examined a number of alternative voting systems. In the end, we came down in favour of the Additional Member System, used in Germany for national elections: half single member constituencies with vote by simple majority, half "topped up" from party lists. Later, when a member of the Parliament myself, I proposed an amendment to introduce this system for the Community as a whole. It was not adopted.

The Right Approach went on to outline the action being taken.

> The parties of the Centre and Right, including the Conservative Party, are therefore intensifying their efforts to come together. The Christian Democrats inside the Community announced recently the formation of a new European People's Party. At the same time we have been holding discussions with a number of important Christian Democrat and Conservative parties inside and outside the Community, in order to form a working alliance. We are not aiming at a single monolithic party, but an alliance of autonomous parties co-operating for a common cause.

Following the death of Sir Peter Kirk in 1977, Geoffrey Rippon had become leader of the Conservative Group in the nominated European Parliament. He had long-standing links with the CD parties through the *Centre Européen de Documentation et d'Information* (CEDI), and negotiations for close links with these parties at various levels progressed very satisfactorily.

It is interesting to note, however, that the main stumbling-blocks at the time had little to do with supposed CD support for "federalism". Rather, it was the CDs who had doubts about whether British Conservatism was truly "Christian"; and problems with the word "Conservative" itself.

Peter Kirk, as the son of a bishop, had perhaps been able to embody the old jibe that the Church of England was "the Conservative Party at prayer" – indeed, he had once suggested a solution to the problem of links between future UK elected MEPs and the national parliament at Westminster: that the MEPs should all become bishops.* It was clear, however, that the Conservative Party in Britain (though not the Ulster Unionists in Northern Ireland) was a secular party, not linked to any one Church, or indeed religion. The free-market philosophy which was to be dubbed "Thatcherism" in fact had more in common with the approach of continental Liberal parties, which also had a tradition of anti-clericalism.

While Leader of the Opposition, however, Mrs Thatcher herself made significant efforts to cement good relations with the Christian Democrat parties. In June 1977 she spoke at the *Centro Italiano di Studi per la Conciliazione Internazionale* in Rome on the subject of "Europe as I see it".[8] She was careful to describe Conservative economic policy in terms which would strike a chord among her audience.

> When we speak of political and economic freedom we do not mean freedom to ignore the rights of others, or freedom to amass wealth without any regard for its use. We accept the moral commitments of a free society, which have been handed down to us from their origins among the Jews and Greeks through the rich development of the Christian tradition.

---

* Bishops have had the distinction of being temporary members of the House of Lords.

She also dealt with the problem of nomenclature.

> When translated into other languages, the word 'Conservative' acquires completely different overtones. In Italian, for example, it is a term of criticism. ... I would ask those who shy away from the word to concentrate their attention on the common ground which exists between the British Conservative Party and the Christian Democrats and other centre right parties in Europe.

In time, a complex of links would grow up between centre-right parties, in progressively wider and looser circles. The largest and loosest circle would be the International Democrat Union (IDU), founded in 1983, which would end up with 45 full or associated parties from around the world, including the US Republican Party. Within this was the European Democrat Union (EDU), founded in May 1976, linking some of the national parties fully affiliated to the European People's Party with the Conservative Party (although, as Crowson describes, there were considerable misgivings on the EPP side that belonging to both the EPP and the EDU might be considered "bigamy"[9]). The closest link would be in the European Parliament itself, when the Conservative Members formally joined the EPP Group in 1992.*

In fact, organisations linking Conservative and other centre-right parties had already existed since the 1960s: for example, the Democrat Youth Committee of Europe (DEMYC) founded in 1964; or the European Democrat Students (EDS), founded in 1961. As early as 1949 YC's had temporarily attended meetings of the CD's youth wing, the *Nouvelles Equipes Internationales* (NEI). Conservatives participated from the start in the European Union of Women (EUW) which was founded in 1953, and the UK's branch of which was fully integrated into the Conservative Party organisation in 1973. These youth and women's organisations formed elements of the equivalent bodies at international level: the International Young Democrat Union, based in London, today linking 80 centre right political youth organisations from 50 countries; and the International Women's Democrat Union.

Organisation and candidates

The political parties' preparations for direct elections were to some extent conditioned by the fact that a national general election was also in the offing. The time available between the confirmation of Euro-constituency boundaries and the election itself also meant that the setting up of the necessary organisation and the selection of candidates needed to be carried out in a very condensed period. In the case of the Conservative Party, Euro-constituency Councils were created, members being nominated by

---

* But *not* the EPP itself – see later.

the Westminster constituency parties in each Euro-constituency; and these then appointed selection committees. Meanwhile, at Conservative Central Office, a Standing Advisory Committee on European Candidates whittled down to a manageable number the well over a thousand hopefuls who put their names forward to become the first elected Conservative MEPs. Panels of interviewers, each containing a sitting MEP, eventually produced an approved list of some two hundred.

Most of those who eventually found themselves sitting on the Conservative benches in Strasbourg in July 1979 could tell extraordinary stories about the candidate selection process that followed. The Euro-Councils' organisation was thorough: selection of about a dozen for interview from the Central Office list; reduction of these to a short-list of five; interview by the full Council; and finally a large meeting of 25 delegates from each of the Westminster constituencies to choose between the final three.

The problem soon emerged, however, that a large proportion of the constituencies were selecting the same small group of candidates for interview; and later, that an even smaller group were appearing in the final three of several constituencies at once. Though the rules allowed applications to fifteen different constituencies, I myself applied only to those where I had family or residence connections: Greater London, the West Country and Kent. Even this involved a hair-raising car journey to Cornwall, and dropping out of one interview for which it was impossible to get back. When it came to the finals, some constituencies found that the candidates they had put on their short-lists had already been selected somewhere else. A number responded by bringing forward their selection meetings to steal a march on rivals. Candidates not initially in the last three, but on the reserve list, found themselves contacted at the last minute to appear at the final selection, with at least one, Amédée Turner in Suffolk, coming out the winner.

I eventually found myself in three finals, fortunately spaced reasonably far apart: Upper Thames, Thames Valley and Kent West. In Upper Thames, Baroness Elles and I were both defeated by Robert Jackson, a Fellow of All Souls who would later enter the House of Commons, and later still defect to the Labour Party. In Thames Valley, I came second to Baroness Elles. Finally, I won the nomination for Kent West ahead of GLC councillor Shelagh Roberts (who was soon selected for SW London).* The third short-listed candidate, Neil Balfour, had earlier been selected in Yorkshire North.

The outcome of all this was a list of Conservative candidates with a very high level of qualifications for the job. Ten of us had experience working

---

* My selection for Kent West, rather than Shelagh Roberts, actually spared the constituency a by-election. It turned out after the election that she should have been disqualified from standing since she held "an office of profit under the Crown" at the time. In September 1979 the election in SW London had to be run again, and, although Shelagh Roberts won comfortably, there was a sizeable swing to the Liberals.

for one of the European Community institutions (though I was the only one to have worked for the Parliament itself). Six were, or had been, MPs, and another six were in the House of Lords. Among seven farmers was the President of the NFU, Sir Henry Plumb; among businessmen Sir David Nicolson from British European Airways (BEA); Basil de Ferranti; former Director General of the National Economic Development Council, Sir Fred Catherwood; and the former Lord Mayor of London, Sir Peter Vanneck. Sir Fred Warner had been British Ambassador in Japan, John de Courcy-Ling in the Paris embassy. There was also a high level of linguistic ability: the successful candidate for Humberside, Bob Battersby, who had appropriately been working in the Commission's fisheries department, spoke a large number of both European and non-European languages, including Mandarin. He was the only MEP, apart from the Member representing Greenland, to speak any Inuit.

A study of the European Elections of 1979 carried out in the following year[10] nevertheless drew attention to the failure of the Conservative Party to select well-known names as candidates, on a par with Labour's Barbara Castle, "no doubt because the most prominent figures in the party were more interested in position in a future Tory government than in a seat in the European Assembly".

The existing Leader of the Conservative Group in the Parliament, Geoffrey Rippon, was expected to stand, but was reportedly unwilling to do so unless given a "bye" into a seat. The obvious "big name", Ted Heath, also declined to put himself forward, though the possibility was mooted that he could become the elected Parliament's first President. But at least one former Cabinet Minister, Paul Channon, tried but failed to find a Euro-seat; likewise another MP spoken of as a possible leader, Sir Eldon Griffiths. James Scott-Hopkins, a former junior agriculture minister who had been the MP for West Derbyshire, gave up his seat at Westminster to stand for the European Parliament in Hereford and Worcester. He became the Group's leader after the elections.

Other sitting MPs elected to the European Parliament *did* retain a dual mandate: Sir Brandon Rhys-Williams, Elaine Kellett-Bowman (whose husband Edward was also elected), Tom Normanton and Jim Spicer. So, of course, did those in the House of Lords: Lord Bethell, Baroness Elles and Lord Harmar Nicholls. There was also the Marquess of Douro, heir to the Duke of Wellington.

In the case of the Peers, the dual mandate was ideal: they provided a useful link between Westminster and Strasbourg. In the case of those in the House of Commons, the link was perhaps even more useful, but was to place an increasing strain on those involved. In flying backwards and forwards between London, Brussels and Strasbourg in order to vote they were always at the mercy of strikes or fog. The Labour Party banned the dual mandate altogether, though the SNP MEP, Winnie Ewing, retained her seat in the Commons. The three Northern Ireland MEPs had dual, at times even triple, mandates.

The failure of more sitting MPs to be selected as candidates – including some like Charles Fletcher-Cooke and John Osborn who were already in the nominated Parliament – has been attributed to a reluctance on the part of selection meetings to approve dual mandates.[11] This, though, was only part of the story. My own experience both having briefed meetings of potential selection committees during the Direct Elections Information Campaign, and having appeared before seven of the actual committees, is that these were looking for something different from Westminster Members. There was, to begin with, a (correct) recognition that the need to commute regularly to Brussels, Luxembourg and Strasbourg – to say nothing of looking after constituencies of county size – would prove a strain, leading to a preference for younger candidates. Those on the preliminary interview panels, moreover, seemed especially pro-European, with the result that they were looking as much for real commitment to the European cause as to the Party itself. The ability to speak European languages was clearly a plus point. This was not true of all Euro-constituencies, as the election of MEPs like Harmar Nicholls indicated; but was probably so in most of the safest seats.*

The effect was the exact opposite of what was to occur twenty years later, when an aspiring candidate's stance more pro-European than that of the Party would prove fatal.

Issues and policies

Although all three main political parties had trans-national political links – those of the Conservatives, however, being considerably looser than those of the Labour Party within the Confederation of Socialist Parties of the European Community, and of the Liberals within the Federation of Liberal and Democratic Parties in the European Community – the election campaign at national level was conducted largely in terms of national concerns. This was in part the result of there having been a general election only a few weeks earlier. *Europe Elects its Parliament* remarks that "the battle between the two major parties was a repetition and an extension of the European dimension of the general election,"[12] and goes on to observe that:

> there was more discussion about Britain in Europe than about Europe itself. Armed with reports about the former European Assembly, Conservatives and Labour competed with each other in their arguments and their oratory to assert from the outset that their respective Euro-deputies had been – and would be – the best defenders of the British people in Strasbourg. Indeed, this was what was promised in the slogans they adopted: 'The Labour Party will fight for you in Europe' and 'For a better deal in Europe, vote Conservative'.[13]

---

* Harmar Nicholls himself would later observe that he had had so little expectation of winning that he hadn't even bothered to attend his own count.

This is certainly a plausible description of the overall campaign, though not necessarily of the campaigns within the individual constituencies (see below).

Commentators also drew attention to the similarity of policies on the most salient issues: the UK's contribution to the EC Budget, agricultural surpluses and fishing. At the general election in May, Margaret Thatcher had already indicated that a Conservative Government would seek a reduction of the net budgetary contribution, a freeze on the price of agricultural support for surplus products and preferential zones for British fisherman. This, of course, remained the policy a month later.

The Conservative manifestos for both the general election[14] and the subsequent European election[15] nevertheless exhibit genuine enthusiasm about the Community and about Britain's place in it. The earlier manifesto promises that a Conservative government "will restore Britain's influence by convincing our partners of our commitment to the Community's success". It also advocates an extension of Community activity beyond a purely "common market". Particular importance was attached to the co-ordination of Member States' foreign policies.

> In a world dominated by the super-powers, Britain and her partners are best able to protect their international interests and to contribute to world peace and stability when they speak with a single voice.

The later manifesto is even more outspoken. "Our belief in Europe," it states, "remains unshaken". Conservatives wanted Britain to demonstrate "her commitment to the Community's true ideals and purposes".

On specific issues, a substantial amount of preparatory work had already been carried out by the Party and by groups within it. In October 1978, for example, a group of MPs published *Europe Right Ahead*,[16] a survey of the main issues which would face the elected Parliament. One proposal to which it drew specific attention was for the creation of a European Ombudsman – an idea which had already been promoted in the nominated Parliament by Sir Derek Walker-Smith, and which would be implemented by the elected Parliament. Three existing Members of the Parliament had outlined a European policy for consumers.[17] Another pamphlet from the European Conservative Group prophetically advocated transforming the CAP into a Community Rural Policy.[18] Michael Shaw MP had outlined policy for controlling the Community Budget.[19] Charles Fletcher-Cooke MP, who was also a QC, outlined how the threat of terrorism required "the closest cooperation ... between national police forces, perhaps on an institutional basis".[20] The future of Community regional policy was covered by an existing MEP, Elaine Kellett-Bowman, and the future cabinet minister Ken Clarke.[21] Lord Reay outlined policy on development;[22] and Lord Bessborough, Tom Normanton and John Osborn on energy.[23] There was even a policy on fish farming.[24]

The Conservative Group for Europe had also been active: for example, in publishing proposals in the field of foreign and defence policy by the future MEP Derek Prag.[25] The former Conservative MP Christopher Tugendhat, who had succeeded Christopher Soames as European Commissioner, also contributed a paper hoping, somewhat nervously, that the elected Parliament would not be *too* bold in its relations with the Commission; but also discussing the issue of future relations between elected Conservative MEPs and Westminster. Two future Foreign Secretaries, Lord Carrington and Douglas Hurd, had already made proposals: the first that MEPs should automatically become members of a reformed House of Lords; the second that they should sit in a joint European Grand Committee.

Some of the specific policies actually in the manifesto are also worth noting. First, it anticipated the campaign that led to the "1992" Single Market. The Community should "sweep away national restrictions on competition and fair trade, liberalise exchange controls, simplify customs procedures and break down protectionist barriers". Where national regulations imposed differing technical requirements and standards in each country and were an obstacle to trade, "we shall support speedy action by the Community to remove them".

There should be no "harmonisation for its own sake". On the other hand, "some industries (such as insurance, building societies, car components and equipment leasing) are anxious to promote constructive harmonisation to increase the opportunities open to them". For the consumer "we want harmonisation that genuinely protects his interests".

Secondly, and more significantly in view of what happened in later years, the manifesto declared that it "obviously makes sense for the Member States to co-operate more closely in the economic sphere."

> That is why we regret the Labour government's decision – alone among the Nine – not to become a full member of the new European Monetary System. We support the objectives of the new system, which are currency stability in Europe and closer co-ordination of national economic policies, and we shall look for ways in which Britain can take her rightful place within it.

A much more comprehensive statement of the Conservative Party's position on Europe at the time is contained in the *Campaign Guide for Europe 1979*.[26] These substantial guides were published by the Conservative Research Department at every election, both national and European. They not only served as briefing for candidates and party workers at the time, but also serve today as valuable reference works. They were in part based on the *Notes on Current Politics* published regularly by the Department, and contained key quotations from party leaders and spokesmen.

The *Campaign Guide for Europe 1979*, for example, quotes Mrs. Thatcher's 1977 speech in Rome.[27]

We are the European party in the British Parliament and among the British people, and we want to co-operate wholeheartedly with our partners in this joint venture.

It also gives detailed background information about the nature of the Community. For example, the section on "Institutional and Legal Development" states clearly that "community law in the fields covered by the Treaties takes precedence over the national law of the Member States, and, in the case of conflict with national law, Community law must prevail".

Hidden in the text are proposals which, when later implemented, would have very significant consequences for the effectiveness of the Parliament: notably a change in the procedures which would allow amendments to, and direct votes on, Commission legislative proposals. The Guide also gives details of the actual issues before the European Parliament and the Council of Ministers, with indications of the positions a Conservative government and Conservative MEPs would adopt. Unsurprisingly, a large section covers reform of the Common Agricultural Policy.

The Preface to the guide ends interestingly.

The decline into sour chauvinism of a party which once had such strong internationalist pretensions is as puzzling to its opponents as it must be grievous to the diminishing group of its friends. …

It was, of course, referring to the Labour Party.

The campaign

While going through the selection process to become a Conservative candidate, I was also involved (in my capacity as deputy head of the Parliament's London Information Office) in the politically neutral campaign to inform British and Northern Ireland voters about the elections. The Commission's Eurobarometer was finding that the British were the least well-informed of any national electorate. In October 1978, it is true, 44% had "read or heard something about the European Parliament"; but only 18% were able to say that it was about the elections. By April 1979 these figures had risen to only 55% and 25% respectively, still significantly below the results in West Germany, France or Italy.

Apart from the information put out by the government's Central Office of Information, and by interested bodies like the European Movement, the Commission and Parliament information offices in Kensington Palace Gardens had a special budget to provide briefing on the elections. This was used for advertising in the press, to disseminate literature, to take parties of opinion formers and party activists to see the European Parliament in action in Strasbourg and Luxembourg, and to organise information stands in major city centres. A special corps of hostesses, more used to promoting cars at motor shows than to politics, was recruited to staff these stands and – having been taken on an intensive briefing visit to Luxembourg – answer voters' questions.

The bulk of this work was contracted out to PR firms, the main contract going to Charles Barker Watney Powell. Community officials like myself concentrated on drafting texts and giving speeches.

However, raising awareness of the coming European elections ("the first international elections in history") was made a great deal more difficult by the national political situation. Callaghan's Labour Government was hanging on by the skin of its teeth in the House of Commons, and was expected to fall at any moment. Moreover, following the 1978–79 "winter of discontent", the Conservative Party was riding high and had every prospect of being in office within months.

During the period following my adoption as a Conservative candidate and the declaration of my result on the 11th June 1979, I kept a diary of day by day events. This shows clearly the effect on the European campaign of the Callaghan Government's resignation at the end of March, following the loss, by one vote, of a "no confidence" motion. I record a meeting of the Kent West Conservative Euro-Council on the 27th March being "hopelessly overshadowed by prospect of U.K. general election". The assassination of Airey Neave on the 30th March further ratcheted up the tension. On the 1st April the Euro-Council scrapped all currently planned meetings, and redefined my role as support speaker for the Westminster candidates.

There were, of course, some advantages in this situation. The party organisation was mobilised for the General Election to an extent that would not have occurred just for the Euro-elections. By polling day on the 3rd May most constituencies had got as near to a 100% canvass as was feasible at any time, with the result that each one had a nearly fully-marked register: that is, one showing, in particular, the "Conservative pledges" to be knocked up on polling day. That register would be equally valid for the Euro-elections on the 7th June. Speaking in support of the Westminster candidates – who in my case included the future Chancellor of the Exchequer, Sir Geoffey Howe, the future Solicitor-General, Patrick Mayhew, and other future ministers John Stanley (now Sir John) and Bob Dunn – meant that I was known to most active party workers, at least, by the end of April. My diary records enthusiastic attendances at meetings, and also considerable interest in Europe (as measured by the number of questions addressed to me alone).

Following the General Election, however, it was clear that generating enthusiasm for another poll a month later would be difficult. *Europe elects its Parliament* observes that "the start of the official campaign, on the 9th May, passed virtually unnoticed";[28] and, indeed, it receives no mention at all in my own diary.

There were, however, some features of the campaign which it is perhaps worth noticing. One is the relative prominence of sections of the Conservative Party which, at the time, were generally more pro-European than the organisation as a whole. My diary illustrates, for example, the active role played by Young Conservatives; and also members of the women's committees, many of whom were also in the Kent branches of the European Union of Women. An especial effort was made to involve individual members of the Conservative Group for Europe living in the constituency. Moreover, in addition to Party literature, the campaign teams distributed very large quantities of leaflets providing purely factual information about the European Parliament. There was, in fact, a double message: "vote Conservative (again)"; and a more idealistic "vote for Europe". This would be a great deal more difficult to carry off in later European elections.

A further detail worth noting is that, at the Kent West eve-of-poll meeting, the guest speaker was a German member of the *Bundestag*, Volker Rühe, who would later become Germany's Minister of Defence. This was in part the legacy of many years of contacts between the Young Conservatives and the CDU equivalent, the *Jung Union*. YC/JU contacts, in fact, went back a long way: in the 1960s I had been part of a visiting group from the Chelsea Young Conservatives to the JUs in Wiesbaden, Heidelberg and Mannheim; and, on another occasion, to West Berlin. Contacts made in the youth movements continued in the elected European Parliament: for example, between the MEP for Derbyshire, later for Surrey, Tom Spencer (from 1971 to 1974 chairman of the European Union of Conservative and Christian Democrat Students, and today Director of the European Centre for Public Affairs), and Elmar Brok, who would become President of the European Parliament's Foreign Affairs Committee in succession to Spencer, and then one of the key politicians behind what is now the Lisbon Treaty.

The results

Although I won the Kent West Euro-constituency comfortably, with some 60% of the vote, my diary records despondency at the end of the campaign. The verification of the ballot – that is, a count of votes cast to compare with the returns from the polling stations – took place on the evening of the poll itself, the 7th June; but the count proper was not possible until the close of poll in those countries voting on Sunday the 10th. My despondency on the Thursday evening was due to the shocking news that, even in the best Conservative constituencies like Sevenoaks, the total poll was only 37.9%. In Rochester & Chatham it was only 25%, with Kent West as a whole polling, overall, 33%. When I phoned Pauline Lloyd, my secretary in the London office of the Parliament, to get the national picture, she told me that the poll in Liverpool had been a mere 15% – though the silver lining was that the Conservative candidate, Gloria Hooper, now Baroness Hooper, had amazingly won the seat.

The low poll had, indeed, proved a winning formula for the Conservative Party. There had been a 5% swing from Labour to the Conservatives since the general election, giving the Party over half the British vote. Labour voters had mostly stayed at home, so that we could win even in constituencies like Liverpool with comparatively few Conservative voters in normal elections. Out of the 81 UK seats, 60 returned Conservative MEPs, with Labour winning a mere 18. The Scottish National Party (SNP) won one: Winnie Ewing. The three N. Ireland seats were shared between the Democratic Unionist Party: Ian Paisley; the Official Unionists: John Taylor; and the Social Democratic and Labour Party (SDLP): John Hume. The Liberal Party, with 12.6% of total votes cast, won no seats at all.

The declaration of the Kent West result on the 11th June improved local morale considerably. For me, nevertheless, it was still dispiriting that all the preparatory information work carried out in the months leading up to the elections had apparently failed. In Germany nearly two-thirds of the electorate had voted, double the UK figure. In the UK there were, of course, special factors, including low morale in the Labour Party after losing power at Westminster, and public weariness of elections. An Opinion Research Centre (OPR) poll carried out for ITV, however, found that a third of those interviewed had failed to vote because of "insufficient information".

Post-election studies identified a number of factors behind the decisive Conservative victory. *Europe Elects its Parliament* notes "the shift to the Right which had already appeared in the general election and which was then spurred on by a kind of dynamic of success".[29] It also observes that "one should not under-estimate the impact of a campaign prepared well in advance and which reflected the relative harmony of views on Europe within the party. The Labour Party, on the other hand, with its internal divisions and an unconvincing campaign, was unable to mobilise the dissatisfaction of public opinion which is nevertheless disposed … to blame the EEC for many of the United Kingdom's ills."

This failure of Labour to mobilise its vote was hardly surprising, given that – as Anthony Forster observes – the anti-Marketeers in the party "did not want any Euro elections at all and were not in favour of taking part in them".[30] The Boundary Commissions had, in addition, given the Conservative party an added bonus by grouping Labour-supporting urban areas together, so concentrating the Labour vote on only a few candidates.

Yet the euphoria in the Conservative Party generated by overwhelming victory disguised some unease about the political consequences. The most immediate, at a European level, was that joining the European People's Party (EPP) Group – assuming that it had been seriously contemplated – was now out of the question. The German Christian Democrats (the CDU) and its allies the Bavarian *Christlich Soziale Union* (CSU) had won forty seats between them. The Italian Christian Democrats had won thirty. Had sixty-four Conservatives and allies joined (there were with us two Danish Conservatives and John Taylor from the official Unionists; a Danish Centre Democrat was also with us for a time), we would have become the dominant force in the EPP Group, with first pick of committee chairman-ships and other perks. Though the Germans would have welcomed us, the Italians and others from smaller countries would clearly have not. Instead, we had enough members and nationalities to form our own Group, the European Democratic Group (EDG), with the right to two committee chairmanships and a Parliament Vice-Presidency.*

The second, more long-term consequence was on the choice of electoral system. The major justification for the choice of "first past the post" in single-member constituencies at national level is that it tends to produce stable governments and an absence of the post-election horse-trading that is endemic under systems of PR. In addition – a factor which applies at European level as well – a Member, once elected, becomes the representa-tive of everyone in the constituency, not just of his or her Party; at the same time, constituents can identify "their" MEP in a way that is not possible under a system of party lists. These are powerful justifications for the traditional British system used in the European Elections of 1979, even if the "stable government" argument applies only embryonically in the case of the European Community/European Union.

The fewer the number of seats in play, however, the greater is the danger of the actual election result diverging from the result if seats had been allo-cated in proportion to votes cast. Under a system of PR, with just over 50% of the vote, the Conservative Party would, in 1979, have won only 40 of Great Britain's 78 seats. Labour would have won 26, the Liberal Party 10 and others 2.† The discrepancies were uncomfortable, and the election was widely felt to be not quite fair.

---

* The method by which committee chairmanships and other posts within the European Parliament are allocated is a subject for a book in itself. Briefly, the d'Hondt system of Proportional Representation is used to allocate a "picking order" between the Political Groups. Within each group, the same system is used to allocate a "picking order" between the different national sections. Supposing that the largest Political Group were, for example, the European People's Party: it would have the first choice of committee chair-manships. Within the EPP, the German section would be the largest and have the right to decide the EPP's first choice. This process would continue until the last Vice-Presidency of the least prestigious delegation was allocated. The system, however, is complicated by the election of the Parliament presidency, which has effects on the "picking order" for other posts like the Vice-Presidencies and Quaestors.

† Since it is not possible to divide the loyalties of a single Member of Parliament between different political parties, no system of PR can produce a mathematically proportionate result (except in freak, virtually impossible circumstances). Various methods of counting have therefore been devised to approximate proportionality, giving more or less advan-tage to smaller parties. The most common is the d'Hondt system used by the European Parliament (see previous footnote), which divides the total number of votes for each party by 1, then 2, then 3, and so on, giving figures which determine the order in which seats are allocated. This is slightly biased in favour of larger groups. One alternative is the Sainte-Laguë method, where the divisors are increased by one, giving a slight bias to smaller parties. The modified Sainte-Laguë method, on the other hand, changes the first divisor to 1.4. All these methods are used in the PR systems of various countries. Both Victor d'Hondt and André Sainte-Laguë were mathematicians, the first Belgian, the second French.

More seriously, the one-sided result in the UK also had significant consequences at European Parliament level. In brief, it heavily weighted the overall result in favour of the Centre-Right. At the time, it seemed that complaints from the Socialists could be safely ignored. Yet the chickens would eventually come home to roost: in the European Elections of 1994 the British results swung the balance of power decisively in the other direction. This, in turn, played a part in souring the whole European enterprise for many, if not most, Conservatives.

Notes

1 *The Right Approach: a statement of Conservative aims* (Conservative Central Office, October 1976).

2 See, for example, *The case for direct elections to the European Parliament by direct universal suffrage: selected documents* (European Parliament, September 1969).

3 For full documentation see *Elections to the European Parliament by direct universal suffrage* (European Parliament, 1976).

4 Speech at Market Drayton on the 6th June 1969.

5 *Direct Elections to the European Assembly* (Cmnd. 6399, HMSO February 1976).

6 *Second Report of the House of Commons Select Committee on Direct Elections to the European Parliament, appendix 15* (1976).

7 *Our Voice in Europe* (CPC), March 1976).

8 *Europe as I see it* by the Rt. Hon. Margaret Thatcher MP (European Conservative Group, August 1977).

9 Crowson *op.cit.* p. 193.

10 *Europe Elects its Parliament* by Geneviève Bibes, Henri Ménudier, Françoise de la Serre and Marie-Claude Smouts (Policy Studies Institute, September 1980).

11 See, for example, Crowson, *op.cit.* p. 202.

12 Bibes, Ménudier, de la Serre and Smouts, *op.cit.* p. 24.

13 *ibid.* p. 30.

14 *The Conservative Manifesto 1979* (Conservative Central Office, April 1979).

15 *Conservative Manifesto for Europe 1979* (Conservative Central Office, May 1979).

16 *Europe Right Ahead* by Peter Blaker MP, Alick Buchanan-Smith MP, Hugh Dykes MP, David Hunt MP, Peter Mills MP and Peter Rees QC, MP, editor Lord O'Hagan (CPC, October 1978).

17 *Consumers in Europe: a Conservative View* by Nicholas Bethell, Jim Scott-Hopkins MP and Jim Spicer MP (European Conservative Group, November 1977).

18 *Towards a Community Rural Policy* by Jim Scott-Hopkins MP and John Corrie MP (European Conservative Group, April 1979).

19 *The European Parliament and the Community Budget*, by Michael Shaw MP (European Conservative Group 1978).

20 *Terrorism and the European Community* by Charles Fletcher-Cooke QC, MP (European Conservative Group, January 1979).

21 *New Hope for the Regions* by Elaine Kellett-Bowman MP and Kenneth Clarke MP (European Conservative Group, April 1979).

22 *The European Community and the Developing World*, by Hugh Reay (European Conservative Group, 1979).

23 *Energy for Europe*, by The Earl of Bessborough, Tom Normanton MP and John H. Osborn MP (European Conservative Group, 1979).

24 *Fish Farming in Europe*, by John Corrie MP (European Conservative Group, 1979).

25 *Foreign Policy and Defence: a role for Europe* by Derek Prag, foreword by Geoffrey Rippon (Conservative Group for Europe, November 1978).

26 *Campaign Guide for Europe 1979* and *Campaign Guide for Europe 1979 Supplement* (Conservative Research Department, January 1979 and April 1979).
27 Thatcher *op.cit. (Europe as I see it).*
28 *Europe elects its Parliament* p. 53.
29 *Europe elects its Parliament* p. 65
30 Forster *op.cit.* p. 66.

7 The Years of "Maggie's Money"

In the EDG

Taking my seat in the first meeting of the elected European Parliament was a curiously unsettling experience. For five years I had looked down on the MEPs from Strasbourg's Palace of Europe* press gallery, where officials from the information offices were entitled to sit. Now I was down on the floor of the chamber, with the press corps looking down on me.

A collection of memoirs by British Members elected in 1979[1] contains pieces by two journalists, David Harris from the *Daily Telegraph* and Alasdair Hutton from BBC Scotland, whose experienced antennae captured the flavour of the first meeting in Strasbourg that summer. For Harris it was like "being at a new school"; for Hutton we were "pioneer settlers".

> There was a feeling of wide open spaces to be tamed, whole areas of policy to explore and leave our mark on. There were traces that some people had been here earlier but had not stayed. We were there to develop this territory and make it great.[2]

Two less idealistic observations appear in the pieces from a number of contributors: that there were no offices and few telephones for Members (I was lucky to be able to use my old office); and that Ian Paisley made the first intervention on record in the new Parliament, complaining that the Union Jack flying outside the Palace of Europe was upside down. My own piece and that of several others also records how the first sitting was dominated by procedural wrangles, to the great distress of those who wanted to get on with (as the late Eric Forth, one of the new MEPs, but subsequently in the House of Commons, always ironically put it) "building Europe".

A number of the Conservatives elected in 1979 would later move to the House of Commons, including David Harris himself. He records that he had never quite adapted to the political culture of the European Parliament,

---

* Though this building had only recently been constructed, it was the headquarters of the Council of Europe, not of the European Parliament. A chamber exclusively for the use of the Parliament was being built in Luxembourg.

in particular "the need to make constant political compromises and to find consensus." Very soon a group dubbed the "H-block" came into existence – five of its prominent members being Harmar Nicholls, Harris, Hord, Howell and on occasions Hutton – which aimed to keep alive the pure light of Conservatism. Being essentially a one nation, one party group, as Harris observed, "gave us an outward appearance of unity and cohesion". But John Palmer, at that time European editor of the *Guardian*, wrote that he "found it fun to monitor the intense hatreds and mutual contempt which marked relations among Tory MEPs".[3]*

Though things were never as bad as that, EDG MEPs very soon found themselves pulled in two incompatible directions. In the Parliament itself, particularly as it acquired real legislative powers, the need to work with allies from other countries and parties became essential. Generally, these allies were to be found in the European People's Party Group; but on occasion among the Liberals, the Gaullists and even the Socialists, Radicals or Communists. In the bodies where the compromises usually had to be reached, the Parliament's specialist committees, Group spokesmen soon became adept at the necessary negotiating skills. Most British MEPs, in fact, found the need to work with non-Brits stimulating: Stanley Johnson records in his autobiography[4] that he "liked the sense of being surrounded by people from very different parliamentary traditions".

At the same time, the Conservative Party in the UK was developing in an entirely different direction. The Thatcher Government was struggling with the legacy of the 1970s, and consensus politics – even within the Party itself, as the "wets" were soon to discover – was definitely out. A new economic strategy was in place, which entirely reversed the Keynesian orthodoxy of previous years. A combination of monetary policy and fiscal tightening was used to squeeze inflation out of the economy and reduce public debt. Trade Union leaders were no longer invited for sandwiches at 10 Downing Street – indeed, they became "the enemy within". The "enemy without" was no longer just the Soviet Union, but also in some respects the European Community, from which the Prime Minister wanted "my money back".

In these circumstances, the earlier fears of a divergence between Conservatives in Westminster and those in Brussels, Luxembourg and Strasbourg were in danger of being justified. Practically nothing, though, was done to prevent it. The Carrington and Hurd proposals were forgotten, and an uneasy tension developed which was ironically described by Harris.

---

* There was, it was noted at the time, also a "P-block" consisting largely of more committed pro-Europeans: Patterson, Pearce, Plumb, Prag, Price, Prout, Provan and Purvis, who sat in a line on the EDG benches, at least until Plumb and Prout were promoted to the front. Curiously, a new "H-block" came into existence after the European Elections of 1999, centred on the Conservative MEPs Daniel Hannan, Roger Helmer and Christopher Heaton-Harris.

The collective attitude of the Commons to this new breed of politicians [the MEPs] was best summed up by the decision that, yes, we could have access to Westminster catering provided it was in the strangers' (i.e. visitors') cafeteria and not at meal times. There seemed to be indecision on whether we presented a threat to the standing of MPs or whether we were powerless nonentities.[5]

I myself found that my press pass, which I had been issued with as an EC information officer and which I retained for as long as possible, was a good deal more valuable at the Palace of Westminster than my MEP pass. It may be that MPs had unconsciously accepted the thesis of Enoch Powell that conflict between the House of Commons and the European Parliament was "inevitable and intended".[6]

As time went by, particularly as the first stirrings of Euroscepticism began to occur at Westminster, mutual criticisms would indeed develop. MEPs would be accused of having "gone native" and voted for legislation which was contrary to Party policy. Our rejoinder would be that Conservative Ministers had also voted for it in the Council of Ministers; and that the job of controlling Ministers was theirs, not ours. Indeed, though there was a formal procedure to scrutinise draft European Community legislation in the House of Commons, its effectiveness was virtually nil – certainly compared with the work of the Danish *Folketing*'s Market Committee, which gave Danish ministers their mandate before they left for Brussels. It was chastening to find that our Danish colleagues in the EDG represented a considerably more democratic system than ours. We soon discovered that the only real parliamentary scrutiny of European Affairs at national level was being done by the House of Lords. The reports of its Select Committee on the European Communities were often masterpieces of analysis.

We also soon discovered, of course, that the Council of Ministers actually operated in much the same way as we did ourselves. The preparatory work for Council meetings, and in practice a large proportion of the decisions, were taken in the Committee of Permanent Representatives (COREPER), where civil servants from UKREP (the UK's permanent representation in Brussels) had to wheel and deal with their equivalents from the other representations. The position of national ministers was later summed up, unforgettably, by the Tory Minister and diarist Alan Clark. "Everything is decided, horse-traded off, by officials at COREPER," he wrote in his diary[7] in 1986. The ministers themselves, "arrive on the scene at the last minute, hot, tired, ill or drunk (sometimes all of these together), read out their piece, and depart".

At constituency level, the situation was a great deal better. I personally got on quite well with the eight MPs in Kent West – some of whom, like Mid-Kent MP Andrew Rowe, were quite enthusiastic about Europe; and also had good relations with Kent County Council (and also Surrey County Council until the boundary commission removed East Surrey from the Euro-constituency) and the Borough and District Councils. Rank-and-file

Conservatives in the 1980s were still content to be "the party of Europe", and found no difficulty in seeing Government, MPs and MEPs as basically all on the same side against Socialism. It helped that the Labour Party, having been taken over by the Bennite Left, was virulently anti-Market and officially in favour of withdrawal from the Community altogether.

Changing the Rules

Within the European Parliament the EDG found itself, initially with 64 Members, the third largest political group. We were, however, only medium-large compared to the Socialists (112) and the EPP Group (108), which between them comprised more than half the Parliament's membership. As it happened, the leaders of both the large groups were from Germany, as was the leader of the 40-strong Liberal and Democrat Group; and the early procedural disputes revolved around a determination of minorities not to be pushed around by the "three big Germans". As EDG spokesman on the Rules and Petitions Committee of the European Parliament, I was extremely surprised to find my first alliances to be with the Communists, the Gaullists and above all a group led by the maverick Italian Radical, Marco Pannella, which, with our help, successfully fought off attempts to disband it.

The most important task of the Committee, however, was to rewrite Parliament's Rules of Procedure; and here we succeeded in pushing through a change which would turn out to be of enormous importance for the future development of the Parliament's powers: to provide for direct votes on the Commission's legislative proposals.

It seems odd now – as it seemed to us then – that any Parliament should prefer to vote on generally long and rambling "Resolutions" rather than on the actual texts of draft laws. French members of the Committee, nevertheless, strongly defended the established principle (based on French practice), that Parliament should "vote on its own text, not the Commission's". It was also true that, legally, the "opinion" of Parliament needed to enact legislation took the form of the Resolution. We argued, however, that Parliament would never achieve true legislative powers until it was able, directly, to amend draft Directives and Regulations.

Eventual victory in this battle was a key element in preparing for the Treaty changes which followed, and which now give Parliament co-decision with the Council of Ministers over almost all legislation. As it happened, another key element was already falling into place: the events leading to the European Court of Justice's ruling in the *SA Roquette Frères v. Council of the European Communities* case, generally referred to as the "isoglucose" case.[8]

This concerned a draft Regulation setting quotas for production of a sweetener (isoglucose). Parliament had been asked for its "opinion", as the Treaty required; but before it could give it, parliamentary activities were suspended in order that direct elections could take place. The Council of

Ministers nevertheless adopted the Regulation on the 25th June, before the new, elected Parliament could convene. Following an appeal by one of the manufacturers (*SA Roquette Frères*), however, the Court struck down the Regulation, ruling that the Treaty required Council to give Parliament reasonable opportunity to act.

The result was, in effect, to provide Parliament with a limited "suspensive veto" over proposed legislation. The Rules were changed to make the most of this opportunity: after votes on a draft Regulation or Directive, the Commission would be asked whether or not it accepted any parliamentary amendments, and whether it would withdraw the proposal if Parliament had rejected it *in toto*.* If it did not, the matter could be referred back to committee before Parliament voted on the Resolution: i.e. gave its "opinion" to Council. Although this invented procedure initially caused the Commission considerable irritation, it gradually became accepted practice. Eventually it became the basis for the formal changes in Parliament's legislative powers incorporated in the Single European Act, later expanded in the Maastricht and other Treaties.

The battle of the Budget

Though the work we did in the Rules Committee would turn out to be very significant, the main political action at the time was elsewhere, more particularly in the Agriculture and Budgets Committees. As former President of the NFU, and later of the Community equivalent, COPA (Committee of Professional Agricultural Organisations), Sir Henry Plumb was an obvious choice to head the Agriculture Committee – although he himself observes that he only got the job after "bare-knuckle politics" and "background manoeuvrings".[9] A major issue of the moment for the media was the growth of "butter, beef and wheat mountains", and the linked scandal of taxpayer subsidies for "butter to Russia". Sir Henry's task of promoting the necessary reforms was enlivened by the presence on the committee of the still anti-Market Barbara (by this time Baroness) Castle.

However, the central European issue of the time, both in the European Parliament and for the British Government, was the Community Budget. This only accounted for 0.9% of Community GDP; but Conservatives at both Westminster and Strasbourg had been elected on a platform of reducing the proportion devoted to the CAP, which in 1979 accounted for 81% of the total. More dramatic was what soon became known as "the war of Maggie's money": the size of the UK's net contribution.

Despatches from this war varied considerably. The news reaching non-British MEPs from the Dublin summit of November 1979 were of an un-ladylike display of tantrums by the new British Prime Minister,

---

* The Treaty provided that "as long as the Council has not acted, the Commission may alter its proposal at any time during the procedures leading to the adoption of a Community act" (Article 250 in current version).

who clearly didn't understand the concept of the Community's "own resources". I remember a senior member of the EPP Group, the former Belgian Economics Minister Fernand Herman, who would later become a great friend, explaining why giving each country a *juste retour* from the Budget – i.e. as much money back as was put in – would destroy the Budget's whole *raison d'être*. Logically, of course, he was absolutely right.

The briefing we got from UKREP and Party sources, on the other hand, were of our Prime Minister pointing firmly but politely to the agreement when Britain joined the Community that if an "unacceptable situation" developed in relation to the UK's net budgetary contribution, something would be done. The prospect of a net contribution of over £1 billion in 1980, almost as large as that of Germany when the UK economy was considerably weaker, was clearly unacceptable – especially as every other Member State, including France, was a net recipient.

Behind the action on the European stage, there were also powerful domestic considerations. In her own account[10] Margaret Thatcher quotes from a speech, the Winston Churchill Memorial Lecture, she gave in Luxembourg on the 18th October, warning that "I cannot play Sister Bountiful to the Community while my own electorate are being asked to forego improvements in the fields of health, education, welfare and the rest".

Moreover, although accounts of the negotiations are apt to refer to the "lady's ferocity",[11] with handbag-swinging much in evidence, the tactics used were in fact carefully calculated. One of her advisers, she recalls, was the very pro-European Conservative, ex-Commissioner Soames, who observed that "the Community had never been renowned for taking unpleasant decisions without long wrangling", and pointed out that "a major country like Britain could disrupt the Community very effectively if it chose." Accordingly, she describes how floating the idea of withholding all British payments to the Community caused "satisfactory anxiety in the Commission", although it was actually ruled out in advance for legal and practical reasons. In the case of the other major government objective, reform of the CAP, she had earlier observed that it would "not be achieved by loud words or sharp tactics".[12]

There is no doubt, however, that – at least when writing about the events over a dozen years later – she saw most of the other Community leaders at the time, particularly Giscard d'Estaing, as enemies to be beaten rather than as colleagues. "It was quite shameless", she recalled. "They were determined to keep as much of our money as they could."[13]

Hugo Young maintains that she also saw enemies to the rear: the Foreign Office and the two Conservative ministers responsible for the negotiations, Lord Carrington and the "super-wet" Ian Gilmour. Geoffrey Howe, at the time Chancellor of the Exchequer, recalls that he "took every opportunity to press the stark arithmetic of our case," but suspects that he "came to be seen as the soft cop is contrast to the hard cop persona" of the Prime Minister. She was, he notes "persuaded, reluctantly", to accept a "two-year ceasefire on the European front", until the whole issue was finally settled at the Fontainebleau summit in June 1984.[14]

The outcome of the war, however, was an enormous boost for the Government and the Conservative Party. The initial deal meant that Britain received rebates amounting to £2 billion over three years, with the result that the net contributions turned out to be only £200 million in 1980 and a mere £6 million in 1981. The anti-Marketeers, including the Labour opposition, were "completely overshadowed by Margaret Thatcher's robust defence of British interests".[15] Some have even viewed the whole episode as a deliberate ploy to distract attention from the unpopular effects of the economic depression at home, and cultivate the "iron lady" image. Europe "provided a suitable scapegoat",[16] according to Turner.

This is not very plausible. Turner himself quotes sufficient evidence from the time and later to indicate that the Prime Minister was passionately sincere about the net contribution issue, as much for economic reasons as on grounds of national sovereignty. The Labour solution to the problem had been, in the words of the Financial Secretary to the Treasury at the time and Chancellor of the Exchequer to be, Nigel Lawson, to favour "almost every conceivable increase in non-agricultural spending, as a potential gain for Britain. ... It did not take me long to stop officials briefing me along these lines. ... It would have made no sense to be striving to curb government spending at home while boosting it at EC level."[17]

In the European Parliament we were also fighting a war over the Budget, though a slightly different one. At this time the Parliament had very limited powers over legislation; but it did have two "nuclear weapons": the power to sack the Commission, and the power to block the Budget. It was generally thought that more would be achieved, as in the case of nuclear weapons, by *threatening* to use these powers rather than by actually using them – and this indeed turned out to be true in the case of the Commission. However, an astute Dutch Socialist, Piet Dankert, who was rapporteur* on the draft 1980 Budget, calculated that early detonation

---

* The job of *rapporteur* in the European Parliament has no real equivalent in British parliamentary practice. Once one of Parliament's specialist committees is made responsible for a particular matter – a Commission draft law, an "own initiative" by the committee itself or, as in this case, the Community Budget – one of its members is appointed to pilot the business through its various parliamentary stages. When only one committee is involved – or, in cases where more than one is involved the lead committee – the appointee is Parliament's *rapporteur*. (Any other committee asked for its opinion appoints a "draftsman"). Thereafter, the *rapporteur* becomes – in theory at least – the non-partisan servant of the committee, preparing its report and introducing this in plenary. There he or she is responsible for explaining the subject matter to the Parliament and advising on votes – a job which at Westminster would be carried out by a minister. Since the coming into force of the Single European Act the *rapporteur* can also play a key role in negotiations with Commission and Council, particularly where the legislative process requires "conciliation" between Parliament and Council. Rapporteurships on important matters like the Budget or major legislation can be extremely influential. There is consequently intense competition to secure them between Political Groups, the national sections within them and individual MEPs. Committees therefore usually allocate rapporteurships on the basis of a complex points system, weighted by size of Group and importance of subject.

of the Budget bomb would show that an elected Parliament had to be taken seriously. In November Parliament adopted amendments lopping £2 million off spending on agriculture, which the French press described as a "victory for the British Conservatives". These amendments were rejected out of hand by the Council of Ministers, as Dankert knew very well that they would be. The sole British Labour member of the Budgets Committee at the time, Richard Balfe – now a Conservative – records that "we were going to reject the budget, whatever compromises the Council offered".[18] In December Parliament threw it out by 288 votes to 64, despite pleas from the Budgets Commissioner, the former Conservative MP Christopher Tugendhat.

The actual effect on Community expenditure was not, in fact, very great. The Treaty provided for a "system of twelfths" to be activated, under which appropriations equal to one twelfth of the 1979 budget were released month by month. However, there were at least three winners.

The Parliament established itself in the media as a credible political force. We Conservative MEPs were able to show that we were doing our bit to support the UK Government in its battles on the Budget. And Piet Dankert became the next President of the European Parliament, beating the expected winner from the European People's Party Group,[*] effectively as a result of many Conservative votes.

Widening and deepening

In September 1982 Conservative Research Department issued an edition of *Notes on Current Politics* summarising the achievements of the Government since coming into office in May 1979.[19] It recorded satisfactory progress on "a wide range of measures important to our trade and industry" during the British presidency of the Community Council of Ministers during the second half of 1981. As well as the success on the Budget rebate, it drew attention to "major reductions in the size of the infamous butter and beef mountains", and to a cut in the proportion of the Budget spent on agriculture to 66% of the total.

The British government had also, especially during the presidency, "played a leading part in improving the Community's effectiveness and cohesion in international affairs". This had brought immediate benefits which "were demonstrated during the Falklands conflict when Britain received invaluable political and economic support from our Community partners. There was an immediate statement of condemnation from the Community on the day of the invasion, followed by an embargo on imports of Argentine goods and a ban on arms sales to Argentina."

Mrs. Thatcher records in her memoirs that "the significance of the Falklands War was enormous, both for Britain's self-confidence and for our

---

[*] The German MEP Egon Klepsch, who finally made the presidency some years later, this time with Conservative support.

standing in the world." Even those on the European left, whose instincts were to condemn a revival of British imperialism, were virtually silent. When it was all over I was in Florence for a meeting of the Education, Youth, Culture, Information and Sport Committee of the European Parliament, where we met a grand old man of the Italian Communist Party. "It was well done," he told me, "the way she dealt with that Fascist Galtieri."

Strangely, *Three Years Work* makes no reference to an event which had taken place at the beginning of 1981: the enlargement of the Community to ten Member States with the accession of Greece. It was strange, because eventually including all the democratic countries of Europe in the process of unity had been a consistent theme of Conservative policy from Churchill onwards (and continues to be so today). In November of the following year, speaking in London, Mrs Thatcher left no room for doubt that the "Common Market" had this crucial *political* dimension, and that she supported it strongly. The Community was "more than a trading organisation".

> It is a large and stable area of freedom and democracy in a world which has need of both. We must work to preserve, perpetuate and extend that freedom. That is why we welcome the accession of the countries which share our democratic ideals.

Some years later she would make an even more definitive statement of this thesis in relation to the countries of Central and Eastern Europe.

The reasoning behind Conservative support for the Greek/Iberian enlargement was elaborated in a European Democratic Group paper, *From Nine to Twelve*, published by the CPC in 1982.[20] It echoed an important philosophical influence of the time on Conservative thinking, the economist Friedrich von Hayek, in perceiving the economic dimension of the Community as primarily the means to a political end: the Treaty provided "an economic framework which guarantees to adherents the possibility of living in freedom and democratic liberty". This, indeed, had been the principal motive of the applicant countries, all three of which were emerging from a period of right-wing authoritarianism; so that, in the Community's consideration of the applications "any refusal or needless postponement would be frustrating and would discourage their efforts to maintain democratic rule".

The paper also highlighted the link with security issues. The defence of Western Europe would be more precarious if "these three countries with their long coastlines and their vital strategic positions, Portugal on the Atlantic, Spain in the Western and Greece in the Eastern Mediterranean, were not to be with us, but alternatively, against us".

The prospect of Community enlargements nevertheless gave rise to a fundamental debate about its future, generally described as one between "wideners" and "deepeners". This had many facets. At one level, the two sides were seen as being in fundamental conflict. The Thatcher

Government's support for widening was attacked as merely a strategy to dilute the Community into the old Conservative goal of a Free Trade Area. On the other side, those arguing for deepening – reform of the institutions to create a more tightly-knit union before enlargement – were accused of really using this as an excuse to keep other countries out. Both charges contained more than an element of truth.

At another level, however, widening and deepening were inevitable partners. As Spanish and Portuguese accession approached, thinking on how to run a Community double the size of the original Six intensified. In the Parliament, for example, increasing the number, not just of its members, but also of its official languages from the original four (Dutch, French, German and Italian) to nine (adding Danish, English, Greek, Portuguese and Spanish) had important consequences for efficiency and cost. In the Council of Ministers, the job of reaching consensus became more complicated, and the number of potential vetoes was doubled. The Greek/Iberian enlargement increased the size of the Commission by four – at the time not seen as a big problem for efficiency, but one which would loom much larger as subsequent enlargements took place. Finally, there were serious budgetary consequences, as the new Member States, poorer than the rest, required considerable Community funding.

The dilemma for Conservatives was that, though enlargement itself was seen as highly desirable, some of the generally-accepted institutional consequences were not. For example, the view of most Members of the European Parliament, other than a number from the UK and Denmark, was that the problem of too many potential national vetoes was logically solved by switching to majority voting in the Council of Ministers. If that resulted in a loss of democratic control by national parliaments, that, too, was logically solved by increasing the power of the European Parliament. Since the Commission was a collegiate body, specifically forbidden to act as national representatives, there was no need to link its size to the number of Member States. And a larger Community of course needed a larger budget.

There was, moreover, no lack of plans to bring about the necessary reforms. The then Prime Minister of Belgium, Leo Tindemans (who would one day chair the EPP Group in the Parliament when the Conservatives joined it) had in 1976 published a report on how to create a real European Union. In 1979 there had been the report of the "Three Wise Men"* on how to improve the Community's decision-making process. In 1981 the Foreign Ministers of Germany and Italy, Hans-Dietrich Genscher and Emilio Colombo, produced a draft "European Act". Two years later Genscher-Colombo became a "Solemn Declaration on European Union", signed by

---

* This had been commissioned in 1978 by the European Council, better known as the "summit" of Heads of State and Government. The three men concerned were Robert Marjolin from France, Barend Biesheuvel from the Netherlands and Edmund Dell, formerly a minister in the Labour Government, from the UK. Opponents of their findings made much of an alleged misprint in the French press describing them as *"les trois singes"*.

the Heads of State and Government – including, of course, Mrs Thatcher – at the Stuttgart Summit of June 1983. The governments thereby resolved "to transform the whole complex of relations between their States into a European Union". This would involve not only institutional reform, but also the extension of Community competences into new fields like "international problems of law and order".

Within the European Parliament, a new Institutional Affairs Committee had been set up in 1981; and in 1984 it produced a "draft Treaty establishing the European Union" The *rapporteur* was the former Italian Commissioner and member of the Communist Group, Altiero Spinelli, who had been interned on the island of Ventotene during the Second World War and who, together with a small group of fellow prisoners, had drafted the Ventotene Manifesto in support of a new European federalist movement.

Crocodiles and Kangaroos

These developments inevitably produced divisions within the European Democratic Group, which reflected those becoming apparent in the Conservative Party as a whole. The majority view was that of the Group's spokesman on the Institutional Affairs Committee, the late Derek Prag, who had the distinction of having worked in Luxembourg as an official of the ECSC in the 1950s. During a debate on the Spinelli Report he had told Parliament that "the burden of proof must be on those who believe that there is no need for institutional reform. There is plenty of evidence to suggest that the institutional arrangements set out in the Treaty of Rome nearly thirty years ago are no longer adequate."

A minority, however, rejected the reforms proposed in the Tindemans, Genscher-Colombo and Spinelli Reports for reasons which would later become far more generally accepted within the Party: that, however justified on grounds of efficiency, they were a step away from national sovereignty towards "federalism". The core of the antis was the "H-block"; but they were joined by a number of others, including myself (whose record thereafter had on it a small but indelible "Eurosceptic" black mark). Yet not long afterwards the Group itself published a pamphlet[21] which effectively justified the anti position. "Conservatives are mistrustful of blueprints" it said.

> They believe that institutions must be allowed to evolve naturally; and Parliaments in particular need first to acquire authority, and so influence, before they can be endowed with substantial formal powers. ... Viewed in this light, the Spinelli proposals adopted by the Parliament on 14 September 1983 look like an attempt to take a short cut. ... This is what really disqualifies them in the Conservative mind.

The five authors included three of the Group's senior lawyers – and also, curiously, Derek Prag.

My own reasons for voting as I did, however, were somewhat different – in fact, on the issue of Parliament's powers, I was on the side of Spinelli. The immediate grounds were that the report supported the possibility of a "two-speed Europe", with the UK inevitably consigned to the slow lane. Behind this, however, lay a much more fundamental point: that, in expending its mental energies on institutional matters, the Community was neglecting a much more important matter, the "costs of non-Europe". By this was meant the failure to eliminate the barriers to internal free movement which were hampering the operation of the internal market, and the consequent comparative stagnation of the Community's economies. Allowing two or more speeds, I thought, would fragment the market even more.

The campaign for "a real Common Market" would soon become the main theme of Conservative European policy. The objective had of course featured in the 1979 manifesto, and in many previous official and unofficial Conservative documents. The then Secretary of State for Employment, Norman (now Lord) Tebbit, declared in 1982 that progress towards "a common market in which industry can operate free from barriers to the movement of people, goods and services" would be "one mark of our success or failure".[22]

But in 1979/80 there had come a new impetus, originating not from national or even European politicians, but from a number of European industrialists, among them Basil de Ferranti, who had been President of the Economic and Social Committee before becoming a Conservative MEP. It was no accident that these industrialists included somebody from consumer electronics, Dr Wisse Deckker of Philips, and de Ferranti from high-tech defence technology and computers. The divisions in Europe between different national markets in these fields were allowing, in the first case Japan, in the second case the United States, to take over those markets.

In the European Parliament, immediately after the European Elections of 1979, de Ferranti, together with two German MEPs – one a Christian Democrat, Karl von Wogau, the other a Social Democrat, Dieter Rogalla – formed the "Kangaroo Group".* This brought together MEPs, Commission and Council of Ministers' officials and leaders in major European companies to intensify the "real common market" campaign. A specific target of the Group was the Parliament's Economic and Monetary Affairs Committee, where a series of reports would call for action. One of the Committee's chairmen during this period was the future Commission President Jacques Delors, then a French Socialist MEP.

At much the same time, another European Parliament "intergroup" (as they were called) had come into being: the "Crocodile Club", so called

---

* Why Kangaroo? The official explanation is that Kangaroos are able to jump over customs and other barriers between markets. Another explanation is that a number of MEPs on the Delegation to Australia came back to the Parliament wearing kangaroo lapel badges given to them by the airline Quantas. The Group immediately adopted them.

because its inaugural meeting had been held at the three-star restaurant of that name in Strasbourg. Its driving force was Altiero Spinelli, and its objective was to campaign for the Treaty changes embodied in his report.

Despite representing the majority opinion among Conservative MEPs, the Conservative Crocodiles had considerably more problems with the Party at home than the Kangaroos. My colleague for Kent East, Christopher Jackson, recalls leading a delegation to Britain from Parliament's Institutional Committee, including its Chairman Altiero Spinelli, for a series of meetings with Conservative, Liberal and Labour MPs, the TUC and the CBI to argue the case for supporting the Parliament's Draft Treaty on European Union. For the Conservatives, the Minister of State at the Foreign Office (later Foreign Secretary) Malcolm Rifkind had arranged a meeting at Church House with "some 20 parliamentary under-secretaries and ministers of state". The atmosphere was "muted, mildly interested and not hostile." But after the meeting, at a lunch which he was hosting, Rifkind insisted that "there was really no need at all to change the treaties". Jackson comments that "Malcolm was a good and intelligent minister, but this reflected the usual stupidity of British administrations in rejecting something at first and then coming along much later to support it".[23]

Jackson was, of course, right about the eventual outcome. It became clear as the "real common market" campaign got up steam that one of the problems in passing the necessary legislation was the decision-making procedure in the Council of Ministers. The Conservative Government would soon come around to support the treaty changes needed, which would be embodied in the Single European Act of 1986.

There were, nevertheless, disagreements building up in another direction, which were omens of bigger conflicts to come. In September 1981 I had become Group spokesman on the Social and Employment Committee, where discussions were taking place on a number of Commission proposals concerning the labour market. Among them was the so-called "Vredeling Directive"[24]* to give employees increased rights of information and consultation throughout the Community, which was linked to the draft 5th Company Law Directive on the structure of companies; and also proposals to regulate the markets in part-time work and temporary work. In the background was a general drive from the Left to limit working hours as a way of creating more jobs. Even British Commissioner Ivor Richard was on record as arguing "the amount of work is not in the short or medium term going to be sufficient to allow everybody to work a 40-hour week for 48 weeks in the year for 40 years of his or her life".[25]

In this area, the Conservative Party could unite – or almost – in opposition. The idea that unemployment would be reduced by cutting hours of work was an elementary mistake in economics, the so-called "lump of

---

* So called after its original proposer, the Dutch Socialist Commissioner Henk Vredeling.

labour" fallacy. Forcing countries with more flexible labour markets to make them more rigid, in the name of fair competition, was a policy of "equal millstones" which would end up making the whole Community uncompetitive. In any case, the Left was not really interested in creating more jobs for the unemployed; the aim was to protect the jobs of those already in employment.

We deployed these arguments vigorously in Committee,[26] as did Conservative Ministers in Council. Our alternative was the "programme for European economic recovery" outlined in a report by the Christian Democrat Fernand Herman, which had been adopted by a massive majority of the Parliament. At the centre of this, of course, was the "consolidation of the internal market".

Consultation of the voting records of Parliament will, however, reveal the surprising fact that the EDG actually voted for the Vredeling Directive when it came before the full Parliament; and also that I myself was *rapporteur* on the draft Part-time Work Directive. This was a classic result of the need to compromise in order to obtain a majority in the Parliament. Our EPP Group allies were not, in principle, against the rights of employees to be consulted; only against those provisions of the measure which might put up costs, especially for SMEs (Small and Medium-sized Companies), the famous German *Mittelstand*. It was on the basis of substantial changes that the centre-right as a whole agreed to support the final text.

None of this, however, was much understood by the Party at home. In the event, Vredeling and the other proposals remained blocked in the Council of Ministers until the following century.

Constituency issues

In any case, as far as Conservative Party members in the constituencies were concerned, most of what went on in Brussels, Luxembourg and Strasbourg was not of very great interest. The great events of the early 1980s were the new "monetarist" economic policies introduced by the Government, the moves to limit the power of the Trade Unions and, of course, the Falklands War. One measure, however, had an immediate impact in the European context: the complete abolition of exchange controls in October 1979. In his memoirs, Howe describes this as a decision to "walk over the edge of the cliff and see what happened". In the event, the decision was completely justified. Sterling rose by 25% in the following year, and it "sent out a message to the world about our commitment to liberal economics as the means of reviving Britain".[27]

But it had a much wider impact than that. When, years later, I have explained exchange controls to conferences in schools and colleges, and even to older audiences, it is clear that they take it with a pinch of salt. Yet I still have old passports in which it is carefully recorded how much foreign currency I had been allowed for trips on the Continent. Imposed at the outbreak of the Second World War in 1939, these limits had remained in force ever since, often making British tourists the subject of pity and ridicule as they ran out of cash. John Major, in a speech in 1993, recalled that twenty years earlier "all you could take to the continent was a limited amount of foreign currency and £25 sterling. Today we go to France much as we might go to Yorkshire."[28]

Well, not quite: Yorkshire and the rest of the UK use the same currency, whereas France and the UK still do not. Yet the final end to fifty years of exchange controls *did* improve the lives of a growing number of ordinary people, as well as liberating British businesses from restraints on their ability to invest and trade abroad. The next measure with similar impact did not occur until the beginning of 1993, when VAT and excise duty controls for individual travellers within the Community were abolished; and, after that, the introduction of euro-denominated notes and coins throughout most of the Community at the beginning of 2001.

During my time in the European Parliament I, like many of my colleagues, distributed a regular Newsletter in the constituency, the readership being largely Conservative Party members. The content consisted, in part, of reports on what was going on in the Parliament itself; and in part of local issues which had been raised with me as having a European dimension. During the 1979–84 Parliament a number of subjects kept coming back; and the list gives an indication of the European issues that actually interested voters.

Not surprisingly, a large number of these subjects concerned agriculture. In rural areas the NFU (to which I myself belong) was the most active of the bodies lobbying MEPs, and also had a strong influence on local Conservative opinion. The Newsletter list includes items on winter feed for bees, apples, abattoirs, the status of vets and environmental health officers, tomato imports, milk quotas, levies on hard wheat imports, sheepmeat aid, promotion of English cheese and wine, many complaints about the Ministry of Agriculture, Fisheries and Food (MAFF) as it was then, and CAP fraud.

As it happens, the first pamphlet[29] published by the new European Democratic Group was in the field of agriculture: a report from the Group's Apple Industry Committee, which had been chaired by Kent East MEP Christopher Jackson, and which was accompanied by a favourable Foreword from the then Minister of Agriculture, Peter Walker. This reflected a high profile issue at the time: the invasion into British supermarkets of French Golden Delicious apples which threatened British growers, particularly those of Kent Cox's Orange Pippins. The first constituency "surgery" I held in Tunbridge Wells after the elections was attended by a determined delegation from the Women's Farming Union, who made it very clear that they expected their MEPs to do something about it.

Almost as frequent, but from an entirely different perspective, were items concerned with animal welfare: the transport of live animals, trade in horses, the protection of migrating birds, rabies, animal experiments and the culling of baby seals. After these, the most frequent topics were transport-related: Heavy Goods Vehicles (HGVs), tachographs (the "spy in the cab"), driving licences, border controls, buying cars abroad and, of course, in Kent, the Channel Tunnel project.

In more urban areas this was the period when Britain's manufacturing industries were shrinking, with the result that interest in "money from Europe" grew markedly among local authorities, chambers of commerce and similar bodies. MEPs were able to point them in the direction of the Community's Regional Fund, which provided money for infra-structure projects or direct investments to provide new employment; the Social Fund which provided money for retraining; funds available separately through the European Coal and Steel Community (ECSC); and also loans from the European Investment Bank, sometimes with interest-rate subsidies attached. In Northamptonshire, for example, the Conservative MEP Anthony Simpson reacted to the closure of the Corby Steel works by organising a visit to the Commission in Brussels for local authority leaders to make contact with the responsible officials. The result was that, after an interchange of visits, a total of £130 million of European funding became available, and Corby was transformed from a one-industry steel town into a community based on a wide variety of new industries.

Attracting European funding in this way nevertheless meant over-coming two basic problems, inherent in the system. The first was the requirement that there had to be "matching money", essentially from the British Treasury, which was not always forthcoming. The second was that European funding could not just replace money that would have been spent anyway: in the jargon, there had to be "addition-ality". Applying this criterion, however, was complicated both by the Government's reluctance to see any overall increase in public spending, and by the dispute over Britain's contribution to the Community Budget. "Additionality", if honestly implemented, inevitably meant a higher level of public expenditure; and if one took the view that it was "our" money anyway, whether it was additional or not was beside the point. The "matching money" and "additionality" requirements have bedevilled the administration of what are now the "Structural Funds" ever since.

Speech notes for constituency and branch meetings, and the added records of questions, also give some indication of what interested Conservative Party members during this period. My own notes from the first half of 1982 show that Community support for the UK during the Falklands war was an important plus point, as was the fact that money from the Community Budget had already helped to equip the hospital in Port Stanley. The notes also reveal considerable interest in the question of languages, either regret that not enough was being done to teach them, or confidence that everyone would soon speak English anyway. Wine lakes and butter mountains were a constant feature, as were media reports of

CAP fraud: for example the manipulation of "Green currency" rates on the border between Northern Ireland and the Irish Republic.*

There were also frequent complaints about a matter that would later become almost an obsession: European "red tape" – but with a difference. Where later the complaints would be about red tape "imposed from 'Brussels'", the complaints then were that not *enough* was being done by "Brussels" to remove nationally-imposed red tape: for example, the procedures if one fell ill abroad. An official "notes for holiday-makers" in 1982 contained the following advice:

> To avoid trouble, apply for a certificate of entitlement to treatment (Form E.111 or 111 for West Germany) before going away.
>
> Form E.111 (and 111) is obtained by filling in form CM1 ...
>
> Form CM1 is found at the back of leaflet SA 30 ...

In the Parliament, the Kangaroo Group was making a particular effort to expose absurdities caused by incompatible national regulations. Examples quoted in my *Newsletter* included the infamous multiplicity of documents needed to move goods between countries (ten separate pieces of paper to get them across the Channel by lorry); but also problems for individuals, such as those faced by a couple married in West Germany who elected to take the wife's maiden name (as they were entitled to under a recent German law) but had problems returning to their home in France because French law still required all documents to be in the husband's original surname. My own constituency cases included a student refused entry to France for not having enough money on him; arrest of a lorry driver by the Belgian police for not possessing documents which had actually been retained by Belgian customs; a refusal to pay compensation after a mugging abroad; conflicting rulings in the courts of different countries on the custody of children; charges of up to one third of value for cashing travellers' cheques. ...

In the face of cases such as these, "harmonisation" did not carry the negative overtones for Conservatives that it would acquire some years later.

---

* The BBC *Panorama* programme popularised this issue with tales of a pig which had been going backwards and forwards across the border collecting £7.50 in Monetary Compensatory Amounts (MCAs) on each circuit. At this time, as a member of Parliament's Budgetary Control Committee, I was charged with preparing an "on the spot" investigative report for the Committee on this issue. As in the case of other such reports (notably one by my colleague Bob Battersby on wine fraud in France) its conclusions were considered sufficiently inflammatory as to be classified "internal".

"True to Britain and true to Europe"

Because the European Parliament has a five-year fixed term, but the House of Commons – until now – does not, elections to the two bodies soon became decoupled after being only a month apart in 1979. Margaret Thatcher's second UK general election as Conservative leader took place in June 1983, the second direct elections to the European Parliament a year later.

In both elections, however, positioning the Party on the issue of Europe was not difficult. As *The Conservative Manifesto 1983*[30] put it: "The Labour Party wants Britain to withdraw from the Community, because it fears that Britain cannot compete inside and that it would be easier to build a Socialist siege economy if we withdrew. The Liberals and the SDP appear to want Britain to stay in but never to upset our partners by speaking up forcefully. The Conservatives reject both extreme views."

By contrast, Conservatives were "determined to make a success of British membership"; but also had "stood up for British interests". They had opposed "petty acts of Brussels bureaucracy"; but also sought "the removal of unnecessary restrictions on the free movement of goods and services between member states, with proper safeguards to guarantee fair competition". Overall, the balance of approach was positive. As the Prime Minister declared in a message celebrating the tenth anniversary of Britain's Community membership at the beginning of 1983: "The unity of Europe as a force for peace, freedom and democracy is a goal for which I pledge my Government to work."

The result of the election was a satisfactory triumph for the Conservative Party, and almost a terminal disaster for Labour, which polled only 2% more than the SDP/Liberal Alliance. Europe had played a small but significant part in the campaign: staying in the Community, while "standing up for Britain" was exactly what most of the electorate seemed to want.

Unsurprisingly, therefore, the Party's stance in the European Parliament elections in the following year was much the same. Margaret Thatcher recalls that she addressed us, the sitting Conservative MEPs, in March 1984[31] in 10 Downing Street, and outlined "the vision on which we were to fight the European Assembly [*sic*] elections later that year. ... " Hers was of "a free enterprise *Europe des patries*".

> A Community striving for free trade, breaking down the barriers in Europe and the world to the free flow of goods, capital and services; working together to make Europe the home of the industries of tomorrow; seizing the initiative on world problems, not reacting wearily to them; forging political links across the European divide and so creating a more hopeful relationship between East and West; using its influence as a vital areas of stability and democracy to strengthen democracy across the world.

The Conservative message at the election was therefore of a Conservative Government at home and Conservative MEPs abroad taking the lead in moving the Community in these directions. "We have shown," the manifesto[32] declared, "that it is possible to be true to Britain *and* true to Europe". It placed especial emphasis on "greater cooperation among the Ten on foreign policy" and "even greater cooperation on defence and security"; and, of course, on making "a reality of the common market". Rapid enlargement of the Community to include Spain and Portugal was welcomed.

My own election address highlighted the Conservative campaign during the previous five years for "two fundamental reforms": "first, to the Common Agricultural Policy, so that money is no longer wasted on 'mountains' of unwanted food; and, secondly, to the way in which the Community is financed – in particular so that Britain no longer pays an unfair share. Both these campaigns – by a Conservative Government backed by Conservative Members of the European Parliament – are succeeding. The EEC is being reformed." And the text concluded with the words: "Mrs Thatcher in Downing Street; a strong Conservative group in Strasbourg – that is Britain's winning combination in Europe."

It is interesting to note that an issue which was later to become of overwhelming importance to the fortunes of the Party – potential British membership of the European Monetary System (EMS) and the Exchange Rate Mechanism (ERM) within it – played only a minimal part in the 1984 election campaign. With the Labour Party still in favour of leaving the Community altogether, the Conservative Government's policy of keeping the pound outside the Mechanism "until the time is right"* was hardly challenged. This was despite the fact that the 1979 manifesto had regretted the Callaghan Labour Government's decision not to join. Geoffrey Howe recalls that some months at the Treasury had persuaded him "that the oil-induced volatility of the pound sterling created difficulties for our immediate membership of the Exchange Rate Mechanism of the EMS".[33]

The 1983 *Campaign Guide* expanded this argument by observing that the pound sterling, still "a major international currency", was "sensitive to a variety of external factors not experienced by most of the EMS currencies".[34] Yet Howe then recalls that "in 1984/5 I was persuaded once again in favour of ERM membership. ... Oil-induced volatility of the pound sterling had paled into insignificance."

Behind the scenes, we now know, the issue was already creating mounting tensions within the Government. The Chancellor of the Exchequer, Nigel Lawson, had been in favour of joining the Exchange Rate Mechanism

---

* This phrase was sometimes rendered as "when the time is ripe". Could whoever first coined the phrase have been thinking of Ira Gershwin's lines in the song *I Can't Be Bothered Now*: "I'll pay the piper, when times are riper"? According to the future Chancellor, Nigel Lawson, "ripe" was the original word used, later changing to "right" – possibly, he thinks, as the result of a typing error. The term actually used in the 1984 Manifesto was "when the conditions are right."

from the start, and was soon to experiment with "virtual membership" by having the pound shadow the D-Mark. Lawson's view was shared by most Conservative MEPs, some of whom were already active in a new pressure group campaigning for a common, or even a single, currency (the difference is to be explained later). For most Conservatives at home, however, the issue did not at the time register high on the scale of priorities.

This time, the low turnout at the European Elections, which was only one percentage point above that in 1979 and again the lowest in the Community, did not come as much of a surprise. It was still higher in Conservative areas than in Labour ones, though to a considerably lesser extent than in 1979. This was reflected in a fall in my Kent West Conservative majority from over 67,000 to under 34,000.

The overall result was also not quite as good as in 1979. The new leader of the Labour Party, Neil Kinnock, had already begun a slow retreat from the straightforward policy of leaving the Community. He had "moved party policy from the 1983 commitment to withdrawal, to a position in 1984 of considering withdrawal".[35] Fifteen seats changed from Conservative to Labour – mostly those which were natural Labour territory except in the extraordinary circumstances of 1979 – so reducing the number of British Conservative MEPs to 45. The SDP/Liberal Alliance polled over two-and-a-half million votes, 19% of the total, but still won no seats. This yet again produced angry letters in the press – not all from members of the Alliance – in denouncing the "outrage" of the voting system.

Notes

1 *Memories of the first elected European Parliament* collected by Bill Newton Dunn MEP (Allendale Publishing, 2007).
2 *Memories of the first elected European Parliament*, p. 37.
3 *Memories of the first elected European Parliament*, p. 57.
4 *Stanley I Presume* by Stanley Johnson (Fourth Estate, 2009) p. 297.
5 *Memories of the first elected European Parliament*, p. 35.
6 Evidence to the House of Lords Select Committee on the European Communities, *op.cit.*
7 *Diaries* by Alan Clark (Phoenix paperback, 1993) p. 139.
8 138/79 [1980] ECR 3333
9 *Memories of the first elected European Parliament*, p. 68.
10 *The Downing Street Years* by Margaret Thatcher (HarperCollins 1993), p. 79.
11 See Hugo Young, *op.cit.* p. 318.
12 Thatcher in *Europe as I see it*.
13 Thatcher *The Downing Street Years* p. 81.
14 Howe, *op.cit.* p. 182
15 Anthony Forster, *op.cit.* p. 66.
16 Turner *op.cit.* p. 106.
17 *The View from No. 11* by Nigel Lawson (Bantam Press, 1992) p. 109.
18 See in *Memories of the first elected European Parliament*, p. 13.
19 *Three Years Work* (Conservative Research Department, 27 September 1982).
20 *From Nine to Twelve* (CPC for the EDG 1982).
21 *Problems, Powers, Opportunities: a Conservative View* by Diana Elles MEP, Derek Prag MEP, Christopher Prout MEP, Alan Tyrrell QC, MEP and Michael Welsh MEP (European Democratic Group, 1984).

22 Speech in The Hague in October 1982.

23 In *Memories of the first elected European Parliament*, p. 41.

24 *Proposal for a Council Directive on procedures for informing and consulting the employees of undertakings with complex structures, in particular transnational undertakings.* Original proposal tabled in 1980 (see *Official Journal* C297 of 15.11.1980). Amended proposal tabled in July 1983 (COM (83)292 final).

25 Speech to the Industrial Society on the 11th July 1983.

26 See *Vredeling and All That: European Community Proposals on Employee Consultation and Information*; and *Europe and Employment: Policies for Economic Recovery and Jobs*, both by Ben Patterson MEP (European Democratic Group 1984).

27 Howe, *op.cit.* p. 143.

28 *Britain at the Heart of Europe* (CPC for Conservatives in the European Parliament, May 1993).

29 *Apples: Report of the EDG Apple Industry Committee* (EDG, 1980).

30 *The Conservative Manifesto 1983* (Conservative Central Office, May 1983).

31 Thatcher, *The Downing Street Years*, pp. 536–7.

32 *A Strong Voice in Europe: the Conservative Manifesto for the European Elections, 14 June 1984* (Conservative Central Office, May 1984).

33 Howe *op.cit*, p. 111.

34 *The Campaign Guide 1983* (Conservative Research Department, April 1983).

35 Forster *op.cit.* p. 69.

8　Towards the Single Market

"1992"

The next European Parliament elections took place five years later, in 1989; and the Conservative Party was then able to claim that, at least during the previous five years, it had been one of the guiding forces leading Europe towards a promised land. The Commission under the Presidency of Jacques Delors, all twelve national governments, and a large majority in the European Parliament had accepted the need to implement what Geoffrey Howe had described as "the revolutionary British suggestion … that the Community should establish a common market".[1]

Whereas before there had been plenty of documents and speeches, but not much in the way of decisions, the difference in the second half of the 1980s was a comprehensive plan and, above all, a timetable. A Single Market by the end of 1992 became established as a vital and achievable goal, popularised simply as "1992".

At the time of the European Elections of 1989, of course, much of the Single Market legislation had still to be adopted, including on such critical and contentious issues as the abolition of tax controls at frontiers. Moreover, even at the beginning of 1993, the Single Market only truly existed in the case of physical goods – barriers to cross-frontier operations remained for most of the services sector, including that of financial services.

"1992" was nevertheless a real achievement. It gave the Community a new momentum after more than a decade of "eurosclerosis". In 1982 the European Parliament's "Group for the Recovery of the European Economy" (which consisted of the chairmen of the six parliamentary committees with economic matters in their terms of reference) commissioned a study on the economic crises then affecting the European Community. The Group's *rapporteur* was the Conservative MEP for Cambridgeshire, Sir Fred Catherwood; and on his initiative two external economists were appointed, Michel Albert, former head of the French *Commissariat au Plan*, and Professor James Ball, Principal of the London Business School. The "Ball Albert report",* entitled *Towards*

---

* It was sometimes referred to afterwards as the "Albert Ball Report", which led some to conclude that it had been written by a single person of that name.

European Economic Recovery in the 1980s,[2] was published in August of the following year. Its most striking finding was to identify the main cause of the Member States' low growth and high unemployment as "the costs of non-Europe". Economic recovery would need a new impetus from the Community, creating a "psychological jolt". This "1992" succeeded in doing.

As important, perhaps, was that "1992" showed that decisions at Community level could really have a positive impact on people's lives. On the evening of the 31st December 1992, for example, the two MEPs for Kent, Christopher Jackson and I, organised a large party on board the cross-channel ferry *The Pride of Kent*. We saw in the New Year at Calais, where I took delivery of some 120 bottles of wine, the price including the small French tax. The ferry immediately returned to Dover, almost making it in time to see in the New Year once again. Then, on the back of the small open-backed truck, the wine, my family, my staff and I were driven through customs – and were not stopped!

At constituency level, "1992" was also a winner. Many Conservative MEPs set up "1992" clubs for local businesses, providing briefing on the progress of the legislation and its consequences. As the magic date grew nearer, there were innumerable "1992" conferences, seminars and workshops, some politically, some commercially organised. All of us wrote regularly on the subject in our local newspapers. Between 1988 and 1994 I contributed regular updating articles to Vacher's quarterly *European Companion*. Moreover, all strands of opinion within the Conservative Party, even those with an impeccable anti-Market record, were able to unite around the Single Market objective.

The key document in the "1992" programme was the Commission's White Paper of the 15th June 1985, *Completing the Internal Market*.[3] It was presented by the Conservative Commissioner Arthur Cockfield, who had replaced Christopher Tugendhat in 1984 (at the same time becoming Lord Cockfield), and who had been allocated the internal market portfolio within the Commission. All accounts of "1992" agree that he played a crucial part in putting it through. Geoffrey Howe goes even further in stating that he "had almost single-handedly imposed and carried well on the way to fulfilment the entire single-market programme".[4]

Cockfield had seized the opportunity given by his portfolio "with characteristic zeal and mastery of detail". He had been selected by Thatcher as "someone entirely after her own heart – 'one of us'", with a record of "singlemindedness in our cause".[5] Moreover he had exceptional qualifications for the job. After graduating from the London School of Economics (LSE) in both law and economics, his career had begun in 1938 in the Inland Revenue, after which he had joined Boots the Chemist as finance director and afterwards, from 1961 to 1967, its managing director and chairman. He had then become an *eminence grise* behind the post-1970 Chancellors of the Exchequer, Iain Macleod and his successor Anthony Barber; had been chairman of the Price Commission between 1973 and 1977; and had served in a number of posts in the Thatcher government after 1979.

Not all were comfortable with the outcome of Cockfield's zeal. Mrs Thatcher herself recalled mixed feelings in her memoirs.

> Arthur Cockfield was a natural technocrat of great ability and problem-solving outlook. Unfortunately, he tended to disregard the larger questions of politics – constitutional sovereignty, national sentiment and the promptings of liberty. He was the prisoner as well as the master of his subject. It was all too easy for him, therefore, to go native and to move from deregulating the market to reregulating it under the rubric of harmonization. Alas, it was not long before my old friend and I were at odds.[6]

As the European Parliament's initial *rapporteur* on the Single Market programme, I retain keen memories of Lord Cockfield's approach to his subject. On one occasion, in the Economic and Monetary Affairs and Industrial Policy Committee of the European Parliament (its remit had been temporarily enlarged), he had no compunction in ruthlessly demolishing the arguments I – the Conservative spokesman in the Committee! – put up in mild criticism of certain of his tax proposals. Prime Minister Thatcher probably had, or should have had, ample warning of what to expect from her experiences in the 1970s as a junior Treasury spokesman, when Cockfield was advising the Treasury; and later when he was in her cabinet. Indeed, rumour had it that Cockfield's appointment to the Commission was partly because the Prime Minister was fed up with being lectured to and corrected by one of her own ministers.

On the substance, Cockfield was of course completely right. The logic of "free trade, fair trade" made it inevitable that some degree of harmonisation would be needed to ensure fair competition. Later objections to the harmonisation of certain health or safety standards nearly always contained a large element of self-contradiction: British businesses should be protected from "cheating" by (usually) the French; but, at the same time, there should be no "interference from Brussels". The solution that the House of Commons should decide on such matters, so preserving national sovereignty, ignored the possibility that all the other national parliaments might want to do the same, so destroying the Single Market which the whole policy was about.

As it happens, the Cockfield approach was, where possible, to sidestep this dilemma by substituting "mutual recognition" for harmonisation. The European Court of Justice had already provided the legal precedent for such a policy in its celebrated 1979 ruling in the "Cassis de Dijon" case.* This created a presumption that if a product was legally produced and marketed in one Member State, it could be legally marketed and sold in another. The Treaty allowed national restrictions "justified on grounds of public safety, public policy or public security; the protection of health and life of humans, animals or plants". But mutual recognition by every Member State of every other Member State's health and safety regulations, quality and environmental standards and professional qualifications would clearly have avoided years of tortuous negotiations. As the White Paper observed, the objectives of national legislation in these fields were usually identical, so that the rules and controls, although taking different forms, "essentially come down to the same thing".

Mutual recognition, however, could only work where there was mutual trust. In the field of the free movement of goods this sometimes existed. In the field of services and of labour it was frequently absent.

The second way in which Cockfield tried to avoid detailed harmonisation was by adopting the "reference to standards" approach. Instead of Directives or Regulations defining the precise characteristics to which a product in free circulation would have to conform – the *locus classicus* of such over-detailed measures was an earlier draft Directive on toys, which had proposed extensive rules on, for example, the combustibility of false beards – the draft legislation would merely establish broad, essential targets, with the detail provided by standards bodies like CEN (*Comité Européen de la Normalisation*) or the electrical product and telecommunications equivalents: the *Comité Européen de Normalisation Electrotechnique* (CENELEC); and the European Conference of Postal and Telecommunications Administrations (CEPT). Even this, however, had its limitations: there was bound to be conflict over what constituted the "essential elements" to be included in the legislation, and a great deal depended on rapid and effective work by the standards bodies themselves.

There is also some truth, however, in Howe's observation that "very soon it was Delors, not Margaret, who was able to rely on Arthur's tenacious commitment to his cause".[7] This was hardly surprising: an honourable man, Cockfield took seriously his Commissioner's oath of independence. It is also true, though, that Delors had an agenda somewhat different from that of Thatcher's Conservative Government. His political credo might perhaps be described as "Christian Socialism" – he was "a tough, *dirigiste* French socialist, out of the Catholic social tradition", as Hugo Young puts

---

* Case C-120/78, *Rewe-Zentral AG v. Bundesmonopolverwaltung für Branntwein*. An importer had been prohibited by the German authorities from importing *Cassis de Dijon*, a French liqueur, into Germany, on the grounds that its alcoholic strength was too low: German law prevented the sale of any drink with an alcohol content between 15% and 25%. The German authorities argued that this measure was not concerned with country of origin at all, and would have applied to domestic as well as to imported products. But the European Court of Justice held that the measure was equivalent to a quota (illegal under the Treaty), because it would have the practical effect of restricting imports, even though it did not directly target imported goods.

it.[8] Though as committed as everyone else to the removal of barriers to trade and the creation of "a real common market", he added to this what he described as "the social dimension of 1992": ensuring "a fair share-out of the advantages deriving from the single market".[9]

Most of this social dimension concerned the labour market, and in particular measures to "solve the serious problem of unemployment and minimize its unequal distribution". In the context of making freedom of movement and establishment a reality, it also meant making sure that "the economic measures to be taken do not affect the standards of social protection attained in Member States". This implied Community initiatives, "flanking" the Single Market programme, not only in the field of the labour market but also in those of health and safety, consumer protection, education and the environment.

Such an agenda inevitably clashed with the view that these were mostly matters that should be left to the choice of individual Member States rather than regulated at Community level: the principle of what came to be called "subsidiarity". For Conservatives, opposing it on these grounds created few problems. However, it was also far from clear how proposals designed to pursue the "social dimension" could be distinguished from those designed to ensure a "level playing field" in the market. For Conservatives, this frequently *did* create problems.

It is also worth noting that Delors himself has, both then and since, been criticised by supporters of closer European integration for having, in the Single Market programme and the Single European Act, sold out to "free-market liberalism". Far from having presided over a "grab for power by Brussels", or having introduced "Socialism by the back door" – as Margaret Thatcher and other Conservatives would maintain – he had allowed the drive towards the Treaty objective of ever-closer union to be fatally watered down. The result had been disillusionment among Europe's citizens, who had rejected the "liberal, Anglo-Saxon model" – the reason, according to this view, that the French eventually voted against the draft Constitution for Europe in 2005.[10]

The Cockfield White Paper

The Cockfield White Paper of 1985 listed some 300 measures programmed to come into effect before the end of 1992. These were presented in what amounted to the form of a grid: on one axis the subject matter, on the other the timetable. The subjects were the removal of physical barriers, subdivided into the control of goods and the control of individuals; the removal of technical barriers, subdivided into the free movement of goods, public procurement, free movement for labour and the professions, a common market for services, capital movements, industrial cooperation and the application of community law; and the removal of fiscal barriers, subdivided into VAT and excise duties. The timescale was divided into two periods: 1985–86 and 1987–92.

It has to be admitted that the White Paper was in many ways a confidence trick. Much of the contents had already been published. In 1983 the Commission had produced an *Assessment of the Function of the Internal Market*; and in the following year Cockfield's predecessor, Commissioner Narjes, had presented *Consolidating the Internal Market* (COM(84)305 final of June 1984) and a second Consolidation document (COM(84)350 final of July 1984) which had observed that "we do not need new ideas, new policies or new Community funds ... ", only political will to implement the proposals already on the table. The Narjes papers had even proposed a timetable, albeit an unrealistic one: some 68 proposals to be adopted in 1984, and another 60 or so in 1985.

It was on these "Consolidation" documents that Parliament's Economic and Monetary Affairs and Industrial Policy Committee (as it was then) appointed me *rapporteur* in 1984; but the preparation of the report was overtaken by the 1985 White Paper, with the result that the final report presented to the Parliament effectively covered the "1992" programme as well. The burden of translation costs had not yet forced the Parliament to limit the length of *rapporteur's* documents, with the result that I was able to present a 124-page "explanatory statement"[11] to the resolution for debate.

In the light of criticisms levelled at "1992" – at the time by Socialists, and later even by Conservatives – it is worth repeating two of the points made. The Single Market, it was sometimes claimed, was really a project designed to create only a "Europe of the multinationals". I therefore quoted from an earlier Parliament report which had pointed out that "for large firms, which have subsidiaries in all Member States, the existing technical barriers to trade are a cost factor and an inconvenience. For small and medium-sized undertakings, however, they are often an insuperable barrier". This is significant because of changes that later took place in business opinion on the Single Market programme.

Secondly, the report observed that the Single Market was "not a matter merely of economics or good business. It is also a matter of human rights and personal freedom". The 1984 Fontainebleau summit, at which the UK budget rebate issue had been settled, had also established a "People's Europe" committee (chaired by an Italian former colleague on Parliament's Rules and Petitions Committee, Pietro Adonino). This was already examining the many bureaucratic restrictions on individuals caused sometimes by malice or maladministration, but also by the incompatibilities of national laws of the kind being documented by the Kangaroo Group and by the European Parliament's Rules and Petitions Committee.

The thrust of my report, therefore, was free market and libertarian; and I have little doubt that it reflected orthodox Conservative opinion at the time.

Looking though the details of the Cockfield White Paper, though, it is not difficult – admittedly with hindsight – to see where problems would arise. One of its key objectives in the case of controls at national frontiers was "not merely to simplify existing procedures, but to do away with internal frontier controls in their entirety". As the Paper immediately admitted, not only would this come up against the issues of controlling terrorism, drug-trafficking, immigration and plant and animal health but also that of taxation: "the problem of removing physical controls," it stated, "is largely related to that of removing fiscal barriers". When the discussions on Cockfield's far-reaching proposals on VAT and excise duties really got under way in 1987, it was clear that the main issue for the national finance ministries, including the UK Exchequer, was not so much the Single Market as whether or not they would lose revenue.

The Cockfield White Paper also indicated that the free movement of persons had far-reaching implications for various policies not normally associated with freedom of trade: rules on the right of residence, the right of asylum and the status of refugees, visa policy, rules on extradition, police cooperation, mutual enforcement of arrest warrants and so on. This "justice and home affairs" dimension would later be tacked onto the Community as a "second pillar" of the European Union, pursued largely through inter-governmental agreement. For Conservatives, however, extending the European Union's competence into such fields proved extremely sensitive, as the Party's reaction to the Lisbon Treaty has more recently shown. On the one hand, cross-border cooperation to catch criminals and prevent illegal immigration was welcome. On the other, there were fears – mostly unjustified, but nevertheless real – about possible interference with the British criminal justice system.

In addition, the limitations on applying the principle of mutual recognition, admitted in the White Paper, opened the way for an unwelcome return to the default solution of harmonisation. This turned out to be particularly true in the case of "non-tangibles" like the services sectors and professional qualifications, where the principle of "home country control" was expected to apply. This meant, in the field of financial services, for example – where the UK had a particular interest in opening up continental markets – that British firms selling financial products in, say, Germany, would be subject to British supervisory regulations rather than German ones. The German view, however, was that British rules were unacceptably lax: applying home country rules would put German consumers in jeopardy, as well as making it impossible for German-based firms to compete. The same problems existed in the field of the professions: if those with a qualification in one Member State had the right to practice in every other Member State, what guarantee was there that professional standards would be maintained? Generally, there was a fear that the Single Market would result in a "race to the bottom".

Opening up markets in these fields, therefore, proved much more difficult than was optimistically predicted in 1985. Financial Services had mostly to be left to a Financial Services Action Plan many years after 1992. The general recognition of qualifications took even longer. In other sectors – notably in the field of consumer protection, where mutual trust was often absent – a return to detailed harmonisation led to the complaints of "excessive regulation from Brussels" which did so much to spread Euroscepticism in the Conservative Party, even before 1993. The massive achievements in removing barriers which actually took place tended to be forgotten.

The Single European Act

The most important obstacle perceived to stand in the way of completing the Single Market, however, was the decision-taking capacity of the Council of Ministers. The legal bases available in the Treaty for Single Market legislation were limited: most measures up to then had been based on what was at the time Article 100, which required unanimity; and the Council had twelve, later fifteen members, which created the potential for that number of vetoes by "one protectionist country after another".[12] Accordingly, the Cockfield White Paper observed that "it is clear than a genuine common market cannot be realised by 1992 if the Council relies exclusively on Article 100".

The obvious answer was to take Single Market decisions by majority vote – or, rather, by Qualified Majority Vote (QMV), under which the voting strength of each Member State was to some extent weighted according to size.* The British Government first proposed that this should be achieved, not by changing the Treaty, but by "gentlemen's agreement", "written but not legally binding" under which single market legislation would be treated "as though the unanimity rule had been set to one side".[13] If the Treaty was to be changed, it would be necessary to hold a preliminary Inter-Governmental Conference (IGC), which "might open the way for uncontrollable constitutional ventures".[14] The Foreign Office also doubted whether it would be possible to get any major changes to the Treaty ratified by all the Member States' parliaments.

One Foreign Office minister, the future Foreign Secretary Malcolm Rifkind, was nevertheless bold enough to disagree. Accepting Treaty changes, he argued, would show that Britain was really serious about the Single Market.[15] This was the view that, ultimately if at first reluctantly, was accepted.

In the European Parliament there was virtually unanimous agreement that, if the Council of Ministers was going to use QMV more frequently, one "constitutional venture" was inescapable: an increase in Parliament's own role. This was not just a bald bid for power. If ministers were sometimes going to be outvoted in Council, not only the national governments they came from but the national parliaments that supported them would have lost sovereignty – a "democratic deficit" would have opened up. This could be closed by increasing the power of those elected at European level.

---

* The considerations governing the original weighting in the Treaties took into account not only population, but also economic importance.

The logic of this position was powerful: in putting it to Conservative audiences both before and after the passage of the Single European Act (SEA) I found broad agreement. It did not appeal so much, however, to MPs at Westminster. When the issue came up again in the run-up to the Maastricht Treaty, the official Conservative reaction was openly hostile – the argument, Chancellor of the Exchequer Norman Lamont would say in 1992, was "the thin end of the wedge. It would lead to further centralisation and more power seeping away to Community institutions".[16]

One result was a further sharp deterioration in relations between Conservative MPs and MEPs.

A certain mythology has grown up about how the SEA came to be passed. According to later Conservative Eurosceptics, Prime Minister Thatcher was somehow tricked at the 1985 Milan summit into agreeing to an Inter-Governmental Conference (IGC); then hoodwinked by Howe and the Foreign Office into signing a document she didn't agree with. Both theories are thoroughly implausible. According to those present at the Milan summit the eventual decision to hold the IGC was more the result of a miscalculation by British officials than of deception. The summit chairman, Italian PM Bettino Craxi, was entitled to have the matter decided by vote, but was not expected to do so.

It can also be argued, however, that Craxi knew exactly what he was doing. Stephen Wall's opinion is that the Italians, "by cleverly outvoting Britain on calling an IGC, had instilled in the British a fear that, if we did not compromise, we would be left behind by the other member states … ".[17]

If this was the case, it worked. Thatcher's reaction, after some initial anger, was not to fight the decision, but to start campaigning for the Treaty changes which would help the Single Market programme. "By this means Mrs. Thatcher, instead of being the chief obstacle to further European union, became one of its chief architects."[18] As far as the extension of Qualified Majority Vote (QMV) was concerned, Howe's own account notes that "we were enthusiastic protagonists of this where it could be seen as necessary for the effective operation of the single market".

Having secured during the IGC negotiations in Luxembourg "all the points which were of real importance", notably the preservation of the veto on tax matters and retention of the right to control immigration from third countries, the Government had no difficulty in getting the treaty through the House of Commons. Hugo Young observes that the outcome "certainly satisfied Mrs Thatcher".

> When she got back home, she called the result 'clear and decisive'. This reflected the general atmosphere in the Conservative Party at the time. Hardly anyone criticized the Act as a piece of crypto-federalism which wasn't all that crypto. The Prime Minister's enthusiastic report to Parliament was accepted in similar spirit.[19]

Moreover, the Prime Minister herself, according to various witnesses,[20] not only read through the final text carefully, but had spent many hours painstakingly talking through the drafts. This gives the lie to later assertions – for example by her foreign policy adviser at the time, Charles (now Lord) Powell – that she was at the time unaware of the SEA's longer-term implications.

The SEA was then presented by the Party as one of the "achievements of the Conservative Government", which had made "significant steps ... towards securing major improvements in the working of the Community: better decision-making, effective cooperation in research and development and closer cooperation on foreign policy".[21]

The whole Single Market package, the Cockfield White Paper and SEA together, was hailed by Conservatives, and denounced by the Labour left, as "Thatcherism on a European scale". "Everyone in the Thatcher Cabinet backed it, and so did almost everyone in the Thatcher Party"[22] Hugo Young correctly observes; and he takes some malicious pleasure in noting that the later *über*-Eurosceptic Bill Cash "warmly supported the Act", even attacking Enoch Powell for opposing it.[23]

Second thoughts

How, then, does one explain the later criticisms of the SEA by various leading Conservatives, including, to a certain extent, the Prime Minister herself? There were, of course, the problems caused by "level playing field" considerations, leading to what was felt to be unnecessary harmonisation. Some, like Cabinet Ministers Peter Lilley and Michael Portillo, reportedly "claimed to have voted for the headline agreement that the government thought the SEA represented, without much concern for the detail of the treaty",[24] which, if true, does not say much for their political judgment. Others began to criticise the SEA not for what it contained, but for what it led to.

Eight years later, Mrs Thatcher herself wrote that "I still believe it was right to sign the Single European Act, because we wanted a Single European Market".[25] On the other hand, she also observed that "the new powers the Commission received only seemed to whet its appetite"; and admitted to having been wrong in believing that the objective of eventual political union meant "a good deal less than some people over here think ... ". Clearly she was regretting having conceded any new powers to the European Parliament – or "Assembly" as she preferred to call it, referring to "that inchoate, inexperienced and frequently irresponsible body". (In fact, the Parliament in the 1980s contained a wealth of experience, with numerous past and future Prime Ministers among its Members; but gave her a rough time when she spoke to it in December 1986.) She also regretted inclusion in the SEA of a reference to future Economic and Monetary Union, a reference which was to cause her acute vexation at the Hanover and Madrid summits in 1988 and 1989 respectively.

Two other perceived consequences of the SEA would also cause second thoughts among many Conservatives. One, very technical, was the application of the "Luxembourg compromise" to the now greatly extended use of QMV. Howe admits in his memoirs that he "had not fully anticipated" the impact which the SEA would have.[26] The compromise was, of course, still a convention rather than in the Treaty, and "after the Single European Act, a nation that needed an exemption from single market rules ... put itself in the hands of the European Court if any other nation launched a challenge".[27]

The increased role of the European Court of Justice as a result of the SEA was, indeed, the second and more general cause for second thoughts. While nothing in the Treaty specifically increased the Court's powers, implementing the Single Market meant an expanded field for Community action and a vast increase in Community legislation. This, in turn, meant that, in the event of disputes about, or failure to implement, Single Market measures, the European Court of Justice (ECJ) would be called upon to rule. More significantly, the Court would sometimes rule that the Treaty was directly applicable, whether there was legislation or not. As a result it became "activist", systematically upholding the objective of free movement in a single market over other considerations.

Such judicial activism should, in principle, have delighted Conservatives. In certain areas where unanimity still prevailed in the Council of Ministers, notably in the field of taxation, a number of barriers to trade would never have been abolished if the Court had not found them incompatible with Member States' Treaty obligations. In a speech in Brussels to the European League for Economic Cooperation (ELEC) in November 1989,[28] Michael Heseltine (then out of Government) warmly welcomed what the European Court of Justice was doing. This ensured that "member states live up to their treaty obligations and actually implement the laws which the Community is making. Thus – with our agreement – the European Court has become the most vigorous force behind the drive to European integration".

There was even pressure from Conservatives to strengthen the powers of the ECJ. Writing at the same time as Heseltine, the Party's spokesman on the European Parliament's Legal Affairs Committee, Lord Inglewood MEP, proposed that the Court should be given power to impose sanctions on Member States; and also suggested strengthening the Commission's powers to bring Member States before the Court for infringing Community Law. If the Single Market was to be a reality, he argued,

the regulations and directives agreed by the national governments in the Council of Ministers, following scrutiny by the democratically elected European Parliament, must be implemented by national authorities and enforced by national courts in the same way as domestic legislation. If this is not done, then far from creating a 'level playing field' for businesses and our citizens, we will be penalizing business in those countries which are law-abiding and denying Europe's citizens the individual and collective benefits which will flow from a true common market.[29]

Inglewood also proposed modifying the procedure whereby Community Directives had to be "transposed" into national law in order to have legal force so that they would automatically become part of national law after a given date.

The Conservative approach to the role of the European Court of Justice at this time, and to Community law in general, was therefore very different from that of Conservative Eurosceptics in later years, when the Court's rulings would often be portrayed as the high-handed action of "politically-motivated, unelected judges", which circumvented both democratic accountability and the decision to retain the veto in sensitive areas. It also rubbed in the fact that European law took precedence over Acts of the British Parliament, most notably, and unfortunately, when the Court effectively overturned Acts protecting the British fishing industry.[*]

In turn, this perception, whether justified or not, had the effect of politicising the one Community institution which had hitherto been virtually immune from criticism. As Eurosceptic Conservatives increasingly saw the situation, the European Court of Justice, like the Commission and the Parliament, was a "federalist" body, intent on taking away British and Westminster's sovereignty. The fact that its rulings were generally in support of Conservative policy was overlooked, or considered of lesser importance.

The final reason for second thoughts about the SEA came later, in particular after the year 1992 had come and gone. This was the belief that it had not delivered what had been promised. As already noted, the Single Market in the services sector – and in particular the financial services sector where the UK was believed to have a strong competitive advantage – was still very much uncompleted in 1993. Unfortunately, too, 1992 coincided with an economic downturn, with the rate of unemployment over 10% in the UK at the end of the year, and rising. This was not what had been predicted in the many optimistic studies published following the launch of the White Paper and the passage of the Single European Act.

The most influential of these, the Cecchini Report of March 1988, had forecast the "broad orders of magnitude" of the Single Market's economic effects as being between +2.5% and +7% on Community GDP, leading to an estimated increase in the Community's wealth of around £150 billion a year. Industrial restructuring as a result of increased competition would lead to some initial job losses; but in the medium term two million new

---

[*] The 1990 decision in the first Factortame case (C-213/89 [1990] ECR I-2433). The UK Parliament had adopted Acts under which a fishing vessel could only be registered in the UK – and hence be allowed to land part of the UK's "total allowable catch" – if it had "a genuine and substantial connection" with the UK.

jobs would be created. The South East of England would particularly benefit, according to another study by the Henley Centre for Forecasting.

Whether such forecasts were or were not fulfilled is not the subject of this study, although plenty of studies *have* been carried out, with widely varying results. In practice, it is impossible to disentangle the effects of the Single Market programme from other national and international economic developments, in particular the consequences of the fall of the Berlin Wall, German re-unification and the following turbulence in the currency markets. The best response to the doubters is to ask whether they would really want to go back to the *status quo ante*, with vast queues of lorries at frontier crossings, endless form-filling to move goods around, and what Kangaroo-founder Dieter Rogalla called "the rubber-stamp fetishists in their little green huts (or possibly hats)" at every internal border. "1992" was a great achievement, of which Conservatives should be proud.

Business opinion

Showing none of the later doubts, indeed, the Conservative Government of the late 1980s threw itself into preparing for "1992" with enthusiasm and energy. I had begun my first *Vacher's* article in November 1988[30] by noting that at the end of 1987 several thousand leading French businessmen attended a conference on "1992" at the UNESCO building in Paris.

> For some months government advertisements on the subject had been appearing on French television, and the polls were showing an 85% awareness of the issues. On this side of the Channel the equivalent figure was 15%.

The response of the Conservative Government was to launch the Department of Trade and Industry's "Europe – Open for Business" campaign. My second *Vacher's* article in February 1989[31] reported that, within a year, the 15% awareness within British industry and commerce had risen to 90%. TV advertisements were commissioned, and a series of "single market breakfasts" for businessmen organised. Detailed information on the effects of Community legislation was provided through the DTI's "1992" hotline or the Spearhead database; and the Department published a *Single Market News*, the first edition of which in October 1988[32] had the headline "Now for action". A survey by the CBI found that 20% of firms were already carrying out strategy reviews (though 31% of firms had at that point done "nothing").

The principal driving force behind the DTI's campaign was a businessman turned (temporary) politician, Lord Young of Graffam – *Private Eye's* "Lord Suit". He had become involved with Conservative politics through the Centre for Policy Studies (CPS), a think- tank set up by Sir Keith Joseph and Margaret Thatcher while the Party was still in opposition before 1979. After the General Election of 1987 he succeeded Norman

Tebbit as Secretary of State for Trade and Industry, with Ken Clarke as his number two.

As it happened, another Clark, Alan, was already at the DTI, and had even chaired the Internal Market Council during the British Presidency of the Community in the first half of 1986. However, his enthusiasm for "1992" was, to say the least, restrained: his Diary recalls a visit to his office by "Boz" de Ferranti and me to discuss the Single Market project, which he describes as "irrelevant balls".[33]

Alan Clark, however, was not alone in being amazingly ignorant of what was, after all, the key element of the Party's European Community policy. Lord Young's memoirs,[34] published a year after he had left the Government and returned to his business career in 1989, describe an early briefing at which he had "come across" the Single European Act. "I, in company with the majority of Britons at the time, had paid little attention to what was happening in Europe. ... None of my friends in industry or commerce had any idea what was going to happen in 1992."[35]

But the "Europe – Open for Business" campaign, in Lord Young's own words, succeeded "beyond our wildest dreams". Twenty "single market breakfasts" convinced even journalists as sceptical as *Daily Mail* editor David English that "1992" was a good idea. Yet it was not long before Young himself began to show signs of doubt. In this context, perhaps the most interesting part of his memoirs is the "Epilogue", in which he admits that "Europe" had been mostly left out of the main text, despite the fact that "there are few more important changes to come in our lifetime, and in the lives of our children". His DTI had tried "to keep the cause of enterprise in Europe alive", but there had "developed a fashion among our commentators in the press and television to assume that we are feet-dragging in Europe, that the Germans and the French are automatically right and Margaret Thatcher and the British Government are insular and automatically wrong".[36]

There then follows a passage which is very reminiscent of the thoughts, quoted earlier in this study, of Eden and Macmillan.

> The Latins, and here Chancellor Kohl is a Latin, have a habit of keeping their gaze fixed firmly on the horizon and building castles in the air. ... The British, on the other hand, keep their gaze firmly on their feet and look carefully where they are going.[37]

His conclusion was that "somehow we need to have more of a Latin outlook, and they certainly need more of ours". Yet later, after becoming President of the Institute of Directors (IoD) in 1993, he began to embrace an increasingly Eurosceptic point of view.

Indeed, the movement of opinion on Europe within the Conservative Party over this period is mirrored by, or mirrors, a similar movement among much of business opinion in the UK; and this is well exemplified in the official attitude of the IoD. Before the European Elections of 1984 the Institute published a "Business Leaders' Manifesto",[38] which called for "complete internal free trade in the Community". The detailed policies it advocated anticipated closely the programme which would appear in the Cockfield White Paper a year later; and the SEA was implicitly supported in the Manifesto's condemnation of "the bureaucracy and indecision that is still the hallmark of the Council of Ministers". Like many other bodies, the IoD published a "Guide to Europe 1992"[39] for its members.

Shortly after the 1984 elections, I became a member of the IoD's European Advisory Council, which was at that time chaired by another MEP, Baroness Elles. Part of our work was to prepare a much fuller Business Leaders' Manifesto for the European Elections of 1989, which was published in April of that year.[40] The IoD, it began, had been "one of the UK's staunchest supporters of a European single market"; and it went on to demand that the "1992" programme should be the Community's absolute priority. "Those items [of legislation] which are essential to create the single market should be put to the top of the list and those which are not essential be put aside until the essentials are enacted."

Within the Single Market programme, the first priority should be the abolition of frontier controls, which would be "the acid test of the political will to create a single market in Europe". This would need to cover people as well as goods. It would be "no use abolishing tax and other controls on goods at international borders if lorry drivers still have to stop and show their passports". It would also mean new systems for collecting Value Added Tax and excise duties.

As it happened, my responsibilities in the European Parliament's Economic and Monetary Affairs and Industrial Policy Committee had by then become concentrated on the taxation issue. In 1987 Lord Cockfield had published his detailed proposals on the "abolition of fiscal frontiers",[41] which envisaged, in the case of VAT, treating goods moving between Member States in exactly the same way as goods moving within them.[*] He had also proposed a partial harmonisation of both VAT and excise duty rates. The IoD manifesto, following some heated internal debates, rejected any harmonisation of rates; and marginally preferred the Postponed Accounting System (PAS) – which the Council of Ministers eventually adopted as a "temporary" solution, together with a minimum VAT rate of 15% – to the Cockfield solution. The Manifesto also called for proposals on company taxation recommending that governments should agree on a series of measures to ensure fair competition, the fair allocation

---

[*] In technical terms, this was a move from the "destination" principle to the "origin" principle. It would have vastly simplified the administration of VAT; but had the disadvantage that some countries (i.e. those with a negative trade balance like the UK at the time) would lose revenue to those with a positive one (mainly Germany). The Cockfield solution was a "clearing system" to reallocate revenues; but it soon turned out that few governments had the necessary trust in the others. The Postponed Accounting System eventually adopted shifted the point of taxation to the place of delivery (with goods travelling untaxed). This avoided revenue loss, but opened the way to large-scale VAT fraud. As Parliament's *rapporteur* I supported the Cockfield proposals to the bitter end (in 1992); and I still do.

of revenues and "that differences in tax systems do not distort company behaviour".[42]

Yet even before European polling day, a sharp change in attitude had been heralded in a speech given by the IoD's Director General, Sir John Hoskyns, to its Annual Convention on 28 February 1989. With the title "Why the Single Market Programme is in Trouble", he declared that "on present indications, '1992' is going to fail"; and the costs of failure would exceed any possible benefits from success.

I remember becoming steadily more aghast as I sat in the Albert Hall listening to this speech – rather as though I was hearing a tirade against the Sermon on the Mount by the Archbishop of Canterbury. Actually, most of Sir John's targets had little to do with the Single Market programme and its success or failure. He had set his sights, rather, on a number of wider, perceived defects in the way the Community was being run – targets which would be aimed at again and again as Euroscepticism took hold.

Number one target was "the Brussels bureaucracy". Hoskyns did not make the usual mistake of adding the adjective "vast" – indeed, noting that there were "only about 15,000 officials in the Brussels Commission", he observed in a later speech to the Institute of Economic Affairs that "we believe that the Brussels bureaucracy may be too small, not too big". But he did not hold back on other accusations. The "Brussels machine" was "becoming corrupted both intellectually and financially". The officials' "mental clocks seem to have stopped at about 1970". The Single Market project was going wrong as a result of "shifting objectives, bad organisation, wrong people, poor motivation, inadequate methods, weak management, personal politics – and pilfering on a heroic scale". The Commission itself was guilty of "muddled thinking on almost everything, including monetary union, tax harmonisation and social policies". Even the Parliament was made up of a "self-selecting sample" of "enthusiasts for Europe" – though here he remembered to add that "we have some outstandingly able MEPs on the Institute's European Advisory Council".

In comparison with this, the mildly critical remarks of DTI Secretary of State Lord Young, who also spoke at the Convention, seemed tame. Yet he, too, observed that "it is no good deregulating here, and then seeing ever more regulations come flooding in from Brussels"; and warned that "1992" might become a "pretext for protectionism".

At this stage, it is doubtful whether Hoskyns represented mainstream business opinion in the UK, which was still reasonably enthusiastic about "1992". The CBI, the City of London, the British Institute of Management (BIM) and most large firms were strongly supportive, and actively engaged in "Open for Business". Nevertheless, among smaller firms – the backbone of the IoD's membership, and also an important element of Conservative support in the constituencies – there were more doubts. *The Times* report of the Convention observed that "Sir John's heresies may yet become tomorrow's orthodoxies".

One irony of this situation was that the Single Market programme was also under attack from the opposite end of the political spectrum, and for totally opposite reasons. The French left, in particular, was bitterly hostile to the imposition of "Anglo-Saxon liberalism". *La Grande Illusion*[43] by French economist, politician and journalist Alain Minc argued that the Single Market would lead to a "Darwinian nightmare", dominated by Germany. When I presented my first report to Parliament on the 12th June 1985 I was attacked for wanting "to cure the evil [of economic decline] with an even greater evil: … the free movement of capital and the removal of exchange protection".

Even the British Labour members of the European Parliament published a study[44] predicting that "1992" would result in higher unemployment rather than economic growth unless the social measures to which Hoskyns objected so strongly were also adopted. In the June 1985 debate the left-wing Labour MEP, Les Huckfield – famous for having, on another occasion, circumvented the disconnection of his microphone by continuing his speech through a loud-hailer* – denounced the whole idea of a Single Market as "pure Euro-Thatcherism".

Lobbying in Brussels

For members of the European Parliament, perhaps the most notice-able effect of business interest in the Single Market programme was to put us on the receiving end of a massive increase in lobbying. In 1983 the British Public Relations Consultants Association (PRCA) asked me to write a paper on the subject (which was published that November[45]) and a second edition was published in 1990.[46] "Over the last few years", I wrote, "there has been a dramatic growth in professional lobbying at European Community level, particularly in Brussels. … Best estimates put the number of those engaged professionally in Brussels lobbying at 'several hundred'; but no-one really knows because there is, so far, no system of registration or accreditation." Two years later a Commission paper estimated that there were "approximately 3,000 special interest groups of varying types in Brussels, with up to 10,000 employees working in the lobbying sector".[47] By 2009 nearly 300 companies, many of them subsidiaries or offshoots of companies based in Britain, were specifically marketing themselves as "Brussels political consultants".

It soon became clear that the rising volume of lobbying activity would have to be regulated in some way. In 1992 itself Parliament tightened up its rules, introducing a register of lobbyists and a code of conduct – though the Commission did not fully follow suit until 2008. By then security consid-erations had also led to much stiffer controls on admission to all premises.

---

* Though the episode gained Huckfield a lot of publicity, the device was largely futile: by cutting off the microphone, the President had also cut Huckfield off from the interpreters, so that most of the Parliament would have had no idea what he was talking about.

The reason for this explosion of interest was of course that "1992" meant that decisions made at Community level were, in many areas of economic life, becoming more important than those at national level. This had been apparent for some time in fields like industrial and technical standards. More recently the emphasis had shifted to the "green" issues of environmental and consumer protection.

For business in general, this largely meant a change of focus; and for businesses based outside the Community a welcome simplification. Instead of trying to influence fifteen different governments elaborating fifteen different systems of industrial and other standards, efforts could be concentrated on one decision-taking centre. In speeches to UK business meetings at this time I would often complain that the best briefings we MEPs were receiving came, not from British or even other European sources, but from US-based companies, efficiently co-ordinated by the American Chamber of Commerce in Brussels.

I would usually add that Americans, despite not being part of the Community, seemed to understand how it worked better than the British. They instinctively understood the separation of powers between independent institutions in way that we, brought up on the doctrine that all power resided in the "Crown in Parliament", did not; and naturally equated the European Parliament with the US House of Representatives, the Council of Ministers with the Senate,[*] the Commission with the President and his cabinet, and the European Court of Justice with the US Supreme Court.

This, as it turned out, was playing with fire. Were we, the questions would then come, on our way to a United States of Europe after all?[†] What made sense to business interests, and to US companies in particular, was decidedly less appealing to British audiences. Those who have written about the period identify a decisive turning-point in July 1988, when President of the Commission Delors, speaking to the European Parliament, forecast that 80% of economic and social decisions might soon be taken at European level.

The response from Margaret Thatcher, and from much of the Conservative Party, was dismay – and also robust.

Notes

1   Speech at Chatham House on the 8th November 1983.
2   *Towards European Economic Recovery in the 1980s* by Michel Albert and Prof. James Ball (European Parliament, August 1983).
3   *Completing the Internal Market: White Paper from the Commission to the European Council* (COM(85)310 final, 14 June 1985).

---

*   Before 1910, the US Senate was appointed by the US State legislatures, roughly in the way EU Council members are appointed by their national parliaments.

†   It was to this perspective on the European Community institutions, allegedly the model which Delors wished to follow, that Prime Minister Thatcher famously said "No! No! No!" in the House of Commons on the 30th October 1990.

4 Howe *op.cit.* p. 535.
5 Howe *op.cit.* p. 405.
6 Thatcher *The Downing Street Years* p. 547.
7 Howe *op.cit.* p. 406.
8 Hugo Young *op.cit.* p. 327.
9 Foreword to *Social Dimension of the Internal Market* (Commission Working Paper SEC(88)1148 final of 14 September 1988).
10 See *L'Europe contre L'Europe* by Olivier Ferrand (Hachette, 2009).
11 *Report drawn up on behalf of the Committee on Economic and Monetary Affairs and Industrial Policy on consolidating the internal market* (European Parliament document A 2-50/85/B of 31 May 1985).
12 Howe *op.cit.* p. 407.
13 Howe o*p.cit.* p. 407.
14 Hugo Young *op.cit.* p. 330.
15 Recalled in a speech to a meeting in London of the International Association of Former Officials of the European Communities (AIACE) on the 19th November 2008 by Sir Stephen Wall, in the early 1980s head of the FO's European Community Department (Internal).
16 *Europe: A Community Not a Superstate* by The Rt. Hon. Norman Lamont M.P. (Conservative Political Centre, October 1992).
17 Wall *op.cit.* p. 150.
18 Hugo Young *op.cit.* p. 332.
19 Hugo Young, *op.cit.* p. 334.
20 Officials David Williamson and Michael Butler, quoted by Hugo Young; and Geoffrey Howe himself.
21 *Nine Years' Work: The Achievements of the Conservative Government* (Conservative Research Department, 6 June 1988).
22 Hugo Young *op.cit.* p. 338.
23 Hugo Young *op.cit.,* p. 382.
24 Forster *op.cit.* p. 74.
25 Thatcher *The Downing Street Years* p. 557.
26 Howe *op.cit.* p. 458.
27 Hugo Young *op.cit.* p. 333.
28 *The Democratic Deficit* by Michael Heseltine MP (Centre for Policy Studies. November 1989).
29 *Making Community Law More Effective* by Lord Inglewood MEP (Conservatives in the European Parliament, October 1990).
30 *Vacher's European Companion*, Number 66, November 1988.
31 *Vacher's European Companion*, Number 67, February 1989.
32 *Single Market News, Issue no.1* (Department of Trade and Industry, October 1988).
33 Clark *op.cit.* p. 143.
34 *The Enterprise Years: a businessman in the Cabinet* by Lord Young (Headline, 1990).
35 Lord Young *op.cit.* p. 241.
36 Lord Young *op.cit.* p. 324.
37 Lord Young *ibid.*
38 *Euro-Election 1984: the Business Leaders' Manifesto* (Institute of Directors, March 1984).
39 *Director's Guide to Europe 1992* (IoD, June 1988).
40 *Euro-Election 1989: Business Leaders' Manifesto* (Institute of Directors, April 1989).
41 The *Global Communication* (COM(87)320), *VAT Rates Directive* (COM(87)321), *Fiscal Frontiers Directive* (COM(87)322), *Clearing Mechanism Working Document* (COM(87)323), *Convergence Directive* (COM(87)324), *Cigarettes Directive* (COM(87)325), *Manufactured Tobacco Directive* (COM(87)326), *Mineral Oils Directive* (COM(87)327) and *Alcoholic Beverages Directive* (COM(87)328).
42 See *Company Tax Harmonisation in the European Community* by John F. Chown (Institute of Directors, June 1989), where the issues were developed in more detail.

43 *La Grande Illusion* by Alain Minc (Grasset 1989).

44 *The Economics of 1992* by Henry Neuberger (British Labour Group in the European Parliament, 1989).

45 *Lobbying in Europe* by Ben Patterson MEP (PRCA Guidance Paper, November 1983).

46 *Lobbying: an introduction to Political Communication in Europe* by Ben Patterson (Countrywide Political Communications, 1990).

47 Quoted in the third edition of *Lobbying in Europe* (GPC 1994).

9   Bruges and After

"A diet of Brussels"

Before the European Elections of 1989 there was the British General Election of 1987, which resulted in a third successive victory for the Conservative Party led by Margaret Thatcher. On Europe, the message was much the same as in 1983 and 1984: the Government had "taken Britain from the sidelines into the mainstream of Europe".[1] Being good Europeans, however, had not prevented us from "standing up for British interests". Attention was particularly drawn to two Conservative achievements: the agreement on the Community Budget, which had "saved Britain £4,400 million since 1984"; and having "led the way in establishing a genuine common market".

This message was repeated for the European Elections two years later. "The Conservative Approach" to the Community, as the 1989 Campaign Guide[2] put it, "combines a firm commitment to Europe with a determination always to secure the best deal for Britain".

The 1989 Manifesto[3] was written by the then head of the Conservative Research Department, Chris Patten, with input from a committee, of which I was member, chaired by the Europe Minister, Lynda Chalker – earlier a colleague of mine on the committee of the Greater London Area Young Conservatives. It outlined Conservative policies in some considerable detail. To a much greater extent than before these reflected the activities of Conservative MEPs themselves, with substantial sections on the Single Market, and on "The Quality of Life". This last section covered the conservation of the countryside, food standards, animal welfare, cleaning up the sea and rivers, reducing acid rain, removing lead from petrol, the ozone layer and greenhouse gases, energy policy, the shipping of hazardous waste and sustainable development. Far from complaining about "interference from Brussels", the Manifesto and Campaign Guide welcomed Community legislation in these areas, with the Government even claiming credit for the ban on lead in petrol.

The European Elections of 1989, indeed, were notable for the prominence of such "green" issues; and also for the rise of the Greens, both in the UK and in other Member States. In Britain, the Greens won 15% of the vote, pushing the SDP/Liberal Alliance into fourth place. In the new

Parliament, the Green Group became the fifth largest, with 30 members, only just behind the European Democratic Group's 34.

Emphasising "green" issues, however, did not help us. Nor did the triumph of Conservative ideas represented by "1992", "Thatcherism on a European scale". The Labour Party, with 40% of the vote, captured 13 Conservative seats, making it the largest component of the British MEPs: 45 as against 32 Conservatives. A disappointing result had been expected: the opinion polls had been predicting Conservative losses, as had the results of the earlier county council elections and by-elections. But the reality was a great deal worse than the forecasts: more than double the number of losses. A *post mortem* was urgently carried out.

The most straightforward explanation was that the bad result was simply a normal "mid-term trough". European Elections had by this time become decoupled from UK elections by more than two years, and the Conservative Government was taking unpopular decisions. The Community Charge (the hated "poll tax" in media and public parlance) was an inevitable issue. At the same time, the Labour Party was openly campaigning on domestic issues. The election, its manifesto[4] proclaimed, "gives us the chance, by voting Labour, to pass judgement on ten years of Mrs Thatcher and an opportunity to demand a new start, a new approach to the way Britain is being governed".

Other suggested explanations, however, referred specifically to the European Election campaign itself. The Conservative Manifesto was considered to have been reasonably positive – "but no-one reads manifestos". By contrast, the stance of major Party spokesmen during the campaign appeared to be openly negative towards the Community. The principal contribution of the national campaign was a poster stating "Stay at home on June 15 and you'll live on a diet of Brussels". At Central Office, the day-to-day Questions of Policy Committee seemed to be functioning well in handling any European issues that came up. But there were persistent rumours that anonymous high officials were "not giving too high a priority to this one", at least at the start of the campaign.

As a result of work on the manifesto and Questions of Policy, my time was to some extent split between the Kent West constituency and the Foreign Office or Smith Square; so my own *post mortem* notes, made at the time, are pertinent.

> In the constituencies ... it almost seemed as though two campaigns were in progress: that being conducted by the candidate and his or her supporters, and that going on at national level. Those [Conservatives] who sit on Euro-Councils and upon whom Euro-candidates have to rely for support tend to be drawn especially from those in the Party with enthusiasm for the European idea. In the 1975 referendum, and again in 1979 and 1984, they have supported the Conservatives as 'the Party of Europe'. It was precisely these key supporters who were most confused, and indeed angered, as the campaign developed.

That the bad result was at least in considerable part due to these special factors, rather than "mid-term blues", was given credence by the findings of Gallup, which had tracked public opinion during the run-up to the campaign and during the campaign itself. It found that "negative Tory campaigning", rather than domestic political issues, was the main cause of the party's heavy defeat.

In the House of Commons, Conservative MPs had been expressing disquiet about certain Community projects on grounds of "loss of sovereignty". One result had been, right at the start of the campaign, a row about the LINGUA programme for promoting the study of foreign languages, and the idea of a European "pensioners' card" – ideas to which, on the face of it, no-one could possibly object, and for which Conservative MEPs had actually campaigned. There was a similar row about the proposal for health warnings on cigarette packets. Gallup found that "Ministerial hostility" towards these measures "dampened enthusiasm for Europe among Tory supporters, and encouraged them to stay at home or back the Greens".

My own conclusion was that the Conservative defeat was in part "the inevitable result of domestic events and decisions taken some time beforehand". On the other hand, specifically European issues had also played a major part: "'green' issues – on which the Government proved surprisingly vulnerable – were correctly identified by voters as genuinely European ones." Finally, "the public impression that the Conservative Party was 'anti-European' had had very damaging consequences in the constituencies, and also handed the Labour Party the initiative. The destruction of our most positive theme, '1992', was especially unfortunate."

The Bruges speech

My post mortem notes on the European Elections of 1989 mentioned two speeches as having contributed to the public's impression of Conservative negativism on Europe. The first was that of Sir John Hoskyns at the 1989 Institute of Directors Annual Convention. The second, of course, was that of Prime Minister Margaret Thatcher to the College of Europe in Bruges on the 20th September 1988.

A great deal has already been written about this speech. It has given rise to a Conservative organisation inspired by and named after it, the Bruges Group, which wages an "intellectual battle against the notion of ever closer union in Europe." Hugo Young describes the to-ing and fro-ing of the draft script between Downing Street and the Foreign Office, and refers to "secret official papers" that "expose ... the mutual contempt" that existed between them. The Foreign Secretary at the time, Geoffrey Howe, is himself scathing about the speech in his memoirs: its depiction of the Community "veered between caricature and misunderstanding" and "was sheer fantasy". He even ventures a psychological explanation for what the Prime Minister said. He had been "driven to conclude that for Margaret the Bruges speech represented, subconsciously at least, her escape from the collective responsibility of her days in the Heath cabinet".[5] Michael Heseltine has a similar explanation: Mrs Thatcher was "getting off her chest all the frustration she clearly felt as, despite herself, she had been forced time and time again to come to terms with our European partners".[6]

There is no doubt that the speech had a huge and lasting impact, both at home and abroad; nor that, as Howe observes, the effect was like "that illustrated in Dukas' overture* to The Sorcerer's Apprentice: where Margaret had drawn the first bucket of Euroscepticism from the well, others were only too ready to follow."[7] The same point is put, with a somewhat different spin, by Crowson: "What Thatcher had done was put public voice to doubts that many had held privately, but dared not speak for fear that it threatened the party's ethos of loyalty and silence."[8]

However, it is worth looking carefully at the actual text of the speech; and also putting it in context. Both its critics like Howe, and the speaker herself in her own memoirs, are perhaps guilty of exaggerating its Eurosceptic message for their own subsequent purposes. Stephen Wall observes that "the shocked reaction to the speech in much of Europe at the time, as well as the iconic status it has achieved among Eurosceptics, owed much to the way it was briefed to the Press by Mrs Thatcher's spokesman, Bernard Ingham".[9]

The most often quoted sentence from the speech is the one about not having "successfully rolled back the frontiers of the state in Britain, only to see them re-imposed at a European level with a European super-state exercising a new dominance from Brussels". This has to be seen, though, in context. First there had been Delors' "80% of legislation" remark to the European Parliament, followed by his assertion of the need for "the beginnings of European government". Even more significant, there had been Delors' speech to the British Trades Union Congress in Brighton only two weeks before Mrs. Thatcher's in Bruges. The brothers had greeted Delors rapturously, singing *Frère Jacques* – not because they had suddenly been converted to a federal Europe, but because they saw in Delors' programme at Community level a way of blocking the domestic policies of Margaret Thatcher's government at national level. Europe, Delors had told them, would bring a major extension of workers' rights and of social policies flanking the Single Market – "the biggest exercise in social engineering since the war" as Ron Todd of the Transport and General Workers' Union subsequently put it.

There is no doubt that Thatcher was goaded beyond endurance by this, as she saw it, completely illegitimate interference in British politics. She observes in her memoirs that by the summer of 1988 Delors had "altogether slipped his leash as a *fonctionnaire* and become a fully fledged political spokesman for federalism".

---

* This is actually a stand-alone symphonic work.

Delors, of course, did not see himself as a *fonctionnaire* at all. In the past he had been French Finance Minister (though appointed by President François Mitterand rather than drawn from elected members of the French parliament). Community orthodoxy was that the Presidency of the Commission had always been a political post, giving its holder as much right to speak out as any Prime Minister. The clash between a strong Commission President and a strong national leader was inevitable – and indeed had a precedent in the relations between Professor Hallstein and President de Gaulle during the early 1960s.

The sentences that follow the one on the "frontiers of the state" are rarely quoted.

> Certainly we want to see Europe more united and with a greater sense of common purpose. But it must be in a way which preserves the different traditions, parliamentary powers and sense of national pride in one's own country; for these have been the source of Europe's vitality through the centuries.

This view was not out of line with a respectable strand of thinking within the Conservative Party; nor with one in other Member States.

Much of the remainder of the speech then covered a number of practical issues: the need for budgetary discipline and the reform of the Common Agricultural Policy; support for the Rome Treaty as a "Charter for Economic Liberty"; the opening up of markets, particularly financial markets; a rejection of protectionism; strengthening Europe's contribution to the defence of the West. All of this was mainstream Conservative policy; and earlier she had re-stated one of her most consistent and far-sighted themes:

> We must never forget that east of the Iron Curtain, people who once enjoyed a full share of European culture, freedom and identity have been cut off from their roots. We shall always look on Warsaw, Prague and Budapest as great European cities.

And yet, and yet. ... Here and there are the phrases which so upset the Foreign Secretary and others: "the dictates of some intellectual concept", "ossified by endless regulation", "waste our energies on internal disputes or arcane institutional debates", "concentrate power at the centre of a European conglomerate", "decisions to be taken by an appointed bureaucracy", "a European super-state". These, as Howe hinted, were essentially Aunt Sallies without much basis in reality, inserted into the speech, it is possible to argue, partly to make the audience of budding Eurocrats' flesh creep. Regrettably, they became the Eurosceptics' stock-in-trade.

Not surprisingly, the reaction among most of our continental colleagues in the European Parliament was that de Gaulle was back; and certainly Thatcher's first guiding principle, that "willing and active cooperation between independent sovereign states is the best way to build a successful European Community," was as clear a statement of the Gaullist model as could be desired. Professor Anand Menon interestingly recalls that, on exactly the same day as the British Conservative Prime Minister delivered her Bruges speech, the Conservative Prime Minister of Denmark, Poul Schlüter, made a speech of his own in London in which he said: "The nation state was born of the industrial society, and like industrial society it is becoming outworn."[10]

The contrast, Menon observes, was indicative of how debates about the future of the EU were already becoming "highly polarized" – even, he might have added, within what up to this point had been thought of as the same political family. As it has turned out, this was an early sign that the British Conservative Party was about to make a decisive break with the Scandinavian Conservative parties. In the case of the Danes, they had been allies in the European Parliament since the formation of the European Conservative Group there in 1973. Following the European Elections of 2009, the Danish and Swedish Conservative Parties declined to follow the British Conservative MEPs out of the European People's Party Group into a new "anti-federalist" group.

It is, nevertheless, worth noting that, just as Thatcher's support for the Single European Act made possible implementation of the Single Market programme, the "inter-governmental" approach advocated in the Bruges speech made possible the next major steps forward in European integration: the Foreign and Security and Justice and Home Affairs "pillars" embodied in the Maastricht and Amsterdam Treaties.

Rise of the Eurosceptics

Whatever the actual content of the Bruges speech, there is no doubt that it re-opened within the Conservative Party divisions on the European issue which had been more or less dormant since the late 1960s. As Heseltine puts it, she had "unleashed the hounds that were to eat away at the vitals of the party from then on – to no discernible political benefit".[11]

John Major's autobiography[12] contains thumbnail portraits of the Conservative Eurosceptics prominent during the passage of the Maastricht Treaty in the House of Commons, including their unofficial whips, the sinister-sounding duo of Gill and Cran. Studies of the period[13] have identified a number of different "camps", broadly divided into "pragmatists" and "fundamentalists".

Among the fundamentalists were those MPs like Richard Body, John Biffen, Roger Moate and Teddy Taylor who had been "anti-marketeers of the first hour", voting against EEC membership in 1972. These had been joined by a second group of "constitutionalists", notably the MP Bill Cash, who had come to oppose the Community and all its works as a threat to national and parliamentary sovereignty. On these groups the influence of Enoch Powell was strong.

There was also an "English populist nationalist group", as Forster calls it, which included the MPs Nicholas Winterton, John Carlisle, Tony Marlow, Rhodes Boyson (who really belongs with the pragmatic free-marketeers described below), Bill Walker and Richard Shepherd, and was substantially composed of the Party's right wing. Finally there were, on exactly the opposite wing of the Party, those like Peter Walker, whose views on Europe had had "somewhat chequered histories" (Forster), but who still looked to the multiracial Commonwealth and other wider international groupings.

In the first group of pragmatists were the free-marketeers. Most had seen the Rome Treaty as a "Charter for Economic Freedom", and welcomed the Single Market campaign as "Thatcherism on a European scale". Then, like Hoskyns and other business leaders, they had begun to feel betrayed by the activities of the Delors Commission. Some were MPs like Michael Spicer and Nick Budgen. Others were one-time campaigners for Community membership like Russell Lewis, and a large majority of members and subscribers to the Institute of Economic Affairs. The same was true of the Selsdon Group, and the free-market think-tank, the Adam Smith Institute. Disillusionment with Europe became a prevailing mood even within the Bow Group, while the Monday Club finally came down firmly for Euroscepticism.

In a linked camp were those who followed wherever Margaret Thatcher led, and who moved into a Eurosceptic position with her: for example, Teresa Gorman in the House of Commons and Norman Tebbit in the House of Lords. Hugo Young believed that their motives had, at least in part, nothing to do with Europe at all: after Thatcher's removal from the leadership of the Party and the Premiership in 1990 "expressing anti-Europeanism … was one way of securing revenge for what the other side had done". This camp overlapped substantially with the "No Turning Back" Group of MPs set up in 1985 to defend Thatcherism, which included Peter Lilley, Michael Portillo, Francis Maude and John Redwood.

Forster notes two important features of this move to Euroscepticism. First, the opposition to European Community membership, once dominated by the Labour left, was effectively taken over by the Eurosceptic right. One result was that the Labour old guard, elected on a platform of leaving the Community altogether – like the MEPs Alf Lomas and Barry Seal – found themselves in an increasingly uncomfortable position. A more fundamental consequence was that it made it easy for the Labour Party as a whole under Neil Kinnock, then John Smith, and finally Tony Blair, to move smartly into the vacant "party of Europe" slot.

The second feature was to draw in "disaffected journalists in the weekly and weekend editions of *The Times* and the *Telegraph*, which now increasingly devoted column space to Eurosceptic writers".[14]

Forster might have added that this development fitted in well with the intentions of those papers' owners, and notably of Rupert Murdoch, whose group of papers included *The Times, Sunday Times, News of the*

World, and, most notoriously, the *Sun*. It soon became a constant problem for pro-Europe Conservatives that the only stories about the Community in the papers seemed to be about daft "Brussels" schemes to straighten out bananas or force fishermen to wear hairnets. That these stories usually turned out to be untrue, or wildly distorted, was no help. As the Tory writer G.K.Chesterton observed, "the truth is … half an hour behind the slander".[15]*

Joining the EPP Group

Meanwhile, circumstances were propelling Conservative MEPs in an entirely different direction. At the beginning of 1986, when Spain and Portugal became Member States, the European Democratic Group in the European Parliament had more than made up for its 1984 election losses by adding to its strength 17 Members of Spain's *Alianza Popular* (AP) Party, including its leader, Manuel Fraga. This had transfigured the Group in a number of ways. Instead of being overwhelmingly British, it now contained another national section of more or less equal stature. Instead of holding Group meetings mostly in London, with occasional trips to Copenhagen, Madrid was added to the regular venues, with León and Valencia also included.

British Conservatives and the AP shared a roughly similar political outlook. Though Fraga had served as a minister under Franco, he had moved his party towards the centre, making it pro-free-enterprise, pro-Western, monarchist and mildly nationalist, with allies among other Spanish centre-right parties. There was some friction over Gibraltar; but the most lively disputes within the Group were on the issue of bull-fighting, AP members clashing with the animal rights faction, and retaliating – through the vehicle of the Group's annual Christmas cabaret – with attacks on fox-hunting.

The preliminary results of the 1989 European Elections showed the ED Group emerging with 48 seats, including 15 Spaniards. At the beginning of the year, however, there had been a major realignment in the Spanish political system, with the AP merging with other parties, including Christian Democrats, to form the *Partido Popular* (PP). The catastrophic result was that, immediately following the European elections, the PP Spanish members announced that they were leaving the EDG to join the European People's Party Group in the Parliament. Many of the AP veterans who had formed part of our group had, in fact, failed to be selected as PP candidates, and had been replaced by mainstream Christian Democrats.

This reduced the EDG to a mere 34 seats, only the fifth largest group after the Socialists (which became the largest), the European People's Party Group, the European Liberal Democrat and Reform Group (ELDR)

---

* Mark Twain made a similar point: "A lie can be halfway round the word before the truth has pulled its boots on".

and the Communists and Far left Group (EUL/LU). It soon became clear that we were peripheral to the main decisions in the Parliament, both organisational and political. Ominously, the one member of the group from Northern Ireland, the Ulster Unionist James Nicholson, soon followed the Spaniards into the European People's Party Group. Soundings indicated that attempts by the rest of the group to follow suit would be rebuffed.

Yet even before the elections there had been moves to merge with the EPP Group. In dealing with the large volume of legislation consequent upon the Single Market programme, all the centre-right groups had made efforts to co-ordinate their voting, both in committee and in plenary; and the closest co-ordination was between the EDG and the EPP Group. "Boz" de Ferranti had even come to the conclusion that attending EDG Group meetings on Single Market matters was a waste of time, and usually attended the EPP discussions instead, where he planned tactics with fellow Kangaroo Group co-founder, the German Christian Democrat (CDU) Karl von Wogau.

In Parliament's Economic and Monetary Affairs and Industrial Policy Committee, which was responsible for the bulk of the Single Market legislation, the EDG and the EPP Group effectively acted as a single unit. The two group "co-ordinators", the Belgian Christian Democrat Fernand Herman and myself – and frequently the co-ordinators from the Liberal ELDR and the European Democratic Alliance (EDA), mostly French Gaullists – would meet before each meeting to go through the agenda and work out a common whip for the votes; and again before the plenaries at which the final votes would be taken. A joint decision had allowed me to become the Single Market *rapporteur* (de Ferranti and von Wogau were of course the first choices, but both declined due to pressure of work).

Significantly, there were seldom any disagreements on policy. At the start, Herman was extremely suspicious, as were most of the Benelux and Italian Christian Democrats. There was even a sharp dispute about the UK's zero rate of VAT, which was widely believed to result in Britain evading a large part of the VAT element of its budgetary contribution.[*] By contrast the German CDU/CSU members, who effectively controlled the EPP Group at the time, were as militant about the Single Market as we were.

Immediately following the European Elections of 1989, moves began to put this alliance with the EPP Group on a formal footing. The first proposal was that there would be an "exchange of hostages": one or more members of each group would transfer to the other, which would avoid upsetting the balance of numbers, important for the selection of committee chairmanships, etc. Because of my experience in EMAC, I was chosen to be the first "hostage" in the EPP.

---

[*] Eventually I was able to persuade them that the zero rate *was* part of our VAT base, unlike VAT exemption. See *VAT: the zero rate issue* by Ben Patterson (EDG, 1988).

There followed, however, an embarrassing row. Picking up a story in the local Kent press, the *Daily Telegraph* announced in July that I had "defected" from the Conservative Party to join the Christian Democrats. I was obliged to write to the papers, and to the Kent West Conservative Euro-Council, explaining the rather complex situation. The "hostage" arrangement, I pointed out, was part of negotiations which had been going on between the EDG and EPP Group with a view to an eventual merger; adding that "I cannot stress strongly enough that the negotiations have the specific approval of the Prime Minister".

The "hostage" scheme was nevertheless quickly shelved.

As had been the case in 1973, the main opposition within the European People's Party to accepting us was not that we were insufficiently "federalist", but that we were insufficiently Christian – that we were a secular party, properly belonging in the tradition of continental liberalism. Some of the Liberals themselves, particularly the Dutch, thought so too, and put out feelers for an alternative merger. In addition, there was still a minority in the Group which believed that our true home was with the Gaullists.

A major effort was therefore launched to explain the philosophical and moral basis of British Conservatism. A paper by the Conservative MEP and journalist Lord Bethell[16] stated that Conservatives "specially revere the family unit and, although religion forms no part of any qualification for party membership, they generally accept the values of Christianity and the Bible." The paper drew attention to the Conservative record of social reform in the 19th century, particularly that of the 7th Earl of Shaftesbury, a founder of the Young Men's Christian Association (the YMCA).

Actually, most of the negotiations were very much more down-to-earth. Precise calculations were made as to whether the two sides would qualify for more European Parliament posts together or as separate groups; whether funding would be more or less after a merger; who would get what posts within the combined secretariat; and how we might affect the balance of influence between the different national sections within the existing EPP Group. The leader of that Group, the German Egon Klepsch, was extremely keen to become President of the Parliament in 1992, and – recalling his failure to be elected to the post in 1981 – wanted to be sure of our votes. The result was an agreement to affiliate in May 1992.

In view of the recent disputes about Conservative MEPs belonging to a "federalist" organisation, it is important to be clear exactly of what we became members in 1992. Neither we, nor the Conservative Party, joined the European People's Party itself, which is a transnational organisation comprising 74 Christian Democrat parties from 38 countries. From the start, Conservative MEPs joined the EPP Group in the Parliament as "associated", non-party members. This position was clarified rather than changed in 1999, when the then leader of the Party, William Hague, negotiated an arrangement under which parliamentary group was renamed the "Group of the European People's Party and European Democrats (EPP-ED)", with the "European Democrat" label returning after a seven-year gap. Within the EPP-ED Group some national sections belonged to the EPP subdivision, others to the ED.

It is true, though, that for important purposes the distinction between full and "associate" members was of little relevance. Although each national section held individual meetings, the Group's managing Bureau, of which I became a member, acted as a unitary body under the chairmanship of the former Belgian Prime Minister Leo Tindemans, a leading campaigner for greater European unity. I also chaired one of the Group's five policy committees, the chairmen of which met over lunch each month in Strasbourg to discuss strategy.

The complexity of this situation would come to a head as preparations began for the European Elections of 1994. As members of the EPP Group in the Parliament, Conservative MEPs were invited to attend the conference of the European People's Party itself, called to prepare a policy statement; and a number of us eagerly joined in, speaking, drafting texts and tabling amendments. It was not until the voting began that our status came into question: not being party members, we were not entitled to participate – even though some of us, notably Derek Prag in the field of foreign and defence policy, were responsible for sizeable chunks of the document. Nor, of course, was the Conservative Party bound by what eventually became the EPP's election manifesto.

Notes

1 *The Next Moves Forward: the Conservative Manifesto 1987* (Conservative Central Office, May 1987).

2 *The Campaign Guide 1989* (Conservative Research Department, March 1989).

3 *Leading Europe into the 1990s: the Conservative Manifesto for Europe 1989* (Conservative Central Office, June 1989).

4 *Meeting the challenge in Europe: Labour's manifesto for the European Elections 1989* (Labour Party, 1989).

5 Howe *op.cit*. p. 538.

6 *Life in the Jungle: my autobiography* by Michael Heseltine (Hodder and Stoughton, 2000) p. 348.

7 Howe *op.cit*. p. 538.

8 Crowson *op.cit*. p. 219

9 Wall *op.cit*. p. 79

10 Menon *op.cit*. p. 70.

11 Heseltine *op.cit*, p. 348.

12 *John Major, the autobiography* by Sir John Major (HarperCollins, 1999). See chapter 15, "The Bastards".

13 For example, those by Hugo Young and Anthony Forster.

14 Forster, *op.cit*. p. 72.

15 In "The Scandal of Father Brown" from *The Father Brown Stories* by G.K. Chesterton (Cassell, 1929).

16 *Moral Aspects of Conservatism* by Lord Bethell MEP (EDG, 1990).

10 ERM and EMU

Werner, Jenkins and Delors

Geoffrey Howe, in his memoirs, recalls wondering in 1988 "why the European agenda seemed always to be unfolding at such breakneck speed. ... We often seem to be on a remorselessly moving carpet." The occasion was the June summit at Hanover where the curtain was raised on "the drama which would dominate Community politics for the next five years – economic and monetary union (EMU)".[1]

It may be useful briefly to set the stage.

In the original 1957 Rome Treaty, there is no mention of monetary union or of a single currency. The first move in this direction came as a by-product of the Common Agricultural Policy in the 1960s, when fluctuating exchange rates threatened to disrupt the principle of common farm prices. The Commission's proposal of fixed exchange rates was, however, rejected in favour of the notorious – and notoriously fraudulent – system of artificial "green" rates, with positive or negative Monetary Compensatory Amounts (MCAs) being paid as produce crossed internal frontiers.

The first serious proposal for monetary union came in 1970 with the Werner Plan[2] for successive steps towards a full monetary union in 1980: convertibility of currencies; the liberalisation of capital markets; a Monetary Cooperation Fund; and finally the irrevocable locking together of exchange rates. In the following years the first steps in the Plan were actually implemented, with Community currencies linked together in what became known as "the snake in the tunnel".*

For the Conservative Government of Ted Heath this did not turn out a happy experience. The pound sterling joined the "snake" even before joining the Community, on the 1st May 1972, but was forced out again less than two months later. In principle, the Accession Treaty signed Britain up to the objective of EMU by 1980; but the post-1973 recession combined

---

* So called from the diagrams describing how the system worked. The participating currencies were locked inside the "snake" where parities could not fluctuate by more than 2.25% up or down. The "snake" then fluctuated within the "tunnel" agreed by members of the International Monetary Fund (IMF) in 1971, with a parity band of 4.5% in either direction.

with inflation – the term "stagflation" came into use to describe the situation – put paid to any such plans. The "snake in the tunnel" blew apart, with every country looking out for itself.

Within five years, however, currency stability was back on the agenda. A new initiative launched by Commission President Roy Jenkins in 1977 was picked up and pushed through by German Chancellor Helmut Schmidt and French President Giscard d'Estaing. The result was the European Monetary System (EMS) and the Exchange Rate Mechanism (ERM). This differed from the "snake in the tunnel" by having substantial funds available for intervention, and the ERM being based on a "grid" of bilateral exchange rates, with fixed margins of fluctuation both between any two currencies and against the "central rate" of the European Currency Unit: the "ecu".* In the event of "fundamental disequilibria" there was provision for realignments. After some initial hesitation from Ireland and Italy, by early 1979 all Community Member States had joined, except the UK.

The official position of the Conservative Party towards EMS/ERM membership has already been described. At this point, the future Chancellor of the Exchequer, Geoffrey Howe, though endorsing "unreservedly the objective of establishing a zone of currency stability in Europe",[3] was not in favour of immediate UK entry. Others, however, were more enthusiastic. In the same Commons debate the then leader of the Conservatives in the European Parliament, Geoffrey Rippon, hoped "that we shall not be absent from the European system in the way that we were absent from the beginnings of the European Economic Community. I take no satisfaction from saying that I expressed these views in 1956 in this House, but I would almost despair if we turned our backs on destiny a second time."[4]

After the European Elections of 1979, the majority of Conservative MEPs continued to support Rippon's view. As the years went by, Conservative ministers visiting British section meetings were increasingly asked exactly what was meant by the phrase "when the time is right/ripe"; and officials of the United Kingdom Representation (UKREP) in Brussels were forced, during the regular briefing meetings which were held with MEPs, to think up ever more tortuous explanations. In their turn, Conservative MEPs had to fend off the same questions at constituency meetings and particularly at meetings with businessmen. Howe recalls that use of the "right/ripe" phrase was often "greeted with open mirth".[5]

At first there was a view that the EMS/ERM would soon go the way of the Werner Plan; and, indeed, in the early years of the system there were frequent realignments, mostly to accommodate the inexorable rise of

---

* The European Currency Unit, or ecu, was an artificial "basket" of Member States' currencies. In 1979 it had replaced the European Unit of Account, which was used for the Communities' budget, and which, in turn, had its origin in the unit of account established by the European Payments Union (EPU) between 1950 and 1958. The orginal Unit was a "pre-Smithsonian Dollar", equivalent to 0.88867088 grams of fine gold. Its exchange rates against the national currencies involved were fixed, most at parities which, over time, grew wildly out of date.

the D-Mark. As the system settled down, however, the "zone of currency stability" objective was increasingly attained, as was another objective: low inflation. In the pre-EMS period of 1975–80 French inflation had run at an annual rate of 10.5%. By the period 1985–90, with the Franc linked to the D-Mark and the policies of the *Bundesbank*, French inflation was down to an annual rate of 2.9%. This provided powerful evidence in favour of Nigel Lawson's "second best" policy of shadowing the D-Mark.

Yet while the Conservative Party and Government continued to debate EMS/ERM entry, the train had already left for the next station. Perceptive, and prescient, economists had long recognised that a system of fixed exchange rates between separate currencies was inherently vulnerable to major shocks, and could only be an interim solution – in the words of Margaret Thatcher's economic advisor, Professor Alan Walters, that the EMS/ERM system was "half-baked".

In addition, the system was "asymmetric": countries were effectively obliged to follow the policies of the *Bundesbank*, while the *Bundesbank* itself was free to conduct policy according to German domestic requirements. Although for smaller countries this is a plausible basis for economic management (what in games theory is called a "Stackleberg Strategy"), for larger countries like France or the UK it can feel, to say the least, politically demeaning. More important as it turned out, the whole system relied on nothing overly dramatic happening to Germany.

In any case, the objective of full economic and monetary union had already been endorsed by the Community Heads of State and Government – including the British Prime Minister – at successive summits, and had even been written into the Single European Act. During the implementation of the Single Market programme the phrase "a single market needs a single currency"[*] began to become current. Geoffrey Howe could not really have been much surprised, though he claims to have been, when it was decided at Hanover to establish a committee of central bank governors, chaired by Commission President Delors, to propose "concrete stages" leading to EMU.

The Delors Report[6] was published in May 1989, in time for both the Madrid summit and the European Elections. It envisaged reaching EMU in three stages, with "a decision to enter upon the first stage" constituting "a decision to embark on the entire process".

During Stage One, which would begin in July 1990, all Community currencies would join the Exchange Rate Mechanism, and a "single financial area" would be created: i.e. restrictions on capital movements would end. In Stage Two there would be a "European System of Central Banks", and the margins of fluctuation between currencies in the ERM would narrow. Stage Three would begin with the irrevocable locking of exchange

---

[*]   In 1990 the Commission published *One Market, One Money* (European Economy no. 44, October 1990), which calculated that a Single Currency would add between 0.3% and 0.4% of GDP to the gains already expected from the Single Market.

rates, a European Central Bank would take over control of monetary policy, and the Stage would end with the replacement of national currencies by a Single Currency, provisionally to be called the Ecu. At the same time, the economic dimension of EMU would involve "binding rules" for national budget deficits and national debt.

Common or single?

The Delors Report represented the orthodox route to monetary union; but there had always been an alternative. Various initiatives to promote the use of the European Currency Unit (the "ecu") as the denominator for financial operations had already resulted in the development of significant "private ecu" markets. Official and private bodies – including from October 1988 the UK Treasury – had issued ecu-denominated loans, bonds or bills. In addition, certain companies operating in more than one country had found it convenient to keep their accounts in ecus. Contracts between borrowers and lenders in different currency areas could be drawn up in ecus to share exchange-rate risk. And even private individuals could have ecu-denominated bank or credit-card accounts.

The ecus used in financial markets, of course, did not involve the creation of "new" money: they came into existence as a "bundle" or "basket" of national currencies, based on the ecu in the Exchange Rate Mechanism. As a kind of average, the ecu was "harder" than its weaker components (though paying a lower interest rate) but "softer" than its stronger components (though paying a higher interest rate). Not surprisingly, ecus were particularly popular in countries with "soft" currencies, a great deal less popular in hard-currency countries like Germany – where, indeed, it was actually illegal for private citizens to hold them.

Among economists, operators in the financial markets and those politicians interested in the subject there were quite a few enthusiasts for developing the European Currency Unit into a full "parallel currency". Under a number of proposed schemes, the ecu would no longer be composed of "bundled" national currencies, but would be issued as a currency in its own right. It would become legal tender in all European Community countries, so becoming a true "common currency". Whether it eventually replaced the national currencies entirely would be up to individuals and the markets.

This alternative route to monetary union had a strong appeal to many Conservatives. *Leading Europe into the 1990s*, while rejecting the full Delors project as involving "a fundamental transfer of sovereignty", and implying "nothing less than the creation of a federal Europe", nevertheless supported most of Delors' Stage One: the abolition of exchange controls, a free market in capital and other measures to "create a single European financial market". The Party had strongly supported the increased use of the ecu, for example, and had "encouraged it to a greater extent than many other Member States. The Government has already successfully issued Ecu Treasury bills and keeps a portion of its reserves in Ecus."

As discussions on the Delors Report got under way in the Community, the "common currency" approach became the official policy of the Conservative Government. Just before his resignation as Chancellor of the Exchequer in October 1989, Nigel Lawson had prepared a paper advocating a system of "competing currencies" as an alternative to the Delors plan. This, however, would have involved only the existing national currencies; and as John Major – who succeeded Lawson, and so was responsible for presenting the paper to the cabinet – observes in his autobiography, this was subject to the objection that the D-Mark would almost certainly have ended up as the winner.

A more detailed proposal, the so-called "Major Plan", was launched before the June Dublin summit in 1990. This had been first outlined in a paper by the British Invisible Export Council[7] – and was based on promoting the ecu, which would be redefined so as to be as the "hardest" rather than the "central" currency in the Exchange Rate Mechanism. The Plan was welcomed as a "constructive contribution to the debate", but received little support except *via* a somewhat similar Spanish proposal.

The "common currency" approach had, in fact, already been the subject of detailed examination by the Delors Committee. Annexed to the main Report was a paper by the then Governor of the *Bundesbank*, Otto Pöhl, which went into the advantages and disadvantages of various options. A pure free-market "Hayekian ecu",[*] competing with and floating against the national currencies, was dismissed as "propagated in scientific circles" but "not realistic". A common currency based on the existing "basket" could never be as attractive as the strongest national currency, and as a result an asymmetric "crowding out" of national currencies would take place, with the *Bundesbank* accumulating ecu holdings.[†]

More serious were "hard ecu" proposals. Though Pöhl thought these "appeared to be quite elegant at first sight", depending as they would on market forces rather than political decisions, he saw a number of objections. If the ecus were "new", rather than bundled national currencies, there was a danger of excessive monetary expansion – though this would not be the case if, as under the "Major Plan", national central banks were obliged, on request, to "buy in" their own currencies using ecus. There was also the "telephone" problem: having a telephone is only useful if others have one too. The more other subscribers there are, the more useful it becomes. In the case of currencies, the greater the number of transactions, the lower the costs of any one transaction. The problem for a parallel currency, which would have no "privileged domain" like a national currency, would be to achieve the critical mass needed to be competitive.

---

[*]   So called from a series of Institute of Economic Affairs publications by the Nobel Laureate Friedrich von Hayek, who advocated a system of competing currencies, with floating exchange rates between them. Citizens would be free to use or refuse to use any currency. (e.g. *Choice in Currency: a way to stop inflation*, first published in 1976).

[†]   Though this system might have ended up with the D-Mark becoming the *de facto* Single Currency – a situation which some people believe has happened anyway.

But the greatest objection was a very simple one: if the objective was to substitute a single currency for the existing twelve, what was the point of creating a thirteenth? The economist Tim Congdon – a strong opponent of monetary union – nevertheless rightly observed in 1990 that "a money is accepted as such because it serves as a common standard of value and medium of exchange in a particular area. Proposals which explicitly envisaged a plurality of standards of value and media of exchange ... always lacked credibility".[8]

Many Conservatives campaigned energetically for the "common currency" approach, as I did. In the constituency, and in Party meetings, it went down well; and explaining the difference between "single" and "common" provided a satisfyingly crushing response to Eurosceptics when they accused us of wanting to "abolish the pound sterling". Even in the European Parliament, where it was generally assumed that the Delors programme would be implemented, it was possible to get a respectful hearing.

Bit by bit, however, we were ground down by the critique of Pöhl and others. Even those who had initially welcomed the proposal concluded that, in the words of Stephen Wall, it was "a brilliant idea whose day was already past".[9] By the time of the Maastricht negotiations the usual response from continental colleagues was "nice try!" It is also worth noting that some early campaigners for greater use of the ecu who had put their money where their convictions were and invested in ecu-denominated securities, ended up making serious losses. This did not make them very keen on the Major Plan.

John Major himself clearly believed in his Plan, though perhaps as much for political as for economic reasons: it "eased the divisions opening up in the Conservative Party" and "put Britain back in the debate". But comments by Prime Minister Thatcher "made people believe that she saw it – quite wrongly so far as I was concerned – as a diversion or a wrecking tactic".[10] In the end the "hard ecu" proposal was quietly dropped in favour of the "opt in" solution eventually incorporated in the Maastricht Treaty.

Into the Exchange Rate Mechanism

If there is one moment which can be said to have turned the Conservative Party off Europe, it was "Black Wednesday" (or "white Wednesday" depending on point of view), on the 16th September 1992, when Sterling fell out of the Exchange Rate Mechanism. As the Chancellor of the Exchequer at the time, Norman Lamont, has put it, "the experience of British ERM membership has come to occupy a very special position in the collective guilt of the Conservative Party".[11]

Most commentators are agreed that the event cost the Party its reputation for economic competence, followed by the General Election of 1997, and possibly two more elections after that. The circumstances which led to the pound sterling joining the Mechanism on the 8th October 1990 are therefore of uncommon interest.

Margaret Thatcher's own memoirs detail a series of meetings between ministers between 1979 and 1982 at which it was agreed that the time for Exchange Rate Mechanism membership had not come. Then, in 1985, Nigel Lawson took over from Howe at the Treasury, and was party to the "Plaza Agreement" for co-ordinated intervention in the currency markets in order to halt a sharp rise in the dollar exchange rate. This, according to the Thatcher account, "gave Finance ministers – Nigel above all perhaps – the mistaken idea that they had it in their power to defy the markets indefinitely".

It was not long, however, before Lawson became more convinced than ever that ERM entry was the best way to ensure monetary discipline. By contrast, Thatcher had become "more convinced than ever of the disadvantages of the ERM". She observes, however, that there was a "fashionable consensus" in support of Lawson, who in March 1987 began the policy of maintaining Sterling at around 3 D-Marks, apparently without the Prime Minister's knowledge (Hugo Young describes the policy as "a private frolic of his own"). She contemplated sacking him; but recognised that "he had the strong support of Conservative back-benchers and much of the Conservative press".

In fact, as Lawson himself notes in his memoirs, this support covered virtually the complete spectrum of Party opinion. A policy group consisting of, among others, Nigel Foreman, Peter Hordern, David Howell, Peter Lilley, John MacGregor, John Major, Cecil Parkinson and John Redwood was "overwhelmingly in favour of Exchange Rate Mechanism entry", the only dissenter being Redwood (who was nevertheless prepared to go along with a unanimous pro-membership recommendation).[12] The Foreign Secretary, Geoffrey Howe, was by this time also strongly in favour of ERM entry. Thatcher writes that he and Lawson were "in cahoots". It is interesting to note that by 1988 Lawson was also in favour of making the Bank of England independent, a proposal of which Thatcher was "dismissive".

Down among the foot-soldiers, there were rumours that all was not well, but little idea that the policy differences were so sharp. Most Conservative MEPs were strongly in favour of Exchange Rate Mechanism membership, but in part for reasons not quite the same as those advanced by Lawson. One element of Delors Stage One, most of which was entirely in line with Conservative policy, was that all currencies should join the ERM; and, even without accepting that being in Stage One committed the country to the other two Stages, keeping options open seemed sensible.

Thatcher recalls that Leon Brittan, now a Commissioner, tried to convince her that joining the ERM would give Britain a stronger say in how EMU developed. Her account then goes on to describe the Howe/Lawson "ambush" before the Madrid summit of June 1989. Under threat of resignation by both ministers, she was induced to outline the conditions for Sterling's entry into the Exchange Rate Mechanism; and at Madrid she did affirm the UK's intention to join, but without saying when. Then Major became Chancellor, with "one great objective: … to keep the Party together. ... To him this meant that we must enter the ERM as soon as possible to relieve the political strains". This argument, it seems, did the trick. On Thursday the 13th June 1990 she told Major that she would no longer "resist Sterling joining the ERM"; and in October the decision to do so was taken.

John Major's own account is somewhat different. He recalls that by 1990 "the pro-ERM tide was strong". A poll of the corporate sector in *Financial Weekly* had revealed that "97 per cent of executives wanted sterling to join the ERM, and 66 per cent did not care at what rate we went in".[13] Like Lawson, he had also come to the conclusion that the ERM entry was inevitable. "We had no alternative anchor for our economic policy. One after another, the possibilities had been knocked away." Monetary targets, the original framework for anti-inflation policy, had proved increasingly difficult to interpret. The only feasible alternative was to link the pound sterling – as the next Chancellor of the Exchequer, Norman Lamont later put it in his 1991 Budget speech – "to other currencies with a proven track record of low inflation. ... We committed ourselves to that discipline after lengthy debate and our decision was widely supported on both sides of the House, and in the country at large." Only the timing and the exchange rate at which to enter remained in question.

The latter – 2.95 D-Marks to the pound sterling – was more or less determined by the markets. Major observes that much opinion at the time, including the CBI, wanted it to be higher. He does, however, also note that "we did ruffle a few feathers" by not negotiating an agreed exchange rate with the Monetary Committee in Brussels, and that the opinion of the *Bundesbank* was for a slightly lower rate. But he also recalls the glowing press the decision received, and the support of the Labour Opposition, not only for the decision to join, but also the D-Mark rate of entry.

What about the timing? According to Hugo Young, this is where the real mistake was made: the "decision was calamitous". The moment of entry was determined not by economic logic, but by "when the leader's resistance at last collapsed". It had thus taken its place "in a category that has become familiar in this history: of climactic moments long postponed, then urgently desired, then achieved at a conjunction of time and place producing less, sometimes much less, advantage than might have been previously attainable".[14]

Geoffrey Howe seems to agree with this criticism of the timing. In 1981, when the Government was considering the Exchange Rate Mechanism issue, but when inflation was at 12%, well above the rate of existing ERM member countries, he was advised that joining "would be seen not as a consequence of success in dealing with inflation but as an important change in policy". He comments that "much the same argument could – perhaps should – have been advanced in respect of the date finally chosen for entry by Margaret Thatcher and John Major in September 1990".[15] And Lawson's view is that the timing "could scarcely have been less right".[16]

My own view, however, is that depicting "Black Wednesday" merely as a consequence of bad timing is misleading. It would certainly have been better to have joined the Exchange Rate Mechanism at an earlier date – specifically in November 1985, when virtually the whole Cabinet (including Norman Tebbit, then Party Chairman), together with the Governor of the Bank of England, Robin Leigh-Pemberton, were in favour. Earlier that year David Howell had written in *Crossbow* that "we should move into the ERM quickly, ideally now, before the next dollar storm breaks. ... The penalties for not [entering] will be very great, both in the near term and further ahead".[17] Indeed an EDG policy paper published in March 1987[18] stated clearly that "we believe the time has been right for some time, and that the UK economy has been paying a significant 'uncertainty premium' (notably higher interest rates) as a result of remaining outside the ERM".

Lawson himself records that not joining in 1985, "when the time really had been right" was a missed "historic opportunity".[19] The Exchange Rate Mechanism in 1985 was considerably more flexible than in the 1990s, with realignments against the D-Mark taking place on average once a year between 1979 and 1987. There would have been little difficulty, he believes, in securing a Sterling realignment, as would have been necessary, in April 1986 (he gives figures of ERM entry at DM3.70, with a re-alignment to DM3.50). There would have followed "a clear run of five or six years during which the Deutschmark would have served us ... as a very satisfactory low-inflation anchor". And as a bonus, "it would have been unequivocally an act of economic policy, clearly distanced from the wider political argument over the future of Europe which later threatened to split the Conservative Party".

Yet "Black Wednesday" can in reality have had little to do with the technicalities of the ERM entry date. Sterling was not alone: the Italian lira met an almost simultaneous fate, and before long most other currencies in the system, in particular the French Franc and the Irish Punt, came under similar pressure. The whole episode was the long-term, and – despite Lawson's confidence that entry in 1985 would have given Sterling time to "bed down" in the system – probably unavoidable consequence of an event that had already taken place by October 1990: the fall of the Berlin Wall.

Changes at home and abroad

If John Major had believed that getting the pound sterling into the Exchange Rate Mechanism would relieve political strains within the Conservative Party, he was unfortunately wrong. Howe recalls the Chancellor telling the 1990 Party conference that "joining the ERM does not mean that we are now on the road leading inexorably to a single currency". He adds, however, that "remarkable as it appears in retrospect, the decision to join the ERM seems to have stirred up rather than quelled the underlying arguments".

It was not really that remarkable. Under the Delors Plan, joining the Exchange Rate Mechanism in Stage One was a necessary step on the way to, and inevitably leading to, Stages Two and Three. Whatever the Government said, a lot of people – both for and against – thought this a strong possibility. Moreover, the case for a Single Currency seemed to have been accepted in principle as a result of the Major Plan – only the method of getting there was different.

Within the Conservative Party there was also a body of support for accepting the whole of Delors. In early 1990 the Conservative Group in the European Parliament had published a pamphlet[20] by Sir Fred Catherwood, by this time a Parliament Vice-President, outlining the case for monetary union. Writing before the decision to join the Exchange Rate Mechanism, he argued, like Lawson, that Britain needed "a credible external currency discipline". Unlike Lawson, however, he thought that even being in the ERM was not enough (as, indeed, proved the case). The merit of a Monetary Union, with an independent banking system, was that it would be a continued external discipline, ruling out the easy option of currency depreciation.

Added to these macro-economic arguments was a simpler case. In 1987 I and my parliamentary research team (of two), carried out a study on exchange costs, which was eventually published in *The Times*.[21] We assumed that a traveller left London Heathrow with £100, and did a complete tour of the Community. At each airport visited, the stock of money was changed into the local currency, but nothing was spent. How much would be left when the balance was changed back into Sterling on return to London? The answer was £55.50. Subsequently a number of similar exercises were carried out yielding even greater losses. There were, interestingly, substantial variations depending upon the order in which countries were visited.

Within the Party as a whole support for a Single Currency was, of course, a minority view. More prevalent was the belief – more accurately, perhaps, the hope – that the Delors Plan would founder once detailed negotiations began, and that the whole problem would go away. I myself have speech notes from the period which include a forecast that the Germans were unlikely to sacrifice the D-Mark – the jewel in the crown of their post-war recovery – for a problematically stable euro.

This turned out to be a bad misreading of the situation. I should have realised this from attending meetings of a monetary union pressure group in the European Parliament which was chaired by an MEP and businessman with links to the German government, Otmar Franz. Although Pöhl was thought to be sceptical, the Chancellor, Helmut Kohl, had already reached an understanding on the matter with French President Mitterand. John Major himself seems to have been similarly misled.

> Our European partners were much more set on implementing the Delors Report … and moving to a single currency than I had realised. Whilst we regarded the move as a fanciful long-term ambition

faced by enormous problems, they were regarding it as more less fait accompli.[22]

Serious negotiations on EMU were already in prospect, therefore, when the political background, both at home and in Europe, changed dramatically. In November 1989 the Berlin Wall had come down, and in March of the following year the first free elections were held in East Germany. Like other German-speaking Conservative MEPs I was asked to address meetings there on behalf of CDU candidates; and have never before or since had such a politically electrifying experience. Though maintaining two separate states was still being discussed, I came away with the conviction that German re-unification was already unstoppable.

Earlier, to show solidarity, the whole EDG had met in Berlin; and, while we debated in a reconstructed hall in the old *Reichstag*, our spouses were taken on a tour of museums and art-galleries in the East. While there, my wife Felicity also had an unforgettable experience. A guide was lecturing authoritatively on the museum's collection of ancient Egyptian artifacts, when she suddenly stopped. "But what do I know?" she said. "All my life I've been studying and talking about these things; and yet I've never been allowed to leave the DDR and see for myself. But now I can!"

In October 1990 re-unification duly happened. As became clear later, it fulfilled one half of an agreement between Kohl and Mitterand, which had, indeed, made it virtually inevitable. Various sources show that François Mitterand had initially shared Margaret Thatcher's reluctance to see Germany re-united; but – unlike the British Prime Minister – had soon agreed to what had become Kohl's overriding political objective. In return he had got German acceptance of EMU.

Before EMU, however, another currency union, "GEMU", had to take place: between the D-Mark and the *Ostmark*, the currency of the GDR. The latter were exchanged for D-Marks at rates which effectively meant a huge subsidy from the West: at par for wages, prices and basic savings up to a limit of 4000 Mark per person, with less for children and more for pensioners; at a 2:1 rate for larger amounts of savings, company debts and housing loans; whilst so-called "speculative money" was converted at 3:1. This, it was widely believed, was a huge economic gamble, but a political necessity.

The political background in Britain also underwent a dramatic change. The trigger was the resignation speech on the 13th November of the, by then, Deputy Prime Minister, Geoffrey Howe, who had "wrestled for perhaps too long" with his disagreements with the Prime Minister over Europe. The occasion, Young records, "propelled Howe to heights of oratory more disdainful and more lethal than he had ever reached before". Perhaps more instructive, though, is Howe's resignation letter of two weeks before. In this he had made it clear that it was "our conduct of policy on the crucial monetary issue in Europe, first on the Exchange Rate Mechanism and now on EMU", that most concerned him. Britain finally inside the ERM had "a great opportunity at last to shape Europe's monetary arrangements in the years ahead".

We can only do that by being and staying on the inside track. ... The risks of being left behind on EMU are severe. All too much of our energy during the last decade has been devoted to correcting the consequences of our late start in Europe.

This was a clear appeal for full British participation in the coming EMU negotiations, even if a later sentence was more equivocal: "None of us wants the imposition of a single currency, but more than one form of EMU is possible."

It is possible that Margaret Thatcher could have withstood the pressure from Howe and others over Europe – on this issue, she had the support of a sizeable and growing proportion of Conservative MPs. She was also vulnerable, however, over the domestic issue of the Community Charge ("poll tax"). The combination gave Michael Heseltine the opportunity he was looking for to mount a leadership challenge. And so, as Major puts it in a chapter heading, "an Empress fell".

The opt-in solution

The two Inter-Governmental Conferences which were preparing the Maastricht summit – negotiations on EMU had been separated from those concerned with the other Treaty changes – began work in December 1990. The European Parliament had, of course, been asked for its "opinion"; and presenting this became the responsibility of a small delegation from the EMAC committee, of which I was a member. We attended a meeting at which we gave our evidence in one room, while the Finance Ministers (including the British Chancellor of the Exchequer, Norman Lamont) deliberated in an adjoining room. Fortunately, we had a spy next door: the Greek representative Efthimios Christodoulou, who, during his career, has moved effortlessly between being an MEP, Governor of the Greek Central Bank and a Greek Minister. We were able to exchange notes as the negotiations progressed.

By this time, the main issue was no longer whether the Delors Plan was to be implemented – that was, as Major had foreseen, a *fait accompli* – but the Economic dimension of EMU, and specifically fiscal policy. The Germans, desperate to ensure that any Single Currency would not be debauched by spendthrift governments, wanted tight rules on the level of national budget deficits and of public debt. The British position was that this could be left to market forces, given a few simple rules on debt financing. When I put this view forward we were subjected to a disdainful lecture by a German minister – one which had already annoyed his colleagues in the next room, including Lamont and Christodoulou.

When the Maastricht Treaty was eventually adopted, both sides seemed have won. The British view was incorporated in three "golden rules": no privileged access to financial institutions for financing public debt; no monetary financing of debt; and "no bail-out" by the Community. The

German view became the "excessive deficit procedure" and the "Stability and Growth Pact".

As it happened, Christodoulou was back in the European Parliament when the Pact came before the EMAC committee, and he was made *rapporteur*. By then, there were doubts whether providing for sanctions on countries running "excessive" budget deficits was altogether a good idea. "Don't worry", Christodoulou told the committee. "When it comes to the crunch, they won't enforce it!" And of course he was soon proved entirely right. Also proved right, it has to be admitted, were those who feared that, even combined, neither the German nor the British approach would prove sufficiently effective in the face of financial crisis. The limits set by the Stability and Growth Pact were massively breached by virtually all governments in response to the 2008–9 credit crunch. Nor did the disciplines of the market – at least until the bond markets very belatedly threatened to pull the plug – prevent Greece from hovering on the edge of default, so bringing the "no bail-out" rule to the test.

A few months later, in July 1991, I found myself in Moscow, giving a lecture to the Soviet Academy of Social Sciences on the subject of "European Monetary Union (*sic*)".[23] The Soviet Union was only weeks away from collapse, and a powerful aroma of *fin de siècle* was about (I often wonder what became of the about a hundred, presumably Marxist, economists who were there); but I did my best to fit in with a front of academic normality.

The main lines of the Maastricht Treaty were already clear: the Community train, as I put it, was going to have first and second-class carriages, with some countries qualifying for the full EMU and sharing a Single Currency, others not. The UK, technically, could "easily afford a first class ticket".

> Our inflation rate will soon fall below that of Germany. We have no problems with budget deficits. And sterling has, in practice, largely been within the ERM narrow band ever since it joined. Only political considerations could lead us to travel second class.

The British Government had already secured the right of opt-out from the final, first-class stage of EMU – or, to be more accurate, the right to opt in at some future date. John Major, I said, "should have no problem in signing".

In the end, as the different stages of the Maastricht Treaty were implemented, the UK elected to sit in a second-class carriage – but with some of its luggage, as it were, in first class. It is not widely realised, for example, that the Governor of the Bank of England today sits as a member of the

European Central Bank's General Council.* The UK has been an enthusiastic participant in those aspects of Delors designed to open up capital markets; and is also bound by the "golden rules", and by the requirement to avoid excessive budget deficits.

EMU, however, was only one part of Maastricht – as it turned out, the easy part. The rest was to drag Major and the Conservative Party into what Hugo Young called "the heart of darkness".

Notes

1 Howe *op.cit.* p. 533.
2 *Report to the Council and the Commission on the realization of economic and monetary union in the Community* (Supplement to the Bulletin of the European Communities, 8 October 1970). Pierre Werner was Prime Minister of Luxembourg from 1959 to 1974 and again from 1979 to 1984.
3 See *Hansard* the 19th November 1978, Cols. 477–80.
4 See *Hansard* the 30th November 1978, Col. 618.
5 Howe *op.cit.* p. 575.
6 *Report on economic and monetary union in the European Community* (Office for the Official Publications of the European Communities, May 1989).
7 *The Next Stage in an Evolutionary Approach to Monetary Union* (British Invisible Export Council, March 1990). The authors of the plan were Paul Richards from Samuel Montagu, Nigel Wicks at the Treasury, and the UK's former ambassador to the Community, Sir Michael Butler.
8 *EMU now? The leap to European money assessed* by Tim Congdon (Centre for Policy Studies, 1990).
9 Wall *op.cit.* p. 103.
10 Major *op.cit.* p. 152.
11 *In Office* by Norman Lamont (Little, Brown and Company, 1999) p. 385.
12 See Lawson *op.cit.* pp. 663–4.
13 Major *op.cit.* p. 153.
14 Hugo Young *op.cit.* p. 366.
15 Howe *op.cit.* p. 275.
16 Lawson *op.cit.* p. 1010.
17 *Crossbow*, April 1985.
18 *Group objectives in the field of Economic, Monetary, Fiscal and Industrial Policy* (EDG, March 1987).
19 Lawson *op.cit.* p. 500.
20 *Europe's Need, Britain's Opportunity: Economic and Monetary Union* by Sir Fred Catherwood MEP (Conservatives in the European Parliament, 1990).
21 *The Times*, Saturday the 5th November 1987.
22 Major *op.cit.* p. 149.
23 Published as *European Monetary Union* by Ben Patterson MEP (Conservatives in the European Parliament, 1991).

---

* This comprises the President and Vice-President of the ECB itself, and the Governors of all 27 national central banks of EU Member States. It participates in the advisory and coordinating functions of the ECB, and, in particular, in preparations for new countries to join the Euro Area.

11 The Battle for Maastricht

"Game, set and match"

Though John Major was thought to be the "Thatcherite" candidate in the Conservative Party leadership contest that followed Mrs. Thatcher's withdrawal (in a straw poll of Conservative MEPs the original challenger, Heseltine, came first), his victory was greeted with enormous enthusiasm by pro-Europeans. Although he himself writes rather dramatically that "few sentiments in recent political history have provoked such havoc or been so misrepresented",* his statement in March 1991 that Britain should be "where we belong; at the very heart of Europe; working with our partners in building the future," seemed to promise a new beginning. The fact that the speech in which this occurred was delivered in Bonn to the CDU think-tank, the *Konrad Adenauer Stiftung*, indicated that the Party and Government at home were at last on the same side as Conservative MEPs and our centre-right allies in the European Parliament. Indeed, Major records that, unlike his predecessor, he got on extremely well with Helmut Kohl.

The Maastricht Treaty that had emerged from the Inter-Governmental Conferences and the Maastricht summit was presented by the Government as – and, indeed, was genuinely believed to be – an "historic triumph" of the Conservative approach to Europe. In the Foreword to a Conservative Research Department briefing in February 1992, the Foreign Secretary, Douglas Hurd, wrote that Britain had done well at Maastricht. "Patient negotiation under the Prime Minister's leadership" had brought an agreement which "met all of our objectives". British initiatives – on the rule of law, subsidiarity, accountability, crime and defence, as well as on the very structure of the Treaty – "shine through in the final text".[1]

In his memoirs, Hurd describes how he and the then Minister for State for Europe, Tristan Garel-Jones, had sketched out a new concept of Europe as "a temple, not a tree".

---

* What he had *meant* to say, he later told his biographer Dr Anthony Seldon, was that Britain should be at the heart of the *debate* on Europe (*Sunday Telegraph*, 30 March 1997). Quoting this is his Bruges Group paper, *John Major and Europe: The Failure of a Policy 1990–7*, Dr Martin Holmes also cites Major's political advisors Sarah Hogg and Stephen Hill in support; but also observes that the clarification was "politically posthumous".

Under the old Monnet doctrine Europe would grow slowly like a tree, with a single central trunk and many branches. We saw the new EU rather as three pillars: one supranational, but the other two (foreign affairs, and home affairs and justice) inter-governmental.[2]

Strengthening the role of the Community in the field of foreign policy, and improving the arrangements for fighting international crime, terrorism and drug-trafficking, but without more supra-nationalism, was felt by the Government to be a key British achievement; and judging by the criticisms of this three-pillar structure by disappointed "federalists", this was almost certainly true – though it was also true that the three pillars came together within the over-arching title of "European Union" (EU). Actually, neither of the new "pillars" constituted a radical departure from what was already taking place. The foreign and security pillar was in effect a formalisation of what had in practice been developing under the heading of Political Cooperation ever since the Fouchet Plan of 1961, a Gaullist proposal for inter-governmental policy coordination outside the framework of the Rome Treaty. The justice and home affairs pillar was likewise a formalisation of the inter-governmental Trevi Group of Community Home Affairs ministers.

Other changes made by Maastricht were also considered in line with Conservative thinking. "Subsidiarity" had been written into the Treaty, providing a "constant counterweight to the natural tendency of the centre to accumulate power", as Delors himself had explained the European Parliament in January 1990. It established the principle that the Community should only act "if, and in so far as, the objectives cannot be sufficiently achieved by the Member States … "; and also that "any action by the Community shall not go beyond what is necessary to achieve the objectives of the Treaty". This was re-enforced by the stipulation that "decisions should be taken as closely as possible to the citizens".*

For its part, the European Parliament moved a step closer to its goal of full "co-decision" on legislation with the Council of Ministers. This would apply in certain fields – notably those concerning the Single Market. In other fields the old "cooperation" procedure would continue to be used; and in others, like tax, the even older "consultation" procedure. In addition an "assent" procedure (in effect a Parliament veto) also applied for such matters as approval of new Member States. This complexity did not make Parliament's legislative powers very transparent.

---

* It was soon pointed out, of course, that "subsidiarity" could apply just as much within individual Member States as within the European Union; and that it could prove a powerful argument for devolution of power to regions and local governments. In fact, the Lisbon Treaty makes this explicit, referring to "regional and local self-government" as part of countries' "fundamental structures, political and constitutional" (Article 3a (2)); and referring to action "either at central level or at regional and local level" when defining subsidiarity (Article 3b(3)).

The Research Department brief, however, concentrated on other changes to Parliament's role: a "European Ombudsman" answerable to Parliament; strengthened budgetary control; and a greater role in monitoring the Commission's activities. Finally, the suspect "Social Chapter" was dropped from the Treaty text itself, and placed into a Protocol under which individual countries could act if they so wished. Britain was not obliged to participate.

In sum, the Maastricht agreement – as the 1992 centenary edition of the Campaign Guide[3] put it – provided "a spring-board for Britain to play a leading role in the Community of tomorrow". In the words of a recent study of the Conservative Party, Major and his negotiating team had "pulled off the seemingly impossible trick of creating a European Union Treaty that avoided mention of federalism, that did not oblige the UK to sign the so-called Social Chapter, that maintained the possibility of national vetoes on foreign and security and justice and home affairs matters, and that enshrined the British opt-out on the single currency".[4]

Major recalls that he was "received with acclaim and the waving of order papers" when he reported on Maastricht to the House of Commons. Britain had won "game, set and match" (a phase which very quickly came to haunt Major, but which he himself never in fact used.) Douglas Hurd and Norman Lamont "were received rapturously at meetings of Conservative backbenchers". "It was the modern equivalent of a Roman triumph."[5]

The Party divides

Two pamphlets by lawyers, both published in 1990, provide evidence of the growing divisions over Europe that were nevertheless soon to plague the Conservative Party. One[6] was by the MP for Stone, Bill Cash; the other[7] by the leader of the British Conservatives in the European Parliament – whose constituency, as it happened, encompassed that of Cash – the late Lord Kingsland (at that time Sir Christopher Prout QC).

Bill Cash has the distinction of having a chapter all to himself in *This Blessed Plot*.[8] It describes how his Euroscepticism was driven by "a sense of existential crisis", a "terrible awakening", when, as a member of the House of Commons Select Committee on European Legislation, he "realised what was really going on": the European Community was on the road to becoming "a political federation". I remember having a long conversation with him in the grounds of the *Konrad Adenauer Stiftung* conference centre on the banks of Lake Como, to which we had both been invited, and trying to convince him that the Community was still about completing the Single Market. He hinted that I was the victim of a conspiracy.

The Cash pamphlet – which, significantly, was published by the Bow Group – indeed begins by hinting at conspiracy. He contrasts the Mitterand/Kohl statement of the 20th April 1990, that "the time has come to transform the nature of the relations between the member states into a European Union" with the 20th May 1990 statement by the French foreign minister that "no country is ready to give up sovereignty over defence and security matters. ... Nobody should be deceived by this use of the tough-guy/soft-guy approach".

The European Community, Cash believed was "at a cross-roads". The federalists' plans for European Union could mean handing over the Community to "an economic and legal order which would be dominated by German interests and influence". Unlike the Rome Treaty and the Single European Act, which were "autochthonous documents", deriving their legitimacy from "the consent of the States which signed them", federalism would compromise "the essential sovereignty of a nation".

It is difficult not to get the impression, however, that Cash's main fears were not so much for national sovereignty as for the sovereignty of his own political stamping-ground, the House of Commons.

> If the European Parliament becomes the central parliament for a federal Europe, the national parliaments, including Westminster, will be reduced to the status of regional assemblies. ... Under the federalists' plan all the traditional powers of national governments (tax, defence, foreign policy) would pass to the federal European Parliament. The national governments would be left with next to nothing.

There follows a list of reasons why the European Parliament could not exercise proper democratic control. The constituencies were too large. There was no two-party system on the Westminster model. There were too many languages. Even Conservative MEPs there had "recently voted for federalism". The Parliament's committee system was "lamentably weak" (an extraordinary charge, this, given that most of those who had been both MPs and MEPs during their political careers usually cited the European Parliament's system of specialised committees as being far superior to the system at Westminster). Voters were "generally not interested in EC affairs" and national parliaments were "the natural focus of each Member State's electorate".

He did not perceive the possibility that, with the vast transfer of power to the European Parliament that he envisaged, voters might change their minds.

The paper by Sir Christopher Prout was less polemical and more analytical – unsurprisingly, since it was based on a lecture at Somerville College, Oxford. He began by trying to define the term "federalism".

> Federalism, as the word is almost invariably used in the columns of newspapers in this country, is taken to be a process which undermines the nation state by removing from it discretionary executive powers and handing them over to be exercised by super state institutions. So far, almost nothing of the sort has been happening. Indeed,

federalism as the concept has developed in the European Community is a doctrine of decentralisation.

Unfortunately, such attempts to explain the separation of powers to different levels of government – the constitutional entrenchment of subsidiarity – were already doomed to failure. "Federalism" was well on the way to becoming a term of abuse in Conservative circles, with the more boorish Eurosceptics rendering it as "federast".

Prout next turned to three uses of the word "sovereignty". In the case of the first, the "sovereignty of Parliament", his view was that "Westminster retains the sovereign legislative authority to take us out [of the Community] tomorrow, however unlikely that eventuality may be." If it did so we should "be in breach of our Rome Treaty obligations; ... but that would be a matter to be resolved by the rules of public international law".

It was public international law, in fact, which defined the second use of the word: the sovereignty of the nation state. When a country signed a treaty it was akin to signing a contract in private life "because we believe that we will be, on balance, better placed in life than before we signed. We limit our freedom of manoeuvre, in one respect, to gain even greater freedom of manoeuvre in another." If we were to reject such treaties because they curtailed national independence, "we would have to repudiate every treaty we ever signed!"

The final use of the word was "Sovereignty in Fact, or the real power of the nation state to control its own economic and political destiny". When German interest rates went up, for example, market forces had obliged Britain to put theirs up too: economic sovereignty had been lost. But "sometimes a nation state can enhance its Sovereignty In Fact by limiting its Sovereignty In Law". This was why the French believed that their power over monetary policy would be increased, not reduced, by merging the power of their Central Bank into a European system.

As in the case of explaining the term "federalism", however, such sophisticated analysis faced an uphill task in confronting the gut feelings of Conservative Eurosceptics. So did the justification for increased powers for the European Parliament, to which Prout now turned, in the face of the resentment felt by many Conservative MPs. The argument that such increased powers were needed to compensate for the fact that "no scrutiny procedure by a national parliament, however effective, can protect a national parliament against the fact that a Minister can find himself outvoted in the Council of Ministers," cut no ice with them. For Eurosceptics, the answer to the "democratic deficit" was the national veto.

Prout concluded that "the preservation of our national identity is fundamental to the political philosophy of the Conservative Party"; and this was best achieved within the Community by "a process of integration with decentralisation, based on the rule of law and administered by the courts". This was what had been embodied in the Single European Act, and would, he believed, be embodied in the Maastricht Treaty.

The General Election of 1992 and after

Before these impending divisions could do any real damage to the Party, the Major Government had an unexpected triumph. The April 1992 general election was won, admittedly only by a majority of twenty-one seats, but with more votes than any British party has ever polled, either before or since. In the weeks before the election Labour had been recording leads in the opinion polls of up to 7 per cent. The morale among party workers, however, was astonishingly high; and in Gravesham, the theoretically marginal constituency in which I spent most of my time in support of the sitting MP, Jacques Arnold – like me, a former Hyde Park Tory – the canvass returns were astonishingly good. Whether the campaign itself changed voters' minds, or whether the opinion polls were wrong is still a matter of dispute. A *post mortem* by the Market Research Society attributed part of the polling errors to a "Shy Tory Factor".* The Murdoch press claimed "It's The Sun Wot Won It".†

During the campaign, according to Major himself, "there was barely a mention of Europe".[9] But Hugo Young observes that the election took place "in the shadow of Maastricht … when the Treaty was still being written about as an unqualified triumph, burnishing Major's name as a man of competence. To that extent, Europe played its role in helping him to win."[10]

The 1992 Conservative manifesto[11] did, in fact, outline policy on Europe in some detail. The section on the European Community began by stating that "the Conservatives have been the party of Britain in Europe for 30 years. We have argued when argument was necessary; but we have not wavered nor changed our views. We have ensured that Britain is at the heart of Europe; a strong and respected partner." The Maastricht Treaty had been "a success both for Britain and for the rest of Europe". British proposals had "helped to shape the key provisions of the Treaty", including an agreement that the European Court of Justice would be able to fine any Member State which failed to fulfil its obligations under Community law.

The manifesto then went on to outline an agenda for the British Presidency of the Council of Ministers, due in the second half of 1992. The priorities would include starting negotiations with those EFTA countries who want to join the Community "so that they can join by 1995"; building on the EC's Association Agreements with Czechoslovakia, Hungary and Poland "so that we can welcome them to full membership by the year 2000"; concluding trade and cooperation agreements with "the main republics of the former Soviet Union"; and completing the single market and extending it to the seven countries of EFTA. After the "deepening" of

---

* A significant number of those polled, it was thought, had intended to vote Conservative, but had been reluctant to admit this to the pollsters.

† The headline that appeared on the front-page of *The Sun* newspaper on Saturday the 11th April. On polling day, Thursday the 9th April, the front page header had been "If Kinnock wins today will the last person to leave Britain please turn out the lights". There is some evidence that the Labour leader, Neil Kinnock, was indeed a liability to his Party.

Maastricht, the main Conservative objective, therefore, was an ambitious programme of "widening" – a policy on which all factions in the Party could unite.

Ironically perhaps, it was a former Communist country in Eastern Europe – but not from the old Soviet system – which produced the first crisis for the re-elected Conservative Government. A decade after the death of Marshal Tito, Yugoslavia had broken up into its constituent parts, with Slovenia and Croatia declaring their independence in June 1991. When Bosnia-Herzegovina followed suit in 1992, the Yugoslav army – in effect the army of Serbia – invaded. Stories of mounting atrocities led NATO to intervene, with Britain immediately sending 1,800 troops.

In the European Parliament the conflict in former Yugoslavia had already produced sharp divisions of opinion within the centre-right. Most CDU/CSU Members had supported Croatian independence (which had, indeed, been sponsored by the German Government), and were anti-Serb. The Greeks and others supported the Milošević Government's right to defend the Serb minority in Bosnia. There were ugly exchanges of view, with the strongly pro-Serb Conservative MEP, Derek Prag, harking back to Croat support for the Nazis during the War,[*] others already talking of "taking out" Milošević.

John Major's autobiography records that, on this issue too, "no party was more split than the Conservatives, which was divided into four camps". This, though, was not on pro- or anti-Serb lines. Some Conservatives wanted nothing to do with the conflict as "there was no British interest involved"; a second group wanted humanitarian aid delivered, provided there was no fighting; the third group wanted the use of air-power only; and the fourth was in favour of ground troops as well.

In view of what was to happen later in the Middle East, Afghanistan, Sierra Leone and elsewhere in the world, these differences of opinion on the direction of Conservative foreign and defence policy deserve some examination. A division has existed between those who want to act for humanitarian or ideological reasons (who would later be described, in the US context, as "neo-Conservatives") and those who want to act only in defence of British interests (who might be described as traditional High Tories), and has a long pedigree. In the 19th century the best-known exponent of the first school was probably Lord Palmerston who began his political career as a Pittite Tory, and later served in Tory, Whig and Conservative governments, as well as his own Liberal governments.[†]

---

[*] It should not be forgotten, though, that Croat partisans also fought the Nazis. Tito (real name Josip Broz) himself was a Croat.

[†] Claiming Palmerston as part of a Tory tradition may appear controversial. In 1856, however, the Conservative leader Lord Derby wrote that Palmerston's apparently unassailable position at the time was because "in short he has been a Conservative Minister working with Radical tools ... ". (see *The Conservative Party from Peel to Churchill* by Robert Blake (Eyre & Spottiswoode, 1970) p.91. Blake himself makes the point that Disraeli – "an instinctive Palmerstonian" – was quick to assume "the mantle of Palmerston" soon after the latter's death.

Motivating his long responsibility for British foreign policy was a desire not only to defend, but also to spread, British power and values throughout the world – with "boldness and dash" and if necessary with the aid of gunboats.

The second school, however, has historically warned the Party to beware of "foreign entanglements", and particularly entanglements on the other side of the Channel. Its principal prime ministerial exponent was probably Lord Salisbury, whose policy has been described as "keeping aloof from continental engagements, while keeping in touch with continental Chancelleries";[12] and who himself described "English" foreign policy as "to float lazily downstream, occasionally putting out a diplomatic boat-hook to avoid collisions".

This second Tory tradition almost certainly lies behind many of the difficulties which the Party has faced in its involvement with Europe, and especially the European Union. Though "defence of British interests" inevitably led to massive British involvement in the First and Second World Wars,* and in the Cold War after that, these could plausibly be thought of as temporary affairs: afterwards, a victorious Britain could return to the *status quo ante*. But membership of the European Union, though likewise justified by defence of the national interest, is – in intention at least – for ever. In addition, it has threatened to become a great deal more than "keeping in touch with foreign Chancelleries" – or "inter-governmentalism", as it would be called today.

What was a reasonable stance for Imperial Britain at the end of the nineteenth century, however, had already become almost impossible to carry off by the second half of the twentieth (as, too, had Palmerstonian activism). That conclusion was reached by Macmillan, with regret; by Heath with enthusiasm; by Thatcher through clenched teeth; and by Major without much choice. All of them, however, were at the head of a Conservative Party where the roots of the old Tory philosophy went deep, even deeper than the championing of Empire and Commonwealth, or of Atlanticism. If a really serious crisis in Britain's Community membership came, the Party was almost bound to be in trouble.

---

* Involvement in the Second World War was not, however, uncontroversial. There were quite a few Conservatives who did not believe that the defence of Poland – one of the "far-off counties, of which we know little" – was a sufficient cause for declaring war on Germany. Had Lord Halifax, rather than Churchill, become Prime Minister after Neville Chamberlain, it is possible that the Government would have accepted Hitler's apparent offer to leave the British Empire alone in return for a free hand in Europe. Even since the war, there has been a school of thought arguing that this would have been the right policy (this was the view, for example, of the historian, diarist and Conservative MP, Alan Clark). The Cambridge historian Maurice Cowling – who has been variously described as a proponent of "black Conservatism", a "rational pessimist" and an "isolationist imperialist" – believed that the Second World War had been a "liberal war which had been entered into in a condition of moral indignation without the resources to fight it". (See *Mill and Liberalism*, by Maurice Cowling p. xv, (2nd edition, Cambridge: Cambridge University Press, 1990); and *The Impact of Hitler: British politics and British policy, 1933–1940* by Maurice Cowling, pp. 391 and 399 (Chicago, London: Chicago University Press 1977).

That crisis duly came on Wednesday the 16th September 1992, when Sterling's participation in the Exchange Rate Mechanism was "suspended".

"Black Wednesday": causes and consequences

Had the Government not made major efforts in September 1992 to keep the pound sterling above its Exchange Rate Mechanism "floor" of DM 2.778, it is possible that the political fallout would have been greatly reduced. Yet even on the morning of "Black Wednesday" itself, the Chancellor of the Exchequer, Norman Lamont, officially announced that the government was "prepared to take whatever measures are necessary to maintain Sterling's parity within the ERM". The Bank of England raised interest rates to 12%, and was raising them again to 15% when the ERM suspension was announced. At the same time the Bank intervened on the foreign exchange markets to support the pound sterling, backed by an over £7 billion foreign currency loan negotiated by Lamont.

By this time, of course, operators on the currency markets – most famously George Soros – had already taken positions against Sterling which threatened to overwhelm any possible Bank of England intervention. That left the interest rate lever; and it is conceivable that a rise to, say, 30–35% would have stabilised the pound sterling's parity. The British domestic economy, however, required lower rather than higher rates, and any rise of this kind was ruled out – for both economic and political reasons, according to Major.

These events have been widely considered, in the words of Hugo Young, "one of the most embarrassing, as well as politically calamitous, episodes in the post-war history of British economic policy".[13]

The newspapers were soon publishing figures of how much money had been "needlessly handed over to the currency speculators" – figures which, much later, were found to be wildly exaggerated. The charge of having raised interest rates to 15% was used against Major and the Conservative Party for years afterwards – although, in fact, the rise to 15% was never implemented, and even the 12% to which they *were* raised was for an insignificant period of time. For the Labour Party the episode was a godsend, destroying in a few hours the hitherto unbreakable Conservative reputation for competent management of the economy.

The episode was also a godsend for the Eurosceptics in the Conservative Party. Major's policy of being "at the heart of Europe" was widely perceived to have been discredited; and the "foreign entanglement" of the Exchange Rate Mechanism could be presented as a symptom of the wider "foreign entanglement" of the European Community itself. Major, in his memoirs, ascribes much of the blame for "Black Wednesday" to the intransigence of the German Government and the *Bundesbank*; but this, of course, was a two-edged defence. For a Eurosceptic it merely proved how little Britain's continental partners were to be trusted.

In the context of economic policy, it also confirmed the position of those who had all along argued against a fixed exchange rate for Sterling. By January 1993 its value had fallen by over 14% against the D-Mark, and reached a low point at a little above 2 D-Marks in November 1996. The recovery in the domestic economy which took place during this period was widely attributed to this "freeing of the pound sterling", though in fact the recovery was already under way earlier in 1992. By 1998 the exchange rate was back to the original ERM central parity of 2.95 D-Marks.

But if a fixed exchange rate for Sterling appeared discredited, the Exchange Rate Mechanism itself became "toxic": the hostility to it at the 1992 Conservative Party Conference exceeded anything expressed about Maastricht. Leaving the ERM in 1992 had been announced as only a temporary measure. Yet neither the Major Government, nor the Labour Governments that succeeded it, felt able to take the risk of re-joining. Moreover, the toxicity of the ERM carried over – understandably, though quite illogically in economic terms – into the debate about the euro.

The events of "Black Wednesday" give rise to two questions: why did they happen? and could they have been prevented? Answering these questions in full is not the purpose of this study. A blow-by-blow account – of course from his own point of view – is contained in Norman Lamont's memoirs.[14] As it happens, however, I found myself preparing the European Parliament's own commentary on the events as *rapporteur* on two pertinent documents: the 1992 Annual Report[15] of the Committee of Governors of the Central Banks of the Member States – the forerunner of the European Monetary Institute and the European Central Bank; and the report on "lessons to be learned from the disturbances on the foreign exchange markets" from the Monetary Committee of the European Community.[16]

As far as the first question is concerned, the Central Bankers and the Parliament report[17] were agreed (as were John Major, Norman Lamont, and most commentators) that the prime cause was German re-unification. The resulting burden of expenditure – financed largely by borrowing – had created a need for high short-term D-Mark interest rates, which, in turn, had resulted in a flow of short-term capital from the dollar into the D-Mark and a rise in the latter's exchange rate. Other currencies in the Exchange Rate Mechanism (like Sterling) could then only keep their parities stable against the D-Mark through interest rates "at odds with the needs of the domestic economy".

If all this had already been obvious at the time, however, why had the "inescapable and clear conclusion" not been drawn? The Bank Governors drew attention to two political events which influenced the situation: the narrow Danish "no" vote on the Maastricht Treaty in June, which had been a "catalyst"; and the impending French referendum which had become "a reference date for a possible realignment" of ERM parities. My own conclusion was therefore that "an orderly realignment of exchange rates within the ERM should have taken place during the second half of 1992, before a 'messy' realignment could be precipitated by the markets".

John Major's account gives one reason why this did not occur. The French were determined to maintain a *franc fort* and were against realignment. Major was against a unilateral realignment unless the French did so too.

> It was not national pride that kept me from devaluing the pound while the franc stayed strong, but a hunch that the markets would ignore such a half-cocked move. That is indeed what happened: Italy's lone devaluation drew the predators in for the kill, and within days the lira was outside the ERM.[18]

Norman Lamont's account reveals that not only a realignment within the Exchange Rate Mechanism, but even Sterling's exit altogether from the mechanism, had been the subject of discussions within the government and the Treasury for some time; and an ERM exit was considered inevitable if the French were to vote "no" to the Maastricht Treaty. For Lamont, the key issue was whether or not such moves could result in lower UK interest rates – and this was by no means certain. Leaving the ERM would only benefit the economy if it led to "sustainably lower interest rates"; but if a Sterling devaluation did "draw the predators in for the kill" it was doubtful whether "a cut in interest rates would be sustainable in anything other than the short run". If the Government's nerve cracked as the pound sterling went into free fall, "interest rates would be forced up to defend the exchange rate".[19]

The bad-tempered meeting of Finance Ministers in Bath earlier in September, chaired by Lamont, had tried to get the *Bundesbank* to reduce *its* interest rates instead. This it had been unwilling to do, since this might have triggered domestic inflation. Yet the communiqué from Bath had stated that a realignment "would not be the appropriate response" – an assertion, the Central Bank Report mildly observes, which "failed to have a lasting impact on market expectations". Why had all fifteen Finance Ministers not resigned? I asked in my speech to the Parliament.

All such explanations, of course, were made with the benefit of hindsight. At the time, Lamont observes, it appeared that a general realignment within the Exchange Rate Mechanism was not on offer. Later he found that there had been some confusion about the German position in particular – partly, he believes, as a result of disagreement between the *Bundesbank* and the German government itself. Had full information been available, and the situation less fraught, the outcome might have been different. Lamont nevertheless concluded that "I do not believe that what is euphemistically called a 'realignment' would have worked".

Following "Black Wednesday" and the currency crises of the following year, there were sharply differing opinions as to what lessons had been learned. The Monetary Committee primly concluded that "when a currency begins to come under speculative attack … the Member State affected must demonstrate its strong will to defend its parity through appropriate measures. ... The other Member States will determine to which extent and how they can support these efforts through appropriate action." The inference, almost certainly reflecting the view of the *Bundesbank*, was that the will of the British to remain in the Exchange Rate Mechanism had been insufficiently strong, so that the *Bundesbank* itself felt excused for not having made a greater effort. Major, indeed, bitterly contrasts German failure to support the pound sterling with the whole-hearted support later given to the French *franc fort*.

More important, however, were the long-term lessons. There was widespread agreement on the basic problem: that, in a world of free capital flows, a system like the Exchange Rate Mechanism was vulnerable to speculative attacks. But at this point opinions diverged sharply.

For a majority in the British Conservative Party, the events proved the case for floating exchange rates. They vindicated the words of Enoch Powell from the 1960s: "The rate of exchange is ... a price, and like all prices represents the point at which supply and demand – in this case the supply and demand for the respective moneys – tend to balance."[20] John Major himself also made the mistake of concluding that the failure of the Exchange Rate Mechanism weakened the case for a Single Currency. In an article published by *The Economist*, he wrote – using words which would also, this time legitimately, come to haunt him – that continuing the EMU programme as if nothing had happened had "all the quality of a rain dance and about as much potency".[21]

The majority conclusion in the European Parliament and among most Member State Governments, however, was that the ERM *débâcle* actually *proved* the case for a Single Currency. They preferred the view of Professor Mundell, that the purpose of money was to be "a convenience", and the fewer the currencies, and the fewer the fluctuations between them the better.[22] Once the separate national currencies had been abolished it would be impossible for speculators to play one off against another.

This view shortly afterwards received unexpected, but telling, support from the man who had done best out of the September 1992 *débâcle*, George Soros. "A single currency", he was reported as saying, "would put me out of business".*

The Maastricht rebellion

Being the catalyst for "Black Wednesday" was not the only damage to be inflicted on the British Government by the Danes. The Maastricht Treaty, Major recalls in his autobiography, had "sailed comfortably through its first and second readings" in the House of Commons; and then, with the result of the Danish referendum, "all hell broke loose". Consideration of the Maastricht Bill had already been delayed by the general election in April. After weighing the options, the Government decided to defer

---

* But it hasn't, of course.

passage of the Bill once again, until the Danish position could be clarified. Adding to the problems, finding a way to ensure the Danes could vote "yes" in a second ballot became the responsibility of the British Presidency of the European Community in the second half of 1992. "Not since the heyday of the Vikings had the Danes precipitated such disruption", Major comments.

The Danish problem was in fact solved with surprising ease. At the December summit in Edinburgh, the Community was "nudged" towards a deal which enabled the Danes to approve Maastricht in a second referendum the following May. Progress was also made in Edinburgh towards the next enlargement of the Community to include Austria, Finland and Sweden. It was "the most successful European summit I attended as prime minister", Major comments, producing "some of the best results of any European Council since Britain joined the Community".[23]

His account nevertheless omits to mention one appalling decision which has had long-term consequences for the reputation of the Community, besides costing an estimated £154 million a year. This was recorded in an Annex to the main presidency conclusions, and ran as follows:

> Article 1(a). The European Parliament shall have its seat in Strasbourg where the twelve periods of monthly plenary sessions, including the budget session, shall be held. The periods of additional plenary sessions shall be held in Brussels. The Committees of the European Parliament shall be held in Brussels. The General Secretariat of the European Parliament and its departments shall remain in Luxembourg.

This is not the place to describe in detail how the European Parliament came to be located in three different cities. The situation was more a consequence of historical accident than of formal decisions. The result, however, has been not only to hamper the work of the Parliament and its Members and incur huge unnecessary costs, but to open the Parliament to considerable popular ridicule: in German, it was early on dubbed the *Wanderzirkus*. What has rubbed salt into the wound, as far as the Parliament itself has been concerned, is the fact that any decision on "the seat of the institutions" is reserved by the Treaty to the national governments alone.* The European Parliament itself has repeatedly voted to meet in one place.

All this could perhaps have been put right at Edinburgh. Stephen Wall records that the decision was a "small price" paid to President Mitterand as part of a "complex package on the site of EU institutions".[24] The evidence, however, indicates that the matter was hardly given any thought. Otherwise, the text would not have referred to "the twelve periods of monthly plenary sessions". The Parliament does not sit in August.

---

* The text of what is now Article 289 reads: *"The seat of the institutions of the Community shall be determined by common accord of the governments of the Member States."*

In other ways, nevertheless, the British Presidency of 1992 was an impressive success. Heroic efforts by the Council of Ministers meant that 95% of Single Market legislation had been adopted by the target date of the 31st December – though it is true that only half of the Directives requiring further legislation at national level had been so "transposed" in all twelve Member States. Paradoxically, the "good boy of Europe" on this score was Denmark, with nearly 100% transposition. The record of the British Presidency is all the more remarkable in having taken place in the shadow of "Black Wednesday", and with the Government on the rack in Parliament as it struggled to approve the Maastricht Treaty.

The passage of the Maastricht Bill through the House of Commons – what Major describes as "the longest white-knuckle ride in recent British politics" – *did* come to a successful end in July 1993, with the Government carrying a Confidence motion by the comfortable margin of thirty-eight votes. During a "year of gruesome trench warfare", however, Major had come close to being forced into resignation; and the Conservative Party had been seen to be openly, and viciously, split. The number of Conservative rebels rose from the twenty-two who voted against the second reading before the first Danish referendum to (according to Major) a hard core of forty, with others "floating in and out of rebellion". They were backed by senior Party figures like Lord Tebbit, and by most of the "Tory Press". Baroness Thatcher, as she had become, herself described Maastricht as "a Treaty too far", and rallied the Conservative right with the memorable but provocative charge that "One Nation Conservatism" meant "No Nation Conservatism".[25]

In Hugo Young's account, the Conservative Eurosceptic rebels are not treated gently. A "confederacy of zealots and lurchers", a "church overflowing with apostates of one kind or another", they "moved in from cranks' corner to establish themselves at the centre of political debate".

> Considered as a group, they were cantankerous, mostly humourless, and acquired a single-mindedness sufficient to elude, in a way the British system cannot readily tolerate, party discipline.[26]

Ted Heath's opinion, as recorded in his memoirs, was much the same: the rebels' "treacherous antics" were unprecedented in British politics.[27]

Major's own depictions, however, are somewhat kinder; and he also draws attention to a feature of the situation demanding an explanation which neither he nor Young fully provide. How is it that this rebellious crew, apparently determined to destroy the Conservative Government, regularly received the support of their constituency Conservative associations? When area chairmen tried to persuade the associations to bring the rebels into line, Major recalls, they resisted. Warnings in late 1992 from Conservative Central Office and Sir Basil Feldman, chairman of the National Union of Conservative and Unionist Associations, that the fate of the government only just elected in April was in the balance, failed to bring sufficient pressure to bear on the rebels.

Major also draws attention to another fact which is germane. The fifty or so Conservative MPs who retired in 1992 had been generally "pro-European". Many of their younger successors elected that year were not. This shift, however, could not have been accidental: the new MPs had been selected as candidates by their constituency Conservative associations, and their attitudes to Europe would have already been examined by the selection committees. Moreover, these seats would, broadly, have been "safe" – that is, the members of the associations would have been mainstream Conservatives.

Activist opinion: conflicting evidence

It is plausible to reach the conclusion that the Eurosceptic rebels were backed by their Conservative associations in large part because those associations had already approved of their views when selecting them. There is evidence, indeed, that efforts by Conservative Central Office to ensure that candidates more in tune with the official line should be chosen had actually been counter-productive. Signs that the pro-Europeans were losing ground among Conservative activists had already appeared at the 1992 party conference, when Norman Tebbit's blatantly Eurosceptic speech received an ecstatic reception from a sizeable proportion of the hall. Conservative Party members, like members of the public in general, claimed not to have been told enough about the Maastricht Treaty, of which they were consequently extremely suspicious. Any support there might have been for the Single Currency, even with the British "opt-in", had been thoroughly destroyed by "Black Wednesday".

The full impact of this apparent change at the Party's grass-roots did not come home to me personally until the European Elections of 1994, when a significant number of active Conservatives defected to the newly-formed United Kingdom Independence Party (UKIP). Earlier, though, there had been plenty of indications that a change was under way even among those who could not claim to have been left in ignorance. In 1993, when Maastricht had already received the Royal Assent, the Bow Group itself published a paper[28] by the future MEP Daniel Hannan (with a foreword by the veteran anti-Marketeer, Sir Teddy Taylor MP), calling for a new direction for party policy. The Major government, it argued, had presented Maastricht as a move away from centralisation; but there would be a backlash against it "as the Treaty's actual provisions become more and more obvious". The "implications of the Maastricht process" would, sooner or later, threaten "the first-past-the-post voting system, the principle of minimum interference in industry, the Atlantic alliance, the maintenance of the Union, even the status of the monarchy".

I also remember addressing a group of Young Conservatives in the Kent West constituency who were almost unanimously hostile to British membership of the Community. Indeed the YCs nationally, once in the vanguard of pro-Europe opinion, were by this time not only shrinking dramatically in numbers, but also becoming a hotbed of extreme right-wing opinion. By 1998, even the by then mildly Eurosceptic leadership of the Party was obliged to close the organisation down.

The shrinking in the membership of the YCs was mirrored by a fall in membership of the Party as a whole. In part this was the continuation of a long-term trend, affecting all political parties. According to official statistics published in 1953, the membership of the Conservative Party in England and Wales alone was then nearly three million. Just before the General Election of 1970, an estimate by Butler and Pinto-Duschinsky[29] put the figure at half of that. By 1992 the figure was down to half of that again. And in 2005 – when a poll on the Party's leadership made it possible to reach a precise figure – the membership was only just above a quarter of a million. In 2010, according the Party's co-chairman, Sayeeda Warsi,[30] the latest records showed that there were only 177,000.

The decline in Party membership in the early 1990s provides one explanation for changing attitudes to Europe in the constituency associations. Large numbers of what Bernard Crick described in the early 1960s as "non-political conservatives"[31] were failing to renew their subscriptions, leaving the branches and constituency associations in the hands of a relatively small number of activists. As in the uncannily parallel case of the Labour Party in the early 1980s, these tended to be more militant in their opinions than Conservative supporters as a whole – and on Europe (just like the Labour Party) this meant Euroscepticism.

Many of these Conservative activists of the 1990s saw themselves as successful revolutionaries. The leader of that revolution had been Margaret Thatcher; and there was an ideology to defend: Thatcherism. From an historical perspective, this was a thoroughly un-Conservative approach. But it goes some way towards explaining the response of those Conservative associations asked to restrain their Eurosceptic MPs: "What is right for Margaret Thatcher is right for our Member".[32]

There is, however, counter-evidence that, at least at this time, Euroscepticism was not yet the prevalent view among the members of Conservative constituency associations. In late 1993 Party members were consulted on preparations for the European Elections of 1994 through the CPC Discussion Programme.[33] The 400 or so groups which reported were overwhelmingly positive about the Community, calling on the Party to give more emphasis to the benefits of membership. The overall message at the election should be positive: as one group (Surbiton) remarked, "we must avoid giving the impression, which was conveyed in 1989, that we have nothing constructive to say about the Community's future – there must be no repeat of 'Brussels Sprouts'".

The groups were keen to emphasise a distinctive Conservative vision of the Community's future, "free-trading, decentralising and deregulating", and based on states "which retain their own individuality". John Major's success in "forcing through the principle of subsidiarity" was applauded (though some groups thought a better word might be found). As far as "regulations from Brussels" were concerned, these should be kept to a minimum; but as important was to ensure that they would be "fairly and universally applied throughout the Community".

Unsurprisingly, there was virtually unanimous support for enlargement of the Community. Some groups emphasised the role this would play in strengthening democracy; others that it might slow down any move to "political and economic union". Quite a few groups advocated giving preference to countries which would be net contributors to the Community Budget. Only a very small minority were in favour of "consolidating" the existing Community before admitting new Member States.

There was no opposition to the increase in the European Parliament's powers embodied in the Maastricht Treaty: the main conclusion of the groups was that this increased the importance of electing Conservative MEPs. The groups also supported Conservative participation in the European People's Party Group "to counterbalance the effects of Socialism". There was an almost 50:50 split, however, on further increases in the Parliament's legislative powers.

On closer cooperation in a Common Foreign and Security Policy (CFSP) the groups were divided: "in theory yes, but in practice no" (Chipping Barnet) summed up the central view. The Bosnian conflict had provided justification for this position: it was "a good example both of why Europe should, eventually, have a European CFSP and why it is impracticable … in the short to medium term". (Bexhill and Battle).

There was no disagreement on the Exchange Rate Mechanism: any pledge to re-join would be "equivalent to a suicide note" (Esher). There was, however, considerable support for a Single Currency, though this was to be achieved through the "Major (i.e. "hard ecu") Plan" rather than through that of Delors. Other groups, though, thought even the Major Plan would be "monetary union by the back door, so the answer is 'no'". (Birkenhead).

Some of the most interesting replies, in view of later events, dealt with reform of the Community's institutions. Groups were generally in favour of reforming the voting system in the Council of Ministers so as to improve the position of larger countries, and of reducing the number of Commissioners below one-per-country. Both reforms, of course, were later incorporated in the Lisbon Treaty.

Several questions arise. How far did the CPC discussion groups reflect the views of Conservative Party activists in general? Were the Maastricht rebels leading or following their Conservative associations? Did Margaret Thatcher's own disillusionment with the Community, as signalled in the Bruges speech, generate Euroscepticism in the Party; or was she reflecting a change that was taking place anyway? Was there, as many academics were soon asserting,[34] a major "ideological fault line" within the Party over Europe? Or was the split not really about Europe at all: perhaps it arose, instead, from a desire on the part of those inclined to One Nation Toryism to remove Thatcher, and of Thatcher loyalists to avenge that removal?

And finally, following the Party's defeat in the General Election of 1997, did Euroscepticism become Conservative orthodoxy because Conservatives were genuinely converted to that position? Or was it because Euroscepticism is the default position for all British Oppositions?

These are questions which will be addressed more fully in Chapter Sixteen.

Notes

1 *Britain at the Heart of Europe* (Conservative Research Department, February 1992).

2 Hurd, *op.cit*. pp. 460–1.

3 *The Campaign Guide 1992: Centenary Edition* (Conservative Research Department, March 1992). The first Campaign Guide, "An Election Handbook for Unionist Speakers", was published in 1892.

4 *The Conservative Party from Thatcher to Cameron* by Tim Bale (Polity Press, 2010).

5 Major *op.cit*. p. 288.

6 *A democratic way to European Unity: arguments against Federalism* by William Cash MP (Bow Group, June 1990).

7 *Federalism, Integration, Sovereignty, Union and all that* by Sir Christopher Prout QC, MEP (Conservatives in the European Parliament, May 1990).

8 Hugo Young *op.cit*. p. 375: Chapter 10, *William Cash: Europe Made Me*.

9 Major *op.cit*. p. 291.

10 Hugo Young *op.cit*. p. 435.

11 *The Best Future for Britain: the 1992 Conservative Party manifesto* (Conservative Central Office, April 1992).

12 "Salisbury" by Sir Geoffrey Butler in *The Tory Tradition* (Conservative Political Centre, 1957).

13 Hugo Young *op.cit*. p. 438.

14 *In Office* by Norman Lamont (Little Brown and Company, 1999).

15 *Second Annual Report of the Committee of Governors of the Central Banks of the European Community Member States* (April 1993).

16 *Lessons to be learned from the disturbances on the foreign exchange markets* (The Monetary Committee of the European Community C3-0170/93).

17 *Report on the second Annual Report 1992 on the activities of the Committee of Governors and on the monetary and financial conditions in the Community*. Rapporteur Mr.Ben Patterson (Committee on Economic and Monetary Affairs and Industrial Policy, Subcommittee on Monetary Affairs, European Parliament, A3-0213/93, 30 June 1993).

18 Major *op.cit*. p. 327.

19 Lamont *op.cit*. p. 223.

20 "Intervention and the exchange rate" in *Freedom and Reality* by Enoch Powell (Elliot Right Way Books, 1969).

21 *The Economist*, 25th September 1993.

22 See "A Theory of Optimum Currency Areas" by Professor R. Mundell in *American Economic Review*, 1961.

23 Major *op. cit*. p. 371 and p. 522.

24 Wall *op.cit*. p. 153.

25 Speech in January 1996.

26 Hugo Young *op.cit*. p. 387.

27 Heath *The Course of My Life* p. 715.

28 *Time for a Fresh Start in Europe* by Daniel Hannan (Bow Group 1993).

29 Butler and Pinto-Duschinsky *op.cit*. p. 279.

30 Speech to the National Conservative Convention in Birmingham on the 3rd. October 2010.

31 *In Defence of Politics* by Bernard Crick (Penguin Books, 1962).

32 Major *op.cit.* p. 362.

33 *Preparing for the 1994 European Elections: Summary of reports* (Conservative Political Centre and Conservatives in the European Parliament Joint Discussion Programme, September/ November 1993).

34 For example, D. Kavanagh: *The Reordering of British Politics* (OUP 1997), John Barnes: 'Ideology and Factions' in *Conservative Century: The Conservative Party Since 1990* (OUP, 1994), D. Baker, A. Gamble and S. Ludlum: 'The Parliamentary Siege of Maastricht 1993: Conservative Divisions and British Ratification of the Treaty on European Union' in *Parliamentary Affairs*, 1994; A. Aughey: 'Philosophy and Faction' in *The Conservative Party* (Prentice Hall 1996); all quoted by Turner, *op. cit.*

12 Into the Cold

"Europe: Right or Left?"

The Conservative Party still fought the 1994 European Parliament election on a platform of keeping "Britain at the heart of Europe". In May 1993 the CPC published a pamphlet by John Major with that title,[1] based on a speech to a Conservative Group for Europe dinner celebrating the twentieth anniversary of UK accession to the Community. This was the speech which ended with the quotation from George Orwell about "old maids bicycling to Holy Communion through the morning mist", much ridiculed subsequently by those with a poor knowledge of English literature.

The speech also responded to a number of criticisms of the Community which were becoming received wisdom within the Party. Douglas Hurd, the Foreign Secretary, had already spoken of European legislation intruding into the "nooks and crannies of everyday life";[2] and "where this is so," Major commented, "we must correct it, … but some intrusion is necessary and is in our interests. For example, if we are to make the Single Market work, there has to be some body of common law." As for the Maastricht Treaty, it had become the "scapegoat for the varied and nameless fears about Europe, most of them wholly unrelated to the Treaty". He related how, at a Conservative constituency dinner, the speaker had asked what objections there were to Maastricht. Thirty-five different points had been raised, thirty-three of which were not related to Maastricht at all, but dated back to the Single European Act or even the Rome Treaty.

Yet in making this point Major unconsciously revealed how dangerous the situation was becoming. Euroscepticism had already taken so firm a grip among many Conservatives that they were questioning not only Margaret Thatcher's main achievement in the Community, the SEA, but the foundations of Community membership itself. The positive message spelled out by Prime Minister was being overwhelmed by the "varied and nameless fears".

The Conservative manifesto for the European Elections of 1994,[3] while still strongly positive about British Community membership, also made an effort to allay these fears. The Introduction by the Prime Minister promised to "fight for the kind of Europe we want: not a European superstate, but a Europe of nation states, working together. ... We want less interference from "Brussels" – not more." There was a pledge not to re-enter the Exchange Rate Mechanism "in the foreseeable future". The strategy was, if possible, to fight the campaign on traditional lines, attacking the unpopular aspects of the Community as the result of having had a "Socialist Parliament" since 1989: "You will not be voting for Europe: Right or Wrong? You will be voting for Europe: Right or Left?"

As in 1989, I spent part of the election campaign at Conservative Central Office on the Questions of Policy Committee; and, once again, there were few problems in dealing with the points referred to us from the constituencies. Yet both at Central Office and in my constituency of Kent West – which had now become marginal as a result of boundary changes – it soon became obvious that the main problem would be persuading Conservative supporters to vote. Those Conservative pro-Europeans who had been alarmed by the 1989 campaign had become even more disillusioned by the activities of the Eurosceptics, and were disinclined to make much effort. Large numbers of Conservatives appeared reluctant to vote for reasons which were analysed by the Conservative leader in the Parliament, Sir Christopher Prout (later Lord Kingsland), in a lecture to the European Union of Women in June 1993.[4]

> Some take the view that the Parliament is of such inconsequence as to be unworthy of a visit to the polling-booth. To them it is not a 'real Parliament'. ... Others, by contrast, see it as a component part of a powerful network of foreign institutions which threaten Britain's sovereignty or identity or interests ... and that, in these circumstances, the most appropriate reaction of loyal Conservatives is to ignore the European Elections in the hope that the Parliament will go away; or, in any case, confer no democratic legitimacy on it by their votes. There are even ... some Conservatives who are capable of holding both these views of the European Parliament at the same time!

To this reluctance to vote was added the disturbing factor, already mentioned, of defections to the United Kingdom Independence Party. This was a foretaste of the much more damaging situation for the Party that would arise once UKIP could benefit from a switch of the election system to Proportional Representation in the European Elections of 1999.

The Conservative Party was, on the whole, better prepared for the election than in 1989, with a massive 771-page Campaign Guide[5] already published in anticipation of a possible British general election. This was supplemented by a loose-leafed Handbook containing regular updates from the Questions of Policy Committee.[6] There was also considerable input from the constituencies through the CPC discussion groups, outlined in the previous chapter.

These documents, however, reveal that the Party had faced a dilemma in deciding on its core election message. Though "Europe: right or left?" was eventually chosen – often firmed up, in reflection of the Bruges speech, as "Don't let Socialism in by the back door!" – there was obvious disquiet that this would appear negative. A (confidential) campaign strategy paper echoed many of the CPC groups in warning against a repeat of the 1989 mistakes. It was "important to present clear, positive reasons for electing Conservatives to the European Parliament. Any campaign which simply attacks our opponents will not engage public interest or enthusiasm."

Conservative candidates found themselves facing another problem. At both open and Party meetings, we found ourselves having to spend time defending the activities of the Community, not only of the Parliament itself, but also of the Commission. This left us wide open to the charge of being more interested in representing "Brussels in Britain than Britain in Brussels". Yet it was difficult to resist making an effort at correcting the misconceptions that were by then virtually the only news about "Europe" getting into the press. It was one of the penalties of having spent fifteen years within the system.

In the event, none of the extensive pre-election preparations made by the Conservative Party prevented it from suffering a massive defeat. The Labour Party was also well prepared, with funding at least equal to that of the Conservatives. Its manifesto was impressively glossy, and began with a strong positive message on Europe, rather than the former concentration on domestic politics.

> The elections to the European Parliament on June 9th are a vital opportunity for the British people to shape the future of Europe. We want to build a Europe of freedom and social justice, a Europe which is open and accountable to all our citizens. … And we want to strengthen Europe by building a strong community and not just a free market – responding to our people's desire for secure employment, for a clean environment, and for a safe and prosperous future for their children.[7]

The Conservative Party's share of the British poll, which had been over 50% in 1979, fell to only 28%, while that of Labour rose to 44% and that of the Liberal Democrats to 17%. Only 18 Conservative MEPs were elected, compared to 62 Labour Members. The Scottish National Party increased their strength to 2, while the Liberal Democrats entered the Parliament for the first time, also with 2 seats.

In Kent West I had expected to hold on despite the boundary changes and the evidence of opinion polls – as candidates do. Using the then modern technology of a computer data-base and mail-merge, the campaign team sent out many hundreds of letters to constituents with whom I had been in contact over the years. There was no shortage of leaflets and other *matériel*. But campaigning was only intermittently the exhilarating experience of previous elections. Party workers were fewer on the ground, and mostly there through a sense of duty rather because of any real enthusiasm. My experienced agent, Anne Moloney, did her best to mobilise the Party throughout the Euro-constituency, but with a success that varied significantly between Westminster constituencies. This was reflected in wide variations in eventual turnout.

On polling day, touring the committee rooms, I soon knew that I had lost; and this was confirmed on Sunday night when the result from Kent East, theoretically a safer seat than mine, came through: Christopher Jackson had narrowly lost to the Labour candidate, Mark Watts. My own count was not due until the Monday; and overnight there was always hope. But my Labour opponent Peter Skinner was of course then declared the winner by a comfortable margin of over 16,700 votes. The Kent West Conservative, Labour and Liberal Democrat shares of the poll were not much out of line with the national figures.

David Butler and Martin Westlake, in their study of the European Elections of 1994,[8] suggest that I might have been one of four sitting Conservative MEPs to have fallen victim to the "spoiling votes of anti-Maastricht candidates". Unlike Kent East, where Mark Watt's majority over Jackson was a mere 635, but where the United Kingdom Independence Party polled 9,414, the Kent West UKIP vote was some 7,000 short of Skinner's majority. But taking into account the likelihood of increased Conservative abstentions Butler and Westlake may well have been right.

In retrospect – and particularly in the light of the even greater defeat of 1997 – the 1994 results had little to do with Europe itself, except in the sense that the Exchange Rate Mechanism *débâcle* and divisions on Maastricht had contributed to a general fall in the Party's standing. Public opinion seemed to match Conservative views on Europe much more closely than those of Labour or the Liberal Democrats, with 40% seeing Europe as a threat, 71% against granting more powers to the European Parliament, 56% against adopting the Single Currency and 68% opposed to a "federal Europe". However, the polls also revealed that Europe – and certainly the complexities of EU institutions – ranked a long way down on the list of issues which concerned people. While the Party tried to fight on genuinely European issues, the electorate was concerned overwhelmingly with domestic politics.

Soon afterwards, under the leadership of Tony Blair, "New Labour" was skilfully exploiting the weaknesses in the Government's position, including the succession of essentially trivial scandals that came to be known as "Tory sleaze". Even had we been able to put over to voters a clear, positive, consistent message, based on our performance in the European Parliament, it is doubtful whether the election result would have been very much different.

This was no consolation, however, to those dozen or so MEPs who had been pioneers in the first elected European Parliament in 1979; who had taken a leading part in making that Parliament more effective; who had blazed the trail for the Single Market; and who had now lost their seats – through no fault, they felt, of their own. The Prime Minister wrote me a personal letter observing that "if there were any justice, you would

Winston Churchill called for "a
United States of Europe".

But his successor, Anthony Eden, found
European integration a bit of a bore.

Harold Macmillan applied to
join the Common Market.

But President de Gaulle wanted
"*L'Europe à l'anglais sans les anglais*".

Enoch Powell. His objective: "destroying British membership of the EEC".

Geoffey Rippon: Monday Club pro-European who negotiated British accession to the EC.

Sir Alec Douglas-Home: was Europe "a dead duck"?

After accession: Peter Kirk (Parliament), Christopher Soames (Commission) and John Davies (Council).

Pro-Europeans in waiting: John Selwyn Gummer and Leon Brittan while at Cambridge University, 1960.

Edward Heath. Didn't hide the consequences of joining the European Community.

Conservative MEPs in the first directly elected European Parliament, meeting in Strasbourg, 1979.

Geoffrey Howe: Bow Group generation

Arthur Cockfield: the man behind the Single Market.

Margaret Thatcher: for "active cooperation" between independent sovereign states.

John Major: putting Britain "at the heart of Europe".

Christopher Prout: defined "federalism".

Michael Howard: for Europe *à la carte*.

Norman Lamont: disillusioned with subsidiarity.

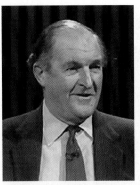

Henry Plumb: first British European Parliament President.

Michael Heseltine: resigned over Westland and challenged Thatcher

Ken Clarke: pro-Europe views cost him the leadership.

Norman Tebbit: opposed to "crazy Socialist schemes".

Bill Cash: "a terrible awakening".

Douglas Hurd: no interference in the "nooks and crannies of everyday life".

Chris Patten: Party
Chairman. A Conservative
Christian Democrat?

Peter Walker: founder
of Anti-Common
Market League.

Malcolm Rifkind: argued
for Single European Act.

Jacques Delors: Christian
Socialist President of
the Commission.

Iain Duncan Smith:
ex-leader who founded
Centre for Social Justice.

Valéry Giscard d'Estaing:
chaired Convention on
the Future of Europe.

William Hague: the "Thatcher's
Children"generation.

David Cameron, Prime Minister, with Timothy
Kirkhope, then leader of Conservative MEPs.

BRITAIN
BRITAIN
BRITAIN
N
T
EUROPE
EUROPE
EUROPE

a BOW GROUP pamphlet

A BOW GROUP PAMPHLET

NO TAME
OR MINOR
ROLE

Two shillings and sixpence

ONE
EUR
OPE

by the One Nation Group of MPs

Britain's place in the world

a
smaller
stage

a Bow Group pamphlet

FOUR SHILLINGS

the
new
EUROPE

Rt. Hon. EDWARD HEATH
Dr HANS VON
EMILE NOËL
WILLIAM CLARK
RICHARD BAILEY

Conservative Political Centre

EUROPE
SHOULD
BRITAIN
JOIN?

Price 2/6

A
EUROPE
OF
NATIONS

a practical policy for Britain

THE
MONDAY
CLUB

HERE
TO
STAY

Britain's
role in the
European
Community

Lord Carrington
Poul Møller
Christopher Tugendhat
Sir Fred Catherwood
David Curry
Adam Fergusson

Foreword by
Margaret Thatcher

OUR FUTURE
IN EUROPE

Rt Hon Geoffrey Rippon

Conservative Political Centre

George Gardiner

A EUROPE
FOR THE
REGIONS

CONSERVATIVE POLITICAL CENTRE
10p

John Biffen

A NATION
IN DOUBT

Conservative Political Centre: 30p

EUROPE
RIGHT
AHEAD

by a group of Conservative MPs

Conservative Political Centre: 85p

European Conservative Group

OUR
EUROPEAN
FUTURE

Speeches on Europe by
The Rt Hon GEOFFREY RIPPON, QC MP

BRITAIN AT
THE HEART OF
EUROPE

POLITICS TODAY
No. 3   7th February 1992   £1.90
CONSERVATIVE RESEARCH DEPARTMENT

P677   £5.00

A DEMOCRATIC WAY
TO EUROPEAN UNITY:
Arguments against
Federalism

William Cash MP

THE BOW GROUP

PEST
PRESSURE FOR ECONOMIC AND SOCIAL TORYISM

Towards a
European Identity

Published by PEST   35p

BRITAIN'S NEW DEAL IN EUROPE

'Her Majesty's Government have decided to recommend to the British people to vote for staying in the Community'

HAROLD WILSON, PRIME MINISTER

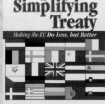

A Simplifying Treaty

Making the EU Do Less, but Better

by Timothy Kirkhope MEP
with a foreword by Rt. Hon. William Hague MP

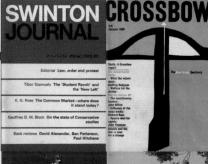

SWINTON JOURNAL

Price 3s 6d   Winter 1968/69

Editorial Law, order and protest

Tibor Szamuely The 'Student Revolt' and the 'New Left'

K. G. Ross The Common Market—where does it stand today?

Geoffrey D. M. Block On the state of Conservative studies

Book reviews David Alexander, Ben Patterson, Paul Hitchens

CROSSBOW

free trade and the euro

Conservative Group for Europe / Tory Europe Association

monday world

Conservative Europe

The 2003 Party Conference Magazine of The Conservative Group for Europe

Featuring...
Foreword
Rt. Hon. David Curry MP
Rt. Hon. Lord Heseltine of Thenford CH CBE
Europe and the Superpower
Damian Green MP
The International Baccalaureate -
An option not a replacement for A Levels
David Eddington MP
British farming getting a fair deal
in the global marketplace
Sir Ben Gill
European Enlargement and
Globalisation: What future for the CAP

TOWARDS A COMMUNITY RURAL POLICY

Jim Scott-Hopkins
John Corrie

EUROPEAN CONSERVATIVE GROUP

Diana Elles   10p

The housewife and the Common Market

CONSERVATIVE POLITICAL CENTRE

Tufton Beamish & Norman St John-Stevas

Sovereignty: substance or shadow

CONSERVATIVE POLITICAL CENTRE 8v

Direct Elections to the European Assembly

Presented to Parliament
by the Secretary of State for Foreign and Commonwealth Affairs
and
the Secretary of State for the Home Department
by Command of Her Majesty
February 1976

LONDON
HER MAJESTY'S STATIONERY OFFICE

IEA
Rome or Brussels . . . ?
W R LEWIS
Hobart Paperback

75p

CPC
new tasks
new techniques

A European Technological Community

by Sir Anthony Meyer, BT

TRADE equals JOBS

The case for a common trade policy for the EEC

by MICHAEL WELSH

Conservative MEPs

Britain's Waste:
the lessons we can learn from Europe

by Caroline Jackson MEP

Conservatives in the European Parliament

AUGUST 1969   2/6

crossbow

THE BOW GROUP QUARTERLY

What We Should Do About Enoch

The author at Speakers' corner, 1967; and demolishing the Berlin Wall, 1990.

Swinton Conservative College in Yorkshire, now no more, where the author was a tutor in the 1960s.

Prime Minister Thatcher meeting Conservative MEPs in Downing Street.

certainly have held the seat", and that "politics can at times be a cruel business" – a truth he himself was soon to experience fully.

The only satisfactory response, I remember thinking at the time, was to recall the words of the former Labour Foreign Secretary, George Brown, when he lost his Belper seat in the General Election of 1970: "That's how democracy democs!".

Luxembourg, CJD and BSE

One of the last important acts of the European Parliament before the elections had been to vote on whether Austria, Finland and Sweden should be admitted as Community Member States. This was carried out using the "assent" procedure under which not just a majority of those voting, but a majority of all MEPs, whether present or not, is required. There was a last-minute panic that Sweden would not be approved as a result of the country's tradition of neutrality; and massive pressure was applied by the British Government to support its key policy of EU enlargement. As far as the Party was concerned, it was also forecast that the arrival of the Swedish MEPs would strengthen the specifically Conservative presence in the Parliament. There need have been no worries. All three applicant states were approved by comfortable margins.

Following the elections, the old Parliament continued with committee work until mid-July, when the newly-elected Members took over. Even afterwards, when no longer a Member, I found myself having to present a report to the EMAC committee on the new Commission's proposals in the field of excise duties.

By this time, however, I had formally made the transition from sitting on the dais at the front chairing the Committee* at its previous meeting, to sitting on the staff benches at the back as the Committee's research officer. By the time I retired in 2004 I had attended virtually every meeting of the Committee, in one capacity or another, for well over twenty years. At the time I remember being very happy to make the transition: having a paid job to go back to after fifteen years' absence was a luxury few defeated MEPs enjoyed.

There were, however, some consolation-prizes to temper the wind. Those Members who had served continuously since the first European Elections of 1979 found that they had a right to the title "Honorary Members of the Europe Parliament", with passes to prove it. This soon created problems in some UK constituencies, with the real MEPs complaining that those styling themselves "Hon. MEPs" were creating confusion, the "Hon." even implying some kind of superiority. It did not help that the "Hons" were, on the whole, from the strongly pro-Europe wing of the Conservative

---

* I was actually a Vice-chairman; but the chairman, the Dutch Christian Democrat Bouke Beumer, was away for some months for personal reasons, and was in any case standing down at the election.

Party, the real MEPs more Eurosceptic. The Parliament soon dropped the practice.

Constituency work, too, tailed off rather than came to an abrupt halt. Over a year and a half later ex-constituents' letters were still arriving at my home in Kent. Some were even addressed to my successor, Peter Skinner – and, as I remarked to the Medway Conservative Association Annual Dinner in March 1996, the oddest thing was that several of these were from the Home Office!

Rejoining the Parliament's staff, however, meant working in Luxembourg. This involved commuting in the reverse direction to meetings in the UK, but made getting to Brussels and Strasbourg much easier. From that point of view, being more or less half way between the two is a good place for the Parliament's secretariat to be located. After Luxembourg plenary sessions of the Parliament were ended in the early 1980s, however, very few actual MEPs went there; and after the opening of the new European Parliament buildings in Brussels in the mid-1990s pressure mounted for most officials to be relocated there. Today, although Parliament's secretariat is still officially based in Luxembourg, the bulk of the personnel there are translators.

In Luxembourg, I found, the Conservative Party had a small but active branch of "Conservatives Abroad", among whose members there was not a trace of Euroscepticism. Some years later the Conservative MEP, Lord Inglewood, addressed a dinner of the branch, and wrote afterwards that "it was all rather reminiscent of the vanished Conservative era of twenty years ago with decent and civilized people without dogma trying to see the way forwards. How things have changed … !"[9]

In the UK itself, support for the Conservative Party had continued to fall. On the 9th June 1995, the anniversary of defeat in the European Elections, I spoke to one of the last meetings of the Kent West Conservative Euro-Council and began by remarking that "we should be grateful for the small mercy that the election was not today: the Gallup Poll in the Daily Telegraph is showing Labour on 59.5% and the Conservative Party on only 20%". The Party's problem was obvious: 85% of the electorate thought it "disunited", as opposed to only 28% in the case of the Labour Party. To blame, of course, were the open and vituperative disagreements on Europe, with Prime Minister Major under open attack from his own backbenchers. The then leader of the Opposition, Tony Blair, records how he had "learned how to play him and his party off against each other".[10]

As the popularity of the Conservative Party declined, so did that of the European Community within it; and both trends were strengthened by yet another misfortune for the Government: the spread of BSE (Bovine Spongiform Encephalopathy) among British livestock. This would lead, week after week, to despairing farmers appearing on television as their cattle were slaughtered and incinerated. In Europe it would lead to the UK threatening a systematic use of its veto on all EU decisions which required unanimity, with the Home Secretary, Michael Howard, finding himself having to veto a proposal which had been a British initiative in the first place.

Whether or not there really was a link between BSE and the human brain disease CJD (Creutzfeldt-Jakob Disease) is still not entirely clear. Until the crisis broke in March 1996, the scientific advice to the British Government was that no link existed. Then the Advisory Committee set up to examine the matter reported that a possible, though unproven, risk might exist. When this was reported to the House of Commons, the EU's Standing Veterinary Committee immediately imposed a complete ban on all exports of British beef and beef products, a ban that would remain in place for years despite the eventual massive cull of British herds.

Major's own view was that the EU's action was "hysterical" and "disproportionate". It would, he correctly forecast, "further inflame British opinion against the European Union".

> There was outrage in the Conservative Party, not just among the Eurosceptics but among pro-Europeans, who until this point had supported our approach of a targeted culling of cattle and of trying to negotiate an end to the ban.[11]

Yet putting faith in governmental assurances that "British beef was safe" – even with the Agriculture Minister, John Selwyn Gummer, feeding his infant daughter a hamburger on television – was surely unrealistic. When the possible BSE/CJD link was first announced, beef consumption in the UK itself fell by 90%, and only recovered slowly. Ordinary people on the other side of the Channel, whose opinions I experienced at first hand, were genuinely angry and appalled on reading reports that the original cause of the outbreak had been cattle-feed made from the carcasses of sheep which had suffered from another brain disease in animals, scrapie. Though there was certainly an element of protectionism, the EU authorities were essentially reacting to the demands of their consumers.

Within the Conservative Party, as Major recalls, "the frustration over the ban became enmeshed in the hostility to European policy as a whole". When he announced the retaliatory policy of using the veto he found it greeted "less as a tactic to force our partners to give priority to the scientific evidence over beef – and hence to agree how to lift the ban – than as a declaration of war on Europe".[12]

Moreover, unlike the row over Maastricht, which had been an issue largely of interest to MPs at Westminster, the BSE crisis was experienced throughout the country, and in particular in rural areas where Conservative support was strong. Euroscepticism became even more entrenched in constituency parties; and one body of opinion which had traditionally been favourable to the EU, the farming industry, became markedly more hostile.

A "vote-free recovery"

Despite the record of splits and dissension since Major's victory in 1992, the policies for Europe on which the Conservative Party fought the General Election of 1997 should have been very attractive to voters. Two neat phases contained in the manifesto[13] were fully in accord with public opinion. "We want to be in Europe but not run by Europe;" and "we also believe the European Union itself should do less, but do it better".

The manifesto placed heavy emphasis on support for "the nation".*

> We believe that in an uncertain, competitive world, the nation state is a rock of security. A nation's common heritage, culture, values and outlook are a precious source of stability. Nationhood gives people a sense of belonging. The government has a positive vision for the European Union as a partnership of nations.
>
> A Conservative Government will seek a partnership of nation states. … The diversity of Europe's nations is its strength. … We will seek more cooperation between national governments on areas of common interest. … We will … prevent policies that would be harmful to the national interest. We will defend the rights of national parliaments and oppose more powers being given to the European Parliament at the expense of national parliaments.

There were specific pledges to retain the veto; to keep the UK's frontier controls; to preserve the inter-governmental nature of cooperation in justice and home affairs; to oppose extending the concept of European citizenship; not to sign the Social Chapter; and, finally – a pledge which actually spooked the Labour Party into making a similar commitment – not to adopt the euro without a prior referendum.

The manifesto also led boldly on what might earlier have been thought a weak point in the Government's record: the economy. A large cross-head at the start of the text proclaimed Britain "The Enterprise Centre of Europe".

- The UK is on course to grow faster than both France and Germany for the sixth successive year in 1998 - a post-war record.
- Inflation has now been below 4% for well over 4 years, the longest period of low inflation for almost half a century.
- Mortgage rates are at their lowest levels for 30 years.

---

* Some of the wording – for example, the paragraph that follows – is even reminiscent of Disraeli's definition of Conservatives as the "national party" (though he meant the phrase to mean a lot more than mere nationalism). "Now, a nation is a work of art and a work of time," he wrote in one of his Runnymede letters to *The Times*. "A nation is gradually created by a variety of influences – the influence of original organisation, of climate, soil, religion, laws, customs, manners, extraordinary accidents and incidents in their history and the individual character of their illustrious citizens. These influences create the nation; these form the national mind. … "

- Unemployment has fallen to its lowest level for 6 years. We now have a lower unemployment rate than any other major European economy. Youth unemployment in Britain has fallen to less than 15% whereas by contrast, in France it has risen to 27% and in Italy to 33%.
- A higher proportion of our people are in work than in any other major European economy – 68% against a Continental average of 57% …

… and so on.

All this was true. From 1993 onwards the British economy had begun to recover, aided by – but only partially because of – the dip in the external parity of the pound sterling. John Major, in his memoirs, argues convincingly that the discipline of Exchange Rate Mechanism membership had lastingly reduced inflationary expectations, with the result that Sterling devaluation boosted exports without stimulating wage-inflation. A "benevolent legacy was passed on to New Labour in May 1997", including a "sparkling economy".

This legacy also comprised much more than favourable statistics. During the Chancellorships of Norman Lamont and Ken Clarke, most of the systems of macro-economic management for which their Labour successor, Gordon Brown, took the credit had already been put in place: inflation-targeting and near-independence for the Bank of England (with hindsight, the arrangement introduced by Clarke – the so-called "Ken and Eddie show"[*] – was a better one than that of Brown, though both Lamont and Clarke did favour full Bank independence). "We should have been popular", Major comments.

How was it, then, that the economic recovery was – as Major puts it – "vote-free"?

One explanation, which he offers, is that the down-side of low wage-inflation was the lack of a "feel-good factor" from rising incomes. Divisions over Europe had also spilled over into economic management, notably when, during the passage of the Finance Bill of 1994, there was a rebellion by eight Conservative MPs over the issue of the UK's contribution to the EU budget. The Party whip was withdrawn from the eight,[†] who became Eurosceptic heroes – the "whipless nine" – when Richard Body joined them in solidarity. There followed an even more damaging rebellion when the Government was forced into a u-turn on the imposition of VAT on fuel and power.

In addition, Norman Lamont's contribution to recovery was undermined both by memories of "Black Wednesday" and a combination of unfortunate remarks ("singing in the bath", "green shoots of economic spring",[‡] "*je ne regrette rien*") and vicious treatment in the press. The manner

---

[*] Eddie George was Governor of the Bank of England at the time.

[†] Nick Budgen, Michael Carttiss, Christopher Gill, Teresa Gorman, Tony Marlow, Richard Shepherd, Teddy Taylor and John Wilkinson.

[‡] In fact, when the definitive figures for 1992 became available, it turned out that Lamont was right.

of his going and his accusation in the Commons that the Government was "in office but not in power" did not help either. Ken Clarke's reputation as Chancellor has risen steadily in the years that have followed, but his support for adopting the euro created tensions within the Party at the time, and have since cost him the Party leadership three times.

Moreover – and despite a persistent belief at this and at subsequent elections that Euroscepticism was a vote-winner – the manifesto commitments on Europe did little to affect the result. The polls were showing, it is true, an apparent match between Conservative and public views on the EU; but they also showed Conservative and Labour virtually level-pegging on who had "the best policies for Europe". As before, this was an issue of far less importance to the ordinary voter than to Conservative activists. Indeed, it did not dawn on the Party leadership until two election defeats later that "banging on about Europe"* was actually a vote-loser.

In the case of the General Election of 1997, well-reported Conservative splits on Europe were certainly a vote-loser. In 1996 a rumour that the Party was to change policy on the euro, and rule out adopting it for the duration of the next parliament, had produced a furious public denial that this was the case from the Chancellor, Ken Clarke. But at the election a significant number of candidates supported the supposed new policy – or went even further in ruling out the euro for ever – in their election addresses. No doubt some were influenced by the offer of Paul Sykes, a Eurosceptic millionaire, to provide money where a prospective candidate had declared against the euro. John Major's account of the election recounts how he went to bed "spitting with anger" at the defections from Party policy, and his frantic efforts to keep the Party together. In fact, breaking with official policy did the defectors no good: the swing against anti-euro Conservatives was no less than against the rest.

A further explanation for the failure of Conservative policy on Europe to make an impact is advanced by Stephen Wall. At the May 1997 election, he observes, "what is interesting is the similarity, rather than the differences, between the manifestos of both parties. ... Both talked about avoiding a federal Europe, of a partnership of nations, of focusing on enlargement, CAP reform, the single market, and foreign policy".[14] Even on the euro the manifestos said roughly the same. Only on the Social Chapter, where the Conservative position was not especially popular, did policies differ much.

Europe did, however, affect the election result in a different way. It is one of the paradoxes of politics – encapsulated in a famous remark by Winston Churchill – that one's most dangerous enemies are often those closest to you. For the Conservative Party, a credible party standing on its right is a significant threat, just as a credible alternative party on the left is a threat to Labour. A party even more Eurosceptic than the Conservatives had already done some damage in the European Elections of 1994. In 1997

---

* A phrase attributed to the Labour strategist, MP and Minister, then European Commissioner, and later a Lord and – briefly – a Minister again: Peter Mandelson.

James Goldsmith's Referendum Party, well-funded, threatened to do the same. Among its candidates were the former Conservative Party Treasurer and leading figure in the "Yes" campaign of 1975, Alistair McAlpine and the once strongly pro-Common Market MP for Reigate, George Gardiner.

In the event, the Referendum Party did badly, most of their candidates losing their deposits. As I had myself discovered in 1994, however, the damaging effect of such parties goes beyond the number of potential Conservatives who actually vote for them. Defection by even a very small number of Party workers can be harmful. Voters who would normally vote Conservative, but sympathise with the more extreme position, can compromise by not voting at all. And at the General Election of 1997 even the threat of the Referendum Party attracting votes clearly influenced the position on Europe adopted by many Conservative candidates. It is plausible, indeed, that the real purpose of Goldsmith's intervention – aided by much of the right-wing press – was not so much to win votes or seats, but to stampede the Conservative Party into moving even further in a Eurosceptic direction. In that he succeeded.

The result of the General Election of 1997 was a devastating defeat. Labour won 419 seats to the Conservatives' 165, with the Liberal Democrats winning 46 and "others" 29. The Conservative share of the vote was only 31%. It was worse than the General Election of 1945, when the Party won 210 seats with nearly 40% of the vote; and even worse than the General Election of 1906 when the Party won only 156 seats to the Liberal Party's 397, but still with 43% of the vote.

It might have been thought that electoral defeat on this scale would have caused the Party to think twice before perpetuating discord on Europe. Major records that, if anything, the opposite was the case. He quotes the former Defence Secretary, Michael Portillo, who had been dramatically shown on television losing his Enfield seat, so giving rise to the symbolic concept of a "Portillo moment". Why, Portillo had asked, had the distinctive right-of-centre Margaret Thatcher "won three spanking election victories in succession", whereas, when led by the middle-of-the-road Major, Clarke, Hurd and Heseltine, "the party was smashed to pieces".[15]

As far as the European issue was concerned, Major comments, "this analysis does not survive examination": of the winning parties Labour had "proclaimed its enthusiasm for Europe" and the Liberal Democrats were "unquestionably committed to a federalist destination". He also rails against a "pernicious" and "determined effort to rewrite history" on the Conservative right.

> Falsehood, distortion and a sort of paranoid inventiveness have contrived to present a picture in which the Eurosceptics are seen as men and women of untarnished honour, fighting to maintain a fixed and principled position against the aggression of a provocative gang of starry-eyed 'Europeanists', ever ready to cheat, whose 'federal' aims betrayed their own country.

Even allowing for some understandable bitterness, and even if half true, a situation described like this did not hold out great promise for rapid political recovery.

Notes

1 *Britain at the heart of Europe* by the Rt. Hon. John Major, M.P. (Conservative Political Centre, May 1993).

2 In Brussels in November 1991 (see his *Memoirs*, p. 459).

3 A *Strong Britain in a Strong Europe: The Conservative Manifesto for Europe 1994* (Conservative Central Office, 1994).

4 *The European Community and the 1994 European Elections* by Sir Christopher Prout QC MEP (Conservatives in the European Parliament, 4 June 1993).

5 *The Campaign Guide 1994* (Conservative Research Department, 1994).

6 *Handbook for Europe 1994* (Conservatives in the European Parliament and Conservative Research Department (May 1994 and after).

7 *Make Europe work for you: Labour's Election Manifesto for the European Elections, June 1994* (The Labour Party, 1994).

8 *British Politics and European Elections 1994* by David Butler and Martin Westlake (St. Martin's Press, 1995).

9 Letter to "Conservatives Abroad", Luxembourg branch.

10 *A Journey* by Tony Blair (Hutchinson, 2010) p. 2.

11 Major *op.cit.* p. 653.

12 Major *op.cit.* p. 654.

13 *1997 Conservative Party General Election Manifesto: You can only be sure with the Conservatives* (Conservative Central Office 1997).

14 Wall *op.cit.* p. 161.

15 Major *op.cit.* p. 697

13 No Longer the Party of Europe

The Party in opposition

The General Election of 1997 marks the point at which the Labour and Conservative Parties can be said to have definitively changed sides on Europe. New Labour, under the new Prime Minister, Tony Blair, became Britain's main "party of Europe". At the same time the Conservative Party became steadily more unsympathetic to the European Union and all its works.

Perhaps an even more precise timing of the change was the date in late June 1997 when William Hague succeeded John Major as leader of the Party. Major had been forced to make compromises on policy towards the EU in order to keep the parliamentary Party together; and this had led to charges from both Europhobes and Europhiles that he had behaved more like a chief whip than a leader. Hugo Young sums up his period in office as "a six-year exercise, painfully unsuccessful, in trying to persuade the Conservative Party that there was a middle way between the anti-Europe passions of its most vocal minority of politicians and the pro-European necessities that came with the task of government".[1] Butler and Westlake, in their account of the European Elections of 1994, quote Major's interview with the *Independent* in April 1994 in which he observed that he was neither a "Eurosceptic" nor a "Euro-enthusiast" but a "Euro-realist"; adding that "I think this is the position of most people in this country". But they add the comment that in seeking to alienate neither the pro-Europeans nor the Eurosceptics, "Mr. Major had alienated both and, in the eyes of his critics, his pragmatic search for support had laid him open to the charges of vacillation, opportunism and lack of leadership".[2]

Yet there *was* a credible middle way which Major might have been able to pursue successfully had circumstances been different. His own speeches, memoirs and actions show that he had a clear view of how the EU should develop, with Britain "at its heart", which was entirely in line with the policies of the Party since the 1960s, and of Mrs Thatcher herself until her final years in office.

William Hague became leader of the Party at the precocious age of 36. Politically, he was of a generation which has been popularly described as

"Thatcher's children" – when she became Party leader, he was in his mid-teens, just eligible to join the Young Conservatives. He was not old enough to have experienced the idealism which had motivated the pro-European Conservatives of the 1960s and early 1970. For his generation such enthusiasm had in any case become suspect.

Enthusiasm for Europe was indeed on its way to becoming a kiss of death within the Conservative Party – clearly, at this point, in the parliamentary party. The most obvious successor to Major (Michael Heseltine being ruled out as a result of ill-health) was Ken Clarke. He had been a minister of one kind or another during the whole eighteen years of Conservative Government between 1979 and 1997, twelve of them in the Cabinet. Despite being Chancellor of the Exchequer only during the turbulent closing period of the Major Government he had managed to build up a solid reputation for competent economic management. He was a great deal more popular with the electorate as a whole than any possible alternative.

Clarke, however, refused to bend his views to the Eurosceptic wind. This was the last Conservative leadership contest conducted on the basis of a vote in the parliamentary party only; and Clarke actually led on the first two ballots. In the final round, however, he formed a rather curious and unwise alliance with the strongly Eurosceptic John Redwood (who had actually stood against Prime Minister Major for the Party leadership in 1995), and was beaten by Hague, 92 votes to 70.

In view of the current widespread belief that the parliamentary party was only reflecting the growing Euroscepticism of Conservatives in general, it is interesting to compare the votes of MPs with those of constituency associations, Conservative peers and MEPs, all of which were formally consulted. In the constituency vote Clarke beat all the other original contenders put together – Hague, Redwood, Lilley and Howard – by a wide margin. Among the peers his total was over two-and-half times that of all the others together; and among the MEPs he secured a clean sweep. These figures suggest that Clarke's pro-European stance was not considered a block to his leadership by Conservatives in general, contrary to Turner's assertion that "a potential leader's position on Europe now transcended any wider competing ideological position".[3] Hague clearly recognised this by including in his team pro-Europeans like Sir Norman Fowler, Stephen Dorrell and former MEP David Curry.

I remember meeting William Hague, then a back-bencher, at one of the dinners organised by the Conservative MEP Michael Welsh to promote constructive dialogue between Conservatives at Strasbourg and Conservatives at Westminster. We on our side spoke eloquently about co-decision, subsidiarity, *Mitbestimmung*, the problems of the central Balkans and so on. Hague spoke little, but gave a distinct impression he thought we were living on a different planet. By that time even Conservative MPs with good pro-Europe credentials like Stephen Dorrell – who was also present at the dinner – had moved in a more sceptical direction. In any case, various commentators estimated that no more than

25 out of the 165 Conservative MPs elected in 1997 could be described as pro-European.

When Hague assumed leadership of the Party, it was therefore hardly surprising that its position on Europe shifted to a new centre of gravity. The clearest change was abandonment of the policy concerning the Single Currency on which – officially at least – the Party had fought the General Election of 1997. Adoption of the euro was not yet ruled out for ever; but ruled out "for the foreseeable future". This shift was made all the more inevitable in that there was a general expectation that the Blair government would soon activate the UK's "opt in", not just to the Social Chapter (which it did), but to Stage Three of EMU as well.

In fact, the expectation turned out to be misguided. Although in 1997 the incoming Labour Government had committed itself in principle to joining the single currency, and although Prime Minister Blair himself was still keen, Chancellor of the Exchequer Gordon Brown had become increasingly hostile.[*] In 2003 the Treasury published a massive, multi-volume study of the issue,[4] concluding that "five economic tests" of suitability for membership had still to be met.

The shift in official Conservative policy did not come without some cost. During the years that followed there was a small but steady seepage of support, as those who could not accept the new position on Europe left the Party. The first former elected Conservative MEP to leave for the Liberal Democrats was Peter Price, who had represented first Lancashire West, then South-East London in the European Parliament, and had for two-and-half years chaired its Budgetary Control Committee. (Hugh Dykes, one of the Conservative MEPs in the nominated Parliament before 1979 had already become a Liberal Democrat, as had the MP for Torridge and West Devon, and vice-chairman of the Conservative Party between 1983 and 1987, Emma Nicholson, who is now Baroness Nicholson and was for some time a Liberal Democrat MEP for the South East). Hague's shift of position on the euro was, for Price, the decisive factor. He would later be joined by James Moorhouse, and later still by John Stevens and Brendan Donnelly *via* the short-lived pro-euro Conservative Party, the sitting MEP Bill Newton-Dunn and another sitting MEP and Vice-President of the Parliament Edward McMillan-Scott.

Others, like my colleague in Kent, Christopher Jackson, publicly resigned from the Conservative Party without joining another. There were also defections to "new Labour" by pro-Europe MPs: in 1997 a contemporary of mine in CUCA, and at this time chairman of the Macleod Group, Peter Temple-Morris (now a Baron); in 2005 the one-time MEP Robert Jackson; and two years later the sitting chairman of the Conservative Group for Europe, Quentin Davies.

---

[*] Although, according to Mandelson, "it wasn't that Gordon was necessarily opposed, it was just that there was no way he was going to allow it to happen on Tony's watch". See *The Third Man: life at the heart of New Labour* by Peter Mandelson (HarperCollins, 2010) p.389.

These defections did not, of course, trouble the Party unduly – most of the original Conservative MEPs had already been written off as having gone irredeemably "native". But ex-MEPs were only the tip of an iceberg. When on visits from Luxembourg, I would sometimes meet former activists from the Kent West Conservatives, to be told that "I'm not actually a member of the party any more". Europe was not the only reason for the sharp decline in party membership that took place in the late 1990s and after; but it was a contributing cause.

The loss of pro-Europe Conservatives might have been offset by attracting back into the Party those who had been put off by Major's perceived lack of Eurosceptic backbone. By this time, however, the various anti-EU parties to the right of the Conservatives were beginning to coalesce around the United Kingdom Independence Party (UKIP). This had been founded in 1993 at the London School of Economics by a group of "anti-federalists", and had already contested 24 out of the 87 British European Parliament seats in 1994. It first leader was a former Conservative MP, Roger Knapman. In the European Elections of 1999 – fought for the first time on a system of Proportional Representation – it won three European Parliament seats. By the European Elections of 2004 it was attracting 16% of the vote, increasing its number of MEPs to 12 (two of which, however, soon left the Party). In the European Elections of 2009 it would do even better, pushing the Labour Party into third place. There is little doubt that these United Kingdom Independence Party successes were predominantly at the expense of the Conservative Party.

Evidence from the CPS

Following the General Election of 1997, very little literature specifically on Europe was published by Conservative Central Office or the CPC, either pro or anti. Despite the new official position of moderate Euroscepticism, it was obvious that anything which unleashed renewed dissension on the subject could only do the Party harm.

For insight into Conservative thinking about Europe during this period, however, one can to turn to the free market think-tank founded by Sir Keith Joseph and Margaret Thatcher in 1974, the Centre for Policy Studies (CPS). Although theoretically "independent of all political parties and special interest groups", the mission of the CPS was to keep alive the principles of "Thatcherism", including on the subject of Europe. Its publications, moreover, are to be found together with official Party documents in the Conservative Party archives at the Bodleian Library at Oxford University.

The CPS published some twenty-five papers on Europe between 1990 and 2005, most of them after the General Election of 1997. The theme of almost all was opposition to the main components of the Maastricht Treaty: Economic and Monetary Union, and moves towards "political union".

Among the papers is the text of a speech at the 1990 Conservative Party Conference by the Canadian Conrad Black, who was then owner of the

Daily Telegraph; who was given a peerage; and who in 2007 began serving time in an American prison having been convicted of fraud. The title of his speech was "Conservatism and the Paradox of Europe".[5] Conservatives, Black argued, had initially supported British membership of the European Economic Community (EEC) because they believed in "Cobdenite" free trade. However "the philosophy of Europe has moved on since then".

> What began as the European Economic Community is now just the European Community. ... It has become a vehicle for removing much of our ability to govern ourselves as an independent sovereign nation.

The main purpose of his speech was therefore "to remind those Conservatives who support European integration of their inherently Tory responsibility to safeguard the constitution of this sovereign nation". Moreover, Black went on to warn, Europe was on the road to "market socialism ... embodying all the evils of intervention, centralisation and unaccountability that have no place in our Conservative philosophy", and "aimed squarely at ... the submergence of our distinctiveness and the marginalisation of our institutions".

This was as clear a statement as any of the thesis which Eurosceptics would advance in the years that followed. Black ended with a prescription for the future: "an inner Europe of full political adherents, probably based on the original six, ... in close association with an outer Europe of common marketers ... which the emerging democracies of eastern Europe could join ... relatively soon".

He did not mention – and perhaps hadn't realised – that this was effectively the Conservative policy of the late 1950s, which had run into the sand with the failed Maudling negotiations. Nor had he apparently noticed something already obvious: that the new democracies would not be prepared to settle for anything less than full EU membership, any more than Austria, Finland and Sweden were prepared to settle for long-term membership of the "free trade only" European Economic Area (EEA). Indeed, when in the summer of 2000 the French and German governments appeared to launch a plan for a "two-tier" Community, with a "core group" moving to political union on their own, and the rest on the outer fringes, the reaction of the candidate countries was distinctly hostile. Nor was the possibility of being relegated to a second division, together with some of Europe's poorest countries, received particularly well in Britain.

Two more sophisticated CPS studies, one published a year before, the other three years later, nevertheless came to much the same conclusion. The first[6] was by a member of Margaret Thatcher's policy unit in the early 1980s, who would, many years later, become Shadow Home Secretary, Shadow Chancellor of the Exchequer, and eventually Minister of State for Policy: Oliver Letwin. The second[7] was by a fellow of Nuffield College, Oxford: Nevil Johnson.

Like many other Conservative Eurosceptics then and since, Letwin begins by stating that he has only just woken up to an awful truth: that Britain was on the way to finding itself in a "federal European Union with a central government in Brussels". The trigger for Letwin's awakening had been "one of the least known facts of modern British history: namely, that on the 14th February 1984 the European Parliament adopted, by 231 votes to 31 with 43 abstentions, a Draft Treaty of European Union". This was the report by Spinelli (wrongly described by Letwin as Parliament's President), covered earlier in Chapter Seven (see sections on "Widening and Deepening" and "Kangaroos and Crocodiles"). Apparently under the malign influence of this document, power was being transferred "slowly but surely, from London to Brussels by means of increasing federal control over laws, taxation, macro-economic policy, micro-economic policy and foreign policy". Even the Single European Act, "under cover" of creating the Single Market, was a step on the way to federal union.

What should Britain's policy be? One option would be to accept the apparently inevitable; and here Letwin quotes Michael Heseltine's book[8] of the same year. "There is no escaping the fact that a fledgling federalism is emerging. ... Many may not like it but it cannot be wished away." British policy under this scenario would be to "seek to create workable federal institutions – a true and democratically accountable government of the union".

The other option, unsurprisingly favoured by Letwin, would be to "adopt an open and plausible non-federalist policy for Britain", the basis of which would be a free-trading "greater European bloc", of which the European Union would be only a part. Norway, Sweden, Finland, Switzerland, Austria, Turkey and the ex-Communist countries of Central and Eastern Europe are mentioned as candidates for the wider grouping. Letwin was indulging in the same wishful thinking as Black – constructing "a pleasant pipe-dream, a mere repetition of EFTA", as he himself puts it (though denying this to be the case).

The later paper, by Johnson, indeed sets out to answer the question of why "at the end of nearly 20 years of [Community] membership, we seem ... to be more or less back with arguments remarkably similar to those which raged at the beginning". One answer was that the political development identified by Churchill as central to European unity – Franco-German reconciliation – had become a "special relationship"; and this meant that "the cards are very often stacked against British initiatives and preferences in Community policy-making".

More important, however, was a fundamental divergence of view about what the Community was for, itself the result of divergent histories and traditions. Where Britain had seen the Community as predominantly about trade and economics, the continental view was that economic integration was only a mechanism for achieving "ever-closer union" – the theory of "functional federalism" or "*l'engrenage*". This was being put into practice not merely through institutional changes, but increasingly through the development of common policies.

The central section of the study contained an analysis of political institutions and traditions of public law. The institutional and administrative structures of the Community were "predominantly French in design and character": that is to say "legalist", "rule-based" and short on accountability. Where the British tradition required legal certainty, the continental tradition relied on broadly-drafted texts, open to varying interpretation, but also to bureaucratic rigidity. "When people in Britain criticise the Community for being 'bureaucratic' they are in effect criticising it for conforming to something like the model just outlined." The whole system within which Britain found itself was, as a result, "alien".

The solution which the paper eventually recommended was the "Common Market approach". Instead of "ever-closer union", the aim should be "freely co-operating states joined in a single market". Though recognising (unlike Black) that a Common Market, still less a Single Market, is not the same thing as free trade, the author noted that it did not require "the equalisation or standardisation of everything", which would, if taken to its logical conclusion, destroy competition. But in campaigning for this approach, the author did recommend "a real effort to show that we do belong to Europe", including a more positive approach to learning other European languages.

By this time, most Conservatives would have wholeheartedly agreed with Johnson. Given the basic premises, however, his conclusions clearly resulted in a dilemma: if the approach of "continentals" (or of the French) was so alien to British traditions, why would they accept a British "Common Market only" approach? If this turned out to be a non-starter, was there not a danger that a more drastic remedy would have to be considered: withdrawal from the Community altogether? This, indeed, was the conclusion reached by those who eventually defected to the United Kingdom Independence Party.

The idea that there are fundamental differences of approach between Britain and "the Continent" is, as we have seen, not uncommon: Eden's island tradition of pragmatism, Macmillan's Aquinas v. Newton, de Gaulle's Europe or the open sea, Lord Young's "Latins" with their gaze fixed on the horizon, as against the British "looking where they are going". What is never entirely explained is why this is so much more of a problem than the traditions of, say, Ireland (also an island) or, for that matter, a non-centralised federation like Germany; and how Scotland, with a different legal system, has co-existed more-or-less happily with England within the United Kingdom. Various academic and other studies, indeed, have described divisions within Europe of a much more far-reaching nature: between the "Protestant North" and the "Catholic South", for example; or between the countries and regions of the "core" and those of the "periphery"; or between "Anglo-Saxon", "Nordic", "Rhineland/ Continental" and "Mediterranean" socio-economic systems – the classification contained in the 2003 report of an Independent High-Level Study Group: the Sapir Report.[9]

In view of the tendency to perceive fundamental differences between countries in this way, it is also worth noting that regional differences *within* countries can be just as great – and in purely economic terms (for example, *per capita* income and unemployment rates) considerably greater than – differences *between* countries.

Establishing a policy

Immediately following the election defeat in 1997, the CPS published a paper[10] on "The Future of Europe" by the next leader but two of the Conservative Party, Michael Howard. He was one of a trio of same-generation Cambridge graduates, members of CUCA in the early 1960s, who went on to occupy senior cabinet positions, the other two being Ken Clarke and Norman Lamont. They formed, with Hugh Dykes, the third wave of what was described in the 1980s and early 1990s as the "Cambridge Mafia", the first and second waves having included MPs John Nott, Leon Brittan, Christopher Tugendhat, John Selwyn Gummer, Norman Fowler, Peter Lloyd, Peter Viggers, Peter Temple-Morris and Nick Budgen (and, in the case of MEPs, myself), all of whom had served together on the Cambridge University Conservative Association committee during 1959–61. Also on that committee at the time were the historian John Barnes and the anthropologist Colin Renfrew, later Master of Jesus College and now in the House of Lords.

Michael Howard's declared objective in the paper was to "establish a position behind which our party can rally"; and in this, bar one or two details, he succeeded. *The Future of Europe* provides a good outline of the policy towards the EU which the Party maintained from then until at least the end of his own period of leadership. In February 2004, having become Party leader, Howard made a speech in Berlin effectively making his approach of six years earlier official policy.

First, Howard defines the enemy: the incoming Labour government had "consciously chosen to swim with the federalist current". Whereas the Conservative government had intended to veto any "closer political integration at the IGC",[*] Labour was set to "allow giant steps to be taken towards the creation of a federal European state".

The paper then defines the Conservative alternative: "an outward-looking, free-trading community which brings nation states together to co-operate in different fields for their mutual benefit". The key to achieving this was "flexibility", or what in the jargon of the time was called "variable geometry Europe". Different groups of Member States would be able to develop common policies in areas on which they were agreed under a procedure known as "enhanced cooperation", making use if necessary of Community institutions. Rather than having an "inner core" and "outer

---

[*] An Inter-Governmental Conference (IGC) was due to draft what became the failed Constitutional Treaty, and later the Lisbon Treaty.

fringe" or first- and second-class membership, the EU would become a much more attractive "series of overlapping circles", with Member States choosing which common policies to adopt *à la carte*.

This "single, coherent and popular Conservative vision of Europe", as a post-1994 European election Party leaflet[11] put it, had in fact already been outlined by John Major during that election campaign in a speech which became known as the "Ellesmere Port Address".

> I have never believed that Europe must invariably act as one on every issue. ... I don't happen to think that it threatens Europe if member states are free to do some things in their own way and at their own speed. ... For nations to work this way, alongside Community arrangements, is a sensible new approach: varying when it needs to be – multi-track, multi-speed, multi-layered.[12]

Howard adds to this that there should be no fixed *acquis communautaire*. Powers ought to "pass up and down between Brussels and Member States as necessary". If the principle of subsidiarity was to mean anything at all "it must allow states to opt out of common policies when doing so would not have a direct and significant impact upon the internal affairs of other members". As far as Britain was concerned, this would mean the "repatriation" of certain areas of policy. One example was EU legislation on the quality of drinking water; there was "no possible European interest in the matter".[*] More serious candidates for repatriation were the Common Fisheries Policy (CFP), and eventually the Common Agricultural Policy itself.

The idea of repatriating powers was not, however, as out of line with orthodox thinking as might be thought. In December 2001 the European Council in Laeken, Belgium, which established the Giscard d'Estaing Convention on the Future of Europe, also adopted the "Laeken Declaration". This, in proposing a clearer division of powers between the EU and Member States, explicitly envisaged "restoring tasks to the Member States" in certain policy areas.

Howard then turned to the European Court of Justice (ECJ), which had by this time become something of a *bête noire* for Conservatives, in sharp contrast to the approaches of Heseltine and Lord Inglewood described earlier. It was essential that the Court operated "within the remit given to it by the Member States", rather than take an activist role in interpreting the Treaties. Linked to this was a need to limit the "direct effect" of EU law: for example, Directives which had been adopted at EU level, but not yet transposed into national legislation. Contrast this, again, with the proposals of Lord Inglewood, outlined in Chapter Eight, for *automatic*

---

* In 1989, at the time of the "environment" European election, Michael Howard was Minister for Water and Planning. He was then responsible for major initiatives to clean up Britain's rivers and coasts and improve water quality, some of which, like improving the quality of bathing water off beaches, had been prompted by EU legislation.

direct effect. Howard also returned to a point earlier raised by Nevil Johnson: the imprecise drafting of EU legislation, which left the door open for the Court to interpret it in a "federalist" way. Finally, a qualified lawyer himself, Howard could not resist a professional put-down: it "would be sensible to require all European judges to be properly qualified".

The last section of the paper dealt with the critical question: how are the other EU Member States to be persuaded that "variable geometry is the only practical way"? The facts that, at the time, Britain was a net contributor to the EU budget, and had a trade deficit with other Member States, gave us, thought Howard, a reasonable bargaining position. We might negotiate the repatriation of certain policies in return for abandoning our veto in other spheres. Changes were in any case on the way: "enlargement is simply not possible without structural changes".

It is interesting that Howard, like Johnson before him, believed that expansion of the EU to take in the ex-Communist countries of Central and Eastern Europe would propel the EU in a non-federalist, Conservative direction. Others – and notably the majority in the Convention on the Future of Europe tasked with drawing up a Constitution for Europe – were at the same time arguing the exact opposite: that managing an organisation of up to thirty countries required much tighter integration. For example, maintaining vetoes for every Member State in significant areas of policy, it was thought, would be intolerable; there would need to be a shift to Qualified Majority Vote (QMV). This, indeed, was the outcome of the Convention, and later of the Inter-Governmental Conference (IGC) and of the European Council which adopted the necessary Treaty changes.

The often-repeated assurance that the new Member States had "not freed themselves from the tyranny of Moscow in order to submit to that of Brussels" also turned out wide of the mark. Instead, EU membership – including full adoption of the *acquis* – was viewed in those countries as a mark of democratic respectability, a guarantee of stability and, of course, a source of funds. Implementation of the "Copenhagen criteria" in order to qualify for EU membership was in most cases the driving force behind vital administrative and legal reforms, which increased the view in those countries that they were "rejoining European civilisation". Ideas like "variable geometry" were viewed with suspicion, as implying second-class status.

I was able to hear these opinions for myself when lecturing at the European Institute in Łódž in Poland in 1998 and 1999, and later when I took over as co-ordinator of an inter-parliamentary Working Group on Macro-economic Research. This had been established by the European Centre for Parliamentary Research and Documentation (ECPRD), a body jointly organised by the European Parliament and the Council of Europe. During my co-ordinatorship, as well as meeting in Brussels, Luxembourg, Strasbourg, Lisbon and Helsinki, the working group visited the parliaments in Prague, Budapest, Bratislava, Vilnius and Bucharest. Those attending all these meetings were drawn from the staff of the EU Member

States' and candidate countries' parliaments, and, in addition, from those of Council of Europe countries like Norway, Croatia, Bosnia-Herzegovina, FYROM,[*] Moldova, Albania, the Ukraine and even Russia. The only opinion I ever heard favourable to "variable geometry" came from the President of the Czech Republic, the impeccably Eurosceptic Václav Klaus.

In 1999 the CPS published the text[13] of the third Keith Joseph Memorial Lecture by the journalist and former special adviser to Margaret Thatcher, John O'Sullivan, who, many years before, had succeeded me as Tutor at Swinton College. His subject was "Conservatism, Democracy and National Identity".

Like Michael Howard, O'Sullivan began by identifying the enemy. It was not possible to give a short answer to the question: what do Tories stand for? And that was "because the Tories cannot give a short answer to the question: what exactly is it that we stand against?" O'Sullivan's answer was not "federalism", but "the gradual undermining of democracy". This was taking place as a result of "the shift of power from legislatures to bureaucratic agencies and the courts … ; the shift of power from nation states to supranational bodies; and the development of anti-democratic ideas … that justify these relatively new political practices".

He cited the incorporation of the European Convention on Human Rights into UK law as a contributing factor to the increased power of judges as opposed to politicians. In the case of the shift of power from nation states, he distinguished between *inter*national bodies like NATO, which are "forums for the exercise of national sovereignty", and *supra*national organisations, "of which the European Union is one", that are "hostile to national sovereignty in principle". Echoing Enoch Powell in the 1970s, he then argued that democracy at EU level – i.e. the European Parliament – could only be "unreal". He even questioned the reality of democracy in those EU Member States using systems of Proportional Representation. One seriously anti-democratic idea was "multiculturalism", which replaced the (democratic) nation state and majority rule by ethnic, cultural or religious identities. Instead of sovereign national parliaments, the outcome was "a wilderness of committees".

The Tory Party should embrace democracy with more enthusiasm, O'Sullivan concluded, and defend "the central democratic institution in British life – namely the House of Commons".

There is no doubt that this view has proved attractive to a large number of Conservatives – in particular to Conservative MPs at Westminster. The Westminster model of democracy, the "rule of the majority", however, is not immune to criticism – particularly since a Labour government was elected at the General Election of 2005 with fewer than a quarter of registered voters. O'Sullivan's thesis has also been somewhat undermined by recent Conservative enthusiasm for "direct democracy", the by-passing of Parliament via referendum.

---

[*] Former Yugoslav Republic of Macedonia, so-called as a result of Greek objections to simple "Macedonia".

Again, O'Sullivan may not have noticed that the European Parliament would, almost contemporaneously with his lecture, secure the resignation of the entire Santer Commission, using, among other powers, that to refuse discharge of the Budget – one element of the classic parliamentary "power of the purse". This cast doubt on the idea that "Brussels" was subject to no democratic control.

"Unelected Commissioners ... "

Scepticism about the European Union on the grounds that it was "undemocratic" was nevertheless a major element of Conservative thinking on Europe during the post-1997 years. In 2000 the Bruges Group published a pamphlet by one of the original campaigners for British Common Market membership, entitled "The Myth of Europe".[14] Its author, frequently quoted earlier, was Russell Lewis.

Lewis' translation from pro-EEC campaigner to Eurosceptic was in part the result, he wrote, of perceiving "four undeniable defects in the EU: its lack of democracy, its excessive regulation, its corruption and its structural bias against British interests". The EU's structure, he argued, was "oligarchic"; and there was the prospect, "under federalism, of unelected bankers and bureaucrats becoming our masters and our General Elections becoming a farce".

The "unelected" status of the Commission is, in fact, a regular theme in Conservative Eurosceptic writing of the period; and it is one, curiously, that was supported by some of the most ardent integrationists. Giscard d'Estaing himself, President of the Convention on the Future of Europe, drew the logical conclusion from his advocacy of a United States of Europe: that the President of the Commission, like his US or French equivalents, should be directly elected, and thus have his or her own independent democratic mandate.* The Convention in fact rejected this US/French model in favour of that at Westminster: that the Commission should reflect majority support in the European Parliament. Given that the Parliament can dismiss the Commission by motion of censure, and already subjects incoming Commissioners to a vetting procedure modelled on that in the US Congress, this is – at least in embryo – already the case.

The description of the Commission as "unelected", however, was shorthand for a more fundamental criticism of that body. Following the resignation of the Santer Commission in 1999 and the nomination of Romano Prodi as Commission President-in-waiting, the CPS published a paper[15] by the former Conservative cabinet Minister, Tom King, calling for a complete rethink of what the Commission should do and who should be appointed to it. Instead of aspiring to be a "government" mostly composed of politicians, it should be no more than an administration composed

---

*   A view repeated more recently by ex-PM Tony Blair.

of civil servants and perhaps "top figures" from industry, the media or Non-Governmental Organisations (NGOs).

Despite its title, King's paper was as much about the role of the Council of Ministers as that of the Commission. The conventional view of the EU's institutions – on the model going back to the idealised views of the English constitution of Locke and Montesquieu, on which that of the United States was based – is that the Council, with the European Parliament, is one half of the legislature. Like the US Senate before 1910, its members represent the Member States, which nominate them from their own State governments and/or State legislatures. Like the US Senate, each State is equally represented, irrespective of size or population. Where the Council of Ministers differs from the US Senate, of course, is the fact that it has different "configurations", with different national Ministers assembling depending on the subject under discussion. Formally, nevertheless, the Council of Ministers consists only of the Foreign Ministers; and there have been suggestions from time to time that it should consist only of full-time "Ministers for Europe".

In King's view, however, the Council of Ministers should not be seen as part of the legislature but – in so far as he believed such a thing should exist – the EU's "government". The "power of initiative" currently exercised by the Commission, "should be returned to its natural political home with the Council". The Commission would then "concentrate on the administration of the Community's activities, as decided by the Council". The Community, indeed, did move sharply in this constitutional direction when the summits of Heads of State and Government became an institution in its own right, the European Council.

Given this alternative understanding of the EU's institutional system, it is not surprising that King and Conservatives who thought like him should have been so antagonistic to the "political" pretensions of the Commission, particularly under the Delors Presidency. As already observed, a good part of the friction between Delors and Prime Minister Thatcher derived from the fact that she thought of him as a *fonctionnaire*, whereas he saw himself as a political leader, a genuine President (if not quite on a par with the Presidents of France and the United States).

Many of the disagreements that exist concerning Europe can, indeed, be attributed to such differences in underlying constitutional concepts. Those who prefer the traditional approach of international law, i.e. "inter-governmentalism", naturally see the Council of Ministers and the European Council as the key political institutions. Those supporting the Community model see the Commission playing a major political role; but also divide into those supporting the "US/French" model, with the Commission having its own independent role (with its President even being directly elected), and those supporting the "British" model, with the Commission resting on (and perhaps even being drawn from the ranks of) a European Parliament majority.

Russell Lewis' second charge against the Commission – that it was "riddled with corruption" – was certainly understandable at the time, given some of the facts that emerged about the Santer Commission prior to, and following, its resignation. The trigger to the crisis was a 600-page dossier describing instances of corruption and fraud compiled by an assistant auditor in the Commission, Paul van Buitinen. This he had sent to the European Parliament at the end of 1998, together with an extensive covering letter. An investigation by a panel of "Wise Men" confirmed a substantial proportion of the allegations, commenting that it was "hard to find anyone in the Commission who was prepared to take responsibility for anything". On the 16th March 1999 the whole Commission resigned before it could be pushed by the Parliament.*

It is also true, as Eurosceptics repeatedly point out (though Lewis himself does not), that the Court of Auditors has year after year failed to sign off the Commission's accounts. However, as both the Court itself and the European Parliament's Budgetary Control Committee have noted, this has usually been not so much the fault of the Commission itself, but rather the result of failure by the Member States (which administer most EU policies, especially the CAP, "on the ground"), to submit adequate accounts. Moreover, if one is looking for corruption, it lies mostly in the administrations of the member nation states, not the EU's own institutions. Since an inflow of EU funds not only helps finance desirable projects, but also improves national budgetary balances, national administrations have indeed had every incentive to turn a blind eye to dubious practices.

There was also, both in the closing months of the Santer Commission and when the Prodi Commission took over in the following year, a determined effort to impose stricter standards within the Commission itself. The Commissioner responsible for reforms was the former leader of the British Labour Party, Neil Kinnock, who had the advantage – from the point of view of identifying the problems – of being one of the very few outgoing Commissioners to be reappointed. Unsurprisingly, most Conservatives were not convinced that this had put everything right.

" ... and unelected bankers"

The complaint that central bankers are unelected seems a strange one. It would not have surfaced had there not been, in the 1990s, a surge in support for central bank "independence", on the model of the German *Bundesbank*. This, in turn, was the result of empirical evidence establishing a correlation between low inflation and central bank independence, and suggesting that politicians could not be trusted to set interest rates and conduct monetary policy in a non-inflationary way: they were too influenced by the electoral cycle and the pressures of US-style "pork-barrel politics". When in 1997 the incoming Chancellor of the Exchequer, Gordon Brown, made the Bank of England independent, this was widely hailed as a masterstroke.

---

*   There was a rumour that the Commissioners were acting on legal advice – if they resigned, they kept their pension entitlements; if they were dismissed as result of a parliamentary motion of censure, they would not.

Maastricht had already, largely at the insistence of Germany, deeply entrenched the independence of the European Central Bank (ECB) in the Treaty. This provides that

> neither the ECB, nor a national central bank, nor any member of their decision-making bodies shall seek or take instructions from Community institutions or bodies, from any government of a Member State or from any other body. The Community institutions and bodies and the governments of the Member States undertake to respect this principle and not to seek to influence the members of the decision-making bodies of the ECB or of the national central banks in the performance of their tasks.[16]

In addition, the ECB's independence was reinforced by two of the "golden rules" on the financing of public debt which had also been written into the Treaty with strong British support: no monetary financing of debt; and "no bail-out" by the Community.

Conservative Eurosceptics, of course, did not want the President of the ECB or the other members of the Board of Governors to be elected in the event of the UK joining the Euro Area. The implication of the "unelected" tag was that they would want the Bank subject to some form of democratic control. In this, however, they were in very suspect company. The political left of many Euro Area countries, and in particular the French Socialists, had been consistently arguing for the ECB to be counterbalanced by, and subordinate to, an "economic government": i.e. the very inflation-prone arrangement which independence was designed to avoid.

Rather than control by politicians, however, it can be argued that what was really being asked for was "accountability". The Bank of England is independent, but is nevertheless required to write an explanatory letter if it fails to meet its inflation target; and the Governor appears from time to time before House of Commons committees. What is not often realised is that the ECB is similarly accountable. The Treaty provides that

> The President of the ECB and other members of the Executive Board may, at the request of the European Parliament or on their own initiative, be heard by the competent committee of the European Parliament.[17]

From the start, by agreement between the ECB and Parliament's Economic and Monetary Affairs Committee* this was interpreted to mean

---

* This arrangement was largely on the initiative of the Committee's first post-EMU chairman, who had earlier chaired its Monetary Sub-committee, the German Socialist MEP, Christa Randzio-Plath. In preparation for the creation of the ECB she had particularly studied the relations between Congress and the US Federal Reserve Bank. The agreement between Parliament and the ECB had the strong support of the Bank's first President, Wim Duisenberg.

a "monetary dialogue": regular quarterly meetings at which the ECB President reported and answered Members' questions on the past conduct of monetary policy, and forecasts for the future. Not only are these meetings open to the media and the public, but verbatim reports are published by both ECB and Parliament on their respective websites. The ECB, in fact, is probably as democratically accountable, if not more so, than any national central bank, including the Bank of England.

"In Europe, but not run by Europe"

The first major electoral test for the Conservative Party under its new leadership, and with its revised policy on Europe, was the European Parliament election of June 1999. Going into the contest, the Party was massively behind Labour in the opinion polls: a gap of between 10 and 20 per cent; and yet it emerged the clear winner, polling nearly 36% of the vote, 8 per cent *ahead* of Labour, and gaining 18 seats. As a result, Labour was the big loser, dropping no fewer than 33 seats, more than half its 1994 total. The Liberal Democrats gained 8 seats. The United Kingdom Independence Party, the Greens and Plaid Cymru (the Welsh Nationalists), entered the Parliament for the first time, with 3, 2 and 2 seats respectively. The Scottish Nationalists kept their two seats, and in Northern Ireland the three seats were shared, as usual, between the Ulster Unionists (UU), the Democratic Unionist Party (DUP) and the Social Democratic and Labour Party (SDLP).

This spread between different parties was the result of a change in the voting system, in England, Wales and Scotland, from "first-past-the-post" in single-member constituencies to Proportional Representation in multi-member constituencies, using "closed" party lists. (Northern Ireland continued to use Single Transferable Vote.) The Blair government had introduced the change partly to show willing as "good Europeans"; but mainly, it was generally believed, as part of a deal with the Liberal Democrat leader, Paddy Ashdown. The European Parliament Elections Act 1999[18] had only received the Royal Assent in the middle of January that year, largely as a result of the Bill having been rejected six times in the Lords.

Both the change of system, and the lateness of its introduction, had major implications for political parties and their candidates. In the case of the Conservative Party it meant that the number of safe or winnable seats in the South and West of England was reduced, while the Party could now expect to win several seats in the North. For the candidates, it was no longer a case of being selected or re-selected for a constituency, but of being placed in a sufficiently high position on a regional party list. Sitting MEPs and prospective candidates who had "nursed" their constituencies over the years were suddenly thrown into a general pot with other aspirants. Moreover, those carrying out the selection process were no longer the constituency activists they knew, but regional committees, and finally

– to determine the critical issue of the order on the list – mass meetings of Party members from every part of a large region. The whole unfamiliar process had to be carried out to a tight timetable.

The South-East region of England, having once been, for a Conservative candidate, the best place to be, had suddenly become the worst. It covered eleven former Euro-constituencies, all of which the Party could have expected to win in a reasonably favourable year. In the event, the PR system returned only five. It also saved the two Labour MEPs, Peter Skinner and Mark Watts, who had won my Kent West and Christopher Jackson's Kent East seat in 1994.

Neither I nor Jackson presented ourselves for election in 1999. Had the two Kent constituencies remained in being, it is possible that we would both have been re-selected. Under the new system, however, we would have been competing in a regional pool with five sitting Members, as well as new, and much younger contenders like the journalist Daniel Hannan. Old age, indeed, had been creeping up on us: at the Conservative South-East regional final one delegate was overheard saying: "We can't have him, he's got grey hair!" In addition, both Christopher and I had records which, while not exactly "federalist", were firmly pro-European in the Ted Heath tradition. In my own case I had also found myself an extremely interesting job in Luxembourg, working in the Monetary Union Task Force which the Parliament had set up to help bring about EMU and the euro.

As it happened, the Single Currency issue had by now become the acid test for Conservatives. For a time following the adoption of the Maastricht Treaty there had been many arguing that, in the end, EMU would prove impossible. The economist Tim Congdon, a Council Member of a "keep the pound sterling" lobby, Business for Sterling, was reported in 1996 as saying of the euro:

> It is nonsense. It is a fantasy and it is not going to happen. Neither the EU nor a subset of its members will have a single currency on January 1st 1999, January 1st 2002, January 1st 2003, or, indeed, at any date in the relevant future.

Congdon was not the only one to have got things wrong. There was also a lot of wishful thinking that no choice on the Single Currency would in the end be necessary. It became clear by March 1998, however, that the euro would come into existence as planned at the beginning of 1999, though without euro-denominated notes and coins as yet being issued. Accordingly, in a move to heal the rift within the Party which had opened up in the 1997 election campaign, Hague held an internal referendum on the new, more Eurosceptical party policies in the autumns of 1998; and an overwhelming majority of those Party members voting, 84%, had supported keeping the pound sterling, at least for the duration of the next two Westminster parliaments.

It was also noted, however, that over half the Party's membership had either voted for joining the Single Currency, or not bothered to vote at all. Two members of Hague's recently appointed team, David Curry and Ian Taylor, had already resigned, arguing that it was foolish to give such long-term commitments when circumstances might have changed completely in ten years' time. Nevertheless, although the main arguments used by opponents of Euro Area membership had been about national sovereignty, the Party's decision soon appeared to have been wise on economic and financial grounds as well. In the early months of 1999 the euro's parity against the dollar fell sharply and unexpectedly on the foreign exchange markets.*

At the Conservative South-East regional final the key question was therefore: "What is your position on the Euro?" and those who replied that they thought the UK should join were given no quarter. Two sitting MEPs, John Stevens (who made the best and bravest speech of the day in support of EMU) and Brendan Donnelly (who is now Director of the Federal Trust), were effectively de-selected. Both then fought the election anyway, but as candidates for a breakaway "pro-euro Conservative Party". The then leader of the British MEPs, Tom Spencer – as far from being a Eurosceptic as it is possible to get – was selected, but was subsequently obliged to drop out for personal reasons. The two new MEPs eventually elected for the region, the former MP Nirj Deva and Daniel Hannan, were from a very different school of thought, but one which was now much more in tune with the views of Party members.

The Party's policies for the election included not only opposition to the euro, but firm support for a "flexible", "variable geometry" model for the EU itself (attacked by Labour as "pick and mix"); no further extension of majority voting in the Council of Ministers; repatriation of certain policies; and curbs on the power of the European Court of Justice. A phrase from the 1997 manifesto became the title of that for the European Elections of 1999: *In Europe, not run by Europe*.[19] The Party's approach was also helped by the exposure of fraud in the Commission, by Conservative MEPs' role in exposing it, and by the involvement in suspect practices of a prominent French Socialist Commissioner, Edith Cresson.

These policies clearly resonated with the voters. Indeed, the resonance was, if anything, too great: in the South-East the election returned the soon-to-be leader of the United Kingdom Independence Party, Nigel Farage, almost certainly at Conservatives' expense. Whereas Conservative views on Europe had been drowned out in the General Election of 1997

---

* After this initial fall, however, it began to appreciate steadily, and at the beginning of 2009 actually reached parity, for a short while, with the pound sterling. A convincing explanation for its dip in value in 1999 was advanced at the time by the Bank for International Settlements (BIS):

" ... the newly created euro may have proved too successful. Larger and more liquid markets, along with relatively low interest rates, encouraged the issue of euro-denominated bonds whose proceeds could then be exchanged and used to finance investment elsewhere".

(BIS 70th Annual Report, Basle, 5 June 2000).

by the blast of the New Labour message, in the purely European Elections of 1999 they got through. Europe and the euro had risen to become the most frequently-mentioned issue. Hague was given credit for having astutely kept the Party together and brought off an unexpected victory. Party morale rose.

Nevertheless, the success of the strategy in 1999 did store up certain problems for the future. As one commentator put it: "while [Hague] may have succeeded in energising his activists and bringing out the Tory core vote on a Eurosceptic platform in a low poll, there can be no guarantee that such an approach would work in a general election".[20] This was prophetic in the light of what was to happen two years later.

The low turnout – at a mere 24% for the UK as a whole, one might say a disgracefully low turnout – was clearly a major, and possibly misleading, determinant of the result. It was also an unexpected refutation of one key justification for the change in electoral system. "First-past-the-post" in single-member constituencies, it had been argued, created the problem of "wasted votes": in constituencies considered safe for one of the parties, there was no real incentive for those supporting other parties to go to the polls. Under PR every vote would count, and more people would turn out. The exact opposite happened.

It is possible to argue, of course, that the low poll in 1999 was due to special factors unrelated to the electoral system. Potential Labour voters were less inclined than Conservatives to think European issues important; and since the Blair government had a comfortable lead in the polls on issues in general, there were more of them. This produced a huge "differential turnout" effect.

As against this, the absence of identifiable candidates for identifiable areas – the system with which voters were familiar – may also have played a part. Academic studies of elections, it is true, indicate that votes are usually cast for parties rather than individual candidates; but voting for a party list – in particular a "closed" list, where the order of candidates cannot be changed – is not quite the same thing as voting for a party's local standard-bearer. Nor is a constituency as amorphous as the South-East region the same thing as the historical counties of Kent, Sussex or Surrey. Whatever the mathematical arguments for PR, there is something to be said for the traditional British system, particularly the tradition that an MP or MEP, once elected, represents *all* his or her constituents, and not just a party or those who support it.

For some Conservatives, indeed, the change of electoral system played a major part in moving them in a Eurosceptic direction: it convinced them that the EU was becoming less rather than more democratic. One of these was John Strafford, chairman of the Campaign for Conservative Democracy – a pressure group with roots in the Greater London Area Young Conservatives of the late 1960s, and having as is main objective a greater say in the running of the Party for ordinary members.

It was also an indication of how complex the views of many Conservatives about the European Union had become that Strafford was also on record as favouring the direct election of the Commission President, a proposal generally advanced by convinced federalists.

Saving the pound

The Conservative Party went into the General Election of 2001 with what it believed would be a winning policy on Europe. The manifesto[21] clearly outlined the policy around which the Party was now united, centred on pledges that "the next Conservative Government will keep the pound sterling. We will maintain our national veto on European legislation."

Emphasising again that Britain should be "in Europe but not run by Europe", it promised to "lead a debate in Europe about its future, promoting our own clear and positive vision". Instead of a becoming a "fully integrated superstate" – the route down which, it asserted, "the Government is taking us" – the EU should be "a Europe of nations coming together in different combinations for different purposes and to different extents. In other words, a network Europe". This would allow other countries to go ahead with closer integration if they so wished under the "reinforced cooperation" procedure (but only if this did not damage "Britain's national interest"). Any further transfer of powers from Westminster to "Brussels" would be subject to referendum; and legislation would be passed to "prevent EU law from overriding the will of Parliament in areas which Parliament never intended to transfer to the EU".

During the election campaign itself, the Party dwelt heavily on the pledge to "keep the pound", a policy for which it knew it had overwhelming public support. For this tactic to be effective, however, the public had also to be convinced that Labour was about to swap the pound for the euro; and this turned out to be an impossible task. Publicity claiming that the election was "your last chance to save the pound" fell largely on deaf or indifferent ears. Indeed it appeared to reinforce the public perception, gleefully encouraged by Labour, that the Party was obsessed with Europe to the exclusion of other, more voter-relevant issues. "'Save the Pound' proved as effective for Hague as 'Ban the Bomb' did for Michael Foot," as Ken Clarke later put it.

An analysis of the Conservatives' 2001 election campaign in *The Conservative Party from Thatcher to Cameron*[22] by Tim Bale quotes two justifications subsequently advanced by Party officials for the time and effort spent on the issue of Europe. First, it "helped divert media (and it was hoped, voter) attention" from issues which favoured Labour. Secondly, it may have minimised the defection of Conservatives to the United Kingdom Independence Party (UKIP). Both tactics may have been valid. But, as Bale himself comments, the Party "managed to grab headlines but ... failed to grab votes"; and the voting figures suggest that the squeeze on UKIP did not make up for defections to the Liberal Democrats.

Indeed, the Conservative Party added only one seat to the total scored in the disastrous General Election of 1997. It made nine gains, including five from Labour; but lost eight, seven of them to the Liberal Democrats. Its share of the vote rose by only 1 percentage point, to 30.9%. As a result, having become the youngest leader of the Party since Pitt the Younger, Hague found himself joining the small group of former Conservative leaders who had been obliged to relinquish the post without ever having been Prime Minister.*

There then followed one of the most unfortunate leadership contests in the Party's history. Over the years the Campaign for Conservative Democracy had been pressing for the rank-and-file of the Party to participate in the choice of its leader; and the rules had at last been changed. The choice between the final two candidates selected by the Conservative MPs would be decided by ballot of all paid-up Party members.

The favourite to win this time was not Clarke, but the Shadow Chancellor, Michael Portillo, who had been Defence Secretary in the Major Government. He had dramatically lost his Enfield seat in the General Election of 1997, but had come back into the Commons two years later, representing Chelsea. There were rumours that he had not been entirely loyal either to Major when in the Cabinet (he was said to be one of those whom Major had described, in an unguarded moment, as "bastards"), nor to Hague while in the Shadow Cabinet; but his Eurosceptic credentials were good, and he emerged from the first ballot of Conservative MPs in the lead.

But at this point stories began to appear in the press that Portillo had admitted having had homosexual experiences at university, and even veiled hints that he was still gay. This was enough, deplorably, to knock him out of the leadership race. In the final vote of MPs it was Clarke – running again, but sticking to his views on Europe – who headed the poll, followed by a candidate virtually unknown outside Westminster, Iain Duncan Smith. Like the man whom he had succeeded as MP for Chingford and Woodford Green, Norman Tebbit, he was an irreconcilable Eurosceptic, and had been a thorn in the side of the Major government during the Maastricht rebellions. He had even been the campaign manager for John Redwood's abortive attempt to replace Major in 1995.

I remember thinking at the time that, with Clarke obviously about to win, Conservative policy on Europe would soon be returning to normal; but I had overlooked some crucial factors. The first was that the Party had got itself into a position very much like that experienced by Labour in the early 1980s. The militant Eurosceptic tendency, having captured the castle, was more interested in doctrinal purity than in winning the next general election. There had already been signs that intolerance was growing towards Conservatives with more traditional, pro-European views: in 2000 the MP for Esher, Ian Taylor – a former

---

* In the 20th century there had been only one: Austen Chamberlain.

minister and later chairman both of the European Movement and of the Conservative Group for Europe – narrowly escaped de-selection by his local party.

As a result, the fact that Clarke was still overwhelmingly the more popular candidate among not only voters as a whole, but even among Conservative voters, counted for nothing. Clarke himself was only too aware of the problems he was up against. Writing in the 2007 Party Conference issue of the Conservative Group for Europe magazine *Conservative Europe*, he observed that "by the first decade of this century sections of the previously pro-European natural governing party of the country, the Conservative Party, had become almost a single issue pressure group, advocating a form of extreme right wing nationalism which we politely call Euroscepticism".[23] Opinion polls taken at the time among the relevant electorate – Conservative Party members – indeed showed them rating the issue of Europe top of their priorities in deciding how to vote, in stark contrast to the views of the electorate in general. This situation was observed with some satisfaction by Labour. The Tories, Peter Mandelson recalls in his memoirs, were retreating to their "comfort zone: Euroscepticism, or perhaps more accurately, Europhobia".[24]

The second error I made was in underestimating how far this membership had shrunk, like that of the Labour Party's in the early 1980s, to its militant core. During the contest, a dinner took place at my house in Kent attended by a number of friends who I thought were Conservative Party members. "I hope", I remember saying, "you will all be voting for Ken?" But not one had paid a Party subscription.

The result was an overwhelming victory for Duncan Smith, by 62% to 38% of the vote. However, he was to remain in the job for little more than two years. In 2003 he was ousted in a *putsch* by the parliamentary party, so joining Hague as another ex-leader who had never been PM. Not nearly as right-wing as he was often portrayed,* Duncan Smith had nevertheless found himself outclassed in the House of Commons by Prime Minister Blair and unable to establish himself in the country as a credible Prime-Minister-in-waiting. As time went by there was mounting dissatisfaction with his leadership; and, despite his pleas to "unite or die", his own record during the Major years did not help in maintaining Party discipline. In October 2003 he lost a confidence vote of Conservative MPs by 90 to 75, and resigned. He was replaced, without a contest, by Michael Howard.

---

* During his leadership the Monday Club was suspended, and action taken to expel extreme right-wingers from the Party. After relinquishing the leadership he in fact pioneered policies more usually associated with the left of the Party, founding a think-tank, the Centre for Social Justice, which worked with charities to discover better ways of tackling poverty and deprivation. Its findings formed the basis of his policies to reform the Welfare State when, in 2010, he became Secretary of State for Work and Pensions in the coalition government.

The defence dimension

However bad the Conservative Party's standing in the opinion polls has been on domestic policies, it has usually been able to maintain a lead over the Labour Party in one area: defence. For many years this advantage was bolstered by Labour's espousal of unilateral nuclear disarmament, and the influence within it of the Campaign for Nuclear Disarmament (CND). The Conservative Party needed only to remind the public of what the leader of the Labour Left in the 1950s, the great Welsh orator Aneurin ("Nye") Bevan, had told his own Party conference in 1957: if Britain unilaterally gave up the bomb "it would send a British Foreign Secretary naked into the conference-chamber". The point was all the more telling in that Bevan had at one time temporarily lost the Labour whip for opposing the construction of the British H-bomb.*

The legacy of the Second World War, combined with the beginning of the Cold War, meant that the foundation of any British defence policy in the 1950s, whatever the party in power, had to be alliance with the United States. For Churchill, bringing America into the war against the Nazis, and then keeping American forces in Europe to counterbalance the Red Army, had been an overwhelming necessity. The Labour Government of Clement Attlee, strongly influenced by Foreign Secretary Ernest Bevin, quickly quashed any notions on the Party's Left of an alliance with the Soviet Union, or of neutrality. Eden's Suez adventure in partnership with the French only made the position more obvious.

As far as Europe was concerned the main defence issue of that time, already outlined in Chapter One, was the German question: how to integrate any new German armed forces safely into the Western alliance. That alliance, based on the North Atlantic Treaty, had firmly committed the US and Canada to the defence of Western Europe, including the key guarantee of a "nuclear umbrella". Any plans for a separate European body, whether the proposed European Defence Community (EDC) or the successfully-created Western European Union (WEU) were seen mainly as devices to ensure a more coordinated contribution by European countries.

None of this, of course, created many problems for Conservatives – except, perhaps, for a small group of MPs like Julian Amery, who suspected the US of actively trying to dismantle the British Empire, and who could not forgive the Americans for undermining the British position at the time of Suez. This suspicion of America later found expression in, for example, the proposals in the Monday Club pamphlet, *A Europe of Nations*, for a joint, fully independent Anglo-French nuclear deterrent, and other features of "Conservative Gaullism".

---

* Various interpretations have been offered as to why Bevan, in his capacity as shadow Foreign Secretary, appeared to reverse so dramatically his previous position on nuclear weapons. The one-time Labour MEP Lord Bruce of Donington, who as Donald Bruce MP had been Bevan's PPS, advanced the view that Bevan had been advised by contacts in the Soviet Union to support retention of a British nuclear capability independent of that of the US, to be used as a bargaining chip in disarmament negotiations.

The central Conservative position on European defence, however, rested firmly on the primacy of NATO, together with – at least until the "East of Suez" debate – CENTO (the Central Treaty Organisation*) and SEATO (the South East Asia Treaty Organisation†). Britain's nuclear deterrent was effectively "assigned" to NATO, making it possible for operational factors like targeting to be coordinated with the United States.

Despite this, however, there was always a reluctance to put all Britain's eggs in the NATO basket. In the case of nuclear weapons, for example, the Conservative position was that it should remain, in the last resort, "independent". As the then Foreign Secretary Lord Home put it to the House of Lords in March 1963, it was assumed that the United States would always, in all circumstances, cover Great Britain with her strategic deterrent. "I profoundly hope that this is true", he added. But this was a large assumption; "and Governments cannot take risks with the national security".[25]

The same logic, of course, applied to other Western European countries; and on his return to power in 1958, de Gaulle had acted on it by creating the French nuclear *force de frappe*. At the time, NATO defence strategists were arguing that a country's nuclear weapons could only be a fully credible deterrent if they constituted a "second-strike capability" – that is, if they could still be launched after an attack by an enemy. With unanswerable Gallic logic, French strategists argued that the French deterrent would be fully credible even if there was only a reasonable possibility of just one second-strike nuclear device getting through: it would damage the aggressor state sufficiently to make it vulnerable to other nuclear powers.‡

It was not just post-Suez anti-Americanism, therefore, that caused Conservatives to examine the case for much closer defence cooperation in Europe. Apart from the need for European countries to contribute more to their own defence, the escalating costs of weapon systems – and especially of any independent nuclear deterrent – made the arguments for cost-sharing and joint procurement strong ones. On the eve of the UK's accession to the European Community, the Bow Group paper *Our Future in Europe* clearly outlined the case for a European defence policy.

> For years the credibility of Western Europe's defences has depended on the presence of 300,000 American troops. It was always a dangerous risk to assume that this state of affairs would be permanent. Now President Nixon's state of the union message, with its reference to other parts of the world shouldering the burdens of their own defence,

---

* This was established under the Baghdad Pact of 1955, and comprised the UK, Iran, Iraq, Pakistan and Turkey. It was dissolved in 1979.

† This was also established in 1955 under the Manila Pact. Its members were Australia, Bangladesh, France, New Zealand, Pakistan, the Philippines, Thailand, the UK, the US and South Vietnam. It was dissolved in 1977.

‡ This was memorably described by a French general as the "strategy of the bee". If two equally-matched men-at-arms were fighting, one of them would be fatally distracted if stung by a bee.

has cleared the air. It has given European governments the ultimatum which many private voices within these countries have been warning would come.

We now have no choice. There must be a more viable, more integrated European defence system. We believe that the British Government should take the initiative towards this, first by approaching the U.S. Government to secure release from the restrictions of the McMahon Act;* second, by negotiating with the French Government to set up a joint Anglo-French nuclear force; and third by establishing for both nuclear and conventional weapons a European Defence Co-ordination Committee composed of all existing and prospective members of the European Communities.[26]

In the European Parliament a report[27] was adopted in June 1978 advocating that arms procurement should form part of the European Community's industrial policy, and received enthusiastic backing from the European Conservative Group, one of whose members, Tom Normanton, tabled a supporting opinion on behalf of the Parliament's Economic and Monetary Affairs Committee.

"No European defence without a federal Europe"

Such a policy clearly commended itself both on grounds of operational efficiency and cost. Yet on returning to power in 1979, the Conservative Party had still not found a way to combine the primacy of the Atlantic Alliance with a specifically European defence policy. The need to strengthen the "European Pillar" of NATO was widely recognised; but exactly how this was to be done remained a matter for discussion. The central dilemma facing Conservatives was that greater integration of national defence policies seemed impossible without greater political integration. As Sir Henry Plumb MEP put it in the Foreword to three papers on European Defence published by the European Democratic Group in 1983:[28] "no European defence without a federal Europe; a federal Europe is out of the question; therefore there can be no European defence".

The first paper, by the Montague Professor of International Relations at Oxford University, Hedley Bull, nevertheless argued that Europe had to do more in the field of defence, if only for the sake of "Western Europe's dignity". There was a "growing divergence of interests between Western Europe and the United States", and the US was in any case pressing for a greater contribution from Europe for its own defence. "The well-known scepticism of many ordinary British people about membership of the European Community" would therefore have to be overcome, and an "appropriate form of political and strategic unity" developed.

---

* The McMahon Act enabled the UK to receive nuclear know-how from the United States on condition that it was not passed on to a third country.

> The idea deeply entrenched in Whitehall that cooperation in political
> and economic areas may continue to develop among the European
> partners, while military matters remain the preserve of NATO, is basi-
> cally unsound.

There remained, however, the dilemma of ensuring "command and
control" without a single political authority. The second paper, by Col.
Jonathan Alford from the International Institute for Strategic Studies,
thought it "possible to imagine the evolution of a federated States of
Europe which would involve the transfer in peace of those instruments of
sovereignty – the armed forces of the state – to supranational authority"
but concluded that this seemed unlikely; and without a federal government "if anything, in the absence of the hectoring presence of the United
States in European military councils, military cooperation may in fact
prove more difficult rather than less".

This did not mean, however, as the final paper by David Greenwood
from Aberdeen University argued, that nothing could be done. While it
was obvious that political integration was a prerequisite for the establishment of a completely cohesive West European defence effort, "it is not at
all apparent that the business of building structures of defence cooperation must inevitably lag behind the creation of Europe's political fabric".
The "increasingly troublesome economic facts of defence life" meant that
greater European cooperation in the provision of arms and armed forces
was "an obvious, indeed *the* obvious, course".

> If Europe were a single market for defence equipment, Western Europe
> could enjoy the benefits which are thought to accrue to the Americans
> through the operation of a single market of this size.

Following the European Elections of 1984, the European Democratic Group
in the European Parliament established a "sub-committee on defence and
security" with British, Danish and Spanish members. In 1988 it published its
findings in a pamphlet,[29] once again emphasising the need for a European
defence identity, but firmly within NATO. Then, one year later, the situation changed dramatically. The fall of the Berlin Wall and the reunification
of Germany was followed by the dissolution of the Warsaw Pact, and then
of the Soviet Union itself, making a complete reappraisal necessary. The sub-
committee re-convened, and, after consulting a wide range of defence experts
from different countries, published its new findings at the end of 1991.[30]

At that time, the authors could only make informed guesses about how
the anticipated "new world order" might turn out. They made an assumption, not only that the Soviet Union was leaving the stage, but also that
in the United States – in a "now parlous economic situation" – a "strong
isolationist impulse" was emerging. The clear implication of this "end of
superpower dominance in the world" was that "the EC must develop a
unified and coherent position in the world". The pamphlet proposed "a

European Community Defence System (ECDS) which would act as the European pillar of NATO, but be capable of independent EC action when necessary". Even in the UK, the pamphlet noted, "54% of people ... believe security and defence policy should be made at the EC level".

As far as forces were concerned, some steps were by then already under way to create autonomous European units. Within NATO it had been decided to set up a "European Rapid Reaction Corps (RRC)" to be used inside NATO territory. The Western European Union was examining the creation of a "European Rapid Reaction Force", which could be deployed "outside the NATO area where explicit US involvement was politically unacceptable, or when European interests were at stake".

Like the earlier studies, the pamphlet finally drew attention to the economic dimension. The European defence industry remained fragmented along national lines, leading to short production runs, duplicated research, and overdependence on unstable export markets. The cumulative effect had been "escalating production costs, and a relative loss of competitiveness particularly against the US". The obvious way out was coordinated defence procurement and an end to "current legal barriers to intra-Community trade in defence equipment". Once again, the broad policy objectives seemed clear enough.

Fourteen years later, however, the CPS published a paper,[31] the starting point of which was that these policies were in the process of being carried out, in part as a result of an Anglo-French agreement between the UK's Labour Prime Minister Blair and French President Jacques Chirac at St. Malo in December 1998. Far from welcoming such a development, however, the paper mounted an attack on "the way that the UK is increasingly turning its back on the US as a source of defence procurement and purchasing equipment from European nations as a back door to integrating European defence".

The Foreword by Major-General Julian Thompson CB OBE, one-time Commander of the British Land Forces in the Falklands War, scathingly warned of "the 'dragging down' effect of integrating Britain's army with low quality European armies". Apart from the French Foreign Legion, marine infantry, and airborne, plus the Dutch marines, he asserted, "Europe's armies are military youth movements". In addition, he believed that "the MoD is often buying inferior or more costly equipment than that which Anglo-US contractors could supply".

Even allowing for the very different provenances of these documents, the switchover in attitude is striking. Its course can be charted in successive Conservative policy statements on the European dimension of defence.

Retrospect: the Westland affair and after

The issue of defence procurement had already, in 1986, produced what Geoffrey Howe thought "the turning point for Margaret Thatcher's administration".[32] The Westland helicopter company, a British supplier to the Ministry of Defence, was in financial trouble, and the government's preferred plan was an arrangement with a US company, Sikorski, under which Westland would be taken over and manufacture American Black Hawk helicopters (in the event, no Black Hawks were ever produced). Heseltine, however, was Defence Secretary and argued that Britain's commitment to European cooperation on defence procurement meant that participation in a Franco-German-Italian joint venture – in which British Aerospace and GEC could also be involved – should be preferred.

Heseltine's own account in *Life in the Jungle* indicates that there was a great deal more to the affair than the simple Europe-or-America issue. So does that of the Home Secretary at the time, Douglas Hurd. There were "military, legal, industrial, but above all political strands which it became impossible to disentangle". The Prime Minister's dual role "as both umpire and passionate protagonist turned a secondary procurement decision into a political crisis".[33]

A leaked letter from the Solicitor General, Sir Patrick Mayhew, and dubious dealings in Westland shares, which gave rise to a Stock Exchange inquiry, created a situation in which even Margaret Thatcher feared she might have to resign. The immediate cause of Heseltine's resignation, moreover, was not the policy issue itself but the way in which the matter was handled by the Prime Minister, who blocked (according to Heseltine) proper discussion of the matter in cabinet. According to Lawson, she was determined to force Heseltine to resign, and "indeed, she had already decided whom she would appoint Defence Secretary in his place".[34] The affair also cost Leon Brittan his job as Trade and Industry Secretary. It is for these reasons that, in retrospect, the Westland affair has been seen, not so much a defence issue, as the beginnings of the rebellion against "Thatcherism" which would later bring the Prime Minister down – though Heseltine records that, at the time, "the thought had simply never crossed my mind".[35]

In the early 1990s the Conservative Party was still officially committed to "developing closer European cooperation on defence".[36] However, as the 1994 *Handbook for Europe* put it, "British interest lies very clearly in ensuring that any emerging European defence identity is firmly rooted in NATO, both from a political point of view, and because of the crucial need to preserve the common resources and force structures of NATO, without competition or duplication". The preferred option was for the WEU to be developed both as "the defence arm of the EU and as the European pillar of NATO".

By the General Election of 2001 European defence cooperation had turned from an objective to a drawback. The Manifesto stated baldly that "our primary alliance, NATO, is being weakened by a concerted drive to create an independent military structure in the EU". Later, it did concede that "Conservatives have always supported stronger European defence cooperation", but this had been "always inside NATO". A Conservative government would not participate in a structure outside NATO, but would insist instead that any European initiative was under the NATO umbrella.

By the General Election of 2005, the manifesto made no mention of European defence cooperation at all. It merely stated that "a Conservative Government will strengthen our Armed Forces within NATO by spending £2.7 billion more than Labour on the front line by 2007–08". And in the European Elections of 2009 the manifesto[37] stated, even more explicitly, that Conservatives would "maintain the UK's independence on foreign affairs and defence, restating our commitment to NATO". The EU was not established for defence purposes and "should not set up expensive and wasteful structures that merely duplicate what NATO does already". The manifesto[38] at the General Election of 2010 was more explicit still.

> We will release spending on unnecessary and bureaucratic EU defence initiatives and spend the money on our Armed Forces. As part of that process, we will re-evaluate our position with the European Defence Agency.

It was already clear at the time, however, that any British government would find it difficult to reverse European cooperation in the defence field. The RAF, for example, was in principle committed to purchasing 232 Eurofighter/Typhoon aircraft, at a cost of £20 billion. Cancellation or reduction in the programme would put thousands of British jobs at risk. Given the pressing need to reduce public expenditure and reduce public debt, the logic of spreading the costs of developing weapon systems between several European countries, rather than trying to go it alone, remained.

For the incoming coalition government in 2010 the best solution seemed to lie in greater bilateral cooperation with France; and this had become a great deal more feasible when, in 2009, President Sarkozy took his country back into the military command structure of NATO. Though early rumours of integrating the nuclear-missile submarine fleets were quickly discounted, there remained many options for cooperation, both in the fields of equipment (e.g. military transports) and research; and many of these were duly incorporated into treaties signed by French President Nicolas Sarkozy and UK Prime Minister David Cameron on the 2nd November 2010.

It is an indication of how coming into office can transform positions taken up in opposition that the negotiations with France were in the hands of one of the Conservative Party's more Eurosceptic ministers, Liam Fox.

Notes

1   Hugo Young *op.cit.* p. 417.
2   Butler and Westlake *op.cit.* p. 75.
3   Turner *op.cit.* p. 221.
4   *UK membership of the single currency: an assessment of the five economic tests* (HM Treasury, Cm. 5776, June 2003).
5   *Conservatism and the Paradox of Europe* by Conrad Black (Centre for Policy Studies, October 1990).

6   *Drift to Union: wiser ways to a wider Community* by Oliver Letwin (Centre for Policy Studies, November 1989).

7   *Britain and Community: the right way forward*, by Nevil Johnson (Centre for Policy Studies, April 1993).

8   *The Challenge of Europe: Can Britain Win?* by Michael Heseltine (London, 1989).

9   *An Agenda for a Growing Europe: making the EU economic system deliver* by André Sapir (European Commission, July 2003).

10 *The Future of Europe* by Michael Howard MP (Centre for Policy Studies, May 1997).

11 *Winning the Argument: the 1994 European Elections* (Politics Today, Conservative Research Department, July 1994).

12 Speech at Ellesmere Port, the 31st May 1994.

13 *Conservatism, Democracy and National Identity* by John O'Sullivan (Centre for Policy Studies, March 1999).

14 *The Myth of Europe* by Russell Lewis (The Bruges Group, 2000).

15 *The European Commission: Administration or Government?* By Tom King MP (Centre for Policy Studies, August 1999).

16 Article 108.

17 Article 113.

18 The long title of which was "*An Act to amend the European Parliamentary Elections Act 1978 so as to alter the method used in Great Britain for electing Members of the European Parliament to make other amendments of enactments relating to the election of Members of the European Parliament and for connected purposes.*"

19 *In Europe, not run by Europe: Conservative manifesto for the 1999 European Parliament elections* (Conservative Party, 1999).

20 Robert Oakley, BBC Political Editor, 14 June, 1999 on *Robert Oakley's Westminster Week*.

21 *Time for Common Sense: 2001 Conservative Party General Election Manifesto* (Conservative Party, 2001).

22 Bale *op.cit.* p. 129.

23 "*Pax Europa* in the Conservative Party" in the 2007 Party edition of *Conservative Europe* (Conservative Group for Europe, October 2007).

24 *The Third Man: life at the heart of New Labour* by Peter Mandelson (HarperCollins, 2010) p. 349.

25 *Hansard*, House of Lords, 14 March 1963.

26 *Our Future in Europe: the long-term case for going in* by Leon Brittan and others (Bow Group, 1970).

27 The Klepsch Report, reproduced, with a Foreword by The Rt. Hon. Geoffrey Rippon MEP, in *Two-Way Street: USA-Europe Arms Procurement* (Brassey's and Crane Russak, 1979).

28 *Thinking again about European Defence* by Hedley Bull, Col. Jonathan Alford and Dr. David Greenwood, with Foreword by Sir Henry Plumb MEP (European Democratic Group, 1983).

29 *Collective Security: the European Community and the Preservation of Peace* by Michel Welsh MEP (European Democratic Group, January 1989).

30 *Defence and Security in the New Europe*, edited by Anthony Forster (European Democratic Group, December 1991).

31 *The Wrong Side of the Hill: The Secret Realignment of UK Defence Policy with the EU* by Richard North (Centre for Policy Studies, 2005).

32 Howe *op.cit.* p. 472.

33 Hurd *op.cit.* p. 396.

34 Lawson *op.cit.* p. 678.

35 Heseltine, *Life in the Jungle*, p. 312.

36 See *The Campaign Guide 1992*.

37 *Vote for Change*, European Election Manifesto (Conservative Party, May 2009).

38 *Invitation to Join the Government of Britain: the Conservative Manifesto 2010* (Conservative Party, April 2010).

14 The Constitutional Treaty

Amsterdam, Nice and beyond

Though focusing on Europe appeared to win few votes, Conservative fears that the EU was moving in an integrationist direction *was* supported by evidence. The Blair government, like that of Major before it, continued to maintain an official position that "Britain is winning the argument". Yet Maastricht proved only a preliminary to two further amending Treaties, and then to an attempt at rewriting the Treaty as a whole to make it a "Constitution for Europe".

The first of these developments, the Treaty of Amsterdam, had been a long time in preparation. The negotiations leading up to it had begun as far back as 1995; it had been signed in 1997; but had only come into effect in May 1999 after a long ratification process. Under its provisions the European Union clearly became a great deal more than a Common or Single Market. On the other hand the "pillar" structure which it developed owed a great deal more to the inter-governmental approach favoured by Britain, and especially by Conservatives, than to any "federalist" agenda. Partly for this reason, Eurosceptic objections to the Treaty were muted.

In any case, the main content of the Treaty – greater cooperation in the fields of foreign policy and security, and in that of fighting crime and illegal immigration – had always been Conservative objectives. There was also a major "tidying up" exercise, with 56 Treaty articles abolished, and the rest renumbered. The legislative powers of the European Parliament were simplified and strengthened, as were the powers of the Parliament to supervise the Commission. In addition the procedures for "enhanced cooperation" by willing groups of countries were spelled out, in accordance with the Conservative policy for a "variable geometry" Europe.

The Amsterdam Treaty nevertheless contained a number of defects. The articles on foreign policy appeared to lay down a clear, "inter-governmental" institutional system, entirely separate from that of the old European Community. The broad guidelines of policy were to be determined by the European Council (the old summit of Heads of State and Government), and implemented by a new "High Representative for the Common Foreign and Security Policy (CFSP)". What was not made clear, however, was how this would be combined with the work of the existing Commissioner for External Affairs, and the Commission's extensive responsibilities in the fields of world trade and development. The Treaty also left in abeyance the looming question of how the EU's institutions were to be adapted in the face of impending enlargement to twenty-five, then twenty-seven Member States. This was the main subject of the next Treaty, that of Nice, which was signed in February 2001, and came into force two years later.

Despite being largely technical in nature, the Treaty of Nice was attacked from all sides. The European Parliament came close to rejecting it, despite the provisions for increased parliamentary powers; and its unpopularity in Member States was emphasised when, in June 2001, the Irish rejected it in a referendum. Only after a second, this time positive Irish vote in October 2002 could it come into effect. British Eurosceptics also viewed the Nice Treaty with deep suspicion. A CPS paper published in October 2001[1] argued that it would be perfectly possible to accommodate the projected enlargements of the EU without the Treaty, and that the bulk of the text was concerned with entirely different matters. One change, for example, was to make industrial policy subject to weighted majority vote rather than unanimity. The Article was "a charter for industrial meddlers" providing "almost infinite scope for intervention in industry".

The author, Brian Hindley, found no substantial reasons to rejoice if the Treaty were to fall, nor any to be greatly upset if it was passed. He did nevertheless comment that the thirty-nine switches from unanimity to majority voting were an example of EU "salami-slicing" tactics, "of making each step in the progress of the EU small enough that objections to that step as such are difficult to mount".

Another CPS paper on the Nice Treaty,[2] published the year before, had been much more wide-ranging and critical, the author being the implacably Eurosceptic journalist, Christopher Booker. One focus of his attention was the proposed change to the "enhanced cooperation" procedure, designed to make it more difficult for countries not involved in a particular group to block its formation. Far from furthering the Conservative objective of "greater flexibility", Booker believed, this was part of a Franco-German plot to isolate Britain in an EU second division or slow lane, while the core countries sped on to full political union.

This, the paper went on, clearly put the Conservative Party on the spot. The Party's real problem was that "just like Mr Blair, they have been caught out by the speed at which the integration process is now moving. Their idea of a perfect European Union seems to be one defined by the single market and no more. But the train is clattering on." In October 1999, Booker then pointedly observed, "Mori found that, for the first time since 1983, a majority of voters, 51%, would favour Britain leaving the EU".

The Nice Treaty itself, as Brian Hindley was surely right in observing, was not much of a clattering train. But the most significant feature of the Nice agreement as a whole was not the Treaty itself, but the decision taken at the same time, and annexed to the Treaty, to establish a "Convention on the Future of Europe", leading to an Inter-Governmental Conference (IGC) in 2004.

The Laeken Declaration of December 2001 had already committed Member States not only to make the EU more efficient, but also to make it "closer to the citizens": more democratic and more "transparent" – i.e. more open to public scrutiny. This was the remit of the Convention on the Future of Europe, which met for the first time in February 2002 under the chairmanship of former French President Valéry Giscard d'Estaing. In carrying out its remit, the Convention was required to consult as widely as possible, especially taking into account opinion outside the EU's own institutions.

Its final product was to be the first draft of a "Constitution for Europe".

The proceedings of the Convention on the Future of Europe

The Conservative Party's official representative on the Convention – strictly speaking, he was a representative from the House of Commons – was David Heathcoat-Amory, whose uncle, Derick Heathcoat-Amory, had been Chancellor of the Exchequer in the early 1960s. He himself had briefly been Minister for Europe, then Paymaster General before resigning from the Major Government in 1996, the issue being Europe. In May 2004 the CPS published his account of the proceedings.[3]

From the start, he reported, there was a certain lack of openness about what the Convention on the Future of Europe was supposed to do. The Labour Government's representative, Peter Hain, was reported to have described the Convention as no more than a "tidying-up exercise"; and it is true that this was something urgently needed. Finding one's way around the basic Treaties, the amending Treaties, the annexed Protocols and Declarations, the extra-Treaty inter-institutional agreements, Council of Ministers resolutions and internal agreements, parliamentary Rules of Procedure, financial regulations, staff regulations and so on presented difficulties even for those working full-time in the field such as myself. Combining a lot of this into a single, easily-readable document would have been a huge step on the way to "transparency".

At the other end of the spectrum, however, was the determination of many Convention participants – led by the chairman, Giscard d'Estaing – to fulfil the much grander aim of writing a constitution for a United States of Europe. Heathcoat-Amory observed that "parallels were soon drawn between the European Convention and the one held in Philadelphia in 1787 which drew up the American constitution".

This latter, he nevertheless added, quoting de Tocqueville, was based on a number of preconditions: "a common language, a habit of self-government, a set of shared moral values amongst the governing class, and a widely held belief in equality and equal liberty." This was not the case with Europe where there were "differences in legal traditions, and attitudes towards the role of the state and the origins of rights." Echoing Enoch Powell over thirty years earlier, Heathcoat-Amory concluded that "there is no European People, no single electorate or coherent public opinion ... there is no European *demos* on which to found a supranational democracy or federation".

His account of the sessions designed to involve the general public is scathing: they were no more than "Brussels talking to Brussels". The "representatives of civic society" who were heard "turned out to be a succession of lobby groups, most of them familiar in Brussels and frequently dependent on EU funding for their existence". The Convention "rapidly became less of a deliberative body and more of an institutional bargaining forum". The representatives of national parliaments, despite being in the majority (56 out of 105) were "the tourists of the Convention and repeatedly failed to act or speak as a coherent body of opinion". Instead, the course of events was determined by the "transnational political groups", which met in advance to determine an agreed line. The two largest, the European People's Party and the Party of European Socialists, had "avowedly federalist aims".

Other accounts certainly agree with much of this description of events, and in particular the role of the political groupings. Indeed there is no doubt that the Convention was to a considerable extent hijacked by the European Parliament representatives, who imposed their working methods on the proceedings. Parliament's President at the time was Pat Cox, an Irish television journalist, who ably coordinated the Parliament's own campaign to be given extra powers. Another EP representative, the German Christian Democrat MEP Elmar Brok, played a major role as the European People's Party co-ordinator, and was actually voted "Mr Convention" afterwards in a poll taken amongst those attending as representatives, academics or journalists.

Nor should this have come as much of a surprise. Many years earlier, when I was still an MEP, an attempt had been made to establish a regular forum for discussion between national parliamentarians and MEPs; and an inaugural meeting had been held in Rome in 1991. Almost at once there had been a procedural dispute about seating: should those attending sit in national groupings or political groupings? The British Conservative MPs assumed that we would be sitting with them as a British Conservative delegation; but we assumed that we would sit, as in the Parliament, with the EPP members from all countries. In the event, the seating turned out completely *à la carte*. All the Members from the House of Lords decided to sit together in their own separate group; and most Conservative MPs, with some others from the House of Commons, formed yet another separate one.

All this was a good indication of how far Conservative MPs and MEPs had already drifted apart, and a warning of troubles to come. I remember attending a meeting of all the Conservatives present at which there was some strong criticism of the decision to sit with the EPP – a foretaste of the pressures that would later build up for Conservative MEPs to leave the Group altogether. One or two of the MPs remembered that I had once worked at Conservative Central Office, and wanted to know what I was doing to stop what they saw as, effectively, a split in the Party.

At the Convention on the Future of Europe, there were also complaints that Giscard d'Estaing appeared to have made up his mind from the start what the final report would contain. One story has him summing up a discussion during which all but one speaker had opposed the text in question. "Well," Giscard is reported to have said at the end, "I think we have a favourable consensus".

The draft Treaty "establishing a Constitution for Europe", submitted in July 2003 and also adopted "by consensus", was certainly more than a tidying up exercise. The preamble, said to have been written by Giscard on his own and which gave rise to a certain amount of ribaldry, begins with a quotation from Thucydides:

Χρώμεζα γὰρ πολιτείᾳ·καὶ ὄνομα μὲν διὰ τὸ μὴ ἐς ὀλίγους ἀλί ἐς πλείονας οἰκείν δημοκρατία κέκληται.

("Our Constitution. … is called a democracy because power is in the hands not of a minority but of the greatest number"); and goes on to proclaim the Convention on the Future of Europe to have been "conscious that Europe is a continent that has brought forth civilisation; that its inhabitants, arriving in successive waves from the earliest times, have gradually developed the values underlying humanism: equality of persons, freedom, respect for reason".

Strangely, this apparently innocuous statement proved a source of some dissension: it mentioned humanism, but not Christianity, which was considered by many to be the main source of European values. The opinions of those, like the British Conservatives, who stressed "national identity and history", and those who were keen to move on to a "common destiny", were combined – and it was hoped reconciled – in the phrase "united in diversity".

Heathcoat-Amory, however, observes that Giscard was not alone is being determined to reach "federalist" conclusions. A "Praesidium" of thirteen members "drew up the agenda … and decided the conclusions". It contained the Convention on the Future of Europe's two vice-presidents, Jean Luc Dehaene from Belgium (whom John Major had once vetoed as Commission President) and Giuliano Amato from Italy, "both former prime ministers and committed federalists". The Convention's secretariat were all "professional insiders, members of the European club".

In fact – though Heathcoat-Amory does not mention this – the Secretary-General of the Convention on the Future of Europe, and in effect the main draftsman of the final text, was not some wild-eyed continental federalist. He was none other than the thoroughly British diplomat, Sir John Kerr. As UK Permanent Representative to the EU, he had helped negotiate Major's "game, set and match" at Maastricht, and was widely considered to be the *éminence grise* behind Giscard and the Praesidium. According to Douglas Hurd, Prime Minister Major christened him "Machiavelli".[4] He would go on to the prestigious post of UK ambassador to the United States.

Heathcoat-Amory was not alone, however, in complaining that the draft Constitution for Europe owed more to private deals than to public debate. His view that "the real debates took place in the Praesidium, or between the Presidency, secretariat and member states in private" in fact received support from the MP representing the Labour Party, Gisela Stuart. A White Paper nevertheless confirmed in September 2003 that the draft Constitution was acceptable to the UK Government, subject to amendments on a number of so-called "red line" issues, of which the most important was retention of the national veto on foreign policy, taxation, social security and Britain's budget rebate.

What the Constitution said

Reading through the texts that emerged from the Convention on the Future of Europe, it is difficult not to conclude that both supporters and opponents, for their own political purposes, considerably exaggerated the texts' importance. On the one hand, the Constitution was hailed as an historic document, the foundation of a new United Europe. Yet it was later found possible (following the rejection of the Constitutional Treaty by referenda in France and the Netherlands) to turn it into a mundane series of amendments to the existing Treaties, like the Single European Act, Maastricht, Amsterdam and Nice.

On the other hand, Conservative opponents also had an interest in exaggeration. For Heathcoat-Amory it would be "outrageous to deny people a vote on a new constitutional settlement changing the way they are governed". An earlier CPS paper[5] went as far as to say that the choices presented by the Constitution "will have perhaps the most fundamental influence on the future shape of Britain since the Norman Conquest". This theme was taken up with gusto by Eurosceptic writers in the press. "You might want to take that vacation in England just as soon as you can – before its 1,000-year run as a sovereign nation comes to an end"[6] one advised American readers.

The official Conservative position was more measured. The manifesto for the European Elections of 2004 declared that, in opposing the Constitution for Europe Conservatives disagreed with "many of its provisions ... but we also oppose the very idea of an EU constitution. Countries have constitutions – nation states make treaties with one another." The Party had already promised to put the matter to a referendum, though the point at issue seemed almost one of mere nomenclature.

The Conservative referendum pledge nevertheless proved a shrewd political move. It panicked the Labour Government, which had initially argued that no referendum was necessary, to do a sharp u-turn, fearful of losing votes on the issue both in the European Elections of 2004, and the general election held in the following year.

Heathcoat-Amory himself had been a member of the working group charged with defining the division of "competences" between the Member States and the Union. Ever since the concept of subsidiarity had appeared in the Maastricht Treaty, there had been demands for more a concrete rules on "who does what", both to give legal certainty and to set clear limits on what the EU could and could not do. The Constitution duly divided areas of policy into those to be handled primarily by the EU; those remaining with Member States; and those for which competence would be "shared". Though it was always possible to argue about which policies should be in which category, the clarification could hardly be objected to. Heathcoat-Amory's main complaint was that defining powers as "shared" did not reveal whether this was to be 50 - 50 or some other proportion.

Many of the articles in the Constitution which aroused hostility were in fact re-statements of what was already the case: the primacy of EU law, the legal personality of the Union, citizenship of the Union, the ability of the Commission to propose legislation without a specialised legal base if this was required to fulfil Treaty objectives, and of the Council to take new powers by unanimity for the same purpose. One, on the face of it completely non-federalist, departure from existing practices – giving national parliaments the possibility of blocking EU legislation on the grounds that it was contrary to the principle of subsidiarity – was considered by opponents to be a question of "too little, too late".

The draft Constitution's most radical proposals were actually in the institutional field. Ironically, one change which originally aroused least opposition, a reduction in the number of Commissioners, would later play a part in the rejection of the Constitution, in its reincarnation as the Lisbon Treaty, by the voters of Ireland. The main institutional change proposed, however, was to end the practice of changing the presidency of the Council every six months, and instead create of the post of a "full time" President of the European Council – actually to be appointed for a once-renewable term of two and a half years. This was intended to answer what had become known as the Kissinger Question: "what is Europe's telephone number?"

This feature of the draft Constitution soon became the subject of criticism, and not just from Eurosceptics. What exactly, it was asked, would be the relationship between the full time President of the European Council, and the equally full time President of the Commission? Whose telephone should Kissinger, or his successors, ring? More seriously, it was envisaged that the presidencies of the specialised Councils of Ministers – and in particular the increasingly important Council of Economic and Finance Ministers (ECOFIN) – would continue to rotate as before. How would this arrangement interconnect with a non-rotating European Council presidency? Finally, there was the relationship of the Council presidency with the new

"European Foreign Secretary" (actually to be called the High Representative of the Union for Foreign Affairs and Security Policy): a new post created by merging the existing posts of High Representative for the Common Foreign and Security Policy (CFSP) and the Commissioner responsible for external relations. Which of the two would actually "speak for Europe"?

There was an even more serious objection, which was to be graphically illustrated some years later. Would a European Council President without the back-up of a national administration, and required to obtain a mandate from twenty-seven Member States, actually be able to act decisively? This problem was highlighted during the French Presidency in 2008, when Nicolas Sarkozy was able to broker a rapid solution to the crisis in the Caucasus directly with his opposite number in Moscow. When later reporting to the European Parliament in Strasbourg, he was accused of having failed to co-ordinate with other Member States. "If I had done that," he replied, "Europe would have been immobilised".

The criminal law and the Charter of Fundamental Rights

One provision of the Constitution for Europe produced a sharp division of opinion between the Labour Government and the Conservative Party. This was the proposal to "communitise" the inter-governmental "third pillar", which covers Home Affairs and Justice: i.e. incorporate it into the general competence of the Union. Prime Minister Blair, speaking in Cardiff in November 2002, had welcomed this as a means of securing "integrated and effective action" against organised crime and drug trafficking, and on asylum and immigration. However, the change would for the first time clearly extend the powers of the Commission and the jurisdiction of the European Court of Justice (ECJ) into the field of criminal law; and for Conservatives this was dangerous.

Heathcoat-Amory had been a member of the Convention on the Future of Europe working party dealing with the subject. His report warned that the result of its conclusions would be the harmonisation of criminal procedures, "including the rules of evidence in trials and the rights of the accused." This had particular significance for the British common law tradition "where jury trial procedures differ greatly from the inquisitorial system on the continent." Harmonisation would mean big changes to distinctive English and Scottish legal systems and there would be no national veto to prevent it. "Criminal justice policy goes to the heart of what a nation state is for."

In the negotiations leading to the Constitution's final version as the Lisbon Treaty, a major effort was made to reassure British opinion on the issue. In spite of this, a conviction had become deeply embedded that the foundations of English justice – Magna Carta, *habeas corpus*, trial by jury and so on – were under threat. Sixth-form and other conferences at which I spoke at the time were being confidently informed by other speakers that, if Lisbon were to be adopted, anyone being prosecuted would be considered guilty until proven innocent.

On one issue, however, the Labour Government and the Conservative Opposition were in agreement: that the Charter of Fundamental Rights, which had been drawn up some years earlier, should not be incorporated directly into any constitution. The original plan had been to annex the Charter to the Treaty of Nice; but instead it had been disseminated only as a "proclamation", and placed on the agenda for the Inter-Governmental Conference of 2004.

As Brian Hindley had pointed out in his 2001 paper, there was a conflict between the claim in the Charter itself that it did not "establish any new power or task for the Community or the Union, or modify powers and tasks defined by the Treaties"[7] and the proposition that it was "in some way fundamental to the future of the Union". Though the Labour Minister for Europe in 2000, Keith Vaz (quoted by Heathcoat-Amory), had claimed that the Charter "would have no more legal effect than a copy of the *Beano*", Hindley's own view was that its wording was "dangerously loose and its effects dangerously unpredictable". The Government was more inclined to support the actual content of the Charter than Conservatives – one article, for example, entrenched an unlimited right to strike. But both were wary of giving the European Court of Justice the right to interpret the Charter, which would be the case if it became a full part of the Treaty.

There was also the question of interaction with the entirely separate European Convention on Human Rights, discussed earlier, which had become directly justiciable in the national courts as a result of the Human Rights Act 1998. Though the rights granted by the Charter and the Convention were in most cases much the same, the case-law of the two relevant Courts, one in Luxembourg, the other in Strasbourg, were not identical – Heathcoat-Amory cited the example of double jeopardy. In the event of future conflict, which jurisdiction would prevail? The answer provided in a Declaration annexed to the Lisbon Treaty was that there would be a "regular dialogue" between the Courts, once the EU as a unit acceded to the Convention.

The Lisbon Treaty also had an annexed Protocol on the "application of the Charter of Fundamental Rights of the European Union to Poland and to the United Kingdom". This stated that

> The Charter does not extend the ability of the Court of Justice of the European Union, or any court or tribunal of Poland or the United Kingdom, to find that the laws, regulations or administrative provisions, practices or action of Poland or the United Kingdom are inconsistent with the fundamental rights, freedoms and principles that it reaffirms.

There nevertheless remained some uncertainty as to the precise legal status of the Charter, even in the Lisbon text. On the one hand, it was not part of the Treaty itself, but annexed. On the other hand, the Declaration appended to the Treaty stated that the Charter had "legally binding force". This uncertainty provided Eurosceptics with a powerful weapon in arguing for rejection of the Treaty as a whole

"A Constitution in all but name"

The document produced by the Convention on the Future of Europe was the basic text considered by the Inter-Governmental Conference (IGC) that took place, as planned, in 2004. The British government's negotiating position was to accept the Constitution, subject to the previously-announced "red lines". Having declared these secure, it stated support for the resulting Constitutional Treaty. The view of the Conservative Party was that this was "Blairite smoke-and-mirrors" – the "red lines" had never really been threatened, and the government was claiming bogus concessions before adopting the Treaty, as it had intended to do all along.

The Government had, however, already conceded a referendum. Opinion polls were showing that Treaty would be decisively rejected. And then Blair was rescued by the results of votes in France and the Netherlands. Both countries, the first on the 29th May 2005, the second on the 1st June, voted "No". Ratification by the seven countries which had still to decide, including the UK, was put on hold, and a meeting of the European Council called for a "period of reflection".

Opinion was divided among both supporters and opponents of the Constitutional Treaty as to whether this was the end of the matter. The general Conservative line was that the democratic decisions of the French and Dutch should be respected, and the whole idea of the Constitution be dropped. A more nuanced Conservative response was that the original idea behind the holding of the Convention – that all the existing Treaties should be replaced by something far more comprehensible, at the same time making the EU more democratic and accountable – should be preserved. The then leader of the Conservatives in the European Parliament, Timothy Kirkhope (who had himself participated in the Convention) published, in 1995, a "Simplifying Treaty"[8] of only 16 pages, including protocols, which the then leader of the Party, William Hague, described in a Foreword as "a proposal whose time has come". It rejected a common Foreign and Security Policy; but supported more co-operation in the field of Justice and Home affairs.

As already noted, it had been argued by its supporters that the Constitutional Treaty was needed to make an EU of twenty-five (shortly to be twenty-seven) Member States manageable; yet the provisions of the Nice Treaty, together with agreements on procedure in the Council of Ministers, seemed to be working perfectly well. There was an expectation among many Conservatives that the Treaty would now die a slow death during the "period of reflection". The more Eurosceptic, on the other hand, maintained that the drive towards a "federal" Europe had only suffered a temporary check, and would be resumed. In this they were proved right.

In France the period of office of President Jacques Chirac was coming to an end, and the heir-presumptive was Nicolas Sarkozy. One of his advisers on Europe, the MEP Alain Lamassoure, was reported to have produced a version of the Constitution for Europe crossing out everything that was already in the Treaties, and reducing the rest to a series of amendments. This, or a similar exercise unofficially carried out by the Commission, became the basis for what was at first known as the "Reform Treaty", published (in French) in June 2007. By this time Sarkozy had replaced Chirac, and immediately reached agreement with the President-in-Office of the Council, German Chancellor Angela Merkel, to proceed on the basis of the new text. Where the Constitution had been some 63,000 words long, the Reform Treaty had only 12,800. After yet another Inter-Governmental Conference (IGC) under the following Portuguese Presidency, the Reform Treaty became the Lisbon Treaty – somewhat longer than the original, with the addition of some 130 pages of clarifying Protocols and Declarations.

This turn of events produced varied reactions in Britain. Eurosceptics were able to claim that this was what they had predicted all along. The Conservative Party as a whole – now having lost yet another general election and subsequently with yet another new leader, David Cameron – was determined to hold the Labour Government to its previous pledge to hold a referendum. The Government certainly was in difficulties: having been spared the embarrassment of a referendum defeat on the Constitutional Treaty, there was every prospect of defeat on the Lisbon Treaty. The new Prime Minister, Gordon Brown, symbolised the problem by turning up late for the signing ceremony in Lisbon on the 13th December 2007. In the end, he decided to tough it out. The Government declared that the Lisbon Treaty was quite different from the old Constitutional Treaty, and could be ratified without a popular vote.

Unsurprisingly, the Conservative reaction was fury; but also some delight that Labour appeared to have put itself in a practically indefensible position. Everything to which Conservatives had objected in the original constitution was there in Lisbon, though now in an almost incomprehensible form – deliberately incomprehensible, it was asserted. Lisbon was the "constitution in all but name", and should be treated in exactly the same way.

The best counter-argument, of course, was that the "Constitution for Europe" had never in fact been a constitution in the first place. It was not quite possible to go back to Hain's original claim that it was only a "tidying up exercise"; but that, in effect, was how the new text was treated. Apart from Hungary, which held a positive referendum, nearly all Member States were able to ratify the Lisbon Treaty by parliamentary procedures. In the UK, despite Conservative objections, it received the Royal Assent on 19 June 2008.

But by this time the whole operation had once again been brought to an unexpected halt. Only the week before, a referendum in Ireland had rejected the Treaty by 53.4% to 46.6%. Not until after a second Irish referendum in October 2009 would there be any possibility of Lisbon coming into effect.

Notes

1 *Nice and After: the EU Treaty and Associated Issues* by Brian Hindley (Centre for Policy Studies, October 2001).

2 *Nice and Beyond: the parting of the ways?* by Christopher Booker (Centre for Policy Studies, October 2000).

3 *The European Constitution and what it means for Britain* by David Heathcoat-Amory MP (Centre for Policy Studies, May 2004).

4 Hurd *op.cit.* p. 462.

5 *A Defining Moment? A review of the issues and options for Britain arising from the Convention on the Future of Europe* by Norman Blackwell (Centre for Policy Studies, February 2003).

6 Stephen Webbe in *The Christian Science Monitor* of 29 March–4 April 2008.

7 Article 51.2 of the Charter

8 *A Simplifying Treaty* by Timothy Kirkhope MEP (Conservatives in the European Parliament, September 2005).

15 The Road to Recovery

Elections in 2004 and 2005

The European Elections of 2004 were in many ways a re-run of those in 1999, with the Conservative Party returning the largest number of MEPs. It was fought on the basis of nine fewer seats for the UK, the result of the EU's enlargement. All the English regions lost one seat, except the East Midlands and, interestingly, the South West, in which the British dependency of Gibraltar – unlike the Isle of Man, within the EU – was included for the first time.

Labour again did badly: after adjusting for the overall reduction in seats, it lost six MEPs to return a total of only 19. On the other hand, the Conservative Party also lost seats, eight on the same basis, falling to a total of only 27. Compared to 1999, indeed, the result was extremely disappointing: the nine percentage point drop in the Party's share of the poll was worse than that of any other.

The Liberal Democrats did well, gaining two seats to a total of 12; and so did the Green Party, with 2 seats. But the clear winner was the United Kingdom Independence Party (UKIP), which came third in number of votes and gained ten seats, also to end with a total of 12. Less well noticed at the time was a significant vote for the right-wing British National Party (BNP), which took nearly five per cent of the poll overall, and up to eight per cent in some regions.

One perhaps surprising feature of the election was the UK turnout, which rose from the pitiful 24% of 1999 to a record 38.4%. There are several possible explanations. In the English regions local elections were held on the same day. For the first time there was a much greater availability of postal ballots – turnout in all-postal ballot areas was 5% higher than in others. Many of those who voted for UKIP were not defectors from other parties, but had previously declined to take part in anything "European". The highest turnout, 56.6%, was in the previously disenfranchised Gibraltar. More generally, the elections were used to register a protest against the political establishment as represented by both the Labour and Conservative Parties, which together failed to achieve even half the poll.

A number of explanations can also be advanced for the success of the United Kingdom Independence Party. The Party achieved huge media coverage as a result of the candidature in the East Midlands of Robert Kilroy-Silk, well-known from his television talk-show. (His membership of UKIP did not last long: in 2005 he left to found another party, from which he also soon resigned.) UKIP was also well-funded. It ran a clever campaign, correctly pointing out that the European Elections ought not to be about national issues, but about European ones; and that this was the British people's first real chance since 1975 to cast a clear vote against continued EU membership.

It is difficult to avoid the conclusion, however, that UKIP was in some measure the creation of the Conservative Party itself – Frankenstein's monster emerging from Eurosceptic experiments. For nearly ten years the message on Europe had been that Britain was in danger of being submerged in a "federal super-state", and that the EU was, in Russell Lewis' words, undemocratic, excessively regulated, corrupt and with a structural bias against British interests. Many people not surprisingly concluded that we should get out while we could.

The Conservative Party, on the face of it, did not fight a bad campaign. The Party's new leader, Michael Howard, had a clear, consistent and long-held policy on the EU which was outlined in his foreword to the Party's manifesto, *Putting Britain First*. The Party believed in

> a Europe that does not demand the sacrifice of independence as the price of participation. A Europe that looks outward. A made-to-measure Europe that accommodates differences. This vision will deliver what British people want from Europe: freedom, stability, and prosperity. It will put Britain first.

A main theme of the Manifesto was "New threats from the EU constitution", together with the promise to hold a referendum on it. The Manifesto also spelt out the position of Conservative MEPs in relation to the European People's Party Group. This was the result of an agreement hammered out after the European Elections of 1999 between European People's Party leaders on the one hand, and Hague, together with the then leader of the Conservative MEPs, Edward McMillan-Scott – of whom more later – on the other. In view of later controversy it is worth quoting in full.

> Conservative MEPs in the European Parliament have worked effectively with other centre-right parties to achieve our stated aims and goals. During the 1999–2004 Session we were allied members of the Group of the European People's Party and European Democrats (EPP-ED). It became increasingly clear, however, that there were substantial differences of view between the EPP and ED elements of the Group on constitutional and institutional issues. This called for a revised relationship with the EPP-ED.

We negotiated, and have secured, two very important changes to the Group's Statutes.

First, we have secured a change in the Statutes of the Group which will enable the ED element to promote and develop its own distinctive position on constitutional and institutional issues in relation to the future of Europe. This change enshrines that right for the first time.

Second, a post of ED Vice-Chairman will be reserved within the Presidency of the Group. We have also secured the right of any Member of the European Parliament to apply to join either the EPP or ED elements of the Group. Centre-right parties, including our sister parties from Central and Eastern Europe, will now have the opportunity to sit with British Conservatives in the ED and follow our distinctive agenda.

When elected, every Conservative Member of the European Parliament will be committed to this position.

This agreement means that Conservative MEPs will remain allied members of the EPP-ED parliamentary group for the duration of the 2004–2009 legislature. It provides us with a powerful platform to promote our distinctive vision of Europe, while at the same time allowing us to work constructively with all parties of the European centre-right against the threat posed by the Left in the European Parliament.

The view of some Conservative candidates and other supporters, however, was that not only the situation *vis à vis* the European People's Party, but the policy of the Party in general, "lacked clarity". One of the sitting MEPs who contested the East Midlands, Chris Heaton-Harris, later wrote that "I had the bizarre experience of Robert Kilroy-Silk standing against me for UKIP, and seeing our Party's best laid plans blown out of the water".[1]

Part of the election strategy was to attract protest votes against the Labour Government, as in 1999; but this time it failed to work. What protest votes there were went either in the direction of the Liberal Democrats – who were to do even better on this score in the following year's General Election – or, in some core Labour areas, the British National Party (BNP).

In sum, the Conservative Party was, in artillery terms, "bracketed". On the one hand it was attacked by Labour and the Liberal Democrats as "extreme", "negative" and "obsessed"; on the other by UKIP as "soft on Europe" and "allied with EPP federalists". The view of the former head of the Minority Parties Unit at Conservative Central Office, Rupert Matthews, was that Michael Howard had wanted to avoid "a massive row which might well end with the EPP expelling the Conservative MEPs and labelling them as extremist zealots. Rather than risk such a dispute, the Conservatives toned down their manifesto and removed from it policies that might have halted the voter drift to UKIP".[2]

What these policies might have been was not stated; and it is unlikely that anything short of a pledge to leave the EU, or at least to re-negotiate

completely the terms of membership, would have made significant
inroads into the UKIP vote. Matthews was right, however, in saying
that the Party suffered from "a major image problem with Europe", the
legacy of past divisions. As a result, it had a "difficult line to tread" in
the European Elections of 2004, persuading UKIP voters to come back to
the Conservatives "without alienating the middle ground nor putting the
party in a position where its opponents in the media can convincingly
portray it as having lurched off to the extremes in a desperate chase for
Eurosceptic votes".

One year later, however, came a General Election, in which the issue
of "Europe" – and with it the United Kingdom Independence Party vote
– faded away. In contrast to the "last chance to save the pound sterling"
message in the General Election of 2001, the Conservative Party concentrated during the 2005 election campaign on domestic issues. Single pages
of the manifesto[3] highlighted what research had shown were messages
echoing voters' concerns: "My taxes keep going up, but what have we
got to show for it?" "What's wrong with a little discipline in schools?"
"I mean, how hard is it to keep a hospital clean?" "Put more Police on
the streets and they'll catch more criminals, it's not rocket science, is it?"
"It's not racist to impose limits on immigration" "Why can't politicians be
more accountable?" The only non-domestic message was "Obviously the
world is more dangerous and we've got to keep up our guard".

The manifesto said little new on the subject of Europe. It promised that a
Conservative Government would hold the referendum on the Constitution
for Europe "within six months of the general election"; and the policy to
keep the pound sterling was now absolute: the manifesto stated concisely
that "We will not join the Euro". This at least answered the criticism that
had been made two years earlier by Ken Clarke (though not, perhaps in
the sense that he had meant it): that Britain would have more influence
on the European agenda if "we could end our semi-detached role that
hovering on the brink of the Single Currency causes".[4] Perhaps the most
controversial item in the manifesto occurred almost as a throw-away
remark: "we will also build on the success of enlargement, making Europe
more diverse by working to bring in more nations, including Turkey".

Most Conservatives firmly supported, in principle, the Party's commitment to enlargement; but there was already evidence that what was called
"enlargement fatigue" was beginning to set in. The media had sounded
warnings that the countries due to join in 2007, Bulgaria and Romania,
were not really ready. In the case of Romania there were unsettling stories
about the number of gypsies who might arrive once there was free movement; and in the case of Bulgaria that corruption and crime were out of
control. In the case of Turkey, the official arguments were that bringing in
a loyal NATO ally would strengthen Western defence, and that rejecting
Turkey might throw the country into the arms of Islamic fundamentalists.
The evidence both from opinion polls and Party meetings, however, was
that Conservatives were largely unconvinced.

The election result, as widely predicted, produced another Labour government, but with a reduced majority. The Conservative Party made a net gain of 33 seats, and the Liberal Democrats of 11, with Labour losing 47. Perhaps the most interesting feature of the result, however, was the low percentage of the vote polled by the winning party. The turnout in the election was 61.3%, slightly up on 2001; but Labour won only 35.3% of votes cast, with the result that the government was returned with a majority of 66, but with the support of well under a quarter of the electorate.

Having done his bit to pull the Party together, and put on a moderately good show in two elections, Michael Howard resigned the Party leadership.

Cameron Conservatism

At the end of April 2004 I had ceased to be an EU *fonctionnaire*, and had officially retired back to the UK. During that summer, however, I spent a considerable time in Brussels, as a member of a panel interviewing economists from the ten new Member States who had applied to work in the EU. The procedures had been changed so that the different institutions no longer organised their own recruitment. Instead, a European Personnel Selection Office (EPSO) had been set up to act for all EU bodies. I was one of two examiners on the economics panel nominated from the Parliament.

The thousands of applicants had been reduced to a manageable number by a preliminary round of multiple-choice questions. The next stage required the candidates to submit essays in an official EU language of their choice. Judging by the composition of the panel, EPSO had assumed that there would be a spread of choices – indeed, it turned out that I was the only native English-speaker, compared to two each for French and German. Yet, in the event, over 85% of the essays were submitted in English. It was a telling sign, perhaps, of how the balance of influence within the EU was about to shift, in the political as well as in the linguistic field: a shift described by the American Secretary of Defence, Donald Rumsfeld, as being from "old" to "new" Europe. The Conservative Party, too, saw the shift as one very much for the better: from the integrationist, *étatist* model of Monnet and Delors to the enthusiasm for free markets and national sovereignty of the post-Communist administrations in the new Member States.

Meanwhile, marking the essays kept me busy through the summer months.

Having retired back to the UK also meant that I could, if I wished, resume active politics; and almost the first Party event to occur was the second Conservative leadership election held under the new rules introduced by Hague. This also produced surprises. The favourite this time was David Davis, who duly led the field after the first ballot of Conservative MPs, but with only 62 votes. Second was David Cameron with 56, and third the most Eurosceptic of the candidates, Liam Fox with 42. The least Eurosceptic, Ken Clarke, polled only 38 votes and was eliminated.

The betting was that David Davis would head the second ballot as before, and that it was evens whether Cameron or Fox would join him for the final. In the event Cameron topped the second poll with 90 votes, Davis fell back to 57 and Fox, with 51, was eliminated.

There has been much speculation since about the role, if any, played by the candidates' views on Europe during the contest. Based solely on the figures, Cameron appeared to have attracted the bulk of Clarke's support. However, he had earlier let it be known that, if elected leader, he would require Conservative Members of the European Parliament to leave the EPP Group, something for which Eurosceptics had been pressing for some time. A similar pledge had been made by Fox even earlier (though not by Davis); and it has been suggested that Cameron's move was largely designed to neutralise Fox's advantage among the more Eurosceptic MPs, and ensure a place in the final with then front-runner, Davis.

This certainly sounds plausible. On the other hand, such a pledge should have put off many former Clarke supporters, which it clearly did not. It is arguable, then, that Europe played little part in the contest, and that Cameron's advantage lay in his "brand image" rather than specific views: he was seen as the candidate of a new school of "Notting Hill Tories", young, forward-looking and untainted by the final years of the Major government.

Playing to this perception proved decisive when the candidates appeared before the 2005 Conservative Party conference. David Davis, still considered the favourite, made a moderately competent but traditional speech from the lectern. Cameron, speaking without notes, addressed the conference from the front of the stage, promising a break with the past, and to make people "feel good about being Conservative again". In the ballot of party members, he defeated Davis by a margin of over two-to-one.

The initial reaction in the media was rather light-hearted: the "toffs" had retaken the Tory Party after forty years of middle-class rule. Not only Cameron himself, but others who were appointed to the shadow cabinet – Oliver Letwin and Boris Johnson – were Old Etonians, and from not very humble backgrounds. Labour tried to make political capital out of this; but it soon became clear that it was very far from a reactionary, right-wing takeover. The new leadership immediately set out to nullify the charge that the Conservatives were the "nasty party" (a phrase used by the then Party chairman, Theresa May, at the 2002 conference, when drawing attention to the need for change). Most notably, the Party became "green". Protection of the environment, reducing greenhouse gases, energy efficiency, reduced waste, became major policy themes, with at least two members of the new leadership making a point of going to the House of Commons on bicycles.

With Hague back as shadow foreign secretary, no change was expected on policy concerning Europe. Indeed whereas the so-called "modernisers" in the Party – notably Michael Portillo in the years following the 2001 defeat – had argued for a return to the centre ground of politics in the field, in particular, of social policy, there was no similar call for a move away from Euroscepticism. Euroscepticism had ceased to be a distinguishing mark of no-turning-back Thatcherism: it had become "a given rather than a touchstone".[5] The word nevertheless went out within the Party that a period of silence on the subject would be welcome. Echoing Basil Fawlty, "don't mention Europe" became something of a catch-phrase at party meetings.

That a policy of avoiding any more dissension on Europe within the Party was now in place appeared confirmed by Cameron's own conduct. In spite of criticism from some MEPs, he avoided formal meetings with the leaders of other parties comprising the EPP-ED parliamentary group. At the same time, strident Euroscepticism was dropped from the Party's electoral message, along with undue concentration on the issues of crime, immigration, unmarried mothers, homosexuality and other matters which had contributed to the "nasty" image. Instead, there was a focus on the underlying causes of a "broken society" – a policy which at one stage became encapsulated in the phrase wrongly attributed to Cameron: "hug a hoodie".

The policy of calming passions on Europe certainly seemed to be working when, in January 2009, Ken Clarke was made shadow Secretary of State for Business, Enterprise and Regulatory Reform. Michael Portillo, writing in the *Sunday Times* of the 14th December 2008, had thought a return by Clarke – though badly needed, given the dramatic turn of events in the economy – would be impossible because of his views on Europe. In the event, these were generally held to be irrelevant.

The new strategy on Europe did have some cost, though. In March 2009 one previous donor to the Conservative Party, spread-betting tycoon Stuart Wheeler, said he was giving £100,000 to the United Kingdom Independence Party "in protest at the Tories' reluctance to talk about the EU". He was also going to vote UKIP at the June European Elections – but would remain a Conservative. The news was received with equanimity by Conservative Campaign Headquarters, but was a reminder of the continuing problems posed by any separate party positioned on the Eurosceptic right.

Where to sit?

In addition, one contentious Euro-issue refused to go away: where Conservative Members of the European Parliament should sit following the upcoming European Elections of 2009. Eurosceptics in the Party were determined to hold Cameron to his pledge during the leadership contest that there should be a break with the EPP Group. For them, the arrangement negotiated by Hague and McMillan-Scott in 1999 had not only lacked clarity, but failed to disentangle the Party from association with avowed "federalist" objectives.

In 2001 the CPS had published a paper[6] claiming that the ED element of the EPP-ED Group was a "convenient fiction",[*] and advocating the creation in the Parliament of a new, centre-right but anti-federalist group. One of those contributing to the paper was an adviser to the MEPs from Philippe de Villiers' French nationalist *Mouvement pour la France*; another Secretary of Conservatives Against a Federal Europe (CAFÉ), one of the many groups which sprang up in the Party to oppose Maastricht. Their central contention was that an alliance with the Christian Democrats in order to strengthen the opposition to Socialism was based on a false premise.

> More than left and right, ... the real divide in the European Parliament is between those who wish to see a greater concentration of power in Brussels and the *souverainistes*, who have a belief in cooperation between autonomous Nation States.

One argument advanced by those supporting exit from the EPP-ED, indeed, was that the European Parliament lacked an "official opposition". Every existing political alliance in Europe – the Communists, the Socialists, the Liberals, the Greens, the Christian Democrats – supported the euro, the constitution, a common foreign policy and an EU criminal justice system. But once there was a mainstream conservative bloc positing a different kind of Europe "the cartel will be broken" and "Euro-federalism will cease to be inevitable, and become one among a series of competing ideas".[7] A *souverainiste* group, the CPS paper suggested, could be formed by combining British Conservatives with the French nationalists, two Portuguese who had been expelled from the EPP-ED, three Dutch MEPs, a Dane, and, improbably, *Fianna Fáil* and some right-wing Italians. Nothing of the sort, of course, happened.

A new group, however, appeared to become a great deal more feasible following the enlargements of the EU in 2004 and 2007. The rules of the Parliament require a political group to be composed of MEPs from several Member States: at the time seven. There were high hopes of finding like-minded parties in several of the twelve new EU countries.

One apparently firm ally was found at once in the Civic Democratic Party (ODS) of the Czech Republic, the Party of the Eurosceptic Czech President, Václav Klaus. In 2006 David Cameron and the Czech prime minister designate, Mirek Topolanek, announced their joint decision to establish a new parliamentary group immediately after the European Elections of 2009. Meanwhile, they set up a "Movement for European Reform" "open to all like-minded parties from EU member states and from

---

[*] It incorrectly described "European Democrats" as "the name of the Eurosceptic Group to which the Conservatives had belonged between 1979 and 1992". Nothing could have been less Eurosceptic than the European Democratic Group (EDG) as a whole, the "H-block" excepted.

EU candidate countries, who share our ideas of a modern, open, flexible and decentralised EU, ready to face the challenges of the 21st century".

The Movement held an inaugural conference in Brussels in March 2007, addressed by Cameron and Topolanek, and attended by 380 people from 17 different countries and 18 different political parties. The only other party which formally joined the Movement, however, was the Bulgarian Union of Democratic Forces (UDF).

It also became clear that the fluidity of politics in many of the only recently established democracies made the task of identifying solid, respectable, like-minded parties far from straightforward. In Poland, for example, splits and mergers had meant that most of the parties were of very recent origin. The most obvious candidate for membership of the new parliamentary group was the Law and Justice Party (PiS), formed in 2001 and tracing its origins back to the *Solidarność* (Solidarity) movement of the 1980s. It was free-market, strongly nationalist and, as its name implies, firmly for law and order. However, its policies during a period in office under the leadership of the Kaczyński twins – one of the brothers, the late Lech, remained as President when the other, Jarosław, ceased to be Prime Minister – were not entirely in line with the liberal, "caring Conservatism" with which Cameron was anxious to be identified in the UK.

Even the alliance with the ODS faced problems. Although Václav Klaus was firmly against the Lisbon Treaty, Prime Minister Topolanek – President-in-office of the European Council during the first half of 2009 – controlled the parliamentary party and secured ratification of the Treaty by the Czech Republic's parliament before his government fell that March (though without there being any clear alternative).

One further problem facing the Party in forming a new parliamentary group was securing an amicable split with the EPP Group; but this was successfully negotiated in advance of the European Elections of 2009. Indeed, as one of the campaigners for the split, Daniel Hannan MEP, observed in March 2009, "it was always the contention of us Get-Outers that relations with the Christian Democrats would improve once we left: the EPP would lose a bad tenant and gain a good neighbour".[8] In a letter to the former Conservative MEP for East Sussex and Parliament Vice-President Sir Jack Stewart-Clark, David Cameron also promised that the new group would "continue to work closely with the remaining EPP Group parties on areas where we agree". The Conservative Party had indeed already set up joint working parties with the German CDU and the *Union pour un Mouvement Populaire* (UMP), the Party of French President Sarkozy.

Despite the agreement, however, breaking with the EPP Group was still controversial within the Party. One sitting MEP and Vice Chairman of the Conservative Group for Europe, Christopher Beazley, asserted that the new Group would be "a political error with appalling consequences ... a cobbled together hotch-potch of mavericks, single member parties, narrow-minded nationalists Canute-like trying to hold international cooperation at bay, right-wing extremists whose domestic policies would be deeply embarrassing to a Centre Right responsible Party like the British Tories".[9] In addition, the Conservative leader would no longer have the right to attend the pre-summit planning meetings of European People's Party leaders "where the real decisions are made".

It was also possible that, as in the case of the Spanish *Partido Popular* in 1989, the lure of being in the largest parliamentary group would prove too great for potential allies. Even with the Group leader sitting on Parliament's "Conference of Presidents", it would have little clout in decision-making compared to the two largest groups, the EPP Group and the Socialists. Ambitious politicians aiming to become Parliament President, or at least chairman of an important committee,[*] would be able to do their calculations.

One further disadvantage of being in a smaller parliamentary group – one not even recognised by most MEPs – is reduced influence on the structure of the European Parliament's own staff, and possibly on that of other EU institutions as well. As I myself quickly discovered in 1973, the idea of Parliament officials being evenhanded servants of the institution, above mere party politics, is a great illusion. The promotion ladder is a complex labyrinth, in which it is important to be of the right nationality and of the right political complexion at the right time. Above all, when major posts are being allocated, it is important to be the candidate of either the EPP Group or of the Socialist Group, which have traditionally divided the top jobs between them. A Socialist Secretary-General of the Parliament, Julian (now Sir Julian) Priestley was, almost as of right, succeeded by a candidate from the EPP, Harald Rømer – as it happened, a Danish Conservative and former Secretary-General of the old European Democratic Group. His chances of getting the job as a Conservative and Reformist (see later), or even a European Democrat, would have been, to say the least, remote.

Finally, the logic of 1992 would remain. My own conclusions as Single Market *rapporteur* during the 1980s and early 1990s, were also reached by the Conservative MEP, Malcolm Harbour, *rapporteur* ten years later, and who in 2009 became chairman of the Parliament's Internal Market Committee. Writing in the Conservative Group for Europe's 2003 Party Conference Magazine, *Conservative Europe*, he noted that "Conservative MEPs working in alliance with other centre-right parties, have had a very significant influence on the direction of Internal Market policy".[10]

Despite such doubts, however, all Conservative candidates in the European Elections of 2009 were required to sign up to the following pledge:

> I hereby agree that if I am elected, I will respect the agreement made by David Cameron and Mirek Topolanek in July 2006, 'that at the commencement of the next legislature period of the European Parliament, following the elections in 2009 our delegations will

---

[*] The application of the d'Hondt system to the allocation of posts between groups means that the largest groups get the first pick of chairmanships (see Chapter 6).

establish a new parliamentary group, which other like-minded parties will be invited to join', and that I will become a member of whichever political group in the European Parliament is decided upon by the Party Leader, in consultation with the leader of the Conservative MEPs, after the 2009 European elections.

Moats and duck-islands: the European Elections of 2009

In the run-up to these elections, held in the UK on 4 June, the Conservative Party had high hopes of making significant gains. It was well ahead of Labour in the opinion polls, and other parties – the United Kingdom Independence Party in particular, which appeared less well organized than in the European Elections of 2004, and no longer had Kilroy-Silk at its head – did not seem to pose a threat. The polls were also showing that the Conservative Party's policy of remaining in the EU, but resisting any further political integration, exactly reflected the views of most voters. Research carried out for *The Economist*, for example, showed that, while about 80% of the electorate wished to remain in the EU, over 30% of the electorate wanted this on the basis of "free-trade only".[11]

Rather like Labour's in 1989, however, the Conservative campaign focused primarily on the domestic political situation. The lead slogan was "It's time for" (or "Vote for") "change", followed by the message: "if you're sick of Gordon Brown's hopeless Government, this is your chance to show it".

Though understandable in terms of British national politics, this was probably a mistake in the context of European elections. It allowed UKIP again to claim that it was the only one clearly addressing the issue of British EU membership, while being as much anti-Brown as the Conservative Party. However, the European poll was coupled with county council elections, in which the Party hoped to capture the few remaining counties under Labour control. The Party was also looking forward to the impending general election, possible within only a few months, but in any case due within a year.

Yet, as polling day approached, the British political scene was thrown into confusion. The *Daily Telegraph* began to publish, day after day, details of Members of the House of Commons' claims for expenses. The most prominent targets were Labour ministers; but several so-called "Tory grandees" also found themselves held up to censure and ridicule, having claimed tax-payers' money for "clearing out the moat" or "purchasing a duck island". The response by MPs that their claims were "within the rules" merely prompted the question: who designed the rules? And when those in the firing line began to pay back money, this was generally seen as an admission of guilt. An extraordinary, genuine wave of anger about "corrupt MPs" grew in both the media and among the general public, with little distinction being made between the main parties. The first casualty was the Speaker of the Commons, Michael Martin; and before long a growing number of both Labour and Conservative MPs were announcing that they would be standing down at the coming general election.

This turn of events had the effect of boosting support for those parties not perceived as being implicated, and which had a chance, under the proportional voting system, of winning European Parliament seats: the Greens, UKIP (although two of the UKIP MEPs elected in 2004 had already been involved in fraud) and the British National Party (BNP). The opinion polls began to show the Conservative Party's projected vote in the European Elections running well below that projected for a General Election.

The political situation became even more extraordinary on the eve of poll, and on polling day itself, when the resignation of several cabinet ministers precipitated a crisis in the Labour Party, with the media openly speculating whether the Prime Minister could stay in office. A cabinet reshuffle was brought forward to the Friday, after the results of the English county council elections had been declared (with Labour failing to win control in any, and the Conservatives making almost a clean sweep), but before the European results were known.

When these were eventually announced on the evening of Sunday the 7th June, they duly reflected the events of the previous weeks. Labour, with under 16% of the vote, had its worst result since 1918, and ended up with only 13 out of the UK's 72 MEPs – the same as UKIP, which overtook Labour in terms of popular vote. The British National Party won two seats off Labour in the north of England. The Liberal Democrats, with a share of the poll 1.2% lower than in 2004, nevertheless went up one seat to 11.* The Greens, with a share of the vote 2.4% higher, nevertheless remained at 2.

For the Conservatives, the result was just satisfactory: 25 seats were won, and the Party's share of the vote, at 28.6%, was slightly higher than in 2004. In Wales the Party for the first time gained more votes than Labour. Yet it was not quite the triumph that had been anticipated earlier in the year. In the South East, for example, we had been confident of making at least one, and possibly two or three gains; but only the four sitting MEPs were eventually returned in the ten-seat region.

As had been predicted, the MPs' expenses scandal had clearly damaged the main parties represented in the House of Commons. For Labour the result was catastrophic, for the Conservative Party it turned what could have been a massive victory into a merely modest one. The Liberal Democrats might have been expected to be substantial beneficiaries, but were limited to holding their own, as were the Scottish National Party (SNP) and Plaid Cymru in Wales. Instead, a sizeable proportion of the electorate voted for parties not represented in the Commons: UKIP, the

---

* At the election the Liberal Democrats in fact already had eleven seats as a result of Bill Newton-Dunn having left the Conservative Party to join them. His re-election as a Liberal Democrat was, technically a LibDem gain.

BNP, the Greens, and a host of smaller parties which did not win seats like the English Democrats (1.8%), the Christian Party-Christian People's Alliance (1.6%) and the Socialist Labour Party (1.1%). Most of the British electorate – almost two-thirds of it – did not vote at all.

Post-election analysis confirmed that many Conservative supporters had split their vote, supporting the Party for county council but UKIP for the European Parliament. There is also anecdotal evidence that this reflected a continuing resentment among certain sections of the Party at the events of November 1990. A recently-published study[12] of opinions and attitudes among grass-roots Conservatives by two under-cover journalists carries a report of a Conservative Way Forward dinner in Mayfair, addressed by Cecil Parkinson. They spoke to a certain Gloria, who

> had always voted for UKIP in the European elections, reasoning that, because MEPs were elected on a list system, there was a danger that a vote cast for the Conservatives might result in the election of a Europhile Tory. … Gloria believed that Margaret Thatcher had been 'got rid of' by her party not because of the poll tax fiasco, but because pro-European Tories had conspired against her in order to hasten the march of a European super-state.[13]

Conservatives and Reformists

The immediate issue for the Conservative Party following the European Elections of 2009 was whether the promised new European Parliament group could be formed. Numbers presented no problem: the 25 British Conservatives (26 with James Nicholson of the United Conservatives and Unionist Party of Northern Ireland) already constituted more than the minimum total for a group. In the Czech Republic the Civic Democratic Party (ODS) won nine seats, and in Poland the Law and Justice Party won fifteen. This meant that the proto-group needed to attract at least one MEP each from four more countries (no Bulgarians, in the end, decided to join).

In fact, there was no shortage of candidates – more than the necessary three parties, indeed, were reported willing to join, including the Italian Northern League and the Danish People's Party (DPP). In these two cases, however, there were grounds for rejection. Both the Northern League and the DDP had an anti-Islamic stance, and were opposed to Turkish EU membership.

As it turned out, one MEP each from the Dutch *ChristenUnie*, the Latvian National Independence Movement (TB/LNNK), the Hungarian Democratic Forum (MDF), the Belgian *Lijst Dedeker* (LDD), the Lithuanian LLRA and a Danish Independent gave the new group members from nine countries. For the first time, supporters of the new group declared, the European Parliament had "an Official Opposition". Its principles and policies had already been outlined in the "Prague Declaration" of 2009, including support for "free enterprise, free and fair trade and competition" and for "the sovereign integrity of the nation state".

However, the successful formation of the group – which took the name European Conservatives and Reformists (ECR) Group rather than re-adopting that of European Democrats – did not silence controversy over the matter. A retiring Conservative MEP, Caroline Jackson, speaking on the BBC's *World Tonight* programme, described as "stupid" exchanging the European People's Party Group for a few "odds and sods, ... random Latvian nationalists and the odd Hungarian that you find under the political hedge". The media in several countries attacked the British Conservatives for linking up with "fascists", prompting the counter-charge that the successors to the actual fascists were Italians sitting in the EPP Group.

The new group, moreover, did not get off to a particularly good start. At the opening session of the Parliament in July 2009, its official candidate for one of the vice-presidencies, the Polish MEP Michal Kamiński, was defeated by the former leader of the British Conservative MEPs, Edward McMillan-Scott, who was expelled from the new group and stood as an independent. As a result, the European Conservatives and Reformists (ECR) Group became the only parliamentary group with no seat on the Parliament's Bureau", a situation which lasted until the unexpected resignation of a Vice-President from the Alliance of Liberals and Democrats for Europe Group (ALDE) in mid-2011 enabled Conservative MEP Giles Chichester to take her place. A further consequence was that the designated leader of the new group, the British Conservative Timothy Kirkhope, had to hand over the leadership to Kamiński in compensation. The Group faced further embarrassment when Kamiński declared himself to be in favour of the Lisbon Treaty. Meanwhile, McMillan-Scott was expelled from the Conservative Party itself, and by the beginning of 2010 was threatening legal action against the Party. In March he resigned from the Party "I have served more or less faithfully for 43 years"[14] and joined the Liberal Democrats.

The formation of the group also came under fierce attack from both pro-Europe and Eurosceptic directions. Articles in the *Guardian*, the *Independent* and the *New Statesman* accused Kamiński of anti-Semitism – in his youth he had been a member of the extremist Polish Revival Party (NOP). Remarks by the Polish chief rabbi, condemning Kamiński's former position but approving of his present support both for Jews and for Israel, were quoted by the Labour leadership to condemn, and by the Conservative Party to vindicate, the alliance in the European Parliament. Conservative MEP Daniel Hannan commented in his on-line *Bulletin* that "from the moment David Cameron announced that he planned to estab-lish a *souverainiste* alliance, the palaeo-federalists started hurling clods of manure at him".[15]

The comments on Hannan's article by militant Eurosceptics, however, were every bit as strongly-worded. "The EU parliament" said one, was

an unjust, undemocratic, centralising, illiberal monster. ... The danger and the irony is that having a strong grouping opposing further integration might in the end legitimise the levels of integration we already have along with the institution that supports it.

It was not therefore certain that leaving the EPP Group to establish the European Conservatives and Reformists (ECR) Group would bring back into the Party those who left it for the United Kingdom Independence Party. It was also clear that the new group was proving a great deal more controversial, and was attracting a great deal more animosity from different sides, than the independent European Democratic Group to which I had once belonged, or the European Conservative Group that preceded it. In addition, the instability of the Polish Law and Justice Party was soon creating further problems. A split between the hard-line leadership and more moderate elements led to the resignation in early 2011 of the ECR leader, Kamiński, to be replaced by Jan Zahradil from the Czech ODS party.

The Lisbon Treaty

Just in time for the 2009 Conservative Party Conference, the Irish voters approved the Lisbon Treaty in a second referendum. Only the signatures of the Polish and Czech Presidents were needed for the Treaty to come into effect; and on the 10th October Polish President Lech Kaczyński signed, as he had promised to do if there were an Irish "Yes".

There remained the hope that Czech President Václav Klaus would hold out until the election of a Conservative Government in the UK, when the Treaty could be killed off in a referendum. On the 18th October, however, Klaus told a Czech newspaper that "the train [of the Lisbon Treaty] is going too fast and has gone so far that it will not be possible to stop it or to send it back". Klaus, it also became clear, had been opposing the Treaty less as matter of principle than in order to extract concessions: notably to ensure that the descendants of Germans expelled from the Sudetenland after the Second World War could not use the Charter of Fundamental Rights to seek compensation from the Czech government.

Czech ratification was therefore more or less assured when the European Council at the end of October adopted a Protocol, to be annexed to the Treaty, extending to the Czech Republic the "opt-out" from the Charter of Fundamental Rights already enjoyed by the UK and Poland. To meet any other lingering doubts some may have had, the Council also specifically confirmed that "the Treaty of Lisbon provides that *'competences not conferred upon the Union in the Treaties remain with the Member States' (Art.5(2) TEU)."* An appeal claiming that the Treaty was incompatible with the Czech constitution was summarily dismissed by the country's constitutional court; and on the 3rd November Klaus signed.

This created a potentially embarrassing problem for the Conservative Party.

Policy before full ratification had been crystal-clear: if the Treaty were still un-ratified when the Party came to power, there was a "cast-iron pledge" that the new government would hold a referendum on it and campaign for a "No" vote. Less clear, however, was what would happen once full ratification had taken place. Not only within the Conservative Party, but also within the country as a whole, there was substantial support for holding a referendum anyway. However, whether rejection of the Treaty could have any effect – besides incurring considerable expenditure – was problematic: UK ratification would stand. Only if the government were willing to break its Treaty obligations, with unknown legal effects, could a "No" vote have any real consequences.

David Cameron therefore found himself obliged to outline a new position, which he did on the day following the Czech ratification. Lisbon, he said, was no longer a Treaty. It had become part of EU law. Holding a referendum on it would therefore serve no useful purpose. Instead, Cameron concentrated on outlining measures to ensure that a similar situation could not arise again. If the Conservatives won the next election, they would amend the European Communities Act 1972 "to prohibit, by law, the transfer of power to the EU without a referendum." Other safeguard measures would include a UK Sovereignty Bill making it clear that ultimate legal authority remained with Parliament, so putting the UK "on a par with Germany, where the German Constitutional Court has consistently upheld – including most recently on the Lisbon treaty – that ultimate authority lies with the bodies established by the German Constitution". Finally, a Conservative Government would make sure that Britain had a renewed "opt-out" from the Social Chapter, a secure opt-out from the Charter of Fundamental Rights and a block on "creeping control over our criminal justice system by EU judges".

Within the Conservative Party as a whole, this new position was generally very well-received. Overt Eurosceptic rebellion was confined to the resignation from their ECR Group "spokesmanships" in the European Parliament of Daniel Hannan and Roger Helmer. Even those who had pressed hardest for a referendum like Cameron's defeated opponent for the leadership, David Davis, conceded that there was no sense in pursuing the matter further. The *Economist* observed that Cameron was only "stating the bleedin' obvious".[16]

Outside the Party and in much of the media, however, Cameron's statement received less favourable treatment. It was described as a "Euro-fudge" or a "climb-down", designed to keep the Party together rather than lay down clear policy. The United Kingdom Independence Party made the most of Cameron's alleged "betrayal" over a referendum, and polls immediately afterwards showed UKIP's potential support at a general election doubling to 4%. The actual content of the statement also appeared to have been taken much more seriously abroad when French Europe Minister Pierre Lellouche was reported in the *Guardian* as having described the policy as "pathetic", and symptomatic of the Conservatives' "bizarre autism" on the subject of

Europe. Later, however, Lellouche claimed to have been misreported.* Both he and French President Sarkozy nevertheless continued to warn that there was no enthusiasm in the rest of the EU for any more institutional changes, and certainly none for changes designed to suit Britain.

The later, more considered opinion of commentators was that Cameron, assuming a Conservative win at the general election, had at least bought time before having to make serious decisions about the Party's European policy. Concentration on clearing up the economic mess left behind by Labour would prevent any upsurge of Eurosceptic rebellion of the kind experienced by John Major. On the other hand, the EU itself would not stand still. A committee chaired by the shadow Foreign Secretary, William Hague, was given the task of preparing for any problems.

In November, the nominations made by the European Council to the two new posts created by the Lisbon Treaty, the President of the Council itself and the High Representative for the Common Foreign and Security Policy (CFSP), were received with some ribaldry in the press, and with some relief by the Conservative Party. The Prime Minister, Gordon Brown, had been widely reported as having pressed the claims of Tony Blair for the first post, and the UK Foreign Secretary, David Miliband, as a fall-back position for the second. Blair, it was argued, had the international clout to "stop the traffic" in Beijing and Washington. He would be a President of the type originally envisaged by Giscard d'Estaing (who clearly saw himself in the job).

In the event, however, the nomination of the hardly-known Prime Minister of Belgium, Herman Van Rompuy, was more in accordance with what insiders believed to be EU's real requirements: a competent and uncontroversial figure to chair the Council and prepare its work. This had been clearly recognised from the start by those actually in power, notably French President Sarkozy and German Chancellor Merkel, if not by Giscard. The whole furore about a "President for Europe" once again seemed to have been an example of both Euro-enthusiasts and Eurosceptics exagerating the issue for their own purposes.

The real problem – and one that had been predicted all along (see Chapter Fourteen) – began to emerge not long afterwards: the EU now had *two* Presidents, Barroso heading the Commission and Van Rompuy the European Council. This had created the potential for rivalry between them as to who really "spoke for Europe", and left the "Kissinger Question" still unanswered.

The nomination of the British Commissioner with responsibility for trade, Baroness Ashton of Upholland, for the post of High Representative was also an example of the practical triumphing over the dramatic. Although she had, reportedly, only been Brown's third choice for the post, she had the important support of re-appointed Commission President Barroso. Since the main objective of the appointment was to unite the

---

* For example, his use of the words *"pathétique"*, which means sad or unfortunate in French, had been misunderstood.

responsibilities of the former High Representative of the Council with those of the Commissioner for External Affairs, and since the post carried with it a Vice-Presidency of the Commission, someone with Commission experience was a strong candidate besides being a Socialist (to balance the Christian Democrat Van Rompuy) and a woman.[*]

Baroness Ashton's nomination, however, received further unfavourable comments when the important Internal Market portfolio in the Commission – including responsibility for the regulation of financial services – went to the French candidate, Michel Barnier. French President Sarkozy unwisely crowed that this would help "continental ideals to prevail over the discredited Anglo-Saxon model"; and a "senior banker" responded by accusing the British Government of having "surrendered control of the City of London to the French in return for some nonentity getting a non-job".[17] Several MEPs, for example James Elles in his on-line Newsletter,[18] also observed that, as nominee for a Commission Vice-Presidency, Baroness Ashton still had to be vetted and approved by the European Parliament (as she eventually was).

Meanwhile, on the 1st December 2009, the Lisbon Treaty came into effect. Few noticed much difference.

The 2010 election and after

The General Election of May 2010 produced a result which few if any political commentators had foreseen: a coalition government of Conservatives and Liberal Democrats. In the early months of the year the Conservative Party had experienced a steady narrowing of its previous massive lead in the opinion polls, leading to speculation that Labour might even retain power, thanks to the bias in its favour produced by variations in constituency electorates. The general expectation, however, was that the Conservative Party would end up with the most seats in the new House of Commons, and would consequently be asked to form a government.

All such conventional predictions unravelled during the election campaign proper, and notably after the first televised debate between the leaders of the Conservative, Labour and Liberal Democrat parties: David Cameron, Gordon Brown and Nick Clegg. Polls taken after the debate showed that Clegg – until then a relative unknown – was considered the winner by a massive margin; and this, in turn, produced an apparent surge in support for the Liberal Democratic Party itself. For

---

[*] Lord Mandelson, reportedly the UK Government's second choice for the post, qualified on the first two counts, but not, of course, on the third. Though he stated that he would have liked the job, it appears he was not seriously considered as a candidate by the Council. In his memoirs, *The Third Man* (HarperCollins, 2010) page 495, he somewhat acidly remarks that "it was an extremely slapdash process by which to fill such an important post." David Miliband, who it seems *was* considered, did not want to leave UK politics, for reasons which became clear after the General Election of 2010 – a decision he might now be regretting. Besides the support of Barroso, Baroness Ashton also had the support of the Socialist Group in the European Parliament and of the various national member parties.

much of the campaign the Party was shown in the polls to be running several percentage points ahead of Labour, and at one point even ahead of the Conservatives. The election was described in the press as a "three horse race", and the probable outcome a House of Commons in which no one party had an overall majority (a "hung parliament"). It was uncertain which of the three main parties would have the most seats.

In the event, the Liberal Democrat surge in the opinion polls turned out to be something of an illusion. Rather than polling over 30% and beating Labour into third place, the final result showed the Party, with 23%, at much the same level predicted before the formal campaign began. In terms of seats there was actually a net loss. Labour, as predicted, polled extremely badly in percentage terms – little more than in the General Election of 1983 – and lost some 90 seats; but benefited from a positive swing in Scotland and a reasonable showing in the Northern England "heartlands" and in London. The Conservative Party emerged as clearly the largest party in terms of both votes and seats; but fell short of the critical overall majority in the House of Commons. Detailed analysis of constituency results revealed that there had been no uniform swings between the parties: in some cases the Conservative Party had won where it had never expected to (Carlisle, Montgomeryshire); but failed to win in others which had been considered almost certain gains (Westminster North, Hammersmith). The commentators concluded that the country had been uncertain about which party it wanted in government, and had voted accordingly.

A blow-by-blow account of the manoeuvres and negotiations that took place once the election result was clear is not necessary here. Though various options appeared to be on the table – a minority Conservative administration with or without support from other parties; a "rainbow" coalition of Labour, Liberal Democrats, various nationalists and the single Green; even an all-party "government of national unity" – the external context, and in particular the economic context, proved decisive. Whatever the ideological positions of the parties, the clear need for a stable government, combined with "the numbers", made a Conservative-Liberal Democrat agreement virtually inevitable – "the only game in town" as the Liberal Democrat negotiators admitted. What was perhaps not inevitable, however, was the form this agreement took: a full coalition government with the ambition of remaining in office for a full five years.

Following the negotiations which led to this solution, both parties announced that they had made concessions on the policies outlined in their manifestos. The document outlining the agreement also showed that the negotiating teams had gone into considerable detail in aligning policies, almost certainly aided by work already carried out by civil servants in the cabinet office in preparation for alternative election outcomes.

At a press conference in the St. Stephen's Club announcing the start of negotiations with the Liberal Democrats, the Conservative leader David Cameron had stated that his party had three "red lines" where no concessions would be made. One of these was policy on the European Union.

In this context, the Party's election manifesto[19] had outlined a number of measures to be taken by an incoming Conservative Government. Any further transfer of powers to the EU, and any proposal to adopt the euro, would be subject to a referendum. A European Sovereignty Bill would be introduced, making it clear that ultimate authority over all legislation rested at Westminster. The law would be changed so that use of the *"passerelle"* or "ratchet" procedure in the Lisbon Treaty transferring powers to the EU without a new Treaty would be subject to a vote of the UK Parliament. National control would be restored over "those parts of social and employment legislation which have proved most damaging to our business and public services". There would be a "full opt-out" from the EU's Charter of Fundamental Rights; and Britain's criminal justice system would be protected from any extension of the European Court of Justice's powers in this area. A Conservative Government would "never sign up to a European Public Prosecutor".

In contrast, the Liberal Democrat manifesto[20] – perhaps deliberately – borrowed a phrase of John Major's by promising to put Britain "at the heart of Europe". There would be a "strong and positive commitment" to European cooperation, with a particular emphasis on joint measures to tackle climate change. The manifesto also supported working through the EU "for stricter international regulation of financial services and banking", and keeping Britain "part of international crime-fighting measures such as the European Arrest Warrant, European Police Office (Europol), Eurojust, and the European Criminal Records Information System, while ensuring high standards of justice." It also, of course, stated the Liberal Democrats' belief that "it is in Britain's long-term interest to be part of the euro" – though only "when the economic conditions are right" and after a referendum.

On the face of it, these positions were some way apart; and there is indeed evidence that policy on Europe was a significant issue in the negotiations. In the parallel negotiations which took place between the Liberal Democrats and the Labour Party Nick Clegg was reported as saying that the outline agreement with the Conservatives "still fell short of what they wanted on Europe".[21] Later, when an agreement was almost concluded, Clegg told Gordon Brown himself that "he was still seeing how far he could push the Tories on Europe".[22] On the other hand, the leader of the Conservative negotiating team, William Hague, reported afterwards that policy on Europe had *not* proved a problem.

David Cameron's words at the St. Stephen's Club had in fact been chosen carefully. The "red line" was the transfer of further powers to the European Union without a referendum, rather than insistence on the "restoration of national control" over existing EU competences. What was in effect a post-Lisbon standstill on the distribution of powers between the EU and the UK was eventually incorporated in the agreement between the Conservatives and the Liberal Democrats – although this did also promise to examine "the balance of the EU's existing competences", "the case for a United Kingdom Sovereignty Bill", to establish "a Commission to investigate the creation of a British Bill of Rights" and to "work to limit the application of the Working Time Directive in the United Kingdom". Joining the Euro Area was not ruled out for ever; only "in this Parliament" – although, since no preparations would be made for joining either, the first feasible date for this to happen would effectively be well into the following Parliament.

Scattered throughout the subsequent and more detailed coalition programme[23] were certain more positive pledges: to "publish details of every UK project that receives over £25,000 of EU funds"; to end the "so-called 'gold-plating' of EU rules"; strong support for EU action in the field of the environment and against climate change; and, of course, support for EU enlargement. The programme also addressed a number of more specialised issues: promising to "stop foreign healthcare professionals working in the NHS unless they have passed robust language and competence tests", fulfilling "our EU treaty obligations in regard to the taxation of holiday lettings", and working towards a new system of charging Heavy Goods Vehicles (HGVs) for road use.

Reaction to the coalition agreement in both the Conservative and Liberal Democrat parties, and in the Labour and other Opposition parties, tended to confirm the view that policy on Europe was viewed as an issue of only limited importance. Attention instead focused overwhelmingly on the economic situation, and in particular on policies to reduce the public sector borrowing requirement and the level of public debt. Even the more Eurosceptic Conservatives raised few objections to the compromise policy – possibly happy that overseeing its detailed implementation could safely be left to the new chairman of the House of Commons European Scrutiny Committee, Bill Cash.

Notes

1 Foreword to *Fighting Off the UKIP Threat: a strategy for success in the 2009 European Elections* by Rupert Matthews (PMS, 2008).
2 Matthews *op.cit.*
3 *Are You Thinking What We're Thinking? It's Time for Action* (Conservative Party, 2005).
4 *Addressing Europe's Real Agenda* by The Rt. Hon. Ken Clarke QC MP in *Conservative Europe, 2002 Party Conference Magazine* (Conservative Group for Europe, October 2002).
5 Bale *op.cit* .p. 379.
6 *Bloc Tory: a new party for Europe?* by Gawain Towler with Emmanuel Bordez and Lee Rotheram (Centre for Policy Studies, August 2001).
7 Daniel Hannan MEP's blog, 4 December 2008.
8 Daniel Hannan's *Euro Bulletin*, 11 March 2009.
9 *Responsibility in Europe: the preparations* by Christopher Beazley MEP in *Conservative Europe* (Conservative Group for Europe, Autumn 2008).
10 "Internal Market reforms must be the EU's top priority" by Malcolm Habour MEP in *Conservative Europe, 2003 Party Conference Magazine* (Conservative Group for Europe, October 2003).
11 *The Economist*, 30th May–5th June 2009.

12 *True Blue: strange tales from a Tory nation* by Chris Horrie and David Matthews (Fourth Estate, 2009).
13 Horrie and Matthews *op.cit.* p. 126
14 Article in the *Observer* of the 14th March 2010.
15 Daniel Hannan's *Bulletin*, the 31st July 2009.
16 Bagehot column in *The Economist* of the 7th November 2009.
17 Reported in *The Times* of the 2nd December 2009.
18 James Elles MEP: *In-Touch Newsletter*, Winter 2009.
19 *Invitation to Join the Government of Britain: the Conservative Manifesto 2010* (Conservative Party, April 2010).
20 *The Liberal Democrat Manifesto 2010: change that works for you; building a fairer Britain* (Liberal Democrats, 2010).
21 As recalled by one of the Labour negotiators, Peter Mandelson: *op.cit.* p. 551.
22 Mandelson *op.cit.* p. 553.
23 *The Coalition: our programme for government* (Cabinet Office; May 2010).

16 1945 to 2010 – An Analysis

Europe and the parties

During my political life, as I observed in the Preface to this study, the Conservative and Labour parties appear to have exchanged policies on Europe on more than one occasion. The most dramatic of such switches has been the most recent, when the Conservatives, the "party of Europe" in the 1970s and 1980s, became steadily more Eurosceptic during the 1990s; while Labour, which had fought elections in the 1980s on a platform of ending Britain's European Community membership, became, under the leadership of Tony Blair from the mid-1990s onwards, a new "party of Europe".

One very plausible explanation is that it all depends on whether one is in government or in opposition. Hugo Young observes that "it is the fate of modern British governments, however sceptic they are in theory, to be in practice 'European'; the facts of life are European".[1] And Anthony Forster comments that "mass scepticism in political parties has been a phenomenon which has coincided with periods of opposition;" and "is part of the radicalisation process parties undergo out of office".[2]

The history of the Labour Party since the 1950s certainly provides strong evidence to support the theory. Gaitskell's passionate opposition to Macmillan's application to join the EEC gave way to the Brown/Wilson application almost immediately after Labour won the General Election of 1964. Equally soon after the Labour Party lost in the General Election of 1970 it rejected the terms of entry negotiated by the Heath government, only to reverse position again on returning to power in 1974, with the Wilson government recommending a "Yes" vote in the 1975 referendum. Following defeat in the General Election of 1979, the official policy became passionate rejection of continued membership; but turned to enthusiastic support once Labour returned to power in 1997.

It is true that these changes in Labour policy do not absolutely coincide with the Party's electoral fortunes: the move from an anti-Europe to a pro-Europe position in the late 1980s and 1990s took place gradually, even before Blair became leader. It can be argued, though, that this was part of a general repositioning of the Party to make it electable: a recognition that, in government, anti-Europeanism is not a viable policy. Now that Labour has returned to opposition, and its leader Ed Miliband has declared New Labour dead, it will be interesting to see whether – and, if so, how quickly – the Party reverts to a Eurosceptic position. There were indeed early signs that some repositioning on Europe was already taking place. In the run-up to the fixing of the EU's 2011 Budget, Labour's shadow Europe minister, Wayne David, accused the Prime Minister of having "thrown in the towel" in the fight to block any rise in EU spending.

In the case of the Conservative Party the evidence is less clear-cut. In the early years after the Second World War, indeed, the position was exactly the reverse: the enthusiasm of Churchill and other leading Party members for a United States of Europe during the years of opposition between 1945 and 1951 became the disdain of Anthony Eden for the whole European project when the Party returned to power. Only after the shock of Suez did the Macmillan government tentatively apply for EEC membership. Likewise, Conservative determination to enter the Community began well before victory in the General Election of 1970, notably after Ted Heath became leader in 1965; and the Party remained pro-European during its spell in opposition between 1974 and 1979.

The rise of Euroscepticism in the 1990s also presents a complex picture. It began to gain a hold in the Party well before defeat in 1997, and can be said, indeed, to have contributed significantly towards it. Turner observes that, when the Conservative Party has been in power, the leadership has usually had little difficulty in maintaining control over policy; and that being in power has "reduced the scope for ideological debate within the party".[3] On the other hand, electoral unpopularity at any time has weakened the leadership's grip, allowing latent factional disputes to surface. From this standpoint it can be plausibly argued that it was the Thatcher Government's troubles with the Community Charge ("poll tax") that opened the way for militant Euroscepticism.

It also has to be remembered that, whatever the official policies at any one time, both parties contained substantial groups within them which throughout maintained strong enthusiasm for, or strong opposition to, participation in European integration. On the Labour side, it was the "Jenkinsites" who made possible passage of the European Communities Act 1972 when Heath was in office, despite the official position of their party rejecting the terms that Heath had negotiated. On the Conservative side there were, from the moment of Harold Macmillan's application to join the EEC in 1961, the die-hard anti-Common-Marketeers, at first unwilling – as they saw it – to abandon Commonwealth and Empire, later unwilling to give up national and parliamentary sovereignty to "Brussels".

Hostility towards Europe has also served as a proxy for disagreements about entirely different matters, or as part of a general political package. Many on the right of the Conservative Party opposed Macmillan's application to join the EEC not so much in order to defend the Commonwealth, EFTA or British agriculture, as because they disliked his perceived left-wing approach as a whole – in particular the "wind of change" and the policies of the Colonial Secretary, Iain Macleod. In the case of Enoch Powell, one wonders whether his dislike of Heath, and his disappointment at being soundly beaten by him for the party leadership, at least played a part in his change of mind on Heath's central policy, the drive for European Community membership. A third, much more clear-cut example has already been noted: the Eurosceptic attacks on John Major's government during the debates on the Maastricht were for many as much a way of obtaining revenge for the dismissal of Margaret Thatcher as an objection to the Treaty itself.

It is also possible to detect swings of the political pendulum, not just between parties, but also within them, with attitudes towards Europe forming part of more general changes. Sometimes the swing can mark the replacement of an old guard by a new generation, with accompanying changes in outlook. One example, perhaps, can be found in the refusal of Macleod and Powell to serve under Sir Alec Douglas-Home, and then the arrival in the leadership for the first time of a Conservative from the post-war intake, the very pro-European Ted Heath. The militant enthusiasm for Europe of the Greater London Area Young Conservatives in the late 1960s and the early 1970s was an element in their battle with the Conservative establishment as a whole. More clear-cut examples, again, were the revolt against Prime Minister Thatcher's growing Euroscepticism which brought Major to power; and then the counter-revolution which brought in Hague and Duncan Smith. The victory of Cameron and the "Notting Hill Tories" can be viewed both as a generation change, and also as a break with the days when the Party seemed to prefer quarrelling about Europe to winning elections.

Switchers

One alternative approach to charting movements of opinion within parties as a whole is to examine the speeches and writing of individual members who switched sides, paying close attention to their reasoning. There are some particularly interesting examples, for example, on the Left of the Labour Party: Wedgwood-Benn (Tony Benn), who was pro-Europe when at the Ministry of Technology for reasons of economic and industrial logic, but who later turned violently anti for constitutional reasons; or Barbara Castle, one of the most powerful voices in the "No" campaign in 1975, who – becoming convinced that "Socialism in one country" was no longer feasible – ended up a supporter of Socialism on a European scale once she had served for a few years as an elected Member of the European Parliament.

Examples of Conservatives who changed their minds on Europe are not in short supply. In some cases the switch has been from one extreme to the other, as in the case of the 1975 Treasurer of Britain in Europe, Alistair McAlpine, who ended up in James Goldsmith's Referendum Party; or that of Beryl Goldsmith, for many years deputy head of the British European Movement, who became PA to Norman Tebbit and equally Eurosceptic. Nicholas Ridley, in the early 1960s a self-declared federalist, was in 1990 forced to resign as Secretary of State for Trade and Industry for saying (among other things) that "giving up sovereignty to Europe was as bad as giving it up to Adolf Hitler".[4] For most part, however, the changes of mind have remained within the bounds of acceptable Party opinion.

A group of particular interest in this context are the members of the Bow Group in the late 1950s and early 1960s who campaigned for British Common Market membership, even when it was not Party policy; but who are now mildly – and some not so mildly – disillusioned. Both my bosses when I worked in the Conservative Political Centre, David Howell and Russell Lewis, fall into this category. Their changes of mind, this group argues, reflect changes that have taken place in the European Union itself – from free trade to *dirigisme*, for example – or in the world as a whole. In a letter to *The Economist*,[5] Lord Howell (as he now is) wrote of a struggle "between the coming realities of a network world – with Asia in the ascendant – and the inward-looking, bloc-iste, over-intervening mentality of the European integrationist Bourbons". Yet in the late 1950s and early 1960s the need to be inside a European "bloc" in a world of "blocs" was being used as a positive argument for joining the Common Market: for example by another similar switcher, William (now also Lord) Rees-Mogg.

Then there is the case of Enoch Powell. Even allowing for hostility to Heath, something more must have led the probable author of the 1965 One Nation Group pamphlet *One Europe* to state thirteen years later that helping to destroy British membership of the EEC had become "my principal object in the remainder of my political life". His change of attitude appears to have occurred over a relatively short period of time, and not long after he had been arguing, as Shadow Minister of Defence, for a withdrawal of British forces from "East of Suez" in order to concentrate on the defence of Europe "with which the security of the British Isles is bound up". The change had the features of a Damascene conversion: like St. Paul, Powell thereafter devoted all his energies to demolishing a cause which he had previously espoused. A similar sudden conversion from orthodox support of Britain's membership of the European Community to an obsession with a perceived threat to British nationhood occurred in the case of Bill Cash.

Such sudden changes of mind do not seem to be typical in the case of those who moved in the opposite direction. Peter Walker moved from being a founder of the Anti-Common Market League to a supporter of Heath's drive for membership during the course of the late 1960s, in part, perhaps, as result of having managed Heath's leadership campaign in 1965. He later became an even more convinced pro-European as a result of attending the Community's Council of Ministers. Similarly, the transformation of Sir Derek Walker-Smith from eloquent opponent of the Macmillan EEC application to respected chairman of the European Parliament's Legal Affairs

Committee took place as he gained experience on the European political scene. There are similar later examples: the Conservative MEP Bryan Cassidy, who arrived in the European Parliament after the 1984 European Elections, and initially shocked many of those who had already served five years by what would later be called his Eurosceptic views. By the time he left the Parliament in 1999, and later as a member of the Economic and Social Committee, he was writing letters in the national press in stout defence of EU policies and British EU membership.

There are several possible explanations for such movements from "anti" to "pro". Working together with people from other countries having a similar political outlook, as in the cases of Walker-Smith and Cassidy, served to modify initial hostility towards the Community: a process often castigated as "going native". Once the UK had joined the Community, continued opposition would also have seemed unrealistic. It can also be argued that, in more recent years, many of those with a more sceptical attitude did not really alter their opinions, but found their classification changed as a result of a shift in the position of the Conservative Party as a whole.

For this reason, the motives of those who changed from "anti" to "pro" are perhaps of less interest than those who moved in the opposite direction.

"I thought we were only joining a Common Market"

Among older members of the Conservative Party, whenever the subject of Europe comes up, there will nearly always be someone who says: "I voted 'Yes' in 1975; but now … ". The thoroughly Eurosceptic Conservative MEP Daniel Hannan (who currently represents me in the Parliament), has written in his newsletter that "in nearly ten years as your MEP, I have had one sentiment expressed to me more often than any other, whether in my mail box, on the doorstep or at public meetings. 'We voted to join a common market,' people say, 'not a European superstate'".[6]

A perception that the European Community was originally only about economics and free trade, but that it has now become something entirely different, is indeed a common theme of those who have turned against it. Powell conceded that he had originally supported joining the EEC "on the grounds of trade", but that it had later become clear to him that it "would be something quite different from a free trade area". Russell Lewis argued in *Rome or Brussels … ?*, published in 1971, that the Rome Treaty was "designed to establish free trade and a free economy in the territory of its members", and that "policies for market freedom predominate over those for planning and control", adding that the Spaak Report, on which the EEC Treaty was based, was "an even more thoroughgoing free economy proposal than the Treaty".[7] While the Common Market might not have lived up to the visionary, free-market expectations of its founders, the danger of it becoming a "collectivist leviathan" could be held at bay. Yet by 2000 Lewis is arguing that the battle has been lost and that freedom and diversity are being crushed in order to create "a super-state called Europe".

A completely different view, however, has also been advanced: that a "super-state called Europe" was the objective all along, which supporters of British membership either overlooked, or were duped into overlooking. One convert to Euroscepticism, the former Chancellor of the Exchequer Norman Lamont, recounts how he was adopted as the Conservative candidate for the 1972 Kingston by-election "partly because I was more pro-European than my rivals". He had "always seen the European Union essentially as an economic venture, though accompanied by increasing political cooperation. While there was some political language in the preamble to the Treaty of Rome, I had never taken those words seriously."[8] Even John Major is reported to have complained that the "Founding Fathers" of the European of the Community "were careful not to disclose their ultimate federal objectives. History will record how we were steadily outsmarted between 1972 and 1992."[9]

In *Nice and Beyond* the inveterate *Daily Telegraph* critic of the EU, Christopher Booker, observed that Lamont and Major were far from being alone in holding such views. For forty years the British had faced "one of the most perplexing challenges of their history".

> The heart of the problem is that there has always been a fundamental difference of perception between Britain and her continental partners as to the real nature of this project. British politicians consistently portrayed it to their fellow citizens as little more than a means of increasing trade and sharing prosperity: a common or single market, through which, as a bonus, she might live in greater political amity with her neighbours. On the continent, however, from the time of its original inspiration in the vision of its founders, Jean Monnet and Robert Schuman, it was always seen as something much more ambitious than that. It was viewed as a long-term project to lead western Europe eventually, step by step, to complete economic and political integration; towards what Winston Churchill, in a series of historic speeches in the immediate post-war years, called a 'United States of Europe', comparable with the United States of America.[10]

Likewise, Oliver Letwin in *Drift to Union* describes "one of the most extraordinary chapters of misunderstanding ever encountered in British history". Despite the repeated denials of various Conservative ministers, the Community was quickly becoming

> what its founders and most powerful advocates have always wanted it to be: a federal European Union. ... Those of us in Britain (and elsewhere) who did not understand this have only our own ignorance and the misinformed statements of our leaders to blame.[11]

Most Conservative Eurosceptics, it must be said, are less apt to blame their own ignorance than the statements of their leaders, more specifically those of Ted Heath. The assurance in the July 1971 White Paper that "there is no question of eroding any essential national sovereignty" is frequently quoted, sometimes (as in the case of Letwin's pamphlet) leaving out the word "essential". Heath himself also pointed out in his autobiography that the phrase was quoted by Eurosceptics "as a complete sentence, followed by a full stop. It was not. There was a semi-colon." As a result, the second, explanatory half of the sentence – "what is proposed is a sharing and an enlargement of individual national sovereignties in the general interest" – was "deliberately and misleadingly omitted".[12]

In addition, as the earlier chapters of this study make clear, it is just not true that the European Community was presented to the British people as nothing more than an economic project. The political dimension – the need for greater European unity in the face of the Soviet threat, or in the face of US technological superiority – was, indeed, frequently presented as being more important. In addition, many Conservatives arguing for EEC membership in the 1960s not only understood that the objective was *"une patrie européenne"*, but welcomed the fact. There were also those like William Rees-Mogg arguing that we were moving into a world of continental blocs, and that we would be safer and better off inside one. Heath consistently made the point that "what Europe is about is redressing the balance on the two sides of the Atlantic – redressing the balance in trade, finance, defence and in political influence".[13]

As far as institutional development was concerned, there were Conservative schools of thought supporting, variously, a full European state, a federal Europe, a confederal Europe or a Gaullist *"Europe des patries"*. The issue was the subject of lively debate rather than swept under any carpet. Moreover, the Rome Treaty, with its phrase about the "ever closer union among the peoples of Europe", was available for all to read, as were thousands of more or less popular publications on the origins, history, structure and policies of the Community. The idea that Monnet, Schuman, de Gasperi, Spaak and Winston Churchill himself somehow concealed what was meant by "a United States of Europe" is ridiculous. Indeed, at the very beginning, the Schuman Declaration of 1950 observed that the pooling of coal and steel production would be "a first step in the federation of Europe".

In *This Blessed Plot* Hugo Young examines in some detail the belief that later "moved powerfully through the Conservative Party that British entry was originally approved on false, even fraudulent, pretences".[14] It was certainly true, he notes, that the possibility of a "close-knit federation" or "the risk of a major or total loss of sovereignty" were discounted in most Conservative quarters.* When recommending the Single

---

* The views of, respectively, Sir Harry Legge-Bourke MP and Angus Maude MP, neither of whom, as it happens, were particularly pro-Common Market.

European Act to the House of Commons in 1986, the Foreign Secretary Sir Geoffrey Howe described such "fearful constitutional fantasies" as "terrors for children".

On the other hand, the same Sir Geoffrey Howe had, when Solicitor General in the early 1970s, clearly spelled out the legal implications of membership, including the supremacy of Community law. Young observes that "the violence with which Heath was later attacked depends on seriously aberrant hindsight".[15] Moreover, the debates in the House of Commons during the late 1960s, when Heath was Leader of the Opposition, show how determined he was that there should be no misunderstandings about what Community membership involved. "Those who say that the British people must realise what is involved in this are absolutely right," he observed in the debate on Europe of the 17th November 1966. Joining the Community meant a surrender of sovereignty; and it was "important that we should frankly recognise this surrender of sovereignty and its purpose".[16]

Both Young and Heath himself cite the opinion of one of the most consistent anti-Europeans of all, Teddy Taylor, who in 1971 resigned from a ministerial post in the Heath government in protest against European Community membership. Much later, in 1997, Taylor wrote in the *Daily Telegraph* that Heath had known what membership meant, and had not tried to conceal it. "He didn't hide the consequences. The tragedy is that few listened."[17] Indeed, in the first of his influential Godkin lectures at Harvard University in March 1967, Heath had warned that people might be misled by the "vernacular phrase 'Common Market'". It conjured up "a vision of a market place in which everything is open to haggling and bargaining; in which the better haggler or bargainer you are the more likely you are to obtain your way". But this was not the case. "This organisation in much more than a Market. It is a Community."

Young does go on, however, to warn against too easy a dismissal of those who claim to have been misled. Pointing out that "it was clear from the start what the country was signing up for; the Rome Treaty says everything; Britain signed it; end of story" showed contempt for honestly-held perceptions; and this had been "the greatest flaw in the prosecution of the pro-Europe cause in British politics for twenty years".[18] A similar view was advanced at the time by the one-time Clerk of the House of Commons, Robert Rhodes James, who criticised Heath's tendency to take pleasure in "flattening" the Conservative anti-marketers "perhaps too totally for his own good. ... Many of his critics were, no doubt, ill-informed and obtuse, but they were voicing a sincerely held, if muddled, apprehension that was seeping through the Party."[19]

A better approach, perhaps, is that there was genuine uncertainty at the time about how the Community would develop, so that no-one could have spelled out precisely how Britain would be affected. Joining, indeed, was rightly presented as a chance to exercise direct influence on that development.

What is a Common Market?

Throughout the debate on Europe within the Conservative Party the terms "free trade", "Common Market" and "Single Market" have also been used somewhat loosely, without much attempt being made to define them. Pure free trade, in which every economy in the world is fully able to exploit comparative advantage, exists as an ideal and an economic model, but hardly as a practical policy in the world as it is. Even if all tariffs and similar distortions were removed, there would still be the myriad non-tariff barriers – differing technical standards, health and safety regulations, levels of environmental and consumer protection, language and culture – which act, either deliberately or by accident, as trade barriers. Even the "1992" programme to eliminate such barriers within the EU has had only partial success.

In the real world, a Free Trade Area is generally defined as one in which all tariffs, quantitative restrictions or measures having similar effect have been eliminated between the participating economies. Judged by these criteria, the so-called European Free Trade Association (EFTA) was only partially a free trade area: it was confined to manufactured goods. The same would have been true had the larger Free Trade Area, the subject of the Maudling negotiations in the late 1950s, come into being.

One important feature of the Common Market was the inclusion of the agricultural sector. The different national mechanisms of agricultural protection were largely replaced by those of the CAP – intervention buying, levies on imports and subsidies for exports – and in principle agricultural products have been, like manufactured goods, in free internal circulation. From time to time the CAP has had to engage in some rather tortuous practices in order to maintain the system, notably artificial "green" exchange rates and Monetary Compensatory Amounts (MCAs). In addition, it was not until the Single Market after 1992 that the barriers due to national animal and plant health regulations were removed (they remain, of course, during outbreaks of particular diseases). Yet, for all its faults, the CAP has succeeded in its major objectives: not just the essential requirement from the post-war years, to enable Europe to feed itself, but also to maintain an internal free market in agricultural products.

The other principal feature distinguishing the Common Market from a Free Trade Area has been the Common External Policy. In trade relations with non-member economies, those within the Market have acted as a single unit, having a Common External Tariff (CET) on imports from third countries, and handing over the power to negotiate trade deals to a single authority, the Commission.

Ironically, both these distinguishing features of the Common Market – the CAP and the CET – have often aroused the hostility of those who appeared happy to vote for it in 1975. It is frequently overlooked that the national policies that preceded the CAP, including the UK's deficiency payment system, would almost certainly now cost the same or more in aggregate, and without the bonus of internal free trade. In the case of the CET the charge has been that the Common Market has been "protectionist", and intent on constructing a "fortress Europe". Again, the CET has probably been consistently lower than the average national tariffs which would otherwise have applied; and certainly stands comparison with the tariffs of rival economies like the US and Japan, even in the case of agricultural products.

When we come to the Single Market, the conflicts and misunderstandings aroused have already been extensively discussed. In essence, many people have willed the end – the removal of non-tariff barriers and other distortions of competition – but without willing the means: the substitution of a single regulatory regime administered by the Commission for fifteen, now twenty-seven, national regimes.

It is certainly true that the original Cockfield approach of relying on mutual recognition rather than harmonisation has not always been applied. But this has usually been less because of a Commission attempt to seize power than because Member States have not quite trusted each other, and have feared a "race to the bottom". Moreover, it has not been unusual to find the same businessmen complaining about "unfair competition from abroad", and then about "over-regulation from Brussels" when legislation is brought in to level the playing field.

The best response to this kind of contradictory thinking came, in my experience, from Lord Young of Graffam at the time he was at the Department of Trade and Industry (the DTI). As *rapporteur* for the Single Market programme, I was approached by a number of UK-based unit trusts, which complained that the imminent opening up of the market would place them at a tax disadvantage compared to trusts based in Luxembourg. I promised to raise the issue with the Government; and the next day had the opportunity to do so with the Secretary of State himself. His reply was brief: "Tell them to go to Luxembourg".

It is nevertheless true that, as Professor Vaubel, Professor of Economics at Mannheim University and a Eurosceptic of long standing, has pointed out in a recent IEA monograph,[20] market integration inevitably promotes some political integration. Trade liberalisation requires some procedure for the settlement of disputes: once international trade and capital movements have been liberalised, they are highly responsive to all sorts of disturbances, notably government interventions.

> Market integration puts the participating national governments under intense competitive pressure. It increases the incentives for them to 'harmonise' or even centralise taxation and regulation at the international level.

A federal super-state?

Are Conservative Eurosceptics right, then, in asserting that the EU is on the way to becoming a "super-state called Europe"?

The argument that this is so rests in part on the cumulative effects of the Single European Act and the Maastricht, Amsterdam, Nice and Lisbon Treaties. These have changed the character of the EU in a number of ways. As far as the institutions are concerned, there has been a steady extension of Qualified Majority Vote (QMV) in the Council of Ministers, linked to a steady increase in the legislative role of the European Parliament. At the same time the EU has become involved in matters beyond the purely economic, notably foreign and security policy, and justice and home affairs. These developments, it can be argued, are both expanding EU powers and centralising them.

However, other changes have made the case less clear-cut. Whereas the original Treaties prescribed a "Community method", whereby the Commission alone proposed and the Council of Ministers and the European Parliament decided, a number of procedures have been introduced which are best described as "inter-governmental". These, moreover, have not been confined to the foreign-and-security and justice-and-home-affairs "pillars". The transformation of the former summits of Heads of State and Government into a full institution, the European Council, has meant that broad strategy no longer rests solely, or even mainly, with the Commission. Indeed, many analysts have asserted that the real power, from the very beginning, has lain with the national governments, and more specifically with those of France and Germany. Today, it is difficult to argue that Commission President Barroso has more real power over EU policies as compared to that wielded, jointly, by Sarkozy and Merkel.

In addition, the Council of Ministers has from time to time taken initiatives of its own, outside the normal institutional framework. One example was the work of the Primarolo Group[*] which was set up by the Council to monitor, and if necessary negotiate the elimination of, "unfair practices" in the field of corporate taxation.

Eurosceptic Conservatives are entirely right, however, when they claim that most continental political leaders, of both the left and the right, wish to create a "federal" Europe. The lessons taught by the 1930s and the Second World War have lasted through the generations; and the influence of the Federalist movement in Europe has rested substantially on the primary motivation of its founders: to prevent war by limiting national sovereignty.[21]

There are, however, large differences in what the word "federalism" is taken to mean in practice. The "F-word" of popular Conservative demonology is believed to be virtually synonymous with "centralism". On the other hand, the German translation of "federal", "*Bund*" – as used in describing the German state as a *Bundesrepublik* – does not imply that power is centralised, rather that it is shared between the centre and the separate *Länder*, which are "bound together" by the constitution. There is

---

[*] So named after the British Treasury Minister who chaired it, Dawn Primarolo.

a "balance between union and diversity", the creation of "a new political body while not abolishing the original constituent elements".[22]

It is of course clear that the Federal Republic, like the United States, Canada, Australia and other federations, is a great deal closer to being a single political unit than it is to a system of – in Mrs. Thatcher's words at Bruges – "willing and active cooperation between independent sovereign states". Interestingly, the German word *"Bund"* is also used to describe this situation: a distinction is made between a *"Bundestaat"* and a *"Staatsbund"*. The first can be translated as "federation"; but also as "confederation". The second can also be translated as "confederation", but, in addition, as something closer to the Thatcher model or the Gaullist *Europe des patries*. From the beginning Germans have debated whether the goal of European integration is a *Bundestaat* or a *Staatsbund*.

Is it more accurate, then, to describe the likely future structure of the EU as "confederal"? If so, this would be in accordance with British and Conservative interests, at least as they appeared to Harold Macmillan. He recorded in his diary for the 3rd September 1954 (recalling a paper that he had circulated to the Cabinet in 1952) that the "federation of Europe" means "the Germanisation of Europe. ... Confederation (if we play our cards properly) should be British leadership of Europe."[23]

Apart from the South during the American Civil War, the best-known example of a Confederation is Switzerland, where the 26 constituent cantons have considerably greater autonomy than the German *Länder*. Until the creation of the Swiss State in 1848, indeed, each canton was fully sovereign with its own army and currency. According to the constitution they remain sovereign today, in so far as powers have not been specifically delegated to the Confederation.

This is a key provision. Broadly, there is a tendency in a Federation for powers to flow to the centre unless specifically reserved to the States. In a Confederation, the States retain all powers not specifically handed over to the centre. The Lisbon Treaty, for example, explicitly provided in Article 3b for a confederal configuration.

> Under the principle of conferral, the Union shall act only within the limits of the competences conferred upon it by the Member States in the Treaties to attain the objectives set out therein. Competences not conferred upon the Union in the Treaties remain with the Member States.

Whether federal or confederal, however, Switzerland today is a single country, and is a long way further down the path to unitary statehood than mere "willing and active cooperation between independent sovereign cantons". Where the phrase "federal super-state" misleads, therefore, is perhaps not so much in use of the word "federal", but in that of the word "state".

The state, the nation and the nation state

This term, "state", can also confuse. When used to translate the German *"Land"*, or in relation to Australia, Canada or the USA, it refers to the constituent components of those countries. When used as in the expression "the State", however, it is a legal term, defining the basic building block of international society. Various attempts have been made at different times to define precisely the characteristics of a State. One such was the Montevideo Convention of 1933.

> The State as a person of international law should possess the following qualifications: (a) a permanent population; (b) a defined territory; (c) a Government; and (d) a capacity to enter into relations with other States.

A more rough and ready definition is that a State possesses "independence" and exercises "sovereignty" over its citizens. Both these terms can also be defined in a more or less strict way. In the most absolute, Hegelian sense a State is subject to no restraints, internal or external, on what it can do. Turner describes it as implying "the total authority and jurisdiction of a state over a given territory"[24] – or, as the Italian dictator Mussolini put it, "nothing beyond the State, above the State, against the State. Everything to the State, for the State, in the State".

In practice, however, as the late Sir Christopher Prout explained in a lecture quoted earlier, few States have possessed such absolute sovereignty, and certainly no democratic ones. States can also voluntarily submit themselves to various codes of conduct and the jurisdiction of external courts: for example, the European Convention on Human Rights and the European Court of Human Rights. International law itself is in part based on such a voluntary surrender of national sovereignty, much of it the result of simple practical arrangements, like the law of the sea and the status of diplomats. As in the case of domestic law, though, there is also a significant element of compulsion, deriving from the determination of other nation states to uphold the generally-agreed rules of international conduct.

Historians usually date the concept of the modern nation state to the Peace of Westphalia in 1648, which brought an end to the Thirty Years War. Recognition of the principle of *cuius regio, eius religio** effectively solved the problem of whether Catholics or Protestants should dominate in any particular region by leaving it up to the relevant sovereign. The result at the time was to link the State not so much to a particular community or nation as to its ruler: as Louis XIV famously put it, *"L'État, c'est moi!"* It was not until the French Revolution over a hundred years later that the concept of the State as an expression of a population's "general will"

---

* "Whose realm, his/her religion". This principle had already been declared over a century before at the Peace of Augsburg. It was now generally recognised.

became current, together with its military aspects, the *levée en masse* and conscription.

In England, meanwhile, a different model was evolving, based on limiting the powers of the State to those which were deemed necessary for reasonably competent government. Though the Conservative Party can trace its origins back to the Cavalier supporters of Charles I and the doctrine of "the divine right of kings", the experience of Lord Protector Cromwell's military dictatorship made the later English Tories – sometimes in the guise of the 18th century "Country Party" – even more in favour of limited government than the Whigs, but combined with strong support for the common law and the national Church. In consequence, the historical legacy to the modern Conservative Party has an element of paradox: support in an international context for the independent nation state, together with its laws and traditions; but suspicion of the State in many (though not all) domestic affairs.

It is also worth noting that the State is not necessarily coterminous with a "nation". Single nations can be divided into more than one State (East and West Germany); a State can comprise more than one nation (the Hapsburg Empire and, arguably, the UK); a nation can have no State (the Polish people for much of their history); and States can cover no nations at all (many countries of Africa, where the basic unit with which people identify is frequently the tribe rather than the nation). In his 1960 study of nationalism, the historian Elie Kedouri[25] describes as a "far from self-evident" the 19th century doctrine that humanity is "naturally divided into nations, that nations are known by certain characteristics which can be ascertained, and that the only legitimate type of government is national self-government".*

It is clearly true, however, that the nation state is still the dominant form of political organisation in the world. The consciousness of being "British" or "French", and the patriotism that this engenders, tend to over-ride all other loyalties. Indeed, the nation state as a form of political organisation partly owes its historical success to the fact that alternative and possibly divisive loyalties – religious, linguistic or regional – were generally suppressed, often ruthlessly. In France, for example, the recently-passed *loi Fillon* has recognised regional languages like Occitan, Breton and Alsatian as valuable elements of the French "cultural heritage". Yet the move has been strongly attacked as betraying the French Revolution

---

* A recent book on the rise of modern China, *When China Rules the World: the Rise of the Middle Kingdom and the End of the Western World* by Martin Jacques (Allen Lane, 2009) – admittedly by a former editor of *Marxism Today* – observes that the nation state, a product of 19th century European dominance, will soon be surpassed by a new model based on the Chinese historical tradition: the "civilisation state", centred on shared philosophical/cultural assumptions. It can be plausibly argued that the EU itself provides an example of such a state, at least in embryo. Another alternative is the Islamic concept of the *Ummah*: the unity of all Islamic countries, and ultimately of the whole world, under the rule of Allah. Finally there are predictions that the internet will create new loyalties not based on any geographical locality or system of government, possibly leading to "virtual" states.

and its establishment of a united, secular, mono-lingual republic. *"Je suis Jacobin"*, as one opponent of the measure has put it.[26] Similarly, the French government and parliament have banned the wearing of the *burqa* by Moslem women, not because of the implications for the status of women, or possible security risks – reasons which have been advanced for similar opposition to the *burqa* in Britain – but because it "challenges national identity".[27]

Support for the nation state can, indeed, contain an uncomfortable element of Jacobinism, which in recent years has produced a reaction in the form of support for regional identities and minority languages; and these, in some cases, have even threatened the integrity of the nation state in question. One example is to be found in Catalonia and Catalan in Spain. But much the most potentially disruptive is that of Belgium, which threatens to split into its French-speaking and Flemish-speaking component parts. In this Belgium would be following the precedent of Czechoslovakia, which split amicably into the Czech Republic and Slovakia; but this was before either became EU Member States. The creation of a new Member State as a result of the splitting of an existing one would certainly create institutional problems. On the other hand, such moves towards greater political and cultural diversity, far from conflicting with the search for greater European unity, fit in well with the objective of "unity in diversity".

Supporters of the nation state can nevertheless deploy one extremely powerful argument: both historically and in practice, national identity is still the basis of democratic government. Electorates are defined primarily on a national basis; and it is a fundamental pre-condition for democratic government that minorities are willing to accept the will of the majority: that loyalty to the whole overrides subordinate loyalties. This link between national identity and democracy has been a key feature of Conservative thinking, at least since Disraeli. Disraeli also described one of his party's goals as upholding "the majesty of the law" – for him, "the laws of England". Indeed, perhaps even more fundamentally than in the case of democracy, the nation can also be the basis of judicial traditions, systems and practices.[*]

---

[*] The political philosopher John Rawls, among many others, has argued that the law embodies a particular society's concept of justice, the outcome of a notional "social contract". Such theories of justice, however, have been subject to criticisism – for example, by the economist and philosopher Amartya Sen, who writes in his 2009 book *The Pursuit of Justice* (Penguin edition, p.71):

> The use of the social contract in the Rawlsian form inescapably limits the involvement of participants in the pursuit of justice to members of a given polity, or 'people' (as Rawls has called that collectivity, broadly similar to that of the nation-state in standard political theory).

> (Sen's main concern, though, is not that definitions of justice can vary between nation states, but that the idea of a notional prior agreement on a "transcendental" theory of justice within a restricted polity is the wrong approach anyway.)

It has followed that Conservatives have generally seen the primary purpose of foreign policy to be defence of the national interest. For some Conservatives, indeed, this has been the sole object. During the debates which took place at the time of the Macmillan application to join the EEC, this view was forcefully put in a Bow Group publication[28] by the Cambridge historian Alec Campbell. The furtherance of national interest was not something immoral; "on the contrary, its deliberate subordination to some other object would be immoral".

This, indeed, was the orthodox view among a school of Cambridge historians associated with Maurice Cowling, who expounded this view in detail to a course on "Britain and the Modern World" at Swinton Conservative College in March 1992.

> What, he asked, should be the object of British Foreign Policy? One view, held both outside and inside the Conservative Party, should be rejected straight away: that our foreign policy should try to increase justice in the world, or reconcile black and white, or maintain world peace, or maintain any other abstract would interest. The object of British Foreign Policy should be to maintain and advance British interests; that alone.

Campbell and Cowling concluded that it might be worth trying to join the Common Market on national interest grounds, but certainly not in any spirit of idealism. It is worth noting, too, that Campbell had little time for any Atlantic alternative: "our special relationship with the United States does not exist, never has existed and, unless the whole nature of international politics changes, never will exist". If it was in the American national interest to oppose Britain they would, "sadly, no doubt, but firmly". And we would do the same.

Such a 19th century view of how nation states should conduct their foreign policies is not today widely held in academic or political circles. There is evidence, however, that voters in most countries still expect their governments to "defend the national interest", even if they also support more idealistic objectives like world peace and the relief of poverty in third-world countries. There are certainly few signs that the nation state is about to be replaced some time soon. China, proposed as an alternative form of organisation by Martin Jacques,[29] is an example of a rising nation state *par excellence.*

Conservatives, however, have usually been careful not to take support for the nation state too far. As the MEP and Fellow of All Souls, Robert Jackson,* pointed out in a pamphlet[30] written partly to challenge the arguments of Enoch Powell, the absolute right of national sovereignty

---

* Jackson later left the European Parliament to become an MP at Westminster; and later still "crossed the floor" to the Labour Party. Interestingly, his wife Caroline Jackson continued as a Conservative MEP until her retirement from the Parliament in 2009.

was never a Tory doctrine. It was certainly true that "the existing order of things constitutes an investment of knowledge and experience" and that "for Conservatives an established state which has existed for some time is therefore a thing to be preserved". The idea of nationality, however, was only one of the principles around which a state could historically be arranged. "The Conservative mind attaches no special virtue to the national state ... "

For Jackson, Powell's position was less in the Conservative or Tory tradition than in that of "national state worship in the German manner".

International society

In any case, States, whether based on nations or some other entity, have for a long time ceased to be the only "persons" of international society and law. Quite apart from the traditional grey areas of colonies, protectorates, territories, places like the Channel Islands and the Isle of Man (which are part neither of the UK nor the EU) and micro-states like Monaco, San Marino, Andorra and the Vatican, there are an increasing number of international bodies which possess "legal personality" in their own right. This does not mean that the rights and duties of an international organisation are identical to those of a State; but that an international body, in the words of the International Court of Justice as early as 1945, "is a subject of international law and capable of possessing international rights and duties, and that it has the capacity to maintain its rights by bringing international claims".

This puts in perspective objections to the provision in the Lisbon Treaty which asserts that the EU has such "legal personality".*

The proliferation over the last century of bodies linking nation states in more or less integrated ways does give rise, though, to a number of questions. At what stage, for example, does an *inter*-national organisation become a *supra*-national organisation? Most *inter*national bodies can

---

* This, of course, raises the question of why it was thought necessary to include in the Treaty an article on legal personality. International law recognises an international organisation as having legal personality where is exercises independent decision-making powers that are separate from those of its constituent states; and this legal personality does not stem from the provisions of any treaty concluded between the states, but is intrinsic to such organisations. This is clearly the case with the European Union when carrying out its functions under the original Treaties. However, under Maastricht and subsequent treaties, the EU's activities were divided among the three "pillars": the existing European Community pillar; foreign and security policy; and justice and home affairs. In each of these decisions and action are taken in slightly different ways: in the first case under the "Community method", in the other two, at least until the Lisbon Treaty transferred much of the justice and home affairs pillar to the Community pillar, on the basis of inter-governmental procedures, under which each constituent State retains autonomy. This resulted in some uncertainty as to whether the concept of legal personality could apply to the Union as a whole. According to prevailing legal opinion, the Lisbon Treaty implies that when the Union acts as a single international entity it is an autonomous legal person; but when the constituent States act individually within the framework of a common policy concluded inter-governmentally, it is the legal personality of the individual States that prevails.

be thought of as existing to co-ordinate the activities of the States that have established them, able to take multinational, but not autonomous decisions. Yet even before the European Community, there were organisations which escaped such a description, such as the World Bank, which was clearly "an entity in its own rather than as an assembly of its many Members".[31] Writing in 1964 of the recently-formed EEC, the Professor of International Law at Columbia University, Wolfgang Friedman, observed that it was "already true to say that the American business man who plans the establishment of a subsidiary in the Community area thinks of the Community as well as the Member States, that the Communities as such incorporate an idea and a purpose going beyond cooperation of the six Member States".[32] From his standpoint as a lawyer, the *supra*-national nature of the Community was established by the fact that Community law took precedence in certain areas not only over the national laws of the Member States, but also over general international law.

It is clear, then, that the European Community was already from the start more than a conventional international organisation; and, as it has developed, supranational characteristics have replaced more traditional international ones: for example, in the field of legislation. This does not mean, however, that the EU is inevitably on the way to becoming a State. It clearly possesses a population and a territory, and can enter into relations – for example, trade deals – with other bodies on the international stage. But it has no single Government. Nor does it possess the coercive powers traditionally attributed to States: for example, to tax (except very indirectly, and to an almost negligible extent, through the Member States) or to conscript. Both its legislative powers and the powers of its Court are limited to areas covered by the Treaties.

In addition, the claims of John Major and Douglas Hurd in the early 1990s that Britain was "winning the argument" over the EU's future were, in a number of significant ways, correct. The inter-governmental "pillar" structure was one example, though it is true that, under the Lisbon Treaty, justice and home affairs will now largely be dealt with under the "Community method". Perhaps more important has been the *de facto* implementation of the Conservative policy outlined by Major in his "Ellesmere Port Address": a "flexible Europe" in which "different Member States decide to co-operate in different fields". This has long been the case in the high-technology field: Concorde was a notable example, as is the European Space Launcher and several joint projects in the defence field. There is the Schengen agreement eliminating passport controls at internal frontiers, which does not cover the UK but *does* cover non-EU countries like Norway; and, of course, the euro.

Such diversity, which could increase in the future through use of "enhanced cooperation", makes it unlikely that EU will develop into a "State" as traditionally defined: in particular, the principle that groups or constituent parts within it cannot "opt out" of policies they don't happen to like. If minorities do not accept the will of the majority, as

John O'Sullivan has observed,[33] democracy cannot function; and when this happens, for religious or other reasons, the result is often a "failed state". Indeed, paradoxically, the criticisms levelled at the directly-elected European Parliament by Enoch Powell and others – that it creates only the *illusion* of democracy, since it is not underpinned by a common *demos* – strengthen the argument that the EU is a long way from becoming a State, let alone a "Super-state".

Where the European Union is actually heading has been the subject of wide-ranging speculation. Writing at the beginning of the long period of discussions which led eventually to the Lisbon Treaty, one academic suggested that "what is taking place in Europe at the moment is a competition between three models of the state to become the model for the European Community as whole".[34] These models were the French, the German and the British. The French model was centralising and bureaucratic: "Power is the name of the game". The German model, by contrast, envisaged "strict constraints on the growth of central power and adherence to the goal of a *Rechtsstaat*, the rule of law": "Authority is the name of the game". The hallmark of the British model was informality: "Custom is the name of the game". It was Siedentop's view that, despite the claims that Britain was "winning the argument", its model suffered from a lack of clarity, making it difficult to get across. The French looked the most likely winners. Equally controversially, Commission President José Manuel Barroso later described the European Union as "the first non-imperial empire".[35]

Interesting though such speculations are, however, it is more plausible to argue that the EU is following no pre-existing model. Clearly it *is* acquiring more extensive supranational aspects than any international body that has hitherto existed. It may even be able to develop the common policies, particularly in the foreign and defence field, which make it a "player" on the world stage comparable to the US or China. Even if, from inside, it does not behave like a State, from the outside it may well look like one.

The best conclusion one can draw, nevertheless, is that the EU is developing in a way that is entirely *sui generis*: in Bob Boothby's words quoted earlier, "something less than a single sovereign State, something more than a League of sovereign States"[36] – or, in German, something less than a *Bundestaat*, something more than a *Staatsbund*.

Ted Heath was fond of recalling a conversation he once had with the then German Foreign Minister, Dr. von Brentano.

> When he (*Brentano*) first took part in the developments in Europe he thought that Ministers should call together the constitutional lawyers and instruct them to produce a blueprint for the constitution of the new Europe.
>
> "But now", he said to me, "I realise there is no possibility of this happening. What is more, I do not believe any longer that it is desirable. Here we are not dealing with some new country taking unto

itself a constitution for the first time. We are dealing with ancient nation states with long traditions, hopes, aspirations and deep-rooted prejudices. What I believe is now happening", he went on, "is that the more closely we work together in economic affairs so gradually will we create the other institutions which are required by a wider European economic unity. And then every ten years I shall invite the constitutional lawyers to tell us which position we have reached – whether it is confederal, federal or something in between."

"That", I replied, "is a typically pragmatic, British approach and very acceptable to us. The only thing is … that by the time the constitutional historians have decided where we have got to we shall have got to somewhere else."[37]

Centralism and subsidiarity

The fact that the EU is unlikely to develop into a traditional State as defined by international law, however, will not end the hostility of many Conservatives. This is for at least two reasons.

The first, as a recently-published textbook on British government and politics[38] perceptively observes, is that if the EU as an international organisation is *sui generis*, then its component parts, the Member States, must also be *sui generis*. They are obliged to adapt their institutions, legal systems and processes of government in a way which differs from the adjustments that other countries make in belonging to international bodies. Eurosceptics argue that, even if no nation state is fully sovereign in the classical sense, EU membership makes Britain less sovereign than countries outside. Moreover, the very lack of firm definitions and precedents arouses suspicion. As Mannin also observes, "dealing with the constitutional 'facts' of EU membership has become, for politicians and also for many academics, an exercise in obfuscation".[39]

Secondly, there are objections not so much to legal form taken by the EU as to the development of any kind of "continental bloc". For Rees-Mogg in the mid-1960s, like Bob Boothby in the 1940s, being part of such a bloc was one of the reasons for British EEC membership. But for Russell Lewis in 2000 – like "Hinch" in the 1960s – the "source of the glory and the greatness of Europe" lay in its diversity. It was a myth that "the great tragedy of Europe" in the past had been its failure to unite. "Freedom of thought, both political and scientific, flourishes where power is dispersed."[40]

Historically, a debate between those who want to centralise power and those who want to disperse it has been a feature of both the Labour and Conservative Parties. In the case of Labour, the centralising, statist tradition has clashed with that of participatory democracy associated with G.D.H. Cole, in which the basic units are the workplace and the community. In the case of the much older Conservative Party, the legacy of Cavalier and Tory paternalists, defenders of King and Constitution, has clashed with that of Burke's "small battalions" and the free-trading legacy of Peel.

Modern Conservatives, brought up to think of their party as standing for free markets and free enterprise, often forget the other tendency – it can come as a shock to learn that Socialism was once described as "the new Toryism". Even the Thatcher Government centralised power through measures such as rate capping.

In the international context, Lewis is certainly right in claiming that over-centralisation of power can have a deadening effect on economic and social progress. The example of Imperial China under its Confucian bureaucracy, once the most advanced and prosperous civilisation in the world, is the most obvious. The historian Paul Kennedy, quoted by Lewis, has advanced the thesis that it is the expenditure involved in running a large power-bloc, "imperial overstretch", that eventually brings it down.[41] This was prophetic in the case of the Soviet bloc – he was writing in 1988 – and could yet be prophetic in the case of the US.

It is also worth reading, however, what Kennedy actually wrote about the European Community at that time. His conclusion was not that there was strength in diversity, but rather the (conventional) opposite. If the European Community could really act together, it might well improve its position in the world, both militarily and economically. If it did not "– which, given human nature, is the more plausible outcome – its relative decline seems destined to continue".[42]

Certainly there is little danger today of the EU being brought down by the weight of its central expenditure and administration, given that its total budget is less than 1% of GDP and that the Commission's "vast Brussels bureaucracy" of popular legend numbers only about 25,000. Kent County Council (which does not even cover the Medway unitary authority) has a staff of nearly 45,000.

Nevertheless, Conservatives are clearly sensible in being vigilant in the face of what has been called "creeping centralisation". Peter Lilley and the other authors of the Monday Club publication *A Europe of Nations* were right to point out that bureaucracies have their own agenda, independent of the interests they theoretically serve. They also have a tendency to expand as a result of Parkinson's Law.* It is for this reason that the concept of "subsidiarity", introduced into the Maastricht Treaty substantially as a result of Conservative pressure, deserves especial attention. The origins of the term lie in the social teaching of the Roman Catholic Church, as developed in *Rerum Novarum* of 1891 and after.

In this theological context, the principle is less about efficiency than about personal and social responsibility. At the basis of society lies the individual human person, unique, and born with free will, with whom accountability for his or her choices should if possible remain.† Under the linked

---

* The two "axiomatic statements" are: "(1) 'An official wants to multiply subordinates, not rivals' and (2) 'Officials make work for each other.'". (See *Parkinson's Law or the Pursuit of Progress* by C.Northcote Parkinson (John Murray, 1958).

† It is perhaps worth noting that this belief also forms the basis of secular philosophies like Existentialism.

principle of solidarity, however, every individual also has duties to others, and should be ready to achieve common goals through the family, local community, workplace or nation. Not only are these duties – for example, the care of the aged – more likely to be carried out effectively if addressed by those closest to the matter in question, but the moral and social responsibilities of families and communities should only be removed to higher levels if any measures carried out by them would clearly be ineffective.[*] Interestingly, a similar concept – though without the moral dimension – also appears in the field of US management techniques as developed in the late 19th and early 20th centuries:[43] P.F. Drucker's seminal work of 1954, *The Practice of Management*,[44] recommended that decisions "be taken as close as possible to the action to which they apply".

At the time of the debates on the Maastricht Treaty there were criticisms that the principle of subsidiarity was "vague and capable of conflicting interpretations".[45] The House of Lords European Scrutiny Committee, which examined the concept in a report published in 2008,[46] concluded that whether a proposal did or did not comply with the principle was "a matter of political judgement ... unlikely to be capable of an entirely objective assessment".

Various commentators also pointed out that subsidiarity, though laying the burden of proof on those wishing to centralise, was not the same thing as *de*centralisation. Indeed, in a lecture at the University of Kent in 1990, my colleague from Kent East, Christopher Jackson MEP – who was largely responsible for including the concept in the Spinelli Report – observed that subsidiarity was "a two-edged sword".

> On the one hand it indicates we should ONLY make decisions at a higher level if they are more effectively made there; but it also suggests that if a decision is more effectively made at the higher level, then it should indeed be made at that level, in the interests of the people.[47]

The force of this point was later illustrated in evidence to the House of Lords Committee, when Professor Simon Hix, from the London School of Economics, observed that "if you follow a purely legal definition of subsidiarity, you would say that defence policy should be done by the EU – scale effects, a collective defence, public goods would be provided more cheaply at central level".

Norman Lamont recalls that several members of the Major government had their doubts. Michael Howard also thought it a "two-edged weapon that could be used by the Commission to achieve more centralisation". Lamont himself states that he "pushed the idea of subsidiarity hard" and that it became "a British objective. ... But I could not have been more wrong about its effectiveness. It achieved absolutely nothing, but was endlessly

---

[*] The principles of subsidiarity and solidarity are treated more fully in Appendix 1 on Conservatism and Christian Democracy.

used by the Government to illustrate they were winning the argument in Europe!"[48] In addition, as local authorities in England know only too well, "the decentralized implementation of a policy whose basic features are decided centrally is not the same as decentralization of the power to decide what that policy should be".[49]

Curiously, the doubts of Eurosceptics about subsidiarity were shared by one of the main driving forces behind the Single Market, Lord Cockfield. Speaking in the House of Lords in November 1990 during a debate on Maastricht, he argued that it "would be a serious mistake to incorporate subsidiarity into the treaty". Subsidiarity was too often "a substitute for thought" rather than "a guide to decisions". In support of this view he cited his experiences in trying to avoid the harmonisation of industrial and other standards at EU level by devolving them to national level under the principle of mutual recognition. "We then found that trade and industry were demanding that we took it back at Community level and operated upon the basis of European standards rather than upon the principle of mutual recognition." No national government was willing to act on its own unless it was certain that all the others would too.

A much more precise outline of how subsidiarity is to be applied in practice – allied to the concepts of "conferral" and "proportionality" – is contained in the Lisbon Treaty, from Article 3b of which it is useful to quote.

> Under the principle of subsidiarity, in areas which do not fall within its exclusive competence, the Union shall act only if and insofar as the objectives of the proposed action cannot be sufficiently achieved by the Member States, either at central level or at regional and local level, but can rather, by reason of the scale or effects of the proposed action, be better achieved at Union level.
>
> Under the principle of proportionality, the content and form of Union action shall not exceed what is necessary to achieve the objectives of the Treaties.

A Protocol expands these provisions further; in particular it places an obligation on the Commission to provide extensive justifications for any proposed legislation.

> Any draft legislative act should contain a detailed statement making it possible to appraise compliance with the principles of subsidiarity and proportionality. This statement should contain some assessment of the proposal's financial impact and, in the case of a directive, of its implications for the rules to be put in place by Member States, including, where necessary, the regional legislation.

It also outlines the role of national parliaments, which, for the first time, are given direct powers – that is, other than through national ministers – over proposed EU legislation.

> Any national Parliament or any chamber of a national Parliament may, within eight weeks from the date of transmission of a draft legislative act … send … a reasoned opinion stating why it considers that the draft in question does not comply with the principle of subsidiarity. … Where reasoned opinions on a draft legislative act's non-compliance with the principle of subsidiarity represent at least one third of all the votes allocated to the national Parliaments [*two votes each to allow for two-chamber parliaments*] the draft must be reviewed.

Even this greater precision is unlikely to satisfy those Conservatives, like Russell Lewis and Norman Lamont, who consider the principle of subsidiarity to be "a fraud". There will always be the problems of deciding what the "objective" of a policy should be and how its "effectiveness" should be assessed, and by whom. The principle also raises legal problems, as the ruling of the German Constitutional Court in Karlsruhe on the Lisbon Treaty demonstrated: if powers over such matters as education and culture are reserved to a lower tier of government (the *Länder*), the ability of the national tier (the Federal Government) to agree any measures in these fields at an EU level is severely limited.

Nevertheless, following the coming into force of the Lisbon Treaty, a body of precedent is already beginning to build up as national parliaments and institutions like the EU's Committee of the Regions examine emerging legislative proposals. The Commission is required to compile a report each year on the application of the principles of subsidiarity and proportionality, on which, in turn, national parliaments and other EU bodies can comment. Moreover, in decisions concerning the relative merits of centralisation and decentralisation, there is nearly always a trade-off between conflicting principles: efficiency and equity as between different groups and regions on the one hand; local democratic involvement and accountability on the other. Hard choices between competing principles are, after all, the stuff of politics.

Conservatives have in recent years expressed a preference for decentralisation; but this is often the case with oppositions. The real test will come, both at home and abroad, now the Party is in government.

Conservative Europeanism examined

Ted Heath began the first of his lectures at Harvard University in 1967[50] by describing "three motive forces behind the desire for a greater European unity". In first place came "the determination to put an end once and for all to the nationalist rivalry and internecine warfare which has ravaged Europe for so long, brought desperate suffering to her people, and almost destroyed her culture and civilisation".

The motives of those Conservatives who campaigned for European unity in the late 1940s and 1950s are indeed easy to understand. Many, like Heath himself and Whitelaw – and like the MP who gave up his seat at Westminster in order to become an MEP in 1979, Tom Normanton – had fought in the Second World War. They had not only experienced the bloody consequences of European political disunity; they also knew that this had been one result of economic and political disunity in the pre-War years.

Moreover, unlike Churchill, "RAB" Butler and those of an earlier generation who were equivocal about how far Britain should participate, Heath had no doubts. For "the new generation", the attitudes which united them were far greater than the nationalist feelings which divided them. "The teenager in Frankfurt has the same feelings and ambitions as the youngster in Manchester."[51]

Such doubt-free commitment was, of course, a minority view within the Conservative Party at the time. Even those, like Harold Macmillan, who were edging their way during the 1950s towards applying for EEC membership, gave the impression of doing so more because all the other options were closing than from any real enthusiasm. The shock of Suez to Britain's finances and self-esteem; the gradual metamorphosis of the Empire into a Commonwealth of states, each increasingly inclined to pursue its own interest rather than Britain's; the resulting decline of Commonwealth trade as that with the EEC countries grew; the failure of the Free Trade Area negotiations; pressure from the United States; all these played a part.

It is also true, however, that a still younger generation of Conservatives, including most founder-members of the Bow Group, were considerably more enthusiastic. Though some, much later, appeared to change their minds, others like Geoffrey Howe played a key role in making the Conservatives the "party of Europe" during succeeding decades. The next generation of Conservatives, my own, likewise contained those like John Selwyn Gummer and Ken Clarke who have maintained a European commitment throughout their careers. Moreover, though the Party as a whole did not match the enthusiasm for Europe of such younger Conservatives in the early 1960s, it was not particularly anti-Europe either. The overwhelming majorities in favour of Macmillan's policy at successive Party conferences, and the small impact made by the militant anti-Marketeers, was not just a matter of loyalty to the leadership. There was a general feeling, even if in some cases mixed with regret, that joining the EEC was probably the right thing to do.

Such acceptance of a policy which the Party had rejected virtually without dissent during the preceding decade nevertheless requires further examination. A number of basic themes can be identified.

In the first place, the implications of Suez for Britain's standing in the world had become as apparent to the bulk of Conservative Party members as to the leadership. So had the implications of de-colonisation and the fact that the Commonwealth was becoming something very different from an Empire. It did not need Dean Acheson to point out the need for a new role.

Accordingly, though much of the debate appeared to about such things as New Zealand butter and agricultural support, the primary reason why Britain entered into the negotiations, as the leader of those negotiations, Ted Heath, later put it, was "political, political in the widest sense".

> The British Government saw that any large, prosperous grouping on the mainland was bound to exert political influence, not only over Europe as a whole but also in its relations with the United States and with the developing countries. Although few thought that this influence would be used to the positive disadvantage of Britain, many believed that the best way for Britain to use her own influence in the modern world was as part of such a grouping.[52]

For Conservatives with an historical perspective, this reasoning was a more positive version of traditional foreign policy: never to let the Continent be dominated by a power-bloc from which Britain was excluded.

A second political argument proved decisive for many Conservatives, and was expressed most consistently by Sir Alec Douglas-Home, earlier and later Lord Home. This was the need for unity in the face of the Soviet threat. Though almost all Conservatives gave priority to NATO in the field of defence, there was a widespread view that Western Europe should also be doing its bit, even becoming – as US President Kennedy had proposed – an (almost) equal "pillar" of the Alliance. Linked to this was the policy left over from the 1950s of tying West Germany firmly into a common defence system. As a result, a persistent Conservative theme during the succeeding decades was that, whatever happened in the economic field, there should be closer European coordination in the fields of foreign policy and defence.

Together with these basic political themes came a host of economic arguments. For pure free-traders, abolishing tariffs and quantitative restrictions between countries could only be positive. Entering the EEC, economists like Russell Lewis argued, would give British industry a competitive jolt, and help Britain match the growth rate of the Six. Outside, British exporters would need to overcome the Common External Tariff (CET) in order sell in their fastest-growing market; inside, they would be part of a large preferential area, a springboard for selling to the rest of the world as well. Inside, Britain would be able to ensure that the Community was "outward-looking". Businesses could operate on a continent-wide basis, producing economies of scale. At the same time "entry into a European market, governed by the strict provisions of the Treaty of Rome forbidding state subsidy of industry, would force our industry to look to itself, not to the state, for the solution to its problems".[53] Finally, only if European countries, including Britain, joined together economically could they resist the *défi américain* in high technology fields like computers and aerospace.

These economic arguments were greatly strengthened by what actually occurred in the years following accession to the Community. Between 1973 and 1983 UK exports to the other EC countries grew twice as fast as to North America, non-EC Europe or the developing countries, to reach 45% of the total. UK exports also gained market share – imports into West Germany from UK, for example, rose from 3.5% of total imports to 7.7%. The CBI estimated in the mid-1980s that two and a half million British jobs depended on Community membership. National wealth (GDP) was reckoned to be about 1.5% higher each year. It was not difficult to demonstrate "the benefits of Europe" (the title of the first Brief for distribution among Conservatives produced by the new European Democratic Group in the European Parliament.[54])

In his introduction to that Brief, however, the leader of the Group, Sir Henry Plumb (now Lord Plumb), who had replaced Sir James Scott-Hopkins at the end of 1980, warned that "building Europe is inevitably a long and complicated business". He hinted that there was a danger of losing sight of the economic benefits outlined as a result of "the clang and din from Brussels". Though he was referring principally to the row over Britain's budget contribution, there was also, in the background, the debate about national sovereignty and political union.

In view of the later excoriation within the Party of "federalism" – incorrectly taken to be synonymous with centralisation – it is interesting to examine how those Conservatives who argued for membership in the 1960s and 1970s saw the institutional future of the Community. As already noted, there were some who not only foresaw an eventual United States of Europe, but welcomed the prospect. Patrick Jenkin, in 1960, thought that this would be "the only entity able to confront the USA, Russia and China on equal terms".[55] In 1972 the left-wing Conservative pressure group Pressure for Economic and Social Toryism was calling for "an integrated European nation".[56]

At the other end of the spectrum were those like the authors of the Monday Club pamphlet *A Europe of Nations*[57] who were, in effect, British Gaullists. Like de Gaulle they were opposed both to federalism in Europe and the Atlanticism of many Conservatives who saw closer ties with the US as a possible alternative to the EEC. Among the proposals which logically followed was the development of an Anglo-French nuclear deterrent.

It has to be admitted, indeed, that the pro-Europe stance of many on the right of the Conservative Party in the 1950s and 1960s was to a considerable extent the reverse side of anti-Americanism. There was resentment at US pressure on British governments to dismantle the Empire* – and, it was suspected, covert US support for "liberation" movements – and, as

---

* And also disillusionment with what the Empire was becoming as a result: a multi-racial Commonwealth, including regimes perceived as neither democratic nor pro-British.

already noted, anger at the US Government's undermining of the British position at the time of Suez. Ironically, this anti-Americanism was an attitude shared by those on the left of the Labour Party who nevertheless were, by contrast, anti-Europe. Conservative right and Labour left also came together in suspicion of the hold American "big business" was acquiring over large sectors of European economies (including the British) – the situation highlighted by the French writer Servan-Schreiber (see the section in 'Wooing Conservatives' in Chapter Four).

Most Conservative pro-Europeans of this period, however, cannot be said to have had precise views on the institutional future of Europe: their position – as Heath pointed out to von Brentano – was one of extreme pragmatism. Despite the anger with de Gaulle himself as a result of his three vetoes, and rejection of his anti-Americanism, the centre of gravity within the Party was almost certainly, from the very start, nearer to support for a *"Europe des patries"* than to any much closer integration. On the other hand, as the passage of the Single European Act demonstrated, Conservative governments have been happy to see closer integration and transfers of power to the Community when it has been in pursuit of an overriding goal – in that case, the Single Market.

This pragmatism is firmly within the Conservative tradition of what A. J. Balfour, nephew and successor as Prime Minister to Lord Salisbury, once described as "the principles of common sense, to do what seems to be the right thing in a given case". Yet, as John Major discovered after the Maastricht negotiations, such a stance is extremely vulnerable to accusations of apostasy from those who are more ideologically motivated. As a result of the upheavals in the Party during this period, Conservative pragmatism had to be modified by a much greater precision about how the Party saw the EU developing in the future: the "flexible" model described by Michael Howard in *The Future of Europe*.[58]

The post-Maastricht problems

The Maastricht upheavals also made it a great deal more difficult to project a single Conservative message on Europe. Even the most Eurosceptic claimed not to be "anti-Europe" – only anti the kind of Europe they believed the EU was becoming. Indeed several elements of the Conservative pro-European case continued to be generally well-received within the Party, and were relatively uncontentious. All sections could unite on the need for the proper control of EU spending, which necessarily involved giving MEPs stronger powers of scrutiny, and attracted Eurosceptic approval of at least one EU body, the Court of Auditors.

The need to co-ordinate the foreign policy of the EU Member States was also widely accepted, partly because it was largely conducted under one of the inter-governmental "pillars". Former Foreign Secretaries like Lord Hurd[59] and Malcolm Rifkind[60] were able to write authoritatively in Conservative Party journals about the complex situations in the Balkans and the Middle East, or on transatlantic relations. The then EU Commissioner for External Relations, the former Conservative Party Chairman Chris Patten, was also able to write convincingly that the EU was the world's "best example of multilateralism, of sharing sovereignty for a common purpose". He believed that the main role of the European Union in international affairs must be "to give teeth and bite to this multilateralism".[61]

With some exceptions like the drinking-water Directive attacked by Michael Howard, the case for EU action in the environmental field also met with general approval; and this strengthened as the issue of climate change came to the fore. Though some still disputed the greenhouse gases/global warming link, most Conservatives recognised that the EU was taking the lead in reducing emissions and promoting "clean" technology, ratifying the Kyoto Protocol (unlike the United States) in 2002. The first example of the European Parliament using its new powers under the Single European Act to overrule the Council of Ministers had, in fact, been in the environmental field, when it tightened up the rules on emissions from motor vehicles. In the case of some related EU measures, like REACH (Registration, Evaluation and Authorisation of Chemicals), where it might have been possible to complain of "interference from Brussels", considerations of public safety were generally recognised to be more important.

Acceptance of EU action in the environmental field carried over into the related field of energy policy. The need for a real Single Market for gas and electricity had always been a Conservative goal, to which was added both the promotion of clean and renewable energy sources and security of supply. A link with the co-ordination of foreign policy was established when the supply of Russian natural gas to Western Europe was cut during a cold snap in early 2009 as the result of Russia's dispute with the Ukraine.

Other issues, however, were dangerously divisive: for example, whether or not the UK should participate fully in EMU. Many Conservatives, like former Vice-President of the Commission, Leon Brittan, saw the Single Currency as a logical development of the Single Market. In 2003 he wrote a paper for the Conservative Group for Europe on "free trade and the euro",[62] arguing that "liberating companies of the costs of exchanging currencies" and "the elimination of exchange risk" meant that: "joining the euro can properly be regarded as removing an obstacle ... to trade". Others, however, saw EMU as a "one-size-fits-all" straightjacket, "the fatally flawed notion that one exchange rate and one interest rate are appropriate for economies with very different and disparate histories, structures, performances and sovereign governments".[63]

Both these position are arguably compatible with a belief in free markets.

Likewise, every Conservative could agree that the EU had a "democratic deficit". Yet there was a wide gulf between those who saw the answer in more democracy at the EU level – more power to the European Parliament, even a directly-elected Commission President – and those who preferred the repatriation of powers to Westminster.

The diverse nature of the message from pro-Europe – or, rather, non-Eurosceptic – Conservatives in the 21st century can be observed in the successive Party Conference editions of the Conservative Group for Europe magazine, *Conservative Europe*. In the 2002 edition, there is an article from Leon Brittan observing that "when Britain plays a positive and constructive role in the EU, and is not hung up by ideological considerations of sovereignty, Britain can often, indeed perhaps usually, persuade its partners to pursue a policy which is immensely to our advantage".[64] The then leader of the Conservatives in the European Parliament, Jonathan Evans MEP, made a similar point in another article in the same magazine; but with a very different spin. Conservatives could unite around an "an unwavering commitment to advance the British national interest", and offer "a more realistic way forward than the grandiose and outdated supranationalist instincts of the Brussels machine".[65]

By 2003, the difficulties faced by pro-Europe Conservatives had grown. In the Foreword to that year's Party Conference edition of *Conservative Europe*, the then Chairman of the Conservative Group for Europe, David Curry MP (who had previously been a Member of the European Parliament) wrote that "we must come to terms with the fact that Euroscepticism is not some irrational aberration which wisdom, time and experience will eventually cure, but the normal environment in which we operate".[66] And in the 2004 edition, John Major himself warned that it would not be easy to "turn around the present hostility to the EU".[67]

Nevertheless, in a spirited article in the same edition, Geoffrey Howe did his best. His target was the widely-held belief that "Brussels" was responsible for the prosecution of traders refusing to use metric measurements. Magna Carta, he pointed out, had already proclaimed that there "should be standard measures of wine, ale and corn throughout the kingdom"; and in 1862 there had been a House of Commons recommendation to adopt the metric system. The decision actually to do so had only been taken in 1965 – but still eight years before the UK joined the European Community.

Indeed, trying to demolish popular myths about the EU, as observed earlier, became an increasingly time-consuming task for pro-European Conservatives. Over the years, the indefatigable Christopher Booker, writing in the *Daily Telegraph* and elsewhere, had popularised a stream of alleged "daft Brussels rules": to abolish London double-decker buses; to make it an offence to sell the acorns of British oak-trees; to ban the transport of whisky by road; to make it illegal to sell a pound of apples. ... All these joined straightening out cucumbers and/or bananas in the public mind.*

In 1981 the consumer magazine *Which?*[68] had published a short quiz on EEC membership. One of the questions had been: "Under EEC rules

---

* Over the years the Commission has kept an inventory of these "myths and rumours", some seventy of the most recent of which are listed and refuted on the Commission web site http://europa.eu.

surplus potatoes are bought by a special agency and dyed green. True or False?" Both at the time, and over the years, I have put this question to meetings and obtained overwhelming votes for "true". The correct answer, of course, is "false"; but that, at the time, the UK's own Potato Marketing Board had been doing it for years. As memories of the old British marketing boards fade, the majority of "trues" has even risen. The same point can be made in relation to Tippex or Brillo-pads constituting a "hazard in the workplace"; banning butchers from giving bones to dogs; or an attempted ban on the sale of second-hand toys at jumble sales.

What can explain the alarming propensity of Conservatives – indeed of the British public in general – to accept such absurd stories as true, so inevitably influencing the political process?

Public opinion ...

The *Eurobarometer* surveys carried out for the Commission over the years have identified two consistent features of British public opinion concerning the European Community/Union, as compared to that in other Member States. It has generally been the most hostile; and generally the least well-informed. The hypothesis of a causal relationship is greatly strengthened by more detailed statistics, which show that the least well-informed groups in all countries tend also to be the most hostile: in 2004, of those saying their knowledge of the EU was low, only 36% thought it was a "good thing", while the equivalent figure for those saying their knowledge was high was 61%. There is also a close correlation with levels of education: those continuing education into their 20s are over 50% more likely to support EU membership than those without higher education.

The "hostility-gap" between Britain and other countries has on occasions been massive. At the time of the first European Elections of 1979, 41% of British voters believed Common Market membership to be "a bad thing". Only Denmark on 28% and Ireland on 16% were even in double figures. Despite the efforts of the UK Government, the Party and the Community itself to stimulate interest, nearly 70% of British voters said afterwards that they had been "very little interested" or "not at all interested" in the campaign. This was reflected in the turnout, with the UK's 32% the lowest by some way (the next lowest was Denmark, on 47%).[69]

The position did not change greatly following the successive enlargements of the EU during the next three decades. A *Eurobarometer*, for which the fieldwork was carried out in late 2006, found the UK, out of all 27 Member States, still with the lowest percentage (34%) thinking membership of the EU "a good thing". The UK also came last in trusting the Commission (22%), with next lowest Latvia on 39%; and trusting the European Parliament (25%), with the next lowest, Latvia again, on 44%.

Given this dismal comparative position, however, changes in UK opinion on Europe over time do seem to have followed discernible patterns.

As already noted, public opinion on the application to join what was still generally called the Common Market was, in the early 1960s, over-whelmingly favourable. By the end of the decade, however, following two French vetoes, it had become overwhelmingly unfavourable. At the begin-ning of 1973, immediately following the successful entry negotiations and actual entry, opinion had shifted back to marginal approval: according to Gallup, 38% in favour, 36% against with 20% "don't know".

Thereafter, between 1974 and 1980 the *Eurobarometer* showed, on average, 35% thinking the European Community a "good thing", 36% a "bad thing" and 22% neither good nor bad. But by Spring 1981 the positive figure was down to 24% and the negative figure up to 41%. Then, in late 1981 and early 1982, the negative figure fell sharply, and the positive figure began a steady climb, reaching a peak of nearly 60% by 1990. In 1991 the position was reversed: the negative figure rose sharply, and the positive began a steady decline – apart from a brief spike in 1997 – to only 29% by late 1999. Between 2005 and 2007 there was another brief rise in positive responses; but for most of the last ten years "good thing", "bad thing" and "neither" have all remained at around 30% each (see Appendix 3).

In *This Blessed Plot*, Hugo Young says of this picture that "there doesn't always seem much rhyme or reason about it".[70] Yet the overall pattern does appear to correlate quite well with the success or failure of policy towards Europe over the years. It was not surprising that, following two failed attempts to negotiate Common Market membership in the 1960s – one by a Conservative government, the other by a Labour one – support for the whole policy should fall away. Nor that eventual success should result in a recovery, albeit a weak one, of favourable opinion. The trou-bles, both domestic and international, in the 1970s once again produced a swing to the negative, as membership appeared to have produced few of the promised benefits.

In the 1980s, Margaret Thatcher's victory in the battle of the budget can be said to have triggered a general perception that things were going Britain's way, a perception soon reinforced by the drive for the Single Market. Then came the Bruges speech (intimating that all was not well after all); Black Wednesday; and the struggle over Maastricht. The 1997 spike corresponds to the arrival in office of New Labour, which was unable, however, to sustain any real long-term pro-European enthusiasm.

Plausible though this may seem, however, British domestic politics can only provide a very partial explanation of the movements in opinion on Europe. The *Eurobarometer* average for all Member States shows those thinking the Community a "good thing" also falling to a low of 50% in 1981, and then rising to a 70% peak in 1990 before falling back in the following decade, and thereafter stabilising at around 50%.

Opinion in the UK, in fact, appears to have followed the same move-ments as that in the rest of Europe – only at a level of approval for

Community/EU membership some twenty percentage points lower. One of the few positive conclusions that can be drawn is that this perhaps casts further doubt on the Powellite thesis that democracy at a European level is impossible because there is no real European *demos*.

... and the media

The figures show, then, that during the years when the Conservatives were still "the party of Europe", support for Community/EU member-ship was rising. The state of public opinion was nevertheless a continuous source of frustration. Canvassers in European election campaigns regu-larly reported that normally loyal Conservatives were not going to vote "because we don't know enough about it", or "nobody tells us what's going on". Unsurprisingly, the conclusion was drawn that a large part of the problem lay with the media.

There is certainly evidence that the press in particular have made little effort to keep their readers systematically informed about the EU. In the period following Britain's accession to the European Community, *The Times* – which at that time still aspired to be Britain's premier journal of record – not only carried reports of the European Parliament's debates in the same way as of those at Westminster, but also featured a parlia-mentary sketch-writer in the person of the paper's European Political Editor, George Clarke. After several years, however, both features were dropped. The *Daily Telegraph*, sometimes described as the Conservative Party's house journal, has never carried systematic reports of European Parliament debates, though between 1979 and 1984 the former *Telegraph* journalist David Harris, at that time himself an MEP, did contribute occa-sional stories to the Peterborough and other columns.

Instead, coverage of EU events in the British press increasingly seemed to concentrate on stories of the "straightening-out-cucumbers/bananas" kind. When a substantial and influential section of the country's newspa-pers, including *The Times* itself, came into the ownership of two declared Eurosceptics, the Australian Richard Murdoch and the Canadian Conrad Black, claims that the public were being misinformed about Europe seemed even more credible. Various commentators have not minced their words: "the British press is infamous for its biased coverage of EU matters;"[71] "the British debate on Europe is ... affected by a raucous popular press that lazily presents the EU as a nefarious plot to do the country down";[72] "years of hostile headlines about the European Union have made sensible public debate of Britain's EU interests almost impossible".[73] In his memoirs, ex-Prime Minister Tony Blair writes of "the near-hysterical – sorry, correct that – truly hysterical behaviour of the Eurosceptic media".

> Papers with a combined daily circulation of around eight million – a situation unique in Europe in terms of pervasion – were totally, wildly and irredeemably hostile to Europe, misrepresented what Europe was

doing and generally regarded it as a zero-sum game: anything that pleased Brussels was bad for Britain.[74]

Politicians, however, need to wary of blaming the press for their problems. It is certainly true that many press barons, like the imperialist Lord Beaverbrook, have used their ownership of newspapers to campaign for a political standpoint. Most, however, have been primarily interested in making money; and readers generally seem to buy those papers which champion their own political and other prejudices. As a result, it has been a longstanding matter of debate whether newspapers mould, or merely reflect, public opinion. The best evidence indicates that newspapers tend to reinforce opinions already held by their readers rather that change them.

Other factors are also relevant. One contributory, and possibly comforting, factor is that the news media are notoriously inaccurate on all subjects, not just on Europe. An analysis of surveys into mistakes in the press, carried out by the American Newspaper Publishers' Association in 1980, concluded that half of all printed news stories included some sort of error, only 10% of them purely typographical.[75] Recent data suggest that only 2% of such errors are ever corrected in subsequent editions.

There are, however, more substantial reasons for apparent press hostility towards Europe. In 1982, the Memorial Fund established to commemorate the first leader of the Conservative Group in the European Parliament, Peter Kirk, commissioned a study of how the EEC was being covered in the media, a matter which was already causing concern. This was published in the following year.[76] Those active and working to make a success of British EEC membership, the study began, firmly believed that "the visionary aims of guaranteeing peace in Europe, and realising a post-war economic revival" were being "diminished and trivialised." At its worst, this was the result of "hysterical, soapbox-style journalism" founded on "the 'Bloody foreigners' paradigm".

The author, Robert Winder – himself a journalist – nevertheless observed that the media, by the very nature of the audiences which they addressed, were inevitably nationalistic, "a nationalism, equally inevitably, paralleled by the respective governments." One of the central characteristics of western journalism was its tendency, "however it may purport to be a conduit of information, to be actually a chronicle of the extraordinary". The EEC was therefore extremely boring for journalists, "chiefly through the complexity and laboriousness of its processes". "There's a limit to the amount of times one can photograph the office blocks in Brussels," the BBC TV's correspondent in Brussels at the time was reported as saying. There were, moreover, no personalities to give stories a human dimension (this was before Delors). "You can't attack people because no-one knows who you're attacking. So attack the whole, faceless enterprise out of sheer frustration".

As editor between 1974 and 1979 of the monthly *European Parliament Report*, issued by the European Community's London Office, I soon became well aware of these problems. Very few readers were interested in long reports of debates. What they wanted was, essentially, gossip; and this was duly provided through an *Unofficial Journal* column. But, in addition, news stories inevitably focused on political conflicts and the exposure of scandals. In June 1977 I actually found my job in jeopardy after making the lead story a speech by the Labour MP Tam Dalyell, a member of the UK delegation to the European Parliament, accusing Parliament's then President, former Italian minister Emilo Colombo, of having been implicated in the disappearance, while it was being shipped from Antwerp to Genoa, of 200 tons of uranium oxide.*

The 1983 study also drew attention to a problem with which journalists are only too familiar. Most of those posted to Brussels, Strasbourg or Luxembourg usually made honest efforts to write or broadcast objective reports on what was going on, even if the result was not very sensational. But programmes and papers as a whole were put together, not in Brussels, but back in London, where sub-editors could make amendments and, in the case of newspapers, wrote the headlines. The study quotes two examples of stories where the headline not merely misrepresented the story, but "completely subverted" it. For the Brussels correspondents this would have been extremely galling. Yet the job of the subs was to ensure that the story was read – and it stood a better chance if "touched with a whiff of scandal and drama".

This natural tendency of the British press to be nationalist and sensationalist was a serious problem for the Conservative Party when it was in office and defending British involvement in Europe. After the defeat in 1997, however, it was seen as a powerful ally, reinforcing the more Eurosceptic stance of the Party in opposition. The problem seemed now to be one for the Blair government, which was quickly forced to drop its initial policy of an early adoption of the euro.

As the European Elections of 2004 and of 2009 showed, however, this apparently happy situation came with a catch: the prevailing attitude of the press seemed to be encouraging a strand of Euroscepticism even more extreme than that of the Conservative Party: that of the United Kingdom Independence Party (UKIP). This faced the leadership with a potential dilemma: should the Party move even further towards Euroscepticism in an effort to forestall UKIP? Or resist the temptation, and risk continued Conservative defections? These were questions of quite a different kind from those facing the Party in the early 1980s, when the main opponent of British European involvement was the Labour Party.

---

* 'That lost uranium – who is to blame?' in *European Parliament Report* no.36 (European Parliament London Office, June 1977). I subsequently discovered that the President's office had blocked my advance on the promotion ladder that year – a move which was rapidly reversed when I became a candidate for election to the Parliament two years later! The uranium oxide was widely thought to have ended up in Israel.

The influence of Labour

During the years immediately following the Macmillan application to join the EEC in 1961, the hostility of the Labour Left provided useful ammunition for the Government in quelling any Conservative dissent. Harold Wilson told the House of Commons in June 1962 that "the whole conception of the Treaty of Rome is anti-planning", while the Victory for Socialism Group attacked Macmillan's policy as a "Tory sell-out". It was not difficult to portray Common Market membership as a useful bastion against Socialist policies for nationalisation and central economic planning.

By the General Election of 1970 the Labour and Conservative Parties were both officially committed to joining the Community, though Labour contained a larger dissident minority. This was drawn mainly, though not exclusively, from the Left, which continued to describe the Community, helpfully, as a "capitalist racket", inspired by the principles of competition and the market economy.

Perhaps less helpful in view of later developments was the document[77] published by the Labour Party's National Executive Committee (NEC) in July 1977 which argued for "a wider and looser European grouping in which each country would be able to realise its own economic and social objectives". The then Shadow Foreign Secretary, John Davies, attacked this proposal as "a veiled way of urging that our EEC membership should be undermined from within". Couldn't Labour understand, he added, that the Community was "a co-operative venture?" If we contributed nothing but abuse to that venture, "our partners will quite understandably feel little enthusiasm for ensuring that we obtain the full benefits of membership".[78]

Twenty-five years later, these statements could well have come from the reverse sides of the House of Commons.

In the mid-1980s, however, the respective party positions were absolutely clear-cut. Labour's policy statement of 1982[79] contained a commitment to withdraw from the Community altogether, the principal reason given being the incompatibility of membership with Labour's domestic programme. Besides enabling the Conservative Party to emphasise yet again the value of Community membership in blocking full-blooded Socialism, this prompted a new, serious analysis of the economic consequences of withdrawal. The idea that Britain could retreat into a comfortable free-trade arrangement was considered improbable even by Labour's own front-bench spokesman. The Conservative Research Department's 1983 *Campaign Guide* concluded that "what they are advocating is Britain's complete isolation from the main international trading powers."[80] In the years 1969–72, it added, the United Kingdom had received on average 22 per cent of the American investment coming into the Nine. In the period 1978–80 this had doubled to about 45 per cent (excluding oil), as US companies took advantage of Britain's free access to the Community market of 260 million consumers.

During the course of the 1980s Labour edged away from a policy of complete withdrawal from the Community. In the 1984 European Elections it proposed, instead, a "fundamental change" in British membership, including the repatriation of powers "ceded by the Tories to the EEC in the European Communities Act 1972" – a policy, ironically, almost identical to that on which the Conservative Party fought the General Elections of 2005 and 2010. By the General Election of 1987 Labour was conceding the need to "work constructively with our partners to produce economic expansion". Finally, following defeat in that election, the Labour Party conference conceded that withdrawal from the Community was no longer feasible, calling instead for the promotion of "democratic socialism" through the Community's institutions.

The shift in Labour's position was matched by a parallel shift in the Conservative response. The Community could no longer be presented as a free-market defence against British Socialism. Instead, there was a possibility that the threat would come from the Community itself. The 1989 Campaign Guide observed that "Labour now sees Europe as a vehicle for imposing the Socialist policies rejected in three General Elections at home".[81]

For the pro-Europe cause in the Conservative Party this double shift was to prove highly damaging, with Prime Minister Thatcher's Bruges speech in 1988 constituting a watershed. A Labour policy document published in 1990[82] implicitly criticised the new Conservative attitude in stating that "Britain must play a positive role in shaping the future of the Community. It is just not good enough to criticise and dismiss our partners' proposals without offering an alternative".

By the General Election of 1992 the main Conservative attack on Labour's European policies was that they were muddled and inconsistent – "U-turn after U-turn". More specifically, however, the *Campaign Guide* singled out for criticism Labour's support for Economic and Monetary Union and its opposition to Major's "opt-in" agreement.

> Whereas the Conservative Government believes that a matter as important as this should be decided by the House of Commons[*] at the appropriate time, the Labour Party would irrevocably commit Britain to a single currency, regardless of whether it made sense at the time.[83]

Full changeover was reached by 1994. The *Campaign Guide* of that year attacked Labour for having "all the blind zeal of the convert. ... Where previously they despised all things European, they would now put "Brussels" in charge."[84] Labour had become party to a Socialist plan for a "centralised European state, with rates of pay, working hours and minimum rates of taxation all decided at a European level".

This brief outline of the Labour Party's policy towards Europe during the last third of the last century, and the Conservative reaction to it, raises

---

[*] N.B. "by the House of Commons", *not* by referendum.

a number of interesting questions. To what extent, for example, was the switch in the policy of one party a consequence of the switch made by the other? And, if so, which should be considered cause, and which effect?

Allowing for a factor already mentioned – changes as a result of being in or out of office – the violent swing in Labour policy during the 1980s can perhaps be seen as, at least in part, a reaction to the policies of the Thatcher Government, and even to the attitudes of Mrs Thatcher personally. On the other hand, the Eurosceptic trend in the Conservative Party can also be seen as a reaction to Labour's espousal of Commission President Delors' "social dimension", and Mrs. Thatcher's own reaction to Delors' speech to the Trades Union Congress.

Both parties, consciously or unconsciously, have slipped easily into the pro or anti stance adopted not so many years before by the other side. The desire of the Labour Left to be free to pursue its own agenda free of Common Market rules is mirrored by the Conservative Party's later wish to be free of interference by "Brussels" in such fields as social policy and taxation. Likewise, Conservative scorn for Labour's lack of "Community spirit" in the late 1970s and early 1980s was turned on the Conservative opposition once Blair had become Prime Minister in the late 1990s and 2000s.

Now that the Conservative Party is in government again, and Labour in opposition, it will be interesting to see whether there will be yet another switchover in attitudes. There were already signs in the run-up to the 2010 General Election that Labour was moving into some of the tactical positions adopted by the Conservatives following the creation of New Labour in the 1990s. The poster depicting Tony Blair with red demon eyes, under the slogan "New Labour, New Danger", was an attempt to show that the new moderate Labour image was an illusion, with old-style Socialism still lurking in the background. Similarly, Labour's reaction to Cameron Conservatism was an attempt to show that nothing had really changed: hence use of the phrase "same old Tories". If the pattern is repeated, it will not be long before Labour accuses the new government of "selling out to Brussels" – as, indeed, they had already begun to do by October 2010 (see earlier under "Europe and the Parties").

Conservative Euroscepticism examined

As de Gaulle correctly observed, the roots of British Euroscepticism – particularly Conservative Euroscepticism – lie deep in British history. The quotation from Harold Macmillan in Chapter One shows that even those generally considered on the pro-Europe side felt that the British way of doing things was fundamentally different from that on the Continent. English history as taught in schools until fairly recently – what has sometimes been called the "Whig Interpretation of History" – tells of "an unbroken thread of liberty and self-government"[85] with its roots in Anglo-Saxon England; Magna Carta; a parting of the ways with Catholic, absolutist Europe beginning with the Reformation and achieving victory in the reign of Elizabeth I; a moment of crisis with the Civil War; and a decisive breakthrough in the Glorious Revolution of 1688.

Thereafter, inevitably, came parliamentary democracy, mastery of the seas, the joint stock company, the industrial revolution, Trafalgar, Waterloo and an Empire on which the sun never set. Like many of my generation, born just before the Second World War, I was brought up on this magnificent tale of "our island race" – especially as one of its greatest popular exponents at the time was my godfather, the historian Sir Arthur Bryant. In the late 1960s Bryant became chairman of the National Common Market Petition Council, the eccentric purpose of which was to get the Queen to veto British membership of the Common Market by using the royal prerogative.

The legacy of Imperialism was particularly powerful within the Conservative Party, even when the Empire itself began to dissolve. It was taken for granted that British rule had been, in the words of Sellar and Yateman,[86] "a good thing". We had sent our finest overseas, often to dreadful climates, to build railways, spread Christianity and impose the rule of law. It was an overriding and permanent determinant of our role in the world. Even Churchill, in his famous wartime speech on the Battle of Britain, had spoken of Britain and her Empire lasting "for a thousand years".[*] It was natural that the most militant organisation opposing Macmillan's application to join Common Market would be called "the League of Empire Loyalists".

There are, of course, very different views about Imperialism in general and the British Empire in particular. By the 1950s, even within the Conservative Party, there were those who were shocked by the measures thought to be necessary in order to maintain British rule. In 1959 Enoch Powell made a speech in the House of Commons protesting after eleven Mau Mau detainees in the Hola Camp in Kenya had been killed for refusing to work, a speech which is generally considered to be the best he ever made.

The less attractive legacy of Imperialism also had unfortunate consequences for the attitudes of some Conservatives towards Europe. As Denis Judd remarks in *Empire: the British Imperial Experience from 1765 to the Present*:

> There was much that was evil, self-absorbed, triumphalist and over-assertive about British rule. The havoc that these characteristics wrought upon the British people's capacity for smug self-satisfaction, including an abiding distrust of all manner of foreigners and foreign ways of doing things – a distrust that helps explain the popular expressions of contempt during the 1980s and 1990s for the organisation and

---

[*] Though he was, of course, indirectly taking a dig at Hitler's claim to have founded "a thousand-year *Reich*".

ordering of the European Economic Community – can only be hesitat-
ingly and uncertainly assessed.[87]

Yet by the time of the Macmillan application to join the Common
Market, opposition from within the Conservative Party was less on behalf
of Empire than of Commonwealth, and couched more in economic than
Imperialist terms. There was, it is true, reference to sticking by "our kith
and kin" in the Dominions; and also the argument from opponents like
Peter Walker that the future lay with the developing countries, especially
those Commonwealth countries of Africa, the Indian sub-continent and
the Far East. When it came to the negotiations, however, the concerns
of the Commonwealth governments themselves turned out to be more
about future access to UK markets than any Imperial idealism. This, in
turn, meant that as the Commonwealth's economic importance to the
UK diminished, while that of the EEC's rose, Conservative opposition to
Macmillan on grounds of Commonwealth solidarity grew steadily less
convincing.

Another, more recent root of anti-Market and Eurosceptic feelings
within the Conservative Party was the legacy of the Second World War.
As Butler and Westlake put it in the Background to their study of the
European Elections of 1994,[88] "Britain was a victor in 1945 and had successfully fought a war to preserve the independence of nation states, whereas
most of the other defeated and/or devastated European countries saw the
pre-eminence of the nation state as a prime cause of the war".

Russell Lewis, for example, questions whether "Europe's down-
fall" really was "due to the folly of its numerous nationalisms … what
some have called 'Europe's civil wars'". Rather, it should be attributed
to "the folly of German nationalism".[89] Such an observation accords
with Crowson's view that there is "a strong strain of anti-Germanism in
Conservative thinking".[90]

However, whatever Conservative views about German nationalism – and perhaps French nationalism, too: Crowson also writes that
"even among the party's pro-Europeans there was a distinct strain
of Francophobia" – Lewis accurately reflects a general view among
Conservatives that nationalism, or at least British nationalism, *is* a positive sentiment. Only recently, with the successes of the Scottish and Welsh
nationalists, and the beginnings of an English nationalist backlash, have
some doubts begun to emerge. It is also worth remembering that there
was little sympathy until very late in the day for nationalist movements
in the British colonies – or, most unfortunately from an historical perspective, in Ireland.

Nationalism as a source of Euroscepticism therefore contains a large
element of double-think: my nationalism good, your nationalism bad. It
can be argued, indeed, that it has been this element of double-think, rather
than nationalism itself, that has lain at the root of most European conflicts,
both between and within States.

A third historical root of Euroscepticism has been, ironically, identical to one source of pro-Europeanism: support for free markets and free trade. The conversion of many Conservatives from support of the Common Market to hostility towards the EU has already been examined in some detail, particularly their perception that the Single Market was no longer about removing barriers, but about imposing controls. From the start, though, there were purists, like the Conservative MP Richard Body, who maintained that the Common Market was a protectionist organisation, their particular targets being the Common Agricultural Policy and the Common External Tariff.

The Commission, in Eurosceptic demonology, has been routinely accused of being "Socialist" or "corporatist", despite its actual record as a defender of competition and the free market against protectionist national governments. Even the most fervent Conservative supporters of membership have often depicted Britain as standing virtually alone in fighting for an "open Europe" against the malign influence of French *étatisme*. Norman Tebbit, revealing one reason for his conversion to Euroscepticism, writes of having to combat in the Council of Employment Ministers "crazy Socialist schemes being proposed by the Commission".[91]

Behind the detailed arguments of Anti-Marketeers and Eurosceptics, then, have been these historical legacies, together creating a conviction that Britain is somehow different. It went against the grain, as Miss Petherick (a deputy area agent in Yorkshire whom I knew well when a tutor at Swinton) put it in 1962 "to think of Britain as part of Europe".[92] Years later, when a newly-elected MEP, this was brought home to me as I was introduced to the AGM of Sevenoaks Conservative Association by the then Conservative MP, Mark Wolfson, a convinced pro-European. "And now Ben Patterson will address you," he said, "Just back from Europe this afternoon".

"I have to tell Mark," I could not resist beginning, "that Sevenoaks is in Europe".

This perception that Britain is different is widely-held. Yet the question has to be asked: is this difference really much greater than that of other countries, each of which also have their unique histories and characters? To the Eurosceptic claim that they do not want Britain to be swallowed up in the uniformity of a European super-state, it has been possible for pro-Europeans to argue that fifty years of Common Market/European Community/European Union membership "have not made the French any less French or the Italians any less Italian". To the Irish, who also live on an island and have a sense of national identity if anything greater than that of Britain, the idea that Britain is too different to be part of Europe is laughable.

The democratic deficit

A more serious objection to British participation in European Union, however, has been that it has weakened democracy, and in particular parliamentary democracy.

At its least sophisticated, this has taken the form of attacks on the "unelected bureaucrats of Brussels". The Commissioners themselves have been dismissed as a body of "elitist civil servants" – or, somewhat contradictorily, "failed politicians" – riding roughshod over the wishes of elected national parliamentarians. As already noted, this view arises in part from a fixation with the Westminster model of democracy, in which the Executive is drawn from, and is part of, the legislature. The alternative model applying in the US, on which the EU's institutional structure is based, is arguably just as democratic – some would say even more so. The view also overlooks the role of the elected European Parliament in holding the Commission to account, if necessary dismissing it, and with an increasing role in its appointment.

Others, however, have analysed the EU's "democratic deficit" differently. Instead of focusing on the Commission, they have directed attention to the institution where most final decisions are made: the Council of Ministers.

In theory, this is composed of elected politicians, each responsible to his or her own national parliament. An obvious limitation on such democratic control nevertheless arises from the use of Qualified Majority Vote (QMV). Where a national minister is outvoted on a measure, the relevant national parliament has no option but to accept that legislation: its theoretical control of the minister is ineffective. To some extent, this possibility is limited by the "Luxembourg compromise" described in Chapter Four, and it remains the case that no country is likely, in practice, to be overruled on a matter of "vital national interest". There are nevertheless two related reasons for taking this weakening of national parliamentary control seriously.

The first is the nature of EU decision-taking itself. Reaching agreement on a measure between twenty-seven sovereign governments inevitably means compromise. Moreover, where a series of measures are being negotiated, the most fruitful approach is often to agree a "package", whereby a country or a group of countries gives ground on one front in order to get its way on another. Arriving at such compromises and packages is usually a complex matter, with negotiations inevitably taking place out of the public eye in what, up until recently, would have been "smoke-filled rooms".

In practice, then, both ministers and national civil servants can effectively escape national parliamentary control as soon as they meet in full Council of Ministers, in the Committee of Permanent Representatives (COREPER) or in one of the many working parties or Council committees. "Commitology", indeed, has become a sub-set of EU studies in itself. There is also a great deal of truth in the comments of Alan Clark recorded in Chapter Seven: ministers have little time to go very deeply into draft EU legislation and necessarily rely on the preparatory work of the civil servants in UKREP and in the home ministries and departments.

Ministers can also be fairly confident that, whatever decisions they are eventually party to, there will be little detailed examination of them in the House of Commons. The Select Committee on European Legislation – now called the European Scrutiny Committee – where Bill Cash had his Eurosceptic awakening, and which he now chairs, is a place for specialists, and can seldom get any issue debated by the full House. The committee, indeed, has only been formally allotted two days of parliamentary time a year! Nor does it make any attempt to follow the example set by the Danish *Folketing*'s Market Committee and "pre-mandate" ministers attending Council of Ministers meetings.

The claim by Eurosceptics that the opacity of the Council's work severely weakens parliamentary control is therefore supported by evidence. It is a criticism, moreover, which has also been made by "federalists", who have campaigned over many years for meetings of the Council at which legislation is to be passed to be held in public. This was incorporated into Article 9C of the Lisbon Treaty – though discussions on non-legislative items will continue, it seems, to be held in secret, as will the meetings of COREPER where quite a number of final decisions are, in practice, taken.

Yet, despite these unsatisfactory procedures, it can be argued in response that they are little different from those of any international body – indeed are the traditional way in which inter-governmental negotiations are carried out. In the case of the UK, relations with foreign countries, including declaring war on them, have historically been the responsibility of the Crown alone.

Some Eurosceptics have therefore gone on to assert that the most damaging consequence of EU membership has been on the constitution of the UK itself. The undemocratic features associated with the conduct of foreign policy have been extended into domestic affairs, in effect enabling the Crown to turn the clock back, and remove from Parliament the powers to control the executive which it progressively won over the course of four centuries. In 2001 the Bow Group published an "audit of who initiates and authors legislation that governs us today",[93] the first conclusion of which was "that every Government since 1975 has diminished, almost by stealth, the powers of the UK Parliament in favour of Ministerial Power exercised in camera through European Institutions".

Government departments, anxious to get some controversial measure adopted, have indeed seemed only too happy on occasion to avoid difficulties at Westminster by legislating at EU level instead, in the last resort, laying any blame on "Brussels". What has been labelled "gold-plating" – adding controls at national level not strictly required by the relevant EU legislation – has also been a frequent feature of the UK's transposition of EU Directives.

The most obvious pro-European response to these Eurosceptic criticisms has been to argue that democratic control lost by the national parliaments can be recaptured at EU level through the European Parliament. For this reason, through successive treaty amendments, the extension of Qualified Majority Vote (QMV) at Council of Ministers level has been matched by an increase in the Parliament's legislative powers, leading to effective "co-decision" on most matters being incorporated into the Lisbon Treaty.

There have been a number of Eurosceptic counter-responses. One has been, simply, that UK MEPs cannot defend UK interests because there are only 72 of them in a parliament of 732. Plausible though this sounds at first, it is of course a criticism that can be made of any parliament: how can Kent's 17 MPs at Westminster, for example, defend Kentish interests in a House of Commons numbering 646? Like Westminster, the European Parliament is organised not on the basis of where the Members come from, but on the basis of parties or party groups; and few if any votes take place on the basis of national origin.

The simplistic argument of relative numbers, however, disguises a much more fundamental point. At Westminster, the MPs from Kent do not have to worry too much about being outvoted on constituency interests because they – and more importantly, most of their constituents – place the interests of the UK as a whole above those of Kent alone. In the European Parliament it is possible that many Members *do* place the interests of the EU as a whole above those of the country from which they come. But is that true of their constituents?

In some cases, the answer might well be "yes". Opinion polls in Italy, for example, have often shown voters having more confidence in the institutions of the European Union than in the politicians and administration in Rome. In the UK, however – and despite the low level of trust enjoyed by MPs, particularly since the recent scandal over expenses – the answer is clearly "not yet". The Conservative Party manifesto at the European Elections of 2004 was entitled "Putting Britain First" because that was the message voters wanted to hear.

As a result, Eurosceptics are able to claim that the European Parliament is not a "real" parliament. This could only be the case, as it was argued by Enoch Powell and others, if the electorate of the EU as a whole felt itself to be "one people", a "polity" or *demos* in which sectional or regional interests would normally be subordinated to those of the whole.

Here, however, one must be careful with the terms used. Parliaments can and have existed without enjoying much popular support, indeed often without the mass of the general public having much idea that they existed at all. Until the extensions of the franchise in the later part of the 19th and the early 20th centuries, most of the UK's population had no say in who represented them at Westminster, neither Lords nor Commons. In so far as they were a "polity", the focus of loyalty was the Crown, if not the monarch him- or herself. The arguments of Powell and others are relevant, not to parliaments as such, but to representative democracy as implemented through parliaments.

Even here, though, powerful rejoinders are available. A Marxist would argue, for example, that for virtually all its history the British Parliament has represented, not the interests of the British people as a whole, but the interests of the classes who happened to have the vote, or of those who paid them. A feminist might well argue that the House of Commons has always been a male-dominated body, representing male interests, even after the franchise was extended to women on equal terms in the 1920s. The rise of nationalism in Scotland has been based on a belief that the interests of Scottish voters have been overlooked by the English-dominated assembly in London.

Whether a parliament is a "real" parliament is, therefore, very much a matter of degree and opinion, with many cross-currents. The message of Commission President Delors to the Trades Union Congress in 1988 which so incensed Mrs Thatcher was that, as a result of the vagaries of British voting, the interest of British workers were now better served at European level. This could also be said in respect of many other fields of policy, particularly those, like the control of greenhouse gases, where unilateral national action is likely to prove futile. In sum, the "all or nothing" position taken by Powell and those arguing in the same vein is largely inapplicable to any political system based either on the principle of subsidiarity – "federalism" as properly defined – or on the constitutional division of powers between executive, legislative and judicial institutions. The European Union incorporates both.

The alternatives

A major problem faced by those Conservatives who have argued for Britain to leave the European Union has been to outline a plausible alternative. Once Joseph Chamberlain's dream of Imperial, later Commonwealth, free trade had faded, and that of a large European Free Trade Area had been blocked, there were few serious options left. The European Free Trade Association (EFTA) was always seen as a stop-gap: the ink was hardly dry on the agreement before Britain began preparing to leave. A Nordic Free Trade Area covering Scandinavia, the UK, Iceland and Canada – the pet project of Reg Simmerson, who would regularly stand at by-elections on an anti-Market ticket, who was a fellow Conservative Member of Hammersmith Borough Council between 1968 and 1971, and with whom I shared a flat for several years – or just joining the United States, were often advanced, but never taken seriously. Creating a North Atlantic Free Trade Area (NAFTA) *was* examined seriously by the Conservative Party on a number of occasions, but never secured the support of any US administration. Members of the United Kingdom Independence Party and others taking a similar position have usually been left with the argument that the UK would have no problems "standing alone – Norway and Switzerland have done all right".

Some Conservatives have nevertheless continued the hunt for a viable alternative to the EU. In the Autumn 2005 edition of *Crossbow* the MEP Daniel Hannan explored the possibility of returning to EFTA. Norway, Iceland, Liechtenstein and Switzerland, he began, were all much richer than the EU average, with "lower inflation, higher employment, healthier budget surpluses and lower real interest rates". They had the benefits of free trade without the burdens of regulation from Brussels (though

Norway, Iceland and Liechtenstein, being within the European Economic Area, did have to accept many Single Market regulations). This was surely what Britain really wanted.

Subsequent events, though, have somewhat altered the situation. The international financial crisis has crippled the Icelandic economy, and both Liechtenstein and Switzerland have come under immense international pressure to abandon a key component of their economic success, banking secrecy. Indeed the lesson of recent years has been that small, free-trading countries and financial centres can prosper when the economic climate is good, but are hard hit economically, and unable to defend themselves politically, when things go the other way. Ireland has experienced much the same economic roller-coaster ride as Iceland, but has benefited from certain stabilising factors as a result of EU and Euro Area membership, harsh though the accompanying conditions may have seemed.

So the idea that Britain would benefit from leaving the EU for EFTA or the EEA has become even less plausible than it was in 2005. As a pamphlet distributed by the Conservative Europe Group and Business for New Europe at the 2009 Party conference[94] put it, "those who advocate Britain's withdrawal from the EU, or who advocate a simpler relationship between the UK and the EU, don't understand how the world works".

The choices made by other European countries should, in any case, give advocates of EEA membership pause for thought. Austria, Finland and Sweden, founder EEA members, rapidly came to the conclusion that full EU membership was a far better option. The ex-Communist countries of Central and Eastern Europe were at one stage offered EEA membership as a kind of "parking area" while the possibility of joining the EU itself was discussed. All rejected the idea as something approaching an insult. The principal reason was clear: EEA countries would be obliged to accept much of the legislation adopted by the EU with only minimal input as to its contents – what was once scathingly described as "government by fax from Brussels".

This is hardly an attractive prospect for Britain.

Leaving the EU would also give rise to certain legal problems. In principle the Treaties are concluded "for an unlimited period", and until the Lisbon Treaty came into effect, there was no provision for a Member State to leave (though Greenland, once part of the European Community as a result of Danish membership, left in 1985 and now has a status somewhat similar to that of the Isle of Man).

It terms of purely domestic law, the UK Parliament is of course free to repeal, unilaterally, the European Communities Act 1972 and any other related legislation (but see the legal opinion in the Bow Group pamphlet *Europe: The First Year*, quoted in Chapter Five). This would, however, put the UK in breach of its Treaty obligations, almost certainly leading to unpleasant repercussions internationally. British businesses and other interests with activities based on an assumption of continuing EU membership would also be likely to take whatever legal action they could to overturn the decision and/or to seek compensation.

Those wanting the UK to leave the EU therefore assume negotiations for an amicable parting. The procedure which would be likely to apply is outlined in the Lisbon Treaty.

ARTICLE 49 A

1   Any Member State may decide to withdraw from the Union in accordance with its own constitutional requirements.

2   A Member State which decides to withdraw shall notify the European Council of its intention. In the light of the guidelines provided by the European Council, the Union shall negotiate and conclude an agreement with that State, setting out the arrangements for its withdrawal, taking account of the framework for its future relationship with the Union. That agreement ... shall be concluded on behalf of the Union by the Council, acting by a qualified majority, after obtaining the consent of the European Parliament.

An important point to note is that any agreement negotiated with the UK could be rejected by a blocking minority in the Council of Ministers, or by half the Members of the European Parliament. Even if there were a general agreement to allow the UK to join, say, the European Economic Area, there could well be many governments and politicians who would resist making any concessions at all to the British defectors.

The point is important because Eurosceptics argue that the main losers from the re-establishment of trade barriers would not be the UK, but other Member States. In his *Crossbow* article, for example, Hannan observes that "over the past 32 years, we have run an average trade deficit with other member states of £30 million per day". Why, then, would they want to cease trading with us? The answer, of course, is that access to the 460 million market of the other 26 EU Member States is a great deal more important economically to the UK than access to the 58 million UK market is to them.

Most Conservative Eurosceptics, however, do not advocate full withdrawal from the EU. Instead there have been proposals to alter the terms of UK membership, ranging from the repatriation of certain policies like that on fishing to wide-ranging opt-outs which would come close to a withdrawal. The approach outlined by Michael Howard in 1997 – that there should be no fixed *"acquis communautaire"* but that powers should "pass up and down between Brussels and Member States as necessary" – in conjunction with the "enhanced cooperation" procedures, could lead to a kind of running renegotiation of Britain's membership terms. The most fruitful approach has indeed been to press for a "variable geometry" EU, in which Member States can choose the policies in which they participate. One particularly successful application was the negotiation of the much-maligned Maastricht Treaty itself, during which Prime Minister Major negotiated a right to "opt in" to the Single Currency if and when Britain felt ready, and an "opt out" from the Social Chapter (later reversed by the Blair government).

There are, nevertheless, practical limits to the application of such flexibility. In the economic, social and environmental fields, freedom to pick and choose which policies to adopt runs up against the "free-loader" problem, as became clear during the detailed implementation of the Single Market programme. Even the principle of mutual recognition, Lord Cockfield's preferred mechanism for opening up markets, often had to be abandoned in favour of general harmonisation in the face of "race to the bottom" concerns. The Lisbon Treaty provisions for enhanced cooperation between groups of countries specifically provide that:

> such cooperation shall not undermine the internal market or economic, social and territorial cohesion. It shall not constitute a barrier to or discrimination in trade between Member States, nor shall it distort competition between them.[95]

It also ensures that:

> any enhanced cooperation shall respect the competences, rights and obligations of those Member States which do not participate in it.[96]

It can be assumed that similar limitations would apply in the opposite case of a Member State, or group of Member States, wishing to opt out of a particular policy.

Conclusions

Various studies by academics – for example, those by Turner and Crowson – have documented the differences in opinion within the Conservative Party created by developments in Europe. Part of the problem, according to Turner, has been that these developments have "challenged the basic assumptions and values of the modern Tory Party. ... Europe is seen as anathema to Tory beliefs in that it is seen as an idealistic and mechanistic imposition which conflicts with the natural and organic development of the nation state."[97] Likewise Crowson writes that "the very idea of European integration challenges traditional Conservative assumptions about sovereignty".[98]

Such theoretical considerations can also be viewed as symptoms of more general troubles. For Turner, the issue of Europe brought into the open "fault lines" already running through the party. Its "ambiguous position on Europe" when Thatcher came to power "emanated from thirty years of policies towards Europe which were as much about party factionalism and ideology as they were about Europe itself".[99]

This view accords with the observations made earlier, that the Maastricht rebels were as much motivated by revenge against those who had removed

Margaret Thatcher from the Party leadership – or who had "usurped" her, as Teresa Gorman put it in her memoirs[100] – as by objections to the Treaty itself; or the anti-establishment, new generation pro-European enthusiasm of the early Bow Groupers and the Young Conservatives of the 1960s.

Pro-Europeanism has also, in general, been strongest on that wing of the Party more associated with One Nation Toryism (what Turner calls the "pragmatic left factions" of the Party), and Euroscepticism with both the traditional "Empire and Commonwealth" and the modern "Thatcherite" right. So, in Turner's view, Europe "became a surrogate issue for attacks on other features of Thatcherism".[101] One example was the Westland affair at the beginning of 1986, which was initially about Europe and defence procurement, but, as it developed, became principally about the Prime Minister's style of leadership.

For Crowson, the fault lines which appeared to emerge after 1997 were in fact a return to the 20th century norm. There were "two ideological strands of thinking on Britain's relationship with continental Europe, each struggling for supremacy within the party",[102] of which the debates about tariff reform sparked by Joseph Chamberlain in 1903 were a symptom, and which went back to the free trade/protection debates of the 1840s and 1850s.

There is also the observation that differences on Europe have been as much between the Party leadership on the one hand, and the membership in the constituencies on the other, as between different wings of the Party. As the *Daily Telegraph* once memorably put it "the Tory Party is a dinosaur with a small head and a large body. The head is Euro-enthusiast and the body is Eurosceptic."[103]

This view, however, is contradicted by much of the evidence contained in the Conservative Party archives in the Bodleian Library, studied by Crowson. The leadership regularly hedged its pro-European stance in deference to perceived opposition within the Party. But "what this study has shown is that the Conservative leadership mistook party ignorance for hostility".

> Even with the growing parliamentary Euroscepticism of the 1990s, it is not clear that this transferred itself to the grass roots. They seem to be largely immune to ideological groundswells: their primary concern is that the Conservatives are electable.[104]

The votes at successive party conferences and the reports of CPC discussion groups, indeed, show that Conservatives have been amazingly willing to follow the leadership's line on Europe, whatever that has happened to be. The regular complaints from Party members about "lack of information", moreover, have been more the result of a (correct) belief that "there are no votes in Europe" than any desire by the leadership or Conservative Central Office or Conservative Campaign Headquarters to deceive.

This view too, however, is subject to certain caveats. The membership of the Conservative Party is not static over time, still less the much smaller groups which are active in the constituencies. My own experience is that the apparent readiness of these to follow the party line can in part be explained by changes in personnel: for example, the reluctance of many who belonged to "the party of Europe" in the 1980s to remain active under the Eurosceptic leaderships after 1997, and the steady and drastic reduction in overall Party membership.

The movements of opinion on Europe within the Conservative Party also have to be seen in the wider political context. One obvious factor, noted earlier, has been whether the Party has been in government or in opposition: since the early 1960s there has been tendency for parties losing office to move in a Eurosceptic direction. Another has been the attitudes adopted by the other parties, in particular the Labour Party. From a tactical point of view, the Conservatives have been in the happiest position when able to claim the middle ground between a Labour Party intent on pulling out of Europe altogether, and a Liberal or Liberal Democrat Party apparently hell-bent on full frontal federalism. Such middle ground, however, has proved much less comfortable when flanked by a moderately pro-Europe Labour Government on the one hand, and a populist Referendum Party or United Kingdom Independence Party (UKIP) on the other.

In addition, the even wider European political context cannot be ignored. The issues debated by the parties at European Parliament elections have generally seemed to be national rather than pan-European, leading commentators to conclude that, rather than a single election, there have been twelve, fifteen or twenty-seven largely unconnected national elections. This has given credence to the claims by Enoch Powell and others that the elections have only provided a semblance of democracy.

Yet analysis of recent results has shown that most of the supposedly isolated national electorates have followed similar broad political trends. Butler and Westlake's study of the European Elections of 1994 noted that parties in power had generally done badly; but found "no overall swing to the left, nor any overall swing to the right".[105] In the European Elections of 2009, however, centre-right parties advanced in almost all countries at the expense of the centre-left; and this occurred whether the centre-right was in power (as in France and Italy), in opposition (as in Britain and Spain) or in coalition (as in Germany). Electorates in almost all EU countries, it appears, were now reacting in a similar way to the "credit crunch" and its consequences.

There have also been discernible pan-European trends over time: for example, the rise of "green" parties as concern about the environment has grown. In the 1979 Parliament there was no Green Group; but following the European Elections of 1984 a "Rainbow" Group was formed consisting of 11 Greens and 9 allies, 4.6% of Parliament's total membership. Today its successor, the Green/European Free Alliance Group has 55 members, 7.5% of the total. A similar, if paradoxical, trend has been the growth of specifically nationalist or anti-integration parties and groupings, a trend of which the British Conservative Party has formed one element.

This indicates that, contrary to the Powellite analysis, we might after all be seeing the beginnings of a genuine European *demos*. If this is so, one provision of the Lisbon Treaty might well enhance the trend: that for "Citizens' Initiatives". The signatures of one million EU citizens (0.2% of the total population) will be enough to invite the Commission to propose a new draft law, to which invitation the Commission is required to respond within three months. The Treaty requires the signatures to be spread over a "significant number" of different countries; and this will give an advantage to political movements or parties that are truly trans-national and have roots in all or most Member States. It might, indeed, prompt the Conservative Party to look again at its relations with the European People's Party.

Notes

1 Hugo Young *op.cit.* p. 412.
2 Forster *op.cit.* pp. 130 and 131.
3 Turner *op.cit.* p. 15.
4 *The Spectator*, 14th July 1990.
5 "Looking beyond Europe": letter to *The Economist* of the 28th November 2009.
6 Daniel Hannon, *Newsletter* (December 2008).
7 Lewis *Rome or Brussels … ?* pp. 8–12.
8 Lamont *op.cit.* p. 124.
9 Quoted in *John Major* by B. Anderson (Headline, 1992) and Turner *op.cit.* p.114.
10 Booker *op.cit.* Chapter One: Approaching Niagara.
11 Letwin *op.cit.* Introduction.
12 Heath *The Course of My Life* p. 716.
13 *Hansard* of the 17th November, 1966, Col. 666.
14 Hugo Young *op.cit.* p. 246.
15 Hugo Young *op.cit.* p. 251.
16 *Hansard* (Commons), Vol. 736, Cols. 653–4.
17 Letter in the *Daily Telegraph*, the 21st January 1997.
18 Hugo Young *op.cit.* p. 253.
19 *Ambitions & Realities: British Politics 1964–1970* by Robert Rhodes James (Weidenfeld and Nicolson, 1972), p.107.
20 *The European Institutions as an Interest Group* by Professor Roland Vaubel (Institute of Economic Affairs, June 2009).
21 See *Federal Union: The Pioneers: a History of Federal Union* by Richard Mayne and John Pinder (Macmillan, 1990)
22 Turner, *op.cit.* p. 147.
23 Macmillan, *Tides of Fortune*, p. 480.
24 Turner *op.cit.* p. 78.
25 *Nationalism* by Elie Kedouri (Hutchinson 1985) p. 9.
26 Reported in *La Dépéche du Midi* of the 24th October 2009 in coverage of a demonstration in favour of Occitan.
27 Immigration minister Eric Besson, as reported in *Le Figaro* of the 26th October 2009.
28 'In the National Interest' by Alec Campbell in *Principles in Practice* (Bow Group, 1961).
29 *When China Rules the World: the Rise of the Middle Kingdom and the End of the Western World* by Martin Jacques (Allen Lane, 2009). See earlier footnote.

30 *Tradition and Reality: Conservative Philosophy and European Integration* by Robert Jackson MEP (European Democratic Group, 1982).

31 *The Changing Structure of International Law* by Wolfgang Friedman (Stevens, 1964).

32 Friedman *op.cit.* p. 293.

33 In *Conservatism, Democracy and National Identity*: the Third Keith Joseph Memorial Lecture (Centre for Policy Studies, 1999).

34 Siedentop *op.cit.* p. 105.

35 At a press conference in Strasbourg on the 10th July 2007.

36 Boothby *op.cit.* p. 370.

37 *Old World, New Horizons* by Edward Heath (Oxford University Press, 1970) p. 57.

38 *British Government and Politics: balancing Europeanization and Independence* by Michael L.Mannin (Rowman & Littlefield Publishers Inc., 2010).

39 Mannin *op.cit.* p. 74.

40 *The Myth of Europe* by Russell Lewis (The Bruges Group 2000).

41 *The Rise and Fall of the Great Powers* by Paul Kennedy (Unwin Hyman, 1988).

42 Kennedy *op.cit.* p. 488.

43 See *The Puritan Gift* by Kenneth and William Hopper (I.B.Tauris paperback, 2007).

44 *The Practice of Management* by P.F. Drucker (Harper Perennial, New York, 1993).

45 *Making Sense of Subsidiarity: How Much Centralization for Europe?* by Prof. David Begg and others (Centre for Economic Policy Research, November 1993).

46 *Subsidiarity, National Parliaments and the Lisbon Treaty* (House of Lords European Scrutiny Committee, thirty-third report of session 2007–08, October 2008).

47 *Shaking the Foundations: Britain and the New Europe* by Christopher Jackson MEP (Conservatives in the European Parliament, October 1990).

48 Lamont *op.cit.* p. 115.

49 Begg *et al. op.cit.* p. 4.

50 Reprinted in *Old World, New Horizons*.

51 *ibid.*

52 Heath *op.cit.* p. 25.

53 Tebbit *op.cit.* p. 94.

54 *The Benefits of Europe*, with foreword by Sir Henry Plumb MEP (European Democratic Group in the European Parliament, 1981).

55 In the Bow Group magazine *Crossbow*, Spring 1960.

56 In *Towards a European Identity* (PEST 1972).

57 See Chapter Three: Finding a Role, Conservative Gaullism.

58 Centre for Policy Studies, 1997.

59 *Europe and the Superpower* by The Rt. Hon. Lord Hurd of Westwell CH CBE in *Conservative Europe, 2003 Party Conference Magazine* (Conservative Group for Europe, October 2003).

60 *EU-US relations: towards deeper cooperation* by The Rt. Hon. Sir Malcolm Rifkind MP in *Conservative Europe, 2008 Party Conference Magazine* (Conservative Group for Europe, October 2008).

61 *EU Foreign Relations: the Next Steps* by The Rt. Hon. Chris Patten CH in *Conservative Europe, 2002 Party Conference Magazine* (Conservative Group for Europe, October 2002).

62 *Free Trade and the Euro* by The Rt.Hon. Lord Brittan of Spennithorne QC (Conservative Group for Europe and the Tory European Network, 2002).

63 *Is the Euro sustainable?* (Bruges Group, March 2009).

64 *The EU and Trade: a benefit for Britain* by The Rt. Hon. Lord Brittan of Spennithorne QC in *Conservative Europe, 2002 Party Conference Magazine* (Conservative Group for Europe, October 2002).

65 *Why Europe needs the Conservatives* by Jonathan Evans MEP in *Conservative Europe, 2002 Party Conference Magazine* (Conservative Group for Europe, October 2002).

66 *Foreword* by The Rt. Hon David Curry MP in *Conservative Europe, 2003 Party Conference Magazine* (Conservative Group for Europe October 2003).

67 *The Wise European* by The Rt. Hon. John Major CH in *Conservative Europe, 2004 Party Conference Magazine* (Conservative Group for Europe, October 2004).

68 *Which?* (Consumers' Association, February 1981).
69 For detailed figures and analysis see *The European Voter: Popular responses to the first Community election* by Jay G. Blumler and Anthony D. Fox (Policy Studies Institute, 1982).
70 Hugo Young *op.cit.* p. 507.
71 Mannin *op.cit.*p. 194.
72 Charlemagne column in *The Economist* of the 22nd to the 28th May 2010.
73 Bagehot column in *The Economist* of the 11th to the 17th September 2010.
74 Blair *op cit.* p. 533.
75 Quoted in "Facts, errors and the Kindel (*sic*)" in *Intelligent Life* (The *Economist*, Autumn 2009).
76 *The EEC and the Media* by Robert Winder (Kirk Scholarship Project 1982/83, DJE International Public Relations Group, 1983).
77 *The EEC and Britain – a Socialist Perspective* (Labour Party National Executive Committee, 12 July 1977).
78 Statement by John Davies MP, the 5th September 1977.
79 *Labour's Programme 1982* (Labour Party, 1982).
80 1983 *Campaign Guide* p. 409.
81 1989 *Campaign Guide* p. 545.
82 *Looking to the future* (Labour Party, My 1990).
83 1992 *Campaign Guide.* p. 656.
84 1994 *Campaign Guide* p. 653.
85 Introduction by Roger Hudson to Green's *A Short History of the English People* (Folio Society edition, 1992).
86 In *1066 and All That.*
87 Judd *op.cit.* p. 429.
88 Butler and Westlake *op.cit.* p. 7.
89 Lewis, *The Myth of Europe* p. 16.
90 Crowson *op.cit.* p. 73.
91 Tebbit *op.cit.* p. 209.
92 Letter from V.B.Petherick to Conservative Central Office, the 6th September 1962, quoted in Crowson, *op.cit.* p. 225.
93 *Who Really Governs Britain ?* by Nirj Deva DL, FRSA, MEP (Bow Group, 2001).
94 *Leading Europe in the Right direction,* by Nick Watts (Conservative Europe Group, supported by Business in Europe, 2009).
95 Article 280A.
96 Article 280B.
97 Turner *op.cit.* p. 82.
98 Crowson *op.cit.* p. 87.
99 Turner *op.cit.* p. 71.
100 *The Bastards* by T. Gorman (Pan, 1993).
101 Turner *op.cit.* p. 107.
102 Crowson *op.cit.* p. 221.
103 *Daily Telegraph* on the 21st April 1996.
104 Crowson, *op.cit.* p. 220/1.
105 Butler and Westlake *op.cit.* p. 275.

17 Conservative European Policy and the Future

Party policy in coalition

If one compares the Conservative Party's policies on Europe contained in the General Election of 2010 manifesto with those that emerged from the subsequent negotiations with the Liberal Democrats – both outlined at the end of Chapter Fifteen – the concessions made by the Party appear, on the face of it, to have been considerable. In particular, the Party was obliged to abandon its ambitions to repatriate a number of powers from "Brussels" and to circumscribe the power of the European Court of Justice. In return, the Liberal Democrats made only one major concession: renouncing Euro Area membership for the lifetime of the Parliament. Their pledge to "an in/out referendum the next time a British government signs up for fundamental change in the relationship between the UK and the EU" was dropped, to the relief of many Liberal Democrats, in favour of the Conservative policy of a referendum on the change itself.

The net result was, in effect, an agreement to maintain the *status quo*.

The Conservative Party's 2010 manifesto, however, had only dealt briefly with policy on Europe. It had concentrated, moreover, on the more Eurosceptic aspects of the Party's position – no doubt to reassure potential Conservative voters who might have been tempted to vote for UKIP. A much more detailed, and balanced, description of the Party's policy towards the European Union had been contained in the manifesto for the previous year's European Elections.[1]

A clear and basic tenet of Conservative European policy, contained in both the 2009 and 2010 manifestos, is that Britain should remain an EU Member State, even an enthusiastic member in terms of the Party's "positive new agenda for Europe" outlined in the 2009 manifesto. This stated that:

> The Conservatives are committed to Britain's membership of the EU. We are proud of the EU's achievements, such as the progress made in widening the freedom to do business, travel and find work, and in anchoring democracy and stability across the continent.

It also reaffirmed the advantages for Britain to belong to a grouping that is an important player on the wider international stage.

> The UK's ability to project our values and advance our interests is enhanced by membership of international organisations, including the European Union. As the world's largest trading bloc the EU's trade policies have a significant impact on global development, as does its handling of the substantial quantities of aid it dispenses.

In contrast to earlier, more Eurosceptic statements, the manifesto went beyond support for EU membership in terms only of "promoting our national interest in Brussels".

> The EU's enlargement policy has been highly successful, facilitating the transformation of countries across Europe for the better over the past thirty years. ... When used well and wisely, the EU's global reach can be employed not just for national and European interests but to achieve ambitious goals such as the alleviation of global poverty.

In addition, in line with the new "green" Conservatism introduced by David Cameron, there was emphatic support for the EU's environmental policies:

> Conservatives have consistently supported and strengthened the EU climate change package and resisted the argument that efforts to tackle climate change should be watered down in the light of the global economic downturn.

It is perhaps of some significance that this policy was very similar to the one on which the Liberal Democrats fought the General Election a year later.

The Conservative manifesto of 2009 also reaffirmed the Party's commitment to the Single Market, "a great achievement which the Conservative Party has always strongly supported". It called for action in a number of areas where internal barriers still exist, such as "energy, communications, financial services and public procurement;" and also to ensure the "proper application and enforcement" of Single Market rules. There was also a new element, coherent with the idea of a "flexible" EU:

> Where we do not believe progress towards fully open markets is moving fast enough, we will consider pressing for the use of the 'enhanced cooperation' mechanism, which would allow a vanguard of countries to pursue further liberalisation at a faster pace.

The manifesto also made it clear that support for the removal of internal barriers to trade did not imply the maintenance or erection of barriers externally: the temptation to strengthen "Community preference", as advocated by the French centre right. In his foreword, David Cameron stated that

> We will be strong defenders of the Single Market within Europe, and free trade with the rest of the world, at a time when calls for protectionism at home and abroad are growing.

Indeed, the manifesto went a step further in proposing the objective of "a transatlantic market by 2015".

It was equally ambitious, if more controversial, in the field of EU enlargement.

> Our MEPs will support the further enlargement of the EU, including to the Ukraine, Belarus, Turkey, Georgia and the countries of the Balkans, if they wish to achieve EU membership, however distant that prospect may be in some cases.

Russia was not mentioned, although the manifesto promised that the Party "will resist efforts ... to draw up a 'final border' for the EU".

Judged by the policies outlined above, therefore, the Conservative Party's claim to be "advancing a modern vision for Europe" is not a fanciful one. The manifesto was especially strong on the external aspects of EU policy: promoting an international "pro-development trade deal", tackling climate change, fighting global poverty and extending the EU's "Neighbourhood Policy" to all potential new Member States in advance of enlargement.

The manifesto also outlined the Party's longstanding policies for EU reform – of the Budget, of the Common Agricultural Policy and of the Common Fisheries Policy. It came down firmly in favour of scrapping European Parliament meetings in Strasbourg (though this can only be brought about through a joint decision of the twenty-seven Member State governments). There was support for a number of EU policies in the economic and industrial field, including the new European Research Council and measures to help small businesses and innovative companies. All proposed new EU legislation should have to pass a "Single Market Test"; and there should be "a more muscular approach to deregulation".

In contrast to these positive themes there were, of course, others of a more Eurosceptic nature. There was the straightforward pledge to "keep the UK out of the euro", and to restore "British control of social and employment legislation". Though stating that new regulation was needed to "make sure that financial services never again subject the global economy to dangerous risks", the manifesto was against "plans for an EU 'super regulator'", preferring "coordination between national regulators". Similarly, "national telecoms regulation" would be defended against Commission plans for a centralised system. EU regulation in general was to be pruned back, with the administrative costs of EU legislation being cut "by 25% by 2012". Plans for the EU to acquire additional powers in the fields of foreign policy and defence were to be opposed, as were any proposals to harmonise policies in the fields of Justice and Home Affairs, and the criminal law.

The manifesto also clearly confirmed both the Conservative Party's opposition to the Lisbon Treaty, and its pledge to hold a referendum on the issue.

> We believe that such a significant handover of powers from Britain to the EU should not be made without the British people's consent. ... If a Conservative Government takes office in time, while the Lisbon Treaty is not yet in force, we will suspend ratification of the Treaty, hold the referendum the British people want and were promised, and recommend that the Treaty is rejected.

Moreover, if the Treaty were to come into force before a Conservative Government came into office, "we would not let matters rest there", though exactly what measures could or would be taken was not spelled out. After the final ratification by the Czech Republic in November Cameron made the statement on the Party's consequent position outlined earlier which, in effect, *did* let the matter rest.

Coherence and contradiction

It is tempting to see the inclusion in the 2009 manifesto of both positive proposals for EU action, and pledges to defend national sovereignty against other EU action, as having been designed chiefly with Party unity in mind. It can also be argued that a major objective was to position the Party on "middle ground" between the ultras of the United Kingdom Independence Party and the BNP on the one hand, and the "federalists" in the Labour and Liberal Democrat parties on the other: a winning formula in the early 1980s (when the anti-Europe ultras were, of course, the Labour Party).

There may be something in both these readings; but it is also true that the policies of the Party on the EU, taken as a whole, *do* have coherence, given the position agreed after the intense debates within the Party at the time of Maastricht and after. Promises to "fight for British interests" do not derive, as opponents have claimed, from insensitive bellicosity towards foreigners, but from the view that the best outcome for the EU as a whole will result from *all* Member States defending their national independence: an international version, it could be said, of Adam Smith's "hidden hand". Rather than adopting uniform practices elaborated at EU level, countries should be as free as possible to work out their own answers to economic and social challenges, in accordance with their own traditions and characters. Out of this variety will come competition; and out of competition will come optimum solutions.

This, in essence, is the rationale behind *"Europe des patries"*, of which the British Conservative Party, together with its Czech and Polish allies in the European Parliament and upholders of undiluted Gaullism in France, is now the principal proponent. Where common action is required – as, for example, in the fields of environmental protection or the regulation of financial markets – the preferred basis is "cooperation between independent nation states" rather than supra-national initiatives. It therefore becomes logical to propose ambitious joint action by Member States in such fields as the fight against world poverty or climate change while at the same time resisting any extension of the powers wielded by "Brussels".

While somewhat different from the stance of the Party in earlier periods, therefore, the policies on which the Conservatives fought the European Elections of 2009 – and which will have formed one element of the negotiations with the Liberal Democrats a year later – were firmly rooted in principle. At a philosophical level, there was a coherent, credible basis for reaching clear positions on day-to-day European issues.

It is nevertheless possible to detect some incoherences at a practical level.

The first area of possible conflict lies in the field of policy towards third countries. This lies not so much in the policy outlined by Hague in his speech at the Birmingham Party Conference of 2010, of conducting collective action through the EU in parallel with independent national action. He was right to observe that the two channels can reinforce each other, provided third parties do not succeed in playing one Member State off against the other. The possible inconsistency lies rather in a suspicious attitude towards the arrangements required for efficient collective action.

Conservatives have accepted in general the need for Europe "to speak with one voice" in international affairs; but this has been combined with deep suspicion of the Lisbon Treaty's provisions to streamline the previous haphazard and confusing responsibilities of the different EU institutions in this field. Not only is there now "a European Foreign Secretary" in the person of Baroness Ashton, but a "EU diplomatic service" has now been created out of the various Commission and other offices: the European External Action Service (EEAS). It is true that these changes give the EU many of the external attributes of a "super-state", yet it is difficult to see how a coherent external policy could be implemented without them. Happily, the coalition government's attitude has been pragmatic: the Minister for Europe, the Conservative MP David Lidington, has welcomed the creation of the EEAS as, among other things, a cost-saving measure.

The second area of possible confusion has already been extensively discussed in earlier chapters. Many Conservatives are reluctant to concede that the creation of the Single Market, by the very fact of abolishing barriers to free movement and banning their re-creation, inevitably leads to restrictions on national sovereignty. Support for a barrier-free Single Market can also conflict with the promotion of a "variable geometry", "flexible" or *"à la carte"* European Union. If countries are free to pick and choose which policies to accept, there is the obvious danger that disparate choices will gradually erode the unity of the market, and even lead to the re-erection of trade barriers.

Thirdly, there is the "widening/deepening" dilemma. Both those who support closer integration, and those who oppose it have often assumed that the more EU Member States there are, the less likely a "European super-state" becomes. In France, where much the same debates on the matter have taken place – though with the balance of opinion more favourable to integration and less to enlargement – this assumption has also been made. As an editorial in the main centre-right daily, *Le Figaro*, put it on the 27th May 2009, *"avec l'élargissement, l'Europe fédérale s'est évanouie et l'Europe des nations s'impose".* *

Yet the need for efficient decision-taking in a steadily expanding union has clearly been one of the main driving forces behind successive "integrationist" treaties. It has become clear, for example, that there is really no need to have twenty-seven Commissioners merely because there are twenty-seven Member States, a problem which was addressed in the Lisbon Treaty, but which has been somewhat compromised through a concession to Ireland.

A fourth area where practical contradictions seem to arise is international trade. True to its belief in free trade, the Conservative Party has supported the removal of trade barriers not only within the EU, but in the world economy as a whole. Many Eurosceptics have nevertheless concluded that membership of the EU, often described as a "protectionist" organisation, is an unnecessary shackle on Britain's freedom to trade internationally. I remember expressing alarm myself when lecturing at Swinton in the early 1960s: Britain within the EEC would no longer have the freedom to conclude a trade agreement with even Australia or New Zealand. That power was to be handed over to the Commission.

Yet the idea that Britain acting alone could negotiate a reduction in world trade barriers was already at that time an example of post-Imperial delusion. Today, faced with not only the still considerable economic power of the United States, but that of rising economic powers like China, the bargaining power of an economy the size of Britain's is negligible. The EU as a whole, however, as the world's largest market for a wide range of products, has massive bargaining strength. Indeed, British EU trade Commissioners like Leon Brittan and Peter Mandelson have wielded international influence every bit as potent as that of any US Secretary of State for Trade, and a great deal more potent than that of any British trade minister. Mandelson – who, like Brittan, has held both the Commission and the UK ministerial posts – makes this very clear in his autobiography, *The Third Man*.

A final area where the Conservative Party's official position may not – at least until recently – have been entirely coherent has arisen as a

---

* "With enlargement, a federal Europe has melted away, and a Europe of nations has become unavoidable."

consequence of the recent international financial crises. Though some countries were in a better position to cope than others, the entire episode demonstrated the reality of globalised financial markets. Prudent fiscal and monetary policies, and conservative regulation of financial markets, did not allow EU Member States like Germany to escape the consequences of, as they saw it, "Anglo-Saxon" laxity. Multinational companies have for long been accused of playing off one government against another by using their power to shift employment and tax revenues. Globalised financial markets have made it possible for banks and other players to do the same using their power to shift between regulatory regimes: regulatory arbitrage or "jurisdiction-shopping", as it is called. Not surprisingly, doubts about the ability of individual nation states to control the situation have grown.

There is certainly a case to be made for the primary job of financial supervision to remain with national regulators, who are in the best position to understand the details of local markets. It is also clear that, as in the recent crises, national taxpayers are the ones who eventually bear the brunt of bail-outs. It is even possible to make the case outlined in a recent Institute of Economic Affairs paper,[2] that regulation is necessary at neither national nor European level: competition between self-regulating markets will produce a better outcome than statutory regulation.

Yet the financial markets make it almost inevitable that problems are contagious across frontiers; and passively accepting the disruption of their own financial systems as a result of such contagion is asking too much of national governments. There is consequently a danger that reliance on separate national supervisory regimes alone will result in the erection of new barriers to cross-frontier financial services, so negating nearly twenty-five years' efforts to remove them.

In addition, the burden of national bail-outs has had the knock-on effect of undermining the standing of some sovereign debt. This was not the primary cause of the funding problems faced by Greece; but rising public debt levels in most Euro Area countries increased the risk of contagion, particularly for other members of the so-called "Club Med". These events have led, first, to various multi-billion euro rescue packages and contingency funds and to the purchase by the ECB itself of national public debt (arguably in breach of the Treaty); and secondly, to renewed calls from France for more centralised economic governance and from Germany for stronger constraints on national fiscal sovereignty. Within the G20 group of leading economies,* the need for a supervisory framework for financial services at a global level has been agreed, and the European Union has taken a lead in implementation.

In this field, therefore, it is probably inevitable that there will be "more Europe" rather than less. As in the case of the Single Market as a whole,

---

* A group of finance ministers and central bank governors from 20 economies: 19 countries plus the European Union.

the price of an open market for financial services would seem to be increased competences for EU institutions, whether this is done openly, or disguised in the form of "Lamfalussy committees".[*] The Commission has tabled extensive proposals; and already there has been agreement between governments on creating new European supervisory authorities, including a Systemic Risk Board. In a generally critical analysis of these developments, the *Economist*[3] warned, not that these would take away national sovereignty, but that they would not give the regulators adequate powers. For example, they would not be able to "wind up cross-border banks in an orderly way to ensure that all depositors are protected, something that is needed to stop countries from simply grabbing what assets they can when big banks fall". Finally, a whole new structure of supervision and support mechanisms is being established within the Euro Area, designed to prevent any future threat to the euro itself from a sovereign debt crisis on the Greek pattern.

All these developments have received the support of the UK government.

Referendum lock and Sovereignty Act

It is also possible that the Conservative Party is getting into deep constitutional waters with its proposals designed to protect national sovereignty. In his speech at the Birmingham Conference in 2010 Foreign Secretary William Hague gave special emphasis to three measures: the so-called "referendum lock"; a UK Sovereignty Act (although in the case of the second, the coalition agreement was only to "examine the case" for the measure); and legislation to ensure that use of the so-called *passerelle* clause in the Lisbon Treaty – whereby, for example, the European Council could decide that a category of Commission proposals could become subject to Qualified Majority Vote rather than unanimity without a Treaty change – would nevertheless be subject to national parliamentary approval.

The "referendum lock", implementing the policy outlined by David Cameron in November 2009 following the final ratification of the Lisbon Treaty, would make it obligatory to have a referendum before any further transfer of competences to "Brussels". A UK Sovereignty Act would assert the primacy of UK over EU law, and make it clear that Parliament at Westminster retained the right, in effect, to amend or repeal the European Communities Act 1972 if so minded. "What Parliament can do, Parliament can also undo", Hague declared.

The first problem with the "referendum lock" is that of deciding exactly which issues it should cover. In some cases this would be clear: major Treaty changes, moving elements of foreign and security policy from the

---

[*] Under the Directives already adopted under the EU's Financial Services Action Plan, regulation of financial markets is carried out by a hierarchy of committees, mostly composed of representatives of national bodies. The system followed the recommendations of a "committee of wise men" chaired by the former President of the European Monetary Institute, forerunner of the European Central Bank, Alexandre Lamfalussy.

"inter-governmental" pillar to the "Community" pillar, as well as joining the Euro Area or abolishing border controls under the Schengen agreement. The coalition government has declared, however, that the "lock" would not apply to Treaty changes consequent upon enlargement, despite the fact that the accession of several new Member States will inevitably bring institutional changes: for example, to the weight of the UK's vote in Council and the number of UK Members of the European Parliament.

The Bill providing for the lock (as well as the Sovereignty Act and the *passerelle* safeguards) was published on the 11th November 2010, and immediately provoked protests from Conservative Eurosceptics. The Bruges Group described the proposed measures as "fig leaves to hide Cameron's blushes" after the failure to hold a referendum on Lisbon. The chairman of the House of Commons European Scrutiny Committee, Bill Cash, called them "milk and water ... a million miles away from what is required". The reason for these complaints was the provision that ministers could decide *not* to hold a referendum where the proposed changes were "insignificant" – for example, increasing the number of official languages. Any decision to hold a referendum, Europe Minster David Lidington observed, needed to pass "a ridicule test". This, the Eurosceptics argued, was a suspicious loophole. The Conservative MP Philip Davies had summed up their fears during a debate on the previous day.

> Ever since we went into the Common Market, the British public have been told at every stage along the way, 'Actually, we're not giving up any sovereignty. This new treaty doesn't give anything away,' but people have found time and again that these treaties have done just that.

A "referendum lock" also creates the problem of what happens if a referendum is lost. For it to have been held in the first place, the government of the day would have to have agreed to the Treaty changes or other measures in question, and so, perhaps, would Parliament at Westminster – which would, of course, remain sovereign. In addition, the precedents set by Ireland in the cases of the Nice and Lisbon Treaties cast doubt on whether the "lock" would hold in the face of political reality: faced with the choice of accepting the Treaty change or precipitating a major crisis in relations with Europe, the electorate might be asked to go on voting until it gave the right answer.

Finally, Hague – no doubt unwittingly – had drawn attention in his Birmingham speech to a paradox. It is highly improbable that the current government will propose any major transfer of power away from Westminster – and certainly not without a referendum. The intention to introduce a "lock" can therefore only be in order to bind future governments. After 2016, however, if Parliament has the power to undo previous Acts like that of 1972, it also has the power to undo the Act providing for a "referendum lock". No Parliament can bind its successor. Such Acts, therefore, can only achieve their objective as long as there is a majority in Parliament to retain them. In practice, for example, a future government wishing to transfer sovereignty *without* a referendum merely has to repeal the referendum Act first, or legislate a derogation from it.

There are a number of theoretical answers to this paradox, generally applied in countries with written constitutions. Certain so-called "entrenched" clauses can only be repealed by special parliamentary majorities, by referendum, or – in the case of federations or confederations – by majorities of both voters and states. Even in such cases a determined government can overturn the blocks – as, for example, the Nationalist government of South Africa did when introducing *apartheid*. Britain, however, has no such written constitution. The "sovereignty of Parliament" is, in theory at least, unconstrained. In the last resort, the "referendum lock" and UK Sovereignty Act measures can be of only declaratory value – unless, of course, the UK were to adopt a written constitution.

In the case of a UK Sovereignty Act, lawyers have already begun to discern, and argue about, unforeseen ramifications. Although a Government statement has asserted that it would "not alter the law on a day-to-day basis", there is a fear that it could create legal uncertainty: for example, in the case of legal rights under Directives adopted at EU level, but not yet transposed at national level. There is a fear that conflicts might arise between the respective jurisdictions of the European Court of Justice and the UK's Supreme Court. And finally, there is the contrasting argument that new legislation is in any case unnecessary, since the national position is already adequately protected by the sovereignty of the Westminster parliament and by common law.

Pragmatism, conservatism and ideology

The closing section of Chapter Sixteen outlined various factors which will influence future Conservative policy towards Europe: whether the Party is in government or opposition; the possible permanent "fault-lines" dating from the free-trade/protection debates of the early 20th century and before; the legacy of struggles for control of the Party's soul between progressives and traditionalists, paternalists and libertarians, "grandees" and "young turks"; tensions between the Party's leadership and its grass roots; the size of the Party's membership and its age profile.

One further element of that context may also need to be examined: the direction in which "Conservatism" itself will develop in the coming years.

There is a substantial body of academic opinion which maintains that "Conservatism" as a political movement – as opposed to "conservatism" which is best described as a disposition or state of mind – does not exist. In this view, the British Conservative Party has historically been a machine for obtaining and retaining power, adapting its policies and rhetoric as circumstances have required. "Conservatism is what Conservative governments do," as some have put it, in imitation of Herbert Morrison's famous description of Socialism. Even Benjamin Disraeli, to whom Conservatives tend to look back for their philosophical roots, described the first characteristic of Conservatism as "an instinct for power".

If there is such a thing as Conservative philosophy, one important element is indeed empiricism: in the already-quoted words of A. J. Balfour, "the principles of common sense, to do what seems to be the right thing in a given case". The main benefit offered by the Party in campaigning for office has accordingly been the simple one of competent government. Moreover, when its reputation for competence has been destroyed for some reason – in the closing years of the Macmillan government, for example, or most spectacularly after "Black Wednesday" in 1992 – it has tended to find itself out of power for some time.

However, as the profoundly conservative political philosopher Michael Oakeshott observed, "we may decry the style of politics which approximates to pure empiricism, because we observe in it an approach to lunacy."[4] For Oakeshott, not only individuals, but also societies, needed to absorb the lessons of experience; and these, rather than being expressed in rational propositions or dogmas, tended to be incorporated in traditions and established institutions, which politicians destroyed at their peril. This is the element of British Conservatism which derives from Edmund Burke, who observed in a much-quoted passage:

> We are afraid to put men to live and trade each on his own private stock of reason; because we suspect that the stock in each man is small, and that individuals would do better to avail themselves of the general bank and capital of nations and of ages. ... [5]

British Conservatism, then, contains elements both of managerial pragmatism and traditional "conservatism", which have sometimes combined so that incoming Conservative governments have been content to run whatever system they have inherited from their predecessors. Indeed the young Disraeli described Conservatism as a desire "to keep things much as they find them as long as they can, and then ... manage them as well as they can".[6] This is certainly a plausible reading of the second Churchill Government elected in 1951, which, despite the "setting the people free" rhetoric, accepted with few modifications the Welfare State and mixed economy created by Labour after 1945 – and also, of course, its policy towards Europe.

It is not, however, a plausible description of the Thatcher government elected in 1979. In this case the Conservative Party not only offered, but actually implemented in the teeth of violent opposition, a programme which was radically different from those of its predecessors, both Labour and Conservative. Certain commentators, it is true, have written off "Thatcherism" as some kind of aberration, not really in the true Conservative tradition at all. But this will not do. The economic reforms introduced in the 1980s can be seen, for example, as following in the steps of the first government actually to call itself "Conservative", that of Sir Robert Peel, whose Bill to repeal to the Corn Laws in 1846 was as radical a move as any before or since. In both cases the moves were motivated by strong philosophical convictions.

Moreover, if there has been a single radical move by a Conservative government to match the repeal of the Corn Laws it is that carried out by Ted Heath after the General Election of 1970: to join the European Community.

It is therefore necessary to explain what lies behind the more activist element of Conservatism, sometimes referred to as Radical Toryism or Tory Radicalism. British Conservatism does seem to have, if not an ideology, at least core principles which take the Party beyond mere pragmatism or support for the *status quo*.

To begin with, in contrast to the doctrine of *laissez faire* with which the Conservative Party is sometimes associated, but which more properly belongs to classical Liberalism, Radical Tories have never been averse to using the power of the State to achieve social or economic objectives. Indeed their historical antecedents are the Cavalier supporters of Charles I, who upheld the rights of the Crown against the determination of Parliament to limit them. This is the element of Conservative philosophy which is generally referred to as "paternalism", and which has from time to time made the Party's policies dangerously authoritarian. Paradoxically, however, the Cavalier/Tory legacy also includes a libertarian strand: resistance to the puritan tradition of trying to stop people enjoying themselves "for their own good", what would today be called the "nanny state".

As far as policies themselves are concerned, a number of consistent themes can be identified. In 1973, the first year of British European Community membership, the Conservative Political Centre published a pamphlet of mine[7] which attempted to outline some of these. One was a predilection for variety and a distrust of monopoly power, whether political or economic, which led the Party to support a programme of spreading private ownership as widely as possible: the creation of a "property-owning democracy". This would later become a key element of the Thatcher government's economic policies, implemented through the privatisation of nationalised industries and the sale of council houses. The principle also leads, more controversially, to a suspicion of state monopolies in social welfare, health provision and education.

A second theme I explored was the Conservative Party's "pursuit of excellence". This has also been potentially dangerous ground, since it has required certain fine distinctions being made as to the meaning of the word "equality", and has laid the Party open to the charge of élitism. I quoted Aristotle's observation that "injustice arises as much from treating unequals equally as from treating equals unequally"; and the literary critic Dr. F. R. Leavis – a couple of whose lectures I once attended – that the word élitism was itself "a product of ignorance, prejudice and unintelligence. ... Unless standards are maintained somewhere the whole community is let down".[8]

I concluded with the better-known principles of Disraelian One Nation Toryism, and the companion objective of "elevating the condition of the people" (both of which are examined in Appendix 1). The Party's sincerity in maintaining these traditions – and, indeed, both the sincerity and record of Disraeli himself – are frequently questioned by the Conservative Party's political opponents, whose caricature of Conservatives as "the Party of privilege" they awkwardly fail to support. This is why the testimony of those in the early labour movement who could actually remember Disraeli's 1870 ministry, like the Scottish miners' leader Alexander Macdonald and the first chairman of the Labour Party itself, Keir Hardie, are of especial significance. Macdonald, who became one of the early "Lib-Lab" MPs, told the House of Commons that the "Conservative Party has done more for the working classes in five years than the Liberal Party in fifty".

Despite the fact that it is possible to identify such long-standing themes in the Party's history, it has been argued that the desire to formulate a consistent Conservative philosophy or ideology is not only futile but actually dangerous. This view was forcefully advanced by the *Bagehot* column in the *Economist*[9], which poured scorn on formulations such as "libertarian paternalism", "communitarian civic conservatism" and even "progressive conservatism". Mistakenly, some Conservatives had a "vain urge ... to think of themselves as philosopher-kings rather than mere technocrats. ... The Tories should stop worrying about whether their view of the world works in theory, and concentrate more on generating ideas that will work in practice."

This may or may not be good advice. A counter-argument is that voters appear to like parties that identifiably "stand for something". In the case of future policy towards Europe, however, whether the pragmatic, managerial tradition dominates ideological concerns is likely to be crucial. If Euroscepticism proves so persistent as to become, in effect, a new element of Conservative philosophy, the task of being in government and managing Britain's relations with Europe will be considerably more difficult.

One obvious drawback of elevating Euroscepticism into a principle is that it can lead to the interpretation of events through a lens of wishful thinking; and this has nowhere been more obvious in recent years than in attitudes towards the euro. As already noted earlier, the Eurosceptic response to plans for a Single Currency was that, for both political and economic reasons, it could not possibly happen. When, against their predictions, the Euro Area came into being – encompassing, moreover, a majority of Member States – the Eurosceptic response was that the whole project would soon collapse. When it did not, the attitude became one of resentful hostility, with every small problem – for example, with the Stability and Growth Pact – highlighted as being a sign of the end. The Greek debt crisis was greeted almost with glee: this time, surely, the Euro Area will break apart?

Eurosceptics have failed to understand, and therefore greatly underestimated, both the political will to create and maintain a Single Currency and the economic logic of doing so. In the Conservative Party, in particular, perceptions were distorted by the experience of Sterling's ejection from the Exchange Rate Mechanism on Black Wednesday. Whereas the lesson drawn throughout most of the European Union was that the crisis proved the case for currency union, Conservatives reached the opposite conclusion: that it proved the case for floating exchange rates.

The lesson of this failure of perception is that parties and politicians need to keep a high degree of open-mindedness. Whatever measures the British government takes to defend the position of "thus far and no further", the European Union as an organisation will not stand still. Britain will need to respond; and an automatic response of, first, trying to block, and if that fails, opting out, is most unlikely to be in the country's best interests.

Three scenarios

Considerations such as those just outlined mean that Conservative European policy could develop in a number of ways.

First, the most likely outcome: that the Conservative Party, now in a coalition with the clearly pro-European Liberal Democrats, will once again practise "the art of the possible".* Given the coalition agreement, the policy will, in effect, be to remain within the European Union on much the same basis as at present. Immediately after the new government took office, indeed, some effort was made to reassure other governments that Britain would be fully engaged in the EU. Prime Minister Cameron's first official visit was to French President Sarkozy; while the new Foreign Secretary William Hague, though promising to be "assertive" in dealings with the EU, also called for more decisive EU action in international affairs, and urged Euro Area governments not to lose confidence in tackling the Area's economic problems.

The Prime Minister himself, having initially got off on the wrong foot with the German Chancellor, Angela Merkel – largely as a result of the decision to pull Conservative MEPs out of the European People's Party Group in the European Parliament – had clearly reached agreement with her at least on budgetary and economic policies by the time of her visit to the UK at the end of October 2010. While possibly still mildly Eurosceptic at heart, Cameron is enough of a pragmatist to adapt to his political environment.

This may or may not be the case with some of his Conservative colleagues. But, judging by past experience, members of the Government attending the Council of Ministers will quickly adapt to the need for compromise (while of course stoutly proclaiming in subsequent press conferences and in the House of Commons that British interests have

---

* The title of the arch-pragmatist "RAB" Butler's autobiography, published in 1971. The phrase is a quotation from Bismarck: *"Die Politik ist die Lehre von Möglichen"* ("Politics is the art of the possible").

been fully protected). The commitment to hold a referendum on any further proposals to transfer more powers to the EU, incorporated into the Conservative/Liberal Democrat agreement, will of course stand; but will probably not be put to the test.

It is true that the repatriation of certain policies from "Brussels" is still a Conservative aim; and it is even possible that some measures in this direction might actually take place – not just in the case of the UK, but for all Member States – if subsidiarity is applied not only to new EU policies, but also to elements of the *acquis communautaire*. This was in fact already agreed in principle during the discussions leading to Lisbon. On the other hand, as Tim Bale observes,[10] the idea that widespread repatriation, or limitations on the reach and competence of the European Court of Justice, would be conceded by other Member States is "tantamount to fantasy politics".

In many ways such a pragmatic approach would be a continuation of the policies of the Blair and Brown Labour governments, but also those of Prime Minister Major and Foreign Secretary Hurd in the years before "Black Wednesday" and the Maastricht rebellions. Within Europe itself, the objective would be to remain on friendly terms with as many other governments, leaders and parties as possible and to avoid making enemies. As *Leading Europe in the Right direction* put it:

> Inter-governmental relations at EU level are still conducted on the basis of the national interest, however much issues may be Europeanised. The key is to work and build up alliances with others and be prepared to compromise and seek trade-offs.[11]

There is always a possibility, however, that the Party will find itself moving in a more openly pro-European direction either by choice or as a result of Harold Macmillan's "events".* One early indication that this might happen was the decision in July 2010 by the Conservative Home Secretary, Theresa May, to exercise the UK's right to "opt in" to measures adopted under the EU's Home Affairs and Justice pillar: in this case the European Investigation Order (EIO), making it easier for the police forces of one Member State to investigate suspects living in another. There were objections from a number of Conservative backbenchers, including the defeated candidate for the Party leadership in 2004, David Davis. But in this case, the practical need to fight crime more efficiently overcame any ideological consideration.

Then, in November 2010, the UK and France signed what was hailed – in France at least – as an historic agreement to cooperate on a wide-range of defence projects, including in the field of nuclear weapons. The "events" in this case were economic: the impossibility of either country

---

* Asked by a journalist what was most likely to blow the government off course, Macmillan replied: "Events, dear boy, events".

retaining a full range of credible forces in the face of the need to restrain public expenditure. The texts of the agreement were careful to declare that French and British sovereignty were not compromised; and there was no question of any connection with the European Union. Nevertheless, as commentators pointedly observed, even this limited cooperation agreement represented a sharp change of direction in British defence policy, which had until then rested overwhelmingly on partnership with the United States.

Relations with the United States could indeed prove a critical factor in UK policy towards Europe. Despite the Conservative Party's long-standing insistence that maintaining the Atlantic Alliance should remain the primary concern of British foreign policy, the interests and objectives of Conservative governments and those of US administrations have not always coincided. Documents from the period following the fall of the Berlin Wall released in 2009, for example, showed that Washington had little sympathy with Margaret Thatcher's objections to German re-unification.

In the context of Europe, indeed, the so-called "special relationship" has had strict limits. In their desire to see the European "pillar" of the Alliance pulling its weight, for example, US administrations since the Second World War have actively encouraged closer European unity, and have generally been impatient with British reluctance to become fully involved. As the then British ambassador to the US, Sir Antony Acland, warned the Thatcher government in February 1990, "the Americans would rather work with Britain than with anyone else in charting the way ahead ... but they will feel able to do so only so long as we are seen to be central to the European debate". At the G20 meeting in Pittsburgh in September 2009 it was clear that US policy was directed towards shifting the balance of power within international economic institutions towards the emerging economies, notably China, at the expense of those countries *in situ*, notably those of western Europe. It is true that the overriding need to combat international terrorism, and the continuing conflict in Afghanistan, mean that the UK and the US are obliged to work closely together. Yet US pressure, or developments in US policy, might nevertheless propel Britain towards closer integration with the EU.

The international economic context might also change significantly, with the EU forced to defend itself a great deal more vigorously against rising competition; or, more happily, act as one of the main players in devising a new international "economic and financial architecture". Even policy towards the euro may change: I know of more than one detached observer who has placed bets on it being a Conservative government that takes Britain into the Euro Area.*

---

* The logic of this apparently illogical forecast is generally known as "Nixon in China". Only a US President with impeccably anti-Communist credentials could restore relations with Communist China – and, as it happens, also bring an end to the Vietnam War.

However, a radical European policy of quite a different kind is also possible. Though the agreement with the Liberal Democrats appears to have ruled out any major disagreements on Europe, at least for the duration of the Parliament elected in 2010, there is always the risk of an unanticipated crisis leading to irreconcilable conflict and the breakup of the coalition.

One possible source of such a crisis lies in the old, but ever-present, issue of the EU budget, and in particular Britain's budget rebate. This was worth about £5 billion in 2009, though it is likely to fall to half of this in 2011. In the view of the Commissioner responsible for the EU budget, Janusz Lewandowski, the justification for the rebate no longer exists.[12] Indeed it is true that one of the most important original arguments for the rebate – that the UK does particularly badly out of the agricultural section of the budget – is less compelling now that spending on the Common Agricultural Policy (CAP) has fallen from 71% of the total in 1984 to about 40% today, and is due to be reduced further. It is difficult, though, to see Conservatives readily agreeing to abolish what is seen as one of the most important jewels in the Thatcher crown. If abolition of the rebate cannot be prevented, a resentful Conservative Party might swing back to open Euroscepticism.

The trigger for a crisis of this kind is unlikely to be any particular year's budget – despite the alarms and excursions about possible increases from one year to another the total sums involved are less than one per cent of the EU's GDP. It is far more likely to be the upcoming negotiations on the 2013–2020 "budget envelope" which sets the framework for what the EU will be doing, and how it will be financed, for those seven years.

Any new proposal for closer EU integration could also prove a final straw, especially if it were (improbably, it has to be admitted) approved in a referendum. The Party might at last break with its policy, maintained for half a century, of full EU membership. This could involve complex negotiations to enable Britain to become an individual national member of the European Economic Area.

Some sections of the Party would clearly welcome such a development: it would seem to accord well with the long-standing Conservative preference for free trade and a Single Market without "political" baggage. Two considerations, however, would cause the Party to think at least twice before taking such a step. The first would be pressure from business interests, which would hardly welcome the disruption and uncertainty involved. The second would be that already outlined earlier: the obligation on EEA countries to implement decisions and laws governing the Single Market with minimal influence over their content. Those who already complain of "government from Brussels" would quickly become disillusioned with an arrangement where the UK would no longer have a vote, let alone a veto, in the EU Council of Ministers. Pressure could then grow for the UK to leave not only the EU but the Single Market as well, creating even greater economic uncertainties.

Fortunately, there are reasons to believe that Lisbon represents the end of the road for grand integrationist schemes. The Greek debt crisis of early

2010, which severely tested the willingness of countries to make economic sacrifices in the name of European solidarity, was described as "Stalingrad for the federalist camp".[13] The original six Member States, which have generally been the main proponents of integration, are now in a small minority within the Union; and, as in the case of the Netherlands, some no longer favour it anyway. Any further Treaty changes are likely to be adjustments to existing arrangements in the interests of efficiency, which could not be portrayed as attacks on essential national sovereignty.

Amendments of this limited sort are most likely in two fields. The first would be that of foreign and security policy, where Lisbon has so far failed to answer the Kissinger Question: "who speaks for Europe?" But this issue lies within the remaining "inter-governmental" pillar of the EU, and is therefore the primary responsibility of national governments rather than "Brussels".

The second would be the tightening up of the "excessive deficit procedure", following the complete failure of the Stability and Growth Pact to prevent some Euro Area countries incurring huge budget deficits and rapidly rising public debt. There is once again talk of economic government (or economic governance, as *gouvernement économique* is less alarmingly translated), even for a "European Finance Minister". Agreement on tightening up the excessive deficit procedure, as well as establishing a standing fund to prevent a reoccurrence of the Greek debt crisis of May 2010, was reached by the governments of France and Germany in late 2010, and later approved by all twenty-seven Member States.

The existing excessive deficit procedure *does* apply to the UK. On the other hand, any tightening would impact chiefly on the national sovereignty of those counties within the Euro Area. The Commission has certainly floated the idea that it should vet national budgets before they are presented to the national parliaments, and the British government made it clear from the start that applying this to the United Kingdom would be unacceptable. David Cameron has stated, however, that any changes to the Treaty which would apply only to the Euro Area would not be opposed by Britain, and would not, it can be assumed, trigger a referendum.

There are, of course, certain dangers in allowing the Euro Area to become an increasingly integrated unit within the looser framework of the EU. Just as EEA countries have had to accept rules made by the EU, so EU countries not in the Euro Area might find themselves obliged to accept decisions made in advance by the more tightly-knit Euro Area. There are, indeed, already signs that this is happening.

It is also possible that further enlargement of the EU will create renewed institutional problems. The potential accessions of Croatia and Iceland should be easily accommodated within current arrangements. Difficulties will nevertheless increase if the rest of former Yugoslavia – Serbia, Bosnia-Herzegovina, FYROM (Macedonia), Montenegro and Kosovo – together with Albania have to be accommodated; and will increase even more with the possible accessions of the Ukraine, Belarus, Moldova and the Caucasus republics, let alone Turkey. Within a decade or two, the EU may have as many constituent states as the USA.

Finally – though nothing at all to do with the European Union – the European Court of Human Rights in Strasbourg can still create problems. In November 2010 David Cameron was obliged to accept its ruling that prisoners should be given the vote, though he was reported as saying that doing so "makes me sick". Eurosceptic critics pointed out that Conservative policy before the election had been to enact a British Bill of Rights, which would supersede rulings of the Strasbourg Court (though some lawyers had argued that this could only work if the UK removed itself altogether from the Court's jurisdiction, repudiating the European Convention on Human Rights and even, perhaps, withdrawing from the Council of Europe itself).

The bottom line

How the Conservative Party's stance on Europe develops is likely to involve tactical as well as ideological considerations. The coalition agreement with the Liberal Democrats means that the Party has, for at least the life of the government, no choice but to adopt a more Europe-friendly stance than in the recent past. This nevertheless creates a risk of internal dissention of the kind which did so much to destroy the Major government in the 1990s. It also risks a haemorrhage of Conservative voters towards the United Kingdom Independence Party or other parties on the Eurosceptic right. There will therefore be a strong temptation to position the Party as far in a Eurosceptic direction as is necessary to prevent such a development.

This strategy, however, also involves serious dangers. The lesson of recent years is that trying to occupy ground captured by anti-EU parties does not have the effect of bringing back supporters, but instead actually strengthens those parties. The policy of leaving the EU, once espoused only by small fringe groups, is made respectable; and Conservatives who have some doubts about the EU are encouraged to go the whole way, and out of the Party altogether.

Whatever the tactical considerations, however, the overriding issue will be the extent to which the Conservative Party as a whole has become locked into a Eurosceptic position. Even if the leadership, now in government, grows more EU-friendly, this will not necessarily be so on the backbenches. A survey of 101 Conservative candidates, carried out before the 2010 General Election by the *New Statesman*, found that 72 per cent of them favoured a "fundamental renegotiation" of Britain's EU membership. If those who are now MPs feel that too much had been conceded as a result of the coalition compromises, they may become restive. On the other hand, when the House of Commons voted on the 10th November 2010 on the proposals for greater economic policy coordination within the EU, this was passed with 296 Ayes and with only a hard core of Eurosceptic Conservatives among the 40 voting against.

Opinions differ as to what the actual situation in the Party as a whole has been. Some, like Hugo Young, have tended to see a "Eurosceptic tail wagging the Conservative dog", a minority faction irresponsibly splitting the Party. Others have seen it differently: for example, *The Times* columnist and head of the Conservative Research Department between 1995 and 1997, Daniel Finkelstein: "The Tory split on Europe at the beginning of the last decade was always misunderstood. The party was not split down the middle. The vast majority were on the Eurosceptic side."[14]

Among most Conservative MPs and activists in the constituencies this has probably been true for some time. There is certainly little of the pro-European idealism which motivated those YCs and Bow Groupers who campaigned for membership of the European Community in the 1960s and early 1970s, and manned the "Yes" campaign committee rooms during the 1975 referendum. Pro-Europeans in the Party have for some time been on the defensive: what was once the Conservative Group for Europe is now no longer "for" Europe, but has been renamed the Conservative Europe Group.

One of the themes of this study, however, is that the stance of political parties towards Europe can change over surprisingly short periods of time. Various explanations have been offered; but one significant factor is that parties tend to rank political issues in different orders of importance from the electorate. For substantial sections of the Labour Party in the 1960s, 1970s and 1980s, unilateral nuclear disarmament was an overriding imperative, but one of far less interest to ordinary voters, including Labour voters, than so-called "bread-and-butter" issues. In 2001 the Conservative Party discovered something very similar when campaigning to "save the pound" in a General Election. "Europe" seldom features highly in surveys of voters' concerns.

The preoccupations of a political party at any one time can therefore be substantially out of alignment with those of the voters. Political parties, however, do not exist on some different plane: their members and leaders are drawn from those same voters. What may seem vital to one generation of activists can be of less significance to the next, which on that matter reverts to the general view of the electorate as whole.

The current stance of the Conservative Party in relation to the European Union is therefore susceptible to change, as was its pro-European stance in the late 1960s, the 1970s and early 1980s. As time goes by the Maastricht and Lisbon Treaties will recede into history, and, as far as the general UK population is concerned, their effects will be seen to be trivial. Exactly which institution does what within the European Union will seem a great deal less important than the overall outcome for people's lives of the decisions actually taken.

Current Conservative policy, now to some extent melded with that of the Liberal Democrats, even contains the seeds of genuine enthusiasm for what the European Union is doing. As Leon Brittan put it in *The Times*, immediately following the formation of the coalition government, "Conservative pragmatism and experience combined with Liberal Democrat idealism could be a winning combination".[15] Once the bogeyman of a "European super-state" is banished, the EU can be recognised for what it really is: a new form of political organisation in which separate nations come together to ensure mutual security and prosperity, while at the same time retaining the variety of their individual characters and traditions.

Insofar as the EU is developing a united policy towards the rest of the world, moreover, this is in sharp contrast to those of most similar bodies in the past, empires or nation states. The EU's main instruments of external policy are what has been called "soft power" – trade, aid and mediation – rather than military might; and to this definition can be added the power of example. The EU is, in the words of the *Economist*'s Charlemagne columnist, "a voluntary group of democracies. For all its faults, more states want to join and none wish to leave".[16] It is not too much to argue, as Chris Patten argued in an article quoted earlier, that the experiment in international community living provided by the European Union, if it continues to succeed, will provide a model for the rest of the world.

What has been missing in the debate on Europe within the Conservative Party, indeed, is a greater element of such forward-looking optimism, perhaps even a bit of idealism. Much of the Eurosceptic opposition, though passionate, has in the last resort been "incorrigibly petty".[17] At the same time, those still supporting the Party's traditional policy have been forced into a defensive and generally minimalist position.

But this can change. We can be proud of the Conservative Party's contribution to building the modern European Union from the inspirational speeches of Churchill in the 1940s and 1950s, to the drive to create the Single Market, the end of the Cold War and enlargement to the former Communist countries of Central and Eastern Europe during the Thatcher and Major years. Conservatives should have the confidence to aim for similar, decisive inputs in the years ahead.

Notes

1   *Vote for Change: European Election manifesto* (Conservative Party, May 2009).
2   *Does Britain Need a Financial Regulator?* by Terry Arthur and Philip Booth (Institute of Economic Affairs, 2010).
3   *The Economist*, 4th–10th July 2009.
4   *Rationalism in Politics and other Essays* by Michael Oakeshott (Methuen 1962).
5   *Reflections on the Revolution in France* by Edmund Burke.
6   In *Coningsby*. He was, of course, attacking the Conservative Party, recently created by Peel.
7   *The Character of Conservatism* by Ben Patterson (CPC 1973).
8   *Nor Shall My Sword* by Dr. F.R.Leavis (Chatto and Windus 1972).
9   *The Economist*, 22nd–28th August 2009.
10 Bale *op.cit*.p. 390.
11 Watts *op.cit*.p.1.
12 "*Briten-Rabatt hat seine Berechtigung verloren*" in *Handelsblatt* of the 5th September 2010.
13 Ambrose Evans-Pritchard in the *Daily Telegraph* of the 22nd March 2010.
14 'Cut it straight: Cameron is a real Eurosceptic' in *The Times* of the 4th November 2009.
15 *The Times* of the 13th May 2010.
16 *The Economist* of 4th–10th September, 2010.
17 As Hugo Young put it, *op.cit*. p. 499.

Appendix 1
Conservatism and
Christian Democracy

The search for allies

When the UK joined the then European Community at the beginning of 1973, the only country with a political party closely equivalent to the British Conservatives was Denmark.*

The European Conservative Group in the European Parliament was accordingly formed by only three parties: the British Conservatives, the Ulster Unionists and the Danish Conservative Party. Following the Iberian enlargement in the 1980s, the by then European Democratic Group was joined by the Spanish *Alianza Popular (AP)*; but this party was soon dissolved, and its successor, the *Partido Popular* joined the Christian Democrats in the European People's Party Group instead. Shortly afterwards, the British and Danish Conservatives did the same.

During the early years, however, there was some disagreement about which of the other main centre-right parties had most in common with British Conservatism. At first sight, the most natural allies appeared to be the French Gaullists, like the Conservative Party more in favour of a *Europe des patries* than a federal union. Two sharp disagreements, however, soon made it clear that this was an illusion. The anti-American stance of the Gaullists was starkly at odds with the Conservative Party's determination, in the field of foreign policy and defence, to give primacy to the Atlantic Alliance. At the same time, Conservative support for reform of the Common Agricultural Policy was seen by the Gaullists as a direct attack on one of France's fundamental national interests.

In any case, in the years before entry into the Community very close links had already been built up with the German Christian Democrats (the *Christlich Demokratische Union* (CDU)). The Young Conservatives and the CDU equivalent, the *Jung Union*, were especially close. The same was true of the university organisations.

Relations with other continental Christian Democrat parties were less intimate. For the Italian and Benelux parties the name "Conservative" proved a problem, taken to indicate a party on the right rather than the

---

* It can, of course, be argued that there were other parties just as close: for example *Fine Gael* in Ireland; but these parties had already been signed up by other Groups.

centre-right. It was also perceived that the Conservative Party was a secular rather than a Christian party, fitting in more appropriately with the continental Liberals. To some extent this was a correct assessment. The Dutch Liberals, for example, were not only secular, but shared with British Conservatism strong support for free markets as opposed to the Christian Democrats' "social market" model.

One often-made mistake, however, has been to link Christian Democracy solely to Roman Catholicism. Many of its policies in the social and economic fields do, it is true, closely follow Catholic social teaching. The parties creating the European People's Party nevertheless included not only those with a Catholic background, but also some, like that of the Dutch chairman of Parliament's Economic and Monetary Affairs Committee in the early 1990s, Bouke Beumer, which were historically Calvinist or Lutheran. In Germany the CDU is as much a Protestant as a Catholic party. Any residual associations between the Conservative Party and the Church of England (once described as "the Tory Party at prayer") therefore raised no problems in Conservative/Christian Democrat relations.

The decision, following the election of David Cameron as Party leader, that the Conservative members of the European Parliament should leave the European People's Party Group to form their own group nevertheless indicated that problems do exist. It is worth examining whether these are fundamental, or merely reflect recent political developments.

Christian Democrat and Conservative philosophies

Though its roots lie in a similar reaction to the development of industrial capitalism in the 19th century, modern Christian Democracy is not, like Marxism, a systematic ideology. As the former leader of the EPP Group in the European Parliament, later the Parliament's President, Egon Klepsch, put it, "we are dealing with a set of convictions, insights and experiences that are not, in the first instance, defined theoretically".[1]

Most studies of British Conservatism have made much the same point. In the words of one, "to put Conservatism in a bottle with a label is like trying to liquefy the atmosphere, for Conservatism is less a political doctrine than a habit of mind, a mode of feeling, a way of living".[2]

In practical terms British Conservatism and Christian Democracy both bring together a number of different strands of political thought, including an element of the free-market liberalism which they both originally opposed. Unlike British Conservatism, however, Christian Democracy is an international movement – indeed arguably the most successful trans-national democratic movement of the post-war world. Not only in Europe, but also in Central and South America, it has played a signifi- cant part in the politics of almost all countries. The actual policies adopted have varied considerably: the cautious conservatism of the *Christlich Demokratische Union* (CDU)/*Christlich Soziale Union* (CSU) in Germany, for example, contrasts markedly with the occasionally revolutionary nature of Christian Democracy in some parts of Latin America. Even so, it has been possible for Christian Democrats to maintain organisations at both a pan-European and international level, with broad agreement on basic principles.

These principles, not surprisingly, derive from Christian teaching, principally that of the Roman Catholic church, but also that of Lutheran and Calvinist churches. At the core has been the concept of "communitarian personalism":* each individual is unique, free, responsible and precious in the sight of God; but each individual also lives in a community, under an injunction to "love one's neighbour".

> Human beings, conceived as persons, and society, conceived as a community of persons, are bound together and cannot be separated, not even conceptually.[3]

In philosophical terms, this is an "organic" view of society: that is, communities are seen as analogous to living organisms. It contrasts with the atomistic school of thought, associated particularly with 19th century Utilitarianism, which sees society as a network of contracts; and also with the tendency of Marxists and Socialists to treat society as a machine, capable of being "engineered".

British Conservatism has also, historically, been based on such an "organic" view, the most eloquent early exponent of which was Edmund Burke. Individual human beings had a basic need for identity: a sense of belonging to something of lasting significance, in Burke's words (already quoted earlier) "a partnership not only between those who are living but between those who are living, those who are dead, and those who are to be born". People also need assurance that reasonable expectations will not be regularly falsified. Hence the need for continuity: institutions which are familiar, laws based on precedent, evolutionary rather than revolutionary change, constitutional government. The need for identity and the need for continuity come together in a respect for national traditions.

Burke's concept of a partnership between the generations has also acquired particular significance today in the context of concern for the environment, reflected in the "green" Conservatism introduced by David Cameron. Christian Democracy has reached much the same conclusion, though by a different route: the belief that mankind has a duty to look after God's creation, rather than merely exploit it.

Conservatism and Christian Democracy have also shared – though again arriving at it by slightly different routes – the objective of "elevating the condition of the people". For Conservatives, seeing society as a living organism implies that if one part of the nation is suffering, the whole will

---

* A phrase coined by the French philosopher Emmanuel Mounier, leader of the "Personalist" movement in the inter-war years.

suffer: as Disraeli put it, there should not be "Two Nations". In the case of early Christian Democracy, personalism and communitarianism combined to interpret Christian compassion for the poor and weak as the justification and basis for social reform. Conditions should be created which preserve the basic dignity of the individual human being and enable him or her to develop, spiritually and materially. This can only be achieved through the harmonious development of community.

Where 19th and early 20th century Christian Democracy differed from One Nation Toryism, however, was in its direct involvement in the workplace: for example, through the creation of specifically Christian trade unions. There was considerable overlap with the thinking of contemporary Christian Socialist movements. Indeed, many parties which form the European People's Party today use the name "Christian-Social" (or "Social-Christian") rather than "Christian Democrat", as in the cases, for example, of the Belgian and Luxembourg parties, or the *Christlich Soziale Union* (CSU) in Bavaria. This perhaps helps explain how modern Christian Democrat and Social Democrat parties – for example, in Germany at both *Land* and national level – have been able to govern in coalition, something which would be almost unthinkable in the case of the modern British Conservative and Labour parties, except in times of acute crisis.

But Christian Democracy has also incorporated a very different nineteenth century tradition: that of confessional conservatism. The primary inspiration of this was not a particular view of society, but an emphasis on the spiritual dimension of Christianity and a rejection of the materialism inherent in both economic liberalism and Marxism. A similar strand of thought has also formed an element of British Conservatism: the chairman of the Party at the time of Harold Macmillan's premiership, Quintin Hogg (Lord Hailsham), memorably wrote in *The Case for Conservatism*[4] that

> Conservatives do not believe that political struggle is the most important thing in life. ... The simplest among them prefer fox-hunting – the wisest religion.

Confessional conservatives, however, *did* take political struggle seriously. They saw secularism as a direct threat to the Catholic Church itself; and this led them, in sharp contrast to those tending towards Christian Socialism, to see preservation of the existing social order, and the position of the Church within it, as vital objectives. Both before the First World War in France, for example, at the time of the Dreyfus affair and in the inter-war years this strand of Christian Democracy was tempted into a position on the authoritarian right, even espousing anti-parliamentarianism, anti-semitism and what has been called "clerical-fascism".

Post-war Christian Democracy contained elements of both these earlier traditions; but also rejected aspects of both. Strict confessional conservatism had been widely discredited by its flirtation with authoritarian anti-parliamentarianism, and links between the political movements and the

Catholic Church itself were loosened. Christian Democrat parties sought to represent not only Catholics and Protestants, but non-believers as well.

At the same time, the tradition of radical Christian Socialism seemed too close for comfort to the Marxist belief that the state should have a monopoly in the field of social action. The Cold War soon became the defining feature of European politics, and Christian Democracy emerged as the main non-socialist alternative to Communism. This meant incorporating elements of classical liberalism, including strong support for private enterprise and a reliance on markets rather than central planning. The effectiveness of this new political synthesis, later described as "Rhineland capitalism", was soon demonstrated in the West German *Wirtschaftswunder* (economic miracle).

In practice, Christian Democracy has nevertheless differed markedly between countries. The now defunct Christian Democrat party in Italy retained its association with the Catholic Church to a far greater extent than the German CDU, and also contained wings both more to the political left and to the political right. The parties in the Netherlands, of both Catholic and Protestant inspiration, found themselves in the centre ground between equally powerful socialist and secular liberal groups, a position which enabled them to become the "pivot" of coalition governments. Christian Democracy in Latin America had to deal with political contexts very different from those in Europe: for example, as part of the opposition to the Pinochet military regime in Chile.

Christian Democrats themselves sometimes define their politics as "a middle way between conservatism, liberalism and socialism".[5] Christian Democracy, in this view, shares with continental conservatism its respect for traditional values and the family; but rejects its "patriarchalism and heirarchicalism". Strong anti-Communism is shared; but, unlike Conservatives (in their view), Christian Democrats "embrace the welfare state openly as a vital and desirable means of promoting social justice and protecting the weak" and guarding against "the disparities of wealth that could endanger social cohesion", concerns which are shared with socialism.

Christian Democrats, on the other hand, reject the socialist emphasis on class divisions, and "the enhancement of state power at the expense of both the individual and the multiplicity of social groups necessary for human spiritual and material development". In the case of continental liberalism, Christian Democracy shares the stress on individual liberty and the market "as a means of generating prosperity". It rejects, however, the "idealisation of capitalism", which can result in "exploitation and growing gaps between rich and poor". For Christian Democrats, "community and social groups" are as important in ensuring freedom as individual rights.

While this characterisation of Christian Democracy may involve a distorted depiction of other political philosophies, it helps explain why disagreements have arisen with apparently like-minded parties on the centre-right. The British Conservative Party, in particular, has been seen as incorporating some of the negative features of traditional continental conservatism. Yet, as the great political historian Sir Ivor Jennings wrote in his *Growth of Parties*,[6] "regarded historically, the Conservative Party has hardly ever been conservative, has usually been liberal, and on occasions socialist". And then there is the bitter complaint attributed to the High Tory novelist Evelyn Waugh: "The trouble with the Conservative Party is that it has never turned the clock back a single second."

Political parties, though, can also be described in terms of those who vote for them and whose interests they represent. Research indicates that, though to a declining extent, there is still a strong correlation between regular attendance at mass by Catholics and voting Christian Democrat. The same is true of devout and practising Protestants – especially in the Netherlands – though, overall, Protestants are less inclined to vote Christian Democrat than Catholics. But Christian Democrat parties are also strongly supported by the traditional middle classes, whether Catholic, Protestant or with no strong religious beliefs. Farmers and those running small businesses are especially important. There is also sizeable working class support, notably among working-class Catholics.

Despite the religious factor, therefore, the basis of support for European Christian Democrat parties is not, in effect, much different from that of the Conservative Party in Britain, where strong support from the middle classes (ABC1) has been historically complemented by between a quarter and a third of the working class vote (C2,D,E): the "Tory working man (and woman)". In both cases the greatest strength has been in the rural areas, least in the industrial cities. In both cases, the interests of small business have been important, and also, despite the relatively less economic importance of the sector in Britain, farming.

The Social Market Economy

Given the similarity of interests supported by continental Christian Democrat parties and the British Conservative Party, it is necessary to examine why divergences appear to have arisen. One prominent field of divergence has been that of economic, social and employment policy.

In the formative years of post-war Christian Democracy, two key internal debates took place. The first concerned the declared religious affiliation of the movement: should it develop its programme exclusively on the basis of Christian teaching and seek to represent primarily practising members of the Christian churches? Or should it, while remaining Christian in inspiration, become more pragmatic in policy-making and widen its appeal to voters in general? This debate was quickly resolved in favour of pragmatism and inclusiveness.

The second debate, however, was less easily resolved: was Christian Democracy a movement on the political "left" or on the political "right"? As one of the theoreticians of Christian Democracy, Roberto Papini, has observed, Christian Democracy grew up in the last century "primarily as a resistance movement".[7]

The German historian, Hans Maier even maintained that the first Christian Democrats were clerics who had adopted the principles of the French revolution and who spoke out against the conservative and anti-democratic attitude of the ruling classes of the Ancien Régime.

This Democratic half of the CD tradition, having been betrayed in some countries during the inter-war years, became of great importance after the war when the movement found itself the main European political force opposing totalitarianism of both left and right. The democratic principle was stressed when the name European People's Party – sometimes translated as "Popular Party" – was established in 1976 as the basis for political action at European level.* Christian Democracy sought to distinguish itself from what it perceived as the tendency of "conservatives" to represent only élites.

As observed earlier, however, Christian Democracy came into existence largely in reaction, not to the aristocratic *anciens régimes*, but to the secular, liberal, "bourgeois" regimes that succeeded them. In 1891 the movement's social and economic policies were most explicitly outlined in the encyclical *Rerum Novarum* issued by Pope Leo XIII.† This argued that capitalism and market forces should be subordinated to moral considerations, and called for political action to end "the misery and wretchedness pressing so unjustly on the majority of the working class". It was subtitled "The Rights and Duties of Capital and Labour", and supported, among other social measures, the establishment of trade unions and wage levels sufficiently high "to support a frugal and well-behaved wage-earner".

This approach to social and employment policy remained central to Christian Democracy, even when, after the Second World War, Christian Democrat parties became defenders of private enterprise and free markets against both Socialist and Communist opposition. The new synthesis, which became known by the German term *Soziale Marktwirtschaft* (Social Market Economy), combined market-orientated economic policies with a high level of social protection, and also the close involvement of workers' representatives in the management of companies (*Mitbestimmung*).

None of this was much out of line with the tradition of One Nation Toryism, a strand of Conservative thinking which remained influential even during the high noon of so-called "Thatcherism". Chris Patten, chairman of the Conservative Party between 1990 and 1992, later Governor of Hong Kong, a European Commissioner, Chancellor of Oxford University and now chairman of the BBC Trust, was generally considered not only an important upholder of the One Nation tradition, but also as near as one

---

* The term "People's Party" was already in use in, for example, in the case of the ÖVP (*Österreichische Volkspartei*) in Austria.

† *Rerum Novarum* was supplemented by later encyclicals, in particular Pius XI's *Quadragesimo Anno* (1931), John XXIII's *Mater et Magistra* (1961), and John Paul II's *Centesimus Annus* (1991).

could get to being a British Christian Democrat. Another Conservative Minister, David Hunt (now a Peer), told a meeting of the Tory Reform Group in July 1993 that "I have always, willingly, described myself as a Christian Democrat as well as a Conservative."

Moreover, the actual policies of the Conservative Governments of Churchill, Eden and Macmillan in the 1950s and early 1960s were not very different from those of Christian Democrat governments. The policies of the Heath Government of the 1970s, in its "Selsdon" phase, possibly diverged; but were moving back to the more traditional path when the Government fell victim to industrial action.

The later economic and industrial policies of the Heath government, however, have entered Conservative demonology as having constituted a fatal "u-turn", a betrayal of Conservative principles. The opposition to Heath in the Party, led first by Sir Keith Joseph, and then successfully by Margaret Thatcher, was specifically aimed at repudiating the change of direction: "You turn if you want to; this lady's not for turning", as Mrs Thatcher memorably put it. The policies put in place by the post-1979 Conservative governments, while not nearly as far from the One Nation tradition as is generally believed, were presented as such; and the successful taming of the trade union movement was certainly far removed from the conciliatory policies of Sir Walter Monckton, Churchill's Minister of Labour in the early 1950s.

In Christian Democrat documents of the period, the policies of the Thatcher Government are therefore usually described, not as "conservative", but as "neo-liberal". The confrontation with the trade union movement was, in particular, contrasted with the Christian Democratic pursuit of industrial democracy and the repudiation of class conflict. Measures to make the labour market more flexible were seen as reducing social protection and driving down wage-levels. Much of this criticism, indeed, echoed the attacks on the Thatcher government by the British Labour Party; and also the message delivered to the British Trades Union Congress by the "Christian Socialist" President of the Commission, Jacques Delors, in 1988.

The perception of the British Conservative Party as "liberal" or "neo-liberal" became, in 1992, one of the main arguments of those Christian Democrats who opposed incorporation of British MEPs into the European People's Party Group. As the President of the wider European People's Party, the former Belgian Prime Minister Wilfried Martens, put it when addressing the Party's conference in Athens in November 1992, British Conservatives were "insufficiently social". Accommodating them in the EPP, he warned, risked "diluting, even repudiating, its identity".

Charity and the voluntary sector

One recent theme of Conservative social policy, however, has brought it a great deal closer to one basic tenet of Christian Democracy: the key role of the voluntary sector as opposed to that of the State. In 1891, Pope Leo

XIII wrote in *Rerum Novarum* that "no human devices can ever be found to supplant Christian charity;" a subject that was greatly expanded in Pope Benedict XVI's encyclical *Deus caritas est*.[8] The Marxist critique of the 19th century reliance on charity to relieve poverty had been that "the poor ... do not need charity but justice." Yet

> love – *caritas* – will always prove necessary, even in the most just society. ... There will always be situations of material need where help in the form of concrete love of neighbour is indispensible. ... We do not need a State which regulates and controls everything, but a State which, in accordance with the principle of subsidiarity, generously acknowledges and supports initiatives arising from the different social forces and combines spontaneity with closeness to those in need.

Very similar themes – somewhat misleadingly grouped together as the "Big Society" – have been stressed for some time by David Cameron; and have now become a leading objective of the coalition government. In his *Forewords* to the Party's social policy document, *Repair: Plan for social reform*,[9] and to a policy "green paper", *A Stronger Society: Voluntary Action in the 21st Century*,[10] Cameron argued that, in building a stronger and happier society, "neither the state nor the market are sufficient". Action in a "post-bureaucratic age"

> must start with every person, in their relations with family and friends, and the making of whole and healthy communities. Then, beyond the sphere of the private and informal, there is a public, organised expression of society: the charities, social enterprises; co-operatives and community groups that make up the voluntary sector – what some would call, quite inaccurately, the third sector. The time has come for us to think of the voluntary sector as the first sector ...

This theme distances the Party not only from Marxist and Socialist thinking – which is not very surprising – but also from that of "continental liberalism", association with which has made Christian Democrats so suspicious of British Conservatism. It is true that certain important differences exist between *Deus caritas est*, which singles out the Church itself as the principal vehicle for charity, and the Conservative Party documents, which remain fully secular in identifying a wide range of charitable and voluntary bodies, in particular co-operative organisations. The implied policies are sufficiently close, however, to form at least the basis for a new dialogue between British Conservatives and continental Christian Democrats, should such a development be sought. Interestingly, figures compiled by Johns Hopkins University, quoted in *A Stronger Society: Voluntary Action in the 21st Century*, show that countries in Northern Europe, particularly the UK and Scandinavia, do especially well in terms of overall voluntary work, possibly reflecting the fact that such work is concentrated in the hands of the Catholic Church in other countries.

Much of the background research for this element of Conservative policy was carried out by the think-tank, the Centre for Social Justice, which was founded by ex-Conservative Party leader Iain Duncan Smith, now Secretary of State for Work and Pensions who, as it happens, is a Roman Catholic.

The federal project

If the economic and social policies of post-war Christian Democracy have differed little from those of One Nation Toryism – and, in practice, from the policies of most Conservative governments – the issue of Europe itself has created a much wider division. In this context, indeed, the One Nation tradition can be seen as a source of divergence from Christian Democracy rather than of connection with it. Where Christian Democratic concern to improve living and working conditions derived from the general communitarian principle, that of Disraelian Conservatism derived principally from a belief in national unity. Patriotism would be the bond that cemented solidarity between the classes. As he himself observed in his celebrated speech to the National Union of Conservative and Constitutional Associations at Crystal Palace on the 24th June 1872: "The people of England, and especially the working class of England, are proud of belonging to a great country, and wish to maintain its greatness." The Conservative Party was "a national party, or it was nothing".

Christian Democracy, however, is not a national movement, even if – as Martens admitted in his November 1992 speech – on many domestic matters national Christian Democrat parties have moved in diverse directions "following the logic of their situations". One goal they have all shared: the "federalist project" for Europe. This was what gave the European People's Party, Martens declared, its particular identity and coherence.

Christian Democrats, indeed, played a predominant role in the post-war drive for European unity. As Clay Clemens puts it

> In many respects Christian democracy grew up together with post-war Europe: the success of the political movement and progress towards peaceful cooperation between the states of a long-divided continent were mutually reinforcing developments. Indeed, the founding fathers of Christian Democracy – Adenauer, de Gasperi, Schuman – doubled as the architects of European reconciliation, cooperation and, eventually, integration.[11]

Support for European integration also accorded with the Christian Democratic tenet of "communitarian personalism".

Just as the Christian-Democratic doctrine has raised the inorganic relationship between the individual and society to the level of a genuine integration of the person with the community, it also commits itself to overcoming nationalism, by applying the communitarian principle to international relations.[12]

This support for integration between European nations on grounds of "solidarity" was, of course, balanced by the companion principle of "subsidiarity" – hence the Christian Democrat objective of a "federal" European Union rather than a centralised state. But the European People's Party 1989 manifesto, for example, left little room for doubt about the general direction of policy.

> The EPP wants the progressive realisation of a United States of Europe, with a government responsible to the democratically elected European Parliament and endowed with all the powers of law making and control of the administration.

The 2004 manifesto, likewise, made it clear that "for us, the EU is more than a common economic space, it is primarily a political community of citizens and their nations."

Closer European integration has also been, for Christian Democrats, an objective going beyond the purely institutional. "For us ... Europe is more than a geographical expression. For us, Europe is a community of common values, political, intellectual and cultural."[13]

Men like Schuman and Adenauer, Clemens observes, were sometimes described as "latter-day Carolingians who longed for the return of a Europe united by the Church rather than divided by the nation-state". Perhaps not quite seriously, one exponent of traditional conservative philosophy, Roger Scruton, has indeed conceded that such a belief in "the restoration of the Holy Roman Empire, the sovereignty of the Church" can be considered a possible definition of "Euro-conservatism" – otherwise a political position he considers "nonsense".[14]

As it happens, though, Europe has often been defined by older generations of Conservatives in very much the same way as by Christian Democrats. Speaking at Oxford University in 1951, for example, the Conservative imperialist Leo Amery commended the statesmanship of his contemporary, Winston Churchill, in working for the "re-emergence of Europe as a unit";

> ... and by Europe I mean all those countries which were once part of Western Christendom, which have embodied in their life and culture the Greek love of political and intellectual freedom, the Roman devotion to law and order, and the Christian sense of the equal value of each human soul.[15]

It is also a mistake, one made by many Conservative Eurosceptics, to assert that the integrationist ambitions of Christian Democracy involve the elimination of national and regional differences: a goal sometimes satirised as the search for a "euro-sausage". As the European People's Party's 2004 manifesto went on to say

> the EPP acknowledges, indeed celebrates, the variety of national and local cultures that have developed over many centuries. We seek unity in diversity. The different cultural traditions in the European Union are an important framework of reference and orientation for people.

This accords almost precisely with the Conservative Party's historic defence of both national identity and of "traditions and established institutions".

The drive for European institutional and cultural union, a central plank of European People's Party policy, is nevertheless some distance away from the views of most modern British Conservatives. This has been most obviously so in the case of those in agreement with Margaret Thatcher's Bruges speech, and the earlier "Conservative Gaullists". But it has also been so, though to a lesser extent, in the case of the pragmatic pro-European Conservatives, like Ted Heath and Sir Geoffrey Howe, who took Britain into the European Community; like the Margaret Thatcher who approved the Single European Act; or like John Major who fought the Conservative "ultras" in the House of Commons to adopt the Maastricht Treaty. The guiding principle for these (Ted Heath possibly excepted) was less a drive for European integration than doing what seemed in Britain's best interests at the time.

For this reason, one of Wilfried Martens' misgivings about British Conservatives' joining the European People's Party Group in 1992 was that they lacked integrationist ambition. "They don't want to undo the European construction. ... But for us it is not a question of just enough Europe, but more Europe!"[16]

Later, in 1994, when Conservative MEPs had already been in the European People's Party Group for over two years, Martens was still suspicious. Both British and Danish Conservatives, he told an audience in Switzerland,[17] seemed happy to make the Single Market a goal in its own right rather than a step towards political union. And enlargement, actively supported by Conservatives – and also, in principle of course, by Christian Democrats – risked diluting rather than reinforcing European integration.

Joining and leaving the EPP Group

Given these apparently fundamental disagreements, how was it that the British Conservative MEPs, together with the Conservative Parties of Denmark and, later, Sweden, were able to integrate into the European People's Party Group in the European Parliament, at first with little difficulty?

The main reason, as I myself discovered as Conservative economics spokesman and Parliament's *rapporteur* on the Single Market, was that in the late 1980s and 1990s British Conservatives and members of the European People's Party Group, particularly those from Germany, shared an interest in institutional reform. Margaret Thatcher herself had already recognised that legislation to create the Single Market would not be adopted unless the Council of Ministers was able to decide more by Qualified Majority Vote (QMV). Moreover, as already outlined earlier, logic dictated that the consequent loss of democratic control at national level had to be retrieved by increasing the legislative powers of the European Parliament.

Conservatives also had other reasons to favour an increase in the powers of the Parliament. The Community Budget remained a running source of irritation for the British government, even with the return of "Maggie's money" under the rebate system. Control of spending was generally accepted to be lax, a perception confirmed by the annual reports of the Court of Auditors. The Council of Ministers seemed unable to act – largely because many of the constituent national administrations themselves, and *not* the Commission, were the principal culprits. This left the other half of the budgetary authority, and the only part of it able to sign off the accounts ("grant discharge"): the European Parliament. British Conservative MEPs therefore made a point of securing the chairmanship of Parliament's Budgetary Control Committee for one of their number, Peter Price; and, years later, it was the determination of that committee to control spending which resulted in the dismissal of the Santer Commission.

Finally, there remained from the days of Sir Peter Kirk and the first Conservative delegation to the unelected European Parliament in the 1970s a belief that the main contribution which Britain could make to the development of European unity was its parliamentary tradition. Both the unelected members in the 1970s like Sir Derek Walker-Smith, and the elected members after 1979 like the late Lord Kingsland (Christopher Prout) and other Conservative members of Parliament's Rules Committee, were responsible for major improvements in the European Parliament's powers and procedures. There was, moreover, an underlying belief that the institutional development of the Community should follow the Westminster model: i.e. that the Commission should not only be responsible to, but should ultimately be chosen by, and even drawn from, the European Parliament.

For all these reasons, and in contrast to more theoretical considerations, the Conservative programme for institutional reform did not, in the 1980s, differ greatly from that of the European People's Party, and hardly at all from that of the European People's Party Group in the Parliament.*

---

* The Group already contained members other than British Conservatives who did not belong to constituent parties of the EPP itself: for example the *NEA ΔHMOKPATIA* (*Nea Demokratia* – New Democracy) members from Greece.

Why, then, did this coincidence of interests break down? Earlier chapters have described how the Single European Act, once accepted as essential for the creation of the Single Market, came to be seen as a vehicle for interference in the "nooks and crannies of everyday life" and the ambitions of Jacques Delors. The Maastricht Treaty, the institutional implications of which were in fact far less revolutionary than those of the SEA, the section on the Single Currency excepted, was felt by those Conservatives who opposed its ratification to be "a Treaty too far". The Conservative Party had grudgingly to accept the Amsterdam and Nice Treaties. But, as described earlier, it moved to a position of strong opposition to the proposed Constitution for Europe and its derivatives, the Constitutional Treaty and the Lisbon Treaty, seeing them as openly "federalist". The Conservative position grew steadily more out of line with that of the European People's Party, which criticised all these Treaties for not being "federalist" enough.

Two domestic political events reinforced this divergence from European People's Party policy: the reaction against the removal of Margaret Thatcher from the premiership; and the loss of office to New Labour in 1997. Once in opposition, and free of the pressure to reach compromise agreements, the Conservative Party felt able to assert what it now believed to be its anti-federalist principles. As the debate on the Constitution for Europe, the Constitutional Treaty and the Lisbon Treaty dragged on, opposition to the European People's Party's integrationist project overwhelmed any agreements on other policies.

It is also worth noting that, as more Eurosceptic Conservative MEPs replaced those pro-Europeans elected in the 1980s, other members of the European People's Party Group grew steadily more uncomfortable with their presence. Already by the turn of the century those I met would look back nostalgically to the "good old days".

The Future

Whatever the disagreements on policy, British Conservatives will inevitably find themselves on the same side as continental Christian Democrats in many of the major European political divides. While the anti- or non-federalist tradition of Gaullism has over the years provided a tempting alternative basis for alliance, its anti-Americanism has always proved a stumbling block. The various Eurosceptic nationalist movements with which the Conservative Party now finds itself linked in the European Parliament, though equally opposed to the "federal project", are in other ways uncomfortably far away from the socially tolerant and libertarian approach of modern Conservatism. By contrast, in the important field of economic policy – support for private enterprise, for limitations on the level of taxation and the size of the public sector, for sound money and a responsible attitude to debt – Conservatives and Christian Democrats are fighting the same battles.

For this reason, now that the Conservative Party is in government, some re-integration with the European People's Party would seem sensible. This does not mean becoming part of the European People's Party, which, despite a widespread mistaken belief among Conservatives, has never been the case. Nor does it even mean that Conservative MEPs should become full members of the European People's Party Group in the European Parliament: the arrangements negotiated by William Hague and Edward McMillan-Scott for an "associated" status fully allowed for disagreements on how far European integration should proceed.

Closer co-operation, however, would reverse one unfortunate outcome of the break with the EPP: the non-attendance of the British Conservative Party leader at "summits" of Christian Democrat and affiliated leaders, especially before meetings of the European Council. As anyone who had ever been in politics from local councils upwards knows, it is in such informal discussions that the bones of subsequent decisions are formed. It makes little sense to exclude David Cameron from a body which currently includes the leaders of France, Germany and Italy.

British Conservatism and continental Christian Democracy also have an interest in maintaining a dialogue on basic political philosophy. Though the end of the Cold War has removed anti-Communism as a fundamental shared position, discussions on how to develop, in modern conditions, the similar "One Nation" and "communitarian personalist" traditions could prove useful for both sides. The waning of interest in further institutional upheavals following the passage of the Lisbon Treaty has also narrowed the gap between Conservatives and Christian Democrats on the divisive issue of "federalism". With new EU enlargements pending, a debate on how a Union of thirty-plus States is to be run, given the principle of subsidiarity, will soon be essential.

Notes

1 Foreword to *Efforts to define a Christian Democratic "Doctrine"* by Egon A. Klepsch (European People's Party 1989).

2 *The Conservative Tradition* by R.J.White (Black, 2nd edition 1964).

3 *The search for the intellectual basis of Christian-Democracy* by Paul Dabin in *Efforts to define a Christian Democratic "Doctrine"* (European People's Party, 1989).

4 *The Case for Conservatism* by Quintin Hogg (Penguin, 1947), later re-issued as *The Conservative Case* by Viscount Hailsham (Penguin, 1959).

5 *Christian Democracy: The Different Dimensions of a Modern Movement* by Clay Clemens (European People's Party, 1989).

6 *Party Politics*, Vol. II by Sir Ivor Jennings (Cambridge University Press, 1961).

7 *The tradition and present-day relevance of Christian-Democratic thought* by Roberto Papini in *Efforts to define a Christian Democratic "Doctrine"* (European People's Party, 1989).

8 *Deus caritas est* (God is love), encyclical of the 25th December 2005.

9 Conservative HQ, 2008.

10 Conservative HQ, 2008.

11 Clemens *op.cit.*

12 Dabin *op.cit.*

13 EPP 1989 manifesto.

14 In the third edition of *The Meaning of Conservatism* (Palgrave, 2001).
15 "The Empire in Mid-century" by the Rt. Hon. L.S.Amery C.H. in *Six Oxford Lectures* 1951 (Conservative Political Centre, 1952).
16 Speech introducing the European People's Party's basic programme at the IXth Congress of the EPP in Athens, 11th–13th November 1992, reproduced in *L'une et l'autre Europe* (Editions Racine, 1994).
17 *European integration*, speech to the Swiss Christian Democrat seminar in Berne on the 19th February 1994, reproduced in *L'une et l'autre Europe* (Editions Racine, 1994).

Appendix 2:
Chronology of Main Events

1946

September: Winston Churchill, speaking at Zürich University, calls for "a kind of United States of Europe".

1947

May: United Europe movement created, followed by parallel Socialist and Christian Democrat bodies.

1948

January: Belgium, Luxembourg and the Netherlands form the "Benelux" customs union.

April: Organisation for European Economic Cooperation (OEEC) established to administer the Marshall Plan for European reconstruction.

May: Hague Conference proposes a Council of Europe.

1949

April: North Atlantic Treaty Organisation (NATO) formed.

August: First session of Council of Europe Assembly in Strasbourg. Churchill addresses a crowd of 20,000 in the Place Kléber.

1950

February: General Election returns Labour government with a majority of 6.

May: "Schuman Declaration": plan for European Coal and Steel Community (ECSC).

June: Conservatives support ECSC membership in Commons vote.

August: Churchill carries resolution in the Council of Europe calling for "a unified European army".

October: French PM René Pleven launches plan for European Defence Community (EDC).

1951

February: Bow Group founded at Bow and Bromley Constitutional Club.

April: Treaty of Paris, establishing ECSC, signed by France, West Germany and the three Benelux countries.

October: General Election returns Conservatives to power with majority of 17. Churchill PM, Eden Foreign Secretary.

1952

May: European Defence Community (EDC) Treaty signed.

July: Treaty of Paris comes into force, creating the ECSC ("the Six").

1953

March: Spaak report proposes a Common Market and a political Community.

1954

August: French National Assembly rejects EDC Treaty.

October: Western European Union (WEU) established.

1955

April: Eden replaces Churchill as Prime Minister.

May: Conservatives win general election with a majority of 59.

June: Messina Conference.

1956

October: Suez.

1957

January: Eden resigns, and is replaced by Harold Macmillan.

March: Treaties of Rome to establish the European Economic Community (EEC) and European Atomic Energy Community (Euratom) signed.

September: Reginald Maudling attempts to negotiate European Free Trade Area.

1958

January: Treaties of Rome enter into force, creating the "Common Market".

December: De Gaulle becomes first President of French Fifth Republic.

1959

October: Conservatives win General Election with majority of 100.

November: De Gaulle's "Atlantic to the Urals" speech in Strasbourg.

1960

January: Stockholm Convention, creating European Free Trade Association (EFTA), signed by Austria, Denmark, Norway, Portugal, Sweden, Switzerland and the UK ("the Seven").

February: Macmillan's "wind of change" speech in South Africa.

December: Organisation for European Economic Cooperation (OEEC) becomes Organisation for Economic Cooperation and Development (OECD)

1961

January: Anti-Common Market League (ACML) founded. Monday Club formed.

August: UK makes formal application to join the Common Market.

1962

April: Commonwealth Immigrants Act.

July: US President Kennedy calls for "declaration of interdependence".

1963

January: De Gaulle vetoes continued membership negotiations with the UK.

October: Sir Alec Douglas-Home replaces Macmillan as Prime Minister.

1964

October: General Election returns Labour to power with a majority of 4.

1965

July: France begins "empty chair" boycott in EEC Council.
Douglas-Home resigns as Conservative leader. In ballot of Conservative MPs, Ted Heath polls 150 votes, Reginald Maudling 133 and Enoch Powell 15.

1966

January: "Luxembourg compromise" ends French boycott of EEC Council.

March: General Election returns Labour with a majority of 97.

1967

February: European Community decides to adopt Value Added Tax (VAT).

May: Labour Government re-applies to join the Common Market. Application approved by 488 votes to 62 in House of Commons.

July:	ECSC, EEC and EURATOM institutions merged under Merger Treaty.
November:	De Gaulle's second veto.

1968

April:	Enoch Powell's "rivers of blood" speech.
July:	All tariffs between EC Member States abolished. Common External Tariff (CET) comes into force.

1969

April:	Resignation of de Gaulle, who is replaced by Georges Pompidou.

1970

June:	Negotiations begin for UK accession to EC. Iceland joins EFTA.
	Conservatives win General Election with a majority of 31. Ted Heath Prime Minister.

1971

March:	Werner Plan for monetary union.
May:	System of Monetary Compensatory Amounts (MCAs) introduced for trade in agricultural products between Member States.
July:	White Paper *The United Kingdom and the European Communities*.
October:	Conservative Party Conference votes 2474 to 324 for joining European Communities. Majority of 112 in House of Commons for joining.

1972

January:	UK signs Treaty of Accession to European Communities.
April:	"Snake in the tunnel" exchange rate system established.
September:	Norway votes against Common Market entry in referendum.
October:	UK Treaty of Accession ratified.

1973

January:	UK joins the European Communities. Conservatives and Liberals take up European Parliament seats.
October:	Yom Kippur war triggers world energy and economic crises.

1974

February:	General Election results in return of minority Labour government.
October:	Second General Election. Labour returned with majority of 4.

1975

February: Heath replaced as Party leader by Margaret Thatcher, who defeats Whitelaw in final ballot of Conservative MPs.

June: Referendum on continued EC membership. 67.2% vote to stay in. Labour, the Scottish National Party and the Ulster Unionists take up their seats in the European Parliament.

1976

January: Tindemans Report on European Union.

April: EEC-ACP (African, Caribbean and Pacific) Lomé Convention.

May: European Democrat Union (EDU) founded.

1977

January: Roy Jenkins becomes Commission President.

1978

December: Summit decides to create European Monetary System (EMS).

1979

February: *Cassis de Dijon* ruling by European Court of Justice.

March: EMS comes into existence.

May: Conservatives returned to power in General Election with majority of 44. Margaret Thatcher becomes Prime Minister.

June: First direct elections to the European Parliament. Conservatives win 60 of the 81 UK seats.
Anglo-Danish European Democratic Group formed in European Parliament.

October: Chancellor Geoffrey Howe abolishes exchange controls.

November: Dublin summit: Thatcher demands British budget rebate.

December: European Parliament rejects the 1980 Budget.

1980

April: Luxembourg summit. Compromise solution of rebate issue rejected.

October: European Court of Justice rules in "isoglucose" case.

1981

January: Greece becomes thirteenth Community Member State.

1982

January: Dutch Socialist MEP Piet Dankert elected Parliament President with some Conservative votes.

March: Falklands War.

1983

June: Conservatives win UK General Election with 144 majority.

Stuttgart Summit adopts "Solemn Declaration" on European Union.

1984

February   European Parliament adopts Spinelli Report.

June: Fontainebleau summit: UK rebate issue settled.

European Parliament elections. Conservatives win 45 seats, Labour 32.

1985

June: Milan summit votes to hold an Inter-Governmental Conference (IGC)

Cockfield White Paper on Single Market; and "People's Europe" (Adonino) Report.

December: Inter-Governmental Conference (IGC) approves Single European Act (SEA).

1986

January: Spain and Portugal join EC. Finland joins EFTA.

Westland affair. Resignations of Michael Heseltine and Leon Brittan.

April: House of Commons approves Single European Act.

1987

January: Conservative MEP Sir Henry Plumb elected Parliament President.

June: Third successive Conservative General Election victory. Majority 100.

1988

March: Cecchini Report on forecast effects of Single Market.

June: Hannover summit sets up Delors Committee on Economic and Monetary Union (EMU).

September: Delors addresses TUC conference.

Prime Minister Thatcher's Bruges speech.

1989

February: Hoskyns' "1992 is going to fail" speech to Institute of Directors.

April: Delors Report on EMU.

May: Conservatives win 32 seats to Labour's 45 in "diet of Brussels" European elections.

June: Madrid summit. Howe/Lawson Exchange Rate Mechanism "ambush".

October: Resignation of Chancellor of the Exchequer Lawson.

November: Fall of Berlin Wall.

1990

June: European Court of Justice overrules UK Act in the Factortame case.

Major Plan for a parallel "hard ecu" launched at Dublin summit.

October: German re-unification.

Sterling enters the Exchange Rate Mechanism (ERM) at 2.95 D-Marks to the pound sterling

Thatcher "no, no, no" speech in the House Commons.

November: Resignation of Howe.

Conservative Party leadership contest. Major replaces Thatcher as PM.

1991

January: Operation "Desert Storm" to end Iraqi occupation of Kuwait.

Liechtenstein joins EFTA

March: Major's "at the heart of Europe" speech.

November: Douglas Hurd's "nooks and crannies of everyday life" remark.

December: Summit agrees draft Maastricht Treaty.

1992

April: Conservatives win fourth successive General Election with majority of 21, and highest ever recorded total vote.

May: Conservative MEPs join European People's Party Group in the European Parliament.

Conflict in former Yugoslavia.

June: Danish referendum rejects Maastricht Treaty.

September: "Black Wednesday". Sterling leaves the Exchange Rate Mechanism .

December: Edinburgh summit.

1993

January: Single Market comes into existence.

May: Danes approve Maastricht Treaty in second referendum.

Clarke replaces Lamont as Chancellor of the Exchequer.

July: Maastricht Treaty approved by Commons after government wins vote of confidence.

November: Maastricht Treaty comes into force. The "European Communities" become the "European Union" (EU)

1994

June: Conservatives routed in European elections, winning only 18 seats to Labour's 62.

July: Blair becomes Labour leader. "New Labour" launched.

November: Eight Conservative MPs lose whip over Europe.

1995

January:	Austria, Finland and Sweden join the EU. European Economic Area (EEA) created, covering the EU, Norway, Iceland and Liechtenstein.
March:	Schengen agreement abolishing most internal EU border controls comes into force.
July:	Redwood unsuccessfully challenges Major for Party leadership.
December:	Timetable for Economic and Monetary Union agreed.

1996

March:	BSE/CJD crisis. Ban on British beef.

1997

May:	Labour wins General Election with majority of 178. Major announces resignation from Conservative leadership.
June:	Clarke leads on first and second ballots of MPs in leadership contest; but William Hague defeats Clarke in third ballot.
October:	Amsterdam Treaty signed. Ian Taylor and David Curry resign from Shadow Cabinet over EMU policy.

1998

October:	"No euro for ten years" policy supported in ballot of all Party members.

1999

January:	Single Currency, the euro, successfully launched.
March:	Santer Commission resigns following report on fraud and Parliament discharge votes.
May:	Amsterdam Treaty comes into force.
June:	European elections on new PR system. Conservatives win 36 seats; Labour 29; Liberal Democrats 10; the United Kingdom Independence Party (UKIP) 3; Greens, Scottish National Party (SNP) and Plaid Cymru 2 each.

2000

September:	First "monetary dialogue" between European Central Bank President and Parliament's Economic and Monetary Affairs Committee. Danish referendum rejects membership of Euro Area.
December:	Summit agrees Treaty of Nice.

2001

January:	Greece joins Euro Area
June:	Irish referendum rejects Nice Treaty. Labour wins General Election with majority of 166.

September: Iain Duncan Smith defeats Ken Clarke for Conservative leadership by 62% to 38% in ballot of Party members.
December: Laeken Declaration on future of European Union, proposes constitutional Convention.

2002

January: Euro-denominated notes and coins go into circulation.
May: EU ratifies Kyoto Protocol on climate change.
July: ECSC Treaty lapses after fifty years.
October: Ireland ratifies Nice Treaty in second referendum.

2003

February: Nice Treaty comes into force.
July: Draft Constitution for Europe adopted by Convention on the Future of Europe chaired by former French President Giscard d'Estaing.
September: Swedish referendum rejects membership of Euro Area.
November: Michael Howard, unopposed, replaces Duncan Smith as Conservative Party leader.

2004

January: The Czech Republic, Estonia, Cyprus, Latvia, Lithuania, Hungary, Malta, Poland, Slovenia, and Slovakia join the EU.
June: European Elections. In Britain the Conservatives win 27 seats, Labour 19, Liberal Democrats and the United Kingdom Independence Party (UKIP) 12, Greens 2, Scottish National Party (SNP) 2 and Plaid Cymru 1.
October: Constitutional Treaty agreed by EU summit.

2005

May: France rejects Constitutional Treaty in referendum.
General Election returns Labour with a 65 majority.
June: Netherlands rejects Constitutional Treaty in referendum.
November: David Cameron defeats David Davis by 64,398 votes to 134,446 in ballot of Party members to succeed Michael Howard as Conservative Party leader.

2006

January: Russia cuts gas supplies to Ukraine following dispute over price.

2007

January: Bulgaria and Romania join the EU. Slovenia joins Euro Area
December: Lisbon Treaty signed.

2008
January: Cyprus and Malta join Euro Area.
June: Ireland rejects Lisbon Treaty in referendum.

2009
January: Slovakia joins Euro Area.
June: Centre-right dominant in European Elections. In Britain the Conservatives win 25 seats, Labour and the United Kingdom Independence Party (UKIP) 13 each, the Liberal Democrats 11, the Greens, the Scottish National Party (SNP) and the British National Party (BNP) 2 each, Plaid Cymru 1.
July: Conservative MEPs and allies form the European Conservatives and Reformists (ECR) Group.
              Iceland applies to join the EU.
October: Ireland accepts Lisbon Treaty in second referendum. Poland ratifies Treaty.
November: Czech President Václav Klaus signs Lisbon Treaty, so completing ratification.
              Cameron re-formulates Conservative policy on Europe.

2010
May: Greek sovereign debt crisis leads to EU/IMF rescue package.. UK General Election: Conservatives become the largest party in the Commons. A coalition government with Liberal Democrats is formed, with Cameron Prime Minister, Nick Clegg Deputy Prime Minister. *Status quo* policy on Europe.

2011
January: Estonia joins Euro Area.

Appendix 3

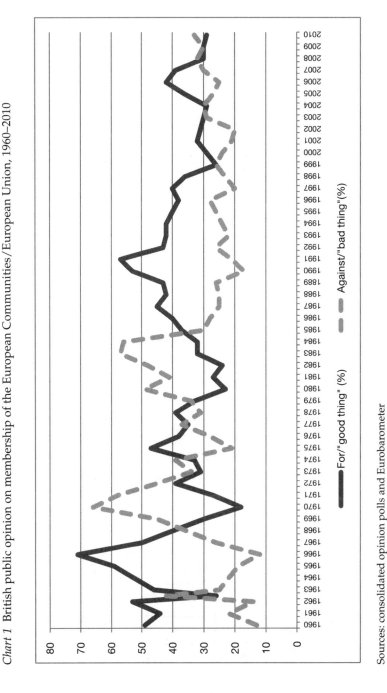

Chart 1 British public opinion on membership of the European Communities/European Union, 1960–2010

Sources: consolidated opinion polls and Eurobarometer

Remaining percentages: "Don't know", plus "Neither" after 1973.

Table 1 Results of Elections to the European Parliament in Great Britain, 1979-2009: seats won and % of votes.

	1979		1984		1989		1994		1999		2004		2009	
	seats	% vote	seats	% vote	seats	% vote	seats	% vote	seats	% vote	seats	% vote	seats	% vote
Conservative	60	51	45	41	32	35	18	28	36	36	27	27	25	28
Labour	17	33	32	37	45	40	62	44	29	28	19	23	13	16
Liberal/SDP/LibDem	0	13	0	19	0	6	2	17	10	13	12	15	11	14
SNP	1	2	1	2	1	3	2	3	2	3	2	1	2	2
Plaid Cymru	0	1	1	1	0	1	0	1	2	2	1	1	1	1
Green	0	0	0	1	0	15	0	3	2	6	2	6	2	9
UKIP							0	1	3	7	12	16	13	17
BNP	0		0		0	0	0	0	0	0	0	4	2	6
Other	0	1	0	0	0	0	0	3	0	5	0	6	0	8

Three Northern Ireland seats not included.
Percentage votes rounded to nearest integer.w

Bibliography of works cited

Albert, Michel; and Ball, Prof. James: *Towards European Economic Recovery in the 1980s* (European Parliament, August 1983).

Amery, the Rt. Hon. L.S., C.H.: "The Empire in Mid-century" in *Six Oxford Lectures 1951* (Conservative Political Centre, 1952).

Anderson, B.: *John Major* (Headline, 1992).

Arthur, Terry and Philip Booth: *Does Britain Need a Financial Regulator?* (Institute of Economic Affairs, 2010).

Bale, Tim: *The Conservative Party from Thatcher to Cameron* (Polity Press, 2010).

Balniel, Lord; with Robert Carr, Paul Channon, Christopher Chataway, William Deedes, Charles Fletcher-Cooke, Ian Gilmour, Philip Goodhart, Brian Harrison, John Hill, John Hobson, Charles Longbottom, Gilbert Longden, James Ramsden, Nicholas Ridley, John Rodgers, Anthony Royle and John Vaughan-Morgan: *One Europe* (Conservative Political Centre, April 1965).

Bathurst, Maurice; with Desmond Miller, Philip Turl, Alan Campbell, Derek Hene and Edward Wall: *Europe and the law* (Conservative Political Centre, February 1968).

Beamish, Sir Tufton; and St John-Stevas, Norman: *Sovereignty: substance or shadow* (Conservative Political Centre, July 1971).

Beaton, Leonard; with Michael McNair-Wilson, Timothy Raison, Geoffrey Smith, John Wakelin and Sir Robin Williams: *No Tame or Minor Role* (Bow Group, 1963).

Beazley MEP, Christopher: *Responsibility in Europe: the preparations* in *Conservative Europe* (Conservative Group for Europe, Autumn 2008).

Beesley, Hugh: *Britain and Europe since the Breakdown* (*Swinton Journal*, March 1964).

Begg Prof. David and others: *Making Sense of Subsidiarity: How Much Centralization for Europe?* (Centre for Economic Policy Research, November 1993).

Beloff, Nora: *The General Says No* (Penguin, 1963).

Bethell, Lord Nicholas; with Jim Scott-Hopkins MP and Jim Spicer MP: *Consumers in Europe: a Conservative View* (European Conservative Group, November 1977).

Bethell MEP, Lord Nicholas: *Moral Aspects of Conservatism* (EDG, 1990).

Bibes, Geneviève; with Henri Ménudier, Françoise de la Serre and Marie-Claude Smouts: *Europe Elects its Parliament* (Policy Studies Institute, September 1980).

Black, Conrad: *Conservatism and the Paradox of Europe* (Centre for Policy Studies, October 1990).

Blackwell, Norman: *A Defining Moment? A review of the issues and options for Britain arising from the Convention on the Future of Europe* (Centre for Policy Studies, February 2003).

Blair, Tony: *A Journey* (Hutchinson, 2010).

Blake, Robert (Lord Blake): *The Conservative Party from Peel to Churchill* (Eyre & Spottiswoode, 1970).

Blumler, Jay G. and Fox, Anthony D.: *The European Voter: Popular responses to the first Community election* (Policy Studies Institute, 1982).

Booker, Christopher: *Nice and Beyond: the parting of the ways?* (Centre for Policy Studies, October 2000).

Booth, Philip (editor) with Samuel Gregg, Robert Kennedy, Denis O'Brien, Dennis O'Keefe, Anthony Percy, Robert A. Sirico, Thomas Woods and Andrew Yuengert: *Catholic Social Teaching and the Market Economy* (Institute of Economic Affairs, 2007).

Boothby M.P., Robert: *I Fight to Live* (Victor Gollancz, 1947)

Britain in Europe: *Why you should vote YES* (HMSO, 1975).

British Invisible Export Council: *The Next Stage in an Evolutionary Approach to Monetary Union* (March 1990).

Brittain, Nick; with Mary Colton, Richard Barber and Nicholas Lyell: *Europe: The First Year* (Bow Group, January 1974).

Brittan, Leon; with Julian Critchley, Hugh Dykes, Russell Lewis and David Walder MP: *A Smaller Stage* (Bow Group, December 1965).

Brittan, Leon; with Jock Bruce-Gardyne, John Macgregor, Archie Hamilton, Howell Harris Hughes and Derek Prag: *Our Future in Europe: the Long-Term Case for going in* (Bow Group, February 1970, reprinted August 1970).

Brittan, The Rt. Hon. Lord: *The EU and Trade: a benefit for Britain* by in *Conservative Europe, 2002 Party Conference Magazine* (Conservative Group for Europe, October 2002).

Brittan, The Rt. Hon. Lord: *Free Trade and the Euro* (Conservative Group for Europe and the Tory European Network, 2003).

Bruce-Gardyne, John (aka Jock Bruce-Gardyne): "Should we join the USA?" in *Crossbow*, April-June 1963 (Bow Group).

Bruges Group: *Is the Euro sustainable?* (March 2009).

Bull, Hedley; with Col. Jonathan Alford and Dr. David Greenwood; foreword by Sir Henry Plumb MEP: *Thinking again about European Defence* (European Democratic Group, 1983).

Burke, Edmund: *Reflections on the Revolution in France*.

Butler, David; and King, Anthony: *The British General Election of 1964* (Macmillan 1965).

Butler, David; and Pinto-Duschinsky, Michael: *The British General Election of 1970* (Macmillan 1971).

Butler, David; and Uwe Kitzinger: *The 1975 Referendum* (Macmillan, 1976).

Butler, David; and Westlake, Martin: *British Politics and European Elections 1994* (St. Martin's Press, 1995).

Butler, R.A. ("RAB"): *The Art of the Possible* (Hamish Hamilton, 1971).

Cameron, David: *Forewords* to *Repair: Plan for social reform* and *A Stronger Society: Voluntary Action in the 21st Century* (Conservative Campaign HQ, 2008).

Campbell, Alec: 'In the National Interest' in *Principles in Practice* (Bow Group, 1961).

Carrington, Lord; with Poul Møller, Christopher Tugendhat, Sir Fred Catherwood, David Curry and Adam Fergusson: *Here to Stay* (European Democratic Group, 1983).

Cash MP, William: *A democratic way to European Unity: arguments against Federalism* (Bow Group, 1990).

Catherwood MEP, Sir Fred: *Europe's Need, Britain's Opportunity: Economic and Monetary Union* (Conservatives in the European Parliament, 1990).

Chesterton, G.K.: *The Father Brown Stories* (Cassell, 1929).

Chown, John F: *Company Tax Harmonisation in the European Community* (Institute of Directors, June 1989).

Churchill, Winston S. *The Second World War, Vol.4: The Hinge of Fate* (Cassell & Co, 1951).

Clark, Alan: *Diaries* (Phoenix paperback, 1993).

Clarke, QC, MP, Rt. Hon. Kenneth: *"Pax Europa* in the Conservative Party" in the 2007 Conference edition of *Conservative Europe* (Conservative Group for Europe, October 2007).

Clemens, Clay: *Christian Democracy: The Different Dimensions of a Modern Movement* (European People's Party, 1989).

Committee of Governors of the Central Banks of the European Community Member States: *Second Annual Report* (April 1993).

Congdon, Tim: *EMU now? The leap to European money assessed* (Centre for Policy Studies, 1990)

Conservative and Unionist Central Office: *Conservative Party: 1951* (1951 Election manifesto, September 1951).

Conservative and Unionist Central Office: *Britain Strong and Free: a statement of Conservative and Unionist policy* (September 1951).

Conservative and Unionist Central Office: *United for Peace and Progress: The Conservative and Unionist Party's Policy* (1955).

Conservative and Unionist Central Office: *The Next Five Years* (1959).

Conservative and Unionist Central Office: *Putting Britain right ahead: a statement of Conservative aims* (October 1965).

Conservative and Unionist Central Office: *Action not Words: the new Conservative Programme* (March 1966)

Conservative Central Office: *A Better Tomorrow: The Conservative programme for the next 5 years* (1970).

Conservative Central Office: *Firm Action for a Fair Britain: the Conservative Manifesto 1974* (February 1974).

Conservative Central Office: *The Right Approach: a statement of Conservative aims* (October 1976).

Conservative Central Office: *The Conservative Manifesto 1979* (April 1979).

Conservative Central Office: *Conservative Manifesto for Europe 1979* (May 1979).

Conservative Central Office: *The Conservative Manifesto 1983* (May 1983).

Conservative Central Office: *The Strong Voice in Europe: the Conservative Manifesto for the European Elections, 14 June 1984* (May 1984).

Conservative Central Office: *The Next Moves Forward: the Conservative Manifesto 1987* (May 1987).

Conservative Central Office: *Leading Europe into the 1990s: the Conservative Manifesto for Europe 1989* (June 1989).

Conservative Central Office: *The Best Future for Britain: the 1992 Conservative Party manifesto* (April 1992).

Conservative Central Office: *A Strong Britain in a Strong Europe: The Conservative Manifesto for Europe 1994* (1994).

Conservative Central Office: *You can only be sure with the Conservatives: 1997 Conservative Party General Election Manifesto* (1997).

Conservative Group for Europe: *Conservative Europe, Party Conference Magazines* (CGE, October 2002, October 2003, October 2004).

Conservative News Letter (Conservative Central Office, July 1961).

Conservative Party: *In Europe, not run by Europe: Conservative manifesto for the 1999 European Parliament elections* (1999).

Conservative Party: *Time for Common Sense: 2001 Conservative Party General Election Manifesto* (2001).

Conservative Party: *Are You Thinking What We're Thinking? It's Time for Action: Conservative Election Manifesto 2005* (2005).

Conservative Party: *Vote for Change, European Election Manifesto* (May 2009).

Conservative Party: *Invitation to Join the Government of Britain: the Conservative Manifesto 2010* (April 2010).

Conservative Political Centre: *The Tory Tradition* (1957).

Conservative Political Centre and Conservatives in the European Parliament Joint Discussion Programme: *Preparing for the 1994 European Elections: Summary of reports* (September/November 1993).

Conservative Political Centre: *Britain's Place in Europe* (Masterbrief 7, May 1967).

Conservative Political Centre: *What Joining Would Mean* (Masterbrief 8, June 1967).

Conservative Political Centre: *Britain, Europe and the World* (Masterbrief 9, August 1967).

Conservative Political Centre: *CPC in Action* (October 1967, republished January 1972).

Conservative Political Centre: *The Common Market*, (Contact Brief 42, September/October 1971).

Conservative Political Centre: *Fitting into Europe* (Contact Brief 51, November 1972).

Conservative Political Centre: *Our Voice in Europe* (March 1976).

Conservative Research Department: *Campaign Guide for Europe 1979* and *Campaign Guide for Europe 1979 Supplement* (January 1979 and April 1979).

Conservative Research Department: *Three Years Work* (27 September 1982).

Conservative Research Department: *The Campaign Guide 1983* (April 1983).

Conservative Research Department: *Nine Years' Work: The Achievements of the Conservative Government* (6 June 1988).

Conservative Research Department: *The Campaign Guide 1989* (March 1989).

Conservative Research Department: *Britain at the Heart of Europe* (7 February 1992).

Conservative Research Department: *The Campaign Guide 1992: Centenary Edition* (March 1992).

Conservative Research Department: *The Campaign Guide 1994* (1994).

Conservative Research Department and Conservatives in the European Parliament: *Handbook for Europe 1994* (May 1994 and after).

Conservative Research Department: *Winning the Argument: the 1994 European Elections* (Politics Today, 22 July 1994).

Conservatives in the European Parliament: *Britain at the Heart of Europe* (Conservative Political Centre, May 1993).

Consumers' Association: *Which?* (February 1981).

Copping, Robert: *The Story of the Monday Club* (Monday Club, April 1972).

Corrie MP, John: *Fish Farming in Europe* (European Conservative Group, 1979).

Cowling, Maurice: *The Impact of Hitler: British politics and British policy, 1933–1940* (Chicago, London: Chicago University Press 1977).

Cowling, Maurice: *Mill and Liberalism* (2nd edition, Cambridge: Cambridge University Press, 1990).

Crick, Bernard: *In Defence of Politics* (Penguin Books, 1962).

Crossbow, Spring 1960, Autumn 1960, New Year 1961, New Year 1962, January–March 1963, April–June 1963, October–December 1964, April–June 1965, July–September 1966, October–December 1969, June 1974, April 1985, Autumn 2005 (Bow Group).

Crowson, N.J.: *The Conservative Party and European Integration since 1945: At the heart of Europe?* (Routledge, 2009).

Curry MP, The Rt. Hon. David : *Foreword* in *Conservative Europe, 2003 Party Conference Magazine* (Conservative Group for Europe, October 2003).

Dabin, Paul: *The search for the intellectual basis of Christian-Democracy* in *Efforts to define a Christian Democratic "Doctrine"* (European People's Party 1989).

Daily Telegraph, 21 April 1996.

Davies MP, John: Statement of 5th September 1977.

De Gaulle, Général Charles : *Mémoires: Le Salut 1944–1946* (Plon, Livre de Poche, 1959).

Delors, Jacques: *Report on economic and monetary union in the European Community (the Delors Report).* (Office for the Official Publications of the European Communities, May 1989).

Department of Trade and Industry: *Single Market News, Issue no.1* (October 1988).

Deva DL FRSA MEP, Nirj: *Who Really Governs Britain ?* (Bow Group, 2001).

Disraeli, Benjamin: *Coningsby.*

Douglas-Home, Sir Alec: *Britain's Place in the World* (Conservative Political Centre, August 1969).

Driscoll, James: *Our Trade with Europe* (Conservative Political Centre, February 1957).

Drucker, P.F.: *The Practice of Management* (Harper Perennial, New York, 1993, first published 1954).

Economist, The: 25th September 1993; 30th May 2009; 4th July 2009; 22nd August 2009; 7th November 2009; 28th November 2009; 22nd May 2010; 4th September 2010; 11th September 2010.

Eden, Sir Anthony: *Full Circle* (Cassell, 1960).

European Democratic Group Apple Industry Committee: *Apples* (EDG, 1980).

Elles MEP, Diana; with Derek Prag MEP, Christopher Prout MEP, Alan Tyrrell QC, MEP and Michael Welsh MEP: *Problems, Powers, Opportunities: a Conservative View* (European Democratic Group, 1984).

Elles MEP, James: *In-Touch Newsletter,* Winter 2009.

European Commission: *Proposal for a Council Directive on procedures for informing and consulting the employees of undertakings with complex structures, in particular transnational undertakings* (the "Vredeling Directive"). Original proposal tabled in October 1980 (see *Official Journal C297* of 15.11.1980). Amended proposal tabled in July 1983 (COM (83)292 final).

European Commission: *Assessment of the Function of the Internal Market* (1983).

European Commission: *Consolidating the Internal Market* (COM(84)305 final of June 1984 and COM(84)350 final of July 1984).

European Commission: *Completing the Internal Market: White Paper from the Commission to the European Council* (COM(85)310 final, 14 June 1985).

European Commission: *The Global Communication* (COM(87)320), *VAT Rates Directive* (COM(87)321), *Fiscal Frontiers Directive* (COM(87)322), *Clearing Mechanism Working Document* (COM(87)323), *Convergence Directive* (COM(87)324), *Cigarettes Directive* (COM(87)325), *Manufactured Tobacco Directive* (COM(87)326), *Mineral Oils Directive* (COM(87)327) and *Alcoholic Beverages Directive* (COM(87)328) (all European Commission, 1987)

European Commission: *Social Dimension of the Internal Market* (Commission Working Paper SEC(88)1148 final of 14 September 1988).

European Commission: *One Market, One Money* (European Economy no. 44, October 1990)

European Court of Justice (ECJ): *Rewe-Zentral AG v. Bundesmonopolverwaltung für Branntwein*, C-120/78 ("Cassis de Dijon" case). *SA Roquette Frères v. Council of the European Communities*, 138/79 [1980] ECR 3333 ("isoglucose" case). *Factortame I*, C-213/89 [1990] ECR I-2433.

European Democratic Group: *From Nine to Twelve* (Conservative Political Centre, 1982).

European Democratic Group: *Group objectives in the field of Economic, Monetary, Fiscal and Industrial Policy* (EDG, 10 March 1987).

European Movement (British Council): *Europe: The Case For Going In* (George G. Harrap & Co. Ltd., 1971).

European Parliament: *The case for direct elections to the European Parliament by direct universal suffrage: selected documents* (September 1969).

European Parliament: *Elections to the European Parliament by direct universal suffrage* (1976).

European Parliament: *Report drawn up on behalf of the Committee on Economic and Monetary Affairs and Industrial Policy on consolidating the internal market* (document A2-50/85/B of 31 May 1985).

European Parliament Report no.36 (European Parliament London Office, June 1977).

Evans MEP, Jonathan: *Why Europe needs the Conservatives* in *Conservative Europe, 2002 Party Conference Magazine* (Conservative Group for Europe, October 2002).

Ferrand, Olivier: *L'Europe contre L'Europe* (Hachette, 2009).

Figaro, Le, of 27 May 2009.

Finkelstein, Daniel: 'Cut it straight: Cameron is a real Eurosceptic' in *The Times*, November 4, 2009.

Fletcher-Cooke QC, MP, Charles: *Terrorism and the European Community* (European Conservative Group, January 1979).

Forster, Anthony (ed.): *Defence and Security in the New Europe* (European Democratic Group, December 1991).

Forster, Anthony: *Euroscepticism in Contemporary British Politics* (Routledge, 2002).

Friedman, Wolfgang: *The Changing Structure of International Law* (Stevens, 1964).

Gardiner, George: *A Europe for the Regions* (Conservative Political Centre, August 1971).

Gilbert, Martin *Churchill: a Life* (William Heinemann, 1991).

Gilbert, Martin: *A History of the Twentieth Century, Volume Three: 1952–1999* (HarperCollins, 1999).

Gorman, Teresa: *The Bastards* (Pan, 1993).

Hailsham, Lord: *The Door Wherein I Went* (Collins, 1975)

Handelsblatt of the 5th September 2010.

Hannan, Daniel: *Time for a Fresh Start in Europe* (Bow Group, 1993).

Hannan MEP, Daniel: blog, Dec. 4. 2008.

Hannan MEP, Daniel: *Newsletter* (December 2008).

Hannan MEP, Daniel: *Daniel Hannan's Euro Bulletin*, 11 March 2009, 31 July 2009.

Hansard, House of Commons (17 November, 1966)

Hansard, House of Lords (14 March 1963).

Heath, The Rt. Hon. Edward; with Dr. Hans Nord, Emile Noël, William Rees-Mogg, William Clark and Richard Bailey: *The New Europe* (Conservative Political Centre, August 1962).

Heath, The Rt. Hon. Edward, MBE, MP: *The Conservative Goal: a call to Action* (Conservative Political Centre, March 1966)

Heath, Edward: *Old World, New Horizons* (Oxford University Press, 1970).

Heath, Edward: *The Course of My Life: the autobiography of Edward Heath* (Hodder and Stoughton 1998).

Heathcoat-Amory MP, David: *The European Constitution and what it means for Britain* (Centre for Policy Studies, May 2004).

Hennessy, Peter: *Having it so good: Britain in the fifties* (Allen Lane, 2006).

Heseltine, Michael: *The Challenge of Europe: Can Britain Win?* (London, 1989).

Heseltine, Michael: *Life in the Jungle: my autobiography* (Hodder and Stoughton, 2000).

Hindley, Brian: *Nice and After: the EU Treaty and Associated Issues* (Centre for Policy Studies, October 2001).

HMG: *Britain and the European Communities – An Economic Assessment* (HMSO, 1970).

HMG: *The United Kingdom and the European Communities* (HMSO Cmnd. 4715, July 1971).

HMG: *Britain's New Deal in Europe* (HMSO, 1975).

HMG: *Direct Elections to the European Assembly* (HMSO Cmnd. 6399, February 1976).

HM Treasury: *UK membership of the single currency: an assessment of the five economic tests* (Cm. 5776, June 2003).

Hogg, Quintin (Viscount Hailsham): *The Case for Conservatism* (Penguin, 1947), later re-issued as *The Conservative Case* (Penguin, 1959).

Holmes, Dr. Martin: *John Major and Europe: The Failure of a Policy 1990–7* (Bruges Group, http://www.brugesgroup.com/news.live?article=75&keyword=23).

Home, The Earl of: *Great Britain's Foreign Policy* (CPC, April 1961).

Hopper, Kenneth and William: *The Puritan Gift* (I.B.Tauris paperback, 2007).

Horrie, Chris and Matthews, David: *True Blue: strange tales from a Tory nation* (Fourth Estate, 2009).

House of Lords Select Committee on the European Communities: *Relations between the United Kingdom Parliament and the European Parliament after Direct Elections* (Vol. II, Minutes of Evidence. HMSO, July 1978).

House of Lords European Scrutiny Committee: *Subsidiarity, National Parliaments and the Lisbon Treaty* (Thirty-third report of session 2007–08, October 2008).

Howard MP, Michael: *The Future of Europe* (Centre for Policy Studies, May 1997).

Howe, The Rt. Hon. Sir Geoffrey, QC, MP: *Conservatism in the Eighties* (Conservative Political Centre, September 1982).

Howe, Geoffrey: *Conflict of Loyalty* (Macmillan, 1994).

Howell, David: 'The Tory Europeans' in *Crossbow,* Autumn 1960 (Bow Group).

Hudson, Roger: Introduction to J.R. Green's *A Short History of the English People* (Folio Society edition, 1992).

Hurd, Douglas: *Memoirs* (Little Brown, Abacus paperback, 2003)

Hurd, The Rt. Hon. Lord, CH CBE: *Europe and the Superpower* in *Conservative Europe, 2003 Party Conference Magazine* (Conservative Group for Europe, October 2003).

Independent (29 April 1994).

Inglewood MEP, Lord Richard: *Making Community Law More Effective* (Conservatives in the European Parliament, October 1990).

Inglewood MEP, Lord Richard: Letter to Conservatives Abroad, Luxembourg branch.

Institute of Directors: *Euro-Election 1984: the Business Leaders' Manifesto* (Institute of Directors, March 1984).

Institute of Directors: *Director's Guide to Europe 1992* (Institute of Directors, June 1988).

Institute of Directors: *Euro-Election 1989: Business Leaders' Manifesto* (Institute of Directors, April 1989).

Jackson MEP, Christopher: *Shaking the Foundations: Britain and the New Europe* (Conservatives in the European Parliament, October 1990).

Jackson MEP, Robert: *Tradition and Reality: Conservative Philosophy and European Integration* (European Democratic Group, 1982).

Jacques, Martin: *When China Rules the World: the Rise of the Middle Kingdom and the End of the Western World* (Allen Lane, 2009).

Jenkins, Roy: *Churchill* (Macmillan, 2001).

Jennings, Sir Ivor: *The Growth of Parties, Party Politics*, Vol. II (Cambridge University Press, 1961).

Johnson, Christopher: "The Common Market: way in for Britain?" in *Crossbow*, New Year 1961 (Bow Group).

Johnson, Nevil: *Britain and Community: the right way forward* (Centre for Policy Studies, April 1993).

Johnson, Stanley: *Stanley I Presume* (Fourth Estate, 2009).

Judd, Denis: *Empire: the British Imperial Experience from 1765 to the Present* (HarperCollins, 1996).

Kedouri, Elie: *Nationalism* (Hutchinson 1960/1985)

Kellett-Bowman MP, Elaine and Clarke MP, Kenneth: *New Hope for the Regions* (European Conservative Group, April 1979).

Kennedy, Paul: *The Rise and Fall of the Great Powers* (Unwin Hyman, 1988).

King MP, Tom: *The European Commission: Administration or Government?* (Centre for Policy Studies, August 1999).

King, Anthony: *Britain Says Yes: The 1975 Referendum on the Common Market* (American Enterprise Institute for Public Policy Research, 1977).

Kirk MP, Peter; Soames, The Rt. Hon. Sir Christopher; and Davies MP, The Rt. Hon. John: *Three Views of Europe* (Conservative Political Centre, December 1973).

Kirkhope MEP, Timothy: *A Simplifying Treaty* (Conservatives in the European Parliament, September 2005).

Kissinger, Henry: *The Troubled Partnership* (McGraw-Hill, 1965).

Klepsch, Egon: The Klepsch Report, reproduced, with a Foreword by The Rt. Hon. Geoffrey Rippon MEP, in *Two-Way Street: USA-Europe Arms Procurement* (Brassey's and Crane Russak, 1979).

Klepsch, Egon: Foreword to *Efforts to define a Christian Democratic "Doctrine"* (European People's Party 1989).

Labour Party National Executive Committee: *The EEC and Britain – a Socialist Perspective* (12 July 1977).

Labour Party: *Labour's Programme 1982* (1982).

Labour Party: *Meeting the challenge in Europe: Labour's manifesto for the European Elections 1989* (1989).

Labour Party: *Make Europe work for you: Labour's Election Manifesto for the European Elections, June 1994* (1994).

Lamont M.P., The Rt. Hon. Norman: *Europe: A Community Not a Superstate* (Conservative Political Centre, October 1992).

Lamont, Norman, *In Office* (Little, Brown and Company, 1999)

Lawson, Nigel: *The View from No. 11* (Bantam Press, 1992).

Leavis, Dr. F.R.: *Nor Shall My Sword* (Chatto and Windus 1972).

Letwin, Oliver: *Drift to Union: wiser ways to a wider Community* (Centre for Policy Studies, November 1989).

Lewis, Russell: *Challenge from Europe: Britain, the Commonwealth and Free Trade Area* (Bow Group, 1957).

Lewis, W. Russell: *Rome or Brussels … ?* (Institute of Economic Affairs, Hobart Paperback, 1971).

Lewis, Russell: *The Myth of Europe* (The Bruges Group, 2000).

Liberal Democrats: *The Liberal Democrat Manifesto 2010: change that works for you; building a fairer Britain* (Liberal Democrats, 2010).

Lilley, Peter (ed.); with Spenser Batiste, Alec Berry, John H. Davies, Anthony Dove, Roger Helmer, Gordon Kingsbury, William Meakin and Charles Tracey: *A Europe of Nations* (Conservative Political Centre for the Monday Club, October 1965).

Lindsay, T.F. and Michael Harrington: *The Conservative Party 1918–1970* (Macmillan, 1974).

Luce MP, Richard; and Ranelagh, John: *Human Rights and Foreign Policy* (Conservative Political Centre, 1977).

Lynn, Jonathan; and Jay, Antony: *Yes Minister: the diaries of a Cabinet Minister by the Rt. Hon. James Hacker MP, Volume One* (BBC, 1981).

Macgregor, John: "Immigration and Europe" by John Macgregor in *Crossbow*, New Year 1962 (Bow Group).

Macmillan, Harold: *The Middle Way: a Study of the Problems of Economic and Social Progress in a Free and Democratic Society* (Macmillan & Co., 1938).

Macmillan, Harold: *Tides of Fortune: 1945–1955* (Macmillan, 1970).

Macmillan, Harold: *At the End of the Day: 1961–63* (Macmillan 1973).

Major, M.P., The Rt. Hon. John: *Britain at the heart of Europe* (Conservative Political Centre, May 1993).

Major, Sir John: *John Major, the autobiography* (HarperCollins, 1999).

Major, The Rt. Hon. John CH: *The Wise European* in *Conservative Europe, 2004 Party Conference Magazine* (Conservative Group for Europe, October 2004).

Mandelson, Peter: *The Third Man: life at the heart of New Labour* (HarperCollins, 2010).

Mannin, Michael L.: *British Government and Politics: balancing Europeanization and Independence* (Rowman & Littlefield Publishers Inc., 2010).

Marr, Andrew: *A History of Modern Britain* (Macmillan, 2007).

Martens, Wilfried: *L'une et l'autre Europe* (Editions Racine, 1994).

Matthews, Rupert: *Fighting Off the UKIP Threat: a strategy for success in the 2009 European Elections* (PMS, 2008).

Mayne, Richard and John Pinder: *Federal Union: The Pioneers: a History of Federal Union* (Macmillan for the Federal Trust for Education and Research, 1990)

Meade, James E.: *UK, Commonwealth and Common Market: a Reappraisal* (Institute of Economic Affairs, 1970).

Menon, Anand: *Europe: the State of the Union* (Atlantic Books, 2008).

Meyer, Sir Anthony BT: *A European Technological Community* (Conservative Political Centre New Techniques series No.7, December 1966).

Meyer, Sir Anthony BT; and Montagu, Victor: *Europe: Should Britain Join?* (Monday Club, November 1966).

Minc, Alain: *La Grande Illusion* (Grasset 1989).

Minoprio, Peter: *The Commonwealth and the Common Market: a brief for CPC discussion groups* (Conservative Political Centre, January 1962).

Mitton, Athony: *A Tax for Our Time* (CPC 1967)

Monday World, Summer 1970 (Monday Club).

Monetary Committee of the European Community: *Lessons to be learned from the disturbances on the foreign exchange markets* (C3-0170/93, 1993).

Morris, James: *Heaven's Command, Pax Britannica* and *Farewell the Trumpets* (Faber and Faber, 1973–78).

Mundell, Professor R.: *A Theory of Optimum Currency Areas* (American Economic Review, 1961).

National Referendum Campaign: *Why you should vote NO* (HMSO, 1975).

Neuberger, Henry: *The Economics of 1992* (British Labour Group in the European Parliament, 1989).

Newton Dunn MEP, Bill (editor): *Memories of the first elected European Parliament* (Allendale Publishing, 2007).

North, Richard: *The Wrong Side of the Hill: The Secret Realignment of UK Defence Policy with the EU (Centre for Policy Studies, 2005).*

Norton, Philip: *Conservative Dissidents: Dissent within the Parliamentary Conservative Party, 1970–1974* (Temple Smith 1978).

O'Hagan, Lord Charles (editor); with Peter Blaker MP, Alick Buchanan-Smith MP, Hugh Dykes MP, David Hunt MP, Peter Mills MP and Peter Rees QC, MP: *Europe Right Ahead* (CPC, October 1978).

O'Sullivan, John: *Conservatism, Democracy and National Identity* (Centre for Policy Studies, March 1999).

Oakley, Robert: *Robert Oakley's Westminster Week* (BBC, Monday 14 June, 1999.

Oakeshott, Michael: *Rationalism in Politics and other Essays* (Methuen 1962).

Orwell, George: *Nineteen Eighty-four* (1949).

Papini, Roberto: *The tradition and present-day relevance of Christian-Democratic thought* in *Efforts to define a Christian Democratic "Doctrine"* (European People's Party, 1989).

Parkinson, C. Northcote: *Parkinson's Law or the Pursuit of Progress* (John Murray, 1958).

Patten, The Rt. Hon. Chris, CH: *EU Foreign Relations: the Next Steps* in *Conservative Europe, 2002 Party Conference Magazine* (Conservative Group for Europe, October 2002).

Patterson, Ben: *Britain & Europe* (Conservative Central Office for the YCs, March 1967).

Patterson, Ben: *The Character of Conservatism* (CPC 1973).

Patterson, Ben (rapporteur): *Direct Elections to the European Parliament: report of an all-Party study group commissioned by the European Movement* (European Movement, 1974).

Patterson MEP, Ben: *Europe and Employment: Policies for Economic Recovery and Jobs* (European Democratic Group 1984).

Patterson MEP, Ben: *Vredeling and All That: European Community Proposals on Employee Consultation and Information* (European Democratic Group 1984).

Patterson MEP, Ben: *VAT: the zero rate issue* (EDG, 1988).

Patterson MEP, Ben (rapporteur): *Report on the second Annual Report 1992 on the activities of the Committee of Governors and on the monetary and financial conditions in the Community* (Committee on Economic and Monetary Affairs and Industrial Policy, Subcommittee on Monetary Affairs, European Parliament. A3-0213/93. 30 June 1993).

Patterson MEP, Ben: *European Monetary Union* (Conservatives in the European Parliament, 1991).

Patterson MEP, Ben: *Lobbying in Europe* (PRCA Guidance Paper, November 1983). *Lobbying: an introduction to Political Communication in Europe* (Countrywide Political Communications, 1990). *Lobbying in Europe: an introduction to Political Communication in Europe* (3rd. edition, GPC 1994).

Patterson, Eric J.: *Poland* (Arrowsmith 1934).

Patterson, Eric J.: *Yugoslavia* (Arrowsmith 1936)

Plumb MEP, Sir Henry (Lord Plumb): foreword to *The Benefits of Europe* (European Democratic Group in the European Parliament, 1981).

Powell, Enoch, edited by John Wood: *Freedom and Reality* (B. T. Batsford, Ltd. 1969).

Powell, Enoch: *The Common Market: the case against* (Elliot Right Way Books, 1971).

Powell, Enoch, edited by John Wood: *Still to Decide* (B. T. Batsford, Ltd., 1972).

Prag, Derek with foreword by Geoffrey Rippon: *Foreign Policy and Defence: a role for Europe* (Conservative Group for Europe, November 1978).

Prout QC, MEP, Sir Christopher (Lord Kingsland): *Federalism, Integration, Sovereignty, Union and all that* (Conservatives in the European Parliament, May 1990).

Prout QC, MEP, Sir Christopher (Lord Kingsland): *The European Community and the 1994 European Elections* (Conservatives in the European Parliament, 4 June 1993).

Reay, Lord Hugh: *The European Community and the Developing World* (European Conservative Group, 1979).

Rhodes James, Robert: *Ambitions & Realities: British Politics 1964–1970* (Weidenfeld and Nicolson, 1972).

Rifkind MP, The Rt. Hon Sir Malcolm: *EU-US relations: towards deeper cooperation* in *Conservative Europe, 2008 Party Conference Magazine* (Conservative Group for Europe, October 2008).

Rippon, The Rt. Hon. Geoffrey Q.C.: *Britain's World Role* (Conservative Political Centre New Tasks series, no.3, March 1965).

Rippon, The Rt. Hon. Geoffrey QC: *Our Future in Europe* (Conservative Political Centre, September 1974).

Roth, Andrew: *Enoch Powell* (Macdonald, 1970).

Russell, William; with Jock Bruce-Gardyne, John Macgregor, Patrick Jenkin, Robert Erith and Talbot Hainault: *Britain into Europe* (Conservative Political Centre for the Bow Group, 1962).

Sapir, André: *An Agenda for a Growing Europe: making the EU economic system deliver* (European Commission, July 2003).

Scott-Hopkins MP, Jim; and Corrie MP, John: *Towards a Community Rural Policy* (European Conservative Group, April 1979).

Scruton, Roger: *The Meaning of Conservatism* (Third edition, Palgrave, 2001).

Sen, Amartya: *The Idea of Justice* (Penguin Books, 2009)

Shaw MP, Michael: *The European Parliament and the Community Budget* (European Conservative Group 1978).

Shearman, William; with Nicholas Beacock and Reginald Watts: *Towards a European Identity* (PEST, 1972).

Siedentop, Larry: *Democracy in Europe* (Allen Lane, 2000).

Smith, Geoffrey: "EFTA" in *Crossbow*, October-December 1964 (Bow Group).

Spaak, Paul-Henri: *Face to Face with Europe* (Conservative Political Centre, May 1967).

Spectator, The: 17 January 1964; 14 July 1990.

Taylor MP, Teddy: Letter in the *Daily Telegraph*, 21 January 1997.

Tebbit, Norman: *Upwardly Mobile* (Weidenfeld and Nicolson, 1988).

Thatcher MP, The Rt. Hon. Margaret: *Europe as I see it* (European Conservative Group, August 1977).

Thatcher, Margaret: *The Downing Street Years* (HarperCollins 1993).

The Times, Saturday 5 November 1987; 4 November 2009; 13 May 2010.

Thompson, Dennis: *The Rome Treaty and the Law* by Dennis Thompson (supplement to *Crossbow*, Bow Group, July-September 1962).

Tombs, Robert and Isabelle: *That Sweet Enemy: the French and the British from the Sun King to the present* (William Heinemann, 2006).

Towler, Gawain; with Emmanuel Bordez and Lee Rotheram: *Bloc Tory: a new party for Europe?* (Centre for Policy Studies, August 2001).

Turner, John: *The Tories and Europe* (Manchester University Press, 2000).

Utley, T.E.: *Enoch Powell: the man and his thinking* (William Kimber, 1968).

Vacher's: *Vacher's European Companion, Number 66* (November 1988).

Vacher's: *Vacher's European Companion, Number 67* (February 1989.

Vaubel, Professor Roland: *The European Institutions as an Interest Group* (Institute of Economic Affairs, June 2009).

Wall, Sir Stephen: *A Stranger in Europe* (Oxford University Press, 2008).

Watts, Nick: *Leading Europe in the Right direction* Conservative Europe Group, supported by Business in Europe, 2009).

Welsh MEP, Michael: *Collective Security: the European Community and the Preservation of Peace* (European Democratic Group, January 1989).

Werner, Pierre: *Report to the Council and the Commission on the realization of economic and monetary union in the Community (the Werner Report)*. (Supplement to the Bulletin of the European Communities, 8 October 1970).

White, R.J.: *The Conservative Tradition* (Black, 2nd edition 1964).

Winder, Robert: *The EEC and the Media* (Kirk Scholarship Project 1982/83, DJE International Public Relations Group, 1983).

Young, Hugo: *This Blessed Plot: Britain and Europe from Churchill to Blair* (Macmillan 1998).

Young, Kenneth: *Sir Alec Douglas-Home* (J.M.Dent & Sons, 1970).

Young, Lord: *The Enterprise Years: a businessman in the Cabinet* (Headline, 1990).

Index

Note: *Where "Brussels" refers to the city itself it is written normally. Where the word is used colloquially, to refer to the Commission or the European Union as a whole, quotation marks are used ("Brussels").*

10 Downing Street, 109, 125
1066 and All That, 321n
1922 Committee, 72
1970 Group, 66
"1992" (*See also* Single Market), ix, 100, 129, 130, 134, 141–6, 150, 277
5th Company Law Directive, 120

Aberdeen University, 230
Accession Treaty, x, 70, 160, 362
Acheson, Dean, 34, 294
acid rain, 149
Acland, Sir Antony, 337
ACP, see African, Caribbean and Pacific (ACP)
acquis communautaire, 41, 213, 214, 315, 336
Action Committee for the United States of Europe, 54, 87
Action not Words, 48
Adam Smith Institute, 155
Additional Member System, 93, 93n
additionality, 123
Aden, 48
Adenauer, Konrad, 1, 28, 29, 352, 353
Adonino, Pietro, 134
A Europe of Nations, 50, 51, 227, 289, 295
Afghanistan, 180, 337
Africa, 12, 38, 49, 76, 282, 308
African, Caribbean and Pacific (ACP), 38, 363
African and Caribbean, 39
Agriculture Committee of the European Parliament, 112
Aitken, Max. *See* Beaverbrook
Albania, 215, 339
Albert Hall, 123
Albert, Michel, 114
Alexander, David, 83
Alexandra Palace, 70
Alford, Col. Jonathan, 230
Algérie francaise, 12
Alianza Popular (AP), 156, 343
Alliance of Liberals and Democrats for Europe Group (ALDE), 260
Alps, the, 8n
Amato, Giuliano, 239
America, 1, 10, 29, 45, 51, 63, 74, 81, 227, 232

American(s), 2, 7, 30, 31, 39, 44, 45, 47, 51, 57, 63, 93, 146, 209, 227, 228, 230, 232, 237, 240, 251, 284, 286, 296, 304, 337
American Chamber of Commerce in Brussels, 146
American Civil War, 280
American Newspaper Publishers' Association, 302
Amery, Julian (Baron Amery of Lustleigh), 3, 49, 227
Amery, Leo, 3, 353
Amsterdam Treaty, 154, 235, 240, 279, 356, 366
anciens régimes, 349
Andorra, 285
Anglo-French nuclear deterrent, 31, 227, 229, 295
Anglo-Saxon(s), 7, 8, 8n, 9, 30, 133, 145, 211, 264, 306, 328
animal welfare, 122, 149
anti-American(ism)/anti-Atlanticism, 51, 53, 228, 295, 296, 343, 356
anti-clericalism, 94
anti-Common Market(eers), 20, 73, 270
Anti-Common Market League (ACML), 19, 65, 66, 272, 361
anti-Communism, 337n, 347, 357
Antwerp, 303
apartheid, 331
Apple Industry Committee/apples, 122, 298
Appleby, Sir Humphrey, 16
Aquinas, St. Thomas of, 9, 211
Archbishop of Canterbury, 144
Argentina, 115
Aristotle, 333
Arnold, Jacques, 179
"art of the possible", 20, 335, 335n
Ashdown, Paddy (Baron Ashdown of Norton-sub-Hamdon), 220
Ashridge (Bonar Law College), 18n
Ashton, Catherine (Baroness Ashton of Upholland), 263, 264, 264n, 326
A Smaller Stage, 47
A Stronger Society: Voluntary Action in the 21st Century, 351
Assemblée française, 68
Assessment of the Function of the Internal Market, 134
Athens, 350, 358n
Atlantic Alliance, 5, 40, 51, 188, 229, 337, 343

Atlantic Payments Union proposal, 40
"Atlantic to the Urals", 8n, 360
Atlantic(ism/ist), 47, 50, 51, 181, 295
Attlee, Clement (1st Earl Attlee), 10, 227
Australia(n), 119n, 228n, 280, 281, 301, 327
Australian soft wheat, 31
Austria, 14n, 186, 197, 209, 210, 314, 349n, 361, 366

baby seals, 123
Bacon, Francis (Viscount Saint Alban), 9
Baghdad Pact, 228n
Bailey, Richard, 29
Baker, Kenneth (Baron Baker of Dorking), 81
Baldwin, Stanley (1st Earl Baldwin of Bewdley), 49n
Bale, Tim, 224, 336
Balfe, Richard, 115
Balfour, A.J.(1st Earl of Balfour), 296, 332
Balfour, Neil, 96
Balkans, 6, 206, 297, 324
Ball Albert report, 129
Ball, Prof. James, 129
Bangladesh, 228n
Bank for International Settlements (BIS), 222n
Bank of England, 166, 168, 172, 182, 201, 201n, 218, 219, 220
banking secrecy, 314
Barber, Anthony (Baron Barber), 131
Barnes, John, 212
Barnier, Michel, 264
Barons Court, 55, 85
Barroso, José Manuel, 263, 264n, 279, 287
Basle agreement, 34
Bath meeting of Finance Ministers, 184
bathing water, 213n
Battersby, Bob, 97, 124n
Battle of Britain, 307
Bavaria(n), 69n, 104, 346
BBC, 10, 124n, 260, 302
BBC Scotland, 108
BBC Trust, 349
Beano, 243
Beaverbrook newspapers, 19
Beaverbrook, Lord (Max Aitken, 1st Baron Beaverbrook), 302
Beazley, Christopher, 255
Bedford, 12n
Beethoven, Ludwig van, 72
Beijing, 263
Belarus, 324, 339
Belfast South, 78
Belgium, 4, 117, 213, 239, 263, 283, 359
Bell, Sir Ronald, 87
Beloff, Nora, 11, 30
Belper, 197
Benedict XVI, Pope, 351
Benelux, 4, 12, 22, 157, 343, 359, 360
Ben-Gurion, David, 6n
Bennite Left, 111
Bentham, Jeremy, 72
Berlin, 103, 141, 170, 212
Berlin Wall, 141, 168, 170, 230, 337, 364
Bessborough, 10th Earl of, 79, 99
Besson, Eric, 319n
Bethell, Nicholas (4th Baron Bethell), 79, 97, 158
Beumer, Bouke, 197n, 344
Bevan, Aneurin ('Nye'), 227, 227n
Bevin, Ernest, 227
Bexhill and Battle, 190

Biesheuvel, Barend, 117n
Biffen, John (Baron Biffen), 61, 61n, 65, 69, 73, 154
"Big Society", 351
Biggs-Davison, Sir John, 49
Birkenhead, 190
Birmingham, 60
Birmingham Conference 2010, 326, 329, 330
bishops, 94, 94n
Bismarck, Otto von, 335n
"black Conservatism", 61n, 181n
Black Hawk helicopters, 232
Black Wednesday, 165, 168, 182–8, 201, 300, 332, 335, 336, 365
Black, Conrad, 208, 209, 210, 211, 301
Blackpool Conference 1968, 56
Blair, Tony, x, 223, 236, 269, 365; "demon eyes" poster, 306; "winning the argument" on Europe, 235; candidate for "President of Europe", 263; drops policy of adopting euro, 303; expectation would activate "opt ins", 207; exploits Conservative weaknesses, 196; introduction of PR for EP elections, 220; keen on single currency, 207; making Labour "party of Europe", 155, 205, 269; opinion on the British media, 301; outclasses Duncan-Smith in Commons, 226; playing Major off against his party, 198; policy on Iraq, 39; pragmatic policy on Europe, 336; rescued by Dutch and French referenda, 244; Social Chapter opt-in, 316; speech in Cardiff, 242; supports elected President of Europe, 216n; St.Malo agreement with Chirac, 231
"Blairite smoke-and-mirrors", 244
Blake, Robert (Lord Blake of Braydeston), 180n
BNP. *See* British National Party (BNP)
Board of Trade, 11
Bodleian Library, 208, 317
Body, Sir Richard, 66, 87, 154, 201, 309
Bognor Regis, GLYC Conference in, 56
Booker, Christopher, 236, 274, 298
Boothby, Bob (Baron Boothby), 8, 26, 287, 288
Boots the Chemist, 130
border controls, 123, 330, 366
Bosnia-Herzegovina, 180, 215, 339
Bosnian conflict, 190
Boundary Commission(s), 93, 104, 110
Bovine Spongiform Encephalopathy (BSE), 198, 199, 366
Bow and Bromley Constitutional Club, 35
Bow Group, 13, 23, 30, 35, 36, 38, 47, 49, 55, 57, 60, 62, 67, 73, 82, 83, 155, 176, 188, 228, 272, 284, 293, 311, 314, 243, 251, 266, 360
Bow Group European Liaison Committee, 82
Bow Grouper(s), 8, 36, 62, 73, 79, 317, 341
Boyle, Sir Edward (Baron Boyle of Handsworth), 6n
Boyson, Sir Rhodes, 155
Bratislava, 214
Bretherton, Russell, 11
Bretton Woods, 82
Brighton Conference 1961, 20
Brighton Conference 1971, 65
Britain in Europe, 12, 53, 55, 86, 87, 88, 271
Britain into Europe, 35, 36, 37
Britain's New Deal in Europe, 86
Britain's Place in the World, 58
Britain, Strong and Free, 5
British Aerospace, 232
British agriculture, 19, 39, 53, 270

British Bill of Rights, 267, 340
British Chamber of Commerce in Paris, 58
British Empire. *See* Empire
British European Airways (BEA), 97
British Institute of Management (BIM), 86, 144
British Invisible Export Council, 164
British National Party (BNP), 247, 249, 258, 368
British Petroleum (BP), 81
British Presidency of 1981, 115
British Presidency of 1986, 142
British Presidency of 1992, 179, 186, 187
British Public Relations Consultants Association (PRCA), 145
Brittan, Leon (Baron Brittan of Spennithorne), 44, 57; "Cambridge Mafia", 212; "Kennedy Toryism", 45; interviews me for Bow Group, 36; member of Commission, 166; on Britain's role in EU, 298; on Conservative/LibDem coalition, 341; on ERM membership, 166; on Single Currency, 297; resigns over Westland affair, 217, 364; Trade and Industry Secretary, 217; trade Commissioner, 327
Broad, Roger, 71
Brok, Elmar, 103, 238
"broken society", 253
Brown, George, x, 51, 197
Brown, Gordon; Ashton "his third choice", 263; Clegg reports "pushing Tories on Europe", 266; "hopeless government" of, 257; hostile to Britain joining EMU, 207; in televised debate 2010, 264; independence of Bank of England, 218; late for Lisbon signing, 245; pragmatic policy on Europe, 336; presses Blair claim to EU Presidency, 263; takes credit for economic management, 201; UKIP attitude to, 257
Bown/Wilson application, 59, 269
Bruce, Donald (Lord Bruce of Donington), 227n
Bruce-Gardyne, Jock (Baron Bruce-Gardyne), 30, 45
Bruges Group, 35, 151, 174n, 216, 330
Bruges speech (Thatcher's), 149, 151, 152, 154, 190, 195, 280, 300, 305, 354, 364
Brussels (city of), 31, 34, 55, 70, 71, 80, 81, 82, 97, 98, 109, 110, 121, 123, 139, 145, 146, 161, 167, 186, 198, 204n, 210, 214, 238, 251, 255, 302, 303
"Brussels", 217; "a diet of", 149, 150, 364; bad for Britain, 302; "Brussels in Britain, Britain in Brussels", 195; Brussels machine corrupted/ outdated, 144, 298; "Brussels Sprouts" not to be repeated, 189; "Brussels talking to Brussels", 238; bureaucrats/ bureaucracy of, 125, 144, 289, 310; clang and din from, 295; democratic control of, 216; foreign & security policy not responsibility of, 339; giving up sovereignty to/selling out to, 270, 306; government by fax from, 314; government by/ run from/power of, 44, 75, 152, 210, 254, 305, 326, 338; grab for power by, 133; interference/ regulation(s)/red tape/daft schemes from/ petty acts of, 124, 125, 131, 136, 144, 149, 156, 190, 194, 278, 297, 298, 306, 313; laying blame on, 311; powers passing up and down from, 213, 315; promoting national interest in, 323; repatriation of powers from, 336; responsibility for prosecution of traders, 298; Single Market without, 15; transfer of powers/ competences to, 75, 210, 224, 329; unelected Commissioners/bureaucrats in, 87, 310; "vast Brussels bureaucracy", 144, 289

Bryant, Sir Arthur, 307
BSE. *See* Bovine Spongiform Encephalopathy (BSE)
Bucharest, 214
Budapest, 153, 214
Budgen, Nick, 155, 201n, 212
budget rebate, UK's, 85, 114, 115, 134, 240, 338, 355, 363, 364
Budgetary Control Committee of the European Parliament, 79, 124n, 207, 218, 355
Budgets Committee of the European Parliament, 112, 115
Bulgaria, 250, 367
Bulgarian Union of Democratic Forces, 255
Bull, Hedley, 229
Bulletin, Daniel Hannan's, 260
bull-fighting, 156
Bundesbank, 162, 164, 167, 182, 184, 185, 218
Bundesrepublik, 279
Bundesstaat, 280, 287
Bundeswehr, 10
Burke, Edmund, 72, 288, 332, 345
Business for New Europe, 314
Business for Sterling, 221
Business Leaders' Manifesto, 143
Butler, Sir David, x, 57, 86, 189, 196, 205, 308, 318
Butler, Sir Michael, 147n, 173n
Butler, R.A. ('Rab') (Baron Butler of Saffron Walden), 20, 20n, 46, 52, 293, 335n
butter mountains, 74, 112, 115, 123
"butter to Russia", 112
buying cars abroad, 123

Calais, 130
Callaghan, James (Baron Callaghan of Cardiff), 88, 92, 93, 102, 126
Calvinist, 344, 345
"Cambridge Mafia", 212
Cambridge University, 6, 6n, 12, 18, 27, 36, 50, 55, 55n, 58, 61, 61n, 72, 181, 212, 284
Cambridge University Conservative Association (CUCA), 12, 72, 207, 212
Cambridge University Federal Union, 55n
Cambridge University Liberal Club, 12
Cambridgeshire, 129
Cameron Conservatism, 251, 306
Cameron, David; and Sarkozy, 233, 335; attitude to European integration, 335; avoiding dissension on Europe, 253; "Big Society", 351; "Cameron's blushes", 330; "caring Conservatism", 255; election as Party leader, 245, 251, 252, 367; euro area Treaty changes not opposed, 339; exclusion from EPP leaders' meetings, 357; foreword to 2009 manifesto, 324; general election 2010, 264; "green" Conservatism, 323, 345; "hug a hoodie", 253; Movement for European Reform, 254, 255, 256; pledge to break with the EPP Group, 253, 260, 344; redefines Conservative policy on Europe, 262, 263, 325, 329, 368; school of "Notting Hill Tories", 252, 271; speech to 2005 Party Conference, 252; St Stephens Club statement, 265, 266; "votes for prisoners" issue, 340
Campaign for Conservative Democracy, 223, 225
Campaign for Nuclear Disarmament (CND), 227
Campaign Guide(s), 54, 100, 126, 149, 176, 194, 304, 305
Campbell, Alec, 284
Canada, 10, 227, 280, 281, 313

CAP. *See* Common Agricultural Policy (CAP)
capitalism, 74, 344, 347, 349
"capitalist plot/club/conspiracy/racket" , 51, 53, 86, 304
Cardiff, 242
Carlisle, 265
Carlisle, John, 155
Carolingians, 353
Carrington, Lord (6th Baron Carrington), 100, 109, 113
Carttiss, Michael, 201n
Cash, Bill; Bow Group pamphlet on Europe, 176, 177; Chairman of House of Commons Scrutiny Committee, 267, 330; "constitutionalist" anti, 154; meeting at *Konrad Adenauer Stiftung*, 176; perceives threat to British nationhood, 272; supports Single European Act, 138; "terrible awakening", 176, 311
Cassidy, Bryan, 273
Cassis de Dijon case, 131, 132n, 363
Castle, Barbara (Baroness Castle of Blackburn), 97, 112, 271
Catalan(onia), 283
Catherwood, Sir Fred, 86, 97, 129, 169
Catholic(s), 19, 132, 211, 182, 281, 289, 306, 344–8, 352
Catholic Church, 289, 345, 346, 347, 352
Catholic social teaching/tradition, 132, 344
Catholicism, 344
"Catholic South", 211
Caucasus, 242
Caucasus republics, 339
Cavalier, 282, 333
Cavalier and Tory, 288, 333
CBI. *See* Confederation of British Industry (CBI)
CDU. See *Christlich Demokratische Union* (CDU)
Cecchini Report, 140, 364
Centesimus Annus, 349n
CENTO (the Central Treaty Organisation), 228
Central and Eastern Europe, 42, 116, 210, 214, 249, 314, 342
Central and South America, 344
Central Office of Information, 101
Centre Européen de Documentation et d'Information, (CEDI), 68, 94
Centre for Policy Studies (CPS), 141, 208, 209, 212, 215, 216, 231, 236, 237, 240, 254
Centre for Social Justice, 226n, 352
Centre for the Study of Social Policy (CSSP), 55n
Centro Italiano di Studi per la Conciliazione Internazionale, 94
Chalker, Lynda (Baroness Chalker of Wallasey), 149
Chamberlain, Sir Austen, 225n
Chamberlain, Joseph, 14, 313, 317
Chamberlain, Neville, 181n
Channel Islands, 70, 285
Channel Tunnel, 123
Channon, Paul (Baron Kelvedon), 97
Charles Barker Watney Powell, 102
Charles I, 282, 333
Charter of Fundamental Rights, EU's, 242, 243, 261, 262, 266
Chataway, Sir Christopher, 73
Chatham House, 146n
Chauvel, Jean, 30
Chelsea, 225
Chelsea Young Conservatives, 40, 55, 56n, 103

Chelwood, Lord. *See* Tufton Beamish
Chesterton, G.K., 156
Chichester, Giles, 260
Chile, 347
China, 13, 26, 282n, 284, 287, 289, 295, 327, 337, 337n
Chingford and Woodford Green, 225
Chipping Barnet, 190
Chirac, President Jacques, 231, 245
ChristenUnie, 259
Christian Democracy, 290n, 343–52, 354, 357
Christian Democratic Students, 82, 103
Christian Democrat(s), 69, 69n, 78, 82, 93, 94, 95, 104, 119, 121, 156, 157, 158, 197n, 238, 254, 255, 264, 343–57, 359
Christian Party-Christian People's Alliance, 259
Christian Science Monitor, 246n
Christian Socialism/ist, 132, 346, 347, 350
Christian trade unions, 346
Christlich Demokratische Union (CDU), 69, 69n, 103, 104, 157, 170, 174, 180, 255, 343, 344, 347
Christlich Demokratische Union (CDU) /*Christlich Soziale Union* (CSU), 69, 157, 180
Christlich Soziale Union (CSU), 69, 69n, 104, 344, 346
Christodoulou, Efthimios, 171, 172
Church of England, 94, 344
Churchill, Sir Winston, 1–7, 29, 72, 116, 275, 293, 353; analysis by in 1940s, 74; article in *Saturday Evening Post*, 2; author of 1951 manifesto, 5; Battle of Britain speech, 307; belief in European Union, 26; bringing in the United States, 227; calls for "a unified European army", 3, 359; "Europe and the open sea", 7; force behind Hague Conference, 2; good starting point, x; imposed on Conservative Party, 46; in pantheon of "founding fathers", 1; joins Liberal Party, 15; leader rather than Halifax, 181n; memo to Eden 1942, 37; "most dangerous enemies", 202; "partnership between France and Germany", 2, 28, 210; post-1951 government, 4, 10, 19, 332, 350, 360; post-war speeches, 274, 342; "prime exponent of British ambiguity", 3; replaced as PM by Eden, 360; son-in-law Christopher Soames, 80; speech at The Hague, 1948, 3; speech to Belgian parliament, 1945, 2; speeches in Strasbourg, 1949, 2, 3, 4, 359; supports Schuman Plan, 3; the "three circles", 4, 5; "with Europe but not of it", 9; Winston Churchill Memorial Lecture, 113; Zurich speech, 1, 2, 359
Churchillian enthusiasm/vision, spirit of Churchill, 8, 16, 19, 270
Citizens' Initiatives, 319
City of London, 144, 264
Civic Democratic Party (ODS), 254, 255, 259, 261
Civil War (American), 280
Civil War (English), 307
Civil War (Spanish), 79
"civil wars" (Europe's), 308
CJD. *See* Creutzfeldt-Jakob Disease (CJD)
Clark University, Boston, Mass., 5
Clark, Alan, 110, 142, 181n, 310
Clarke, George, 301
Clarke, Ken; alliance with Redwood, 206; Bow Group and PEST, 73; Chancellor of the Exchequer, 201, 365; "Cambridge Mafia", 212; opposes policy of ruling out euro, 202; favours Bank of England independence, 201; "Ken and

Eddie show", 201; leadership contest 1997, 206, 366; leadership contest 2001, 225, 226, 367; leadership contest 2005, 251, 252; maintains commitment to Europe, 293; "middle-of-the-road", 203; "obvious successor" to Major, 206; on "Save the Pound", 224; refuses to bend to Eurosceptic wind, 206; regional policy pamphlet, 99; reputation as Chancellor, 202; "semi-detached role" on EMU, 250; shadow Secretary of State for Business, 253; Trade and Industry minister, 142

classical liberalism, 333, 347

Clegg, Nick, 264, 266, 368

Clemens, Clay, 352, 353

"clerical-fascism", 346

climate change, 266, 267, 297, 323, 324, 326, 367

"Club Med", 328

Cobden, Richard, 14, 72

Cobdenite, 209

Cockfield, Arthur (Baron Cockfield); abolition of fiscal frontiers, 143, 143n; advises Treasury, 131; appointed to Commission, 130, 131; memories of his approach, 131; mutual recognition, 131, 278, 316; "natural technocrat", 131; on subsidiarity, 291; predecessor (Narjes), 134; Single Market programme, 130; proposals on VAT, 135; "reference to standards" approach, 132; right on harmonisation, 131; "seizes opportunity", 130; takes oath seriously, 132; Thatcher's mixed feelings on, 131

Cockfield White Paper, 133, 134, 135, 136, 138, 143, 364

co-decision, 111, 175, 206, 311

Colbert, Jean-Baptiste, 75

Cold War, 5, 9, 21, 44, 181, 227, 342, 347, 357

Cole, G.D.H., 288

College of Europe in Bruges, 151

Colombo, Emilio, 117, 303

Colton, Mary, 83

Columbia University, 286

combustibility of false beards, 132

COMECON (Council for Mutual Economic Assistance), 34, 37

Comité Européen de la Normalisation (CEN), 132

Comité Européen de la Normalisation Electrotechnique (CENELEC), 132

Commissariat au Plan, 129

Commissioner for External Affairs, 236, 264

Commissioners, 80, 81, 87, 190, 216, 218, 218n, 241, 310, 327

Commitology, 310

Committee of Governors of the Central Banks of the Member States, 183

Committee of Permanent Representatives (COREPER), 110, 310, 311

Committee of the Regions, 292

Common Agricultural Policy (CAP), 25, 74, 81, 83, 88, 99, 101, 112, 113, 122, 124, 126, 153, 160, 202, 213, 218, 277, 309, 324, 338, 343, 132, 139, 174, 184, 188, 237, 264, 278, 290, 297

common currency, 163, 164, 165

Common External Policy, 277

Common External Tariff (CET), 11, 38, 42, 74, 277, 278, 294, 309, 362

Common Fisheries Policy (CFP), 213, 324

Common Foreign and Security Policy (CFSP), 190, 235, 242, 244, 263

Common Market Campaign Committee, 12

Common Market Safeguards Committee, 65, 66

Commonwealth, 1, 3, 4, 5, 7, 9, 13, 19, 20, 21, 22, 23, 23n, 26, 27, 32, 34, 38, 39, 40, 41, 42, 44, 46, 49, 51, 59, 73, 81, 155, 181, 270, 293, 294, 295n, 308, 313, 317

Commonwealth Immigrants Act, 23n, 361

Commonwealth Economic Consultative Council, 21

Commonwealth fellow, 5

Commonwealth Preference, 15, 53

Commonwealth Prime Ministers, 27

Commun/ism/ist/ists, 21, 39, 65, 79, 109, 111, 116, 118, 157, 180, 210, 214, 251, 254, 314, 337n, 342, 347, 349, 357, 300

Communists and Far left (EUL/LU) Group, 157

communitarian personalism/ist, 345, 346, 352, 357

Community/EEC/EU Budget, 44, 64, 65, 79, 83, 85, 99, 112, 113, 114, 114n, 115, 117, 123, 149, 161n, 190, 201, 214, 216, 270, 289, 324, 338, 355

Community Charge ('poll tax'), 150, 171, 270

Community Heads of State and Government. *See* Heads of State and Government

Community Rural Policy, 99

Community's "own resources", 113

Completing the Internal Market, 130

Concorde, 42, 51, 286

concours, 70

confederation, 24, 50, 280, 331

Confederation of British Industry (CBI), 81, 120, 141, 144, 167, 295,

Confederation of Socialist Parties of the European Community, 98

conferral, principle of, 280, 291

confessional conservatism, 346

Congdon, Tim, 165, 221

Coningsby, 342n

Conservative(s) and Reformist(s), 256, 259, 260, 261, 368

Conservative Campaign Headquarters (CCHQ), 72, 253, 317

Conservative Central Office, 35n, 52, 55, 56, 62, 70, 71, 72, 87, 96, 150, 187, 188, 194, 208, 239, 249, 317

Conservative Club in the Kings Road, 55

Conservative Europe, 226, 256, 298

Conservative Europe Group, 314, 341

Conservative Future, 55

Conservative Gaullism/ist, 50, 53, 227, 354

Conservative Group for Europe (CGE), 66, 68, 71, 93, 100, 103, 193, 207, 226, 255, 256, 297, 298, 341

Conservative Group in the European Parliament, 49, 69, 78, 79, 80, 94, 97, 99, 126, 154, 169, 229, 261, 302, 343

Conservative News Letter, 16

Conservative Party from Thatcher to Cameron, 224

Conservative Political Centre (CPC), 8, 22, 23, 26, 34, 35n, 47, 52, 55, 57, 58, 60, 65, 66, 67, 71, 73, 80, 88, 116, 193, 208, 317

CPC discussion group reports: 53, 65, 189, 190, 194, 195

Conservative Research Department, 52, 66, 70, 100, 115, 149, 174, 176, 304, 341

Conservative Way Forward, 259

Conservatives Abroad, 198

Conservatives Against a Federal Europe (CAFÉ), 254

Conservatives Against the Common Market, 87

Consolidating the Internal Market, 134

Constitutional Treaty, the (see also Lisbon Treaty),
    212n, 235, 240, 244, 245, 256, 367
Constitution for Europe, 133, 214, 235, 237, 239,
    240, 242, 245, 250, 256, 367
consumer protection, 133, 135, 146, 277
continental liberalism, 158, 347, 351
continentalism, 40
Convention on the Future of Europe/the
    European Union, 213, 214, 216, 237, 239, 240,
    242, 244, 367
Co-ordinating Committee on Europe, 66
COPA (Committee of Professional Agricultural
    Organisations), 112
Copenhagen, 72, 156
Copenhagen criteria, 214
Corby Steel, 123
COREPER. *See* Committee of Permanent
    Representatives (COREPER)
corgis, 89n
Corn Laws, repeal of, 14, 333
Cornwall, 71, 96
corporal punishment, 88, 89, 90
Corrie, John, 79
Council of Agriculture Ministers, 64
Council of Economic and Finance Ministers
    (ECOFIN), 241
Council of Employment Ministers, 309
Council of Europe, 2, 9, 69, 78, 79, 89, 89n, 108n,
    214, 215, 340, 359
Country Party, 282
Court of Auditors, 79, 218, 296, 355
Cowling, Maurice, 61n, 181n, 284
Cox, Pat, 238
CPC. *See* Conservative Political Centre (CPC)
CPC Monthly Report, 52
CPS. *See* Centre for Policy Studies (CPS)
Cran, James, 154
Craxi, Bettino, 137
crypto-federalism, 137
Cresson, Edith, 222
Creutzfeldt-Jakob Disease (CJD), 197, 199, 366
Crick, Sir Bernard, 189
criminal justice system, 133, 242, 254, 262, 266
Croatia, 180, 215, 339
Crocodile Club/Crocodiles, 118, 119, 120, 210
Cromwell, Oliver, 282
Crossbow, 13, 23, 30, 35, 42, 43, 44, 45, 47, 56, 57, 67,
    168, 313, 315
Crossman, Dick, 51
Crown in Parliament, 146
Crowson, N.J., 4, 25, 35, 35n, 66, 85, 95, 152, 308,
    316, 317
Crystal Palace, 352
CUCA. *See* Cambridge University Conservative
    Association (CUCA)
cuius regio, eius religio, 281
Curry, David, 206, 222, 298, 366
Cyprus, 367, 368
Czech, Czech Republic, 215, 254, 255, 259, 261,
    262, 283, 325, 326, 367, 368
Czechoslovakia, 63, 179, 283

d'Hondt system, 105n, 256n
d'Hondt, Victor, 105n
Daily Express, The, 19
Daily Mail, The, 20, 89n, 142
Daily Mirror, The, 20
Daily Telegraph, The, 20, 59, 79, 108, 155, 158, 198,
    209, 257, 274, 276, 298, 301, 317

Dalyell, Sir Tam (11th Baronet), 89, 303
Danes (see also Denmark), 154, 185, 186, 365
Danish and Swedish Conservative Parties, 154
Danish Centre Democrat, 104
Danish independent, 259
Danish People's Party (DPP), 259
Danish referendum, 185, 187, 365, 366
Dankert, Piet, 114, 115, 363
David, Wayne, 270
Davies, John, 81, 304
Davies, Philip, 330
Davies, Quentin (Baron Davies of Stamford), 207
Davis, David, 251, 252, 262, 336, 367
de Courcy Ireland, Caroline, 68
de Courcy-Ling, John, 97
DDR See *Deutsche Demokratische Republik* (DDR)
de Ferranti, Basil ('Boz'), 97, 119, 142, 157
de Gasperi, Alcide, 1, 275, 352
de Gaulle, Charles; admiration for "way he
    played his cards", 47; anger with over vetoes,
    296; "Atlantic to Urals" speech, 8, 360;
    British application "just a game", 31; creates
    force de frappe , 228; "de Gaulle is back",
    153; dismisses Giscard d'Estaing, 55; Dutch
    provide opposition to, 28; effect of veto on
    Conservative opinion, 29–32; "empty seat"
    policy, 29; *Europe des patries*, 42, 211, 295;
    fears Britain is American "fifth column", 30;
    impregnable position in France, 28; "in favour
    of Confederation", 24; loses referendum
    and resigns, 54, 362; not alone in doubting
    British credentials, 13, 30, 45; roots of British
    Euroscepticism, 306; Peyrefitte his confident,
    24; Rambouillet meeting with Macmillan,
    30; reading of Suez episode, 7; relations with
    Hallstein, 29, 153; remembers Churchill's
    remark, 7; return to power, 12, 360; signs treaty
    with Adenauer, 28; Soames affair, 51; studied
    by Heath, 30; "trumps Macmillan's ace", 28;
    vetoes Free Trade Area, 13; vetoes Macmillan
    EEC application, x, 29, 40, 41, 361; vetoes
    Wilson/Brown EEC application, 51, 59, 362;
    "wants kind of Europe we could join", 29
de Tocqueville, Alexis, 237
de Villiers, Philippe, 254
Deckker, Dr. Wisse, 119
Défi Américain, Le, 63, 295
Dehaene, Jean-Luc, 239
Dell, Edmund, 117n
Delors Committee on Economic and Monetary
    Union (EMU), 162, 164, 364
Delors Report/Plan, 162–9, 171, 173, 190, 364
Delors, Jacques, 302 ; activities of Delors
    Commission, 155, 217; agenda different from
    Thatcher's, 132; ambitions, 356; and Lord
    Cockfield, 132; cause of Thatcher's "no, no,
    no", 146n; chairs Parliament's Economic
    Committee, 119; "Christian Socialist", 350;
    Commission President, 129; criticised for
    "selling out" to Anglo-Saxons, 133; decisions
    to be taken at European level, 146, 152; *étatist*
    model, 251; explains "subsidiarity", 175;
    friction with Thatcher, 217; seen as way of
    blocking Thatcherism, 152; "slipped leash as
    fonctionnaire", 152, 153; social dimension of
    Single Market, 306; speech to TUC conference,
    152, 306, 313, 364
Democrat Youth Committee of Europe (DEMYC),
    95

democratic control, 3, 26, 43, 117, 177, 216 219, 310, 311, 355
democratic deficit, 84, 136, 178, 297, 309–13
Democratic Forum (MDF), 259
Democratic Unionist Party (DUP), 104, 220
Denmark (see also Danes), 14n, 68, 117, 154, 187, 299, 343, 354, 361
Denning, Lord (Baron Denning), 44
Department of Trade and Industry (DTI), 141, 142, 144, 278
Dépêche du Midi, La, 319n
Derby, Lord (Edward Stanley, 14th Earl of Derby), 180n
Derbyshire, 97, 103
Deus caritas est, 351
Deutsche Demokratische Republik (DDR), 170
Deutschmark/D-Mark, 127, 162, 164, 164n, 166, 167, 168, 169, 170, 183, 365
Deva, Nirj, 222
direct elections (to the European Parliament), 38, 91–107, 111, 105, 363; attitude of Labour Party to, 92; Callaghan pledge on PR, 93; conclusion drawn by Conservatives, 93; Direct Elections Information Campaign, 98; European Movement study on, 93n; preparations for, 95
directly elected MEPs, 43, 71, 73, 91, 287
directly elected Commission President, 216, 217, 297
Disraeli, Benjamin (1st Earl of Beaconsfield), 6n, 14, 20, 180n, 200n, 283, 332, 334, 346
Disraelian Conservatism/Toryism, 334, 352
D-Mark. See *Deutschmark*/D-Mark
Dodds-Parker, Sir Douglas, 21, 79
Donnelly, Brendan, 207, 222
Dorrell, Stephen, 206
Douglas-Home, Sir Alec (also the Earl of Home and Baron Home of the Hirsel); becomes Lord Home of the Hirsel, 73; "emerges" as leader, 46; Europe a "dead duck", x, 34; Foreign Secretary, 73; Macleod and Powell refuse to serve under, 58, 271; on the need for unity in face of Soviets, 294; on the nuclear deterrent, 228; outlines policy towards Europe, 74; PEST a reaction to, 72; resigns as Conservative leader, 361; shadow foreign secretary, 58; takes over as Prime Minister, 361
Douro, Marquess of (Charles Wellesley), 97
Dover, 130
Draft Treaty on European Union, 118, 120, 210
Dreyfus affair, 346
driving licences, 123
Drucker, P.F., 290
DTI. See Department of Trade and Industry (DTI)
Dublin summit of 1979, 112, 363
Dublin summit of 1990, 164, 365
Duisenberg, Wim, 219n
Duke of Wellington. See Wellington, Duke of
Duncan Smith, Iain, 225, 226, 271, 352, 367
Dunn, Bob, 102
Dutch (the), 28, 71, 91, 114, 117, 120n, 158, 197n, 231, 244, 254, 259, 344, 363
Dykes, Hugh (Baron Dykes), 47, 47n, 73, 79, 207, 212

Earl of Home. See Douglas-Home, Sir Alec
Earl of Lauderdale. See Maitland, the Hon. Patrick
Earldom of Sandwich, 49n
East Africa, 88
East Germany (*See also* DDR), 170

"East of Suez" question, 48, 53, 59, 228, 272
ECJ. *See* European Court of Justice (ECJ)
Economic and Monetary Affairs and Industrial Policy Committee of the European Parliament, 131, 134, 143, 157
Economic and Monetary Affairs Committee (EMAC) of the European Parliament, 119, 157, 171, 172, 197, 219, 229, 334, 366
Economic and Monetary Union (EMU), 71, 138, 160, 162, 163, 166, 170–3, 185, 207, 208, 219n, 221, 222, 297, 305, 364, 366
Economic and Social Committee (EcoSoc), 102, 234
economic government/governance, 219, 328, 339
Economist, The, 86, 185, 257, 262, 272, 329, 334, 342
ECSC. *See* European Coal and Steel Community (ECSC)
Ecu. See also European Currency Unit (ecu), 161
EDC. *See* European Defence Community (EDC)
Eden Plan, 9
Eden, Anthony (1st Earl of Avon), 8–11; and participation in Spaak Committee, 11; Churchill memo to, 2; disdain for Europe project, 9, 270; foreign policy left to, 4; Foreign Secretary, 360; government of, 350; Germany main issue for, 10; "heir apparent" to Churchill, 46; "island tradition" of pragmatism, 9, 211; on British attitude to Europe, 9; Prime Minister, 9, 360; promotes "three circles", 5; reference to Messina in memoirs, 9; resigns as PM, 360; "saves the day" by creating WEU, 10, 11; speech in Strasbourg, 4; Suez adventure, 6n, 227; views on Europe, 20, 40, 142
Edinburgh summit of 1992, 186, 365
Education, Youth, Culture, Information and Sport Committee of the European Parliament, 116
EEA. *See* European Economic Area (EEA)
EEC. *See* European Economic Community (EEC)
EFTA. *See* European Free Trade Association (EFTA)
Egypt/Egyptian, 6n, 170
Eliot, T.S., 72
Elizabeth I, 307
Elles, Diana (Baroness Elles), 79, 96, 97, 143
Elles, James, 79, 264
Ellesmere Port Address, 213, 286
Ellis, Tom, 61
EMAC. *See* Economic and Monetary Affairs Committee (EMAC) of the European Parliament
Empire (British), 4, 5, 6, 7, 19, 26, 34, 44, 59, 181, 181n, 227, 270, 293, 294, 295, 295n, 307, 308, 317
Empire (Hapsburg), 282
Empire (Holy Roman), *See* Holy Roman Empire
Empire (Roman), *See* Roman Empire
empire, "first non-imperial", 287
Empire: the British Imperial Experience from 1765 to the Present, 7, 307
"empty chair" boycott, 29, 361
EMS/ERM "half-baked", 162
EMU. *See* Economic and Monetary Union (EMU)
energy policy, 149, 297
Enfield, 203
English Democrats, 259
English, Sir David, 142
English-speaking peoples, 4, 5
engrenage, 210
enhanced cooperation, 212, 235, 236, 286, 315, 316, 323

entrenched clauses, 331
EPP. *See* European People's Party (EPP)
EPP Group. *See* European People's Party (EPP) Group
EPP-ED Group, (Group of the European People's Party and European Democrats (EPP-ED), 158, 159, 248, 249, 253, 254
Erasmus, Deciderius, 72
Erhard, Ludwig, 28
ERM. *See* Exchange Rate Mechanism (ERM)
Esher, 190, 225
Estonia, 367, 368
étatist/étatisme, 251, 309
Eton and Slough, 47
EU budget. *See* Budget of the EEC/EC/EU
Euratom, x, 12, 47, 54n, 360
Euro Area, 173n, 219, 222, 267, 314, 322, 328, 329, 330, 334, 335, 337, 339, 366, 367, 368
euro, the, ix, 183, 200, 202, 207, 221, 222, 223, 224, 250, 254, 266, 286, 297, 303, 324, 329, 334, 337, 366
Eurobarometer, 101, 299, 300, 369
"Euro-conservatism", 353
Euro-constituency Councils, 95
euro-denominated bonds, 222n
euro-denominated notes and coins, 122, 221, 367
Eurofighter/Typhoon aircraft, 233
Eurojust, 266
"Europe as substitute for Empire", 26
Europe des patries, 24, 28, 42, 68, 125, 275, 280, 296, 326, 343
"Europe – Open for Business", 141, 142, 144
Europe: the Great Debate, 92n
European 'Tactical' Group, 66
European "pensioners' card", 151
European Advisory Council of the Institute of Directors, 143, 144
European Arrest Warrant(s), 135, 266
European Assembly, 38, 97, 98, 125, 107, 138
European Assembly Election Bill, 93
European Central Bank (ECB), 163, 173n, 183, 219, 219n, 220, 328, 329n, 366
European Central Banks, 34
European Central Bank's General Council, 173
European Centre for Parliamentary Research and Documentation (ECPRD), 214
European Centre for Public Affairs, 103
European Coal and Steel Community (ECSC), ix, 3, 4, 8, 9, 10, 11, 19, 37, 47, 54n, 59, 118, 123, 359, 360, 362, 367
European Communities Act 1972, x, 61, 70, 83, 84, 84n, 262, 270, 305, 314, 329
European Communities Bill, 67
European Community Defence System (ECDS), 231
European Community Department (Internal), 147n
European Community's London Office. *See* London Office
European Company, 48
European Conference of Postal and Telecommunications Administrations (CEPT), 132
European Conservative Group. *See* Conservative Group in the European Parliament.
European Conservatives and Reformists (ECR) Group, 259, 260, 261, 368
European Convention for the Protection of Pet Animals, 89n

European Convention on Human Rights, 67, 89, 215, 243, 281, 340
European Council (see also Heads of State and Government) , 117n, 186, 213, 214, 217, 235, 241, 242, 244, 255, 261, 263, 279, 315, 329, 357
European Court of Human Rights, 88, 90, 281, 340
European Court of Justice (ECJ), 15, 67, 84, 89, 90, 111, 131, 132n, 139, 140, 146, 179, 213, 222, 242, 243, 266, 322, 331, 336, 363, 365
European Criminal Records Information System, 266
European Currency Unit (ecu), 161, 161n, 163, 164, 165
European Defence Community (EDC), 3, 10, 11, 19, 36, 227, 359, 360
European Defence Co-ordination Committee, 229
European Democrat Students (EDS), 82
European Democrat Union (EDU), 85, 363
European Democratic Alliance (EDA), 157
European Democratic Group (EDG)/ European Democrats, 32n, 105, 108, 109n, 110, 111, 116, 118, 121, 122, 150, 156, 157, 158, 229, 230, 248, 254n, 256, 260, 261, 295, 343, 363
European Documentation and Information Centre, 68
European Economic Area (EEA), 209, 314, 315, 338, 339, 366
European Economic Community (EEC), ix, 4, 6, 7, 12–16, 18, 19, 21–4, 29, 30, 35, 35n, 37, 38–42, 47, 48, 49, 51, 53, 54, 54n, 59, 60, 61, 68, 74, 83, 104, 126, 154, 209, 216, 269, 270, 272, 273, 275, 284, 286, 288, 293, 294, 295, 298, 302, 304, 305, 327, 360, 361, 362, 363
European Elections of 1979, 95–106, 119, 127, 161, 197, 299, 363
European Elections of 1984, 126, 126n, 142, 143, 149, 150, 156, 230, 273, 305, 318, 364
European Elections of 1989, 129, 143, 144, 149, 151, 156, 157, 189, 194, 195, 213n, 257, 305, 353, 364
European Elections of 1994, 106, 159, 188, 189, 193, 196, 202, 203, 205, 208, 213, 221, 305, 308, 318, 365
European Elections of 1999, 109n, 194, 208, 220–3, 247, 248, 249, 366
European Elections of 2004, 208, 240, 241, 247–50, 257, 303, 312, 353, 354, 367
European Elections of 2009, 154, 208, 233, 253, 254, 255, 256, 257, 259, 303, 318, 322, 323, 325, 326, 368
European External Action Service (EEAS), 326
European Free Trade Area, 13, 313, 360
European Forum, 66
European Free Trade Association (EFTA), 14, 19, 22, 23, 26, 31, 37, 40, 44, 46, 47, 48, 53, 179, 210, 270, 277, 313, 314, 361, 362, 364, 365
European Institute in Łódź, 6n, 214
European Integration Department of FO, 54
European Investigation Order (EIO), 336
European Investment Bank (EIB), 83, 123
European League for Economic Cooperation (ELEC), 3, 86, 139
European Liberal Democrat and Reform Group (ELDR), 156
European Monetary Institute (EMI), 183, 329n
European Monetary System (EMS), 100, 126, 161, 162, 363
European Movement, 2, 8, 12, 54, 55, 62, 66, 93n, 101, 226, 272
European Ombudsman, 99, 176

European Parliament Information Office in London. *See* London Information Office of the European Parliament
European Parliament Report, 302, 303n
European Payments Union (EPU), 161n
European People's Party (EPP), 94, 95, 95n, 158, 159, 238, 249, 319, 344, 346, 349, 352–7
European People's Party (EPP) Group, 69, 95, 104, 105, 105n, 109, 111, 113, 115, 117, 121, 154–9, 190, 238, 248, 249, 252–6, 260, 261,335, 343, 344, 350, 354–7, 365
European Personnel Selection Office (EPSO), 251
European Police Office (Europol), 266
European Public Prosecutor, 266
European Rapid Reaction Corps (RRC), 231
European Rapid Reaction Force, 231
European Research Council, 324
European Socialists, Party of, 238
European Space Launcher, 51, 286
European System of Central Banks, 162
European Technological Community (ETC), 47
European Union of Conservative and Christian Democrat Students, 103
European Union of Women (EUW), 79, 95, 103, 194
European Unit of Account, 161n
Europhobia, 226
eurosclerosis, 129
Euro-Thatcherism/Thatcherism on a European scale, 138, 145, 150, 155
Evans, Jonathan, 255
Evans-Pritchard, Ambrose, 342n
Evening Standard, The, 19
Ewing, Winnie, 88, 97, 104
excessive deficit procedure, 172, 339
exchange controls, 100, 121, 122, 163, 363
Exchange Rate Mechanism (ERM), 126, 160–72, 182–5, 190, 194, 196, 201, 335, 364, 365
excise duties, 81, 133, 135, 143, 197
Exeter/Exeter University, 5, 18
Existentialism, 289n
Expanding Commonwealth Group, 21

Fabian Society, 36
Factortame case, 140n, 365
"Fagin of Euroscepticism", 62
fair trade, 14, 15, 61, 100, 131, 259
Falklands War, 115, 121, 123, 231, 363
Farm Price Review, 64
Farage, Nigel, 222
Fawlty, Basil, 253
Feather, Vic (Lord Feather), 87
Federal Republic (West Germany), 10, 101, 124, 280, 282, 294, 295, 360
Federal Trust, 55, 222
Federal Union, 12
"federal"/"federalism"/"federalist", 24, 38, 41, 47, 50, 53, 72, 74, 92, 94, 118, 140, 152, 158, 163, 176, 177, 178, 196, 202, 203, 210, 212, 214, 215, 216, 221, 229, 230, 235,238,239, 244, 248, 253, 272, 274, 275, 278, 279, 280, 288, 295, 313, 318, 327n, 339, 343, 352, 353, 356, 357
Federalist movement, 118, 279
Federation of Liberal and Democratic Parties in the European Community, 98
Federation of University Conservative and Unionist Associations (FUCUA), 18, 36
Feldman, Sir Basil (Baron Feldman), 187
Fell, Anthony, 20

Fianna Fáil, 69, 254
Fifth Republic, 28, 360
Figaro, Le, 327
Finance Bill of 1994, 201
Financial Regulation, 39
financial services, 129, 135, 140, 264, 266, 323, 324, 328, 329
Financial Services Action Plan, 135, 329n
Financial Times, The, 23, 30, 44
Financial Weekly, 167
Fine Gael, 343n
Finkelstein, Daniel, 341
Finland, 14n, 186, 197, 209, 210, 314, 364, 366
Firm Action for a Fair Britain, 84
First World War, 6, 346
first-past-the-post, 92, 188, 223
fiscal sovereignty, 328
Fletcher-Cooke, Sir Charles, 98, 99
Florence, 72, 116
Folketing's Market Committee, 110, 256, 311
Fontainebleau summit 1984, 114, 134, 364
food prices, 22, 27, 54, 65, 83, 88
Foot, Michael, x, 224
force de frappe, 228
Foreign Office, 11, 16, 47n, 51, 54, 55, 68, 70, 113, 120, 136, 137, 150, 151
Foreman, Nigel, 166
Form E.111, 124
Forster, Anthony, 21, 58, 104, 155, 269
Forth, Eric, 108
Foster Dulles, John, 7
Fouchet Plan, 38, 175
Fowler, Norman (Baron Fowler), 73, 206, 212
Fox, Liam, 233, 251, 252
fox-hunting, 156, 346
Fraga, Manuel, 156
franc fort, 184, 185
France, 2, 6n, 10, 12, 22, 28, 29, 37, 41, 47, 51, 68, 87, 101, 113, 117n, 122, 124, 124n, 162, 200, 201, 217, 228n, 233, 240, 244, 245, 254, 279, 282, 318, 326, 327, 328, 336, 339, 346, 357, 360, 361, 367
Franco, Francisco, 156
Franco-German axis/plot, 28, 236
Franco-German reconciliation, 210
Francophobia, 308
Frankenstein's monster, 248
Frankfurt, 60, 293
Franks, Oliver (Baron Franks), 10
Franz, Otmar, 169
fraud(ulent), 122, 124, 124n, 143n, 160, 209, 218, 222, 258, 275, 292, 366
free market(s), free-market, 14, 15, 28, 53, 74, 75, 83, 94, 133, 134, 155, 163, 164, 195, 208, 251, 255, 273, 277, 289, 297, 305, 309, 344, 349
free trade(er), free-trade, 13, 14, 15, 40, 61, 66, 125, 131, 143, 209, 211, 257, 272, 273, 277, 278, 294, 297, 304, 309, 313, 317, 324, 327, 331, 338
Free Trade Area, 13, 14, 15, 19, 36, 40, 60, 117, 273, 277
Freiburg University, 6
French (the), 6n, 10, 29, 30, 31, 39, 54, 55, 62, 63, 64, 67, 68, 68n, 69, 71, 74, 82, 105n, 111, 115, 117, 117n, 119, 124, 129, 130, 131, 132, 132n, 133, 141, 142, 145, 153, 157, 162, 177, 178, 183, 184, 209, 211, 216, 217, 219, 222, 227, 228, 228n, 229, 244, 245, 251, 254, 262, 263n, 264, 282, 283, 287, 296, 300, 308, 309, 324, 337, 343, 345n, 359, 360, 361
French Foreign Legion, 231
French franc, 168

French Golden Delicious, 122
French overseas territories, 26
French Parliament, 10, 28, 153
French President(s), 28, 161, 169, 231, 233, 237, 242, 255, 263, 335, 367
French Revolution, 281, 282, 349
Friedman, Wolfgang, 286
Fulham Young Conservatives, 40
FYROM (Former Yugoslav Republic of Macedonia), 215, 339

G20, 328, 337
Gaitskell, Hugh, x, 28, 269
Gallup poll, 21, 31, 54, 151, 198, 300
Galtieri, General, 116
Gardiner, George, 65, 66, 203
Garel-Jones, Tristan (Baron Garel Jones), 174
GATT. *See* General Agreement on Tariffs and Trade (GATT)
Gaullism/ist(s), 50, 51, 53, 54, 62, 68, 69, 109, 111, 154, 157, 175, 227, 275, 280, 295, 326, 343, 354, 356
GDR (German Democratic Republic). *See* DDR
GEC, 232
"GEMU", 170
General Agreement on Tariffs and Trade (GATT), 34, 40, 44, 51, 67, 74
General Election of 1906, 203
General Election of 1945, 203
General Election of 1955, 10, 360
General Election of 1959, 12, 14, 360
General Election of 1964, 22, 269, 361
General Election of 1966, 47, 48
General Election of 1970, x, 57, 61, 62, 65, 74, 83, 86, 189, 197, 269, 270, 304, 333, 362
General Elections of 1974, 60, 78, 79, 85, 362
General Election of 1979, 88, 102, 125, 269, 332, 363
General Election of 1983, 125, 149, 265, 363
General Election of 1987, 141, 149, 305, 364
General Election of 1992, 179, 191, 200, 305, 365
General Election of 1997, ix, 1, 165, 191, 196, 200, 202, 203, 205, 207, 208, 212, 221, 222, 225, 366
General Election of 2001, 224, 232, 250, 251, 253, 366
General Election of 2005, 215, 233, 247, 250, 305, 367
General Election of 2010, 233, 264, 264n, 305, 306, 322, 338, 340, 368
Geneva, 72
Genoa, 303
Genscher, Hans-Dietrich, 117
Genscher-Colombo Report, 117, 118
George, Eddie (Sir Edward George), 201, 201n
Georgia, 324
German(s), 28, 36, 37, 39, 41, 69, 71, 103, 104, 105, 105n, 111, 115n, 117, 119, 121, 124, 132n, 135, 142, 157, 158, 161, 162, 169, 170, 171, 172, 177, 178, 180, 182, 184, 185, 186, 209, 210, 218, 219n, 227, 232, 236, 238, 245, 251, 261, 262, 263, 279, 280, 281, 285, 287, 308, 335, 343, 347, 349
German Constitutional Court, 262, 292
German question, 10, 36, 227
German re-unification, 141, 170, 183, 337, 365
Germany, 2, 6n, 8, 10, 12, 22, 29, 37, 46, 47, 69n, 87, 93n, 101, 103, 104, 111, 113, 117, 124, 132n, 135, 143n, 145, 162, 163, 170, 172, 181n, 200, 211, 219, 230, 262, 279, 282, 294, 295, 318, 328, 339, 344, 346, 355, 357, 360
Gershwin, Ira, 126n

Ghana, 39
Gibraltar, 156, 247
Gill, Christopher, 154, 201n
Gilmour, Ian (Baron Gilmour of Craigmillar), 73, 113
Giscard d'Estaing, Valéry; author of preamble to Constitution, 239; chairs Convention on Future of Europe, 213, 237, 367; complaints against chairmanship of, 239; dismissed by de Gaulle, 55; leads Independent Republican Party, 55; not alone in federal ambitions, 239; pushes through EMS, 161; seen as "enemy" by Thatcher, 113; sees himself as EU President, 263; Sir John Kerr "eminence grise" behind, 240; sits with Liberals in EP, 55; supports election of Commission President, 216; wants Constitution for US of Europe, 237
Giscardiens, 55, 62
Gladstone, William, 14
Gladwyn, Lord (Gladwyn Jebb, 1st Baron Gladwyn), 12, 79
Gloria, 259
Glorious Revolution of 1688, 307
Godkin lectures (Heath's), 276
Goethe, Johann Wolfgang von, 72
"gold-plating", 267, 311
Goldsmith, Beryl, 272
Goldsmith, Sir James, 86, 203, 271
Gorman, Teresa, 155, 201n, 317
gouvernement économique. See economic government/governance
Grande Illusion, La, 145
Gravesham, 179
Greater London Area Young Conservatives (GLYC), 30, 55, 56, 82, 149, 223, 271
Greece, 116, 172, 328, 355n, 363, 366
Greek(s), 94, 116, 117, 171, 180, 215n, 329, 353
Greek Central Bank, 171
Greek debt crisis, 334, 238, 339, 368
Greek/Iberian enlargement, 117
"green" Conservatism, 252, 323, 345
"green" currency/exchange rates, 124, 160, 277
Green Party/Greens, 149, 151, 220, 247, 254, 258, 259, 265, 366, 367, 368
Green/European Free Alliance Group, 150, 318
greenhouse gases, 149, 252, 297, 313
Greenland, 97, 314
Greenwood, David, 230
Griffiths, Sir Eldon, 97
Grimond, Jo (Joseph Grimond, Baron Grimond), 12
Group for the Recovery of the European Economy, 111
Group of the European People's Party and European Democrats (EPP-ED). *See* EPP-ED Group
Guardian, The, 109, 260, 262
Guildford, 8
Gummer, John Selwyn (Baron Deben), 56, 73, 199, 212, 293

habeas corpus, 242
Habib-Deloncle, Michel, 68
Hacker, James, 16
Hague, The. *See* The Hague
Hague Conference, 2, 359
Hague, William; and Portillo, 225; beats Clarke for leadership, 206, 366; brought in by "counter-revolution", 271; chairs committee on

European policy, 263; credit for holding Party together, 223; Foreign Secretary, 329; holds Party referendum on Europe, 221; includes pro-Europeans in team, 206; introduces rules for choosing Party leader, 251; leads negotiating team with Lib-Dems, 266; leaves leadership without becoming PM, 225, 226; met when back-bencher, 206; negotiates MEPs' relations with EPP, 158, 248, 253, 357; on "Simplifying Treaty" proposal, 244; "'Save the Pound' campaign ineffective", 224; shadow Foreign Secretary, 252, 335; shift of position on Europe under leadership, 207; speech to 2010 Party Conference in Birmingham, 326, 329, 330; succeeds John Major, 205; "Thatcher's children" generation, 205/6; two members of team resign, 222

Hailsham, Lord. *See* Hogg, Quintin (Lord Hailsham)

Hain, Peter, 85, 237, 245

Halifax, Lord, 181n

Hallstein, Prof. Walter, 37, 153

Hamilton, Willie, 43

Hammersmith/London Borough of/ Borough Council, 56, 85, 265, 313

Handbook for Europe, 194, 232

Hannan, Daniel, 109n, 183, 221, 222, 255, 260, 262, 273, 313, 315

Hanover summit of 1988, 138, 160, 162, 364

Hansard, 67

Hapsburg Empire, 282

Harbour, Malcolm, 256

"hard ecu", 164, 165, 190, 365

Hardie, Keir, 334

Harlech, Lord. *See* Ormsby-Gore, David

Harmar Nicholls (Baron Harmar-Nicholls), 70, 97, 98, 98n, 109

harmonisation, 75, 100, 124, 131, 132, 135, 138, 143, 144, 242, 278, 291, 316

Harris, David, 108, 109, 301

Harris, Ralph (Baron Harris of High Cross), 27

Harvard University, 276, 292

"H-block", 109, 109n, 118, 254n

Heads of State and Government, 117n, 118, 162, 217, 235, 279

Heath, Sir Edward (Ted); and Enoch Powell, 58, 271, 272; and Peter Walker, 272; and President Pompidou, 68; and Resale Price Maintenance, 46; and the Second World War, 3, 293; autobiography, 20; becomes Party leader, x, 41, 46, 52, 270, 271, 361; Chief Whip at time of Suez, 6n; conversation with Chauvel, 30; conversation with de Gaulle, 31; conversation with von Brentano, 287, 296; declines to stand for European Parliament, 97; Economic and Monetary Union, 71; "full-hearted consent of the British people", 58; General Election of 1970, 54, 57, 62, 333; General Election of February 1974, 84; Harvard University lectures, 292; Heath tradition, 221; Madron Seligman university friend, 29; maiden speech, 3; Minister of State for Europe/chief negotiator for EEC entry 24, 25, 27, 29, 31, 46; negotiations with Liberal Party, 85; no doubts about Community entry, 181, 293; "no question of eroding essential national sovereignty", 275; not concealing what membership meant, 276; on Eurosceptics, 187; on political dimension/ political union, 38, 294; on redressing Atlantic balance, 275; on surrender of sovereignty, 276; opposition to, attacks on, reputation in the Party, 83, 276, 350; pleasure in flattening anti-marketeers, 276; pragmatic pro-European Conservative, 354; Prime Minister, 270, 362; replaced as Conservative Party leader, 87, 362; Selsdon phase of government, 350; speech at 1962 Conservative Party Conference, 20; speech to 1966 YC national conference, 48; speech to British Chamber of Commerce in Paris, 58; Sterling in "snake in the tunnel", 160; studies de Gaulle, 29/30; terms of EC membership, 85, 269, 270; Teddy Taylor on, 276; Thatcher in Heath government, 152; votes for PR, 93; waiting in the wings, 8

Heathcoat-Amory, David, 237–43

Heathcoat-Amory, Derick (Viscount Amory), 237

Heaton-Harris, Christopher, 109n, 249

Heavy Goods Vehicles (HGVs), 123, 267

Hegel(ian), 63, 281,

Helmer, Roger, 50, 109n, 262

Helsinki, 214

Henley Centre for Forecasting, 141

Hennessy, Peter, 4, 5, 10

Hereford and Worcester, 97

Herman, Fernand, 113, 121, 157

Heseltine, Michael (Baron Heseltine); backed by MEPs, 174; Defence Secretary, 232; "fledgling federalism emerging", 210; ill-health rules out leadership candidacy, 206; mounts leadership challenge, 171; on Thatcher's Bruges speech, 152, 154; PEST, association with, 73; Portillo on, 203; resigns, 364; speech to ELEC in 1989, 139; Thatcher "determined to force resignation", 232; "thought (of leadership challenge) never crossed my mind", 232; welcomes work of ECJ, 139, 213; Westland Affair, 232

High Representative (of the Union) for the Common Foreign and Security Policy (CFSP), 235, 242, 263, 264, 235

High Tories, 180

Hill, Stephen, 174n

Hinchinbrooke, Viscount ('Hinch'), 49, 49n, 50, 288

Hindley, Brian, 236, 243

Hitler, Adolf, 181n, 272, 307n

Hix, Professor Simon, 290

Hogg, Quintin (Baron Hailsham of St Marylebone), 3, 26, 346

Hogg, Sarah, 174n

Hola Camp, 307

Holmes, Dr. Martin, 174n

Holy Roman Empire, 353

home country control, 135

Home of the Hirsel, Lord. *See* Douglas-Home, Sir Alec

Home Office, 198

Hong Kong, 349

"Honorary Members of the European Parliament", 197

Hooper, Gloria (Baroness Hooper), 103

Hord, Brian, 109

Hordern, Sir Peter, 166

Hornsby-Smith, Dame Patricia, 34

Hoskyns, Sir John, 144, 145, 151, 155, 364

House of Commons Select Committee on Direct Elections, 93

House of Commons Select Committee on European Legislation /European Scrutiny Committee, 110, 176, 267, 311, 330

House of Lords Select Committee on the European Communities/European Scrutiny Committee 60, 95, 109, 290

Howard, Michael (Baron Howard of Lympne); "a position behind which our party can rally", 212; attacks drinking water Directive, 297; "Cambridge Mafia", 212; Home Secretary, 199; leadership candidate 1997, 206; Minister for Water and Planning, 213n; "no fixed *acquis*", 213, 315; on enlargement, 214; on subsidiarity, 290; on the ECJ, 213, 214; Party leader, 212, 226, 367; resigns Party leadership, 251; speech in Berlin, 212; *The Future of Europe* paper, 212, 248, 296; "wants to avoid massive row", 249

Howe, Geoffrey (Baron Howe of Aberavon); abolishes exchange controls, 121, 363; Bow Group generation, 36; Chancellor of the Exchequer, 36, 113; Deputy Prime Minister, 170; EMU, views on, 160, 162; ERM entry, views on, 126, 161, 166, 167; Foreign Secretary, 151; key role in making Conservatives "party of Europe", 293; metric system, introduction of, 298; on establishing a Common Market, 129; on loss of sovereignty, 276; on Lord Cockfield, 130; on supremacy of EU law, 276; on Thatcher's Bruges speech, 151; pragmatic pro-Europe Conservative, 354; pressure on Thatcher, 271; recalls Chancellor at 1990 conference, 268; resignation letter, 170; resignation speech, 170; seen as "soft cop", 113; Solicitor General, 67, 276; Westland Affair, views on, 231

Howe/Lawson "ambush", 166

Howell, David (Lord Howell of Guildford); *Crossbow* article 1960, 8, 24; Director of CPC, 52, 272; disillusioned with EU membership, 272; in favour of ERM entry, 166, 168; letter to *the Economist*, 272; Minister, 8; MP for Guildford, 8; PEST association, 73; young Bow Grouper, 8

Howell, Paul, 79, 109

Howell, Sir Ralph, 79

Huckfield, Les, 145, 145n

Hugo, Victor, 72

Human Rights Act 1998, 89, 243

Human Rights and Foreign Policy, 88

Hume, John, 104

Hungarian Democratic Forum, 259

Hungary/Hungarian, 179, 245, 260, 367

Hunt, David (Baron Hunt of Wirral), 350

Hurd, Douglas (Baron Hurd of Westwell); "a temple not a tree", 174; Foreign Secretary, 100; heads Leader of Opposition office, 68; Home Secretary, 232; Major's view of Sir John Kerr, 240; "middle-of-the-road", 203; "nooks and crannies" remark, 44, 193, 365; on Maastricht Treaty, 174; on MEPs' links with Westminster, 100, 109; on Thatcher's views on Europe, 87; on Westland affair, 232; pragmatic approach to Europe, 336; "received rapturously" by backbenchers, 176; "winning the argument" claim, 286; writing on Foreign Policy issues, 296

Hutton, Alasdair, 108

Hyde Park Tory/ies, 56, 179

Iceland, 14n, 313, 314, 339, 362, 366, 368

IEA. *See* Institute of Economic Affairs (IEA)

Imperial Chemical Industries (ICI), 18

"imperial overstretch", 289

Imperial Preference, 14/15

Imperialism/ist, 3, 20, 116, 181n, 302, 307, 308, 353

incomes policy, 59, 82

Independent, The, 205, 260

Independent High Level Study Group, 211

Independent Republican Party, 55

industrial democracy, 350

industrial revolution, the, 307

Industrial Society, 128n

Ingham, Sir Bernard, 152

Inglewood, Lord (Richard Fletcher-Vane, 2nd Baron Inglewood), 139, 140, 198, 213

Inland Revenue, 130

Institute of Directors (IoD), 142, 143, 144, 151, 364

Institute of Directors' European Advisory Council, 143, 144

Institute of Economic Affairs (IEA), 15, 27, 66, 74, 144, 155, 164n, 278, 328

Institutional Affairs Committee of the European Parliament, 118, 120

inter-governmental(ism), 9, 10, 11, 44, 135, 291, 154, 175, 181, 200, 217, 235, 242, 279, 285n, 286, 296, 311, 330, 336, 339

Inter-Governmental Conference(s) (IGC), 136, 137, 171, 174, 212n, 214, 237, 243, 244, 245, 364

Internal Market Committee of the European Parliament, 256

Internal Market Council, 142

International Association of Former Officials of the European Communities (AIACE), 147n

International Court of Justice, 285

International Democrat Union (IDU), 95

International Institute for Strategic Studies, 230

international law, 83, 178, 217, 281, 285, 285n, 286, 288

International Law of God, 14

International Monetary Fund (IMF), 34, 160n, 368

International Women's Democrat Union, 95

International Young Democrat Union, 95

Inuit, 97

IoD. *See* Institute of Directors (IoD)

Iran, 228n

Iraq, 39, 228n, 365

Ireland, 14, 14n, 68, 161, 211, 241, 245, 299, 308, 314, 327, 330, 343n, 367, 368

Irish, (the), 69, 70, 89, 92, 124, 236, 238, 245, 261, 309, 366

Irish Punt, 168

Iron Curtain, 5, 63, 153

Isle of Man, 70, 89, 90, 247, 285, 314

isoglucose case. See *SA Roquette Frères v. Council of the European Communities*

Israel, 6n, 260, 303n

Italian(s), 39, 71, 95, 105, 111, 117, 118, 134, 137, 232, 254, 259, 260, 281, 303, 309

Italian Christian Democrats, 104, 157, 343, 347

Italian Communist Party, 116

Italian lira, 168

Italy, 8, 12, 22, 23, 87, 101, 117, 161, 184, 201, 239, 312, 318, 357

ITV, 104

Jackson, Caroline, 260, 284n

Jackson, Christopher, 120, 122, 130, 196, 207, 221, 290

Jackson, Robert, 96, 207, 284, 284n, 285

Jacobinism, 283

Jacobitism, 14

Jacques, Martin, 282n, 284

Japan, 74, 97, 119, 278

Jay, Douglas (Baron Jay), 51
Jenkin, Patrick (Baron Jenkin of Roding), 13, 73, 295
"Jenkinsites", 270
Jenkins, Roy (Baron Jenkins of Hillhead); biography of Churchill, 2, 3; chairs Britain in Europe, 86; ensures passage of European Communities Act 1972, x, 70; launches European Monetary System, 161; leadership of Labour pro-Europeans, x, 51, 70; on Churchill and British participation in European integration, 3; on Churchill and Hague conference, 2; on Churchill's speech in Place Kléber, 3; on Macmillan, 19; President of the Commission, 88, 363
Jennings, Sir Ivor, 348
Jesus College, Cambridge, 212
John Paul II, Pope, 349n
John XXIII, Pope, 349n
Johns Hopkins University, 351
Johnson, Boris, 70, 252
Johnson, Christopher, 44
Johnson, Nevil, 209, 210, 211, 214
Johnson, Stanley, 70, 109
Johnston, Russell (Baron Russell-Johnston), 88
Joseph, Sir Keith (2nd Baronet and Baron Joseph), 16, 141, 208, 215, 350
Judd, Denis, 7, 307
judicial activism, 139
Jung Union, 103, 343
Junior Imperial League, 5
jurisdiction-shopping, 328
juste retour, 113

Kaczyński, Jarosław, 255
Kaczyński, Lech, 255, 261
Kamiński, Michal, 260, 261
Kangaroo(s), Kangaroo Group, 118, 119, 119n, 120, 124, 134, 141, 157, 210
kangaroo meat, 39
Kant, Emmanuel, 72
Kedouri, Elie, 282
Keeler, Christine, 27
Keep Britain Out, 15, 66
Kellett-Bowman, Edward, 97
Kellett-Bowman, Dame Elaine, 79, 97, 99
"Ken and Eddie show", 201
Kennedy, Paul, 289
Kennedy, President, 7, 40, 45, 294, 361
Kennedy Round, 34, 40, 51
"Kennedy Toryism", 45
Kensington Palace Gardens, 71, 82, 101
Kent, 96, 123, 130, 158, 198, 207, 221, 223, 226, 312
Kent County Council, 110, 289
Kent Cox's Orange Pippins, 122
Kent East, 120, 196, 221, 290
Kent EUW, 103
Kent West, ix, 96, 96n, 103, 104, 110, 127, 150, 188, 194, 195, 196, 208, 221
Kent West Conservative Euro-Council, 102, 158, 198
Kenya, 307
Kerr, Sir John, 239
Keynesian orthodoxy, 109
Kilmuir. *See* Maxwell Fyfe, Sir David (1st Earl of Kilmuir)
Kilroy-Silk, Robert, 248, 249, 257
King, Tom (Baron King of Bridgwater), 216, 217
Kinnock, Neil (Baron Kinnock), 127, 155, 179n, 218

Kirk, Sir Peter, 8, 68, 78, 79, 80, 94, 302, 355
Kirkhope, Timothy, 244, 260
Kissinger Question, 241, 263, 339
Kissinger, Henry, 30, 241
Kitzinger, Uwe, 86
Klaus, Václav, 215, 254, 255, 261, 368
Klepsch, Egon, 115n, 158, 344
Knapman, Roger, 208
Kohl, Helmut, 142, 169, 170, 174, 176
Konrad Adenauer Stiftung, 174, 176
Kosovo, 339
Kyoto Protocol, 297, 367

Labour left, 53, 86, 138, 155, 227, 271, 296, 304, 306
Labour Party, (*see also* New Labour), ix, x, 8, 28, 46, 51, 54, 61, 66, 71, 78, 80, 83, 85, 88, 92, 96, 97, 98, 101, 104, 111, 125, 126, 127, 150, 151, 155, 182, 189, 195, 198, 200, 208, 218, 226, 227, 240, 258, 266, 269, 284n, 303, 305, 318, 325, 334, 341, 350
Labour Party's National Executive Committee (NEC), 304
Laeken Declaration, 213, 237, 367
Laeken European Council, 213
laissez faire, 333
Lamassoure, Alain, 245
Lambeth, London Borough of, 56
Lamfalussy, Alexandre, 329n
Lamfalussy committees, 329
Lamont, Norman (Baron Lamont of Lerwick); at Maastricht negotiations, 171; Black Wednesday, 182, 183; Budget speech 1991, 167; candidate for Kingston, 274; chairs Finance Ministers meeting in Bath, 184; Chancellor of the Exchequer, 137, 171, 182, 201; contribution to recovery undermined, 201; "Cambridge Mafia", 212; favours Bank of England independence, 201; "never taken those words seriously", 274; on subsidiarity, 290, 292; on ERM membership, 165; on re-alignment within ERM, 184; on the "democratic deficit", 137; proved right on recovery, 201n; "received rapturously" by backbenchers, 176; replaced as Chancellor, 365
Lancashire West, 207
Länder, 279, 280, 292
Latin America, 345, 347
Latvia(n), 260, 299, 367
Latvian National Independence Movement (TB/LNNK), 259
Law and Justice Party (PiS), 255, 259, 261
Lawson, Dominic, 41
Lawson, Nigel (Baron Lawson of Blaby); Chancellor of the Exchequer, 126, 166; ERM "best way to ensure discipline", 166, 169; ERM entry timing wrong, 167, 168; father of Dominic Lawson, 41; favours Bank of England independence, 166; favours joining EMS/ERM, 126, 167; Financial Secretary to the Treasury, 114; "in cahoots" with Howe, 166; Madrid summit "ambush", 166, 364; on Heseltine resignation, 232; party to Plaza Accord, 166; proposes competing currencies, 164; rejects Labour solution to budget problem, 114; shadows D-Mark, 127, 162, 166; succeeded by Major, 164; supported by complete spectrum of Party/"fashionable consensus", 166; "when the time is ripe", 126n
Leading Europe into the 1990s, 163

League of Empire Loyalists, 6, 20, 32, 307
Leavis, Dr. F.R., 333
Legal Affairs Committee of the European
    Parliament, 20, 139, 272/3
legal personality, 241, 285, 285n
Legge-Bourke, Sir Harry, 275n
Leigh-Pemberton, Robin (Baron Kingsdown), 168
Lellouche, Pierre, 262, 263
Leo XIII, Pope, 349
León, 156
Letwin, Oliver, 209, 210, 252, 274, 275
Levy, David, 57
Lewandowski, Janusz, 338
Lewis, Russell; attacks "anti-European backlash",
    57; Commission "riddled with corruption", 217,
    218; Director of CPC, 34, 35, 57; disillusioned
    with EU membership, 272; "fillip of increased
    competition", 36, 294; free-marketeer, 155;
    greatness of Europe its diversity, 288, 289; in
    London Commission office, 55; Swinton lecture
    on Britain and Commonwealth, 34; on defects
    of EU, 248; on nationalism, 308; on Treaty of
    Rome, 75; *Rome or Brussels…?*, 74, 75, 273;
    subsidiarity "a fraud", 292; supports Monetary
    Union, 75; *The Myth of Europe*, 216
Liberal Democrat(s), ix, 47n, 73, 195, 196, 203,
    207, 220, 224, 225, 247, 249, 251, 258, 258n, 260,
    264–7, 318, 322, 323, 325, 326, 335, 336, 338, 340,
    341, 366–8
Liberal Democrat 2010 manifesto, 266
Liberal Party/Liberal(s), 6, 12, 14, 15,16, 54, 55, 62,
    78, 79, 85, 88, 92, 93, 94, 96n, 98, 104, 105, 120,
    125, 180, 203, 318, 334, 347, 348, 349, 350, 362
Liberals (and Allies) in Europeal Parliament, 55,
    78, 95, 109, 158, 254, 260, 344
liberalism, 15, 133, 145, 158, 333, 344, 346, 347, 351
Lib-Lab, 334
Lidington, David, 326, 330
Liechtenstein, 14n, 313, 314, 365, 366
Lijst Dedeker (LDD), 259
Lilley, Peter, 50, 81, 138, 155, 166, 206, 289
Lincoln, 78
LINGUA programme, 151
Lisbon, 214, 245
Lisbon Treaty, 39, 43, 67, 103, 135, 175n, 190, 212n,
    241–6, 255, 260–4, 266, 279, 280, 285, 285n, 286,
    287, 291, 292, 311, 314–16, 319, 325–7, 329, 330,
    336, 338, 339, 341, 356, 357, 367, 368
Lithuania, 367
Lithuanian LLLRA, 259
Liverpool, 103, 104
Liverpool University, 5
Llandudno Conference of 1962, 20
Lloyd, Pauline, 103
Lloyd, Sir Peter, 212
Lloyd, Selwyn. *See* Selwyn Lloyd (Baron
    Selwyn-Lloyd),
Locke, John, 217
Łódź, 6n, 214
loi Fillon, 282
Lomas, Alf, 155
Lomé Convention, 363
London, 27, 30, 55–7, 65, 70, 72, 82, 95, 96, 96n, 97,
    116, 154, 156, 169, 207, 210, 265, 298, 303, 313
London and Paris Agreements, 10
London Business School, 129
London, City of. *See* City of London
London (Information) Office of the Community/
    Commission, 55, 70, 87, 302
London Information Office of the European
    Parliament, 71, 82, 101, 103, 303n
London School of Economics (LSE), 18, 49n, 130,
    208, 290
Louis XIV, 281
Luce, Richard (Baron Luce), 88, 89
"lump of labour" fallacy, 120/1
Lutheran, 344
Lutheran and Calvinist churches, 345
Luxembourg, 4,70, 71, 80, 81, 82, 89, 90, 98, 101,
    102, 108n, 109, 113, 118, 121, 137, 173n, 186, 197,
    198, 208, 214, 221, 243, 278, 303, 346, 359
Luxembourg compromise, 64, 139, 310, 361
Luxembourg summit, 363
Lyon, 55, 60

Maastricht Bill, 185, 187
Maastricht negotiations, 165, 174, 296
Maastricht rebels/rebellion, 70, 185, 190, 196, 225,
    316, 336
Maastricht summit of 1991, 82, 171, 174
Maastricht Treaty, 54n, 72, 112, 137, 154, 165,
    171–80, 183–8, 190, 193, 196, 199, 208, 219, 221,
    235, 240, 241, 254, 271, 279, 285n, 289, 290, 291,
    300, 315, 325, 341, 354, 356, 365
Macdonald, Alexander, 334
MacGregor, John (Baron MacGregor of Pulham
    Market) , 23, 166
Machiavelli, Niccolò, 240
Macleod Group, 73, 207
Macleod, Iain, 36, 46, 56, 58, 72, 131, 271
Macmillan, Harold (1st Earl of Stockton); and
    the Kennedy administration, 45; application/
    negotiations to join EEC, ix, 6, 12, 16, 18, 19,
    21, 31, 73, 269, 270, 272, 284, 293, 304, 307,
    308; attacked by Gaitskell, x; Continental and
    Anglo-Saxon traditions, 9, 20, 40, 142, 211,
    306; "Conservative planning", 59; "customary
    processes", 46n; de Gaulle's veto, 7, 28, 31, 40;
    decolonisation policy, 49; discussion of tactics
    with Heath, 29; ECSC, views on, 3; election
    victory, 1959, 12; "emerges" as Conservative
    Party leader, 46; "events", 336, 336n; Foreign
    Secretary, 11; genuine support for European
    vision, 19; Messina Conference, views on,
    11; Nassau agreement, 30; "night of the long
    knives", 27; "never had it so good", 12n; "no
    Disraeli to my Peel", 20; on de Gaulle, 30; on
    federation and confederation, 280; on Imperial
    tradition, 181; on the anti-Marketeers, 20; on
    the press, 20; "only partially a European", 19;
    Prime Minister, 346, 350, 360; Rambouillet
    meeting with de Gaulle, 30; reputation for
    competence destroyed, 332; son-in-law Julian
    Amery, 3; succeeded by Sir Alec Douglas-
    Home, x, 34, 361; *The Middle Way*, 72; visitor to
    Swinton, 19; "wind of change" speech, 12, 361;
    would "lead country back to Europe", 8; US
    pressure on, 15
Madden, Martin, 24
Madrid, 156
Madrid summit of 1989, 138, 162, 166, 364
Magna Carta, 242, 298, 306
Maier, Hans, 340
Maitland, the Hon. Patrick (17th Earl of
    Lauderdale), 21
Major, Sir John; "all the quality of a rain-dance",
    185; and Helmut Kohl, 174; "at the heart of
    Europe", 174n, 182, 193, 266, 365; "bastards",

225; "behaved like a Chief Whip", 205; belief in Major Plan, 165; Black Wednesday, 182, 183, 184, 185; BSE, 199; challenged by Redwood, 206, 225, 366; Chancellor of the Exchequer, 164, 166; *Conservative Europe*, article in, 298; Conservative leadership, 174, 271; credible middle way, 205; Edinburgh Summit, 186; Ellesmere Port Address, 213, 286; ERM legacy, 183, 201; "Euro-realist", 205; Eurosceptic attacks/rebellion, 198, 263, 271; "federal objective" of EU, 169, 274; "game, set and match", 82, 176, 240; general election 1997, 201, 202, 203; joining the ERM, 166, 167, 168; "lack of Eurosceptic backbone", 208; Maastricht negotiations/Treaty, 176, 185, 187, 296, 315; Major government/years, 179, 183, 188, 206, 225, 237, 252, 290, 340, 342; "middle-of-the-road", 203; objective "keeping the Party together", 166; on break-up of Yugoslavia, 180; on Eurosceptics, 154, 187, 188, 298; on exchange controls, 122; on moves to a single currency, 171, 185; on "interference in nooks and crannies", 193; on the Danes, 186; on Sir John Kerr, 240; "opt-in" agreement on EMU, 172, 305, 315; pragmatic approach to Europe, 336, 354; subsidiarity principle, 189; succeeds Thatcher, 365; succeeded by Hague, 205, 206, 366; vetoes Dehaene, 239; "vote-free" recovery, 200, 201; "winning the argument", 235, 286, 287, 291; wins 1992 general election, 179, 200; Young Conservative and Lambeth councillor, 56
Major Plan, 164, 165, 169, 190, 365
Malta, 367, 368
Manchester, 293
Manchester Tory Reform Group, 73
Mandarin, 97
Mandelson, Peter (Baron Mandelson), 202n, 207n, 226, 264n, 327
Manila Pact, 228n
Mann, Thomas, 72
Mannheim University, 278
Mannin, Michael, 288
Margate Conference 1953, 5
Marjolin, Robert, 117n
Market Research Society, 179
Marlow, Tony, 155, 201n
Marr, Andrew, 28
Marshall Plan, 7, 359
Marten, Neil, 66, 87, 92n
Martens, Wilfried, 350, 352, 354
Martin, Michael, 257
Marxism/ist, 15, 172 , 312, 344, 345, 346, 347, 351
Marxism Today, 282n
matching money, 123
Mater et Magistra, 349n
Matthews, Rupert, 249, 250
Mau Mau, 307
Maude, Angus (Baron Maude of Stratford-upon-Avon), 275n
Maude, Francis, 155
Maudling, Reginald/Maudling negotiations, 13, 46, 209, 277, 360, 361
Maxwell Fyfe, Sir David (1st Earl of Kilmuir), 4, 11, 24, 25, 89
May, Theresa, 252, 336
Mayhew, Christopher (Baron Mayhew), 62
Mayhew, Sir Patrick (Baron Mayhew of Twysden), 56, 102, 232

Mayne, Richard, 87
McAlpine, Alistair, 86, 203, 271
McLaughlin, Diarmid, 55, 55n
McMahon Act, 229, 229n
McMillan-Scott, Edward, 207, 248, 253, 260, 357
media, the, 80, 82, 112, 115, 123, 150, 217, 220, 224, 248, 250, 252, 257, 258, 260, 262, 301–3
Medway unitary authority, 289
Medway Conservative Association, 198
Menon, Prof. Anand, 15, 154
mercantile tradition, 40
Merger Treaty, 54n, 362
Merkel, Angela, 245, 263, 279, 335
Messina Conference, 9, 11, 12, 360
Meyer, Sir Anthony (3rd Baronet), 47–50
Middle East, 48, 82, 180, 297
Mid-Kent, 110
Milan summit 1985, 137, 364
Miliband, David, 263, 264n
Miliband, Ed, 270
Milošević, Slobodan, 180
Minc, Alain, 145
Ministry of Agriculture, Fisheries and Food (MAFF), 122
Minoprio, Peter, 32n
Minority Parties Unit, 249
Mitbestimmung, 206, 349
Mittelstand, 121
Mitterand, President François, 153, 169, 170, 176, 186
Moate, Sir Roger, 154
Moldova, 215, 339
Mollet, Guy, 6n
Moloney, Anne, 195
Monaco, 285
Monckton, Walter (1st Viscount Monckton of Brenchley), 350
Monday Club, 35, 49, 50, 51, 72, 155, 226n, 227, 289, 295, 361
Monday World, 49, 57
Monetary Committee of EC, 167, 183, 184
Monetary Compensatory Amounts (MCAs), 124n, 160, 277, 362
Monetary Cooperation Fund, 160
Monetary Union (*see also* Economic and Monetary Union), 75, 144, 160, 163, 165, 169, 172, 190, 362
Monetary Union Task Force, 221
Monnet, Jean, 1, 11, 37, 40, 54, 175, 251, 274, 275
Montagu. *See* Hinchingbrooke, Viscount ('Hinch')
Montenegro, 339
Montesquieu, Charles Louis de Secondat, Baron de, 217
Montevideo Convention, 281
Montgomeryshire, 265
Moorhouse, James, 207
Mori poll, 236
Morris, James, 6
Morrison, Herbert (Baron Morrison of Lambeth), 331
Moscow, 172, 214, 242
Mounier, Emmanuel, 343n
Mouvement pour la France, 254
Movement for European Reform, 254
multiculturalism, 215
Mundell, Prof. Robert, 185
Murdoch, Rupert, 155, 179, 301
Mussolini, Benito, 241
mutual recognition, principle of, 131, 132, 135, 278, 291, 316

NAFTA. *See* North Atlantic Free Trade Area (NAFTA)
nanny state, 333
Narjes, Karl-Heinz, 134
Nassau Agreement, 30, 31
Nasser, Gamal Abdel, 6n
nation state(s), 26, 43, 61, 74, 76, 154, 177, 178, 194, 200, 212, 215, 218, 240, 242, 254, 259, 281–5, 288, 308, 316, 326, 328, 342, 353
National Common Market Petition Council, 307
National Economic Development Council (NEDC or 'Neddy'), 35n, 37, 97
National Farmers Union (NFU), 87, 97, 112, 122
National Incomes Commission (NIC or 'Nicky'), 37
national parliament(s), 40, 44, 45, 67, 91, 92, 94, 117, 131, 136, 146n, 177, 178, 200, 215, 238, 41, 292, 310, 311, 329, 339
National Referendum Campaign, 87, 88, 90
National Union of Conservative and Constitutional Associations, 352
National Union of Conservative and Unionist Associations, 187
Nationalist government of South Africa, 331
NEA ΔHMOKPATIA (Nea Demokratia – New Democracy), 355n
Neave, Airey, 102
Neighbourhood Policy, the EU's, 324
neo-Conservatives, 180
neo-liberal, 350
Netherlands, 4, 6n, 117n, 240, 244, 339, 347, 348, 359, 367
new Commonwealth, 23
New Labour, ix, 196, 201, 205, 207, 223, 270, 300, 306, 356, 365
New Statesman, The, 260, 340
New Zealand, 13, 26, 228n, 327
New Zealand butter, 19, 294
News of the World, The, 155/6
Newsletter (my), 122
Newton, Sir Isaac, 9, 211
Newton-Dunn, Bill, 207, 258n
NFU. *See* National Farmers Union
Nice and Beyond, 274
Nice Treaty, 235, 236, 240, 243, 244, 279, 330, 356, 366, 367
Nicholson, Emma (Baroness Nicholson of Winterbourne), 207
Nicholson, James (Jim), 157, 259
Nicolson, Sir David, 97
Nigeria, 39
Nineteen Eighty-four, 40
"Nixon in China", 337n
Nixon, President Richard, 228
"No Turning Back" (Group), 155, 253
Non-Governmental Organisations (NGOs), 217
"non-political Conservatives", 189
"nooks and crannies of everyday life", 44, 193, 356, 365
Nordic, 211
Nordic Free Trade Area, 313
Norfolk/Norfolk North, 79
Norman Conquest, 240
Normanton, Sir Tom, 79, 97, 99, 229, 293
North Atlantic Free Trade Area (NAFTA), 57, 313
North Atlantic Treaty, 10, 227
North Atlantic Treaty Organisation (NATO), 10, 31, 40, 48, 74, 180, 215, 228–33, 250, 294, 359
Northam, Sir Reginald, 18

Northamptonshire, 123
Northern Ireland, 69, 85, 88, 89, 92, 93, 94, 97, 101, 104, 124, 157, 220, 259
Northern League, 259
Norway, 14n, 68, 210, 215, 286, 313, 314, 361, 362, 366
No Tame or Minor Role, 35, 38, 39, 44, 60, 73
Notes on Current Politics, 100, 115
Nott, Sir John, 81, 212
Notting Hill Tories, 252, 271
Nouvelles Equipes Internationales (NEI), 95
nuclear energy, 47
"nuclear umbrella", 227
nuclear weapon(s)/deterrent, 9, 29, 30, 31, 41, 51, 114, 227, 227n, 228, 229, 233, 295, 336
Nuffield College, Oxford, 209
Nutting, Sir Anthony, 6n

O'Hagan, Charles (4th Baron O'Hagan), 79
O'Neill, Sir Con, 62
O'Sullivan, John, 215, 216, 287
Oakeshott, Michael, 332
Oakley, Robert, 223
Occitan, 282, 319n
ODS. *See* Civic Democratic Party
OEEC. *See* Organisation for European Economic Cooperation (OEEC)
official languages, 117, 330
Old Etonians, 252
One Europe, 41, 42, 272
One Nation Conservatism/Toryism, 72, 187, 190, 317, 334, 346, 349, 350, 352, 357
One Nation Group, 21, 35, 41, 272
"Open for Business" campaign, 141, 142, 144
Opinion Research Centre (OPR) poll, 104
organic view of society, 345
Organisation for Economic Cooperation and Development (OECD), 47, 361
Organisation for European Economic Cooperation (OEEC), 7, 9, 11, 359, 361
Ormsby-Gore, David (5th Baron Harlech), 63
Orwell, George, 40, 193
Osborn, John, 98, 99
Österreichische Volkspartei, 349n
Ostmark, 170
Oswestry, 61, 63
Our Future in Europe, 88
Our Future in Europe: the long term case, 57
Oxford University, 11, 27, 177, 208, 209, 229, 349, 353
ozone layer, 149

Paisley, Ian (Baron Bannside), 104, 108
Pakistan, 228n
Palace of Europe, 108
Palace of Westminster, 110
Palmer, John, 109
Palmerston, Lord (Henry John Temple, 3rd Viscount Palmerston), 180, 180n
Palmerstonian, 180n, 181
pan-Germanism, 37
Pannella, Marco, 111
Panorama, 124n
Papini, Roberto, 348
parallel currency, 163, 164, 365
Paris, 12, 23, 30, 44, 51, 58, 67, 71, 72, 80, 82, 97, 141
Paris Agreement, 10
Paris, Treaty of, 360
Parkinson, Cecil (Baron Parkinson), 166, 259

Parkinson, C. Northcote, 289n
Parkinson's Law, 289, 289n
Parliamentary Group on the Common Market, 66
Parliament (European) officials, 256
Partido Popular (PP), 156, 256, 343
Part-time Work Directive, 121
Party Conference of 1971, 62
passerelle, 266, 329, 330
Patijn, Schelto, 91
Patten, Chris (Baron Patten of Barnes), 149, 297, 342, 349
Patterson, Ben, 109n, 157n, 309
Patterson, Dr.Ethel (*née* Simkins), 5
Patterson, Prof. Eric, 5
Patterson, Felicity (*née* Raybould), 56n, 61, 85, 170
"P-block", 109n
Peace of Augsburg, 281n
Peace of Westphalia, 281
People's Europe (Adonino) Report, 364
People's Europe committee, 134
Pearce, Andrew, 109
Pears, Gordon, 42, 43, 44
Pearson, F.F., 28, 31
Peel, Sir Robert, 14, 20, 288, 333, 342n
Personalist movement, 345n
Perspectives et Réalités, 55
PEST. *See* Pressure for Economic and Social Toryism (PEST)
Peterborough column, 301
Petherick, Miss V.B., 309
Peyrefitte, Alain, 24
Philadelphia, 237
Philippines, 228n
Philips, 119
Picasso, Pablo, 72
Pilsudski, Marshal Józef , 6
Pinder, John, 55
Pinochet, Augusto, 347
Pinto-Duschinsky, Michael, 57, 189
Pitt, William, 7, 7n, 180, 225
Pittite Tory, 180
Pittsburgh, G20 meeting in, 337
Pius XI, Pope, 349n
Plaid Cymru (Welsh Nationalists), 220, 258, 308, 366, 367, 368
"Plan G", 13
Plantagenets, 34
Plaza Agreement, 166
Pleven Plan, 3, 10
Pleven, René, 359
Plumb, Sir Henry (Baron Plumb); candidate in first EP elections, 87, 97; chairs EP Agriculture Committee, 112; in "P-block", 109n; leads European Democratic Group, 295; on European defence, 229; President of European Parliament, 87, 364; President of NFU, 97
Pöhl, Otto, 164, 165, 169
Poland, 5, 6n, 179, 181n, 214, 243, 255, 259, 261, 267, 368
Polaris, 26, 27
Policy Studies Institute (PSI), 48
Polish, 6, 6n, 260, 261, 282, 326
Polish chief rabbi, 260
Polish Revival Party (NOP), 260
Political and Economic Planning (PEP), 55, 55n
political consultants in Brussels, 145
Pompidou, Georges, 54, 68, 362
Port Stanley, 123
Portillo, Michael, 138, 155, 203, 225, 252, 253

"Portillo moment", 203
Portugal, 14n, 116, 126, 156, 361, 364
Portuguese, 117, 245, 254
Postponed Accounting System (PAS), 143, 143n
Potato Marketing Board, 299
Pounder, Rafton, 78
pound sterling/Sterling, ix, 71, 121, 122, 126, 127, 160, 165–9, 172, 182–5, 201, 221, 222n, 224, 250, 335, 341, 365
Powell, Charles (Baron Powell of Bayswater), 138
Powell, Enoch; "apologist for amnesia", 61; analysed by Utley, 59; attacked by Cash over SEA, 138; author of *One Europe*, 41; Biffen his disciple, 61; convert to anti-Market cause, 60; defeated by Heath in leadership contest, 46, 271, 361; in shadow cabinet, 58; influence on economic policy, 56, 58; need for "common allegiance", 60, 215, 238, 287, 301, 312, 319; on direct elections to the European Parliament, 92, 110, 287, 313, 318; on exchange rates, 185; on sovereignty, 25, 40, 154, 284; opposes Common Market membership, 65, 69, 73; principal objective "to destroy British membership of the ECC", 60, 272; no illusions about Empire/ Commonwealth, 59; refuses to serve under Douglas-Home, 271; "rivers of blood" speech, 60, 362; speech on defence to 1967 Conservative Party conference, 59; speech on Mau Mau detainees, 307; speeches in European cities, 60; "state worship in the German manner", 285; support for EEC membership "on grounds of trade", 273; supports my candidature in Wrexham, 61; Ulster Unionist MP, 86; votes for Wilson-Brown EEC application, 59
"Power of the Purse", the, 44, 216
"pound in your pocket", the, 52n
PR. *See* Proportional Representation (PR)
Practice of Management, The, 290
Prag, Derek, 55, 57, 100, 109n, 118, 159, 180
Prague, 152, 214
Prague Declaration, 259
"Prague Spring", 63
Pressure for Economic and Social Toryism (PEST), 35, 72, 73, 295
Price Commission, 131
Price, Peter, 109n, 207, 355
Price, Roy, 55
Pride of Kent, The, 130
Priestley, Sir Julian, 256
Primarolo Group, 279
Primarolo, Dawn, 279n
Prior, James (Baron Prior of Brampton), 27, 28
private ecu, 163
Private Eye, 66, 141
Prodi Commission, 218
Prodi, Romano, 216
Pro-euro Conservative Party, 207, 222
Profumo, John/Profumo Affair, 27
property-owning democracy, 333
Proportional Representation (PR), 93, 105n, 194, 208, 215, 220, 258
proportionality, principle of, 291, 292
Protection(ism/ist), 14, 15, 74, 100, 136, 144, 153, 199, 277, 278, 309, 317, 324, 327, 331
Protestant(s), 281, 344, 347, 348
"Protestant North", 211
Proust, Marcel, 72

Prout, Christopher (Lord Kingsland), 109n, 176–8, 194, 281, 355
Provan, Jimmy, 109n
"pursuit of excellence", 333
Purvis, John, 109n
Putting Britain First, 248
Putting Britain Right Ahead, 48
Putney, 85
Pyrenees, the, 8n

Quadragesimo Anno, 349n
Quai d'Orsay, 16n
Qualified Majority Vote (QMV), 136, 137, 139, 214, 279, 310, 311, 315, 329, 355
Quantas, 119n
Questions of Policy Committee, 150, 194

Radical Toryism/Tory Radicalism, 333
Raison, Sir Timothy (Tim), 73
Rambouillet, 30
Randzio-Plath, Christa, 219n
Ranelagh, John, 88, 89
rapporteur, 93n, 114, 114n, 118, 121, 129, 131, 134, 143n, 157, 172, 183, 256, 278, 355
Rawls, John, 283n
REACH (Registration, Evaluation and Authorisation of Chemicals), 297
realignment (in ERM), 161, 168, 183, 184
Reay, Lord (Hugh William Mackay, 14th Lord Reay), 79, 99
Rechtsstaat, 287
red tape, 124
Redwood, John, 155, 166, 206, 225, 366
Rees-Mogg, William (Baron Rees-Mogg), 25, 26, 27, 272, 275, 288
"reference to standards" approach, 132
"referendum lock", 329, 330, 331
Referendum Party, 65, 86, 203, 271, 318
Reform Treaty, 245
Reformation, the, 307
Regional Fund, 123
regional party lists, 93
Regions, Committee of. *See* Committee of the Regions
regions, devolution of power to, 175n
Reith Lecture, 10
Renfrew, Colin (Baron Renfrew of Kaimsthorn), 212
Repair: Plan for social reform, 351
repatriation of powers (from EU), 84, 213, 214, 222, 297, 305, 336
representative democracy, 312
Republican Party, 95
Rerum Novarum, 289, 349, 349n, 351
Resale Price Maintenance, 46
Rewe-Zentral AG v. Bundesmonopolverwaltung für Branntwein (Cassis de Dijon case), 132n
Rhine, the, 8n
Rhineland (capitalism), 211, 347
Rhodes Boyson, Sir. *See* Boyson, Sir Rhodes
Rhodes James, Sir Robert, 276
Rhodesia (Southern), 49, 56, 80,
Rhys-Williams, Sir Brandon (2nd. Baronet), 79, 97
Ricardo, David, 14
Richard, Ivor (Baron Richard), 85, 120
Richards, Paul, 149
Ridley, Nicholas (Baron Ridley of Liddesdale), 41, 83, 272
Rifkind, Sir Malcolm, 120, 136, 296

Rippon, Geoffrey (Baron Rippon of Hexham), 8, 48, 49, 59. 62, 68, 88, 94, 97, 161
Robert Oakley's Westminster Week, 234n
Roberts, Dame Shelagh, 96, 96n
Rochester & Chatham, 103
Rodgers, Sir John, 21–24, 26
Rogalla, Dieter, 119, 141
Roman (Empire), 2, 176, 352
Roman Catholic(ism), 289, 344, 345, 352
Romania, 250, 367
Rome, 94, 100, 238, 312
Rome or Brussels..?, 74, 75, 273
Rome Treaty/Treaty of Rome, 8, 12, 24, 36, 38, 41, 42, 70, 74, 75, 83, 91, 118, 153, 155, 160, 175, 177, 178, 193, 273–6, 294, 304, 360
Rome Treaty and the Law, The, 67
Rømer, Harald, 256
Roosevelt, President, 29
Rossini, Gioachino Antonio, 72
Roth, Andrew, 41
Rousseau, Jean-Jacques, 72
Rowe, Andrew, 110
Royle Committee, 93
Royle, Sir Anthony (Baron Fanshawe of Richmond), 93
Rühe, Volker, 103
Rules and Petitions Committee of the European Parliament, 43, 111, 134
Rules of Procedure of the European Parliament, 111, 237
Rumsfeld, Donald, 251
Russia(n), 1, 13, 37, 40, 112, 215, 295, 297, 324, 367
Rutherford, Malcolm, 48

SA Roquette Frères v. Council of the European Communities (isoglucose case), 111, 112, 363
Saffron Walden, 78
Sainte-Laguë, André/Sainte-Laguë method, 105n
Salisbury, Robert Cecil, 3rd Marquess of, 14, 181, 296
Salisbury, the 5th Marquess of ('Bobbety'), 46
Samuel Montagu, 173n
San Marino, 285
Sandys, Duncan (Baron Duncan-Sandys), 2, 8, 62, 63, 64, 68, 70
Santer, Jacques /Santer Commission, 80, 216, 217, 218, 355, 366
Sapir Report, 211
Sarkozy, President Nicolas, 233, 242, 245, 255, 263, 264, 279, 335
Saturday Evening Post, 2
Scandinavia(n), 37, 154, 313, 351
Schengen agreement, 286, 330, 366
Schlüter, Poul, 154
Schmidt, Helmut, 161
Schuman Plan, 3, 9, 59
Schuman Declaration, 16n, 275, 359
Schuman, Robert, 1, 3, 274, 275, 352, 353
Scotland/Scottish, 53, 92, 108, 211, 220, 265, 313, 334
Scott, Nick, 73
Scott-Hopkins, Sir James, 79, 97, 295
Scottish National Party (SNP), 78, 88, 104, 195, 220, 258, 363, 366, 367, 368
scrapie, 199
Scruton, Roger, 353
SDP/Liberal Alliance, 125, 127, 149
SEA. *See* Single European Act (SEA)
Seal, Barry, 155

SEATO (the South East Asia Treaty Organisation), 228
Second World War, x, 2, 3, 6, 18n, 50, 118, 121, 181, 181n, 227, 261, 270, 279, 293, 307, 308, 337, 349
Seldon, Dr. Anthony, 174n
Seligman, Madron, 29
Sellar and Yateman, 307
Selsdon phase (of Heath government), 350
Selsdon Group, 35, 83, 155
"Selsdon Man", 83n
Selwyn Lloyd, (Baron Selwyn-Lloyd), 16
Sen, Amartya, 283n
Sénat (French), 68
Senate (Belgian), 2
Senate (US), 146, 146n, 217
Serbia, 180, 339
Sermon on the Mount, 144
Servan-Schreiber, Jean-Jacques, 63, 296
services sector, 129, 135, 140
Sevenoaks, 21, 103, 309
Sevenoaks Conservative Association, 309
"shadowing the D-Mark", 127, 162
Shaftesbury, 7th Earl of, 158
Shakespeare, William, 72
Shaw, Michael (Baron Shaw of Northstead), 99
Shell Mex, 81
Shepherd, Richard, 155, 201n
shipping of hazardous waste, 149
Siedentop, Larry, 287
Sierra Leone, 180
Sikorski, 232
Simmerson, Reg, 313
Simmonds, Hugh, 87
"Simplifying Treaty", 244
Simpson, Anthony, 123
Single Currency, ix, 41, 127, 160–5, 168, 169, 171, 172, 176, 185, 188, 190, 196, 207, 221, 222, 250, 297, 305, 315, 334, 356, 366
Single European Act (SEA), 61, 112, 114n, 120, 133, 136–40, 142, 154, 162, 177, 178, 193, 210, 240, 279, 296, 297, 354, 356, 364
single financial area, 162
Single Market, ix, 15, 51, 75, 81, 84, 100, 129–45, 149, 152, 154, 155, 157, 162, 162n, 175, 176, 179, 187, 193, 196, 202, 210, 211, 230, 235, 236, 256, 274, 277, 278, 291, 296, 297, 300, 309, 314, 316, 323, 324, 326, 328, 338, 342, 354, 355, 356, 364, 365
Single Market News, 141
Single Transferable Vote (STV), 92, 220
Skinner, Peter, 196, 198, 221
Skybolt, 30n
Slovakia, 283, 367, 368
Slovenia, 180, 367
Small and Medium-sized Companies (SMEs), 121
Smedley, Oliver, 15, 66
Smith Square, 71, 150
Smith, Adam, 14, 75, 155, 325
Smith, Ian, 49, 56
Smith, John, 155
"snake in the tunnel", 71, 160, 160n, 161, 362
"Soames Affair", 51
Soames, Christopher (Baron Soames), 51, 80, 81, 86, 100, 113
Social and Employment Committee of the European Parliament, 120
Social Chapter, 176, 200, 202, 207, 262, 316
Social Democrat/Social Democrat Party (SDP), 61, 78, 119, 346

Social Democratic and Labour Party (SDLP), 104, 220
"social dumping", 15
Social Fund, 123
Social Market Economy (*Soziale Marktwirtschaft*), 344, 348, 349
Social Tory Action Group, 73
Socialism/ist(s), 36, 53, 78, 91, 106, 109, 111, 114, 119, 120n, 125, 132, 134, 156, 190, 194, 209, 219, 219n, 222, 254, 256, 264, 271,289, 304, 305, 306, 309, 332, 345–51, 359, 363
"Socialism by the back door", 133, 195
"Socialism in one country", 271
Socialist Group (in the Parliament), 78, 111, 238, 256, 264n
Socialist Labour Party, 259
Society of Conservative Lawyers, 67
Solemn Declaration on European Union, 117, 364
Solidarność (Solidarity), 255
Somerville College, Oxford, 177
Sorcerer's Apprentice, The, 152
Soros, George, 182, 185
South Africa, 12, 331, 361
South America, 344
South Vietnam, 228n
South East Asia Treaty Organisation. *See* SEATO
South-East London, 207
South-East Region(al), 221, 222, 223
Southern Rhodesia, *See* Rhodesia
souverainiste, 254, 260
Soviet Academy of Social Sciences, 172
Soviet bloc, 34, 37, 289
Soviet Union, 6n, 10, 37, 56, 63, 109, 172, 179, 227, 227n, 230
Soziale Marktwirtschaft. See Social Market Economy
Spaak, Paul-Henri, 1, 11, 24, 30, 56, 275
Spaak Committee, 11
Spaak Report, 12, 13, 273, 360
Spain, 116, 126, 156, 283, 318, 364
Spanish, 117, 156, 164, 230, 256, 343
Spanish Civil War, 79
Spearhead database, 141
"special relationship" (with US), 4, 6, 7, 30, 44, 210, 284, 337
Spectator, The, 41, 46, 48, 59
Spencer, Tom, 103, 222
Spicer, Sir James (Jim), 71, 97
Spicer, Michael (Baron Spicer), 72, 73, 155
Spinelli Report, 118, 210, 290, 364
Spinelli, Altiero, 118, 119, 120
Spitfire, 18
St John-Stevas, Norman (Baron St John of Fawsley), 67
St. Malo Anglo/French agreement, 231
St. Oswald, Rowley (4th Baron St Oswald), 79
St. Paul, 272
St. Stephen's Club, 265, 266
Staatsbund, 280, 287
Stability and Growth Pact, 172, 334, 339
Stackleberg Strategy, 162
Standing Advisory Committee on European Candidates, 96
Standing Veterinary Committee of the EU, 199
Stanley, Sir John, 102
Sterling. *See* pound sterling
Sterling Area, 6
Sterling crisis, 6n
Stevens, John, 207, 222

Stewart-Clark, Sir Jack, 255
Stewart-Munro, Christine, 82
Steyning, 55
Stockholm Convention, 14, 361
Strafford, John, 223, 224
Strasbourg, 2, 3, 4, 79, 80, 81, 82, 88, 89, 96, 97, 98,
    101, 108, 109, 112, 120, 121, 126, 159, 186, 198,
    206, 214, 242, 243, 303, 324, 340, 359, 360
Stuart, Gisela, 240
Stuttgart Summit 1983, 118, 364
subsidiarity, 133, 174, 175, 175n, 178, 189, 206, 213,
    241, 288–92, 313, 336, 351, 353, 357
Sudetenland, 261
Suez, 6, 6n, 7, 12, 46, 51, 227, 228, 270, 293, 296, 360
Suez, East of, *See* "East of Suez" question
Suffolk, 96
Sun, The, 156, 179, 179n
Sunday Express, The, 19
Sunday Telegraph, The, 174n
Sunday Times, The, 155, 253
Sunningdale Agreement, 85
Supreme Court (UK), 331
Supreme Court (US), 146
Surbiton, 189
Surrey, 103, 110, 223
Surrey County Council, 110
"suspensive veto", 112
Sussex, 223, 255
Sweden/Swedish, 14, 44, 186, 197, 209, 210, 314,
    354, 361, 366, 367
Swedish Conservative Party, 154
Swinton Conservative College, 18, 18n, 21, 23, 26,
    29, 34, 83, 215, 284, 309, 327
Swinton, Earl of (Philip Lloyd-Graham/Philip
    Cunliffe-Lister), 18
Switzerland/Swiss, 1, 14n, 44, 210, 280, 313, 314,
    354, 361
Sykes, Paul, 202
Systemic Risk Board, 329

tachographs, 123
Tanganyika, 39
Taverne, Dick (Baron Taverne), 78
tax harmonisation, 144
Taylor, Ian, 222, 225, 366
Taylor, John (Baron Kilclooney), 104
Taylor, Sir Teddy, 49, 87, 154, 188, 201n, 276
Tebbit, Norman (Lord Tebbit of Chingford); backs
    Conservative rebels, 187; Beryl Goldsmith
    PA to, 272; "crazy Socialist schemes", 309;
    "enjoys challenge" of Community, 82; moves
    to Eurosceptic position, 155; Party Chairman,
    168; Secretary of State for Employment, 119;
    Secretary of State for Trade and Industry,
    142; speech at 1992 Party Conference, 188;
    succeeded by Duncan Smith at Chingford, 225;
    supports ERM entry, 168
Telegraph, The, See *Daily Telegraph*
Temple-Morris, Peter (Baron Temple-Morris),
    207, 212
Thailand, 228n
Thames Television, 92n
Thatcher, Margaret (Baroness Thatcher); "a Treaty
    too far", 187; address to Conservative MEPs,
    125; becomes Prime Minister, 363; Biffen in her
    government, 61; Bruges speech, 146, 151–4,
    190, 280, 305, 354, 364; budget rebate issue, 99,
    113, 300, 338, 363; campaigns for Single Market,
    137; centralises power, 289; Centre for Policy

Studies (CPS) established, 141, 208; "chance
    to pass judgement on", 150; "chief architect"
    of European union, 137; disillusionment with
    Community/growing Euroscepticism, 190, 271;
    Delors different agenda from, 132, 133; ERM
    entry, 166, 167; Falklands war, 115; "fashion
    that Thatcher wrong", 142; Howe/Lawson "in
    cahoots", 166; Imperialism impossible, 181;
    "leader of a revolution", 189; Letwin in policy
    unit, 209; loses office, 171, 174, 259, 356, 365;
    Meyer "stalking horse" against, 47n; Milan
    Summit, "tricked at", 127; "Mrs Thatcher in
    Downing Street", 126; "no, no. no!", 146n, 365;
    on Bank of England independence, 166; on
    cooperation with centre-right parties/Christian
    Democrats, 93, 94; on Delors/Delors' TUC
    speech 217, 306, 313; on Lord Cockfield, 130,
    131; on Major Plan, 165; on Nigel Lawson, 166;
    O'Sullivan special adviser to, 215; overshadows
    Labour opposition, 114; policies of government,
    205, 306, 332, 333, 350; policy statement 1976,
    91; political dimension of the Common Market,
    116; reluctance to see Germany re-united, 170,
    337; replaces Heath as leader, 87, 350, 363;
    revenge for removal of, 155, 190, 271, 317;
    Ridley resigns from her government, 41; "right-
    of-centre" election winner, 203; second election
    as leader, 125; Single European Act, 137, 139,
    193, 354, 355; signs "Solemn Declaration on
    European Union", 117/118; speech in Rome
    1977, 101; supports enlargement /"widening",
    117, 342; "successfully rolled back the frontiers
    of the state", 152; "the lady's not for turning",
    350; third election victory, 149; Thorneycroft her
    Party Chairman, 3; vulnerability on "poll tax",
    171, 270; Walters her economic advisor, 162;
    warned by Acland on US attitide, 337; Westland
    Affair, 231, 232; "what's right for Thatcher's
    right for our MP", 189
"Thatcherism/ite", 15, 94, 138, 145, 150, 155, 174,
    189, 208, 232, 253, 317, 332, 349
"Thatcher's children", 206
The Hague, 2, 3, 60
The Future of Europe, 212, 296
The Right Approach, 91
The Third Man, 327
The Times, 20, 25, 87, 144, 155, 169, 200n, 301, 341
The United Kingdom and the European Communities,
    69, 362
Thirty Years War, 281
This Blessed Plot, 61, 62, 67, 176, 275, 300
Thompson, Major-General Julian, CB OBE), 231
Thomson, George (Lord Thomson of Monifieth),
    71, 80
Thorneycroft, Peter (Baron Thorneycroft of
    Dunston), 3, 15, 87
Thorpe, Jeremy, 62, 85
Three Views of Europe, 79, 81
"Three-Way Contact Programme", 52
"Three Wise Men", 117
Thucydides, 239
Tindemans Report, 118, 363
Tindemans, Leo, 117, 159
Tippett, Sir Michael, 72
Tito, Marshal, 6, 180, 180n
Todd, Ron, 152
Topolanek, Mirek, 254, 255, 256
Torridge and West Devon, 207
Tory European, 66

Tory Radicalism, *See* Radical Toryism
Tory Reform Group (TRG), 35, 73, 350
"Tory sleaze", 196
Towards a European Identity, 72
Towards European Economic Recovery in the 1980s, 129/130
Trades Union Congress (TUC), 87, 120,152, 306, 313, 350, 364
Trade Union(s), 109, 121, 346, 349, 350
Trafalgar, 307
Transport and General Workers' Union, 152
Treasury, the, 6n, 11, 13, 70, 114, 123, 126, 131, 163, 166, 184, 207, 279n
Treaty of Accession, 70, 362
Treaty of Lisbon. *See* Lisbon Treaty
Treaty of Maastricht. *See* Maastricht Treaty
Treaty of Nice. *See* Nice Treaty
Treaty of Paris. *See* Paris, Treaty of
Treaty/Treaties of Rome. *See* Rome Treaty
Trevi Group, 175
trial by jury, 242
Triboulet, Raymond, 68
Triffin Plan, 34
Trinity College, Cambridge, 58
TUC. *See* Trades Union Congress
Tufton Beamish, Sir (Lord Chelwood), 66, 67, 79
Tugendhat, Christopher (Baron Tugendhat of Widdington), 100, 115, 130, 212
Tunbridge Wells, 122
Turin, 60
Turkey/Turkish, 210, 228n, 250, 259, 324, 340
Turner, Amédée, 96
Turner, John, 4, 22, 114, 192n, 206, 270, 281, 316, 317
Turton, Sir Robin, 66, 87
Twain, Mark, 156n

UK Council of the European Movement, 12, 54
UK monetary area, 14
UK Permanent Representative to the EU, 239
UK Sovereignty Bill/Act, 262, 329, 331
UK's net budgetary contribution, 64, 112, 113
UKIP. *See* United Kingdom Independence Party (UKIP)
Ukraine, the, 215, 297, 324, 339, 367
Ulster Unionist(s), 60, 69, 78, 85, 86, 94, 157, 220, 343, 363
UN. *See* United Nations
Unilateral Declaration of Independence (UDI), 49, 56
unilateral nuclear disarmament, 227, 341
Union Jack, 108
Union of Democratic Forces (UDF), 255
Union pour un Mouvement Populaire (UMP), 255
United Conservatives and Unionist Party of Northern Ireland, 259
United Kingdom Independence Party (UKIP), 188, 194, 196, 208, 211, 220, 222, 224, 247–50, 253, 257, 258, 259, 261, 262, 303, 313, 318, 322, 325, 340, 366, 367, 368
United Kingdom Representation (UKREP), 110, 113, 161, 310
United Nations (UN), 34, 51, 67
United States (of America), (US/USA), 4, 6, 6n, 7, 26, 30, 31, 41, 44, 45, 63, 68, 119, 217, 227, 228, 229, 229n, 230, 237, 240, 274, 280, 284, 293, 294, 297, 313, 327, 337
United States of Europe, 1, 2, 13, 54, 87, 146, 216, 270, 274, 275, 295, 353, 359
Universities of Cambridge and Oxford, 27

University of Kent, 290
"unity in diversity", 283, 354
Unofficial Journal, 303
uranium (oxide), 303, 303n
US/USA. *See* United States
US Congress(ional), 80, 93, 216, 219n
US Federal Reserve Bank, 219n
US House of Representatives, 146
US Senate, 146n, 217
US State legislatures, 146n
US Supreme Court, 146
USA. *See* United States
USSR (United Soviet Socialist Republics) See also 'Soviet Union', 26, 37n
Utilitarianism, 345
Utley, T.E. (Peter), 58, 59

Vacher's quarterly European Companion, 130, 141
Valencia, 156
Value Added Tax (VAT), 35, 44, 81, 122, 133, 135, 143, 143n, 157, 157n, 201, 361
van Buitinen, Paul, 218
Van Rompuy, Herman, 263, 264
Vanneck, Sir Peter, 97
"variable geometry", 212, 214, 215, 222, 235, 315, 326
VAT. *See* Value Added Tax (VAT)
Vatican, The, 285
Vaubel, Prof. Roland, 278
Vaz, Keith, 243
V-bombers, 30n
Venice, 72
Ventotene Manifesto, 118
Victory for Socialism Group, 304
Vietnam, South. *See* South Vietnam
Vietnam War, 56, 337n
Viggers, Sir Peter, 212
Vilnius, 214
von Brentano, Dr. Heinrich, 287, 296
von Hayek, Friedrich, 116, 164n
von Wogau, Karl, 119, 157
Vredeling Directive, 120, 121
Vredeling, Henk, 120n

Wadham College, Oxford, 11
Wales/Welsh, 92, 189, 220, 227, 258
Walker, Bill, 155
Walker, Peter (Baron Walker of Worcester); abandons opposition to Common Market, 82, 272; believes future lies with developing countries, 308; "chequered history" of views on Europe, 155; created Baron Walker, 19n; foreword to Apples pamphlet, 122; founds Anti-Common Market League, 19; Minister of Agriculture, 64; patron of PEST, 73; reports to House of Commons on "vital national interest", 64; Secretary of State for the Environment, 65
Walker-Smith, Sir Derek (Baron Broxbourne); chairs EP Legal Affairs Committee, 20, 272; co-leads anti-Market "1970 Group", 66; defends obligation to hold direct elections, 91; former Minister of Health, 20; initial hostility to Community modified, 272, 273; member of UK delegation to EP, 79, 355; moves amendment at 1992 Conference, 20; promotes European Ombudsman, 99; proposes Council meet in public, 80; speaks against EEC membership, 69

Wall, Sir Stephen, 64, 137, 152, 165, 186, 202
Walters, Prof. Sir Alan, 162
Wanderzirkus (wandering circus), 186
Warner, Sir Fred, 97
Warsaw, 153
Warsaw Pact, 230
Warsi, Sayeeda, 189
Washington, 9, 263, 337
Waterloo, 34, 307
Watts, Mark, 196, 221
Waugh, Evelyn, 348
Wedgwood-Benn, Anthony (Tony Benn), 271
Welfare State, 226n, 332, 347
Wellington, Duke of, 97
Welsh, Michael, 206
Welsh Nationalists. *See Plaid Cymru*
Werner Plan, 71, 160, 161, 362
Werner, Pierre, 173n
West Berlin, 103
West Indian, 39
West Indian sugar, 19
Western Christendom, 353
Western European Union (WEU), 10, 11, 42, 48, 78, 227, 231, 232, 360
West Germany. *See* Federal Republic (West Germany)
Westlake, Martin, 196, 205, 308, 318
Westland Affair, 231, 232, 317, 364
Westminster (Parliament), 112, 221, 284n; attitude to EP powers, 137; avoiding difficulties at, 311; catering at, 110; "central democratic institution", 215; constituencies, 96, 198; Eurosecptic stirrings at, 110; give up seats at, 97, 293; IDS virtually unknown outside, 225; Kent MPs at, 312; Labour loses power at, 104; Maastricht, interest in, 199; "museum's at", 43; need for pre-legislative/specialist committees, 80, 177; no say who represents at, 329; power to repeal European Communities Act, 84n, 87, 178, 329; press pass for, 110; public accounts system, 79; Question Time, 79; "reduced to status of County Council/ regional assembly", 92, 177; relations with MEPs, 94, 97, 100, 109, 206; repatriation of powers to, 297; report of debates at, 301; role of Ministers at, 114n; "something different from MPs", 98; sovereignty of, 140, 266, 330, 331; support speaker for candidates to, 102; transfer of powers from, 224, 330; two-party system at, 177; Westminster model, 216, 310, 355
Westminster North, 265
"wets", 109
WEU. *See* Western European Union (WEU)
WEU Assembly, 78
Wheeler, Stuart, 253
Which?, 298
Whig(s), 180, 282
Whig Interpretation of History, 306
"whipless eight/nine", 201
Whitelaw, Willie (1st Viscount Whitelaw), 85, 293, 363
Wicks, Sir Nigel, 173n
Wiesbaden, 103,
Wight and Hampshire East, 70
Wilkinson, John, 201n
Williamson, David, 147n

Wilson, Harold (Baron Wilson of Rievaulx); belief in sovereignty of Parliament, 86; Commonwealth Immigration Act 1968, 23n; European Technological Community idea, 47; hands over to Callaghan, 88; introduces import surcharge, 28; loses 1970 election, 54, 57; popularity wanes, 56; Prime Minister, 54; private poll on EC, 86; pupil of Russell Bretherton, 11; referendum on EC membership, x, 86, 87, 269; renegotiates EC membership, 39, 85; returns to office in 1974, 85; sanctions on Rhodesia, 56; "Selsdon Man" jibe, 83n; opens negotiation to join EC, x, 51, 59, 268; "the pound in your pocket", 52n; tours capitals of Europe, x; "Treaty of Rome anti-planning", 304
wine lakes, 123
"winning the argument", 235, 286, 287, 291
Winterton, Sir Nicholas, 155
Wirtschaftswunder (economic miracle), 22, 28, 347
Wistrich, Ernest, 55
Wolfson, Mark, 309
Women's Farming Union (WFU), 122
working class vote, 348
Working Group on Macro-economic Research, 214
Working Time Directive, 267
World Bank, 286
World Tonight, 260
Wrexham, 61

YCs. See Young Conservatives (YCs)
Yes Minister, 16
Yom Kippur, 82, 362
Yorkshire, 18, 19, 65, 71, 122, 309
Yorkshire Imperial Metals (YIM), 18
Yorkshire North, 96
Young Conservatives (YCs), *See also* Greater London Area Young Conservatives, 5, 18, 19, 40, 48, 55, 56, 103, 188, 189, 206, 317, 341, 343
Young European Left (YEL), 85
Young Men's Christian Association (the YMCA), 158
Young, David (Baron Young of Graffam), 141, 142, 144, 211, 278
Young, Hugo; "a conspiracy of like-minded men", 54; attacks on Heath, 275, 276; Black Wednesday, 182; Bruges speech preparations, 151; cabinet welcome for the SEA, 138; "Eurosceptic tail wags Conservative dog", 341; "facts of life are European", 269; Howe resignation speech, 170; Lawson shadows D-Mark, 166; on Churchill, 3; on Delors, 132; on Enoch Powell, 61; on Eurosceptics, 155, 187; on John Biffen, 62; on Macmillan, 19; on Major premiership, 205; on Russell Bretherton, 11; opinion polls on Europe, 300; Powell's authorship of *One Europe*, 41; relies on account of Sir Con O'Neill, 62; supremacy of EU law, 67; Thatcher and the SEA, 137; Thatcher's "enemies to the rear", 113; the 1992 election, 179; "the heart of darkness", 173; "the moment that decided everything", 67; timing of ERM entry, 167
Yugoslav(ia), 5, 180, 215, 339, 365

Zahradil, Jan, 261
Zurich speech, Churchill's, 1, 2, 236

Госплан (Gosplan), 37n